Commentary on Thomas Aquinas's *Treatise on Divine Law*

Thomas Aquinas's classic *Treatise on Divine Law* is brought to life in this illuminating line-by-line commentary, which acts as a sequel to Budziszewski's *Commentary on Thomas Aquinas's Treatise on Law*. In this new work, Budziszewski reinvestigates the theory of divine law in Aquinas's *Summa Theologiae*, exploring questions concerning faith and reason, natural law and revelation, the organization of human society, and the ultimate destiny of human life. This interdisciplinary text includes thorough explanations, applications to life, and ancillary discussions that open up Aquinas's dense body of work, which tends to demand a great deal from readers. More than a half-century has passed since the last commentary on Thomas Aquinas's view of these matters. Budziszewski fills this gap with his consideration of not only the medieval text under examination, but also its immediate relevance to contemporary thought and issues of the modern world.

J. Budziszewski is Professor in the Departments of Government and Philosophy, University of Texas at Austin. Especially known for books on classical natural law and commentaries on Thomas Aquinas, he is also keenly interested in virtue ethics, conscience, self-deception, family and sexuality, religion in public life, toleration, and the unravelling of our common culture.

Commentary on Thomas Aquinas's
Treatise on Divine Law

J. BUDZISZEWSKI
University of Texas at Austin

Ante Studium (*Before Study*)

Ineffable Creator, Who out of the treasures of Your wisdom appointed treble hierarchies of Angels and set them in admirable order high above the heavens; Who disposed the diverse portions of the universe in such elegant array; Who are the true Fountain of Light and Wisdom, and the all-exceeding Source: Be pleased to cast a beam of Your radiance upon the darkness of my mind, and dispel from me the double darkness of sin and ignorance in which I have been born.

You Who make eloquent the tongues of little children, instruct my tongue and pour upon my lips the grace of Your benediction. Grant me penetration to understand, capacity to retain, method and ease in learning, subtlety in interpretation, and copious grace of expression.

Order the beginning, direct the progress, and perfect the conclusion of my work, You Who are true God and Man, Who live and reign forever and ever.
Amen.
Thomas Aquinas

CAMBRIDGE
UNIVERSITY PRESS

University Printing House, Cambridge CB2 8BS, United Kingdom

One Liberty Plaza, 20th Floor, New York, NY 10006, USA

477 Williamstown Road, Port Melbourne, VIC 3207, Australia

314–321, 3rd Floor, Plot 3, Splendor Forum, Jasola District Centre, New Delhi – 110025, India

79 Anson Road, #06–04/06, Singapore 079906

Cambridge University Press is part of the University of Cambridge.

It furthers the University's mission by disseminating knowledge in the pursuit of education, learning, and research at the highest international levels of excellence.

www.cambridge.org
Information on this title: www.cambridge.org/9781108831208
DOI: 10.1017/9781108923576

© J. Budziszewski 2021

This publication is in copyright. Subject to statutory exception and to the provisions of relevant collective licensing agreements, no reproduction of any part may take place without the written permission of Cambridge University Press.

First published 2021

A catalogue record for this publication is available from the British Library.

ISBN 978-1-108-83120-8 Hardback

Cambridge University Press has no responsibility for the persistence or accuracy of URLs for external or third-party internet websites referred to in this publication and does not guarantee that any content on such websites is, or will remain, accurate or appropriate.

*To those, now in glory,
who patiently spoke to me of God
when I was not listening*

Analytical Table of Contents

All selections are from the *Prima Secundae* (First Part of the Second Part) of the *Summa Theologiae*; St. Thomas's titles for the sections are paraphrased.

Outline of the Summa *on the Topic of Divine Law*	page xvii
The Decalogue	xxi
The Two Great Commandments	xxiii
Architecture of Law in General	xxv
Detailed Architecture of Divine Law	xxvii
Preface: On Discovering Thomas Aquinas	xxix
Commentator's Introduction	xxxiii

I PRELIMINARY CONSIDERATIONS

The Types of Law (Question 91)   1

Was a Divine Law Needed? (Article 4)   3
Is the Divine law a distinct kind of law, alongside what St. Thomas calls the eternal, natural, and human laws, or is it merely a rehashing or recapitulation of one of the other kinds of law? Does it provide anything that the other kinds don't?
    Text, Paraphrase, and Commentary   3
    Discussion: The Relation between Natural and Divine Law   19

Does Divine Law Come in One Edition or in Two, Old and New? (Article 5)   22
According to the tradition, there is more than one Divine law, for there is the law of the Old Testament, called the Old Law, given to the

chosen nation, the Jews, and the law of the New Testament, called the New Law or the Law of the Gospel, given to the Church. One might hold that there could not have been two laws because God would have done just as He intended to do the first time, or that the Old Law and New Law are not two different laws but two different promulgations of the same law. Is this the case? Or are they somehow different?

    Text, Paraphrase, and Commentary   22
    Discussion: Revelation – Says Who?   33
    Discussion: By No Other Name than Christ?   35

II THE OLD DIVINE LAW

What Kinds of Precepts the Old Law Contains (Question 99)   41

Were Any of the Old Law's Precepts Moral? (Article 2)   43
According to an influential argument, the Old Testament law included three different kinds of precept: moral, ceremonial, and judicial. Is this classification correct? At first, the question would seem to be easy to answer: Just look and see whether there are any moral, any ceremonial, or any judicial rules. However, the "look and see" approach begs the question of which rules are of which kind.

    Text, Paraphrase, and Commentary   43
    Discussion: How Many Kinds of Precepts Are There?   58
    Discussion: Correcting Aristotle   61

Were Any of the Old Law's Precepts Judicial? (Article 4)   64
Judicial rules should be of broad interest, even among those who do not share St. Thomas's faith tradition, because they concern rulers and governance, relations among citizens, relations with foreigners, and relations among members of a household.

    Text, Paraphrase, and Commentary   64
    Discussion: What Difference Does It Make?   77

Were the Promises of Benefits and Threats of Penalties Appropriate? (Article 6)   80
Although the Old Law is rich with promises of blessings in the present life for obedience to God's law and warnings of calamities for faithlessness, in this respect the New Law is quite different. Yet the claim is that both laws come from God. What is going on? St. Thomas believes that although God devised the best law possible given the initial condition of the Hebrew people, His intention in giving them the law was not that they remain in this condition, but that they advance – that their minds be more faithfully shaped by His.

    Text, Paraphrase, and Commentary   80
    Discussion: So What Are These Promises and Threats?   97
    Discussion: Does the New Law Also Contain Promises and Threats?   100

Analytical Table of Contents xi

The Old Law's Moral Precepts (Question 100) 102
Are All of the Old Law's Moral Precepts Also Included in the Natural Law? (Article 1) 102
If all the moral precepts of the Old Law belong to natural law, then we could have known them all by reason alone. In that case, why was it necessary for God to add words? But if any of the moral precepts of the Old Law do not *belong to natural law, then they would seem arbitrary to us – unintelligible decrees without any basis other than that they were decreed. In that case, how could they count as true law? For in order to be true law, doesn't an edict have to be recognizable as an ordinance of reason?*
    Text, Paraphrase, and Commentary 102
    Discussion: Does What Holds for the Old Law Hold for the New Law Too? 113
Why Does the Old Law Contain Just *These* Moral Precepts? (Article 5) 115
In the present Article we are concerned with the Decalogue, which is a summary of the Old Law. At first glance, what these Ten Commandments include and leave out might seem a bit quirky. For example, since we are forbidden even to consider *possessing our neighbor's wives and husbands, why aren't we forbidden* even to consider *lying and murdering, acts that are also wrong? After compiling a thorough list of such puzzles, St. Thomas shows that far from being arbitrary or idiosyncratic, the Commandments are organized and systematic.*
    Text, Paraphrase, and Commentary 115
    Discussion: The Moral Architecture of the Decalogue 148
    Discussion: The Rest of the Moral Precepts 149
Were the Old Law's Moral Precepts Appropriately Formulated? (Article 7) 151
Certain principles of composition apply with equal force to each of the commandments. At stake is whether the Decalogue is just a collection of good ideas, haphazardly expressed, or a clear and systematic body of principles truly sufficient to serve as the foundation of the Old Law.
    Text, Paraphrase, and Commentary 151
    Discussion: Sins of the Fathers 171
    Discussion: Does the Old Law Recognize the Natural Law? 173
Can Any Exceptions Be Made to the Old Law's Moral Precepts? (Article 8) 176
A precept is "dispensable" if the authority that issues it can allow an exception to the duty of obedience. Are the Ten Commandments dispensable? For example, could any person ever be allowed to dishonor his parents, steal or murder, or be unfaithful to his wife?

Text, Paraphrase, and Commentary	176
Discussion: False Difficulties	191
Discussion: Real Difficulties	192

Was It Enough to Obey the Old Law's Moral Precepts or Did They Have to Be Obeyed in a Certain Way? (Article 9) — 197

I may perform a just deed because it is ingrained in me to do the right thing the right way, but I may also perform it merely because people are watching. Does the law require only that certain things be done? Or does it also require that they be done "according to the mode of virtue" – in the way that a just person would perform them?

Text, Paraphrase, and Commentary	197
Discussion: Do Legislators Really Aim at Making Men Virtuous? Should They?	215

Did the Old Law's Moral Precepts Have to Be Obeyed According to Love in the sense of Charity? (Article 10) — 218

We have already considered whether the precepts of Divine law require doing the deeds that they perform as a virtuous person would perform them. However, the complete development of the virtues lies in that loving friendship between man and God which is called charity. In fact, without charity, even the ordinary moral excellences are virtues only "in a restricted sense," because although they direct us to good purposes, they do not have the power to place these purposes in right relationship to our ultimate purpose, which is God. These facts force us to broaden our inquiry. If even acts of virtue are not all that they should be unless motivated by charity, then do the precepts of Divine law require acting from this motive?

Text, Paraphrase, and Commentary	218
Discussion: Love is Complicated	235

How Are the Moral Precepts of the Decalogue Related to the Old Law's Other Moral Precepts? (Article 11) — 237

Besides the Ten Commandments, the Old Testament contains a host of other moral precepts. Were they really needed? Why isn't the Decalogue enough? Unlike the previous two Articles, which focus on the manner in which the Old Law must be followed, this one focuses on its architecture: On the relation among love of God and neighbor, the Decalogue itself, and all the other Old Law moral rules.

Text, Paraphrase, and Commentary	237
Discussion: Is "Determination" Arbitrary?	260
Discussion: False Teachers	261

Did the Moral Precepts of the Old Law Make Man Just and Acceptable in the Sight of God? (Article 12) — 265

The question of this Article is whether a person can earn his way into God's approval by doing the sorts of good "works" or deeds

Analytical Table of Contents xiii

which were commanded by the Old Law. One of the difficulties theologians confront is that some New Testament passages seem to suggest that obedience to the Old Law's moral precepts does have the power to do this, but others seem to suggest that it does not. How we can be justified – how we can be made just in God's sight and acceptable to Him – is one of the great doctrines of Christianity, and was also one of the great fault lines during the Protestant Reformation.

Text, Paraphrase, and Commentary	265
Discussion: St. Thomas and the Reformers	281

The Old Law's Ceremonial Precepts – Reasons for Them (Question 102) — 284

Were the Old Law's Ceremonial Precepts Arbitrary or Given for Intelligible Reasons? (Article 1) — 284

The vast majority of the ceremonial precepts are what St. Thomas calls "determinations" of the three commandments of the Decalogue concerning the worship of God. In his view, they do not depend on "the very dictate of reason," because although it could not be other than right to worship God, He might have enacted different modes of worshipping Him. But this fact does not imply that there were no reasons for enacting these modes rather than others. Were there such reasons? Or did the Divine legislator flip a coin?

Text, Paraphrase, and Commentary	284
Discussion: So What Was the Problem with Mixing Linen with Wool?	303
Discussion: Another Example: Avoiding Blood	305
Discussion: Can Anything Still Be Learned from the Ceremonial Precepts?	306
Discussion: Does God Have a Sense of Humor?	308
Discussion: Does St. Thomas Have a Sense of Humor?	308

The Old Law's Judicial Precepts – Reasons for Them (Question 105) — 311

Reasons for Old Law Judicial Precepts about Relations between Citizens and Rulers (Article 1) — 311

St. Thomas holds that although the ceremonial precepts of the Old Law passed away with the coming of Christ, their underlying rationale continues to have much to teach us. This is even more true of the judicial precepts, which were the civil law of the ancient Jewish people, a commonwealth of human beings united under God. The first category of judicial precepts is "precepts concerning rulers," which is almost equivalent to what we call "constitutional laws." The Israelite community had the special characteristic of being united in subjection

to God – as all communities ought to be – but most of what we find
here has implications for any community whatsoever.
    Text, Paraphrase, and Commentary   311
    Discussion: What St. Thomas Really Means by Kingship   332
    Discussion: The Peril of Tyranny   334

Reasons for Old Law Judicial Precepts about Relations among Citizens
(Article 2)   336
*Having considered the reasons for the rules about the structure of
governance, St. Thomas now turns to the reasons for the rules about
the relations among members of the community. Because this Article is
extremely long, I have summarized the Objections and Replies,
devoting the usual line-by-line commentary only to the* sed contra *and
the* respondeo.
    Text, Paraphrase, and Commentary   336
    Discussion: Commonwealths Considered Ideally and Considered
    as They Are in Real Life   336
    Discussion: On Whether the Lower is Really the More Solid   356

Reasons for Old Law Judicial Precepts about Relations with
Noncitizens (Article 3)   359
*Besides addressing relations among persons of the Chosen Nation, the
Old Law also addresses their relations with foreigners, or "strangers,"
both inside and outside their borders. Some of these aliens were
friendly, others hostile. Some lived in the cities and towns of other
lands, some were sojourners passing through the land, and some,
though not Israelites, were residents of the land.*
    Text, Paraphrase, and Commentary   359
    Discussion: Building Families and Transmitting Faith   389
    Discussion: Harm to Innocents   390

III THE NEW DIVINE LAW, OR LAW OF THE GOSPEL

The New Law in Itself (Question 106)   395

Is the New Law a Written Law, or Is It Poured into Us? (Article 1)   395
*St. Thomas argues that although in one sense the New Law is a written
law, something outside of us, in another sense it is the very grace of the
Holy Spirit, instilled into us. The latter sense is primary, but,
surprisingly, this does not make the former sense superfluous. We still
need written instructions too.*
    Text, Paraphrase, and Commentary   395
    Discussion: The Relevance of the Gospel to Philosophy   406
    Discussion: The Relation between Nature and Grace   406

Does the New Law Make Men Just and Acceptable in the Sight of
God? (Article 2)   408
*In some places the New Testament plainly speaks of justification as the
beginning of the process of becoming just; in other places as its*

Analytical Table of Contents

continuation, lest it be lost; and in still other places as its fulfillment. Not only does the God of Truth declare His followers just, but also, through the perfect integrity of the Savior with whom He joins them, He makes them just. St. Thomas considers Objections from various points of view, exploring how this could be. This Article should be read together with Question 100, Article 12.

Text, Paraphrase, and Commentary	408
Discussion: The Letter That Kills	423
Discussion: The Scandal of This Teaching	425

The Contents of the New Law (Question 108) — 427

Is It Appropriate that the New Law Includes Not Only Precepts but Also "Counsels"? (Article 4) — 427

The Tradition has always distinguished between precepts and evangelical counsels. The precepts are the moral commands of the Decalogue, interpreted in the light of the New Testament teaching about love. These are utterly necessary for entering into redeemed life. The counsels, such as perpetual poverty and perpetual virginity, are directions for those who wish to progress even more swiftly and with a minimum of distractions to the fullness of that life. Is this distinction reasonable? Considering certain remarks of Christ Himself, the answer would seem to be yes. On the other hand, over the course of history many have answered no. St. Thomas considers the objections and proposes solutions.

Text, Paraphrase, and Commentary	427
Discussion: Does the Recommendation of Perpetual Virginity Imply that Marriage Is Bad?	451
Discussion: The Evangelical Counsels as the Foundation of the Consecrated Religious Life	453

Afterword: Implications of St. Thomas's Teaching for the World of the Present — 456

By the light of natural law, even nations that have never heard of Divine law may be able to achieve more or less decent rules of conduct and systems of civil law. Yet apart from grace, in our fallen state we fall far short of admitting what in principle we are capable of knowing, and doing what in principle we are capable of doing. We need Divine guidance to mend and correct us. Why then does the very mention of such guidance arouse such strong resentment? Can this resentment be overcome?

Index of Scriptural References	459
Index of Persons and Topics	465

Outline of the *Summa* on the Topic of Divine Law

All selections are from the *Prima Secundae* (First Part of the Second Part) of the *Summa Theologiae*; capitals indicate selections included in this commentary; titles are given using St. Thomas's phrasing.

Preliminary Considerations (Question 91)

    (ARTICLE 4) WHETHER THERE WAS ANY NEED FOR A DIVINE LAW?

    (ARTICLE 5) WHETHER THERE IS BUT ONE DIVINE LAW?

THE OLD LAW

The Old Law in Itself (Question 98)

    Prologue to Question 98

    (Article 1) Whether the Old Law was good?

    (Article 2) Whether it was from God?

    (Article 3) Whether it came from Him through the angels?

    (Article 4) Whether it was given to all?

    (Article 5) Whether it was binding on all?

    (Article 6) Whether it was given at a suitable time?

How the Precepts of the Old Law Are Distinguished from One Another (Question 99)

    Prologue to Question 99

    (Article 1) Whether the Old Law contains several precepts or only one?

(ARTICLE 2) WHETHER THE OLD LAW CONTAINS ANY MORAL PRECEPTS?

(Article 3) Whether it contains ceremonial precepts in addition to the moral precepts?

(ARTICLE 4) WHETHER BESIDES THESE IT CONTAINS JUDICIAL PRECEPTS?

(Article 5) Whether it contains any others besides these?

(ARTICLE 6) HOW THE OLD LAW INDUCED MEN TO KEEP ITS PRECEPTS

EACH KIND OF OLD LAW PRECEPT

Of the Moral Precepts of the Old Law (Question 100)

Prologue to Question 100

(ARTICLE 1) WHETHER ALL THE MORAL PRECEPTS OF THE OLD LAW BELONG TO THE LAW OF NATURE?

(Article 2) Whether the moral precepts of the Old Law are about the acts of all the virtues?

(Article 3) Whether all the moral precepts of the Old Law are reducible to the ten precepts of the decalogue?

(Article 4) How the precepts of the decalogue are distinguished from one another?

(ARTICLE 5) THEIR NUMBER

(Article 6) Their order

(ARTICLE 7) THE MANNER IN WHICH THEY WERE GIVEN

(ARTICLE 8) WHETHER THEY ARE DISPENSABLE?

(ARTICLE 9) WHETHER THE MODE OF OBSERVING A VIRTUE COMES UNDER THE PRECEPT OF THE LAW?

(ARTICLE 10) WHETHER THE MODE OF CHARITY COMES UNDER THE PRECEPT?

(ARTICLE 11) THE DISTINCTION OF OTHER MORAL PRECEPTS

(ARTICLE 12) WHETHER THE MORAL PRECEPTS OF THE OLD LAW JUSTIFIED MAN?

OF THE CEREMONIAL PRECEPTS OF THE OLD LAW

The Ceremonial Precepts in Themselves (Question 101)

Prologue to Question 101

(Article 1) The nature of the ceremonial precepts

(Article 2) Whether they are figurative?

(Article 3) Whether there should have been many of them?

(Article 4) Of their various kinds

The Cause of the Ceremonial Precepts (Question 102)

Prologue to Question 102

(ARTICLE 1) WHETHER THERE WAS ANY CAUSE FOR THE CEREMONIAL PRECEPTS?

(Article 2) Whether the cause of the ceremonial precepts was literal or figurative?

(Article 3) The causes of the sacrifices

(Article 4) The causes of the holy things

(Article 5) The causes of the sacraments of the Old Law

(Article 6) The causes of the observances

The Duration of the Ceremonial Precepts (Question 103)

Prologue to Question 103

(Article 1) Whether the ceremonial precepts were in existence before the Law?

(Article 2) Whether at the time of the Law the ceremonies of the Old Law had any power of justification?

(Article 3) Whether they ceased at the coming of Christ?

(Article 4) Whether it is a mortal sin to observe them after the coming of Christ?

OF THE JUDICIAL PRECEPTS OF THE OLD LAW

The Judicial Precepts in General (Question 104)

Prologue to Question 104

(Article 1) What is meant by the judicial precepts?

(Article 2) Whether they are figurative?

(Article 3) Their duration

(Article 4) Their division

The Reasons for the Judicial Precepts (Question 105)

Prologue to Question 105

(ARTICLE 1) CONCERNING THE REASON FOR THE JUDICIAL PRECEPTS RELATING TO THE RULERS

(ARTICLE 2) CONCERNING THE FELLOWSHIP OF ONE MAN WITH ANOTHER

(ARTICLE 3) CONCERNING MATTERS RELATING TO FOREIGNERS

(Article 4) Concerning things relating to domestic matters

THE NEW LAW

The Law of the Gospel, Called the New Law, in Itself (Question 106)

> Prologue to Question 106
>
> (ARTICLE 1) WHAT KIND OF LAW IS IT? I.E. IS IT A WRITTEN LAW OR IS IT INSTILLED IN THE HEART?
>
> (ARTICLE 2) OF ITS EFFICACY, I.E. DOES IT JUSTIFY?
>
> (Article 3) Of its beginning: should it have been given at the beginning of the world?
>
> (Article 4) Of its end: i.e. whether it will last until the end, or will another law take its place?

The New Law in Comparison with the Old Law (Question 107)

> Prologue to Question 107
>
> (Article 1) Whether the New Law is distinct from the Old Law?
>
> (Article 2) Whether the New Law fulfills the Old?
>
> *(Article 3) Whether the New Law is contained in the Old?*
>
> (Article 4) Which is the more burdensome, the New or the Old Law?

The Things Which Are Contained in the New Law (Question 108)

> Prologue to Question 108
>
> (Article 1) Whether the New Law ought to prescribe or to forbid any outward works?
>
> (Article 2) Whether the New Law makes sufficient provision in prescribing and forbidding external acts?
>
> (Article 3) Whether in the matter of internal acts it directs man sufficiently?
>
> (ARTICLE 4) WHETHER IT FITTINGLY ADDS COUNSELS TO PRECEPTS?

The Decalogue

AS GIVEN IN EXODUS 20:3–17
(RSV-CE)

1. You shall have no other gods before me. You shall not make for yourself a graven image, or any likeness of anything that is in heaven above, or that is in the earth beneath, or that is in the water under the earth; you shall not bow down to them or serve them; for I the Lord your God am a jealous God, visiting the iniquity of the fathers upon the children to the third and the fourth generation of those who hate me, but showing steadfast love to thousands of those who love me and keep my commandments. (20:3–6)
2. You shall not take the name of the Lord your God in vain; for the Lord will not hold him guiltless who takes his name in vain. (20:7)
3. Remember the sabbath day, to keep it holy. Six days you shall labor, and do all your work; but the seventh day is a sabbath to the Lord your God; in it you shall not do any work, you, or your son, or your daughter, your manservant, or your maidservant, or your cattle, or the sojourner who is within your gates; for in six days the

AS GIVEN IN DEUTERONOMY 5:7–21
(RSV-CE)

1. You shall have no other gods before me. You shall not make for yourself a graven image, or any likeness of anything that is in heaven above, or that is on the earth beneath, or that is in the water under the earth; you shall not bow down to them or serve them; for I the Lord your God am a jealous God, visiting the iniquity of the fathers upon the children to the third and fourth generation of those who hate me, but showing steadfast love to thousands of those who love me and keep my commandments. (5:7–10)
2. You shall not take the name of the Lord your God in vain: for the Lord will not hold him guiltless who takes his name in vain. (5:11)
3. Observe the sabbath day, to keep it holy, as the Lord your God commanded you. Six days you shall labor, and do all your work; but the seventh day is a sabbath to the Lord your God; in it you shall not do any work, you, or your son, or your daughter, or your manservant, or your maidservant, or your ox, or your ass, or any of your cattle, or the

Lord made heaven and earth, the sea, and all that is in them, and rested the seventh day; therefore the Lord blessed the sabbath day and hallowed it. (20:8–11)

sojourner who is within your gates, that your manservant and your maidservant may rest as well as you. You shall remember that you were a servant in the land of Egypt, and the Lord your God brought you out thence with a mighty hand and an outstretched arm; therefore the Lord your God commanded you to keep the sabbath day. (5:12–15)

4. Honor your father and your mother, that your days may be long in the land which the Lord your God gives you. (20:12)

4. Honor your father and your mother, as the Lord your God commanded you; that your days may be prolonged, and that it may go well with you, in the land which the Lord your God gives you. (5:16)

5. You shall not kill. (20:13)
6. You shall not commit adultery. (20:14)
7. You shall not steal. (20:15)
8. You shall not bear false witness against your neighbor. (20:16)
9. You shall not covet your neighbor's house; (20:17a)
10. you shall not covet your neighbor's wife, or his manservant, or his maidservant, or his ox, or his ass, or anything that is your neighbors. (20:17b)

5. You shall not kill. (5:17)
6. Neither shall you commit adultery. (5:18)
7. Neither shall you steal. (5:19)
8. Neither shall you bear false witness against your neighbor. (5:20)
9. Neither shall you covet your neighbors wife; (5:21a)
10. And you shall not desire your neighbor's house, his field, or his manservant, or his maidservant, his ox, or his ass, or anything that is your neighbors. (5:21b)

The Two Great Commandments

All of the moral precepts of Divine law flow from the general precepts of the love of God and neighbor.

    A. Love of God in the Old Law:

> Hear, O Israel: The Lord our God, the Lord is One;[1] and you shall love the Lord your God with all your heart, and with all your soul, and with all your might. And these words which I command you this day shall be upon your heart; and you shall teach them diligently to your children, and shall talk of them when you sit in your house, and when you walk by the way, and when you lie down, and when you rise. And you shall bind them as a sign upon your hand, and they shall be as frontlets between your eyes. And you shall write them on the doorposts of your house and on your gates. And when the Lord your God brings you into the land which he swore to your fathers, to Abraham, to Isaac, and to Jacob, to give you, with great and goodly cities, which you did not build, and houses full of all good things, which you did not fill, and cisterns hewn out, which you did not hew, and vineyards and olive trees, which you did not plant, and when you eat and are full, then take heed lest you forget the Lord, who brought you out of the land of Egypt, out of the house of bondage.[2]

    B. Love of neighbor in the Old Law:

        1. Toward the neighbor who is part of the community:

> You shall not hate your brother in your heart, but you shall reason with your neighbor, lest you bear sin because of him. You shall not take vengeance or bear

---

[1] Substituting "The Lord our God, the Lord is One" for the RSV-CE's "the Lord our God is one Lord."

[2] Deuteronomy 6:4–12 (RSV-CE); compare Deuteronomy 11:1, 11:13, 13:3, and 30:6; Joshua 22:5 and 23:11; and Psalm 31:23.

any grudge against the sons of your own people, but you shall love your neighbor as yourself: I am the Lord.[3]

2. Toward the neighbor who is not part of the community:

The stranger who sojourns with you shall be to you as the native among you, and you shall love him as yourself; for you were strangers in the land of Egypt: I am the Lord your God.[4]

C. This teaching as confirmed in the New Law:

1. Love of God:

And one of them, asked a question, to test him. Teacher, which is the great commandment in the law?" And he said to him, "You shall love the Lord your God with all your heart, and with all your soul, and with all your mind. This is the great and first commandment.[5]

2. Love of neighbor:

And a second is like it, You shall love your neighbor as yourself. On these two commandments depend all the law and the prophets."[6]

---

[3] Leviticus 19:17–18 (RSV-CE).
[4] Leviticus 19:34 (RSV-CE).
[5] Matthew 22:35–38 (RSV-CE); compare Mark 12:30 and Luke 10:27.
[6] Matthew 22:39–40 (RSV-CE); compare Matthew 19:19, Mark 12:31, Luke 10:27 (as amplified by Luke 10:29–37), Romans 13:8–10, Galatians 5:14, and James 2:8. See also the Golden Rule, Matthew 7:12 and Luke 6:31–33.

Architecture of Law in General

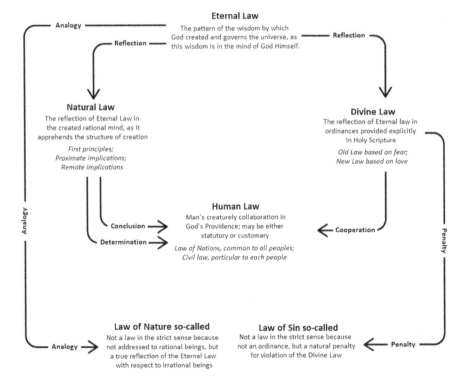

Detailed Architecture of Divine Law

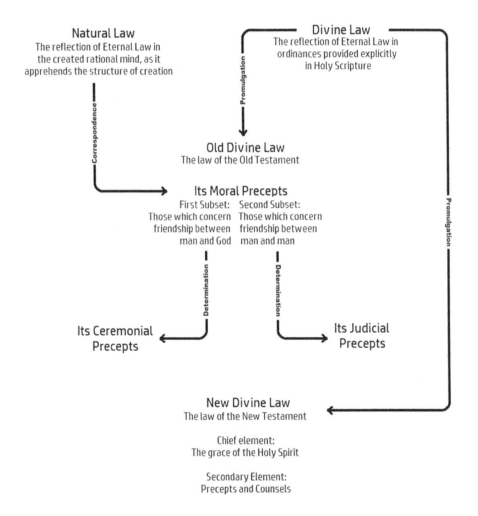

Just as the principal intention of human law is to create friendship between man and man; so the chief intention of the Divine law is to establish man in friendship with God.

Thomas Aquinas

Preface

On Discovering Thomas Aquinas

I first heard of Thomas Aquinas when I was ten years old, in a novel by Wilmar H. Shiras about an unusual child. Not until graduate school did St. Thomas cross the horizon of my awareness again, when a professor for whom I served as a teaching assistant gave exactly one lecture to the great thinker in an undergraduate survey. I am pretty sure the professor, who considered faith and reason implacable competitors, did not believe a word that St. Thomas said, but I am grateful for the exposure.

Not long after that, I read Dante for the first time, my interest piqued by a book about teaching literature, the author of which mentioned the souls frozen in ice at the center of Dante's *Inferno* – for although they were imprisoned there for different sins than mine, I too, a young nihilist, felt myself frozen in ice. Dante, of course, was so profoundly influenced by St. Thomas that his *Comedy* has been called "the *Summa* in verse."[7] It will not be surprising, then, that when I began my own teaching, I devoted a good deal more than one lecture to St. Thomas, nor will it be astonishing that I sometimes illuminated his points by quoting lines from Dante's poem.

It amazed me that so many scholars in my own field of ethical and political philosophy, scholars who ought to have known better, jumped over the Middle Ages as though they had produced nothing worth noting and were nothing but darkness and obscurantism – or even as though they had never taken place. Some teachers crossed the entire two millennia between Aristotle and Thomas Hobbes without taking a breath. The idea seemed to be to get to Nietzsche as quickly as possible. We have no need to discuss the reasons for this deliberate

---

[7] This widely quoted expression seems to have been coined by a student, W. F. X. R. Freeman, in "Sources of Dante's Inspiration," *Fordham College Monthly* 40:2 (November 1921), p. 76.

oblivion. Suffice it to say that even while I was still attracted to Nietzsche, it seemed to me both unaccountable and strangely wrong.

Though still a nihilist, I was powerfully drawn to what I devoutly told myself was merely the *appearance* of truth in St. Thomas's arguments – so much so that one of my students remarked after class one day, "I've been listening carefully, and I figure that you're either an atheist or a Roman Catholic. Which one is it?" After my return to Christian faith, though not yet of St. Thomas's communion, I began studying his work still more carefully, making, of course, all the mistakes that an autodidact makes, but perhaps having some of the advantages of an autodidact too, since I considered him the greatest authority on himself instead of viewing him through the blurry lenses of numerous secondary sources. Not that this commentary is anything other than a secondary source, but at least his own words are included.

Everyone who aspires to think seriously should try to understand how his own mind works. Most people, I think, cannot teach anything until they understand it. May God deliver me from ever teaching what I do *not* understand, but my bent is somewhat different, for the way I come to understand something is to work out how I could teach it. Despite the convenience of technical terms, which I certainly use sometimes, I am convinced that unless one can put something in everyday language, he still does not grasp it. Learning how to put St. Thomas in everyday language took some years, during which time I discovered that I had to learn a lot of other things as well before I could grasp his thought.

At a certain level, the Angelic Doctor is highly intuitive because classical thinkers always begin with what we dimly know already – where else could one begin? – and then try to clarify and elevate it. His apparatus for clarifying and elevating, however, is most difficult. To understand his theory of law I had to grasp his ethics, to understand his ethics I had to grasp his understanding of the good, to understand his understanding of the good I had to understand his metaphysics, and ultimately – though of course this goes beyond what we can know without God's help – I had to understand his theology. Needless to say, in order to understand any of these things I had to understand his own sources, and of course, given my quirk, I could not understand any of *those* things until I knew how I might teach them too.

Of course I am a scholar, writing in large part for scholars. A good many persons outside academia also write to me; I delight that they find my work worth reading, and I hope they will continue to do so. In trying to elucidate St. Thomas's writing, however, I consult the memory of all of my own former difficulties – and of course the difficulties of my students. Teaching young persons who are considering these matters for the first time has been enormously helpful, not only because I teach to understand but also because the so-called silly questions that some students ask are often the most helpful of all. This is because they are the hardest to answer, requiring the most searching consideration of first principles. One may think that one understands something – right up to the point when someone asks a question about a point that seems obvious to oneself but is not obvious *to him*. In the process of trying to make it obvious to the questioner too, one discovers all kinds of things – not least about the mysteries of knowledge. By God's mercy, I hope I have made some things clear.

I am grateful for the example of friends who mirror to me the life of the mind under God. First among these are Hadley Arkes, Francis Beckwith, Kenneth L. Grasso, John P. Hittinger, F. Russell Hittinger, Christopher Kaczor, and Robert C. Koons. Moreover, I have been blessed by graduate and law students whom I did not deserve, who took the sorts of things this book discusses much more seriously than I would have done at that stage of my life. Among those whom I once had the honor to teach I list my friends and colleagues Christina Bambrick, Thomas Rives Bell, Kody W. Cooper, David A. Crockett, Paul DeHart, Justin Dyer, William McCormick, SJ, Kevin Stuart, and Matthew D. Wright. But there are so many.

The opportunity to test-fly several of the arguments in this book came to me when I was invited to make a presentation at the conference "Aquinas and the Development of Law" held at the Aquinas Institute, Blackfriars, Oxford, in March 2018. The conference was illuminating, the Blackfriars were gracious, and I am especially grateful for the hospitality shown to both me and my wife by Fr. Richard Conrad, OP, the director, and Dr. Ryan D. Meade, of Loyola Chicago School of Law, another participant in the conference, who was there as a visiting scholar. After the manuscript of this book was finished, Richard Conrad offered immeasurably helpful suggestions. I am also grateful to Robert Dreesen, Robert Judkins, and Hilary Hammond, who were crucial in bringing this book to light.

To declare the fiftieth part of what I owe my wife, Sandra, would be a task too high for me. She so overflows with charity, however, that to her it seems no debt.

Commentator's Introduction

During the first half of the twentieth century, philosophy of religion was widely viewed as dead, not even a domain of serious questions but only of "pseudo-questions." A pseudo-question has the grammatical form of a question but does not actually mean anything. For example, among logical positivists the question "Is there a God?" was considered meaningless because such sentences as "God exists" and "God does not exist" are neither true by definition nor verifiable by reference to sense data. This view of meaning is rather obviously hoist by its own petard, for the statement "A sentence is meaningful only if it is either true by definition or verifiable by reference to sense" is itself neither true by definition nor verifiable by reference to sense data. So if the criterion is true, then it is meaningless, and therefore *not* true. Perhaps it is not surprising that philosophy of religion, that supposed corpse, rose from the dead. In fact religion, along with other supposedly dead fields of inquiry such as ethics, has become one of the most active lines of philosophical investigation.

Then, during the second half of the twentieth century, social scientists, philosophers, and even some theologians touted what was called the "secularization thesis," which held that religious influence and authority were in terminal decline. A corollary was that to survive at all, religions would have to embrace secularity and become as little like themselves as possible.[8] These claims have not fared well either, for renewed religious faith is bursting out all over the world – sometimes, unfortunately, faith in gravely defective religions, but sometimes, fortunately, not – while the denominations and religious groups that did gamble on accommodating themselves to the surrounding secular culture have been suffering shrinkage and evanishment. We may say one thing

---

[8] See for example Harvey Cox, *The Secular City: Secularization and Urbanization in Theological Perspective* (Princeton, NJ: Princeton University Press, 1965; rev. ed. 2016).

xxxiv   *Commentator's Introduction*

for the secularization thesis. Although it is not universally true, it does give an accurate description of the upper strata of Western society, so that religious and supposedly nonreligious views have come to *contest* the Western public square.[9] A remark widely attributed to sociologist Peter Berger makes the piquant observation that if the people of India are the most religious on the planet, and the people of Sweden the least, then America is a country of Indians ruled by Swedes.

In that sense, this book is for the Indians. If interested Swedes read along too, my joy will be complete. It offers a line-by-line discussion and analysis of some of what Thomas Aquinas writes about Divine law in the *Summa Theologiae*. In doing so it fills out and deepens what I have written in my earlier Cambridge books, *Commentary on Thomas Aquinas's Treatise on Law* and *Companion to the Commentary* (both 2014) (as well as my commentaries on his views of virtue and of happiness and ultimate purpose, although in their cases the connection is less direct). With some additional detail, small portions of those books have been recycled here so that the book is self-contained, but most of the work is new. One may think of those small portions as a promissory note, since they undertook the obligation that the present work attempts to pay.

I cannot include everything St. Thomas writes about Divine law, or this volume would be three or four volumes. However, I have chosen carefully. Two Articles are included from the First Part of the Second Part (hereafter I-II), Question 91, where St. Thomas establishes the reality of various kinds of law including eternal, natural, Divine, and human. The rest of the selections are from Questions 98 to 108, where he undertakes close scrutiny of Divine law itself. Since the division of the *Summa* into treatises was devised by later scholars rather than by St. Thomas himself, the titles of the treatises vary somewhat. I am calling Questions 90 to 108 the *Treatise on Law*, but Questions 98 to 108 the *Treatise on Divine Law*.

THE OBJECTION TO GOD

Some of my students protest whenever St. Thomas mentions God, and even more when he mentions Holy Scripture. Why must he "drag God into things"? Shouldn't an atheist be able to make just as much sense of ethics as anyone else? One answer is that St. Thomas isn't dragging God into the picture. God is in it already. Human nature wouldn't exist without God; natural goods wouldn't exist without God; in fact, there wouldn't be anything without God. The moral order depends on God in the same way that everything depends on God.

---

[9] I say "supposedly" because the worldviews and ways of life commonly called nonreligious have decided views about religion. Not only do they pass hostile judgment on the worldviews and ways of life that admit to being religions, but also, just like admitted religions, they too embody claims about matters of unconditional loyalty or ultimate concern.

And this answer is good so far as it goes, but it is incomplete. Although it shows how natural law depends ontologically upon God, it doesn't show how it depends *practically* upon God. After all, someone might suggest that for practical purposes, God can be ignored. Even conceding that He made our nature, still, now that we have been made, we should seek what is naturally good for us just because it is good. Yes, He commands it, the protestor says, but surely that is not the reason why we seek it. Who made Him the boss?

However, the notion that we can ignore God and still seek the good rests on the facile and unconsidered assumption that that God is one thing, and good another.

For what if God *is* our good? What if, in some sense, friendship with Him is our *greatest* good? That is exactly what St. Thomas proposes. But in that case, even if we do pursue the good "just because it is good," it isn't redundant that He commands it. Now "friendship with God" might mean either natural friendship with God, which lies in the concordance of wills, or supernatural friendship with God, which lies in a loving union. Supernatural friendship with God lies beyond anything we can reach by human power alone. But even natural friendship with God would be a colossal good, if only it could be achieved. Consider just the good and beauty of mortal friendship. We enjoy it, yes. But we also appreciate it, and this fact itself is a good; it reflects and thereby doubles the original enjoyment. Did I say doubles? Say rather triples, quadruples, quintuples, as the enjoyment of friendship reverberates in the strings of memory, gratitude, and delight. If we never remember our friends, have no gratitude for them, and are never moved to joy just because they *are*, we can scarcely be said to have experienced friendship at all. We are diminished, impoverished, mutilated; something is wrong with us.

But if all that is true even in the case of goods like mortal friendship, then shouldn't it be still more deeply true in the case of friendship with God? If we cannot take joy in remembering Him, being grateful to Him, and delighting in the thought of Him, aren't we missing the very note on which the chord of good is built?

We are missing it, and this fact alters and deepens the motive for listening to all the rest of those notes. True, the law directs us to nothing but our good. The Objector responds, "Then we should have done it anyway, even apart from God's command." But is it possible that part of what makes it good for us lies in doing it just because He commands it?

What lover has not known the delight of doing something, just because the beloved asked? What child has not begged Daddy to give him a job to do, just so he could do it for Daddy? What trusted vassal did not plead of a truly noble lord, "Command me!" just in order to prove himself in loyal valor? If in such ways, even the commands of mere men can be gifts and boons, then why not still more the commands of God?

Even so, it may seem that such a book as this puts the cart before the horse: How do we even know that there is a Divine law?

We take a step toward the answer by remembering that in St. Thomas's view, faith is not a constriction of reason by blind dogma, as it is so often viewed in our own time. Rather, it is the unshackling of reason by grace and its enlargement by the data of Revelation, so that reason is not only set free from sin but given more to work with. Those who say "Don't speak to me of faith! I follow reason alone!" have a shallow, shabby view of reason itself.

But to say this does not fully answer the question. After all, the whole point of Revelation is that it exceeds what we could have figured out for ourselves. How can it be *reasonable* to submit to help from *beyond* human reason? This is a good question, but it has an answer. Submitting to Divine help is reasonable in at least five ways.

1. Since the reality, power, wisdom, and goodness of God can be philosophically demonstrated, it is reasonable to consider Revelation *possible*.
2. Since, even though we have a natural inclination to seek the truth about God, our finite minds could never equal His infinite mind, it is reasonable to consider Revelation *necessary*.
3. Since He who gave us the inclination to seek Him must desire us to find Him, it is reasonable to consider Revelation *likely*.
4. Since the record of Revelation is well attested by miracles, it is reasonable to believe Revelation *authentic*.
5. Since faith is accompanied by the experience of grace, it is reasonable to believe Revelation *confirmed*. The psalmist cries, "O taste and see that the Lord is good!" Expressing the same thought in a different key, St. Paul exhorts, "test everything; hold fast what is good."[10]

By the light of Revelation, the mind is able not only to see more clearly those things that lie within its natural reach but also to understand and explain many other features of the world that would otherwise have remained utterly baffling, such as why our hearts are so divided against themselves. Thus, when reason rejects Revelation, it is not being more true to itself, but more. Only illuminated by God can it come into its own.

The hope of faith is that one day our thoughts may be lit not only by the reflected light of Revelation, but by the direct illumination of the face of God Himself: That although now our minds only smolder, one day they will blaze with fire.

FOR WHOM THIS BOOK IS WRITTEN

I intend this book for scholars, for students, and for serious general readers, and I reject the view that although a book can be either scholarly or accessible to nonscholars, it cannot be both. Obviously this book will interest Christians

---

[10] Psalm 34:8; 1 Thessalonians 5:21 (RSV-CE).

Commentator's Introduction

and those inquiring into Christianity. However, I am not writing for Christians alone.

On the contrary, this book is for all who are interested in ethics, law, political theory, and jurisprudence; in metaphysics, psychology, and philosophy of nature; in history of ideas, history of reception, and medieval studies; in systematic theology, philosophy of religion, and the relation between Scripture and doctrine; in the relation between St. Thomas and his predecessors, whether pagan, like Aristotle, Jewish, like Maimonides, or Christian, like Maximus the Confessor and Augustine of Hippo; and in the relation between faith and reason. May God grant that the book will also contribute to dialogue between Christians and Jews, Christians and Muslims, and Catholics and various sorts of Protestants, especially Lutheran. Moreover, I keenly hope it will contribute to conversation between Christians and persons who do not count themselves as believers of any sort, including those sometimes called post-Christians. Crucial to this hope is the fact that although St. Thomas quotes Holy Scripture, he doesn't just thump it and say "The Bible says!" He offers philosophical arguments for such things as the reality of God and the reasonableness of Revelation, and he makes further use of the tools of reason to investigate what he believes God has revealed.

It is curious how often even Christians assume that one must already be Christian to be interested in what St. Thomas has to say. I confess that this seems irrational to me. Christians read books by atheists; why shouldn't even the most resolutely secular reader engage with a thinker like St. Thomas? In a case familiar to me, an external reviewer praised a book manuscript by saying that it had challenged all his most deeply held assumptions, but then complained that in the fourth chapter it had mentioned God. "God," he said, "does not belong in political theory." It would have been better had the reviewer allowed the manuscript to challenge that assumption too. How curious that the Lord of the Universe might exist, yet not be important enough to think about.

The argument is sometimes made that a secular point of view is the only one for a self-respecting thinker to adopt because it is theologically *neutral*. No, it isn't. To exclude consideration of God from our thinking would be reasonable only if either there were no God or, even if there were, He could not make a difference to anything else, or even if He did, we could not know anything about Him. These assumptions are not neutral about the God of Revelation; they reject Him. For Revelation proposes that God does exist, He makes all the difference to everything else, and we can know a great deal about Him.

While we are reconsidering our assumptions, let us reconsider a few more of them. One, usually unconscious, is the supposition that the present condition of human nature *simply is* human nature. St. Thomas does not think it is. In his view, we have not always been as we are, we are not meant to be as we are, and we do not have to be as we are. Yet he also disagrees with secular thinkers who suppose that what ails us can be cured by human powers alone. From earliest times we have been disordered by the abuse of free will, and free will alone is insufficient to heal the disorder. To think so is even more absurd than to think that a surgeon who had cut off his marvelous hands could marvelously sew them back on. What we require is final reconciliation with God, the healing of the breach brought about by sin – not only the dislocation between man and God but the interior dislocation within ourselves. Only God Himself can bring this about, but one must accept the scandalous offer.

Another such supposition, this one usually conscious, is that nothing in Divine law that seems odd to us requires investigation. Our own biases, we imagine, are simply truth; the last twenty minutes are what all history was aiming at. Now it is true, and a wise maxim of study, that nothing should be believed without reason. But it is unreasonable to regard, say, an Old Testament rule about what to eat, what to wear, or how to deal with foreigners as unreasonable just because we don't immediately perceive the reason for it. St. Paul gets it right, I think, in the passage we saw above, when he writes, "Do not despise prophesying," but adds, "test everything."

The danger of not questioning the outlook of our own time is twofold. Being heirs of the Law, we imagine that we may kick away the ladder by which we climbed. Having kicked it away, we fall from our supposed height. Thinking ourselves better than the Law, we fall beneath it. For example, we despise the wars of the Old Testament on grounds of their cruelty, forgetting that we are heirs of the long lesson in mercy that God gradually taught a cruel people. But then, secure in the delusion of our mercy, we think nothing of firebombing Dresden.

DIVINE LAW AS REAL LAW

Before jumping into St. Thomas's arguments, it may be good to clarify some of the ideas we will be dealing with, starting with Divine law. This is important, not only for students and general readers but also for scholars, because the nineteenth- and twentieth-century revival of interest in St. Thomas was highly selective, giving especially scant attention to his detailed examination of Torah, which he calls the Old Law. The present time provides an opportunity to rectify that omission.

To begin, Divine law is really law – it is not just an incomprehensible edict of someone with a big stick. To be genuine law, an enactment must "bind the conscience." This means that it must be capable of laying a duty upon us, that it must be a suitable rule and measure of the acts of a rational being. To do this, it must be an ordinance of reason, it must be for the common good, it must be made by competent public authority (not just blind power), and it must be promulgated or made known. Divine law satisfies these criteria, for the mind can see that it makes sense, it promotes both our temporal and eternal good, it is made by the public authority of the whole universe, and, unlike natural law, which is promulgated through the deep structure of the created intellect, it is promulgated in words.

Among the various kinds of law, we find a certain order. We recognize that it is wrong to disobey just laws. But human beings cannot whip up entire new moral obligations all by themselves; even an ordinance such as "drive only on the right side of the road," which could have required driving on the other side instead, does not come from nowhere, for it presupposes a duty to take care for the safety of our neighbors. But where does this preexisting duty to take care for the safety of our neighbors come from? There is no sense in calling it a "social construction," for in that case we could change it to suit ourselves, and the whole point of morality is that duties are binding whether we like them or not – we don't invent right and wrong, we discover them. The place where we discover them is in the kind of being that we are – the constitution of the human person – for among other things, a person is by nature a proper thing for other persons to care for. So human law must be rooted in the natural law.

But where does *that* come from? If the kind of being that we are is merely a meaningless and arbitrary result of a process that did not have us in mind, then morality is meaningless. Granted that what conscience presents to us as law really is law, and not just a collection of urges, then I think we must believe that the process did have us in mind. Of course we are contingent beings; we did not have to exist. But however far back we must go, at last contingent realities must be explained by realities that are not contingent. Effects presuppose a First Cause, contingent beauties presupposes a First Beauty, and contingent meanings – including the meaning of human nature – presupposes a First Meaning. This is what we call God, and the pattern by which He created and governs the universe is called the eternal law. So for human law to be real law there must be a natural law, and for natural law to be real there must be an eternal law.

Now suppose that there were no eternal law. Then natural law would be arbitrary, which means it would not really be law. But in that case human law would be merely blind power, so that it would not really be law either. So one must either accept the whole package – or reject it. If we accept it, everything makes sense. If we reject it, nothing does.

DIVINE LAW AND NATURAL LAW

Just now we were speaking of human, natural, and eternal law, but the book is about *Divine* law. Where does *that* come in?

It is easy to become confused about this question. St. Thomas presents his main discussion of natural law in I-II, Question 94, long before the portions of the *Summa* included in this commentary. Yet it would be a dreadful mistake to think of his theories of natural and Divine law as separate and disconnected. In fact, his theory of Divine law *completes* his discussion of the natural law, tying up strings and answering questions that would otherwise have gone unanswered. This becomes especially clear in I-II, Question 100, Articles

1 and 3. Article 1 is included in this commentary, and although Article 3 is not included, I discuss it in detail in the chapter on Question 100, Article 11.

According to St. Thomas, both natural and Divine law are reflections of eternal law, the former in the structure of the created order, the other in the words of Revelation, as though these were a pair of mirrors. Why then do we need two reflections, two mirrors? Why isn't natural law enough? The most fundamental reason is that God intended us for a supernatural purpose which our natural reasoning is insufficient to fathom without help. But there are other reasons too. For example, because of the uncertainties of human reasoning, it is all too easy to make mistakes about the remote implications of the natural law and even to lie to ourselves about its basics. Divine law removes such deceptions and uncertainties.

Since Divine law comes to us by Revelation rather than by unaided reason, one might suppose that it would be a bolt out of the blue with no discernible connection with what our minds can recognize as good. The great surprise (though it should not be a surprise) is that this is not so. Even though reason could not have worked all of it out ahead of time, it is intelligible to reason. Having received it, we can understand it; we get the point.

I do not mean that once we accept Revelation, what reason can work out for itself is cast aside. One of St. Thomas's most important and characteristic teachings is that reason is a *preamble* to Revelation. He writes,

> The existence of God and other like truths about God, which can be known by natural reason, are not articles of faith, but are preambles to the articles; for faith presupposes natural knowledge, even as grace presupposes nature, and perfection supposes something that can be perfected. Nevertheless, there is nothing to prevent a man, who cannot grasp a proof, accepting, as a matter of faith, something which in itself is capable of being scientifically known and demonstrated.[11]

For if it were unreasonable even to believe that God exists, then how could we believe that this God really had revealed Himself?

Echoing Christ, St. Thomas holds that all the moral content in Divine law flows from the Two Great Commandments, to love God and to love our neighbor. But these Two Great Commandments turn out to grow from the same great spine as natural law – that good is to be done and evil avoided. For to what is love directed? To what is good. And what is good? This turns out to be twofold, for the Supreme Good is God Himself, our final end, but our neighbor is a created image of that good. So loving God and loving our neighbor go together, and the notion of loving one of them but not the other is simply nonsense:

> Now since good is the object of dilection and love, and since good is either an end or a means, it is fitting that there should be two precepts of charity, one whereby we are

---

[11] I, Q. 2, Art. 2, ad 1.

Commentator's Introduction xli

induced to love God as our end, and another whereby we are led to love our neighbor for God's sake, as for the sake of our end.[12]

Before going on we must take care not to fall into a mistake. Loving our neighbor for God's sake does *not* mean loving our neighbor merely as a tool, an instrument, or a ladder for climbing up to God. Far from it. The idea is to love our neighbor *as God Himself loves him* because by His grace we are enabled to share in His own love for our neighbor. A human analogy may be helpful here. If I love my wife, then just because I do care for her, I share in her care for all those for whom she cares. In much the same way, if I love God, then just because I love Him, I share in His love of all those whom He loves. This is more than loving having natural love for our neighbors, for one who loves his neighbor for God's sake actually participates in Divine love.

But we were talking about the reasonableness of accepting Revelation. Consider then the passage in which Moses is commending God's commandments to the Hebrews. He asks the people, "And what great nation is there, that has statutes and ordinances so righteous as all this law which I set before you this day?"[13] There would be no point in daring them to make the comparison unless they were able to make it – unless the human mind can recognize the body of laws being set before it as a more perfect expression of what it already dimly knows.

So the natural law and the Divine law are complementary. Should we not have expected this? Don't both reflect the same eternal wisdom in the mind of God? Perhaps these connections should not be pushed too hard; the Divine law does have a much higher source of illumination, directing us not only to goods within reach of our natural powers but also to the Supreme Good, God Himself, who is not to be attained by any means but His own grace. Without grace, the natural mind is forlorn, bereft of all hope of knowing its author. Yet even so, it knows *about* Him; it experiences both inward and outward pricklings of the light of a Sun it cannot see. It recognizes that it comes from Him; it perceives its debt to Him; it desires to know the truth about Him; it feels its own desperate incompleteness. The ancient Athenians, who inscribed an altar To AN UNKNOWN GOD, were much to be pitied that they did not know Him.[14] Yet how much more fortunate they were than beasts and atheists, for they knew how the altar should be inscribed!

One who reflects seriously will see further into the Divine law by considering the natural law – and he will see further into the natural law by considering the Divine.

---

[12] II-II, Q. 44, Art. 3. See also ad 3: "To do good is more than to avoid evil, and therefore the positive precepts virtually include the negative precepts. Nevertheless we find explicit precepts against the vices contrary to charity."
[13] Deuteronomy 4:8 (RSV-CE).
[14] Acts 17:23.

THOMAS AQUINAS AND HIS ENLIGHTENED CRITICS

The thinkers of the Enlightenment, which in many ways was more like an endarkenment, denied what we have just been saying. For various reasons – in some cases religious skepticism, in other cases fear of religious wars – they tried to sever the connections between reason and faith, between philosophy and theology.[15] Their aim was to make ethics theologically *neutral*. It was to be a body of axioms and theorems which any intelligent, informed mind would consider obvious once they were properly presented – so obvious it would make no difference what religion or wisdom tradition the mind followed, what the mind thought of Revelation, or whether it had experienced Divine grace.

This was a mistake, for neutrality is impossible. Have human beings a common moral ground? Yes, because there is one God, one human nature, and one natural law. But is our common ground a neutral ground? No. In fact, it is a very slippery one. Not all views of God, not all views of the structure of reality, not all views of human nature itself are equally adequate. Some make it harder to see the common ground and harder to stand on it. Some may even prevent us from *wanting* to stand on it. Consider, for example, the view that God or human nature can change. St. Thomas holds that whatever in us can change is not in fact our nature, and that any god that can change is not in fact God. Beliefs in a human nature that can change in its essence, or in a God who can become what He is not, make it very difficult to see what really is our nature and to acknowledge what really is God.

In its failure to recognize the fact that the common ground is not a neutral ground, the Enlightenment project crumbled. As a result of this error, the very idea of a universal ethics came into disrepute. The older and more classical approach to universal ethics, which St. Thomas represents, does not make such an error. This is one of the many reasons why it is now enjoying a modest revival and renaissance, although the secular world tries hard not to notice.

What might such a revival and renaissance mean? The Enlightenment thinkers believed that we could speak with each other only by setting aside our traditions and regarding them as irrelevant. By contrast, St. Thomas recognizes that we *must* speak from within our traditions, because only these give us something to say to each other.[16] Paradoxically, for insight into what

---

[15] The following paragraphs are adapted from the preface to the second edition of my book *What We Can't Not Know: A Guide* (San Francisco: Ignatius, 2011).

[16] What, specifically, does Christian revelation give us to say? We say that the natural law can be known by "unaided" reason, but while not wrong, this way of speaking leaves something to be desired, for as we see later, even the natural law may be grasped by our minds only dimly and reluctantly without additional light. I have discussed five modes of the Divine illumination of natural knowledge in "Nature Illuminated," which is chapter 3 of *The Line Through the Heart: Natural Law as Fact, Theory, and Sign of Contradiction* (Wilmington, DE: ISI Books, 2009). A highly condensed version of the argument is presented in "Natural Law Revealed," *First Things* 188 (December 2008), www.firstthings.com/article/2008/12/natural-law-revealed.

we hold in common, we must fall back on what we do not hold in common. Consequently, rather than being divorced from theology, natural law theory must be reintegrated with it – not because we do not seek common ground, *but just because we do*. There is no need to pretend that conversation among Christians, Jews, Muslims, and atheists is an easy undertaking. However, the attempt will be much more fruitful if these Christians, Jews, and Muslims are not required to impersonate the atheist.

THOMAS AQUINAS AND THE JEWS

Several sections ago I spoke of God teaching a long lesson in mercy to a cruel people. Something we dare not forget is that in St. Thomas's view, *all* of the peoples of Old Testament times were cruel. The distinction of the Hebrew people was not that they were more cruel than the others, but that they had been separated from the others so that alone among the nations, they could be gradually weaned of their cruelty by God Himself. In Torah, Moses reminds the people that God did not set them apart them because they were better than other nations, but to instruct them in better ways:

Do not say in your heart, after the Lord your God has thrust [the pagan nations] out before you, "It is because of my righteousness that the Lord has brought me in to possess this land"; whereas it is because of the wickedness of these nations that the Lord is driving them out before you. Not because of your righteousness or the uprightness of your heart are you going in to possess their land; but because of the wickedness of these nations the Lord your God is driving them out from before you, and that he may confirm the word which the Lord swore to your fathers, to Abraham, to Isaac, and to Jacob. Know therefore, that the Lord your God is not giving you this good land to possess because of your righteousness; for you are a stubborn[17] people.[18]

In similar recognition of fault, St. Paul writes, "God shows his love for us in that while we were yet sinners Christ died for us."[19] One of the Church's eucharistic prayers asks God to admit the communicants into some share and fellowship with the holy Apostles, martyrs, and all the saints, "not weighing our merits, but granting us your pardon."

St. Thomas believes that the Revelation of God to the Jewish people was authentic, so that they are true heirs of the Old Testament covenants. He insists that they must be allowed to practice their rites,[20] strongly opposes taking

---

[17] Literally, "stiff-necked." The Old Testament uses this expression frequently. For example, in the Law, see Exodus 32:9, 33:3,5, and 34:9; in the Prophets, Jeremiah 7:26, 17:23, and 19:15; and in the historical books, 2 Chronicles 30:8 and 36:13 as well as Nehemiah 9:16–17 and 29.
[18] Deuteronomy 9:4–6 (RSV-CE). Compare the words of God in the second chapter of the book of the prophet Ezekiel.
[19] Romans 5:8 (RSV-CE).
[20] II-II, Q. 10, Art. 11.

Jewish children to baptize them against their parents' will,[21] and treats the great Jewish commentator Maimonides with deep respect. As we see later on, he views the basic moral precepts of Jewish law as a supreme reflection of natural law, treats its judicial precepts as a model from which all nations can learn, and believes that by anticipating the Messiah, its ceremonial precepts teach even Christians how to think about the sacrifice of Christ.

DIVINE LAW AS DIVINE PEDAGOGY

A point about Divine law which is often missed is that it is an exercise in Divine pedagogy. According to St. Thomas, the Old Law is, so to speak, the first edition of Divine law, given by God to the Hebrew people, and its chief purpose is to direct external actions. Though it was good, it was incomplete – a preparation for the coming of the Messiah.

The New Law, or Law of the Gospel, is the second edition. It is the fulfillment of Divine law, given to the Church by Jesus, who is that messiah. According to St. Thomas, it cleanses human nature, uplifts it beyond what it can achieve by its own resources, and transforms the interior motive with which exterior actions are performed, so that human beings can be brought into fellowship with God.[22]

At the time when the Divine law of the Old Testament was given, the ancient Israelites were a violent and uncouth people. God Himself calls them stubborn, reminding them that He has not chosen them because of their righteousness. During the periods of gravest disobedience, he allows them to suffer setbacks, defeats, and disasters to return them to their senses. Consequently, we must not assume that everything recorded in the Old Testament is approved by the Old Testament. The Law itself was provisional, a teaching device intended to impart the first steps toward righteousness and give the people a sense of what it might mean to be truly holy. It is not that any of the Ten Commandments could be repealed – but there is a lot more to the Law than the Decalogue, and some of it anticipated later developments.

Ordinary human law can develop over time in several ways, for in the first place the understanding of the legislators may become better or worse, and in the second place the people for whom they are legislating may become better or worse. Well-made laws help the people under them to *become* better, so that eventually they will be able to bear better laws.

Can Divine law also develop? Considering the cautions expressed in the previous section, it might seem that the answer should be a sharp no. Divine

---

[21] II-II, Q. 10, Art. 12.
[22] The next few paragraphs are adapted from my lecture "Of Course Human Law Develops: Can Natural and Divine Law Develop?" delivered at the symposium "Aquinas on the Development of Law", sponsored by the Aquinas Institute and held at Blackfriars, University of Oxford, March 2018.

wisdom is perfect; it can no more improve than decay. Moreover, not only is our creational design unchanging but the supernatural destiny to which Divine law directs us is fixed; whether or not each of us gets there, God made us for beatitude. And yet in certain other surprising ways St. Thomas maintains not only that change and development are possible in Divine law but that they have actually taken place.

Are these changes and developments of such a nature as to give comfort to those who deny the reality and stability of moral basics? No, but they are real. Consider, for example, the change in the rule about divorce. The Divine law of the Old Testament, which St. Thomas calls Old Law, permitted the repudiation of wives. According to Christ, divorce was never pleasing to God, but the Old Law permitted it "because of the hardness of their hearts" – that is, to avoid a still worse fault. According to ancient Christian opinion, the worse fault was that if these ancient men had not been permitted to divorce their wives, *they would have murdered them.* Christ instituted a development of Divine law by putting an end to the Old Law's dispensation from the indissolubility of marriage.[23]

From this point of view, the Old Law was not God's final word, and was never intended to be. Yet the giving of the Old Law *nurtured the people and brought them to greater maturity* so that they could one day be given a better law still, as babies can grow up and eat meat.

The change in certain precepts is only part of the difference between the Old Law and the New. According to Thomas Aquinas, the greatest contrast is that unlike the Old, the New is not primarily a written code at all. Of course it also sets certain precepts and counsels in words, and these are crucial. But its chief element is the healing grace of the Holy Spirit, to which the doors were opened by the atoning death and resurrection of Christ – grace which finally enables human beings not only to understand the law but also to follow it. But this difference must not be misunderstood, for according to St. Thomas such grace was also available to those who lived in the ages before He came and who longed for the Christ who was to come.

LANGUAGES, TERMS, AND TRANSLATIONS

As in my previous Cambridge commentaries, in each Article I follow the same order of presentation. I offer the well-known translation of the Fathers of the English Dominican Province, now in the public domain, in the left-hand column; my own paraphrase, always consulting the Latin, in the right-hand

---

[23] The Old Law on divorce: Deuteronomy 24:1–4. The New Law on divorce: Matthew 5:31–32, 19:3–12. St. Thomas on the danger of wife murder: Supp., Q. 67, Art. 4, ad 4, and Art. 6; *Summa Contra Gentiles*, book III, chapter 123. St. Thomas cites the *Opus Imperfectum*, an incomplete fifth-century commentary on Matthew believed in his day to have been composed by Chrysostom.

column; then line-by-line commentary; and finally brief discussions of selected themes.

Because the Blackfriars translation tends to be quite literal – at least in the sense that it prefers to render Latin terms with English cognates when they are available – my paraphrase is rather free. Occasionally, though, when the Blackfriars translation itself is somewhat free, as well as in those cases when I think it is misleading, my paraphrase is more literal, just so that none of St. Thomas's nuances are lost. When St. Thomas's prose is awkward and complex, I sometimes even rearrange whole sections of text, but since the readers can always compare my wording with the original, it is always clear what I have done.

Many of St. Thomas's transitions are puzzling. Sometimes his arguments place premises and conclusions in a different order than we would normally place them. Sometimes he even buries a conclusion, implying but not stating it. Besides trying to clarify such obscurities, I try to present my explanations in such a way that the reader is habituated to the way St. Thomas's language and arguments work. I also modernize archaisms, although I retain them occasionally, especially when God is addressed or when altering the archaisms would cause confusion. Because so much depends on keeping track of his various distinctions, I have also made somewhat greater use of italics than is customary in a book of this kind.

The Blackfriars translation often inserts quotation marks, although they are not present in the Latin. This is misleading because, except in the case of Holy Scripture, St. Thomas is not usually quoting word for word. Although I have allowed these quotation marks to remain in the Blackfriars text, my own paraphrase omits them except when I am actually quoting. Moreover, whenever any variation of St. Thomas's words from the passage he is citing is significant, I comment on it. Another quirk of the Blackfriars translation is that it capitalizes the word "Divine" in the phrase "Divine law," but not, for example, the word "eternal" in the phrase "eternal law." Simply to forestall the confusion that might result if the translation capitalized "Divine" but the commentary did not, I have retained the capital D. I have also retained the capitals for the two types of Divine law, Old and New.

Typically, the Blackfriars translation completes, or even supplies, St. Thomas's fragmentary citations. Although these additions are generally most helpful, they are occasionally erroneous. For this reason, I have omitted them from the Blackfriars text so that the wording shows only what St. Thomas actually wrote. This leaves for the commentary the details of the passages to be discussed. Where I think the citations inserted into the Blackfriars translation are mistaken, I say so.

Where pronouns are concerned, I generally follow the traditional English convention – the one everyone followed before politically motivated linguistic bullying became fashionable – according to which such terms as "he" and "him" are already "inclusive." Except where the context clearly indicated the masculine, they were always used to refer to a person of either sex. Readers who choose differently may write differently; I ask only that they extend the same courtesy to me. In the meantime, since my language includes masculine, feminine, neuter, and inclusive pronouns, any rational being who feels excluded has only him-, her-, or itself to blame.

Since I am writing not only for scholars but for others as well, I take certain troubles for the convenience of the others. In particular, in quoting from works other than the *Summa Theologiae* (such as the writings of Aristotle and St. Augustine of Hippo), I try to use reliable editions that are in the public domain and available on the Internet. Sometimes this is impossible or inconvenient. The specialists, of course, will have their own favorite translations.

When I provide quotations from the Bible, I most often use either the Douay-Rheims American version or DRA (an American English translation of the Latin Vulgate that St. Thomas used, and that is also employed by the Dominican Fathers translation of the *Summa*), or the Revised Standard Version Catholic Edition or RSV-CE (which is sometimes more clear and often more beautiful). Which translation I am using is always indicated in footnotes. When the chapter and verse divisions of the DRA differ from those of more recent translations, I indicate this fact in the notes as well. Although the DRA is full of archaisms and is rather awkwardly phrased, it has certain significant advantages. For example, the distinction among the different kinds of Divine law precepts is often obscured by the proliferation of Bible translations which do not use a standardized vocabulary. In particular, the Vulgate (and the DRA) lend themselves to the threefold distinction among "precepts," "ceremonies," and "judgments" which is so important to St. Thomas's understanding of Divine law's architecture. By contrast, contemporary translations may use any of the terms "laws," "rules," "commandments," "decrees," "statutes," "ordinances," "teachings," "judgments," "rites," or "regulations," leaving things in a state of confusion. Sometimes, too, the Vulgate gives a different meaning to a passage than some contemporary translations do, so that in order to understand what St. Thomas himself is talking about, the newer ones are not helpful and we must stick to the DRA.

Since a portion of my readers may be encountering St. Thomas for the first time, it may be helpful to explain the method by which I refer to other sections of the *Summa Theologiae*. The *Summa* is divided into the *Prima*, or First Part, the *Prima Secundae*, or First Part of the Second Part, the *Secunda Secundae*, or Second Part of the Second Part, the *Tertia*, or Third Part, and finally the *Supplementum*, or Supplement, which was completed after St. Thomas's death using works he had written earlier. These main parts are abbreviated as "I," "I-II," "II-II," "III," and "Supp." A question, abbreviated "Q." in the singular and QQ. in the plural, followed by a numeral, is not one query but a set of related queries; each of the individual queries is addressed in an article, abbreviated "Art." with a numeral. Usually, though not always, an article phrases the query in such a form that the traditional answer is yes. Possible objections to giving a yes answer are enumerated as "Obj. 1," "Obj. 2," and so forth; St. Thomas's Replies to the Objections are enumerated as "ad 1," "ad 2," and so forth. Although the Objectors are hypothetical persons, not real ones, it is remarkable how far St. Thomas goes to present their arguments forcefully, and, sometimes, how much he lets them get away with in order to make their arguments seem plausible – for example, they often quote Scripture selectively, tearing it out of context and ignoring other passages that might bear on the point at issue. In the spirit of this exercise, I often write as though they were real persons, for example, speaking not only of "the first Objection," but also of "the first Objector." The *sed contra* or "On the other hand" is usually a brief restatement of the view to which the Objectors are objecting. Sometimes it merely cites a representative authority, but sometimes it goes a little further by presenting a brief argument. However, the *responde*, or "Here is my response" – sometimes also called the *solutio* – is St. Thomas's own argument, which is sometimes rather different and always more complete.

I

PRELIMINARY CONSIDERATIONS

QUESTION 91, ARTICLE 4

Whether There Was Any Need For a Divine Law?

TEXT	PARAPHRASE
Whether there was any need for a Divine law?	Is Divine law a distinct kind of law that provides something the other kinds don't?

In the *Prima Secundae*, which is the First Part of the Second Part of the *Summa Theologiae*, Question 91 concerns the *kinds* of law:

- Eternal law, which is the pattern of the wisdom by which God created and governs the universe, as it is in the mind of God Himself;
- Natural law, which is the reflection of eternal law in the created rational mind, as it apprehends and shares in the structure of Creation;
- Divine law, which is the reflection of eternal law in ordinances and teachings explicitly contained in the Holy Scripture;
- Human law, whether statutory or customary, which is man's creaturely collaboration in God's providence;
- And the so-called law of sin, which is not a law in the strict sense because it is not an ordinance – "Do this" – but a natural penalty for violation of Divine law – "This will happen."

For context, the question preceding 91 is about the essence of law, and the questions immediately following 91 are about eternal, natural, and human law in themselves. We do not reach a detailed discussion of Divine law in itself until we come to Questions 98–108, from which most of the selections in the present book are taken. Although I have dealt with Questions 90–97 in a previous book, *Commentary on Thomas Aquinas's Treatise on Law*, the present book cannot be self-contained unless these two articles of Question 91 are repeated and amplified as well. However, it cannot be said too often that St. Thomas's discussion here in Question 91 is preliminary. Many of the matters it broaches – about natural law, and Divine law, and about Divine law in relation to natural – are fully clarified only much later.

As to the present article: In the Prologue to Question 91, St. Thomas indicated that the *utrum*, or "whether," for Article 4 would be whether there *is* a Divine law. But doesn't Revelation say there is? Yes, and St. Thomas has no intention of second guessing Revelation; he is asking something different. Even conceding the authenticity of Revelation, one might still wonder whether the Divine law of which it speaks is a distinct *kind* of law, alongside the eternal, natural, and human laws – or merely a rehashing or recapitulation of one of the other kinds of law. For just this reason, the question of whether there is a Divine law boils down to whether a Divine law was *needed* – whether it provides anything that the other kinds don't.

| *Objection 1.* [1] *It would seem that there was no need for a Divine law. Because, as stated above (2), the natural law is a participation in us of the eternal law. But the eternal law is a Divine law, as stated above (1).* [2] *Therefore there was no need for a Divine law in addition to the natural law, and human laws derived therefrom.* | Objection 1. Apparently, what the Sacred Tradition calls Divine law is superfluous. Considering its origin in God, the eternal law is already, so to speak, a Divine law. True, there must be some way for us to participate in the eternal law, but we have that in the natural law. True, more detailed dispositions of affairs need to be derived from the natural law, but we already have those in human law. Since nothing is left for a supposed Divine law to do, it is not a distinct *kind* of law at all. |

[1] In its special sense, the expression "Divine law" actually refers to the law – or what seems to be a law (that is what is in question) – contained in Revelation, in the Old and New Testaments of the Bible. But the Objector is taking the expression "Divine law" in a much broader sense, as though it meant "any law the authority of which is rooted in God" (many first-time readers, and even some second- and third-time readers, make the same mistake). But the authority of all true law is rooted in God, so using the term in that sense, all law would count as Divine. The eternal law would count as Divine because it is in the mind of God, the natural law would count as Divine at one remove because it is our participation in eternal law, and the human law would count as Divine at two removes because it is a more detailed articulation of natural law as applied to local circumstances.

[2] The hypothetical Objector has fallen into something of a rut. In Question 91, Article 2, Objection 1, he had said that there was no need for a natural law because man is governed sufficiently by the eternal law; in Article 3, Objection 1, he said that there was no need for a human law because man is governed sufficiently by the eternal law *through* the natural law; now he says there is no need for a *Divine* law because man is governed sufficiently by the eternal law through the natural law.

| *Objection 2.* [1] *Further, it is written (Sirach 15:14) that "God left man in the hand of his own counsel."* [2] *Now counsel is an act of reason, as stated above (14, 1).* [3] *Therefore man was left to the direction of his reason. But* | Objection 2. Moreover, Scripture teaches that "God left man in the hand of his own counsel." What this means is that God allows man to reason out for himself |

a dictate of human reason is a human law as stated above (3). Therefore there is no need for man to be governed also by a Divine law.	what to do. This is done through human law, so any so-called Divine law would be superfluous.

[1] St. Thomas cites Sirach 15:14 no less than seven times in the *Summa*.[1] Two of the citations occur in *sed contras*, which are restatements of the traditional view, one of them affirming free will, the other defending it against the claim that we act by necessity. Another citation occurs in a Reply to an Objection, arguing that because the first man had free will, he could have resisted temptation. Interestingly, the other four citations occur in objections. In one way or another, these four objectors keep missing what St. Thomas views as the passage's point – they deny that everything is subject to Divine providence, deny the need for a Divine law, deny the need to coercively restrain wrongdoers, or deny that any man must ever obey another. It would seem that St. Thomas is not only taken by Sirach's teaching but concerned to make sure that we get it right.

[2] In I, Question 14, Article 1, St. Thomas remarks that "man has different kinds of knowledge, according to the different objects of his knowledge. He has 'intelligence' as regards the knowledge of principles; he has 'science' as regards knowledge of conclusions; he has 'wisdom,' according as he knows the highest cause; he has 'counsel' or 'prudence,' according as he knows what is to be done." Counsel, then, means the conclusions of *practical* reasoning.

[3] At first the Objector seems to be arguing that since God allows man to reason out for himself what to do, *no* law but human law is needed. That would be radical indeed. But in that case, one would have expected the objection we meet here to have turned up much earlier, in Article 1. It doesn't. Probably, then, the Objector is conceding here the need for eternal and natural law, and merely arguing that human reason does not need any help from *yet another* kind of law to work out more detailed conclusions.

Objection 3. [1] *Further, human nature is more self-sufficing than irrational creatures.* [2] *But irrational creatures have no Divine law besides the natural inclination impressed on them.* [3] *Much less, therefore, should the rational creature have a Divine law in addition to the natural law.*	Objection 3. Still further, human beings are by nature more fully equipped to direct themselves than such creatures as plants and animals are. We have the help of reason and the guidance of natural law; they have neither. Considering that even they can get by without a Divine law, surely we can. There is simply no need for such a thing.

---

[1] I, Q. 22, Art. 2, Obj. 4; I, Q. 83, Art. 1, *sed contra*; I-II, Q. 10, Art. 4, *sed contra*; I-II, Q. 91, Art. 4, Obj. 2; II-II, Q. 65, Art. 3, Obj. 2; II-II, Q. 104, Art. 1, Obj. 1; and II-II, Q. 165, Art. 1, ad 2.

[1] What the Objector means is that humans are better equipped than lower creatures for the practical needs of life. He does not mean they are better equipped in *all* respects. Wolves, for example, have fur, so they are better equipped to stay warm; they have fangs and claws, so they are better equipped to hunt and defend themselves; and they have four legs, so they are better equipped to run swiftly. Yet even in these respects, we are not altogether deficient. We do find ways to stay warm, hunt, defend ourselves, and run swiftly. Moreover we have something that wolves do not have at all: the power to reason.

[2] The Objector is not claiming that their natural inclinations are the only *law* irrational creatures possess because law is an ordinance of reason. He is saying that their natural inclinations are the only *guide* they possess. Animals are not subject to either natural *or* Divine law, and they don't need to be. No crow was ever told not to steal, no cat not to kill mice, nor was any shark ever commanded to honor its father and mother.

[3] The argument runs like this:

1. If creatures less well equipped to direct themselves than we are can get along without a Divine law, then certainly we can get along without it.
2. But such creatures *can* get along without it.
3. Therefore so can we.

On the contrary, David prayed God to set His law before him, saying (*Psalm 118:33*):[2] "Set before me for a law the way of Thy justifications, O Lord."	On the other hand, we see the Old Testament hero, David, imploring God in prayer to teach him His decrees. If the Divine law were unnecessary, why would David beg for it?

In the course of answering one question, the *sed contra* may seem to raise another, for in some sense David already knew the Divine law: Torah had already been revealed. Why then would he ask God to instruct him in it? Because to "know" the law may be taken in two ways. As we read in the prophet Jeremiah,

I will make a new covenant with the house of Israel, and with the house of Juda: Not according to the covenant which I made with their fathers, in the day that I took them by the hand to bring them out of the land of Egypt ... I will give my law in their bowels, and I will write it in their heart: and I will be their God, and they shall be my people.[3]

In one sense, to know the law is merely to have intellectual knowledge of it, if not a present awareness, at least in the tendency to be aware of it. David had that already. In another sense, to know the law is to have the power to fulfill it,

---

[2] Contemporary translations number the psalm as 119.
[3] Jeremiah 31:31–33 (returning to DRA).

to have it inscribed on the heart. In that sense, David did not yet have it, but begged for it. If he was right to beg for it then he needed it; so there is a need for Divine law.

I answer that, [1] Besides the natural and the human law it was necessary for the directing of human conduct to have a Divine law. And this for four reasons. First, because it is by law that man is directed how to perform his proper acts in view of his last end. [2] And indeed if man were ordained to no other end than that which is proportionate to his natural faculty, there would be no need for man to have any further direction of the part of his reason, besides the natural law and human law which is derived from it. [3] But since man is ordained to an end of eternal happiness which is inproportionate to man's natural faculty, as stated above (5,5), therefore it was necessary that, besides the natural and the human law, man should be directed to his end by a law given by God.

Here is my response. To complete the guidance of human life – to complete man's engagement with the eternal law – Divine law is needed because it accomplishes four things that natural and human law cannot do by themselves. The first has to do with the fact that man was created for *two* ends: not just the happiness of this life, but the happiness of the life to come. We are naturally equipped to direct ourselves to temporal happiness because our power of reasoning suffices both to grasp the natural law and by its light to work out suitable human laws. But our power of reason is utterly inadequate to steer us toward eternal happiness or beatitude, which exceeds all our natural experience. In order for us to reach that second, higher end, we need God to tell us directly what to do, through Revelation. His revealed commands are Divine law.

[1] St. Thomas shows in I-II, Question 91, Article 2 that even in a limited and natural sense our happiness requires good will toward God. However, now he is about to make an even greater claim: that we were made for a yet higher end that *transcends* our natural experience, one that exceeds what our natural powers can achieve or imagine. For the happiness of the life to come is not simply a longer-lasting version of the happiness of this life but an infinitely higher happiness, the complete joy and friendship of *union* with God, of knowing Him as we are known.[4]

[2] At first it seems puzzling that two different things, one lower and one higher, could both be called "ends" or goals. One is tempted to say that only the higher thing is truly an end – that the lower thing is not an end at all but only a stage on the way to our end. This is not correct. In St. Thomas's view, temporal happiness is a real end in the sense that it is desirable in itself, not just

---

[4] St. Paul writes "For our knowledge is imperfect and our prophecy is imperfect; but when the perfect comes, the imperfect will pass away. When I was a child, I spoke like a child, I thought like a child, I reasoned like a child; when I became a man, I gave up childish ways. For now we see in a mirror dimly, but then face to face. Now I know in part; then I shall understand fully, even as I have been fully understood." 1 Corinthians 13:9–12 (RSV-CE).

as a means to something else. But it cannot be our *final* end because for that it would have to be completely satisfying, leaving nothing further to be desired. Eternal happiness, or beatitude, has both of these properties. It is the "sweetness" of "the ultimate and most complete participation in [God's] goodness," which lies in "the vision of His essence, so that we live together in His company, as His friends."[5]

Even if we do have two ends, why do we need two laws? Couldn't the same law direct us to *both* our natural and our supernatural ends, to both temporal and eternal happiness? This question may be taken in several ways.

1. Do natural and Divine law agree with each other? Yes. It would be impossible for them to contradict each other, for they have the same author, God, whose perfect wisdom is wholly self-consistent.
2. Do natural and Divine law overlap? Yes. Many of the precepts of Divine law are included in natural law too, for example the prohibition of murder, and many of the teachings of Divine law promote temporal happiness, such as commandment "Do not commit adultery" and the advice in the book of Proverbs, "Go to the ant, O sluggard; consider her ways, and be wise."[6]
3. Could God then have guided us without natural law, employing only Divine law to direct us to both our natural and supernatural ends? No. The question supposes that we might have been just as we are, naturally endowed with a power to deliberate, yet without knowing any of its first principles. This supposition is inconsistent. Divine law presupposes natural law.
4. Could He have guided us without *Divine* law, employing only *natural* law to guide us to both our natural and supernatural ends? No. This time the question supposes that we might have been able to use our natural powers to grasp things that are beyond natural experience. Again the supposition is inconsistent. Natural law is exceeded by Divine law.

It follows that to direct true human beings to both their natural and supernatural ends requires both natural and Divine law. We can think of this in terms of a ship: Not only does it need to be preserved in good condition, which requires the knowledge of the ship's carpenter, but it also needs to be guided to its destination, which requires the knowledge of its pilot.[7]

---

[5] *Ultima autem et completissima participatio suae bonitatis consistit in visione essentiae ipsius, secundum quam ei convivimus socialiter, quasi amici, cum in ea suavitate beatitudo consistat.* Thomas Aquinas, *Commentary on the Sentences of Peter Lombard*, III, dist. 19, q. 1, art. 5, qc. 1.
[6] Proverbs 6:6 (RSV-CE).
[7] St. Thomas develops this analogy in *On Kingship*, especially chapter 15, sections 102–107. Thomas Aquinas, *De Regno: On Kingship, to the King of Cyprus*, translated by Gerald B. Phelan, revised by Thomas Eschmann, reedited by Joseph Kenny (Toronto: Pontifical Institute of Mediaeval Studies, 1949).

Was a Divine Law Needed?

One more thing: Although human law does not concern itself with man's supernatural end per se, it does not follow that supernatural matters have no bearing whatever on his natural end. Several of St. Thomas's remarks in the *Treatise on Law* shed light on what human law *does* and *does not* do concerning God. What he says in Question 99, Article 2 is much like what he says here: "[J]ust as the principal intention of human law is to create friendship between man and man; so the chief intention of the Divine law is to establish man in friendship with God." But in Article 3 he goes further: "Hence human laws have not concerned themselves with the institution of anything relating to Divine worship *except as affecting the common good of mankind*: and for this reason they have devised many institutions relating to Divine matters, according as it seemed expedient for the formation of human morals, as may be seen in the rites of the Gentiles."[8] In our day an analogy might be found in the fact that although human law sets aside a day of Thanksgiving to acknowledge Divine blessing and protection, it does not set forth instructions about baptism, holy communion, or the worship of God as the Trinity. To put it another way, the public expression of gratitude to God encourages good moral character on earth, but it does not carry us to heaven. The sort of goodness that makes us fit to live in the community, which we can achieve by our natural powers, falls far short of the purity of heart that makes us fit to see God, whom we cannot even approach without His help.

[3] How do we know that man *is* ordained to a supernatural end? From Revelation, of course, but not only from Revelation. This is the also conclusion of a long and complex but brilliantly illuminating philosophical argument, most of which is contained in the *Treatise on Happiness and Ultimate Purpose*, which is placed right at the beginning of the same major subdivision of the *Summa* which contains the *Treatise on Law*. Here we may only touch on a few high points.

Everything we do is for the sake of an end. The end we seek is final and perfect happiness that leaves nothing else to be desired. Since we desire such happiness, and since God and nature do nothing in vain, it is impossible that such happiness *not* be possible. After knocking down a series of other hypotheses – that final and perfect happiness lies in wealth, fame, power, pleasure, and so on – St. Thomas concludes that it does not lie in any created good whatsoever, so it must lie in union with God. Now man cannot be united with God through his body or his senses, so he must be united to God through his mind (though he remarks that the body and the senses do receive a certain completing "overflow").[9] But since the mind could not be satisfied by anything less than

---

[8] Emphasis added.
[9] I-II, Q. 3, Art. 3.

seeing God as He is, that is how it beholds Him. Final and perfect happiness consists in nothing else than this vision of God in His essence.

But how do we know that the attainment of this end lies beyond our natural powers? The gist of the answer is given in the First Part of the *Summa*, Question 12, Article 4. It begins with the observation that our natural knowledge begins from sense experience. This being the case, our natural knowledge cannot go further than what we can learn from sensible things. Now although God is the cause of such things, He is infinitely greater than all of them taken together. Therefore, even if we knew everything that could be known from them – even if we worked out His existence and goodness and so on – we would still fall short of knowing *Him*. It follows that the vision of God cannot be attained by our natural powers, but requires supernatural grace.

[4] *Secondly, because, on account of the uncertainty of human judgment, especially on contingent and particular matters, different people form different judgments on human acts; whence also different and contrary laws result.* [5] *In order, therefore, that man may know without any doubt what he ought to do and what he ought to avoid, it was necessary for man to be directed in his proper acts by a law given by God, for it is certain that such a law cannot err.*	The second thing Divine law provides is practical certainty. A moment ago, we said above that human reason suffices to direct man to temporal happiness. In one respect, that is an overstatement. For it is one thing for human reason to grasp the general principles of natural law, but it is quite another for it to apply them to matters of detail, where the fallibility of human judgment is all too evident. The further we descend into details, the more likely it is that different people will reach different judgments about what to do and not do. Worse yet, the same is true of lawmakers; consequently, the laws are filled with confusion and contradiction. Divine law replaces the fallibility of human judgment with the certainty of instructions given directly by God.

[4] St. Thomas puts this uncertainty in historical context in remarks he offers later in the *Summa* about the condition of human beings after the Fall but before the coming of Christ: "[A]s time went on sin gained a greater hold on man, so much so that it clouded man's reason, the consequence being that the precepts of the natural law were insufficient to make man live aright, and it became necessary to have a written code of fixed laws, and together with these certain sacraments of faith."[10]

His remarks in this Article about the uncertainty of human judgment are easy to misunderstand. Perhaps because our culture has been so deeply influenced by moral skepticism, many first-time readers leap to the conclusion that St. Thomas thinks people reach different judgments about *general principles*.

---

[10] III, Q. 61, Art. 3.

Was a Divine Law Needed?

One person judges stealing to be right, and another judges it to be wrong. This interpretation fails, for although St. Thomas considers our reason fallible, he does not consider it *that* fallible. Notice that in the remark about the clouding of man's reason, quoted above, he does not say man stopped *knowing* the precepts of natural law; he says only that the precepts became insufficient to make him live aright. But *could* he have stopped knowing them? No, for as he insists,[11] "there are certain things which the natural reason of every man, of its own accord and at once, judges to be done or not to be done: e.g. 'Honor thy father and thy mother,' and 'Thou shalt not kill, Thou shalt not steal': and these belong to the law of nature absolutely."

All this leaves us with a certain puzzle. Just what is it, then, that we are uncertain about? Could we wiggle out of the puzzle by saying that St. Thomas is not speaking of how we recognize rules, but about how we apply them? On this hypothesis, everyone does know deep down that stealing is wrong, but they give different answers when asked whether *this act* is theft. Unfortunately, this interpretation falls short too, because in this case Divine law would have been provided as a corrective to applying rules incorrectly, but in fact, it does not prevent that kind of error.

The solution is that St. Thomas is speaking neither of general rules nor of their application to particular acts, but of the intermediate rules which stand between these two poles. For there are three issues: whether stealing *in general* is wrong; which *categories* of acts count as stealing; and whether *this particular* act is stealing. Divine law does not rectify uncertainty about the first point because we are not really uncertain; though we may need reminders and challenges to our self-deception, we all really know that stealing is wrong. Nor does it rectify uncertainty about the third point, because the number of particular acts is infinite; to set them all down in writing would be impossible. The sort of uncertainty that it rectifies concerns the second: "This sort of thing is to be regarded as stealing, and that sort of thing is to be regarded as stealing, but these other four kinds are not." For example, the Divine law given to the Hebrew people instructs that they may eat grapes in their neighbors' vineyards so long as they do not carry any of them out with them, and that they may pluck ears of his standing grain and eat the kernels, but that if they reap them with a sickle, they are going too far.[12]

Such ordinances gave full weight to both the wrong of theft and the need of the poor to have something to eat. They also provided data points to which later ethical thinkers could fit their curves: Is stealing simply taking what belongs to another? Not quite. Is it taking what *rightly* belongs to another? Not quite. Is it taking what rightly belongs to another *against his will*? Not quite. Is it taking what rightly belongs to another against his *reasonable* will?

---

[11] Q. 100, Art. 1.
[12] Deuteronomy 23:24–25.

Yes, that's it. To refuse to allow a poor man to pluck a few grapes would be unreasonable.

[5] By this means human laws are substantially protected from error. Then is St. Thomas suggesting that *all* differences in human laws are due to error? No. If one commonwealth punishes petty theft with imprisonment, and another makes the thief pay a fine, it does not necessarily follow that one of these laws is a bad one, for the best way to apply a general rule often depends on circumstances. This brings us to a related question: Does St. Thomas think every nation must follow precisely the same civil laws as those given in Divine law to the Hebrews? We will have more to say about this later but, briefly, the answer is no. Things that follow by "conclusion" from general principles should be the same everywhere; for example, we should drive carefully everywhere. But things that follow by "determination" of the details may vary from place to place; for example, in the United States we might be required to drive on the right but in the UK to drive on the left. The Divine law contains a mixture of different types of material. Its underlying moral principles are valid everywhere, but the details of its application to the Hebrew nation are not.

[6] *Thirdly, because man can make laws in those matters of which he is competent to judge. But man is not competent to judge of interior movements, that are hidden, but only of exterior acts which appear:* [7] *and yet for the perfection of virtue it is necessary for man to conduct himself aright in both kinds of acts. Consequently human law could not sufficiently curb and direct interior acts; and it was necessary for this purpose that a Divine law should supervene.*	The third reason we need Divine law has to do with the fact that not all of the acts required for complete virtue are outwardly detectable – some are interior movements of the heart, like wishes, intentions, beliefs, and desires. Human law cannot directly command or forbid such acts because no one who tried to enforce such a command or prohibition would be able to tell who was in compliance and who was not. For the complete direction and discipline of human life, Divine law is necessary, because it is free from this limitation. The enforcer is not a human authority, but God Himself.

[6] How can human law command or prohibit what is undetectable? The authorities would have no way to know whether or not you were in compliance. Thus it makes sense for human law to forbid me from getting into a drunken brawl, because brawling can be seen, but not to command me to have a love of sobriety, because love cannot be seen. It makes sense for it to command me to pay child support, because child support can be seen, but not to command me to take an interest in how my children are doing, because interest cannot be seen. Notice too that interior movements of the heart include movements of the intellect. Thus it makes sense for human law to forbid me from taking innocent human life, because killing can be seen, but not to command me to believe in the sacredness of human life, because belief cannot be seen.

St. Thomas is not suggesting that human authority is unable to judge which kinds of interior movements of the heart ought to be performed. Nor is he suggesting that it may not *encourage* their performance. But it may not try to *command* them because it cannot tell whether or not they are being performed. This distinction is subtle. Morally speaking, I do not have a "right" to believe or not believe, love or not love, take an interest or not take an interest in whatever I please; nevertheless the law cannot forbid me from having the beliefs or loves or interests that I shouldn't.[13]

One might object that it would be an injustice for the law *not* to look into interior acts. In Anglo-American common law, for example, one of the elements in the legal definition of murder is that the killer must have *intended* to kill; the principle is *actus non facit reum nisi mens sit rea*, which means "the act does not make guilty unless the mind is also guilty."[14] Even though the intention to kill is hidden and cannot be seen, juries are expected to be able to infer its presence from other circumstances. Notice, however, that in such a case public authority is not trying to detect an interior act *directly*; rather, it is inferring its presence *from* "exterior acts which appear."

It turns out that St. Thomas agrees. Not only does he permit such inferences, he requires them. "What a man does in ignorance," he writes, "he does accidentally. Hence according to both human and Divine law, certain things are judged in respect of ignorance to be punishable or pardonable."[15] Again he explains, "according to jurists, if a man pursue a lawful occupation and take due care, the result being that a person loses his life, he is not guilty of that person's death: whereas if he be occupied with something unlawful, or even with something lawful, but without due care, he does not escape being guilty of murder, if his action results in someone's death."[16]

Considering that conclusions about ignorance and due care require drawing inferences about invisible inward acts *from* visible outward acts, what does St. Thomas's stricture about the inability of human law to detect an interior act actually mean? Apparently it concerns the very different case in which the inward act is *not* accompanied by a visible outward act: "For human law does not punish the man who wishes to slay, and slays not: whereas the Divine law does, according to Matthew 5:22: 'Whosoever is angry with his brother, shall be in danger of the judgment.'"[17]

---

[13] I discuss the question of whether we have rights of other sorts, or in other senses, in *Commentary on Thomas Aquinas's Treatise on Law* (Cambridge: Cambridge University Press, 2014), especially Question 94, "Before reading," and Question 96, Article 4.

[14] Shamefully, in contemporary criminal regulatory law, the element of *mens rea*, guilty mind, is often violated. A person may be convicted of a regulatory offense even if it is conceded that he had no intention of doing wrong.

[15] I-II, Q. 100, Art. 9.

[16] II-II, Q. 64, Art. 8.

[17] I-II, Q. 100, Art. 9. Concerning intention, see also I-II, Q. 7, Art. 4; I-II, Q. 19; I-II, Q. 20, Art. 5; and II-II, Q. 64, Art. 8.

[7] Having hateful or covetous wishes is just as vicious, just as contrary to virtue, as carrying them out. Yet so long as they are not carried out, the human law must ignore them; the ticklish experiment of peering into souls, even with the circumstantial evidence of outward acts, is not to be too often repeated. The Divine legislator, who sees directly into hearts, has no need of experiments, no necessity to make inferences, risky or otherwise; hence the Divine law can stride confidently into regions where the human law should not, commanding "Thou shalt not covet."

Yet this limitation of merely human law is easily misunderstood. True, it would be foolish and pointless to enact a law requiring those who nourish covetousness to pay a fine. In a certain sense such a law would be impossible; one could go through the motions of enacting it, but the resulting so-called law would be a dead letter. But would it be so foolish to enact a law requiring teachers in public schools to warn their young charges against covetousness? That would be a different kettle of fish. The law would not be forbidding something that is not detectable, but commanding something that is detectable, for though covetousness cannot be observed, teacherly warnings can be. So we must not say that law may not *take an interest* in the interior movements of the heart, but only that it may not command or prohibit them per se.

In fact St. Thomas does think the law should take an interest in the movements of the heart. This is its *raison d'être*. He thinks the law should cherish the virtues as a hen does her chicks.[18]

[8] *Fourthly, because, as Augustine says, human law cannot punish or forbid all evil deeds: since while aiming at doing away with all evils, it would do away with many good things, and would hinder the advance of the common good, which is necessary for human intercourse.* [9] *In order, therefore, that no evil might remain unforbidden and unpunished, it was necessary for the Divine law to supervene, whereby all sins are forbidden.*	The fourth and final reason Divine law is needed is that even in the case of exterior acts that *can* be seen, it is impossible to inflict human penalties and prohibitions on every single kind of wicked deed. The attempt to suppress every single evil by human authority would end up crushing a great many goods. So although such sweeping laws might be intended to improve the moral condition of the community, they would actually cause its moral condition to deteriorate. We see then that human law cannot forbid every sin. But Divine law can and does.

[8] If the cardinal error of the Puritan understanding of government was to confuse the functions of Divine and human law, then we see here how far St. Thomas is from being a Puritan. All sin is dreadfully harmful to us, but that

---

[18] See I-II, Q. 92, Art. 1, "Is it an effect of the law to make men good?"

Was a Divine Law Needed?

does not make all of it the business of the government. Do we reach this conclusion by suspending judgment about goods and evils? On the contrary, we reach it by judging them more intelligently – by soberly asking which evils the blunt instrument of human law *can* do something about.

The principle that an overambitious war on evil can also damage good is not pagan; Christ himself taught it in the parable of the "tares" or weeds.[19] If wheat and weeds are matted together, an ill-advised yank on one may uproot the other too. Chide the nobility for pursuing glory, and they grow slothful.[20] Punish the merchants for being greedy, and they grow indolent. Forbid the craftsmen from boasting of their skill, and they let their standards slip. Flaunting, greed, and boasting are bad, but he who criminalizes them will pay a mighty price. Men must be not only directed in their actions but also transformed in their motives, and human law cannot do this for them. Divine law is different because it is coupled with God's grace. Indeed, as St. Thomas argues in I-II, Question 106, Article 1, the very essence of the New Law is God's grace.

The Puritans of every age demand, "If human law cannot repress every evil, then what good is it?" In the passage that St. Thomas cites, St. Augustine gives the answer: "For it seems to you that the law that is enacted to govern states tolerates and leaves unpunished many things, which are nevertheless redressed by divine providence (and rightly so). Yet it does not follow that just because the law does not accomplish everything, we should disapprove of what it *does* accomplish."[21] St. Thomas takes this point up at greater length in I-II, Question 96, Article 2.

[9] Divine law is enforced by God, not by the government. The penalty of human law is the loss of temporal goods, such as liberty if I am imprisoned, comfort if I am scourged, or wealth if I am made to pay a fine. The penalty of Divine law is that by destroying love within us, we separate ourselves from God, "in whom alone man can have the life and happiness for which he was created and for which he longs."[22] If human law tries to forbid every evil, it ends up destroying many goods. No such consequence follows from the fact that the Divine law forbids every sin.

---

[19] Matthew 13:24–43.
[20] I am thinking of St. Augustine's argument in *The City of God*, book v, chapters 12–21, that in the time of the Republic, the Roman nobility performed acts of conspicuous benefit to the commonwealth only for the sake of glory, that is, the opinion of others who thought well of them. We return to this argument in the discussion at the end of I-II, Q. 105, Art. 2.
[21] *Augustine: On the Free Choice of the Will, On Grace and Free Choice, and Other Writings*, translated by Peter King (Cambridge: Cambridge University Press, 2010), p. 11. St. Augustine is summarizing, clarifying, and approving some remarks of his friend, Evodius.
[22] Catechism of the Catholic Church, section 1057.

And these four causes are touched upon in Ps. [19:7],[23] where it is said: "The law of the Lord is unspotted," i.e. allowing no foulness of sin; "converting souls," because it directs not only exterior, but also interior acts; "the testimony of the Lord is faithful," because of the certainty of what is true and right; "giving wisdom to little ones," by directing man to an end supernatural and Divine.	The same four final causes or purposes of Divine law are briefly mentioned in a verse of the Psalms, "The law of the Lord is unspotted, converting souls: The testimony of the Lord is faithful, giving wisdom to little ones." Its *unspottedness* refers to its fourth purpose, forbidding all sins; its *conversion of souls* refers to its third purpose, setting in order even the hidden movements of the heart; its *faithfulness* refers to its second purpose, providing practical certainty; and its *giving of wisdom to little ones* refers to its first purpose, directing us to our ultimate supernatural goal, which natural reason alone cannot attain.

The verse of the Psalms that St. Thomas is citing makes use of the Hebrew poetic device of parallelism, for the second half of the sentence duplicates the structure and echoes the thought of the first. By taking the verse apart in four pieces, St. Thomas obscures the parallelism. However, as though to do homage to the lost Hebrew trope, he substitutes a Latin trope, *chiasmus*, or reversal; for the first purpose in the *respondeo* corresponds to the fourth purpose in the verse, the second to the third, the third to the second, and the fourth to the first. Reversal is out of fashion today, perhaps because one needs a good memory to enjoy it. To St. Thomas's original readers, who had far better memory training, its cadence and anticadence would have been elegantly simple, like unrolling a carpet and then rolling it up. The reversal has the further merit of keeping the reader from thinking that the order in which St. Thomas discusses the four purposes corresponds to their order of importance. Sometimes he makes the order of presentation match the order of importance, but not always.

This particular Psalm is especially well chosen for St. Thomas's purposes in Question 91. The first three articles of the Question show how God's Providence is reflected in nature, while the last three articles show how it is reflected in Revelation. As we see in the following translation, the two halves of the Psalm reflect exactly the same dual purpose:[24]

The heavens are telling the glory of God; and the firmament proclaims his handiwork. Day to day pours forth speech, and night to night declares knowledge. There is no speech, nor are there words; their voice is not heard; yet their voice goes out through all the earth, and their words to the end of the world. In them he has set a tent for the sun, which comes forth like a bridegroom leaving his chamber, and like a strong man runs its

---

[23] The English translation gives the number of the psalm as 118:8, but this is a typo for 18:8. Adding to the confusion, most modern translations of the Bible list the verse as 19:7.

[24] Psalm 19 (RSV-CE), verse divisions suppressed.

Was a Divine Law Needed?

course with joy. Its rising is from the end of the heavens, and its circuit to the end of them; and there is nothing hid from its heat.

The law of the Lord is perfect, reviving the soul; the testimony of the Lord is sure, making wise the simple; the precepts of the Lord are right, rejoicing the heart; the commandment of the Lord is pure, enlightening the eyes; the fear of the Lord is clean, enduring for ever; the ordinances of the Lord are true, and righteous altogether. More to be desired are they than gold, even much fine gold; sweeter also than honey and drippings of the honeycomb. Moreover by them is thy servant warned; in keeping them there is great reward. But who can discern his errors? Clear thou me from hidden faults. Keep back thy servant also from presumptuous sins; let them not have dominion over me! Then I shall be blameless, and innocent of great transgression. Let the words of my mouth and the meditation of my heart be acceptable in thy sight, O Lord, my rock and my redeemer.

Reply to Objection 1. [1] *By the natural law the eternal law is participated proportionately to the capacity of human nature.* [2] *But to his supernatural end man needs to be directed in a yet higher way. Hence the additional law given by God, whereby man shares more perfectly in the eternal law.*

Reply to Objection 1. True, we already share in eternal law through the natural law. But this mode of sharing in eternal law is incomplete because it is limited by our natural powers; it can direct us only to our natural end, not to our supernatural end. To complete our participation in eternal law, we need additional instruction, which God provides through Divine law.

---

[1] The Objector had pointed out that through natural law man already shares in the eternal law. What the Objector overlooks is that every created being shares in the eternal law only in the mode that its nature makes possible. Although the rational mode in which humans share in it is far nobler than the irrational mode in which flatworms share in it, there remains an infinite gap between our minds and God's.

[2] However finite, our minds are certainly capable of working out that we *have* a supernatural end. They can even work out in a limited sense *what it is* – that it must lie in union with God, however inconceivable such union is to us. As we saw above, these conclusions can be drawn just from natural experience – from our longing for happiness, the insufficiency of created things to satisfy us, the fact that nature makes nothing in vain, and so on. The problem is that natural reason cannot *direct* us to union with God because none of our natural powers can achieve it. God must lift us beyond ourselves, so to speak, and only He can tell us how to hold onto the rope – what we must to do to cooperate with supernatural grace.

Reply to Objection 2. [1] *Counsel is a kind of inquiry: hence it must proceed from some principles.* [2] *Nor is it*

Reply to Objection 2. What does it really mean that man is left in the hands of his counsel? That he must look into the goal, inquire into what he must do, yes – but how does that work? All

enough for it to proceed from principles imparted by nature, which are the precepts of the natural law, for the reasons given above: [3] *but there is need for certain additional principles, namely, the precepts of the Divine law.*	seeking needs starting points to get it going and guide it in the right direction. As we have seen, the starting points for looking into our natural goal are implicit in our nature and contained in the commands of natural law. But natural law cannot provide the additional starting points needed for looking into our *supernatural* goal. For these, we need Divine law.

[1] The term "counsel" refers to conclusions of practical reasoning, as we have seen above. But we cannot reach conclusions without premises; we cannot get anywhere without starting somewhere.

[2] An inclination to seek those things we recognize as good and shun those things we recognize as evil is part of our natural equipment. As a principle of practical reason, it can be expressed as "good is that which all things seek after," and as a precept of law, "Good is to be done and pursued, and evil avoided" (I-II, Question 94, Article 2). If our minds didn't already know this, deliberation about what to do could never get started. It would never occur to us that there is something to deliberate about; we would not even grasp what deliberation is. The other starting points of practical reason are implanted in us in the same way, for we are designed with a view to seeking certain goods, in certain ways, in a certain order.

[3] Our natural inclinations get us started on the pursuit of temporal happiness, direct us for instance to make friends, to form families, and to pursue truth. That is fine so far as it goes, but it does not go far enough because our natural inclinations are insufficient to tell us how to reach our supernatural good. Divine law is needed after all.

Reply to Objection 3. Irrational creatures are not ordained to an end higher than that which is proportionate to their natural powers: consequently the comparison fails.	**Reply to Objection 3.** The Objector argues that since we are better equipped than irrational beings to direct ourselves, and *they* get by without Divine law, surely we don't need Divine law. But direction is always direction to some end. True, we are better equipped than irrational beings to direct ourselves to our *natural* end. But this is where the analogy breaks down because irrational creatures have *only* a natural end. We don't.

A plant is driven by automatic processes to take in nutrition, grow, and propagate; that is its natural end. An animal is prompted by instinct and sense perception to pursue its necessities and to procreate; that is its natural end. A man is guided by reason to seek not only the ease of the senses but the fulfillment of the rational soul – to live well as reason understands living well, which includes seeking the truth and living in communities patterned by it; that is *his* natural end. Is this the conclusion of the story? For plants, animals, and other irrational beings (viruses, procaryotes, what have you), it is. For us, it is not. The Objector is not mistaken about our excellent equipment; he is quite right about it. Granted reasonably favorable circumstances, if we do not attain temporal happiness, we have only ourselves to blame. Yet there is something more to be said, isn't there? All that satisfaction is strangely unsatisfying, and we find ourselves asking, "Is this all there is?" With our well-equipped minds, we can find out a great many truths, even the truth that we were made by an all-good and all-powerful Creator. Yet in its way, that knowledge is the most unsatisfying of all – for it is one thing to know *of* God, but quite another to *know God*. For knowing *of* God, our natural powers are enough. For *knowing God*, they fall infinitely short. All this is a hint that we were made not only for a natural end, like the irrational beings, but also for a supernatural end that transcends all our powers. So what that *they* have no need of Divine law? What has that to do with *us*?

DISCUSSION

The Relation between Natural and Divine law

How does Divine law differ from the natural law? Certainly there is a great deal of overlap. As we see later, St. Thomas holds that all the *moral* precepts of Divine law (to be distinguished from its judicial and ceremonial precepts) belong to the law of nature too, though "not all in the same way." As he explains,

> For there are certain things [in Divine law] which the natural reason of every man, of its own accord and at once, judges to be done or not to be done: e.g. "Honor thy father and thy mother," and "Thou shalt not kill, Thou shalt not steal": and these belong to the law of nature absolutely. And there are certain things which, after a more careful consideration, wise men deem obligatory. Such belong to the law of nature, yet so that they need to be inculcated, the wiser teaching the less wise: e.g. "Rise up before the hoary head, and honor the person of the aged man," and the like.[25]

Of course not everything in the natural law is promulgated by words in the Divine law; the task would be endless. But everything in the natural law is *presupposed* in Divine law. Consider, for example, the natural law principle that we owe gratitude to those who have done us great good. It is never explicitly stated in Divine law. Yet the words with which God prefaces the Decalogue, or Ten Commandments, "I am the Lord thy God, who brought thee out of the land of Egypt, out of the house of bondage,"[26] would make no sense

---

[25] Question 100, Article 1.
[26] Exodus 20:2.

unless the people knew the law of gratitude; the whole force of the statement is that because He saved them from slavery, *they owe it to Him to listen.*

According to centuries of custom, the first several commandments of the Decalogue, concerning our duties to God Himself, are called the First Tablet, and the rest of them, concerning our duties to our neighbors, who are made in God's image, are called the Second Tablet. Each of the examples of moral precepts St. Thomas gives above is from the Second Tablet. Do the precepts of the First Tablet also belong to the natural law? Certainly not all of them:

> And there are some things, to judge of which, human reason needs Divine instruction, whereby we are taught about the things of God: e.g. "Thou shalt not make to thyself a graven thing, nor the likeness of anything; Thou shalt not take the name of the Lord thy God in vain."[27]

On the other hand, St. Thomas makes clear that human reason can work out many things about God: not just that He exists but also that because He is the first source of all that is, we owe Him the special kind of honor called worship:

> Since virtue is directed to the good, wherever there is a special aspect of good, there must be a special virtue. Now the good to which religion is directed, is to give due honor to God. Again, honor is due to someone under the aspect of excellence: and to God a singular excellence is competent, since He infinitely surpasses all things and exceeds them in every way. Wherefore to Him is special honor due: even as in human affairs we see that different honor is due to different personal excellences, one kind of honor to a father, another to the king, and so on.[28]

It seems then that the underlying moral principles of the First Tablet, as well as their implications, can be worked out by human reason and belong to natural law. These include the principle that God and only God is to be worshipped as God. Why then does St. Thomas say that about certain other precepts concerning God, we need Divine instruction? For at least two reasons.

One reason – to anticipate a distinction we have so far only mentioned but discuss in detail later on – is that some precepts are "determinations" of natural law rather than "conclusions" from it. "Determination" occurs when more than one way of doing things might have been compatible with the underlying principles, and public authority – in this case, God's own authority – settles which of them is to be followed. The prohibition of making visible images of the invisible God seems to be a precept of this kind. For on the one hand natural reason alone, even without Revelation, is able to work out that God is both real and invisible; but on the other hand it does not follow *as a conclusion from premises* that He may not be worshipped with visible images. He might, for example, have been worshipped with visible images that have a symbolic rather than a literal intent. God, then, seems to have chosen this mode of worship

---

[27] Ibid.
[28] II-II, Q. 81, Art. 4.

Was a Divine Law Needed?

from among several possible modes, perhaps to keep the Hebrew people from falling back into the ways of their idolatrous neighbors. The bearing of this ordinance changes with the Incarnation, of course, because the Son of God visibly assumed human nature.

Another reason is that some precepts concern not our natural but our supernatural end, and these exceed what natural reason could have worked out by itself. Only with the additional data of Revelation, made available by faith, do they become evident to our natural powers of reason. Only Divine law tells us about the inward grace that flows to man from the Holy Spirit, through faith, without which we cannot reach the supernatural destiny that God has appointed for us. Only Divine law instructs us in the outward acts that God has chosen as channels through which that grace is poured.[29]

---

[29] Question 108, Article 1.

QUESTION 91, ARTICLE 5

Whether There Is but One Divine Law?

TEXT	PARAPHRASE
Whether there is but one Divine law?	Are the laws of the Old and New Testament different kinds of Divine law, or merely repetitions of the same Divine law?

How many editions of Divine law are there? St. Thomas is not merely floating the notion of there being more than one as an abstract possibility. Had that been his intention, he would have followed Article 2 with an Article asking "Whether there is but one natural law?" and Article 3 with an Article asking "Whether there is but one human law?" Rather, the *utrum* is posed against the background of the tradition that there *is* more than one Divine law – the law of the Old Testament, called the Old Law, given to the chosen nation, the Jews, and the law of the New Testament, called the New Law or the Law of the Gospel, given to the Church. One might hold that there could not have been two laws because God would have done just as He intended to do the first time; this is a common protest from Muslims. One might also hold that the Old Law and the New Law are not two different laws, but two different promulgations of the same law. Is this the case? Or are they somehow different?

Objection 1. [1] *It would seem that there is but one Divine law. Because, where there is one king in one kingdom there is but one law.* [2] *Now the whole of mankind is compared to God as to one king, according to Ps. 46: "God is the King of all the earth." Therefore there is but one Divine law.*	Objection 1. Apparently, the answer to the query is no. Even in earthly government, we see that a single kingdom has a single king and a single law. Psalm 47 suggests that the entire human race is one kingdom, and God its one king. It follows that the Divine law is its one law.

[1] St. Thomas emphasizes the need for unity of rule in his practical work, *On Kingship*:

[S]everal persons could by no means preserve the stability of the community if they totally disagreed. For union is necessary among them if they are to rule at all: several

Does Divine Law Come in One Edition, or in Two, Old and New?

men, for instance, could not pull a ship in one direction unless joined together in some fashion. Now several are said to be united according as they come closer to being one. So one man rules better than several who come near being one.[1]

He is not, by the way, claiming that the head of human government should rule absolutely. As we see later, he argues that the best form of human rule is partly monarchy, partly aristocracy, and partly democracy.

[2] Psalm 47:8 (in the Vulgate, 46:8) declares in parallel half-verses "God reigns over the nations; God sits on his holy throne." The English translation of the Objector's remark about the verse, "the whole of mankind is compared to God as to one king," is misleading because it seems to us to suggest that mankind is being compared with God. I prefer Freddoso's rendering of the line, "the whole human race is related to God as to a single king."[2]

Notice how the analogy works. We do not *project* what we see in earthly kingship onto God; He is the one true King, from whom all earthly kings take their name.

Objection 2. [1] Further, every law is directed to the end which the lawgiver intends for those for whom he makes the law. [2] But God intends one and the same thing for all men; since according to 1 Tim. 2: "He will have all men to be saved, and to come to the knowledge of the truth." Therefore there is but one Divine law.	Objection 2. Moreover, different kinds of laws are distinguished according to the purposes intended by the legislator in making them. But as we see in St. Paul's first letter to Timothy, God's purpose does not vary; he intends the same thing, salvation, for everyone. Since all of God's law has the same intended purpose, it is all the same law.

---

[1] We know from Question 90, Article 2 that the end or purpose of all genuine law is the common good of those ruled. Law is an ordinance of reason, for the *common* good, made by competent public authority, and promulgated, or made known.

[2] The biblical idiom of *salvation* refers to deliverance or safety; to be saved is to be rescued or redeemed from some great peril or danger. The Bible speaks of being saved or delivered from slavery or captivity, enemies, violence, extinction, trouble, temptation, unrighteousness, guilt, punishment, and death, both physical or spiritual.[3] In the passage St. Thomas cites, which is 1 Timothy 2:4,

---

[1] Thomas Aquinas, *De Regno: On Kingship, to the King of Cyprus*, translated by Gerald B. Phelan, revised by Thomas Eschmann, reedited by Joseph Kenny (Toronto: Pontifical Institute of Mediaeval Studies, 1949).
[2] Thomas Aquinas, *Treatise on Law: The Complete Text*, translated by Alfred J. Freddoso (South Bend, IN: St. Augustine's Press, 2009), p. 15.
[3] Exodus 6:6, Jeremiah 30:10, Psalm 18:3, 2 Samuel 22:3, 2 Kings 14:27, Psalms 37:39, Proverbs 2:16, Isaiah 45:8, Psalm 51:14, Joshua 22:31, Psalm 68:20, and James 5:20.

St. Paul is thinking of rescue from spiritual death and futility, so that instead of eternal exile, one may experience the eternal joy of His presence.

> *Objection 3.* [1] *Further, the Divine law seems to be more akin to the eternal law, which is one, than the natural law, according as the Revelation of grace is of a higher order than natural knowledge.* [2] *Therefore much more is the Divine law but one.*

Objection 3. Still further, although Divine law and natural law both come from eternal law, the former is closer to eternal law than the latter is. For consider how much higher the revealed knowledge of grace is than the knowledge imparted by nature! So if even natural law is one, how much greater the reason to think that Divine law is one.

[1] The knowledge in the mind of God Himself is more exalted than the knowledge human beings can attain through Revelation, which in turn is more exalted than the knowledge they can attain through their created powers of reasoning. For this reason, the Objector suggests that eternal law is a closer neighbor to Divine law than it is to natural law.

[2] With the tacit premises restored, the argument works like this:

1. God is in the highest degree one.[4]
2. Since God is not composed of different things,[5] God is one with His knowledge; so His knowledge is one.
3. Since eternal law lies in His knowledge, eternal law is one.
4. Now the more a law is like eternal law, the greater the reason we have to think it too is one.
5. Since Divine law is even more like eternal law than natural law is, there is even greater reason to think Divine law is one than to think natural law is one.
6. Yet even natural law is one. So Divine law *must* be one.

> *On the contrary,* [1] *The Apostle says, in Hebrews 7: "The priesthood being translated, it is necessary that a translation also be made of the law."* [2] *But the priesthood is twofold, as stated in the same passage, viz. the Levitical priesthood, and the priesthood of Christ. Therefore the Divine law is twofold, namely the Old Law and the New Law.*

On the other hand, the Apostle[6] teaches in his letter to the Hebrews that "when there is a change in the priesthood, there is necessarily a change in the [Divine] law as well."[7] But as he teaches a little later in the same letter, there *has* been a change in the priesthood: although the Hebrew people were served by the Levitical priesthood, the Church is served by the priesthood of Christ. Since there were two priesthoods, old and new, there must be two Divine laws, Old Law and New Law.

---

[4] St. Thomas has established this in I, Question 11, Articles 2 and 3.
[5] I, Q. 3, Art. 7.
[6] Normally St. Thomas reserves this respectful title for St. Paul, whom he probably considers the author of the letter, a view that is no longer generally held.
[7] Hebrews 7:12 (RSV-CE).

[1] The reason why a change in the priesthood necessitates a change in Divine law is that Divine law *institutes* priesthood and contains its rules, and the reason why Divine law does these things is that the priest is a *mediator* between man and God.

[2] Christ, who is both truly man and truly God, is the true and perfect mediator between man and God. The priests of the Levitical priesthood – the priesthood ordained in the book of Leviticus – offered gifts and sacrifices for sins, but these actions merely symbolized and foreshadowed Christ's gift and sacrifice of Himself. The meaning of the change in the priesthood is that when Christ, the reality that the Levitical priesthood symbolized and foreshadowed, finally came, the symbol and shadow was retired.

The meaning of Christ's sacrifice may be obscure to those who are not of St. Thomas's faith. Brutally condensing, it may be explained as follows. To be acceptable to God, we need to put to death the sinful and selfish things we have made of ourselves. This is the price of our rebellion; we truly owe it, but just because we are so sinful and selfish, we are unable to pay it. In lovingly offering Himself for our sins, Christ offered on our behalf the perfect sacrifice that we cannot. If we are united with Him – as we are in the Church, the Body of which He is the Head – then we are united with His sacrifice too. Thus, through His death we can die to our sins, and through His resurrection we can experience new life, the kind He intends for us. In this connection, St. Thomas refers to St. Augustine of Hippo's work *On the Trinity*, book IV, chapter 14, where Augustine writes,

And what could be so acceptably offered and taken, as the flesh of our sacrifice, made the body of our priest? In such wise that, whereas four things are to be considered in every sacrifice – to whom it is offered, by whom it is offered, what is offered, for whom it is offered, – the same One and true Mediator Himself, reconciling us to God by the sacrifice of peace, might remain one with Him to whom He offered, might make those one in Himself for whom He offered, Himself might be in one both the offerer and the offering.[8]

I answer that, [1] *As stated in the First Part, distinction is the cause of number.* [2] *Now things may be distinguished in two ways. First, as those things that are altogether specifically different, e.g. a horse and an ox. Secondly, as*	Here is my response. I explained much earlier in the *Summa* that how many things of a given kind there are depends on the differences or distinctions among them. There are two ways to make distinctions. One way is to indicate that one species, such as *horse*, is different from another species, such as *ox*. The other way is to indicate that an incompletely developed member of a

---

[8] St. Thomas's allusion is in III, Q. 48, Art. 3, "Whether Christ's Passion operated by way of sacrifice?" I am taking the English text of Augustine's words in *On the Trinity* from www.newadvent.org/fathers/130104.htm.

perfect and imperfect in the same species, e.g. a boy and a man: and in this way the Divine law is divided into Old and New. [3] *Hence the Apostle in Galatians 3 compares the state of man under the Old Law to that of a child* [4] *"under a pedagogue"; but the state under the New Law, to that of a full grown man, who is "no longer under a pedagogue."*

species, such as *boy,* is different from a fully developed member of the same species, such as *man.* There really are two Divine laws, but the difference between them is of the latter kind, not the former; they are not different species, but incomplete and complete members of the same species. St. Paul has the same idea. That is why his letter to the Galatians says that people under the Old Law were like children being led to school by their custodian, but that people under the New Law are like adults who no longer need a custodian because they have already arrived.

[1] The idea that "distinction is the cause of number" seems obscure, but it is really very simple. If there is no distinction to be made, we speak of one thing; if there is one distinction to be made, we speak of two things; two distinctions, and we speak of three; and so on. The reference is to I, Question 30, Article 3.

[2] "Imperfect" means "incomplete" or "not fully developed." To say that the Old Law was imperfect does not mean that there was a flaw in it, so that God could have done better. The Old Law was perfectly adapted to an as yet immature people.

[3] St. Thomas speaks of the state of man in general. Initially the chosen nation was like the Gentiles; through centuries of Divine instruction, it gradually became more mature.

[4] In English, the word "pedagogue" means teacher. But the Greek word that it comes from, *paidagogos,* literally "boy-leader," refers to a custodian – a servant who accompanies the children at all times, makes them behave and mind their manners, and sees to it that at the right time, they get safely to the real teacher, who instructs them in his home. St. Paul explains in Galatians 3:23-26 that the Old Law – the law of Moses – acted as the custodian who escorted the people of Israel to the teacher, Christ. When he says that the people under the New Law no longer need a custodian, he is not saying that they no longer need a *teacher,* but rather that they no longer need to be *led* to the teacher because they are already in His presence.

[5] *Now the perfection and imperfection of these two laws is to be taken in connection with the three conditions pertaining to law, as stated above.* [6] *For, in the first place, it belongs to law to be directed to the common good as to its end, as stated above. This good may be twofold. It may be a*

The completeness of the New Law, and the incompleteness of the Old, can be seen in three ways. First, as we saw in Question 90, Article 2, every true law's purpose is to guide us to the common good. But the expression "common good" may be taken in two senses, one lower and one higher. It may refer to a good of the earthly life, something experienced by the senses – or it

sensible and earthly good; and to this, man was directly ordained by the Old Law: [6] *wherefore, at the very outset of the law [in Exodus 3], the people were invited to the earthly kingdom of the Chananaeans.* [7] *Again it may be an intelligible and heavenly good: and to this, man is ordained by the New Law.* [8] *Wherefore, at the very beginning of His preaching, Christ invited men to the kingdom of heaven, saying (Matthew 4:17): "Do penance, for the kingdom of heaven is at hand."* [9] *Hence Augustine says (Contra Faust. iv) that "promises of temporal goods are contained in the Old Testament, for which reason it is called old; but the promise of eternal life belongs to the New Testament."*

may refer to a good of the heavenly life, something experienced by the mind. The Old Law set the Hebrew people on the path to the former sort of good; from the moment the Old Law was first promulgated to them, God invited them into the earthly kingdom that had previously been held by the Canaanites. But the New Law set the people on the path to the latter sort of good; from the moment he first began to preach, Christ invited men into His heavenly kingdom, telling them to turn away from their sins and be converted because the kingdom of heaven is near and easily reached. St. Augustine gives the same explanation in his book *Against Faustus*. There he remarks that the Old Testament is called *old* because its promises have been surpassed by the New; the former promised only the goods of this life, while the latter promises life eternal.

[5] The translation "three conditions pertaining to law" gives the impression that St. Thomas is speaking of the elements in the definition of law – the conditions that must be satisfied for a supposed law to be truly lawful. But as we saw earlier, there are *four* such elements, not three: law is an ordinance of reason, for the common good, made by competent public authority, and promulgated. So why the discrepancy? The solution to the riddle is that there is no discrepancy. The Latin, *tria quae*, does not mean "three conditions" for law, but "three things" about law. Only one of the "three things" St. Thomas mentions is taken from the four elements in law's definition.

[6] As to this "sensible and earthly good," St. Thomas is probably thinking of the words spoken after the Old Law was given to the people, which read in part,

If you obey the commandments of the Lord your God which I command you this day, by loving the Lord your God, by walking in his ways, and by keeping his commandments and his statutes and his ordinances, then you shall live and multiply, and the Lord your God will bless you in the land which you are entering to take possession of it. But if your heart turns away, and you will not hear, but are drawn away to worship other gods and serve them, I declare to you this day, that you shall perish; you shall not live long in the land which you are going over the Jordan to enter and possess. I call heaven and earth to witness against you this day, that I have set before you life and death, blessing and curse; therefore choose life, that you and your descendants may live[.][9]

---

[9] Deuteronomy 30:15–20, quoting 16–19.

[7] In Exodus 3:16–17 (RSV-CE) God instructs Moses as follows:

Go and gather the elders of Israel together, and say to them, "The Lord, the God of your fathers, the God of Abraham, of Isaac, and of Jacob, has appeared to me, saying, 'I have observed you and what has been done to you in Egypt; and I promise that I will bring you up out of the affliction of Egypt, to the land of the Canaanites, the Hittites, the Amorites, the Perizzites, the Hivites, and the Jebusites, a land flowing with milk and honey.'"

[8] The intelligible and heavenly good to which St. Thomas is referring is epitomized by the words of Christ, for example "Repent, for the kingdom of heaven is at hand." To the same effect is the Beatitude, "Blessed are the pure in heart, for they shall see God."[10] St. Paul speaks of the same heavenly good when he exclaims, "For now we see in a mirror dimly, but then face to face. Now I know in part; then I shall understand fully, even as I have been fully understood."[11]

In the DRA, the wording of Christ's exhortation is not "Repent" but "Do penance." This is a mistranslation, for the Latin, like the Greek, actually means "repent." However, the two meanings are inseparable, for to repent is to turn sorrowfully from sin, and to do penance is to show the sorrow of repentance by performing an act that symbolizes this repentance and cooperates with God's grace in the mending of the heart.

[9] The expressions "eternal life" and "kingdom of heaven" refer to the superabundant life that is the blessed experience of union with God. Although it culminates in heaven, St. Thomas holds that Christ's followers have a foretaste of this in the life of faith. As he remarks about Hebrews 11:1, "faith is said to be the 'substance of things to be hoped for,' for the reason that in us the first beginning of things to be hoped for is brought about by the assent of faith, which contains virtually [*virtute*, in potentiality] all things to be hoped for."[12]

---

[10] *Secondly, it belongs to the law to direct human acts according to the order of righteousness (4):* [11] *wherein also the New Law surpasses the Old Law, since it directs our internal acts,* [12] *according to Mt. 5:20: "Unless your justice abound more than that of the Scribes and Pharisees, you shall*

As we saw in the previous Article, another feature of the way law guides us is that it changes *how* we act, uplifting and purifying our motives so that we are not only externally but internally upright – so that we become thoroughly just, wholly virtuous people. In this respect, the New Law goes much farther than the Old because it instructs us not only in outward acts but also in the inward movements of the heart. This is what Christ meant when He taught His followers that

---

[10] Matthew 4:17, 5:8 (RSV-CE).
[11] 1 Corinthians 13:12 (RSV-CE).
[12] II-II, Q. 4, Art. 1.

not enter into the kingdom of heaven." [13] Hence the saying that *"the Old Law restrains the hand, but the New Law controls the mind" (Sentent. iii, D. xl).*	they could not share in His heavenly kingdom unless their justice surpassed even the justice of the experts in the law of Moses and the members of the strict Pharisees. As Peter Lombard put it in his *Sentences*, "The Old Law regulates the hand, the New the rational soul."

[10] The term *iustitiae*, translated as "righteousness," refers to the wholly just and lawful, to the complete rightness or integrity which is pleasing to God. "According to the order of righteousness" means "in accordance with righteousness" or "directed by righteousness."

[11] Although at many points the Old Law seems to direct interior acts – for example, forbidding the interior act of covetousness and commanding the interior act of love – St. Thomas thinks that on closer consideration the Old Law turns out to have been commanding the exterior acts of these virtues, not the virtues themselves. We will consider his view of this matter more closely later on – both defending and qualifying the claim.

[12] The Scribes were a professional class. They were not just copyists but legal experts who applied themselves to the detailed requirements of the Old Law. The Pharisees were a rigorist sect which believed in both the written and the oral Law and emphasized strict observance. Christ was not demanding an even more punctilious *external* observance than theirs, but a transformation of the heart: "Woe to you, scribes and Pharisees, hypocrites! for you tithe mint and dill and cumin, and have neglected the weightier matters of the law, justice and mercy and faith; these you ought to have done, without neglecting the others. You blind guides, straining out a gnat and swallowing a camel!"[13] To "tithe" is to give a tenth of, as directed by the Old Law.

[13] St. Thomas takes the saying that the Old Law regulates the hand but not the soul from a passage in the *Sentences* of Peter Lombard about the Old Law's prohibition of coveting. Lombard writes as follows:

Why the law is said to restrain the hand, but not the soul. But since here the desire of another's wife and another's thing is forbidden, why is the Law said to restrain the hand, but not the soul, while the Gospel restrains both? – *Solution.* That is said of the law in regard to the ceremonial mandates, not in regard to the moral ones. Or because in the Law there is not the same general prohibition of all death-dealing desire, as there is in the Gospel.[14]

As we see, St. Thomas takes the saying in the second of the two senses Peter Lombard considers plausible. Later on, he returns to the question of whether the Old Law directed the manner in which its precepts were to be followed.

---

[13] Matthew 23:23–24 (RSV-CE).
[14] Peter Lombard, *The Sentences*, translated by Giulio Silano (Toronto: Pontifical Institute of Mediaeval Studies, 2008), book III, distinction 40, chapter 1 (p. 169).

| [14] Thirdly, it belongs to the law to induce men to observe its commandments. [15] This the Old Law did by the fear of punishment: but the New Law, by love, which is poured into our hearts by the grace of Christ, bestowed in the New Law, but foreshadowed in the Old. [16] Hence Augustine says (Contra Adimant. Manich. discip. xvii) that "there is little difference between the Law and the Gospel – fear [timor] and love [amor]."[15] | Finally, the law persuades people to *carry out* what it commands. The Old Law persuaded by fear of punishment; the New Law persuades by love. This love is infused into our hearts by Christ as an undeserved gift. Although the Old Law looked forward to it, expressing its anticipation by way of symbols, the New Law actually confers it. In his book *Against Adimantus, a Disciple of Manichaeus*, St. Augustine expresses the difference in a pun: "There is only a small difference between the [Old] Law and the [New Law of the] Gospel – the two-letter difference between *timor* and *amor*, fear and love." |

[14] This recalls the rough and ready definition of law from Question 90, Article 1, which St. Thomas then goes on to unpack into the four conditions we have seen. This rough and ready definition is that "Law is a rule and measure of acts, whereby man is induced to act or is restrained from acting."

[15] In a certain type of symbolism, something that comes earlier, usually called the *type*, foreshadows or prefigures something higher that comes later, usually called the *antitype*. The Old Testament contains numerous prophesies about the coming of the Messiah (translated as "Christ"), but Christian tradition holds that many things even in the nonprophetic parts of the Old Testament anticipate the New. For instance, the sanctuary of the ancient Jewish Temple is a *type* or foreshadowing of heaven, the Old Testament sacrifice of animals is a *type* or foreshadowing of the sacrifice of the Messiah, and the mysterious priest of God, Melchizedek, who ministers to Abraham centuries before the institution of the Levitical priesthood, is a *type* or foreshadowing of Christ Himself. St. Thomas holds that this typological relationship holds between the Old Law as a whole and the New Law as a whole.

[16] By "Law," St. Augustine means the Old Law, and by "Gospel" he means the New Law.[16] Readers of some Protestant traditions may object to the fact that St. Thomas describes the Gospel in terms of *law*, but apparently Christ had no hesitation in doing so. At the Passover meal he shared with his disciples before His death, He announced, "A new commandment I give to you, that you love one another; even as I have loved you, that you also love one another."[17] To someone who objects, "That is grace, not law," St. Thomas would reply

---

[15] I have reworked the interpolations. The Dominican Fathers translation somewhat confusingly renders the passage as "there is little difference between the Law and the Gospel – fear and love," phrasing that does not work in English, inserting the parenthetical explanation, "The 'little difference' refers to the Latin words 'timor' and 'amor' – 'fear' and 'love.'"

[16] We return to this passage in I-II, Q. 100, Art. 7.

[17] John 13:34 (RSV-CE).

Does Divine Law Come in One Edition, or in Two, Old and New? 31

that it is the law that describes the very life of grace. For although grace is offered freely, there is no way to receive it except by cooperating with it, by letting it pass into us, and this is done by loving one another in the way we are loved by Christ.

Here and elsewhere in Question 91, St. Thomas almost gives the impression that the Old Law had nothing to say about love, and that the New Law had nothing to say about fear. He is perfectly aware that this is not the case, and in other places he writes to forestall such a view. However, we must remember that in Question 91 he is giving only a quick preview of topics he will discuss in greater detail later on. In Question 108 he takes up the objection that the New and Old Laws cannot be distinguished with reference to fear and love, because even the Old Law included such precepts as "Thou shalt love thy neighbor" and "Thou shalt love the Lord thy God."[18] Though St. Thomas concedes the importance of these precepts to the Old Law, he insists nonetheless that between Old Law and New Law there is a radical shift in orientation. In the Old Law even the precepts of love were backed up by fear of penalties, penalties which were tangible and belonged to this life; although people were commanded to perform the *exterior acts* of love, few people would have been performing them *because of the interior virtue* of love. By contrast, in the New Law the motive for performing the acts of love is love itself. To be sure, the New Law promises rewards and threatens penalties, but even these concern love: For what does it mean to enjoy eternal life? Simply to be united with God, who *is* love, and who is loved for His own sake. And what does it mean to be damned? Simply to be separated from that God forever.

St. Thomas adds in Question 107 that even so, some people mentioned in the Old Testament were moved by love, "and in this respect," he says, "they belonged to the New Law." In the same way, some people mentioned in the New Testament were *not* moved by love, and these people had to be moved by fear of punishment and by promises of things in this life. Quoting St. Paul in Romans 5:5, he concludes, "But although the Old Law contained precepts of [love], nevertheless it did not confer the Holy Ghost by Whom '[love] ... is spread abroad in our hearts.'"[19]

| *Reply to Objection 1. As the father of a family issues different commands to the children and to the adults, so also the one King, God, in His one kingdom, gave one law to men, while they were yet imperfect, and another more* | Reply to Objection 1. From the fact that there is a single realm and a single ruler, it does not follow that there must be a single law. Do we say "One family, one father, one directive"? No, for the father directs the children of the household in one way but directs the adults in another. In the same way, we should not say "One kingdom, one king, one law," for the one King, God, in His one |

---

[18] Question 108, Article 1, Obj. 2 and ad 2. The internal references are to Leviticus 19:18 and Deuteronomy 6:5.
[19] Question 107, Article 1, ad 2.

> *perfect law, when, by the preceding law, they had been led to a greater capacity for Divine things.*

> kingdom, mankind, gave one law to men when they were spiritually immature, in order to prepare them, by this means, for another, more complete law, when they were ready to take it in.

Just to forestall confusion, we should notice that St. Thomas is careful to say that although household regulations really are commands or injunctions, they are not laws in the strict sense. As he explains in Question 90, Article 3, "he that governs a family can indeed make certain commands or ordinances, but not such as to have properly the force of law." This is because although the family does have a certain authority of its own, which must not be taken away, nevertheless it is not the whole community.

> *Reply to Objection 2.* [1] *The salvation of man could not be achieved otherwise than through Christ, according to Acts 4:12: "There is no other name ... given to men, whereby we must be saved."* [2] *Consequently the law that brings all to salvation could not be given until after the coming of Christ. But before His coming it was necessary to give to the people, of whom Christ was to be born, a law containing certain rudiments of righteousness unto salvation, in order to prepare them to receive Him.*

> Reply to Objection 2. The Objector is right to say that God's unchanging purpose in all law is to lead men to salvation, but salvation is brought about only through Christ. Obviously, the New Law, which leads people to Christ, could not be promulgated until Christ came. Even so, the Old Law was not useless; it *prepared* them to receive Christ by starting them on the road to the consummate integrity of salvation.

[1] St. Thomas does not disagree with the Objector's view that all Divine law must be one in purpose; he only points out that to achieve this one purpose, people in different spiritual conditions must be governed in somewhat different ways. To say that men can be saved by no other name than Christ is to say that men can be saved only through appeal to the One who is *truly called* the Messiah or Christ. The reason no other means but these suffice is that Christ took the burden of human sin and guilt upon Himself to accomplish what we could not accomplish for ourselves.

[2] In Latin, the term *rudimenta*, rudiments, refers to the beginnings or first attempts at something. Holding back from adultery and murder, performing the outward acts of love, limiting revenge to "an eye for an eye and a tooth for a tooth" – such things were beginnings, but the New Law goes much further. Not only adultery and murder but also lustful fantasy and murderous anger are forbidden. Revenge is not just limited but banned. Men are commanded to perform the acts of love not only toward neighbors but even toward enemies.[20]

---

[20] Old Law: Exodus 20:13–14 (cf. Deuteronomy 5:17–18), Exodus 21:23–24, Leviticus 19:18. New Law: Matthew 5:21–22, 27–28, 43–45.

Does Divine Law Come in One Edition, or in Two, Old and New?

The meaning of "receiving" Christ is epitomized by St. Paul's statement that "I have been crucified with Christ; it is no longer I who live, but Christ who lives in me; and the life I now live in the flesh I live by faith in the Son of God, who loved me and gave himself for me."[21] This is a fundamental reorientation of life, requiring our cooperation with the grace of God.

Reply to Objection 3. [1] *The natural law directs man by way of certain general precepts, common to both the perfect and the imperfect: wherefore it is one and the same for all.* [2] *But the Divine law directs man also in certain particular matters, to which the perfect and imperfect do not stand in the same relation. Hence the necessity for the Divine law to be twofold, as already explained.*

Reply to Objection 3. The reason there is only one natural law is that the general rules by which it steers us are the same for everyone, both mature and immature. But the Divine law includes not only general rules but also instructions about certain details of conduct that are *not* the same for everyone; the mature and immature must be directed differently, and so they need two different laws.

---

[1] The natural law directs the spiritually immature and the spiritually mature by the same rules. People in both conditions should pay honor to their parents; people in both conditions should abstain from stealing; and so on.

[2] Perhaps the most conspicuous example of a difference between how the Old Law directs the spiritually immature and how the New Law directs the spiritually mature lies in the ordinances for matrimony. The Old Law explicitly allowed men to divorce their wives "because of the hardness of their hearts"; as St. Thomas suggests, if they had not been allowed to divorce them, they would have killed them. But the New Law reveals that in its very nature, matrimony is indissoluble.[22]

DISCUSSION

Revelation – Says Who?

A student in one of my classes insisted one day that when St. Thomas speaks of Divine law, he means "one's own Divine law": Torah for Jews, the Gospel for Christians, Shari'a for Muslims, Sheilaism for Sheila,[23] whatever it may be.

---

[21] Galatians 2:20 (RSV-CE).
[22] The Old Law on divorce: Deuteronomy 24:1–4. The New Law on divorce: Matthew 5:31–32, 19:3–12. St. Thomas on the danger of wife murder: S. T., Supp., 67, Article 6; *Summa Contra Gentiles*, III, chapter 123. We return to this matter later.
[23] In his book *Habits of the Heart: Individualism and Commitment in American Life* (1985; Berkeley: University of California Press, 2008), p. 221, sociologist Robert N. Bellah reports his interview with a young nurse he calls "Sheila," who received a lot of therapy, made up her own religion, and actually named it after herself: "My own Sheilaism." The term "Sheilaism" is now used generically for personally invented mix-and-match religions.

She was quite offended by the suggestion that this is not what St. Thomas has in mind.

But it isn't. What St. Thomas means by Divine law is what *really is* Divine law. Whether he is right about the authenticity of Christian Revelation is not a matter of indifference. If a purported Revelation is not really from God – if it is merely a product of the human mind that imagines that it is from God – then it is wholly incapable of instructing us about matters that transcend what natural reason can work out for itself. It is worse than a harmless mistake; it is a blind guide. As St. Paul writes, "If for this life only we have hoped in Christ, we are of all men most to be pitied."[24]

Now the various purported revelations (there aren't many, for only a few of the world religions claim Divine Revelation in actual historical time) cannot all be from God because they disagree with each other. There is no "your truth" and "my truth" for St. Thomas; we inhabit the same reality whether we like it or not. What then is his judgment? That the Old Law, given to the chosen nation, is truly from God, but preparatory, and that the New Law, given to the Church, is truly from God, and is its fulfillment. It follows that even if Shari'a included some good things – after all, even the pagans knew some good things, so there is no reason why it could not – nevertheless, it is a regression from that fulfillment, and it is not from God.

If St. Thomas is right that the truth about Revelation is simply a matter of fact – like the fact that the nucleus of an atom really does contain protons, or that gravity really is weaker than electromagnetism – then there is no reason for anyone to be offended by this fact. Suppose we are at the buffet, and Gertrude is about to dip into the tuna salad. Felix says, "Better not. The last three people who ate it got sick." Gertrude replies, "Stop judging me!" Is her response reasonable? Of course not, because the truth about the tuna salad is not about personal preferences; it is about how things stand in reality. Even if Felix is mistaken about the tuna salad, he has not offered Gertrude an insult. In fact, he has exercised concern for her. *She needed to know* that the tuna salad might be spoiled.

Someone might say, "The analogy with tuna salad is nonsense because we can know something about tuna salad but we cannot know anything about God." Why can't we? If the agnostic says that religious truth is especially resistant to rational inquiry, he contradicts himself, for to know God's rational unknowability would be to know something about Him. Indeed, it would be to know a great deal about Him. First one would have to know that even if He exists, He is infinitely remote, because otherwise one could not be so sure that knowledge about Him were rationally inaccessible. Second one would have to know that even if He exists, He is unconcerned with human beings, because otherwise one would expect Him to have provided the means for humans to

---

[24] 1 Corinthians 15:19 (RSV-CE).

know Him. Finally one would have to know that even if He exists, He is completely unlike the biblical portrayal of Him, because in that portrayal He does care about us, and has already provided such means, not only through Revelation but even, in part, through the order of creation itself. So, in the end, the so-called agnostic must claim to know quite a number of things about God just to prop up his claim to not knowing anything about God. The problem is that, on his assumptions, he cannot rationally justify any of these things. If he really knows nothing about God, then he does not know any of those things that allow him to assert that he knows nothing about God.

The hypothetical someone may go on, "But even if we *can* know a good many things about God by rational inquiry, as St. Thomas claims, we cannot know what to make of purported revelations, which go beyond rational inquiry." But we can.

In the first place we can say something negative. Any purported revelation that *contradicts* what reason can tell us must be false. For example, we must not believe a religion which denies the unity of God's wisdom and goodness, any more than we may believe a religion which denies that two things equal to a third thing are equal to each other. As St. Thomas explains, though these truths of reason are not articles of faith, they are "preambles" to the articles, "for faith presupposes natural knowledge, even as grace presupposes nature, and perfection supposes something that can be perfected."[25]

In the second place, even about teachings to which we cannot apply philosophical reasoning we can apply historical reasoning. For example, we can ask whether the original witnesses to God's alleged revelatory deeds are credible.

In the third place, even in cases in which an alleged revelation goes beyond the matters we could have figured out without it, even so we should expect it, if authentic, to provide deeper insight into these matters. And so we can apply a test: Does it? Christian faith forbids "putting God to the test" in the sense of presumption, but in another sense, it encourages it. The psalmist of the Old Testament implores, "O taste and see that the Lord is good!" St. Paul instructs, "Do not despise prophesying, but test everything; hold fast what is good."[26]

Suppose, then, that I live *as though* I believed the New Law. I ardently try to follow it; I live, pray, and worship as it directs; I rely utterly on the grace of Christ that is said to make this possible; I seek Him with all my heart; and I say to Him, "If you are real, you may have me." What happens?

By No Other Name than Christ?

In the Reply to Objection 2, St. Thomas quotes St. Paul's statement that "There is no other name ... given to men, whereby we must be saved." Indeed the

---

[25] I, Question 2, Article 2, ad 1.
[26] Psalm 34:8, 1 Thessalonians 5:21 (RSV-CE).

Church has always taught that we cannot be "saved" – meaning rescued from our alienation from God and reconciled with Him – except through Christ, who died for us. This doctrine cannot be abandoned.

But it does not necessarily follow that we must *explicitly* place our faith in Christ to be saved through Christ. That is a much more difficult question. According to St. Thomas, the holy people of Old Testament times were saved through Christ even though they lived centuries before Christ was born and did not know of Him.[27] With the Angelic Doctor, the Church has always believed that these holy people were saved not apart from Christ and His Church, but because, in some sense, they placed their faith *implicitly* in the Christ whom they were expecting but did not know, and were implicitly in communion with His Church.

This raises the question of whether others too – even in our times – could be saved through implicit faith.

The Church does not hurry her deliberations about such questions. However, because of the mercy of God, some version of the yes answer seems increasingly plausible to most of the thinkers in St. Thomas's tradition. Yet the possibility that implicit faith might suffice for salvation provokes several subsidiary questions. One, of course, is what would count as placing one's faith implicitly in Christ. Another is why – if implicit faith might suffice – evangelization is necessary at all, for it may seem that there is no need to share the faith with others. Let us consider these questions one at a time.

As to the first: Although the answer is far from clear, at least something can be said about what would *not* suffice for salvation. In an interview, Pope Emeritus Benedict XVI rejects the "anonymous Christian" hypothesis offered by the theologian Karl Rahner, according to which placing one's faith implicitly in Christ involves no more than subjectively accepting one's self, or perhaps making some kind of existential choice for good over evil.[28]

Why was Rahner wrong? One reason seems to be that no one chooses against himself as such. It is one thing for me to be for myself as what I really am, a child of God made in His image, but, as Benedict suggests, it is another for me to be for whatever I take myself to be. Even Satan was "for himself" in this distorted sense. A second reason is that no one chooses evil as such. In fact, no one commits any sin except for the sake of something he considers good, but this does not make sin itself good. A third reason is that Rahner's answer does not seem to require conversion or change of heart, with all this implies about

---

[27] I-II, Q. 106, Art. 1, ad 3.
[28] "Full Text of Benedict XVI's Recent, Rare, and Lengthy Interview," Catholic News Agency, 17 March 2016, www.catholicnewsagency.com/news/full-text-of-benedict-xvis-recent-rare-and-lengthy-interview-26142.

acknowledging one's sinfulness and one's inability to save oneself. One listens in vain for Rahner's "anonymous Christian" to cry out like the man in the Temple, "God, be merciful to me, a sinner!"

Benedict mentions a fourth reason too, which is most profound. As he points out, the theologian Henri de Lubac emphasized that following Christ involves becoming conformed to Him in His loving sacrifice. This is why, as Christ said, we must take up our own crosses too. Then is what Christ did for us not enough? No, the reason we must be joined to what He did is precisely that it is enough. We are saved by the Atonement; therefore we must be united, somehow, with the Atonement.

As to the second subsidiary question: Why is evangelization necessary at all? Christ and the Apostles considered preaching the gospel a matter of life and death importance. Yet if even implicit faith in Christ might suffice for salvation, then why must people be told?

Although Benedict does not consider possible answers to the question, he says further reflection is needed on all these issues. I suggest that every serious Christian knows a small part of the answer. For we know all too well, by our experience of following Christ, that taking up our crosses is difficult even if we do know who Christ is. Yes, just as He said, His yoke is easy and His burden light – but this is true only because He provides grace sufficient for the task. The way of the person whose faith in Christ is merely implicit will be precarious and difficult, because he does not know about that grace, and does not know where to find the channels through which it pours.

For example, suppose such a person falls into grave sin. Obviously he needs to repent, but complete repentance involves being sorry not just for fear of the consequences of sin but for the very love of God. Think how difficult this would be for him, considering that what makes grave sin so grave is precisely that it destroys that bond of love. How badly he needs the help of the sacrament of reconciliation, but he does not even know such help exists.

Consider too that it would be more difficult for him to recognize his sins in the first place. There are some general principles about right and wrong that everyone really knows deep down, but it is quite another thing to be honest with ourselves about them, and we need to be confronted. There are also more detailed matters of right and wrong, which are difficult to work out, and we need to be instructed in order to understand them. Scripture, Sacred Tradition, and pastoral care do confront and instruct us. I am not here thinking of a person who knows of these things but neglects them, for a person who rejects the things of faith certainly cannot be said to have implicit faith. Rather, I am thinking of someone who would accept them if they were made known to him, but he has never heard of them. The fact remains that he does not have their assistance.

So it is one thing for salvation through merely implicit faith to be possible, but it is quite another for it to be easy. Implicit faith in Christ desperately needs to develop into explicit faith in Christ. This requires knowledge, and knowledge requires evangelization. This is why Isaiah and St. Paul cry, "How beautiful are the feet of those who bring good news!"[29]

A fascinating scene in C. S. Lewis's Narnia story, *The Last Battle*, illustrates the possibility – but at the same time the difficulty – of implicit faith in Christ.[30] Emmeth, the worshipper of the false god Tash, has come to a place which might be called the vestibule of heaven. Meeting there several followers of the great lion, Aslan – who is Christ as he appears in Narnia – Emmeth tells them his story:

I looked about me and saw the sky and the wide lands, and smelled the sweetness. And I said, By the Gods, this is a pleasant place: it may be that I am come into the country of Tash. And I began to journey into the strange country and to seek him.

So I went over much grass and many flowers and among all kinds of wholesome and delectable trees till lo! in a narrow place between two rocks there came to meet me a great Lion. The speed of him was like the ostrich, and his size was an elephant's; his hair was like pure gold and the brightness of his eyes like gold that is liquid in the furnace. He was more terrible than the Flaming Mountain of Lagour, and in beauty he surpassed all that is in the world even as the rose in bloom surpasses the dust of the desert. Then I fell at his feet and thought, Surely this is the hour of death, for the Lion (who is worthy of all honour) will know that I have served Tash all my days and not him. Nevertheless, it is better to see the Lion and die than to be Tisroc of the world and live and not to have seen him. But the Glorious One bent down his golden head and touched my forehead with his tongue and said, Son, thou art welcome. But I said, Alas, Lord, I am no son of thine but the servant of Tash. He answered, Child, all the service thou hast done to Tash, I account as service done to me. Then by reasons of my great desire for wisdom and understanding, I overcame my fear and questioned the Glorious One and said, Lord, is it then true, as the Ape said, that thou and Tash are one? The Lion growled so that the earth shook (but his wrath was not against me) and said, It is false. Not because he and I are one, but because we are opposites, I take to me the services which thou hast done to him. For I and he are of such different kinds that no service which is vile can be done to me, and none which is not vile can be done to him. Therefore if any man swear by Tash and keep his oath for the oath's sake, it is by me that he has truly sworn, though he know it not, and it is I who reward him. And if any man do a cruelty in my name, then, though he says the name Aslan, it is Tash whom he serves and by Tash his deed is accepted. Dost thou understand, Child? I said, Lord, thou knowest how much I understand. But I said also (for the truth constrained me), Yet I have been seeking Tash all my days. Beloved, said the Glorious One, unless thy desire had been for me thou wouldst not have sought so long and so truly. For all find what they truly seek.

Then he breathed upon me and took away the trembling from my limbs and caused me to stand upon my feet. And after that, he said not much, but that we should meet again, and I must go further up and further in.

---

[29] Isaiah 52:7, Romans 10:15.
[30] C. S. Lewis, *The Last Battle* (New York: Macmillan, 1956), pp. 154–157. This is one of those children's books that has much to commend it to adults.

So in Lewis's story, Emmeth could be saved by implicit faith in the true God; but eventually he had to meet Him in person, go further up and further in. It might be protested that Emmeth did not meet the criteria suggested above. Maybe not. Still, I think this may be something like what the Pope Emeritus was suggesting in the interview.

II

THE OLD DIVINE LAW

QUESTION 99, ARTICLE 2

Whether the Old Law Contains Moral Precepts?

TEXT	PARAPHRASE
Whether the Old Law contains moral precepts?	Are any moral rules included in the Old Law, the law of the Old Testament?

St. Thomas is thinking of an influential argument that the Old Testament law included three different kinds of precept: moral, ceremonial, and judicial. What he wants to know is whether this classification is correct. At first, the question would seem to be easy to answer: Just look and see whether there are any moral, any ceremonial, or any judicial rules. However, the "look and see" approach begs the question of which rules are of which kind. Someone might say, for example, that *all* of the precepts are moral: for aren't they all right to obey? So although, in the *respondeo*, St. Thomas does look and see that some of the precepts in the Old Law are moral, he does more. As we see in the Discussion at the end of the Article, St. Thomas is not the originator of the distinction among moral, ceremonial, and judicial precepts, but besides putting it to powerful use, he may be the first to have recognized that the moral precepts include not only the ten great commands of the Decalogue but others as well.[1]

Objection 1. [1] *It would seem that the Old Law contains no moral precepts. For the Old Law is distinct from the law of nature, as stated above.* [2] *But the moral precepts belong to the law of nature. Therefore they do not belong to the Old Law.*	**Objection 1.** The Old Law does not seem to include any moral rules, for as we have seen earlier in the *Summa*, the Old Law is different from the natural law. Moral precepts concern the latter, not the former.

[1] It has been rightly said that St. Thomas tries to meet his opponents at their highest points; he sometimes states their arguments more cogently than they do themselves. Yet as we see here, sometimes even their highest points are not very

---

[1] His expansion of the category of moral precepts was brought to my attention by Fr. Richard Conrad, OP.

high. In basing his case on what is "stated above," the hypothetical Objector is playing fast and loose with what St. Thomas has actually said previously. For yes, he has certainly stated that the Old Law and the natural law are *different*, but he has also insisted that they are related. Consider for example the way the relation between them is described in Question 98, Article 5, where he says,

> The Old Law showed forth the precepts of the natural law, and added certain precepts of its own. Accordingly, as to those precepts of the natural law contained in the Old Law, all were bound to observe the Old Law; not because they belonged to the Old Law, but because they belonged to the natural law. But as to those precepts which were added by the Old Law, they were not binding on save the Jewish people alone.

From this it seems not that the Old Law and natural law have nothing in common, but that the Old Law illuminates, enlarges upon, and derives some part of its force from the natural law.

[2] But if we assume with the Objector that the Old Law and the natural law really are entirely dissimilar, then from the fact that the natural law is made up of moral rules, it follows that the Old Law cannot include any moral rules. So the answer to the query "Does the Old Law contain any moral precepts?" is no.

Objection 2. [1] Further, the Divine law should have come to man's assistance where human reason fails him: [2] as is evident in regard to things that are of faith, which are above reason. [3] But man's reason seems to suffice for the moral precepts. Therefore the moral precepts do not belong to the Old Law, which is a Divine law.	Objection 2. Moreover, Divine law, both Old and New, exists to compensate for the deficiencies of human reason. Plainly, the teachings of faith do this, because they exceed what reason could have figured out by itself. However, since man's reason seems quite able to work out the moral rules by itself, these are not included in the Old Law.

---

[1] The Objector assumes that God employs two methods for the instruction of human beings. God endowed man with reason, by which he can find out some things, and He provided Divine revelation, by which he is told other things. So far, so good.

[2] However, by the Objector's theory, there is no redundancy in God's method of instruction, no overlap between what man can find out just by using his mind and what he is told by God directly. For example, assuming that the Objector agrees with St. Thomas that the existence of God can be demonstrated philosophically, the Objector would not expect Divine revelation to teach God's existence. Taking for granted that the recipient of revelation would know that already, it would confine itself to teaching other things about God.

[3] The argument works like this.

1. One of the things man can find out just by the use of his mind is how he should live.
2. Therefore, it would be redundant for God to provide rules to man about how he should live.

3. But God's methods of instruction are never redundant.
4. Therefore, the Old Law could not have included rules about how to live.

This is a little bizarre. Surely it makes no sense to say that such precepts as "Do not murder" are not part of the Old Law. Are we then to say that they are part of the Old Law, but not *moral* rules? What are they? Sheer, arbitrary dictates?

Objection 3. [1] *Further, the Old Law is said to be "the letter that killeth" in 2 Cor. 3.* [2] *But the moral precepts do not kill, but quicken,* [3] *according to Ps. 118, "Thy justifications I will never forget, for by them Thou hast given me life."* [4] *Therefore the moral precepts do not belong to the Old Law.*

Objection 3. Besides, St. Paul describes the letter of the Old Law as bringing death, but moral rules bring life, not death. This is why the psalmist writes that he will never forget God's cleansing precepts, for through them God has given him life. It follows that the moral rules have nothing to do with the Old Law.

---

[1] St. Paul describes the Old Testament law as good:

Now we know that the law is good, if any one uses it lawfully, understanding this, that the law is not laid down for the just but for the lawless and disobedient, for the ungodly and sinners, for the unholy and profane, for murderers of fathers and murderers of mothers, for manslayers, immoral persons, sodomites, kidnapers, liars, perjurers, and whatever else is contrary to sound doctrine, in accordance with the glorious gospel of the blessed God with which I have been entrusted.[2]

Yet St. Paul thinks that in some way the Law is also problematic:

If it had not been for the law, I should not have known sin. I should not have known what it is to covet if the law had not said, "You shall not covet." But sin, finding opportunity in the commandment, wrought in me all kinds of covetousness. Apart from the law sin lies dead. I was once alive apart from the law, but when the commandment came, sin revived and I died; the very commandment which promised life proved to be death to me. For sin, finding opportunity in the commandment, deceived me and by it killed me. So the law is holy, and the commandment is holy and just and good. Did that which is good, then, bring death to me? By no means! It was sin, working death in me through what is good, in order that sin might be shown to be sin, and through the commandment might become sinful beyond measure.[3]

In the passage the Objector is using, St. Paul clarifies: It is not the "spirit" of the Old Law which kills but its "letter":

Not that we are competent of ourselves to claim anything as coming from us; our competence is from God, who has made us competent to be ministers of a new covenant, not in a written code but in the Spirit; for the written code kills, but the Spirit gives life. Now if the dispensation of death, carved in letters on stone, came with such splendor that

---

[2] 1 Timothy 1:8–11 (RSV-CE), emphasis added.
[3] Romans 7:7b–13 (RSV-CE).

the Israelites could not look at Moses' face because of its brightness, fading as this was, will not the dispensation of the Spirit be attended with greater splendor?[4]

As St. Thomas explains in *Treatise on Law*, Question 96, Article 6, in ordinary human legislation the letter of the law is taken to be its literal meaning, by contrast with its spirit, which is taken to be its intention. That seems to be how the Objector is using the terms here. A problem the Objector overlooks is that in speaking of a covenant "in the Spirit," St. Paul seems to be referring not to the intention of the law but to the inspiration of the Holy Spirit. If so, then he is *not* using the terms as they are used in human legislation.

[2] The life-giving quality of God's moral instructions is one of the Old Testament's most pervasive themes. After announcing them to the people of Israel, Moses declares,

> I call heaven and earth to witness against you this day, that I have set before you life and death, blessing and curse; therefore choose life, that you and your descendants may live, loving the Lord your God, obeying his voice, and cleaving to him; for that means life to you and length of days, that you may dwell in the land which the Lord swore to your fathers, to Abraham, to Isaac, and to Jacob, to give them.[5]

[3] The Objector is quoting from a psalm of praise in which the Divine poet implores God to help him follow God's instructions. In the following verses, presented here in another translation, he rings changes on the theme of how these teachings enliven him:

- [Verse 17.] Give bountifully to thy servant, *enliven* me: and I shall keep thy words.
- [Verse 50.] This hath comforted me in my humiliation: because thy word hath *enlivened* me.
- [Verse 93.] Thy justifications I will never forget: for by them thou hast given me *life*.
- [Verse 116.] Uphold me according to thy word, and I shall *live*: and let me not be confounded in my expectation.
- [Verse 144.] Thy testimonies are justice for ever: give me understanding, and I shall *live*.
- [Verse 175.] My soul shall *live* and shall praise thee: and thy judgments shall help me.[6]

For the Objector, everything depends on the "words," "justifications," "testimonies," and "judgments" of God's moral instructions being something different from commandments of His law. This is a highly dubious

---

[4] 2 Corinthians 3:5–8 (RSV-CE).
[5] Deuteronomy 30:19–20 (RSV-CE).
[6] Psalm 119 (DRA), verses as indicated; emphasis added. The Vulgate numbers this psalm as 118. This is one of the "alphabetical" psalms, with one stanza for each letter of the Hebrew alphabet.

claim, for in numerous other passages of the same psalm we have been dealing with, the psalmist identifies these instructions explicitly with the Law:

- [Verse 1.] Blessed are the undefiled in the way, who walk in the *law* of the Lord.
- [Verse 18.] Open thou my eyes: and I will consider the wondrous things of thy *law*.
- [Verse 29.] Remove from me the way of iniquity: and out of thy *law* have mercy on me.
- [Verse 33.] Set before me for a *law* the way of thy justifications, O Lord: and I will always seek after it.
- [Verse 34.] Give me understanding, and I will search thy *law*; and I will keep it with my whole heart.
- [Verse 44.] So shall I always keep thy *law*, for ever and ever.
- [Verse 51.] The proud did iniquitously altogether: but I declined not from thy *law*.[7]

[4] Bearing in mind that the Objector takes the "letter" of the Old Law to be the literal meaning of its precepts, his argument may be put as follows.

1. The letter of the Old Law deadens us.
2. Yet the moral precepts of God enliven us.
3. Therefore His moral precepts are not part of the Old Law.

If the Old Law does *not* contain moral precepts, then what kinds of precepts that "kill" does it contain? The Objector seems to think that it includes only ceremonial precepts, such as the requirement for circumcision and the prohibition of consuming blood. It is certainly true that St. Paul does not think the ceremonial precepts have any value in themselves. To the Christians in the city of Galatea, he writes, "For in Christ Jesus neither circumcision nor uncircumcision is of any avail, but faith working through love."[8]

On the other hand, we see in one of Paul's letters to the Christians in Corinth that what faith working through love involves is following the law:

- For neither circumcision counts for anything nor uncircumcision, but keeping the commandments of God.[9]
- Circumcision indeed is of value if you obey the law; but if you break the law, your circumcision becomes uncircumcision ... [R]eal circumcision is a matter of the heart, spiritual and not literal.[10]

---

[7] Ibid., verses as indicated, emphasis added. See also verses 53, 57, 61, 70, 72, 77, 85, 92, 97, 102, 109, 113, 126, 136, 142, 150, 153, 163, 165, and 174.
[8] Galatians 5:6 (RSV-CE).
[9] 1 Corinthians 7:19 (RSV-CE).
[10] Romans 2:25, 29 (RSV-CE).

What could this law be but the Old Law, and what could its commandments be but its moral precepts?

On the contrary, [1] *It is written in Ecclesiasticus 17: "Moreover, He gave them discipline [Douay: 'instructions'] and the law of life for an inheritance."* [2] *Now discipline belongs to morals; for this gloss on Heb. 12: "Now all chastisement [disciplina]," etc., says: "Discipline is an exercise in morals by means of difficulties."* [3] *Therefore the Law which was given by God comprised moral precepts.*	**On the other hand,** the Old Testament book of Sirach teaches that God bestowed discipline upon human beings, bequeathing to them the law of life. But "discipline" refers to moral discipline. This is why the Ordinary Gloss describes it as the teaching of morals by means of vexation. So the law which God bestowed was a body of moral rules.

[1] The *sed contra* is referring to a passage in Sirach, one of the Wisdom books of the Old Testament, about the mercy of God to the human beings whom He had created:

> He set his eye upon their hearts to shew them the greatness of his works: That they might praise the name which he hath sanctified: and glory in his wondrous acts, that they might declare the glorious things of his works. Moreover he gave them discipline, and the law of life for an inheritance.[11]

[2] The letter to the Hebrews is so named because it was addressed to Jewish rather than Gentile Christians. In the passage of the letter to which the Objector refers, its unknown author declares, "Now all chastisement for the present indeed seems not to bring with it joy, but sorrow: but afterwards it will yield, to them that are exercised by it, the most peaceable fruit of justice."[12] Here is the context of the statement in a more recent translation:

> It is for discipline that you have to endure. God is treating you as sons; for what son is there whom his father does not discipline? If you are left without discipline, in which all have participated, then you are illegitimate children and not sons. Besides this, we have had earthly fathers to discipline us and we respected them. Shall we not much more be subject to the Father of spirits and live? For they disciplined us for a short time at their pleasure, but he disciplines us for our good, that we may share his holiness. For the moment all discipline seems painful rather than pleasant; later it yields the peaceful fruit of righteousness to those who have been trained by it.[13]

The gloss on the passage which the *sed contra* cites is the medieval scriptural commentary called the *Glossa Ordinaria,* or Ordinary Gloss, which was a

---

[11] Sirach 17:7–9 (DRA), replacing "instructions," in verse 9, with "discipline," on the basis of the Latin text, *addidit illis disciplinam, et legem vitae haereditavit illos.* Sirach is also known as Ecclesiasticus, not to be confused with Ecclesiastes. In most contemporary translations, the verses numbered 7–9 in the DRA are divided differently and numbered 8–11.
[12] Hebrews 12:11 (DRA), replacing "seemeth" with "seems."
[13] Hebrews 12:7–11 (RSV-CE).

Were Any of the Old Law's Precepts Moral?

compilation of remarks on passages of Scripture by various writers, especially the Fathers of the Church. In it we read that discipline is *erudition per molestias, quando pro peccatis suis mala quis patitur, ut corrigatur prout hic intelligitur* – paraphrasing freely, that it is teaching by means of vexation, because through it a man suffers evils for his sins in order that his understanding may be corrected.

[3] The reasoning of the *sed contra* is as follows. After each premise I give its source in parentheses.

1. God gave humans discipline (Sirach).
2. The intention of this discipline was moral (*Glossa Ordinaria*).
3. But this discipline was associated with the precepts of the Old Law (Sirach).
4. Therefore, the Old Law includes moral precepts.

As always, the *sed contra* merely restates the tradition. For St. Thomas's own argument, we turn now to the *respondeo*.

I answer that, [1] *The Old Law contained some moral precepts; as is evident from Ex. 20:* "*Thou shalt not kill, Thou shalt not steal.*" [2] *This was reasonable: because, just as the principal intention of human law is to create friendship between man and man; so the chief intention of the Divine law is to establish man in friendship with God.* [3] *Now since likeness is the reason of love, according to Ecclus. 13:* "*Every beast loveth its like*"; [4] *there cannot possibly be any friendship of man to God, Who is supremely good, unless man become good:* [5] *wherefore it is written in Lev. 19:* "*You shall be holy, for I am holy.*" [6] *But the goodness of man is virtue, which* "*makes its possessor good.*" [7] *Therefore it was necessary for the Old Law to include precepts about acts of virtue: and these are the moral precepts of the Law.*

Here is my response. The Old Law did contain certain moral rules. This is obvious from the twentieth chapter of the book of Exodus, in which we read, for example, the prohibitions of murder and theft. It was reasonable for the Old Law to include such things, for just as human law aims chiefly at friendship among men, so Divine law aims chiefly at friendship between man and God. Now the reason for love is similarity between the lover and the beloved. This is why the book of Sirach remarks that every beast loves its like. Consequently, there cannot be friendship between man and the supremely good God unless man becomes good too. The book of Leviticus confirms this when it depicts God as commanding, "Be holy, for I am holy."
But what makes us good is virtue. Therefore, it was fitting for precepts about the acts of virtue to be given by the Old Law – and these are the Old Law's moral rules.

---

[1] St. Thomas begins by stating the obvious: Of course the Old Law included some moral rules. The two precepts he cites as examples are from the Decalogue or Ten Commandments, which was the keystone of the Law.[14]

---

[14] The Ten Commandments were declared in both Exodus 20:3–17 and Deuteronomy 5:6–21.

It might seem that no more needs to be said, but St. Thomas goes on to *justify* the fact that the Law includes moral precepts – to show why it needed to do so.

[2] St. Thomas is *not* saying that human law regulates relations between man and man, but that Divine law does not. Plainly, some of the moral precepts of Divine law do regulate relations between man and man. For example, no man is to steal from another. His point is that even when Divine law does regulate relations between man and man, it does so for a different reason than human law. Human law forbids stealing in order to make men friends with each other; Divine law forbids stealing in order to make men friends with God, for man's neighbor is made in God's image, and friendship with God implies sharing His own love for those whom He places in our care.

[3] We have just seen that man is to be established in friendship with God, but friendship is a relation of love. However, love requires some likeness between the two friends, otherwise there is no point of contact. In support of this point St. Thomas quotes again from Sirach:

> Every creature loves its like, and every person his neighbor; all living beings associate by species, and a man clings to one like himself. What fellowship has a wolf with a lamb? No more has a sinner with a godly man. What peace is there between a hyena and a dog? And what peace between a rich man and a poor man? Wild asses in the wilderness are the prey of lions; likewise the poor are pastures for the rich. Humility is an abomination to a proud man; likewise a poor man is an abomination to a rich one.[15]

Whether the passage really means what St. Thomas takes it to mean might be questioned – a problem to which we return in Question 105, Article 3. However, even if this is not the meaning of the passage, the point that love requires some kind of likeness seems unquestionable.

The prior necessity of some likeness between the two friends is not the *whole* truth about love. For example, husband and wife love each other not only because of their similarity as rational beings but also because of their complementary difference as procreative partners. Since each sex possesses something that the other lacks, they are able to complete each other. At present, however, we are considering only the factor of similarity, not the factor of complementary difference. Nor, at the moment, are we considering the important fact that those who love each other are not only drawn to each other but are moved to care for each other.

[4] Reading that love between man and God requires some similarity between man and God provokes the question: Doesn't man already bear God's image, in the sense that he is an intellectual being who can choose freely, one whose very nature is endowed with the power of self-direction? Yes, but this is only a prerequisite. For *in what way* does he direct himself? With God's help, he can yield himself to God so that his friendship with God is perfected.

---

[15] Sirach 13:15–20 (RSV-CE). In the DRA, the corresponding verses are numbered 19–24.

Were Any of the Old Law's Precepts Moral?

On the other hand, it lies within his power to resist God so that his friendship with God is destroyed.

[5] To be holy is to be consecrated, to be set aside for God, to be entirely devoted to Him and at His disposal, yielded entirely to him in thoughts, words, and acts. St. Thomas cites a single chapter of Leviticus for this demand; the Blackfriars translators add one more. Actually, the demand appears repeatedly in the Old Law:

- 11:44 For I am the Lord your God; consecrate yourselves therefore, and be holy, for I am holy
- 11:45 For I am the Lord who brought you up out of the land of Egypt, to be your God; you shall therefore be holy, for I am holy [re-emphasis of the preceding exhortation]
- 19:2 Say to all the congregation of the people of Israel, You shall be holy; for I the Lord your God am holy.
- 20:7 Consecrate yourselves therefore, and be holy; for I am the Lord your God.
- 20:26 You shall be holy to me; for I the Lord am holy, and have separated you from the peoples, that you should be mine.[16]

The New Law confirms the Old Law's demand for holiness, for St. Peter writes in the New Testament, "As he who called you is holy, be holy yourselves in all your conduct; since it is written, 'You shall be holy, for I am holy.'"[17]

[6] The sense in which virtue "makes" man good is that virtue is the difference between a good man and a bad one. If he is virtuous he is good, and if he is not virtuous he is not good. This relationship holds not only for moral good but for all kinds of good; it holds not only for the moral excellences but for every kind of excellence; and it holds not only for man but for all things whatsoever. What dispositional qualities make a horse a good racehorse? Whatever they are, they are the virtues – the proper excellences – of the racehorse. What makes a man a good man? Whatever they are, they are the virtues – the proper excellences – of the man.

St. Thomas does not credit Aristotle with the point here, but he does in other places, so the Blackfriars translators are justified in inserting a reference to Aristotle's *Nicomachean Ethics*, book II, chapter 6, where the philosopher says,

We must consider not only that virtue is a habit but also what kind of habit. We must explain, therefore, that virtue perfects everything of which it is the virtue, rendering both the possessor good and his work good. Thus the virtue or power of the eye makes good both the eye and its operation, for it is by the power of the eye that we see well. Likewise the virtue or excellence of a horse makes the horse good and also makes him good for

---

[16] All quotations from Leviticus (RSV-CE), chapters and verses as indicated.
[17] 1 Peter 1:15–16 (RSV-CE).

running, riding and awaiting the enemy. If this be true in all other things, then human virtue will be a habit making man good and rendering his work good.[18]

To forestall a possible misunderstanding, we return to these matters in the Discussion at the end of the Article.

[7] All law is established for some kind of community. As St. Thomas writes in Question 100, Article 2,

> The community for which the Divine law is ordained, is that of men in relation to God, either in this life or in the life to come. And therefore the Divine law proposes precepts about all those matters whereby men are well ordered in their relations to God. Now man is united to God by his reason or mind, in which is God's image. Wherefore the Divine law proposes precepts about all those matters whereby human reason is well ordered.
>
> But this is effected by the acts of all the virtues: since the intellectual virtues set in good order the acts of the reason in themselves: while the moral virtues set in good order the acts of the reason in reference to the interior passions and exterior actions. It is therefore evident that the Divine law fittingly proposes precepts about the acts of all the virtues.

Among the cardinal virtues, prudence is an intellectual excellence, temperance and fortitude are moral excellences that regulate interior passions, and justice is a moral excellence that regulates exterior actions. St. Thomas also distinguished between "precepts," which concern matters apart from which virtue is not possible at all, and "counsels," which help virtue to develop to perfection more readily. We return to this distinction in Question 108, Article 4.

| *Reply to Objection 1.* [1] *The Old Law is distinct from the natural law, not as being altogether different from it, but as something added thereto.* [2] *For just as grace presupposes nature, so must the Divine law presuppose the natural law.* | Reply to Objection 1. Yes, the Old Law differs from the natural law, but how? Not as something completely alien to the natural law, but as something added to it. For it is fitting that just as grace presupposes nature, Divine law presupposes natural law. |

[1] The Objector had argued that the Old Law and the natural law are two different things. St. Thomas does not disagree; he merely points out that the Objector is mistaken about how they differ. The Objector had thought they were different in the sense that they have no content in common; St. Thomas says they do have content in common, but the Old Law adds something extra. We might say that according to the Objector, the difference between natural law and Old Law is like the difference between water and oil, but that according to St. Thomas the difference between them is like the difference between water and wine. Wine is water with something added.

---

[18] I am taking Aristotle's wording from Thomas Aquinas, *Commentary on Aristotle's Nicomachean Ethics*, translated by C. I. Litzinger (Chicago: Henry Regnery, 1964).

Were Any of the Old Law's Precepts Moral?   53

What, then, does Divine law add to the natural law (and to human law which is based on it)? As we saw in Question 91, Article 4, Divine law adds not one thing but four:

- Natural law directs us to the fragmentary and incomplete happiness of this life, the attainment of which is within our natural powers. By contrast, Divine law directs us to the utter and complete happiness of the vision of God in His Being, the attainment of which exceeds our natural powers and requires Divine grace.
- Although the general principles of natural law are evident to the minds of all people, human reason can easily make mistakes about the details, and this difficulty plagues human law too. By contrast, the Divine law is immune from error because it comes directly from God.
- There are certain interior movements of the heart which human authorities can know, by the natural law, to be wrong, yet which they would be foolish to try to prohibit, because they cannot tell whether people are committing them. The Law of God does not suffer from this limitation, because God sees everything.
- There are certain exterior acts which human authorities can know, by the natural law, to be wrong, yet which they would be imprudent to forbid, because the attempt to eliminate them would do away with many good things too. The Divine law is free of this restriction.

[2] God endows us with our nature by creating us. The nature with which He endows us is a rational nature capable of understanding and reflection; therefore, simply by giving it to us, He also gives us the means to know the natural law, which may be viewed as the set of principles by which our nature is fulfilled. In turn, God purifies and uplifts our nature by the superadded gift of Divine grace. Since the Divine law is the set of principles by which we cooperate with this grace, we could not have worked it out by our natural powers alone. Consequently, he reveals the Divine law to us by announcing it to us.

Thus, just as wine presupposes water, grace presupposes nature, for we cannot experience the purification and elevation of human nature unless, in fact, we possess human nature. In the same way, Divine law presupposes natural law, for if we did not already know the natural law, the Divine law could not even make sense to us.

Reply to Objection 2. [1] *It was fitting that the Divine law should come to man's assistance not only in those things for which reason is insufficient, but also in those things in which human reason may happen to be impeded.* [2] *Now human reason could not go astray in the abstract, as to the universal principles of the natural law; but through being*

Reply to Objection 2. Quite properly, Divine law comes to the rescue not only in matters in which man's reason utterly falls short but also in matters in which it is merely hindered or obstructed. Let us consider this more closely.

Regarding the natural law, it is not possible for human reason to fall short of knowing the universal moral precepts

habituated to sin, it became obscured in the point of things to be done in detail. [3] But *with regard to the other moral precepts, which are like conclusions drawn from the universal principles of the natural law, the reason of many men went astray, to the extent of judging to be lawful, things that are evil in themselves.* [4] *Hence there was need for the authority of the Divine law to rescue man from both these defects.* [5] *Thus among the articles of faith not only are those things set forth to which reason cannot reach, such as the Trinity of the Godhead; but also those to which right reason can attain, such as the Unity of the Godhead;* [6] *in order to remove the manifold errors to which reason is liable.*

which everyone shares – although the habit of sin can cast a shadow on human reason with respect to particular applications of these precepts. On the other hand, regarding the other moral precepts – the ones which are deduced, like conclusions, *from* the universal, shared precepts – the reason of many people goes astray, so that they deem certain evil things lawful.

So the articles set before us for belief include not only those which human reason cannot by its own powers reach at all, such as that God is Three Persons, but also those which rightly ordered reason can attain, such as that God is one Being. In this way it cleanses human reason of the many errors to which it would otherwise succumb.

---

[1] The hypothetical Objector seemed to think that in every situation about which a decision is necessary, man's reasoning is either entirely adequate or entirely helpless. Either it can work out everything without assistance, or it cannot work out anything without assistance. St. Thomas points out that this is not true, for a third situation is possible. In some matters, even though man's reasoning is not entirely helpless, it faces obstacles; although it is able to work things out, it is prone to make mistakes.

The idea of God enlightening human reasoning, reminding the Hebrew people of what they already know, pointing out to them things which they should have figured out for themselves, and correcting their reasoning when it errs, is pervasive in Scripture. Moses asks them, "And what great nation is there, that has statutes and ordinances so righteous as all this law which I set before you this day?"[19] At a later point in their history, God chastises them, saying through the prophet Isaiah, "Cease to do perversely, learn to do well: seek judgment, relieve the oppressed, judge for the fatherless, defend the widow. And *then* come and accuse me."[20] There would be no point in the former challenge unless their minds were capable of recognizing the body of laws being set before them as a more

---

[19] Deuteronomy 4:8 (RSV-CE).
[20] Isaiah 1:16b–18a (DRA), modernizing the punctuation and adding emphasis. Where DRA has "Then come, and accuse me, saith the Lord," RSV-CE has "Come now, let us reason together, says the Lord." According to Strong's Concordance, the Hebrew word underlying the translations "reason" and "accuse" means to decide, adjudge, or prove.

perfect expression of what it already dimly knew; there would be no point in the latter unless they could recognize the force of argument.

[2] In all fields of reasoning, there exist certain universal "first" principles, like axioms, which the mind spontaneously accepts as its starting points. An example of a first principle of practical reason is the wrong of murder. Now first principles hold universally, both with respect to their rightness and with respect to the knowledge of them.[21] For example, murder is wrong for everyone; moreover the wrong of murder is known to everyone.

However, there are two difficulties. The first, which St. Thomas considers here, lies in the application of the universal principles to detailed circumstances. Just as in theoretical reasoning, someone who knows the properties of triangles but must still ask "But is this figure a triangle?" so in practical reason someone who is perfectly aware of the wrong of murder must still ask "Would doing this be murder?" It is easy to see that a violent person is much more likely to err in such matters, and St. Thomas generalizes the point: Even though the mind cannot err about the universal moral principles,[22] habituation to sin does bring about error in the application of these principles to actual cases.

[3] The second difficulty concerns not the straight application of the universal principles to particular cases but the derivation of *subordinate rules, for certain kinds of cases*, from the universal principles. Just as in geometry from the universal properties of triangles we derive more detailed theorems about triangles, so, in morality, from the prohibition of stealing we derive the more detailed rule that if someone has left his property in my keeping, then I ought to return it when he asks.

Now the theorems of theoretical reasoning hold just as universally as the axioms. In practical reasoning, however, the more detailed conclusions do *not* hold as universally as the axioms. For example, if my friend asks for the return of his car keys when he is falling-down drunk, refusing to return the keys until he is sober is *not* stealing; in this case the rule about returning property does not hold. More to the point, *not everyone knows* the rule about returning property. The wrong of stealing is not the sort of thing that people get mixed up about (even though they may steal anyway). However, people do become confused about such things as whether one must return property that has been left in one's keeping when the owner demands it. Habitual sin makes error more likely here too. Even though someone knows the universal rules, he may be confused about their more detailed implications.

---

[21] I-II, Q. 94, Art. 4.
[22] Now and then one does run across someone who says "But *I* don't know murder is always wrong." However, the most likely explanation of such a person is not that he really doesn't know, but either that he is confused about what murder is in the first place, or that he knows the wrong of murder and pretends to himself that he doesn't.

However, in view of what St. Thomas says elsewhere about the relation between prudence and experience, we should probably distinguish between innocent and guilty confusion. Anyone may be confused about the *remote* implications of the universal principles, especially in matters about which he has not had much experience – some things are clear only to the wise. But in the case of the *proximate* implications of the universal principles, the chief reason for confusion is our vices. A habitual drunkard is more likely to be deceived about the wrong of drunkenness. A sexual libertine is more likely to be confused about the rights and wrongs of sex. A violent man is more likely to be confused about the difference between murder and just war.[23] It is not just that we sin because of poor judgment; we also have poor judgment because we sin.

[4] Considering what he has just been talking about, it may seem that by the expression "both of these defects," St. Thomas means (1) errors about applying universal rules, and (2) errors in deriving more particular rules. No, he is returning to his original point. One defect of finite human reason is that some things lie entirely beyond it; the other, which he has just been discussing, is that it makes errors even about some things which do not lie entirely beyond it.

[5] Now St. Thomas offers an analogy. The fact that God is one in Being can be worked out by human reason (even though it is possible to become confused). However, the fact that God is *three Persons in* one Being lies entirely beyond human reason. The Objector would have expected that Divine revelation would have told the latter truth but left it to us to work out the former. In fact, just to keep our minds straight, it tells us both of them.

[6] The reason why Divine revelation tells us of the Trinity of God is that we need to know it but could not have learned it just by reasoning. The reason why it tells us of the Unity of God is different: Even though we *can* work it out by reasoning, we are prone to confusion. What the Objector overlooks is that Divine revelation tells us some of the moral precepts of the Old Law for the same reason.

Reply to Objection 3. As Augustine proves in De Spiritu et Litera, *even the letter of the law is said to be the occasion of death, as to the moral precepts; in so far as, to wit, it prescribes what is good, without furnishing the aid of grace for its fulfillment.*

Reply to Objection 3. As St. Augustine demonstrates in his book, *On the Spirit and the Letter,* even the letter of the moral precepts of the law can be described as killing, just because it commands what is good without providing the grace which is needed to do it.

---

[23] Although even in just war there is such a thing as murder. It is licit to shoot at the attacking enemy soldiers, but it is not licit to shoot a disarmed prisoner of war.

Were Any of the Old Law's Precepts Moral?

St. Augustine takes a radically different view of the difference between the spirit and the letter of Divine law than the Objector does. According to him, its spirit is how we experience the command under the influence of Divine grace, and this gives life. But its letter is how we experience it apart from such grace – and this kills, because although we do not have the power to obey the commandment for the sake of God, we are judged for not following it:

> For that teaching which brings to us the command to live in chastity and righteousness is "the letter that kills," unless accompanied with "the spirit that gives life" ... Now from this you may see what is meant by "the letter that kills" ... When the Holy Ghost withholds His help, which inspires us with a good desire instead of this evil desire (in other words, diffuses love in our hearts), that law, however good in itself, only augments the evil desire by forbidding it. Just as the rush of water which flows incessantly in a particular direction, becomes more violent when it meets with any impediment, and when it has overcome the stoppage, falls in a greater bulk, and with increased impetuosity hurries forward in its downward course. In some strange way the very object which we covet becomes all the more pleasant when it is forbidden. And this is the sin which by the commandment deceives and by it slays, whenever transgression is actually added, which occurs not where there is no law.[24]

Augustine also makes very clear that the expression "the letter that kills" refers not only to the ceremonial precepts, as we have seen that the Objector thinks, but to the moral precepts too:

> Is it possible to contend that it is not the law which was written on those two tables that the apostle describes as "the letter that kills," but the law of circumcision and the other sacred rites which are now abolished? But then how can we think so, when in the law occurs this precept, "You shall not covet," by which very commandment, notwithstanding its being holy, just, and good, "sin," says the apostle, "deceived me, and by it slew me?" What else can this be than "the letter" that "kills"?[25]

A little later Augustine emphasizes that St. Paul "does not mean even there any other 'letter' to be understood than the Decalogue itself, which was written on the two tables."[26]

This suffices for refuting Objection 3, for the fact that God's moral instructions give life but "letter" of the Law "kills" does not imply that His moral instructions are not part of the Law, but that we need the grace of God to follow them.

---

[24] St. Augustine of Hippo, *On the Spirit and the Letter*, chapter 6, section 4, www.newadvent.org/fathers/1502.htm.
[25] Ibid., chapter 14, section 23. We return to this passage in I-II, Q. 100, Art. 12.
[26] Ibid., chapter 14 (24).

DISCUSSION

How Many Kinds of Precepts Are There?

Torah contains hundreds of different precepts – according to rabbinical tradition, 613. Because the Old Law does not provide its own system of classification, one might suggest that these precepts should not be classified at all. Without some sort of framework, however, it is difficult to wend one's way through them. Various classifications have been suggested. For example:

- Some rabbinical commentators associate a certain subset of the precepts with each of the Ten Commandments.
- Just as with the "two tablets" of the Decalogue itself, one might divide the precepts into duties to God and duties to neighbor.
- As we will see later, St. Augustine distinguishes between precepts which are meant to put our lives in order, and precepts which are meant to symbolize something which God will reveal later – as the sacrifice of a lamb foreshadows the sacrifice of Christ.

At the other extreme from such twofold distinctions, the great medieval Jewish thinker Moses Maimonides[27] – whom St. Thomas respectfully calls "Rabbi Moses," short for "Rabbi Moshe Ben Maimon" – suggests that the precepts may be grouped into fourteen different classes according to subject matter. This approach, found in the scholar's *Guide for the Perplexed*,[28] merits a closer look, not only for its intrinsic value but also to provide background for what St. Thomas was trying to do.

First are the "fundamental" precepts, which are the very basis of the Law, the *raison d'être* for all the others. In another of his works, *Mishneh Torah*, in the section called *Hilchot Yesodei Ha-Torah* (meaning Laws of the Foundations of Torah), Maimonides argues that these include the duties to recognize God, to forbear from even speculating that there might be any other God, to recognize His unity, to love Him, to fear Him, to honor the holiness of His Name, to forbear from desecrating His Name, to forbear from destroying things on which His Name is written, to listen to prophets who speak in His Name, and to forbear from testing Him. In the *Guide for the Perplexed*, Maimonides adds to the fundamental precepts the commandments about fasting and repentance.

Second are precepts connected with the prohibition of idolatry, which have as their purpose the fixing of certain truths in the minds of the people. Third come precepts related to the improvement of morals. Here, Maimonides gives

---

[27] Also known by the acronym Rambam.
[28] I am following Moses Maimonides, *Guide for the Perplexed*, translated by Michael Friedländer (1904), www.sacred-texts.com/jud/gfp/gfp171.htm. Except where indicated, my comments are based on part III, chapter 35.

as the reason the need to bring to perfection those social relations which are indispensable to the well-being of mankind. Fourth, precepts related to such things as charity, loans, and gifts, which benefit people "by turns": "He who is rich today may one day be poor – either he himself or his descendants; and he who is now poor, he himself or his son may be rich tomorrow."

Of precepts in the fifth category, which concern the prevention of wrong and violence, Maimonides says simply that "their beneficial character is evident." Sixth are precepts related to fines, false witnesses, and compensation for injuries, for if wrongdoers were not punished, "injury would not be prevented at all," and if compensation were not exacted for injuries, "it would be perfect cruelty and injury to the social state of the country." Seventh are precepts concerning monetary transactions, for without regulations, for example standards of equity, the necessary conduct of business would be impossible.

Eighth are precepts about certain days, such as Sabbaths and holy days, which have two purposes. Some of them provide bodily rest; some fix important principles in the minds of the people; and some do both. Ninth are precepts pertaining to religious ceremonies, for example concerning prayers.[29] These "firmly establish the love of God in our minds, as also the right belief concerning Him and His attributes."

The precepts in the tenth category are related to the sanctuary, its vessels, and its ministers, and those in the eleventh are related to sacrifices, which concern the worship of God. Twelfth are precepts concerning to ritual purity and impurity, the clean and the unclean. The chief effect of these precepts, says Maimonides, is to discourage people from entering the sanctuary too often, so that their minds may be impressed with its greatness and they approach it with proper reverence.

Finally come precepts related to temperance. Category thirteen includes those pertaining to forbidden foods, as well as vows about food and drink, while category fourteen comprises those pertaining to forbidden sexual intercourse. These temperance rules restrain the growth of desire, the excessive indulgence of pleasure, and the disposition to view eating, drinking, and carnal relations as the purpose of life. Maimonides explains that intemperance not only impedes man's moral and spiritual development but disturbs the order of society, both in the country and in the family.[30]

"As is well known," says Maimonides – and as we saw above – the precepts may also be divided into two classes, "precepts concerning the relation between man and God, and precepts concerning the relation between man and man." Of the fourteen categories, he says that the fifth, sixth, seventh, and *part* of the third concern the relation between man and man. All the rest concern the relation between man and God – not just regarding worship but regarding

---

[29] Interestingly, Maimonides excludes from this category the command to circumcise male infants, the place of which is not clear.
[30] Maimonides, *Guide for the Perplexed*, part III, chapter 33.

man's moral and intellectual condition and development. He emphasizes that in reality these too are beneficial to our fellow men, but their benefit is felt only indirectly, through many intermediate steps.

St. Thomas would agree with much of this. With some of it, though, he would sharply disagree. Consider for example the purposes Maimonides gives for the precepts in his tenth, eleventh, and twelfth categories – regulations for the Temple, its sacrifices, and ritual purity. By this time in history, although the synagogue continued, centuries had passed since the Romans destroyed the Temple, and the Temple sacrifices had ceased. Maimonides argues that the precepts for Temple and sacrifice had value only because they made it easier to wean the people from their former pagan practices. It would seem to follow that once they had been weaned from them, their value would be ended. As he writes in an earlier chapter,

> It was in accordance with the wisdom and plan of God, as displayed in the whole Creation, that He did not command us to give up and to discontinue all these manners of service; for to obey such a commandment it would have been contrary to the nature of man, who generally cleaves to that to which he is used; it would in those days have made the same impression as a prophet would make at present if he called us to the service of God and told us in His name, that we should not pray to Him, not fast, not seek His help in time of trouble; that we should serve Him in thought, and not by any action. For this reason God allowed these kinds of service to continue; He transferred to His service that which had formerly served as a worship of created beings, and of things imaginary and unreal, and commanded us to serve Him in the same manner; viz., to build unto Him a temple ...
>
> All these restrictions served to limit this kind of worship, and keep it within those bounds within which God did not think it necessary to abolish sacrificial service altogether. *But prayer and supplication can be offered everywhere and by every person.*[31]

St. Thomas agrees that *one* of the purposes of requiring sacrifices to the true God was that "thereby men were withdrawn from offering sacrifices to idols." In fact, he points out that the rules of sacrifice were not given to the Hebrew nation until they had relapsed into idolatry by worshipping the golden calf: "as though those sacrifices were instituted, that the people, being ready to offer sacrifices, might offer those sacrifices to God rather than to idols."

However, St. Thomas thinks that there was much more to Temple sacrifices than that. For in the first place, sacrifice to the true God was valuable because it fixed the mind of the worshipper on his debt to His Creator: he gave things of his own to God, "as though in recognition of his having received them from God." In the second place, the regulations about the Temple and its sacrifices were valuable for symbolic reasons. "All the other sacrifices of the Old Law were offered up," says St. Thomas, to foreshadow the "one individual and

---

[31] Ibid., part III, chapter 32, emphasis added.

Were Any of the Old Law's Precepts Moral?

paramount sacrifice," the sacrifice of Christ for the sins of the world.[32] Moreover, the earthly sanctuary foreshadowed the life of the redeemed in the world to come:

> In the condition of the blessed in the next life, nothing in regard to worship of God will be figurative; there will be naught but "thanksgiving and voice of praise." Hence it is written concerning the city of the Blessed: "I saw no Temple therein: for the Lord God Almighty is the Temple thereof, and the Lamb."[33]

Maimonides' fourteenfold classification is also very unwieldy. Yet in defense of its unwieldiness, it might be suggested that none of the simpler, twofold distinctions do quite enough. Is there a happy medium between the two and the fourteen?

Some medieval theologians thought yes. A little more than a decade before St. Thomas, the Franciscan compilers of the *Summa Fratris Alexandri*, including Alexander of Hales and his students, John of La Rochelle and William of Middleton, suggested that the precepts of the Old Testament law were best regarded as being of three basic kinds, moral, ceremonial, and judicial.[34]

Essentially, St. Thomas scrutinizes, accepts, and improves upon this suggestion. For example, he gives further clarity to how the moral precepts are related to the natural law; he recognizes that the judicial precepts pertain to much more than the restraint of wrongdoers, for among other things they include what today would be called "constitutional" law; and he shows with great precision how the three categories are related. As he goes along, he folds in finer distinctions, for example showing that some, though not all, of the ceremonial precepts foreshadow things which come later in the history of salvation.

Correcting Aristotle

We saw earlier that St. Thomas embraces the Aristotelian view that the goodness of a person lies in his virtue, for virtue "makes its possessor good." This point is easy to misconstrue, because St. Thomas holds a much more complete view of virtue than Aristotle does, and distinguishes between nature and grace. In this sense, he corrects him.

In the first place, St. Thomas holds that in order to be truly good, it is not enough to possess the inward inclination to do the right things, for one's

---

[32] I-II, Q. 102. Art. 3.
[33] I-II, Q. 103, Art. 3; the internal references are to Isaiah 51:3, which is part of the Old Testament, and Apocalypse of John 21:22, which is part of the New, both quoted from the DRA. The title of the Apocalypse is sometimes given as Revelation, or Revelations.
[34] For discussion, see Matthew Levering, *Christ's Fulfillment of Torah and Temple: Salvation According to Thomas Aquinas* (Notre Dame, IN: University of Notre Dame Press, 2002), pp. 5–7, and Beryl Smalley, "William of Auvergne, John of La Rochelle and St. Thomas Aquinas on the Old Law," in *St. Thomas Aquinas 1274–1974: Commemorative Studies*, edited by A. A. Maurer et al. (Toronto: Pontifical Institute of Medieval Studies, 1974), vol. II, pp. 11ff.

character and motives must be transformed by God Himself. We do not earn our way into God's approval; rather, He accepts us because we have submitted to the ongoing surgery of His grace – a submission which is itself made possible only by His grace!

Consequently, we must distinguish between virtues the development of which require nothing more than our natural powers, and virtues the development of which require the influx of grace. The former are called "acquired," because they are attained by moral sweat, and the latter are called "infused," because they are poured into us by the grace of the Holy Spirit, though not without our cooperation. The acquired virtues are summarized and epitomized by fortitude, temperance, justice, and prudence, often called the "cardinal" virtues, and the infused virtues are epitomized by faith, hope, and charity or love, often called the "theological" or "spiritual" virtues.[35]

If we do cooperate with God's grace, then not only do we develop the spiritual virtues, but new forms of the cardinal virtues take root in us. The difference lies in orientation. Thus,

- Acquired prudence helps us to make good decisions for the sake of earthly life, such as marriage and education, but infused prudence helps us make good decisions for the sake of eternal life with God.
- Acquired justice helps us respect the rights of others as seen in the light of reason, but infused justice helps us to respect their rights as seen in the additional light of love.
- Acquired fortitude helps us to face frightening things for the sake of the goods of this life or to resist what endangers them, but infused fortitude helps us to face frightening things, even martyrdom, for the sake of the kingdom of heaven.
- Acquired temperance helps us to moderate our desires for the sake of earthly goods like health, but infused temperance helps us to moderate our desires for the sake of spiritual purity.

The infused virtues transform human psychology, not in the sense that they are contrary to human nature – for human nature was prepared ahead of time to receive them – but in the sense that this transformation exceeds the capacities which human nature possesses in itself. This vast change affects all aspects of the human person, including intellect, appetite, and will. From this point of

---

[35] For general discussion, see J. Budziszewski, *Commentary on Thomas Aquinas's Virtue Ethics* (Cambridge: Cambridge University Press, 2017). For discussion of the precise relation between acquired and infused virtues, see Michael Sherwin, OP, "Infused Virtue and the Effects of Acquired Vice: A Test Case for the Thomistic Theory of Infused Cardinal Virtues," *The Thomist* 73.1 (January 2009), pp. 29–52, and Richard Conrad, OP, "Human Practice and God's Making-Good in Aquinas' Virtue Ethics," in *Varieties of Virtue Ethics*, edited by David Carr, James Arthur, and Kristján Kristjánsson (London: Palgrave Macmillan for the Jubilee Centre for Character and Virtues, 2017), pp. 163–179.

Were Any of the Old Law's Precepts Moral?

view, says St. Thomas, the infused virtues "deserve to be called virtues simply," since they direct us to our ultimate end in God. By contrast, the acquired virtues are virtues only *secundum quid*, "in a restricted sense," because although they direct us with respect to a particular kind of action, doing so in a way that is *compatible with* our ultimate end in God, they do not actually direct us *to* this ultimate end.[36]

In one of St. Thomas's major early works, he also remarks that the acquired virtues make us fit for the life of the civil community, but the infused virtues make us fit for the spiritual life of that community which is the Church.[37] Similarly, in the *Summa* I-II, Question 61, Article 5, following the writer Macrobius Ambrosius Theodosius, he distinguishes among the forms which the cardinal virtues take at different levels of spiritual development: as "social" virtues, they enable us to conduct ourselves well in the community; as "cleansing" virtues, they incline us to God; and as virtues of the fully cleansed soul, they find their rest in God. The social virtues are acquired, but all these other virtues are infused.[38]

---

[36] I-II, Q. 65, Art. 2. This makes it likely that in most places where St. Thomas refers to the virtues, he is speaking of infused virtues.

[37] I am freely paraphrasing the Latin, *unde et in alia vita hominem perficiunt, acquisitae quidem in vita civili, infusae in vita spirituali, quae est ex gratia, secundum quam homo virtuosus est membrum Ecclesiae.* Thomas Aquinas, *Commentary on the Sentences of Peter Lombard*, III, dist. 33, q. 1, art. 2, qc. 4. For the Latin text of the work see www.corpusthomisticum.org/iopera.html.

[38] In this context he also mentions the "exemplar" virtues, but these the virtues as they preexist in God Himself. They are not human virtues, however; they are the Divine templates that finite human virtues imitate or reflect.

QUESTION 99, ARTICLE 4

Whether, Besides the Moral and Ceremonial Precepts, There Are Also Judicial Precepts?

TEXT	PARAPHRASE
Whether, besides the moral and ceremonial precepts, there are also judicial precepts?	The Old Law is held to include judicial rules, distinct from both moral and ceremonial rules. Is this correct?

I-II, Question 99, Article 3, omitted from this book, is whether in addition to the moral rules, the Old Law contains ceremonial rules. It does, for example rules about foods. Here we turn to the judicial rules, which are of more general interest, even among those who do not share St. Thomas's faith tradition. Judicial rules are about rulers and governance, about relations among citizens, about relations with foreigners, and about relations among members of the household.

What difference does it make whether the provisions of Old Testament law are all the same kind of precept, or different kinds? Since they are what they are no matter how we classify them, this may seem like hair-splitting. It isn't. We return to why it isn't in the Discussion at the end of the Article.

Objection 1. [1] *It would seem that there are no judicial precepts in addition to the moral and ceremonial precepts in the Old Law. For Augustine says in* Contra Faustum *that in the Old Law there are "precepts concerning the life we have to lead, and precepts regarding the life that is foreshadowed."* [2] *Now the precepts of the life we have to lead are moral precepts; and the precepts of the life that is foreshadowed are ceremonial. Therefore besides these two kinds of precepts we should not put any judicial precepts in the Law.*	Objection 1. The view in question seems to be mistaken, for consider what St. Augustine says in his book criticizing the Manichaean heretic Faustus. Augustine remarks that the Old Law includes certain rules about how to conduct ourselves in this life, and other rules which foreshadow the next life. But by the ones which show us how to act in this life, he means the moral precepts, and by the ones which foreshadow the next life, he means the ceremonial precepts. Augustine knew what he was talking about, and since these are the only two categories of precept he mentions, we should not describe any precepts as judicial.

Were Any of the Old Law's Precepts Judicial?

[1] In his book *Against Faustus the Manichaean*, among St. Augustine's criticisms is the fact that Faustus

did not know the difference between the precepts of the life that we must lead, and the precepts of the life that is foreshadowed. For example, *You shall not covet*[1] is a precept of the life that we must follow, but *Every male shall be circumcised on the eighth day*[2] is a precept of the life that is foreshadowed.[3]

The point of distinguishing between precepts of the life that is to be followed and precepts of the life that is foreshadowed is not that the latter are *not to be followed*, but that the reason they were to be followed was to symbolize or prefigure something yet to come. Physical circumcision stands for spiritual circumcision; the external mark on the flesh stands for an internal change which must occur in the heart. Thus, God promises the Israelites,

And the Lord your God will circumcise your heart and the heart of your offspring, so that you will love the Lord your God with all your heart and with all your soul, that you may live.[4]

According to St. Paul, this promise is fulfilled under the New Law:

For he is not a real Jew who is one outwardly, nor is true circumcision something external and physical. He is a Jew who is one inwardly, and real circumcision is a matter of the heart, spiritual and not literal. His praise is not from men but from God.[5]

So the purpose of this precept of the Old Law is to anticipate something about the New Law; the Hebrew people were taught about what was to come through being commanded to do something which symbolized it. This is distinct from the purpose of a precept such as "You shall not covet," which does not symbolize anything.

[2] The first kind of precept Augustine mentions corresponds to moral precepts and the second kind corresponds to ceremonial precepts. Augustine does not mention a third category, that is, judicial precepts. Therefore, holds the Objector, there aren't any.

Objection 2. [1] *Further, a gloss on Ps. 118, "I have not declined from Thy judgments," says, i.e. "from*	Objection 2. Moreover, the inspired author of one of the Psalms says he has not fallen away from God's "judgments." In a commentary,

---

[1] Exodus 20:17 (RSV-CE).
[2] Paraphrase of Genesis 17:10–12.
[3] My rendering of St. Augustine of Hippo, *Against Faustus, the Manichean*, book VI, chapter 2, [Faustus] *nescire quid intersit inter praecepta vitae agendae, et praecepta vitae significandae. Exempli gratia: Non concupisces praeceptum est agendae vitae; Circumcides omnem masculum octavo die praeceptum est significandae vitae.* I am taking the text from www.augustinus.it/latino/contro_fausto/index2.htm.
[4] Deuteronomy 30:6 (RSV-CE).
[5] Romans 2:28–29 (RSV-CE).

the rule of life Thou hast set for me." [2] *But a rule of life belongs to the moral precepts. Therefore the judicial precepts should not be considered as distinct from the moral precepts.*	we read that by God's judgments, the psalmist means the rule of life that God has instituted for him. But as we said above, a rule of life is a moral precept. Consequently, judicial precepts are not something different from moral precepts.

[1] Verses 101-102 of Psalm 118 read as follows:

> I have restrained my feet from every evil way, that I may keep thy words.
> I have not declined from thy judgments, because thou hast set me a law.[6]

From the latter verse we see that the "judgments" are part of the Old Law – but what kind of precepts are they? To solve this puzzle, the Objector draws upon the gloss, or commentary, of Flavius Magnus Aurelius Cassiodorus Senator. Cassiodorus views verse 102 in the light of verse 101. In his view, the psalmist's statement that he had not declined from God's judgments means that he has kept his feet from following the wicked path – that he has not swerved from the rule of life that God has ordained.[7] Thus, the Objector reasons that the phrase "Thy judgments" refers precisely to this rule of life.

The Objector's reasoning would have been much clearer had he quoted both the psalm and its interpreter more fully. Here is what Cassiodorus says in context:

> *I have not declined from thy judgment, because thou has set me a law.* The people clarified their earlier statement: *I have restrained my feet from every evil way*, so that they might not decline from his judgments to the slightest degree ... *From thy judgments*, then, means: "What Your holy will has appointed and given to us as our rule of life." Not to decline from them means precisely to stick fast to the right way ... There follows the reason which they approve: *Because thou hast set me a law.*[8]

[2] The argument works something like this:

1. The Old Law contains judgments.
2. Judgments are rules of life.
3. Rules of life are precepts of the life that is to be followed.
4. But as we saw in the previous Objection, the precepts of the life that is to be followed are moral precepts.
5. So any precepts which we might be tempted to designate as judicial, distinguishing them from the moral precepts, must really be just a kind of, or a subset of, moral precepts.

---

[6] DRA. In verse 101, I have changed a colon to a comma.
[7] *Sic prohibui pedes a via eorum quod non declinavi ab his que constituisti ad regulam vivendi.* Cassiodorus, *Explanation of the Psalms*, translated by P. G. Walsh, volume III (on Psalm 118:102) (New York: Paulist Press, 1991), pp. 219-220. "Senator" was part of his name.
[8] Ibid. As is customary, the italicized words are from the psalm and the other words are by Cassiodorus himself.

Objection 3. [1] Further, judgment seems to be an act of justice, [2] according to Ps. 93: "Until justice be turned into judgment." [3] But acts of justice, like the acts of other virtues, belong to the moral precepts. [4] Therefore the moral precepts include the judicial precepts, and consequently should not be held as distinct from them.	Objection 3. Besides, one of the Psalms promises the people of Israel that one day justice will be turned into judgment, implying that judgment is the deed by which justice is actualized or fulfilled – it is the "act" of justice. But just like the acts of the other virtues, the acts of justice concern the moral precepts. Therefore, the judicial precepts are entirely enclosed in the moral precepts, and should not be distinguished from them.

[1] The *act* of a virtue is that by which the virtue is *actualized*, for each virtue is a disposition or habit of performing certain kinds of acts. Consequently, with each virtue certain characteristic acts are associated. It is by means of these acts that the virtue in question is exercised, and it is by reference to them that it is understood. So what actualizes justice – what is its characteristic act? Earlier in the *Summa*, St. Thomas has devoted an entire Article to the defense of the proposition that its characteristic act is judgment.[9]

I take the issue to be not whether judgment is "an" act of justice, as the Blackfriars translators would have it, but whether it is "the" act of justice. Latin does not have definite or indefinite articles, and in most cases, such as this one, whether to translate by "a" or by "the" must be understood from context.[10] In one sense "an" is perfectly correct, for like each of the cardinal virtues, justice is a compendium of a number of subordinate virtues, for example truth and gratitude. Since each subordinate virtue also has its own characteristic act, these acts are subordinate acts of justice. Here, though, St. Thomas is making a point about the act of justice *as such*.

[2] The psalm from which these few words are taken is a plea to God to save His people from the wicked and restore the reign of justice. Verses 14–15 read: "For the Lord will not cast off his people: neither will he forsake his own inheritance, Until justice be turned into judgment: and they that are near it are all the upright in heart."[11]

In English, to speak of justice *turning into* judgment seems strange. St. Thomas would probably follow St. Augustine, who took the passage to mean that although the just must endure oppression now, one day, by God's authority, they will judge the oppressors. This judgment will come only in God's time;

---

[9] II-II, Q. 60, Art. 1.
[10] There are exceptions. Sometimes, demonstratives or reflexives ("that P," "P itself") are used where we would use the definite article ("the P"), and sometimes adjectives ("one P") are used where we would use the indefinite article ("a P"). Neither is the case here.
[11] Psalm 93:14–15 (DRA), rendering *Quia non repellet Dominus plebem suam, et haereditatem suam non derelinquet, quoadusque justitia convertatur in judicium: et qui juxta illam, omnes qui recto sunt corde*. In most contemporary translations, this psalm is numbered 94.

for now they must bear suffering with patience. Appealing to the reader, Augustine writes,

> Listen now, and gain righteousness: for judgment you cannot yet have. You should gain righteousness first; but that very righteousness of yours shall turn unto judgment. The Apostles had righteousness here on earth, and bore with the wicked. But what is said to them? You shall sit on twelve thrones, judging the twelve tribes of Israel. Their righteousness therefore shall turn unto judgment. For whoever is righteous in this life, is so for this reason, that he may endure evils with patience: let him suffer patiently the period of suffering, and the day of judging comes.
>
> But why do I speak of the servants of God? The Lord Himself, who is the Judge of all living and dead, first chose to be judged [on the Cross], and then to judge. Those who have righteousness at present, are not yet judges. For the first thing is to have righteousness, and afterwards to judge: He first endures the wicked, and afterwards judges them. Let there be righteousness now: afterwards it shall turn again unto judgment ...
>
> He spares sinners: you wish Him at once to destroy sinners. Your heart is crooked and your will perverted, when your will is one way and the will of God another. God wishes to spare sinners: you do not wish sinners spared.[12]

The passage bears out the point that justice is fully actualized in the act of judgment. St. Thomas concurs with this point, although he does not draw the same conclusion concerning the judicial precepts.

[3] The moral precepts command us to perform the acts of the corresponding moral virtues. From this fact, the Objector concludes that any precept which does so command is a moral precept.

[4] Therefore, since the judicial precepts command us to perform the act of the moral virtue of justice, they too are moral precepts. Notice that the Objector does not deny that there are such things as judicial precepts. He merely holds that they are not independent of the moral precepts, but one of their proper subsets.

The Latin word *includunt* is rendered by the Blackfriars translators as "include," but the term can also mean "imprison" or "shut up in," which is more forceful. My paraphrase "entirely enclose" reflects this.

On the contrary, [1] *It is written in Dt. 6: "These are the precepts, and ceremonies, and judgments":* [2] *where "precepts" stands for "moral precepts" antonomastically.* [3] *Therefore there are judicial precepts besides moral and ceremonial precepts.*	**On the other hand,** the sixth chapter of Deuteronomy declares that the body of rules about to be announced is made up of precepts, ceremonies, and judgments – that is, of moral precepts, ceremonial precepts, and judicial precepts. It follows that judicial precepts are a different kind than either moral or ceremonial.

---

[12] St. Augustine of Hippo, *Exposition on Psalm 94* (today 93), verse 14, www.newadvent.org/fathers/1801.htm. I have modernized two instances of "thou dost."

[1] Quoted more fully, Deuteronomy 6:1 declares, "These are the precepts, and ceremonies, and judgments, which the Lord your God commanded that I should teach you, and that you should do them in the land into which you pass over to possess it."[13] The pronoun seems to refer to *all* of the commandments that God gave the Hebrew people. Since the "ceremonies" must be ceremonial precepts, and the "judgments" must be judicial precepts, it would seem that the term "precepts" must refer, not to precepts in general but only to precepts which are neither ceremonial nor judicial – as though the sentence had begun, "These are the ceremonies, judgments, *and other* precepts." Taking it to refer to precepts per se would make the classification redundant, as though we were to speak of "civil engineers, electrical engineers, and engineers."

[2] According to the *sed contra*, the book of Deuteronomy is exchanging a descriptive term for a class (the class of moral precepts) with just one of the attributes of that class (that they are precepts). It may seem odd to call a subset by the name of a larger set, just because we do not often speak that way in English. Then again, perhaps in English we speak that way more often than we think. The figure of speech called antonomasia is the type of metonymy in which something is called by a proper name or title because of something with which it is associated. Thus, using antonomasia, we might give a red-haired boy the name "Red" because he is so strongly associated with red.

Now in the example of the red-haired boy, the associated thing is a color, but of course another thing with which something may be associated is the class to which it belongs. This is why St. Thomas gives Aristotle the title "the Philosopher," for even though he is but a single philosopher, he is so strongly representative of philosophers in general.[14] According to the *sed contra*, the book of Deuteronomy is doing something similar. It gives moral precepts the title "precepts" because, even though they are but a single kind of precept, they are so strongly representative of precepts in general.

[3] Even if we agree that the statement in Deuteronomy divides all of the precepts into three, the *sed contra* is not quite satisfying because we haven't been given any explanation of how these three classes of precepts are related. Without it, we inevitably wonder "Why just these three? Why shouldn't there be six, or seven, or fourteen?" This is the matter to which St. Thomas turns in the *respondeo*.

I answer that, [1] *As stated above, it belongs to the Divine law to direct men to one another and to God.* [2]

Here is my response. As we have found, Divine law puts the relations among men in order and directs men to God. But each of these

---

[13] DRA.
[14] Antonomasia can work in the other direction too. Thus, philosophers in general might be nicknamed Aristotles.

Now each of these belongs in the abstract to the dictates of the natural law, to which dictates the moral precepts are to be referred: [3] yet each of them has to be determined by Divine or human law, [4] because naturally known principles are universal, both in speculative and in practical matters. [5] Accordingly just as the determination of the universal principle about Divine worship is effected by the ceremonial precepts, [6] so the determination of the general precepts of that justice which is to be observed among men is effected by the judicial precepts. [7] We must therefore distinguish three kinds of precept in the Old Law; viz. "moral" precepts, which are dictated by the natural law; "ceremonial" precepts, which are determinations of the Divine worship; and "judicial" precepts, which are determinations of the justice to be maintained among men. [8] Wherefore the Apostle (Rm. 7) after saying that the "Law is holy," adds that "the commandment is just, and holy, and good": [9] "just," in respect of the judicial precepts; [10] "holy," with regard to the ceremonial precepts (since the word "sanctus"—"holy"—is applied to that which is consecrated to God); [11] and "good," i.e. conducive to virtue, as to the moral precepts.

purposes belongs not only to the Divine but also to the natural law, which is the basis of the moral precepts. Moreover, because naturally known principles are *universal*, both in the realm of what is and in the realm of what is to be done, each of these duties also requires more detailed specification, whether in Divine law or in human law.

So, just as the universal principle requiring Divine worship is given more detailed specification by the ceremonial precepts, the universal principle requiring justice among men is given more detailed specification by the judicial precepts.

It follows from all this that we must distinguish among three kinds of rules in the Old Divine law:

1. Moral precepts, which are prescribed by the natural law;
2. Ceremonial precepts, which further specify the worship to be given God; and
3. Judicial precepts, which further specify the justice to be observed among men.

This is why St. Paul adds to his declaration that the law is *holy* the further explanation that it is *just, holy and good*. For indeed:

1. It is just in the sense that its judicial precepts pertain to justice;
2. It is holy in the sense that its ceremonial precepts pertain to the dedication of things to God; and
3. It is good in the sense that its moral precepts pertain to all that is honest and honorable.

---

[1] St. Thomas remarks in I-II, Question 99, Article 3, "The Divine law is instituted chiefly in order to direct men to God; while human law is instituted chiefly in order to direct men in relation to one another." But as we saw in Article 2, "Just as the principal intention of human law is to create friendship between man and man; so the chief intention of the Divine law is to establish man in friendship with God." So the kind of direction which St. Thomas has in mind is the kind which establishes a *communion of friendship*, both among men and between man and God.

[2] St. Thomas says that these two purposes of Divine law belong "in common" (*in communi*) to the dictates of the natural law. The Blackfriars translators represent this as meaning that these purposes belong to it "in the abstract." It seems to me, however, that St. Thomas is saying something different: that they belong to the Divine law *as well as* to the natural law, as my paraphrase reflects. Not only does Divine law direct us to God but also, up to a point, even natural law directs us to God.[15] For "to love God above all things is natural to man," says St. Thomas.[16] Moreover,

> natural reason tells man that he is subject to a higher being ... and whatever this superior being may be, it is known to all under the name of God. Now just as in natural things the lower are naturally subject to the higher, so too it is a dictate of natural reason in accordance with man's natural inclination that he should tender submission and honor, according to his mode, to that which is above man.[17]

But we must be careful not to misunderstand this claim. St. Thomas explains elsewhere that as a result of the Fall, "man falls short of this in the appetite of his rational will, which, unless it is cured by God's grace, follows its private good." It isn't that the natural longing for God is absent from our hearts, but that we do not follow it. Therefore, "in the state of corrupt nature man needs ... the help of grace to heal his nature."[18] Now the grace that heals our nature exceeds the power of our nature, so we could not have known by natural reason alone how to avail ourselves of it. Only Divine law provides the needed instruction; therefore, only with the help of Divine law can we attain our supernatural end – the eternal vision of God in His own Being, the supreme happiness which is enjoyed by the redeemed in the next life. The problem, then, lies not in natural law per se, but in the corruption of our nature by the Fall.

[3] As we have seen, a precept can be derived from a more general precept in two different ways, *conclusion* and *determination*. In I-II, Question 95, Article 2, where he is speaking of the derivation of human law from natural law, St. Thomas explains the two ways like this:

> Some things are therefore derived from the general principles ... by way of conclusions; e.g. that "one must not kill" may be derived as a conclusion from the principle that "one should do harm to no man": while some are derived therefrom by way of determination; e.g. ... the evildoer should be punished; but that he be punished in this or that way, is a determination.

In both modes of derivation, the more general precept gives us a principle or starting point, "something to go on," as we say in English. In the first mode,

---

[15] For discussion, see Sean B. Cunningham, "Aquinas on the Natural Inclination of Man to Offer Sacrifice to God," *Proceedings of the American Catholic Philosophical Association* 86 (2013), pp. 185–200.
[16] I-II, Q. 109, Art. 3.
[17] II-II, Q. 85, Art. 1.
[18] I-II, Q. 109, Art. 3.

conclusion, the principle operates like an axiom in geometry. From it we can draw precise inferences about what to do, just like theorems. In the second mode, determination, the principle operates more as a consideration; even though we must follow the general precept without exception, it does not prescribe every detail of how we are to do so. Determination is pinning these details down, filling in the blanks.

In human law, determination is accomplished by the authority that God delegates to lawmakers. For example, although safety on the roadways might have been accomplished in any of several ways, lawmakers in the United States determined that vehicles are to drive only on the right. In Divine law, however, determination is accomplished by God Himself. For example, although care for the poor might have been accomplished in several ways, God decreed that the corners of fields are to remain unharvested and the poor are to be permitted to glean.

[4] St. Thomas is explaining why the naturally known principles are not enough – why we must pin them down – why determination is necessary. Our minds *naturally* recognize the truth of certain universal principles which serve as the starting points for all other reasoning. This is true both in "speculative" or theoretical matters, *what is*, and in practical matters, *what is to be done*. For example, in theoretical reasoning, we naturally know that equals added to equals are equal, but we do not naturally know whether Farmer Brown has an equal number of horses and cows; perhaps he has an unequal number. Likewise, in practical reasoning, we naturally know that we should do what is needed for the common good, but we do not naturally know that we should drive on the right; perhaps the common good could just as well be secured by the requirement to drive on the left, as in England. In all positive law, whether human or Divine, the purpose of determination is precisely to nail down the details in those cases where a single choice must be made for everyone, but in which the universal principles do not tell us which one to choose.

[5] The moral precepts of the Old Law express the universal dictates of the natural law. Some concern the love of God. For example, we naturally know that we should give reverence to God; this moral precept is universal and unchangeable. But how shall we give Him reverence? Shall we represent His invisible being with visible images, or not? Shall we offer Him sacrifices, or not? Shall we set aside special times to worship Him, and if so, shall we observe them on the seventh day, the tenth, or the thirtieth?

Presumably, God could have arranged some of these things differently. The ceremonial precepts express the details of His arrangements; they are determinations of the moral precepts which direct us to God Himself. In fact, not only could God have arranged some of these things differently, but according to Christian tradition, He has. For example, to commemorate God's rest from creation, the Old Law commands worship on the seventh day of the week, but to commemorate Christ's resurrection from the dead, the discipline of the Church ordains worship on the first day of the week.

[6] Now St. Thomas turns to the other moral precepts, those which direct us in our relations with other human beings. For example, we naturally know that we should be faithful to the marriage bond; this moral precept too is universal and unchangeable. But may I marry one wife, or more than one? If my wife displeases me, can the bond between us be dissolved? And what should be done with me if I am unfaithful to her – should I be punished, or get off scot-free?[19]

Presumably God could have arranged some of these things differently too. Again, Christian tradition holds that He has. For example, Christ teaches that "from the beginning," that is, by God's creational arrangements, marriage was indissoluble, and so it is to be among His followers; He says that the Old Testament law permits husbands to repudiate their wives because of their "hardness of heart,"[20] an expression which is sometimes taken to mean "because otherwise they would have killed them." The *intention* of the law did not change. However, the actual requirement did.

[7] We now perceive the relations among natural law and Divine law, among Old and New Divine Law, and among the moral, ceremonial, and judicial precepts of the Old Divine Law. New Divine Law will be explored later on. All these relations are presented in a pair of diagrams at the head of this book, one, which draws from earlier Articles, labeled *Architecture of Law in General*, the other *Detailed Architecture of Divine Law*. Further discussion of natural law is found in a previous work.[21]

[8] In the passage from which St. Thomas is quoting, St. Paul has been explaining that our sinful inclinations find opportunity to manifest themselves even in response to God's law: "I should not have known what it is to covet if the law had not said, 'You shall not covet.'" Does this mean that there is something wrong with the law? Not at all, St. Paul says, for "the law is holy, and the commandment is holy and just and good." Then does what is good bring about what is bad? "By no means!" he replies. "It was sin, working death in me *through* what is good."[22]

---

[19] Such are the times that in order to forestall the taking of offense, an author who does not wish to submit to the language police must defend the use of many innocent expressions. In Middle English, a *scot* was a tax, fee, or payment. Thus, the term "scot-free" means getting off without payment, or, by extension, without penalty. It is not a slur on the Scots – their name has a different origin, in the late Latin word *Scottus*. So far as I know, the Scots are just as burdened by taxes as any other nation.

[20] Matthew 19:8.

[21] J. Budziszewski, *Commentary on Thomas Aquinas's Treatise on Law* (Cambridge: Cambridge University Press, 2014), especially the discussion of I-II, q. 94, arts. 1–6.

[22] Romans 7:7b, 12–13 (RSV-CE), emphasis added.

St. Paul does not confine himself to saying that the Old Law is good; he goes further, specifying the ways in which it is good. Using the broad term "law," he says that all of it is "holy." Then, using the more particular term "commandment," he says it is holy, just, and good. Someone might take this to mean that *every* precept is holy, *every* precept is just, and *every* precept is good. St. Thomas takes it to mean that in their various ways, some of the precepts promote holiness, some justice, and some goodness. Obviously, the sense in which *certain* precepts promote holiness must be different from the sense in which the whole Law is holy, and the sense in which *certain* precepts promote goodness must be different from the sense in which the whole Law is good. Therefore, St. Thomas goes on to explain.

[9] The precepts which promote justice are the ones we call judicial. This is straightforward.

[10] In one sense, the entire Law is holy, for it all *comes* from God. However, some of the precepts are holy in the more particular sense that they concern things which are *dedicated* to God, for example the regulations for worship and Sabbath rest. These are the ones we call ceremonial precepts.

[11] St. Thomas says that another category of precept is *bonum*, that is, *honestum*. In one sense, the entire Law is good (*bonum*), because it directs us to God, who is the source and final end of all good. However, some of the precepts are good in the more particular sense (*honestum*) that they promote *moral* goodness. These are ones we call moral precepts.

The word *honestum* has no precise parallel in English. Because St. Thomas is using it to embrace the whole of morality, the Blackfriars translators render it as "conducive to virtue." More precisely, it refers to the honest and honorable, taking the honest in the double sense of truthfulness and good faith, and the honorable in the double sense of receiving honor and being worthy to receive it.

Reply to Objection 1. [1] *Both the moral and the judicial precepts aim at the ordering of human life:* [2] *and consequently they are both comprised under one of the heads mentioned by Augustine, viz. under the precepts of the life we have to lead.*	Reply to Objection 1. The judicial precepts pertain to the direction of human life no less than the moral precepts do. Therefore, when Augustine speaks of rules about how to conduct ourselves in this life, he is including both.

[1] The Objector had argued that when Augustine spoke of precepts pertaining to the direction of human life, he meant moral precepts. St. Thomas responds that judicial precepts pertain to the direction of human life just as much as moral precepts do.[23]

---

[23] There are a number of Latin words which express the idea "both." *Tam*, however, more precisely expresses the idea "all the same," "just as much," or "to the same degree." Thus,

[2] Thus, both moral precepts and judicial precepts are proper subsets of Augustine's category "precepts of the life we have to lead."

Reply to Objection 2. [1] *Judgment denotes execution of justice, by an application of the reason to individual cases in a determinate way.* [2] *Hence the judicial precepts have something in common with the moral precepts, in that they are derived from reason;* [3] *and something in common with the ceremonial precepts, in that they are determinations of general precepts.* [4] *This explains why sometimes "judgments" comprise both judicial and moral precepts, as in Dt. 5: "Hear, O Israel, the ceremonies and judgments";* [5] *and sometimes judicial and ceremonial precepts, as in Lev. 18: "You shall do My judgments, and shall observe My precepts," where "precepts" denotes moral precepts, while "judgments" refers to judicial and ceremonial precepts.*

Reply to Objection 2. The term "judgment" refers to the execution of justice, by applying reason to particular instances, in such a way as to settle what is to be done.
We see from this that the judicial precepts have something in common with the moral precepts because both are derived from reason, but they also have something in common with the ceremonial precepts because both pin down how certain general rules are to be applied.
Therefore, sometimes the term "judgments" refers to both judicial and moral rules, for example in Deuteronomy 5, where Moses says "Hear, O Israel, the ceremonies and judgments [which I speak in your ears this day]" – and sometimes it refers to both judicial and ceremonial rules, for example in Leviticus 18, where the Lord says through Moses "You shall do my judgments, and shall observe my precepts, [and shall walk in them]."
In the latter passage, bear in mind that the word "precepts" refers to moral rules, as in the *sed contra*, while the word "judgments" refers to judicial and ceremonial precepts, as just explained.

[1] The Objector had argued that since God's judgments are rules of life, and rules of life are moral precepts, therefore judicial precepts are not distinct from moral precepts, but a kind or subset of them. However, St. Thomas points out that the term "judgment" does not refer to all rules of life; it has a more particular meaning. "Judgment denotes execution of justice, by an application of the reason to individual cases in a determinate way."

In the first place, then, judgment is an exercise of reason in order to preserve justice. Judgment is not the kind of intellectual operation involved in grasping the truth of universal principles and their corollaries, such as not stealing and returning borrowed property. Rather it is the kind involved in determining how such principles are to be applied when more than one way would be possible.

---

although the correlative *tam ... quam* can be taken in the sense "both this and that," as in the Blackfriars translation, I take it in the slightly stronger sense "just as this, so to the same degree that."

For example, Exodus 22:1 directs that "If a man steals an ox or a sheep, and kills it or sells it, he shall pay five oxen for an ox, and four sheep for a sheep," but it might have been four or six oxen for an ox, or three or five sheep for a sheep, or a certain amount of money.[24]

Principles like not stealing and returning borrowed property, then, are moral precepts. However, subordinate regulations which "determine" or pin down how the moral precepts are to be applied are judicial precepts.

[2] We saw above that we arrive at moral and judicial precepts in different ways. Nevertheless, we arrive at both by the exercise of reason.

[3] We have also seen above that some of the moral precepts, such as "You shall not steal," concern the relation of man and man, while others, such as "You shall have no gods before Me," concern the relation of man and God. Just as the judicial precepts determine how the former are to be applied, so the ceremonial precepts determine how the latter are to be applied. Thus, both judicial and ceremonial precepts are determinations of more general precepts.

[4] Just because both judicial and moral precepts are derived by reason, sometimes Holy Scripture uses the term "judgments" to refer to both categories of precept. We see this, for example, in the passage of Deuteronomy which declares, "And Moses called all Israel, and said to them: Hear, O Israel, the ceremonies and judgments, which I speak in your ears this day: learn them, and fulfill them in work."[25]

[5] Again, just because both judicial and ceremonial precepts are determinations of more general principles, sometimes Holy Scripture uses the term "judgments" to embrace both of them. We see this, for example, in the passage of Leviticus in which God commands, "You shall do my judgments [both judicial and ceremonial precepts], and shall observe my precepts [moral precepts, as in Deuteronomy 6:1, discussed above], and shall walk in them. I am the Lord your God."[26]

The concluding remark, "I am the Lord your God" is worthy of special notice, for it is interesting how often, just before or after giving a command or a series of commands, God reminds His people of who He is. Consider for example the context of the quotation just above, a passage in which various abominations and atrocities are listed and forbidden:

And the Lord spoke to Moses, saying: Speak to the children of Israel, and thou shalt say to them: *I am the Lord your God.* You shall not do according to the custom of the land of Egypt, in which you dwelt: neither shall you act according to the manner of the country of Canaan, into which I will bring you, nor shall you walk in their ordinances. You shall do my judgments, and shall observe my precepts, and shall walk in them. *I am the Lord your God.* Keep my laws and my judgments, which if a man do, he shall live in them. *I am the*

---

[24] In the trial of an accused person, judgment is exercised in a different way, by applying a rule to a singular fact: For example, we know that stealing is forbidden, but did this man steal? Here, though, we are speaking of judgment in the context of legislation.

[25] Deuteronomy 5:1 (DRA).

[26] Leviticus 18:4 (DRA).

Lord ... Keep my commandments. Do not the things which [the pagan nations] have done, that have been before you, and be not defiled therein. *I am the Lord your God.*[27]

The point of this repetition is to reinforce the sense of God's holiness, and His insistence that His worshippers keep themselves wholly apart from the customs of the surrounding pagan nations, such as casting infants into the fire as a fertility rite: "Thou shalt not give any of thy seed to be consecrated to the idol Moloch, nor defile the name of thy God: I am the Lord."[28] Of course these practices would be unthinkable to us. In that day, infants were sacrificed to the gods of fertility to insure that there would be more infants later. By contrast, in our day they are sacrificed to the gods of infertility to insure that there will not be any now.

| *Reply to Objection 3. The act of justice, in general, belongs to the moral precepts; but its determination to some special kind of act belongs to the judicial precepts.* | Reply to Objection 3. The moral precepts command doing justice in general. However, the judicial precepts pin down *how* to do justice, by commanding particular kinds or "species" of act. |

The Objector had rightly argued that the moral precepts concern the acts of all of the moral virtues. But the moral virtues include the virtue of justice, so he should have argued that precepts concerning the act of justice are moral precepts too. This would include every one of the commandments of the Decalogue. For justice is giving to others what we owe to them, and as we will see when we get to I-II, Question 100, Article 5, all of the commandments of the Decalogue concern what we owe to others – the first three what we owe to God, and the last seven what we owe to our neighbors.[29]

But that is not quite St. Thomas's point. The reason is that as "determinations," the judicial precepts go beyond general commandments of justice. They fill in the blanks of how these commandments are to be applied to particular kinds of situations, for example punishment of crime, buying and selling, compensation for injury, and loans and repayment of loans.

DISCUSSION

What Difference Does It Make?

Would it make any difference if we got the classification of Old Testament precepts wrong? It may make a difference in a number of ways, but here we consider only two, one of them practical, the other theoretical.

---

[27] Leviticus 18, verses 1–5 and 30, adding emphasis, substituting "the pagan nations" for "they," and modernizing spelling.
[28] Leviticus 18:21.
[29] See also my discussion of II-II, Q. 122, Art. 1, "Whether the precepts of the Decalogue are precepts of justice?", in *Commentary on Thomas Aquinas's Virtue Ethics*.

The practical issue is whether any of those precepts could have been different than they were. Answer: some couldn't, some could; it depends on which kind of precept one has in mind. None of the moral precepts could have been different because they reflect general precepts of natural law. Having created the good of creaturely life, for example, God will not now say "Go ahead and murder if you like." The wrongness of murder is in inherent in the nature of the things that He made.

But the ceremonial and judicial precepts could have been different because they are "determinations" of the moral precepts: by divine authority, they pin down the precise way in which the moral precepts should be observed, in cases in which more than one possibility may have existed. Ceremonial precepts pin down the details of our duty to worship God Himself. Judicial precepts pin down the details of our duties of justice to man in God's image.

Human law is like this too. The lawmakers cannot release us from the duty to take care for the safety of others. On the other hand, they can pin down whether we are to drive on the right or the left. In much the same way, not even God Himself can release us from the duty to worship Him alone, for the rightness of worshipping Him inheres in *Who He Is*. Nor could he release us from the duty to do justice to our neighbors. On the other hand, some of the details of divine worship and executing doing justice might have been arranged differently than they were. This is why, for example, it was possible for Jesus to modify the Jewish Passover so that it became Holy Communion, and why, although adultery is as dreadfully wrong as it ever was, we are no longer bound to punish it by stoning. There were good reasons for the old ceremonial and judicial regulations – but by divine authority, certain changes were possible, and there were good reasons for these too. By the way, by considering these good reasons for the old regulations, Christians too can learn from the ceremonial and judicial precepts of Old Testament law. The fact that Christians are not required to obey them does not mean that they should be indifferent to them. These precepts were part of the divine pedagogy.

The theoretical issue is why it matters whether we get *any* definition or classification right. Answer: it matters because the mind makes use of classifications to engage the shape of reality. Do we wish to understand how things really are, or don't we? A dog is not a cat, nor a triangle a rhombus, nor a person, thank God, a thing. Contrary to the views of postmodernists and some Justices of the Supreme Court, we cannot change the basic structures of reality just by defining them perversely. At stake is the rational mind's privilege and calling to know *what is*.

Now at the bottom of *what is*, we find eternal law: the pattern in the mind of God, by which He created and governs the universe. Although we cannot know it as His own infinite intellect knows it, we can certainly know it through its reflections – by reason in natural law, and by direct verbal proclamation, comprehensible to reason, in biblical law. This is how He imparts it to us.

Thus, even if there were no practical reason to know how many kinds of Old Testament precepts there are, it would be worthwhile to know the answer simply because knowing is our vocation. By doing what we are made for, we are fulfilled, and we give homage to the Author of our minds.

QUESTION 99, ARTICLE 6

Whether the Old Law Should Have Induced Men to the Observance of its Precepts, by Means of Temporal Promises and Threats?

TEXT	PARAPHRASE
Whether the Old Law should have induced men to the observance of its precepts, by means of temporal promises and threats?	The Old Testament law motivated men to obey its rules by promising benefits and threatening penalties which would come in the present life. Was that appropriate?

The Old Law is rich with promises of blessings in the present life for obedience to God's law and warnings of calamities for faithlessness:

> See, I have set before you this day life and good, death and evil. If you obey the commandments of the Lord your God which I command you this day, by loving the Lord your God, by walking in his ways, and by keeping his commandments and his statutes and his ordinances, then you shall live and multiply, and the Lord your God will bless you in the land which you are entering to take possession of it. But if your heart turns away, and you will not hear, but are drawn away to worship other gods and serve them, I declare to you this day, that you shall perish; you shall not live long in the land which you are going over the Jordan to enter and possess. I call heaven and earth to witness against you this day, that I have set before you life and death, blessing and curse; therefore choose life, that you and your descendants may live.[1]

Nothing like this can be found in the New Law, yet the claim is that both laws come from God. What is going on?

One of the themes of the study of law is the development of law over time. Although law can degenerate as well as advance, usually the history of law is studied with a view to how laws and legal institutions have become better, for instance through improvements in the rules of evidence. St. Thomas writes that there are two reasons why a human law might change for the better:

> Thus there may be two causes for the just change of human law: one on the part of reason; the other on the part of man whose acts are regulated by law. The cause on the part of reason is that it seems natural to human reason to advance gradually from the

---

[1] Deuteronomy 30:15–19 (RSV-CE).

imperfect to the perfect ... On the part of man, whose acts are regulated by law, the law can be rightly changed on account of the changed condition of man, to whom different things are expedient according to the difference of his condition.[2]

But how could that apply here? At present we are speaking not of human law, but of Divine law. According to St. Thomas, the law of the Old Testament is the product of authentic Divine inspiration, not just an invention of human beings. If it did come from God, does that mean that it was already perfect and incapable of development?

The answer is no, because although one of the two reasons for change in human laws does not apply to Divine legislation, the other one does. The infinite mind of God knows all things perfectly; it does not need to advance in understanding, as human minds do. Consequently, Divine law will never change because God came up with a better idea. On the other hand, in some respects even Divine law may change because of the changed condition of the human beings who must be governed by it. St. Thomas believes that although God devised the best law possible given the initial condition of the Hebrew people, His intention in giving them the law was not that they remain in this condition, but that they advance – that their minds be more faithfully shaped by His. St. Thomas makes use of this insight in answering the question posed in the *utrum*.

Objection 1. [1] *It would seem that the Old Law should not have induced men to the observance of its precepts, by means of temporal promises and threats. For the purpose of the Divine law is to subject man to God by fear and love:* [2] *hence it is written* (Dt. 10): *"And now, Israel, what doth the Lord thy God require of thee, but that thou fear the Lord thy God, and walk in His ways, and love Him?"* [3] *But the desire for temporal goods leads man away from God: for Augustine says (Qq. lxxxiii, qu. 36), that "covetousness is the bane of charity."* [4] *Therefore temporal promises and threats seem to be contrary to the intention of a lawgiver:* [5] *and this makes a law worthy of rejection, as the Philosopher declares (Polit. ii).*	Objection 1. It seems wrong for the Old Law to have made use of temporal promises and threats. Why? Because the intention of all Divine law is that man become amenable to God's rule by loving Him and regarding Him with fearful awe. This is why, in the book of Deuteronomy, Moses asks the people of Israel, "And now what does the Lord your God require of you, but to fear the Lord your God, walk in all His ways, and love Him?" By contrast, the greed for temporal goods seduces man away from God. Augustine confirms this, writing that covetousness is love's poison. It seems to follow that the intention of the lawmaker precludes the use of temporal promises and threats. Even Aristotle knew that any law which does make use of them should be censured.

---

[2] I-II, Q. 97, Art. 1.

[1] St. Thomas closely analyzes the relations among the love of God and the various kinds of fear of God. The sort of love to which this passage refers is charity, "the friendship of man for God" – loving God for God's own sake – loving God not just to avoid an evil other than separation from God, or to gain a benefit other than the presence of God, but because God is God.[3] The measure of charity is unity with God, so the more one is united with God, the more complete charity is.[4] Although charity is a genuinely voluntary act, a true act of the will, it transcends the will's natural power, so it requires the assistance of the will by God's grace.[5]

As to fear, there are two different kinds, servile and filial. They are given these names because they are like the fear that a servant has for his master and the fear that a child has for his father. If someone turns to God and clings to him because he is afraid of God's punishment, then his fear is servile. But if he stands in awe of God and avoids whatever would separate him from God, then his fear is filial, because it is appropriate for a child to fear giving his father offense.[6] Filial fear is one of the seven gifts of the Holy Spirit – in fact, in one sense, it is the first of them. Every gift of the Holy Spirit makes the soul receptive to the inflow of God's grace, but the first condition that must be satisfied for the soul to welcome this inflow is that it lay down all resistance, and "this is what filial or chaste fear does."[7]

Filial fear is inseparable from charity, and the full development of charity puts an end to servile fear.[8] This servile fear is what St. John had in mind when he wrote, "There is no fear in love, but perfect love casts out fear. For fear has to do with punishment, and he who fears is not perfected in love."[9] On the other hand, beginners in faith, who have only the beginning of charity, have only the beginning of filial fear too. This immature condition is sometimes called "initial fear."[10] Although In such immaturity, beginners retain a degree of servile fear, it does open the way for filial fear. St. Thomas calls it "the herald of charity, just as the bristle [or needle] introduces the thread,"[11] borrowing the metaphor of the bristle from St. Augustine, who writes as follows:

Fear, so to say, prepares a place for charity. But when once charity has begun to inhabit, the fear which prepared the place for it is cast out. For in proportion as this increases,

---

[3] II-II, Q. 23, Art. 1.
[4] Supp. Q. 93, Art. 3, *sed contra*.
[5] II-II, Q. 23, Art. 2.
[6] I-II, Q. 67, Art. 4, ad 2; II-II, Q. 19, Art. 2.
[7] II-II, Q. 19, Art. 9.
[8] II-II, Q. 19, Arts. 9 and 6, respectively.
[9] 1 John 4:18 (RSV-CE). See II-II, Q. 19, Art. 8, ad 2; III, Q. 7, Art. 6, ad 3; and Supp., Q. 4, Art. 1, ad 2.
[10] II-II, Q. 19, Arts. 2 and 8.
[11] II-II, Q. 19, Art. 8.

that decreases: and the more this comes to be within, is the fear cast out. Greater charity, less fear; less charity, greater fear. But if no fear, there is no way for charity to come in. As we see in sewing, the thread is introduced by means of the bristle; the bristle first enters, but except it come out the thread does not come into its place …

Fear does goad: but fear not: charity enters in, and she heals the wound that fear inflicts. The fear of God so wounds as does the leech's knife; it takes away the rottenness, and seems to make the wound greater … it smarts more under the healing operation, but only that it may never smart when the healing is effected … Fear is the healing operation: charity, the sound condition.[12]

[2] In Deuteronomy 10:12, just after reminding the Israelites about their former disobedience, Moses asks them this question about God's requirements. As recounted in Exodus 32, the first time Moses had climbed Mt. Horeb to receive the tablets of the Decalogue, inscribed upon stone by the finger of God, he had been gone so long that the Israelites revolted, reverting to idolatry by making a golden idol of a calf and worshipping it. Upon coming down from the mountain and witnessing their revels, Moses broke the tablets of the law before their eyes, prostrated himself, fasted from food and drink, implored God to turn aside from anger and have mercy upon them, and ground the golden calf into powder, throwing the dust into the water of the brook that flowed from the mountain, and making the people drink it. Relenting, God instructed Moses to hew two tablets of stone like the first, climb again to the height, and receive the commandments again. When again Moses descended from the mountain, God instructed him to resume his position at the head of the journey, so that the people could enter and possess the land promised to them.

Recalling the minds of the people to these past events, Moses says, "And now, Israel, what doth the Lord thy God require of thee, but that thou fear the Lord thy God, and walk in his ways, and love him, and serve the Lord thy God, with all thy heart, and with all thy soul: And keep the commandments of the Lord, and his ceremonies, which I command thee this day, that it may be well with thee?"[13]

[3] In the following passage, Augustine explains that the perfection of charity strengthens the filial and drives out the servile kind of fear, but that the craving for the goods of this life beguiles us so that we lose sight of eternal God and charity is destroyed:

[T]he poison of charity is the hope of getting and holding onto temporal things. The nourishment of charity is the lessening of covetousness, the perfection of charity, the absence of covetousness. The lessening of fear is the sign of its progress, the absence of fear, the sign of its perfection. For *"the root of all evils is covetousness,"* and *"love made*

---

[12] St. Augustine of Hippo, *Homilies on the First Epistle of John*, homily 9, section 4, www.newadvent.org/fathers/170209.htm.
[13] Deuteronomy 10:12–13 (DRA).

perfect casts out fear." Accordingly whoever wants to nourish charity in himself, let him pursue the lessening of covetous desires.[14]

A little later he continues,

Once this kind of covetousness is overcome, there is need to watch out for pride. For it is difficult for him who no longer desires to please men and who considers himself to be fully virtuous to think the company of men worthwhile. Consequently fear is still necessary that even that which he seems to have may not be taken from him,[15] and that with hands and feet bound he may not be cast into outer darkness.[16] For this reason, the fear of God is not only the beginning of the wise man's wisdom, but the completion of it as well.[17]

[4] The Objector argues that temporal promises and threats appeal to servile fear. Since God desires that human beings obey Him through love and filial fear, this is inappropriate.

[5] My paraphrase inserts the word "even," which is not in the text, to emphasize the Objector's point. Aristotle, a pagan, knew nothing of Divine law and was speaking only of human law. Yet even he knew that reliance on servile fear makes law defective. True, Aristotle does not say so explicitly. However, the Objector is drawing an inference from Aristotle's statement that what lawgivers intend is not merely that the citizens obey, but that they become formed in virtue. Here is what Aristotle actually says:

Neither by nature, then, nor contrary to nature do the virtues arise in us; rather we are adapted by nature to receive them, and are made perfect by habit ... we become just by doing just acts, temperate by doing temperate acts, brave by doing brave acts ... legislators make the citizens good by forming habits in them, and this is the wish of every legislator, and those who do not effect it miss their mark, and it is in this that a good constitution differs from a bad one.[18]

| Objection 2. [1] Further, *the Divine law is more excellent than human law.* [2] *Now, in sciences, we notice that the loftier the science, the higher the means of persuasion that it employs.* [3] *Therefore, since human law employs temporal threats and promises, as* | Objection 2. Moreover, Divine law is loftier than human law. Speaking generally, we find that the more elevated a branch of knowledge, the more elevated its methods. Therefore, since human law motivates man by means of temporal promises and |

---

[14] St. Augustine of Hippo, *Eighty-Three Different Questions*, translated by David L. Mosher (1982; Washington, DC: Catholic University of America Press, 2002), question 36, "On Nourishing Charity," section 1, p. 68. The internal quotations are respectively from 1 Timothy 6:10 and 1 John 4:18.
[15] Alluding to Matthew 25:29.
[16] Alluding to Matthew 22:13.
[17] Augustine, *Eighty-Three Different Questions*, question 36, section 4, p. 71.
[18] Aristotle, *Nicomachean Ethics*, translated by W. D. Ross (public domain), book II, chapter 1. The Blackfriars translators take St. Thomas to be referring to book II, chapter 6.

Were the Old Law's Promises and Threats Appropriate? 85

means of persuading man, the Divine law should have used, not these, but more lofty means.	threats, Divine law should have used not these methods, but greater ones.

[1] To say that the Divine law is more excellent is to say that its subject matter is loftier or more noble. Divine law is more excellent than human law because the latter directs us only toward our natural good (our friendship with man), but the former also directs us to our supernatural good (our friendship with God).

[2] The term "sciences" is used here in an extremely broad way for all systematic bodies of knowledge whatsoever, whether theoretical, like mathematics, or practical, like agriculture. In general, the Objector suggests, the means by which a given science teaches must be adapted to its subject matter; for example, in agriculture we might only point out what works, but in mathematics we employ syllogisms.

[3] According to the Objector, since Divine law deals with higher matters than human law, we should expect it to use higher methods of teaching. He does not say what methods of teaching actually would be suitable for so lofty a subject matter, but he argues that the carrot and the stick – promising benefits for obedience, and threatening punishments for disobedience – are base and unbefitting the loftiness of the matters to be inculcated.

Objection 3. [1] *Further, the reward of righteousness and the punishment of guilt cannot be that which befalls equally the good and the wicked.* [2] *But as stated in Eccles. 9, "all" temporal "things equally happen to the just and to the wicked, to the good and the evil, to the clean and to the unclean, to him that offereth victims, and to him that despiseth sacrifices."* [3] *Therefore temporal goods or evils are not suitably set forth as punishments or rewards of the commandments of the Divine law.*	Objection 3. Besides, things which happen equally to the good and the wicked cannot be viewed as a reward of justice or a punishment of guilt. Yet we read in one of the Old Testament Wisdom books, Ecclesiastes, that all things do happen equally: to the just and the impious, to the good and the evil, to the clean and the unclean, to those who sacrifice to God and to those who hold sacrifice in contempt. "All things" means all temporal goods and evils, so temporal things are unworthy to be set forth by Divine law as rewards and punishments for obeying or disobeying its commandments.

[1] This statement is an allusion to a passage in the Gospel of Matthew in which Christ teaches that we should imitate God's patience with those who do wrong:

You have heard that it was said, "You shall love your neighbor and hate your enemy." But I say to you, Love your enemies and pray for those who persecute you, so that you may be sons of your Father who is in heaven; for he makes his sun rise on the evil and on the good, and sends rain on the just and on the unjust. For if you love those who love you, what reward have you? Do not even the tax collectors do the same? And if you salute only your brethren, what more are you doing than others? Do not even the Gentiles do the same? You, therefore, must be perfect, as your heavenly Father is perfect.[19]

If the sun and rain come equally to the righteous and the unrighteous, then the sun and rain can be regarded neither as rewards for virtue nor as punishments for vice.

[2] The phrase used in the Vulgate, *iusto et impio*, which the DRA translates as "the just and the wicked," actually means "the just and the impious." Impiety is not just any kind of wickedness, but wickedness in opposition to piety – the wickedness of ingratitude to all those to whom we especially owe reverence, including our parents, ancestors, and countrymen, but especially including God. Here is the passage in context:

All these things have I considered in my heart, that I might carefully understand them: there are just men and wise men, and their works are in the hand of God: and yet man knows not whether he be worthy of love, or hatred: But all things are kept uncertain for the time to come, because all things equally happen to the just and to the wicked, to the good and to the evil, to the clean and to the unclean, to him that offers victims, and to him that offers sacrifices. As the good is, so also is the sinner: as the perjured, so he also that swears truth.[20]

Notice that although in the passage from the Gospel of Matthew, Christ portrays the fact that the sun and rain come equally to the just and the unjust as a token of God's patience with sinners, the dour author of Ecclesiastes portrays it as a source of dread, for the passage continues in the next verse, "This is a very great evil among all things that are done under the sun, that the same things happen to all men: whereby also the hearts of the children of men are filled with evil, and with contempt while they live, and afterwards they shall be brought down to hell."[21] Can the two passages be reconciled? Yes. For on the one hand, the fact that those who persist obstinately in sin are *not yet* brought to final ruin is an expression of God's mercy. But on the other, the prolongation of His mercy deepens the blame and eventual suffering of those who do persist in injustice, and in the meantime, it sorely tries the patience of their victims.[22]

---

[19] Matthew 5:43–48 (RSV-CE).
[20] Ecclesiastes 9:1–2 (DRA), modernizing archaic verb forms such as "sweareth."
[21] The phrase "down to hell" renders the Latin of the Vulgate, *ad inferos deducentur*. Based on the Hebrew, which is less explicit, some translations say "down to the dead."
[22] See Apocalypse (Revelation) 6:9–11, where St. John, writing of his vision, describes the souls of those who had been slain for their witness as crying out to God, asking Him how much longer He will wait to judge and avenge their blood. St. John reports that they are told to rest a little longer, until their number is complete.

Were the Old Law's Promises and Threats Appropriate? 87

[3] The argument works like this:

1. God rewards only the just, and punishes only the unjust.
2. But the goods and evils of the present life come to the just and the unjust equally.
3. Therefore, it was inappropriate for the Old Testament law to promise temporal goods to the just, and to threaten the unjust with temporal evils.

On the contrary, It is written (Is. 1): "If you be willing, and will hearken to Me, you shall eat the good things of the land. But if you will not, and will provoke Me to wrath: the sword shall devour you."	**On the other hand,** God says through the prophet Isaiah that if the people submit their wills to God and listen to Him, they will feed upon the good things of the land, but if they refuse and provoke Him to wrath, the sword will instead feed upon them.

The quotation in the *sed contra* is from the opening chapter of the book of the prophet Isaiah. God accuses His people of abandoning Him and wallowing in iniquity: "The ox knows his owner, and the ass his master's crib: but Israel has not known me, and my people have not understood."[23] He explains that their present suffering is a consequence of their sins: "Your land is desolate, your cities are burnt with fire: your country strangers devour before your face, and it shall be desolate as when wasted by enemies."[24] He warns them that He will not listen to their hypocritical prayers: "And when you stretch forth your hands, I will turn away my eyes from you: and when you multiply prayer, I will not hear: for your hands are full of blood."[25] Finally he offers hope, but it comes with a price:

Wash yourselves, be clean, take away the evil of your devices from my eyes: cease to do perversely, Learn to do well: seek judgment, relieve the oppressed, judge for the fatherless, defend the widow ... If you be willing, and will hearken to me, you shall eat the good things of the land. But if you will not, and will provoke me to wrath: the sword shall devour you because the mouth of the Lord hath spoken it.[26]

My paraphrase of the two verses quoted in the *sed contra* attempts to illuminate the parallel between the people who devour the land's fruits and the sword which devours the people. In the Hebrew Bible (though not in the Vulgate), the same verb for eating is used in both cases.

Taking into account both its express and its tacit premises, the argument of the *sed contra* might be represented as follows:

1.

---

[23] Isaiah 1:3 (DRA), modernizing archaic verb forms.
[24] Isaiah 1:7.
[25] Isaiah 1:15.
[26] Isaiah 1:16–17, 19–20.

Whatever one might have expected the Old Law to have done, it did, in fact, promise temporal goods to the just and threaten the unjust with temporal evils.
2. But these promises and threats came from God.
3. God does everything fittingly.
4. Therefore, the promises and threats must have been appropriate.

Someone might object that if God does everything fittingly, yet the Old Law included temporal promises and threats, then the tacit premise is incorrect: The Old Law was not from God! For this reason, St. Thomas cannot rest with the *sed contra*'s restatement of the traditional view. He must go on to explain *just how* the promises and threats of the Old Law were fitting. This he does in the *respondeo*, to which we are about to turn.

I answer that, [1] *As in speculative sciences men are persuaded to assent to the conclusions by means of syllogistic arguments,* [2] *so too in every law, men are persuaded to observe its precepts by means of punishments and rewards.* [3] *Now it is to be observed that, in speculative sciences, the means of persuasion are adapted to the conditions of the pupil:* [4] *wherefore the process of argument in sciences should be ordered becomingly, so that the instruction is based on principles more generally known.* [5] *And thus also he who would persuade a man to the observance of any precepts, needs to move him at first by things for which he has an affection;* [6] *just as children are induced to do something, by means of little childish gifts.* [7] *Now it has been said above that the Old Law disposed men to (the coming of) Christ, as the imperfect in comparison disposes to the perfect, wherefore it was given to a people as yet imperfect in comparison to the perfection which was to result from Christ's coming:* [8] *and for this reason, that people is compared to a child that is still under a pedagogue (Gal. 3).* [9] *But the perfection of man consists in his despising temporal things and cleaving to things spiritual,* [10] *as is clear from*

Here is my response. Just as the theoretical sciences must move us to accept their conclusions, so the law must move us to obey its precepts. The motivating role which syllogisms play in the former is played by rewards and punishments in the latter.

Let us continue this analogy. We see that the theoretical sciences set forth their propositions according to the ability of the listener to take them in. Therefore instruction must follow a certain order, beginning from what is already familiar. In the same way, in order to motivate someone to obey the precepts of the law, one must begin by appealing to what he likes (or perhaps fears). This is how we deal with children, when we draw them into doing what they ought to do by promising trinkets in return.

Earlier we saw that the Old Law used an imperfect rather than perfect method to encourage men to look forward to Christ. This was appropriate because it was given to a people who were still immature; they had not yet come into the complete maturity which was to be imparted through Christ later on. For this reason St. Paul compares them to a child who is still under the authority of the escort who leads him to school.

But the full and appropriate development of man lies in holding temporal things in contempt, clinging instead to things

the words of the Apostle (Phil. 3): "Forgetting the things that are behind, I stretch [Vulg.: 'and stretching'] forth myself to those that are before ... Let us therefore, as many as are perfect, be thus minded." [11] *Those who are yet imperfect desire temporal goods, albeit in subordination to God:* [12] *whereas the perverse place their end in temporalities.* [13] *It was therefore fitting that the Old Law should conduct men to God by means of temporal goods for which the imperfect have an affection.*

spiritual. Paul explains this in another passage, where he says that he is stretching himself forward to the things yet to come, forgetting those that are past. He concludes, "Let those who are mature think like this." Now those who are perverse crave temporal goods as their ultimate purpose – but although, by contrast, the merely immature accept God as their director, they do still desire such goods. We see, then, that the Old Law was quite right to lead men to God by means of the temporal things of which immature persons are so fond.

[1] Here is an example of a syllogism from Aristotle's *Physics*:[27]

1. If a series culminates, then all the preceding steps are for the sake of the final one.
2. In plants, all the preceding steps in growth have their culmination in the production of the fruit.
3. Therefore, in plants, all the preceding steps in growth are for the sake of the production of the fruit.

[2] The difference between persuasion in the theoretical sciences and persuasion in law is not that the former employ syllogisms and the latter does not, but that the former employ theoretical syllogisms and the latter employs practical syllogisms. Thus a person subject to a law might reason something like this:

1. Good is to be done and evil is to be avoided.
2. If I violate the law, evil will come to me.
3. Therefore, I avoid violating the law.

Notice that the conclusion is not that I *should* avoid violating the law, but that I *do* avoid violating it. Theoretical syllogisms end in conclusions, but practical syllogisms end in deliberate acts.

The syllogism stated here is a great simplification, of course. In real life all sorts of things might complicate a person's assent to the syllogism. For example, the reasoner might deny that evil will come to him for violating the law ("I won't be caught"), or he might suppose that greater good would come to him than evil ("even if I am caught, I'll only be in the slammer for thirty days"). On the other hand, no one can rationally deny that good is to be done and evil is to be avoided. The universal propositions with which practical

---

[27] Book II, chapter 8.

syllogisms begin, such as "seek life," have the nature of law. They are not always in the mind as thoughts, but they are always in the mind as dispositional tendencies.[28]

[3] We rightly teach arithmetic before calculus; trigonometry before optics; and the classical laws of motion before relativistic frame-shifting.

[4] Generally speaking, we do grasp that students must be introduced to general principles before being expected to work out complex conclusions. Of course students are sometimes taught *false* general principles; for example, many young people are taught the wholly spurious idea that the human race is in complete disagreement about all the elementary points of right and wrong.

There are some notorious exceptions, for some contemporary pedagogies actually deny that instruction should begin with simple and general principles. For example, according to the "whole language" approach to teaching reading, students are taught to recognize words by seeing them over and over, without learning the sounds of individual letters so that they can work them out for themselves. A similar approach to mathematics encourages students to speculate about the answers to mathematical problems before they have learned methods of solution or mathematical reasoning. And in teaching ethics, the so-called quandary method encourages students to discuss their views about baffling moral dilemmas without first having been taught the elementary principles of right and wrong. It is as though we were to ask schoolchildren to work out difficult problems in orbital mechanics before learning arithmetic. One speculates that they would all become orbital relativists.

[5] Just as in teaching theoretical matters, *what is*, we begin with what students already know and gradually inculcate the knowledge of what they do not yet know – so in teaching conduct, *what is to be done*, we begin with what students already desire and gradually inculcate the love of what they do not yet desire.

[6] The expression *puerilbus munusculis*, translated as "little childish gifts," refers not to bribes, but to trivial rewards given as signs of approval. For example, a child may be motivated to behave well by the promise that for each day that he behaves well he will receive a gold star, and that when he receives ten gold stars, he may choose from a box of small toys and baubles. At the beginning, the child behaves well only for the trinket. However, once the habit of behaving well is established, better motives, and better understandings of good behavior, can be built on it.

[7] In English, the word "perfect" does not always convey the sense of the Latin term *perfectum*. We think of the perfect as the flawless, but in most cases a closer rendering of *perfectum* would be "complete," "mature," or "fully and

---

[28] I-II, Q. 90, Art. 1, ad 2.

appropriately developed." Like those of a child, the dispositions and understanding of the people to whom the Old Law was first given were immature, but the intention of the law was to move them toward maturity. In this respect, the law might also be compared with medicine for a sick man. The purpose at which the medicine of human law aims is chiefly the prohibition and punishment of outward wrongdoing. However, the purpose at which Divine law aims goes much further: to heal every tendency to sin, whether outward or inward, so that God can bring man to the everlasting joy of knowing Him.

Sometimes a sick man is not yet capable of receiving the treatment which would cure him; for example, his condition may have to be stabilized before surgery is performed. So it is with the medicine of Divine law. The full achievement of its purpose is brought about by the grace of love, imparted to our souls through Jesus Christ. This is the essence of the New Law, and this is why St. Thomas calls it perfect. Although the Old Law contributed toward the fulfillment of this purpose, it could not bring it about. It was essentially preparatory, and in this sense imperfect.

According to St. Thomas, one way in which the imperfect medicine of the Old Law prepared for the perfect medicine of the New Law was that it drew the people away from the worship of false gods, enclosing or enfolding them "in the worship of one God, by Whom the human race was to be saved through Christ." The other was that it bore witness to the future coming of this Christ, for the Law, the Prophets, and the Psalms all foretold his coming.[29] As Jesus said to certain bitter critics who were teachers of the Old Law,

You search the scriptures, because you think that in them you have eternal life; and it is they that bear witness to me; yet you refuse to come to me that you may have life ... If you believed Moses, you would believe me, for he wrote of me. But if you do not believe his writings, how will you believe my words?[30]

[8] We have encountered this passage before. In English, "pedagogue" means "teacher," but in Latin and in Greek, the cognate terms have the literal meaning "child-leader." The child-leader was not a teacher but a servant, custodian, and guardian who escorted the children to the teacher so that they would get to his house safely. Here is how the passage to which St. Thomas is referring reads in a contemporary translation:

Now before faith came, we were confined under the [old] law, kept under restraint until faith should be revealed. So that the law was our custodian until Christ came, that we might be justified by faith. But now that faith has come, we are no longer under a custodian; for in Christ Jesus you are all sons of God, through faith.[31]

---

[29] See Q. 98, Arts. 1–2.
[30] John 5:39–40, 46–47 (RSV-CE).
[31] Galatians 3:23–25 (RSV-CE).

Reliance on faith does not mean that we no longer have to live a holy life, but that the grace which makes it possible to live this life comes, through the doors of "faith working through love," from Christ.[32]

[9] One "despises" the goods of this life, not in the sense that he considers them evils or denies that he needs them, but in the sense that he trusts in God rather than in things, and considers that all such goods are ultimately worthless if we lack the eternal Good, God Himself. Christ taught,

> Look at the birds of the air: they neither sow nor reap nor gather into barns, and yet your heavenly Father feeds them. Are you not of more value than they? And which of you by being anxious can add one cubit to his span of life? And why are you anxious about clothing? Consider the lilies of the field, how they grow; they neither toil nor spin; yet I tell you, even Solomon in all his glory was not arrayed like one of these. But if God so clothes the grass of the field, which today is alive and tomorrow is thrown into the oven, will he not much more clothe you, O men of little faith? Therefore do not be anxious, saying, "What shall we eat?" or "What shall we drink?" or "What shall we wear?" For the Gentiles seek all these things; and your heavenly Father knows that you need them all. But seek first his kingdom and his righteousness, and all these things shall be yours as well. Therefore do not be anxious about tomorrow, for tomorrow will be anxious for itself. Let the day's own trouble be sufficient for the day.[33]

[10] Paul is speaking of "the righteousness from God that depends on faith."[34] Using another translation, here is the context of the passage to which St. Thomas is referring:

> Brethren, I do not consider that I have made it my own; but one thing I do, forgetting what lies behind and straining forward to what lies ahead, I press on toward the goal for the prize of the upward call of God in Christ Jesus. Let those of us who are mature be thus minded; and if in anything you are otherwise minded, God will reveal that also to you.[35]

[11] St. Thomas distinguishes between those who are "perfect" or spiritually mature, those who are "imperfect" or spiritually immature, and those who are "perverse" and not even on the path toward spiritual maturity. The imperfect still desire the goods of this life, but to at least some degree they grasp that these are not their ultimate purpose, and they pursue them only in the ways God allows.

[12] The perverse desire the goods of this life and pursue them *instead* of God; they make a god of their temporal goods.

[13] Since even on the way to spiritual maturity the immature are still attached to temporal goods, it was appropriate that the Old Law appeal to this attachment. By promising goods and threatening punishments, which

---

[32] Galatians 5:6 (RSV-CE).
[33] Matthew 6:26–34 (RSV-CE).
[34] Philippians 3:9.
[35] Philippians 3:13–15 (RSV-CE).

they overrate because they are not yet grown up, it helps them to grow up. This is a paradox, but as we have been reminded, it is a familiar one. A version of it is confronted by every father or mother who has ever disciplined a child.

Reply to Objection 1. [1] *Covetousness whereby man places his end in temporalities, is the bane of charity.* [2] *But the attainment of temporal goods which man desires in subordination to God is a road leading the imperfect to the love of God,* [3] *according to Ps. 48: "He will praise Thee, when Thou shalt do well to him."*	Reply to Objection 1. The greed or covetousness which leads man to set up temporal things as his ultimate purpose is indeed love's poison. But when the immature pursue the temporal goods which they desire *under God's direction*, they are traveling the first steps of a road which at last leads to loving God Himself. The inspired poet of the psalms is thinking of such persons when he writes that a man gives praise when God has blessed him.

[1] The Objector erred in failing to distinguish between the imperfect and the perverse – between the lingering desire of the former for temporal goods in subjection to God, and the idolatrous craving of the latter for temporal goods in place of God. Calling them both by the same name, covetousness, he invoked the authority of St. Augustine, who had argued that covetousness is the death of that love which unites us to God.

[2] The covetousness which poisons charity is the sort of desire for temporal goods which is possessed by the perverse. By contrast, although the merely immature still desire temporal goods, their willingness to subordinate this desire to God makes it possible to use it to lead them further along the road at the end of which their anxieties about temporal goods will fall away.

[3] Having completed his argument, St. Thomas adds that Scripture confirms one of his premises. With its context, here is how the passage he quotes reads in the DRA:

Be not thou afraid, when a man shall be made rich, and when the glory of his house shall be increased. For when he shall die he shall take nothing away; nor shall his glory descend with him. For in his lifetime his soul will be blessed: and *he will praise thee when thou shalt do well to him.* He shall go in to the generations of his fathers: and he shall never see light.[36]

These words seem to mean that we should not be discouraged just because someone else is more richly blessed in this life, for such blessings are transient. Yet they have a certain value because even in an imperfect condition, men tend to acknowledge God as the source of the blessings of this life. Consequently,

---

[36] Psalm 48:17–19 (DRA), emphasis added. The chapter and verse numbers are different in most contemporary translations.

such blessings encourage them to love Him even though they may have no clear idea of the fate of souls in the life to come – and this is St. Thomas's point. The words "He shall never see light," by the way, are not about punishment, but simply about death; in the Psalms, the condition of souls in the afterlife is obscure.

Not all translations of the Bible lend themselves to St. Thomas's interpretation of the verse. Consider how the same passage is rendered in the RSV-CE:

Be not afraid when one becomes rich, when the glory of his house increases. For when he dies he will carry nothing away; his glory will not go down after him. Though, while he lives, he counts himself happy, and *though a man gets praise when he does well for himself*, he will go to the generation of his fathers, who will never more see the light.[37]

This wording still conveys the idea that we should not be discouraged because others receive the transient blessings of this life in greater measure than we do. However, instead of describing how a man praises God when God does good to him, the passage now seems to describe how he receives praise from other men when he does well for himself. Because of this change, the lesson that St. Thomas draws from the passage disappears. However, his argument is complete without it; the passage was only frosting on the cake.

| *Reply to Objection 2. Human law persuades men by means of temporal rewards or punishments to be inflicted by men: whereas the Divine law persuades men by means of rewards or punishments to be received from God. In this respect it employs higher means.* | Reply to Objection 2. Human law prompts men to obey through the prospect of temporal rewards and punishments meted out by other men. Divine law prompts men to obey through the prospect of rewards and punishments that come from God. So Divine law uses loftier methods after all. |

[1] The Objector had complained that it was inappropriate for the Old Law to induce obedience by promising rewards and threatening punishments in this life, because these are the means used by human law, and Divine law ought to use loftier ones. St. Thomas replies that the Old Law does use loftier ones, for its rewards and punishments are given by God rather than by mere men.

| *Reply to Objection 3.* [1] *As anyone can see, who reads carefully the story of the Old Testament, the common weal of the people prospered under the Law as long as they obeyed it; and as soon as they departed from the precepts of the Law they were overtaken by many calamities.* [2] | Reply to Objection 3. To anyone who reflects on the history set forth in the Old Testament, it is plain that the well-being of the people under the Law thrived when they followed it, and that the moment they swerved from its precepts, they fell into numerous adversities. But particular persons did fall into various |

---

[37] Psalm 49:16–19 (RSV-CE), emphasis added.

> *But certain individuals, although they observed the justice of the Law, met with misfortunes –* [3] *either because they had already become spiritual (so that misfortune might withdraw them all the more from attachment to temporal things, and that their virtue might be tried) –* [4] *or because, while outwardly fulfilling the works of the Law, their heart was altogether fixed on temporal goods, and far removed from God,* [5] *according to Is. 29: "This people honoreth Me with their lips; but their hearts is far from Me."*

afflictions, even some who practiced the justice of the law. This could happen for two different reasons. One was that they were already spiritual; in this case their adversities could only detach them even further from temporal things, and their virtue would be proven by trial. The other was that even though they performed the outward deeds required by the Law, their hearts were utterly stupefied and absorbed by the things of this life, and they were far away from God. Referring to such persons, God says through the prophet Isaiah, "With their lips these people glorify Me, but their hearts are far away."

---

[1] The Old Testament is composed of several kinds of book: Law, History, Wisdom, and Prophets. St. Thomas refers to its *historia*, or history. These writings are devoted largely to showing how the temporal goods and evils which were promised and threatened in the Law actually came to pass, and the other writings also deal frequently with the consequences of faithfulness and unfaithfulness. We should remember that prophecies are not necessarily about the future; often they are interpretations of contemporary events.

The reason this observation is pertinent is that St. Thomas is about to explain why, despite the blessings described in the Old Law, sometimes bad things did happen to good people. The reasoning he offers is of the sort philosophers call an "argument to the best explanation." Given everything we know about God and man, including God's goodness, justice, and desire for our sanctification, his hypothesis explains these events better than any alternative hypothesis. It does acknowledge that there were exceptions to the temporal blessings, but it shows how these exceptions were more than compensated for by spiritual blessings.

[2] The Objector had argued that temporal goods and evils cannot be rewards and punishments because they come equally to the righteous and unrighteous. Although, unlike the Objector, St. Thomas holds that good fortune for faithfulness and misfortune for unfaithfulness was the general pattern of the whole nation's history, he agrees that at the level of individuals, there are exceptions. As reflected in the narratives themselves, however, the exceptions fall into two categories which he is about to explain.

[3] The first category of exceptions to the general pattern is made up of individuals who have already begun disentangling their desires from temporal things and fixing them on God instead. As we have seen, those who have taken only the first steps toward purity of heart may be most effectively encouraged to fix their hearts on God by the promise of His temporal blessings, like children

promised trinkets. Paradoxically, though, for those who have advanced further in the love of God, it may be more advantageous to experience adversity. Suffering reminds them that ultimate confidence cannot be placed in any of the goods of this life, but only in Him. Although St. Thomas does not mention it here, those who are under the New Covenant of Christ have a second reason to submit to affliction, because by doing so, they may be more closely conformed to Him who has suffered for them.

The notion of "trying" or "testing" the virtue of righteous persons is often misunderstood. Why must God put them to the test? Doesn't He already know their hearts? Yes, but they may not know their own hearts. God sends trials not to find out something, but to teach something to those being tried. The classical Old Testament example is Abraham, who was tried by the long interval of time which elapsed before God's promise of a son was fulfilled by the birth of Isaac, and then further tried by God's command to give Isaac up (although this command was withdrawn the instant that Abraham's obedience was clear). Another is Job, a righteous man who clings to God, though demanding a hearing in God's court, even though every conceivable disaster befalls him, his friends wrongly accuse him of having committed secret sins, and even his wife urges him to curse God and die. In the end, both Abraham and Job are vindicated.

[4] The second category of exceptions is made up of individuals who gave the appearance of loving God, but whose love was really given to the things of this life. They hypocritically performed the outward acts commanded by the law, such as offering sacrifice in the Temple, but only in an effort to buy God off. Thus God says through the prophet Amos,

I hate, I despise your feasts, and I take no delight in your solemn assemblies. Even though you offer me your burnt offerings and cereal offerings, I will not accept them, and the peace offerings of your fatted beasts I will not look upon. Take away from me the noise of your songs; to the melody of your harps I will not listen. But let justice roll down like waters, and righteousness like an ever-flowing stream.[38]

The Blackfriars translation tends to render Latin words by English cognates whenever they are available. Thus, *totum habebant in temporalibus defixum* has become "altogether fixed on temporal goods." Although this phrasing is not incorrect, it does not quite convey the force and range of the Latin word *defixum*, which can convey not only the idea of being fastened or attached to something but also the ideas of being focused on it, planted or embedded in it, bewitched or enchanted by it, dumbfounded or astonished by it, or even stupefied by it. Hence my paraphrase employs the stronger phrase, "utterly stupified and absorbed by the things of this life."

---

[38] Amos 5:21–24 (RSV-CE).

[5] St. Thomas is quoting Christ, who is in turn quoting Isaiah. Christ's purpose is to criticize certain teachers of the Law whom he accuses of violating authentic Divine ordinances, yet at the same time presenting their own rules as though they were from God Himself:[39]

> Hypocrites, well has Isaias prophesied of you, saying: This people honor me with their lips: but their heart is far from me. And in vain do they worship me, teaching doctrines and commandments of men.[40]

Here is the passage in Isaiah to which Christ is referring:

> And the Lord said: Forasmuch as this people draw near me with their mouth, and with their lips glorify me, but their heart is far from me, and they have feared me with the commandment and doctrines of men: Therefore behold I will proceed to cause an admiration in this people, by a great and wonderful miracle: for wisdom shall perish from their wise men, and the understanding of their prudent men shall be hid.[41]

Had these teachers of the Law really loved God, they would not have confused His ordinances with their own rules. Thus, St. Thomas uses the passage to highlight the difference between inward devotion to God and the mere appearance thereof.

DISCUSSION

So What Are These Promises and Threats?

St. Thomas assumes that his reader knows all about the blessings and curses of the Old Law. Today, most readers are probably unfamiliar with them. Because no summary can convey the power and poetry of the originals, I will quote liberally. The following passage is from the third book of the Law, which is Leviticus. God is speaking. First come the blessings:

> If you walk in my statutes and observe my commandments and do them, then I will give you your rains in their season, and the land shall yield its increase, and the trees of the field shall yield their fruit. And your threshing shall last to the time of vintage, and the vintage shall last to the time for sowing; and you shall eat your bread to the full, and dwell in your land securely. And I will give peace in the land, and you shall lie down, and none shall make you afraid; and I will remove evil beasts from the land, and the sword shall not go through your land. And you shall chase your enemies, and they shall fall before you by the sword. Five of you shall chase a hundred, and a hundred of you shall

---

[39] Although he refers to Isaiah, St. Thomas is following, not the wording of the Vulgate for the book of Isaiah itself, but its wording for the passage in Matthew where Christ is thus quoting Isaiah. However, the difference in wording is trivial. Where the Vulgate has Isaiah saying "glorifies" (*glorificat*), it has Christ saying "honors" (*honorat*). The RSV-CE uses "honors" in both places.
[40] Matthew 15:7-9 (DRA), modernizing archaic verb forms.
[41] Isaiah 29:13-14 (DRA).

chase ten thousand; and your enemies shall fall before you by the sword. And I will have regard for you and make you fruitful and multiply you, and will confirm my covenant with you. And you shall eat old store long kept, and you shall clear out the old to make way for the new. And I will make my abode among you, and my soul shall not abhor you. And I will walk among you, and will be your God, and you shall be my people. I am the Lord your God, who brought you forth out of the land of Egypt, that you should not be their slaves; and I have broken the bars of your yoke and made you walk erect.[42]

Next come the curses:

But if you will not hearken to me, and will not do all these commandments, if you spurn my statutes, and if your soul abhors my ordinances, so that you will not do all my commandments, but break my covenant, I will do this to you: I will appoint over you sudden terror, consumption, and fever that waste the eyes and cause life to pine away. And you shall sow your seed in vain, for your enemies shall eat it; I will set my face against you, and you shall be smitten before your enemies; those who hate you shall rule over you, and you shall flee when none pursues you.[43]

The catalogue of catastrophes continues, following a pattern fit to make the stoutest heart quail. If the people will not listen, then so much will follow; if still they will not listen, then so much more will follow; if even then they will not listen, then even more than that; if in spite of all they will not listen, then much more still. Calamity is piled upon calamity, until finally,

if in spite of this you will not hearken to me, but walk contrary to me, then I will walk contrary to you in fury, and chastise you myself sevenfold for your sins. You shall eat the flesh of your sons, and you shall eat the flesh of your daughters. And I will destroy your high places, and cut down your incense altars, and cast your dead bodies upon the dead bodies of your idols; and my soul will abhor you. And I will lay your cities waste, and will make your sanctuaries desolate, and I will not smell your pleasing odors. And I will devastate the land, so that your enemies who settle in it shall be astonished at it. And I will scatter you among the nations, and I will unsheathe the sword after you; and your land shall be a desolation, and your cities shall be a waste.[44]

Yet the passage concludes with reassurance. No matter how unfaithful the people may be, God's promises to them are unbreakable. They may break the Covenant, but He will not; He is inexorable in discipline because He is inexorable in love.

But if they confess their iniquity and the iniquity of their fathers in their treachery which they committed against me, and also in walking contrary to me, so that I walked contrary to them and brought them into the land of their enemies; if then their uncircumcised heart is humbled and they make amends for their iniquity; then I will remember my covenant with Jacob, and I will remember my covenant with Isaac and my covenant with Abraham ... I will not spurn them, neither will I abhor them so as to destroy them

---

[42] Leviticus 26:3–13 (RSV-CE); compare Deuteronomy 28–30.
[43] Leviticus 26:14–17.
[44] Ibid., verses 27–33.

utterly and break my covenant with them; for I am the Lord their God; but I will for their sake remember the covenant with their forefathers, whom I brought forth out of the land of Egypt in the sight of the nations, that I might be their God: I am the Lord.[45]

To illustrate how these blessings and curses work out in history, we may consider the beginning of the book of Isaiah. The people have been unfaithful to God and disobedient to His commandments, placing their reliance not in Him, but in strong pagan nations with which they are allied. Therefore the prophet proclaims the imminent fall of the nation's two kingdoms, Israel and Judah, already tragically divided. Here he describes the events which are soon to come to pass as though they were present already:

Ah, sinful nation, a people laden with iniquity, offspring of evildoers, sons who deal corruptly! They have forsaken the Lord, they have despised the Holy One of Israel, they are utterly estranged. Why will you still be smitten, that you continue to rebel? ... Your country lies desolate, your cities are burned with fire; in your very presence aliens devour your land; it is desolate, as overthrown by aliens. And the daughter of Zion is left like a booth in a vineyard, like a lodge in a cucumber field, like a besieged city.[46]

The people remain ceremonially observant – scrupulously so. But because their hearts are not converted, their rituals are disgusting to God:

What to me is the multitude of your sacrifices? says the Lord; I have had enough of burnt offerings of rams and the fat of fed beasts; I do not delight in the blood of bulls, or of lambs, or of he-goats. When you come to appear before me, who requires of you this trampling of my courts? Bring no more vain offerings; incense is an abomination to me ... When you spread forth your hands, I will hide my eyes from you; even though you make many prayers, I will not listen; your hands are full of blood. Wash yourselves; make yourselves clean; remove the evil of your doings from before my eyes; cease to do evil, learn to do good; seek justice, correct oppression; defend the fatherless, plead for the widow.[47]

He appeals to His people directly:

Come now, let us reason together, says the Lord: though your sins are like scarlet, they shall be as white as snow; though they are red like crimson, they shall become like wool. If you are willing and obedient, you shall eat the good of the land; but if you refuse and rebel, you shall be devoured by the sword; for the mouth of the Lord has spoken.[48]

Yet the intention of these punishments is not to destroy the chosen nation, but to purify it – to burn away its sins, as a smelter burns away impurities from molten ore:

---

[45] Ibid., verses 40–45.
[46] Isaiah 1:4–8 (RSV-CE).
[47] Ibid., verses 11–17.
[48] Ibid., verses 18–20.

Therefore the Lord says, the Lord of hosts, the Mighty One of Israel: Ah, I will vent my wrath on my enemies, and avenge myself on my foes. I will turn my hand against you and will smelt away your dross as with lye and remove all your alloy. And I will restore your judges as at the first, and your counselors as at the beginning. Afterward you shall be called the city of righteousness, the faithful city. Zion shall be redeemed by justice, and those in her who repent, by righteousness.[49]

A crucial point is this: God promises not only that He will restore the nation if it becomes faithful, *but that it will, in fact, become faithful.* As we read in the book of Deuteronomy, "the Lord your God will circumcise your heart and the heart of your offspring, so that you will love the Lord your God with all your heart and with all your soul, that you may live."[50] Some new grace will be provided which will make the people able to do what they could not do before. In this way, St. Thomas believes, the Old Law points ahead to the New.

Does the New Law Also Contain Promises and Threats?

Are there promises and threats in the New Law too? Yes, but its blessings and curses are not about the goods of this life. As we saw previously, Christ teaches that anxiety has no place because God knows what we need. Yet lest we misunderstand this assurance, He also explains that we will suffer: "If any man would come after me, let him deny himself and take up his cross and follow me. For whoever would save his life will lose it, and whoever loses his life for my sake will find it."[51] To the followers of the risen Lord, St. Peter writes, "do not be surprised at the fiery ordeal which comes upon you to prove you, as though something strange were happening to you. But rejoice insofar as you share Christ's sufferings, that you may also rejoice and be glad when his glory is revealed."[52]

The guarantee of the New Law is that nothing can sever God's people from Him, and that He will turn even their afflictions to good use. Thus St. Paul exclaims,

We know that in everything God works for good with those who love him, who are called according to his purpose ... neither death, nor life, nor angels, nor principalities, nor things present, nor things to come, nor powers, nor height, nor depth, nor anything else in all creation, will be able to separate us from the love of God in Christ Jesus our Lord.[53]

St. Peter goes so far as to say that God's promises are given so that His people might become "partakers of the divine nature."[54]

---

[49] Ibid., verses 24–27.
[50] Deuteronomy 30:6 (RSV-CE).
[51] Matthew 16:24–25 (RSV-CE).
[52] 1 Peter 4:12–13 (RSV-CE).
[53] Romans 8:28, 38–39 (RSV-CE).
[54] 2 Peter 1:3–4 (RSV-CE).

In short, for fidelity to God the Old Law promises the goods of this life, and for infidelity, their loss. But in the New Law, what God promises is Himself. The blessing for following Him is to possess Him; the penalty for separating is separation. No other good could be greater, nor any evil more appalling. To those whose hearts are engrossed in this world, this seems nothing. To those who hunger and thirst for Him, it is everything.

QUESTION 100, ARTICLE 1

Whether All the Moral Precepts of the Old Law Belong to the Law of Nature?

TEXT	PARAPHRASE
Whether all the moral precepts of the Old Law belong to the law of nature?	Is every moral precept in the Old Law also a precept of natural law?

Eternal law is the wisdom in the mind of God by which He created and governs the universe. This infinite wisdom is brought within the range of our intellects by its finite reflections. One of these reflections lies in the words of Holy Scripture, which, as interpreted by Sacred Tradition, constitute Divine law. The other reflection lies in the order of our nature, including that of our created minds, which is natural law. Usually, only the former is called Revelation, though in a certain sense they are both revealed by God, for the Scriptures unfold His will and wisdom to those who are willing to enter the community of faith, but our nature unfolds them, in part, to all human beings.

Divine law in turn has two parts, corresponding to the commands God gave to the Hebrew nation under the Old Covenant, which is Old Law, and the commands He gave to the Church under the New Covenant, which is New Law. The New Law brings to completion the project which the Old Law begins. Now the precepts of the natural law are *moral* precepts, such as "Do not steal," the truth of which can be known to us by the use of our natural powers. This raises a question: Are the moral precepts in the Old Law also precepts of the natural law? We are compelled to ask this question by a dilemma:

- If all of the moral precepts of the Old Law do belong to natural law, then we could have known them all by reason alone. In that case, why was it necessary for God to add words?
- But if any of the moral precepts of the Old Law do not belong to natural law, then they would seem arbitrary to us – unintelligible decrees without any basis other than that they were decreed. In that case, how could they count as true law? For in order to be true law, doesn't an edict have to be recognizable as an ordinance of reason?

Of course, to ask whether all the *moral* precepts of the Old Law belong to the natural law is not the same as asking whether all the *precepts* of the Old

Do All Old Law Moral Precepts Coincide with Natural Law?

Law belong to it, because the Old Law contains not only moral precepts, concerning virtue, but also ceremonial precepts, concerning worship, as well as judicial precepts, concerning government.

Objection 1. [1] *It would seem that not all the moral precepts belong to the law of nature. For it is written (Sirach 17):*[1] *"Moreover He gave them instructions, and the law of life for an inheritance."* [2] *But instruction is in contradistinction to the law of nature; since the law of nature is not learnt, but instilled by natural instinct. Therefore not all the moral precepts belong to the natural law.*	Objection 1. Apparently, the moral precepts of the Old Law are *not* all precepts of natural law. Speaking of how God revealed the Old Law, the book of Sirach says that He taught His people discipline, so that they possessed the law of life as their heritage. Now something that is *taught* is different than the natural law, because natural law is not learned by teaching; nature itself moves the mind to hold it. So not all Old Law moral precepts are precepts of natural law.

[1] The seventeenth chapter of Sirach is about God's goodness to man in general, but especially his care for Israel, with whom He established an everlasting covenant. So "them" refers to the people of the covenant, and the "law of life" refers to the Old Law.

[2] In the Objector's view, the knowledge of natural law is preinstalled in us; we don't need *additional* teaching because it has already been taught to us by our own natural inclinations. So if the Old Law moral precepts did require additional teaching, they couldn't be part of natural law.

To explain the rationale of the paraphrase: The Objector does not actually say that the law of nature is *instilled* by natural instinct, but that we *have* it by natural instinct. Moreover, the Latin term *instinctu* does not have the mechanical connotations of its English cognate "instinct." It can refer to any sort of impulsion or incitement, including the impulsion of reason.

Objection 2. [1] *Further, the Divine law is more perfect than human law.* [2] *But human law adds certain things concerning good morals, to those that belong to the law of nature: as is evidenced by the fact that the natural law is the same in all men, while these moral institutions are various for various people.* [3] *Much more reason therefore was there why the Divine law should add to the law of nature, ordinances pertaining to good morals.*	Objection 2. Moreover, Divine law is more complete than human law. But human law makes certain provisions for virtuous conduct over and above what natural law prescribes. We see this from the fact that although natural law is the same for everyone, these customary arrangements vary among nations. So if even human law, which is less complete, adds to natural law for the sake of virtuous conduct, then how much more should Divine law do so!

---

[1] Sirach 17:9 (DRA); in most modern translations, this verse corresponds to Sirach 17:11. The word in the Vulgate translated "instructions" is *disciplinam*, discipline or training.

[1] The primary meaning of the Latin term *perfectior* is "more fully accomplished" or "more complete." The purpose of moral discipline is more fully accomplished in Divine law than in human.

[2] The term *mores*, from which we get the English term "morals," refers to customs or conduct; *bonos mores*, or good morals, refers to virtuous conduct. By the things human law "adds" to natural law to promote virtuous conduct, the Objector is referring to those things derived from natural law by "determination" – designation of one among a number of possibilities. For example, natural law commands courtesy in general, but human law, either enacted or customary, may require specific acts of courtesy such as pulling over one's automobile if one is moving slowly and other vehicles need to pass. Specific institutions of courtesy may also vary among nations and peoples. For example, a gesture which is used to show respect in one culture might signify disrespect in another.

[3] The Objector reasons that since human law finds it necessary to "add" things over and above natural law in order to accomplish its moral purpose, and since Divine law accomplishes its moral purpose still more fully, we should expect Divine law to "add" things over and above natural law too. In this case, we should not expect all of the moral precepts of the Old Law to belong to the natural law.

Objection 3. [1] *Further, just as natural reason leads to good morals in certain matters, so does faith:* [2] *hence it is written (Galatians 5:6) that faith "worketh by charity."* [3] *But faith is not included in the law of nature; since that which is of faith is above nature. Therefore not all the moral precepts of the Divine law belong to the law of nature.*

Objection 3. Still further, not only does natural reason introduce certain kinds of virtuous conduct, but faith does too. This is what St. Paul means when he writes in his letter to the Galatians that faith works through jubilant love. But since faith is above natural reason, it is not part of natural law. Consequently, not every moral precept of Divine law is part of natural law.

---

[1] The argument works like this:

1. We are led to certain aspects of good conduct just by natural reason; such are the moral precepts of the natural law.
2. But we are also led to certain aspects of good conduct just by faith; such are the moral precepts of the Old Law.
3. The aspects of good conduct prompted by faith must be different from the ones prompted by reason.
4. Therefore the aspects of good conduct prompted by faith do not belong to natural law.

[2] The Objector may seem to have chosen a surprising passage to make his point, because St. Paul is *contrasting* the New Law of love with the Old Law of

works: "For in Christ Jesus neither circumcision nor uncircumcision is of any avail, but faith working through love."[2] Now the "working" of love is the *activity* to which love prompts us, and love of God and neighbor is the root not only of the New Law but also of the moral precepts of the Old. So although St. Paul is contrasting the activity prompted by love with the *ceremonial* conduct required by the Old Law, such as circumcision, he is certainly not contrasting the activity prompted by love with the *moral* precepts commanded by the Old Law. Rather he is speaking of a shift in motivation. Although both Laws command the works of love, the Old Law urged these works by blessings and curses, the New Law prompts them by imparting the grace of love itself, to which faith in Christ opens the door.[3]

The Blackfriars translation obscures an interesting minor point. St. Paul uses the Greek word, *agape*, for love. The Vulgate translates this by the Latin term *caritatem*, from which we get "charity" – love in the sense of holding the beloved dear. But the word for love which St. Thomas puts in the Objector's mouth here is actually *dilectionem*, love in the sense of taking delight in the beloved, which is why I have paraphrased the word as "jubilant love." Of course, holding the beloved dear and taking delight in the beloved are closely connected.

[3] Faith is an infused rather than an acquired virtue. Although the human will must cooperate with divine grace, the actual cause of the virtue of faith is grace, not human will. The very ability to cooperate is a gift of grace.

| On the contrary, [1]*The Apostle says (Romans 2) that "the Gentiles, who have not the Law, do by nature those things that are of the Law": which must be understood of things pertaining to good morals.* [2] *Therefore all the moral precepts of the Law belong to the law of nature.* | On the other hand, in his letter to the Romans, St. Paul speaks of Gentiles who do not have the law, but who do *by nature* what it requires. We must take his statement as referring to the conduct which *the moral precepts of the Old Law* require. It follows that all the moral precepts of the Old Law are precepts of natural law too. |

[1] The *sed contra* takes the "things that are of the law" in the same sense that the third Objector took the "works of the law." Both expressions refer to the *moral conduct* required by the precepts of the Old Law – to what they instruct us to *do*. Here are St. Paul's words in a more recent translation:

> When Gentiles who have not the law do by nature what the law requires, they are a law to themselves, even though they do not have the law. They show that what the law requires is written on their hearts, while their conscience also bears witness and

---

[2] Galatians 5:6 (RSV-CE).
[3] See Deuteronomy 30:15–20.

their conflicting thoughts accuse or perhaps excuse them on that day when, according to my gospel, God judges the secrets of men by Christ Jesus.[4]

[2] If, when Gentiles follow the moral precepts of the Old Law, they do so by nature, then these moral precepts must also be precepts of natural law.

I answer that, [1] *The moral precepts, distinct from the ceremonial and judicial precepts, are about things pertaining of their very nature to good morals.* [2] *Now since human morals depend on their relation to reason,* [3] *which is the proper principle of human acts,* [4] *those morals are called good which accord with reason, and those are called bad which are discordant from reason.* [5] *And as every judgment of speculative reason proceeds from the natural knowledge of first principles, so every judgment of practical reason proceeds from principles known naturally, as stated above:* [6] *from which principles one may proceed in various ways to judge of various matters.* [7] *For some matters connected with human actions are so evident, that after very little consideration one is able at once to approve or disapprove of them by means of these general first principles:* [8] *while some matters cannot be the subject of judgment without much consideration of the various circumstances, which all are not competent to do carefully, but only those who are wise: just as it is not possible for all to consider the particular conclusions of sciences, but only for those who are versed in philosophy:* [9] *and lastly there are some matters of which man cannot judge unless he be helped by Divine instruction; such as the Articles of faith.*

Here is my response. The moral precepts of the Old Law differ from its ceremonial and judicial precepts in that *in their very nature they promote virtuous conduct.* Now human conduct is designated as having the qualities it has by its relation to reason, which is the distinctive starting point of human acts. So, morals concordant with reason are designated as having the quality "good," and morals discordant with it as having the quality bad.

Now just as every judgment of theoretical reason develops from naturally known first principles, so it is in practical reason too – a point I have explained previously. But the way human reason gets from first principles to judgments differs according to the sorts of things that we judge:

1. In the light of first principles, the moral character of some human actions is so obvious that one can approve or disapprove them right away, without much reflection.
2. Other human actions need a great deal of reflection to be judged properly, because all of their various circumstances need to be considered. Not everyone is able to do this, but only those who have wisdom – just as not everyone is able to reflect upon the findings of the fields of knowledge which proceed by demonstration, but only philosophers.
3. Still other human actions can be judged only if man is assisted by Divine teaching. Such are those which pertain to the domain of faith.

---

[4] Romans 2:14–16 (RSV-CE).

[1] St. Thomas has explained in Question 99, Article 2 that the moral precepts are the ones that command acts of virtue. For "the chief intention of the Divine law is to establish man in friendship with God," and "there cannot possibly be any friendship of man to God, Who is supremely good, unless man become good."

[2] The Dominican Fathers translation is a bit misleading here. *Humani mores dicantur in ordine ad rationem* does not mean that human conduct *depends* on its relation to reason but that it is *designated* by its relation to reason – it is called virtuous or vicious according to whether it is rightly or wrongly ordered to reason.

[3] Why *should* human conduct be called what it is called according to its relation to reason? Because, as St. Thomas has explained in Question 90, Article 1, the governing ordinance and measuring rod of distinctively human acts is the source from which they spring. Because reason is the source of distinctively human acts, it is also their criterion of judgment.

[4] To say that human conduct is called what it is called *according to its relation* with reason is to say that it is called good or bad *according to whether it is well ordered or badly ordered* in relation to reason.

[5] St. Thomas often compares practical with theoretical reason. Throughout this passage he uses the expressions "first principles" and "principles" interchangeably; in this case no significance should be attached to the difference. A principle, *principio*, is something that comes first.

[6] As we are about to see, reason may proceed either immediately or only after pondering, and it may proceed without help or with the help of Revelation.

[7] Some acts can be evaluated easily and quickly, without any special qualifications. A normal, intact human mind leaps right away from first principles to the correct judgment about these acts.

[8] Some acts are more difficult to judge, not everyone is qualified to judge them, and the process of judgment takes more time. The Latin term paraphrased "fields of knowledge which proceed by demonstration" is *scientiarum*, which has a somewhat different meaning than its English cognate, "science." St. Thomas did not share our view that science and philosophy are different things; he would have said that the sciences include all of the theoretical disciplines. He calls those who practice the theoretical disciplines philosophers.

[9] Notice that St. Thomas does not say these acts are judged by Revelation *instead* of by reason; rather, reason judges them *with the help* of Revelation. The idea is not that reason is shut out from the process, but that in order to do its work it needs additional data, data that it cannot supply by itself.

---

[10] *It is therefore evident that since the moral precepts are about matters which concern*	With this light the picture becomes clear, for from these three facts – (a) that the moral precepts of the Old Law concern the promotion of good

good morals; [11] and since good morals are those which are in accord with reason; [12] and since also every judgment of human reason must needs be derived in some way from natural reason; [13] it follows, of necessity, that all the moral precepts belong to the law of nature; [14] but not all in the same way. [15] For there are certain things which the natural reason of every man, of its own accord and at once, judges to be done or not to be done: e.g. "Honor thy father and thy mother," and "Thou shalt not kill, Thou shalt not steal": and these belong to the law of nature absolutely. [16] And there are certain things which, after a more careful consideration, wise men deem obligatory. Such belong to the law of nature, yet so that they need to be inculcated, the wiser teaching the less wise: e.g. "Rise up before the hoary head, and honor the person of the aged man," and the like. [17] And there are some things, to judge of which, human reason needs Divine instruction, whereby we are taught about the things of God: e.g. "Thou shalt not make to thyself a graven thing, nor the likeness of anything; Thou shalt not take the name of the Lord thy God in vain."

morals, (b) that good morals are morals concordant with reason, and (c) that every judgment of human reason is somehow drawn forth by our *natural* powers of reasoning – it follows necessarily that all of the moral precepts of the Old Law are also precepts of natural law. However, we must add that *they do not all belong to the natural law in the same way.*

Why not all in the same way? Because though every judgment is drawn forth by reason, a given judgment may be drawn forth by it in more than one way. Thus,

1. There are some things which each man, by his own natural reason, immediately judges as things to be done or not to be done, for example "Honor your father and your mother," "You shall not kill," "You shall not steal." Things of this sort belong to the natural law *absolutely.*
2. There are other things which the wise judge as things to be done only after subtle consideration. These too belong to the natural law, yet in such a way as to require training, with those with greater wisdom teaching those with less: For example, "Rise in the presence of white hair, and honor the person of the aged man" – things of that sort.
3. And there are still other things which human reason can judge, but only with the Divine teaching mentioned previously, teaching which educates us about matters pertaining to God, for example "You shall not make for yourself a graven image, or any likeness of anything [as an idol]" and "You shall not speak the name of the Lord your God in a futile and irreverent way."

---

[10] St. Thomas begins to tie up the strings of his argument. He begins his peroration merely by reminding us that moral precepts are precepts that promote virtuous conduct.

[11] Now he reminds us of the criterion by which conduct is deemed virtuous, which is reason. St. Thomas means *human* reason (something he might have made a little plainer). True, the ultimate standard is the Wisdom

of God. But unless, to some degree, the judgments of the Divine Intellect could be reflected in our finite reason too, we would not be able to grasp the Divine commands *as law;* they would be opaque to us, whimsical edicts of a power able to hurt us if we disobey. But our finite minds *can* to some degree trace the Divine Reason, because He has made us in His image.

[12] Here we are reminded that all human reasoning depends on the intellectual powers given us by God through His creation of human nature.

[13] As we learned in Question 91, Article 3, natural law is nothing but the participation of the created rational being in eternal law. Only by this rational participation do we recognize the moral precepts of the Old Law as law; in fact, only by this rational participation *are* they law for us, because law is among other things an ordinance of reason that is promulgated or made known (Question 90, Articles 1 and 4). If it is not an ordinance of reason, or not made known, then it is not truly law. Here St. Thomas says that the moral precepts of the Old Law *do* have these qualities, and so they belong to the natural law.

[14] But they do not all belong to it in the same way, because, as we saw earlier in the *respondeo,* from first principles our minds proceed in *various* ways to judge of various matters. The three classes of moral precept St. Thomas is about to list correspond to the three ways in which reason reaches judgments.

[15] Here he speaks of the judgments reason reaches in the *first* way. Everyone grasps them, without any need for special training; moreover everyone grasps them immediately, without lengthy pondering. St. Thomas's examples show that contrary to a common, but gross misinterpretation of his view, these obvious moral basics include not only such ultra-general precepts as "Good is to be done, and evil avoided," but also such precepts as the ones in the Decalogue.

[16] Here he speaks of the judgments reason reaches in the *second* way – only after pondering. Only those with wisdom recognize/acknowledge them on their own. It is not that those who are imperfect in wisdom wise cannot grasp them, but that to do so they need the training of the wise – training which may either help them to see why they are true, or encourage them to take them to heart.

[17] Here he speaks of the judgments reason reaches in the *third* way – only with the help of Revelation. As usual, St. Thomas quotes only enough of the two prohibitions he mentions to spur memory. For poor modern memories like ours, this can be troublesome. The full text of the former prohibition reads, "You shall not make for yourself a graven image, or any likeness of anything that is in heaven above, or that is on the earth beneath, or that is in the water under the earth; you shall not bow down to them or serve them." Thus the Old Law prohibited not all images, as the truncated quotation may seem to suggest, but only idols. Indeed, the Old Law includes detailed instructions for a pair of golden cherubs to adorn the Ark of the Covenant, containing the two tablets of the Law, which was placed in the sanctuary of the tabernacle. As to the latter prohibition, the full text reads, "Thou shalt not take the name of the Lord thy

God in vain: for he shall not be unpunished that taketh his name upon a vain thing." To take God's name in vain is to invoke Him or speak of Him in a futile and irreverent way.

Notice that these prohibitions are *moral* precepts, concerning virtue, not ceremonial precepts, concerning the fitting mode of worship of the true God. To worship a creature instead of the Creator, to take God's name in vain – to do such things is not merely to reverence God in an unfitting manner, but to turn away from reverencing Him, and by doing so to practice evil. It is to commit treason not just against an earthly king but against the King of Kings, the Author of our being, to whom loyalty is owed beyond anything we could render.

At this point we may seem to have hit a wall. If natural reason hasn't even an inkling of the wrong of worshipping idols or speaking irreverently of God – if all our knowledge of them comes from Revelation – then how could such precepts belong to natural law? But St. Thomas doesn't say that natural reason hasn't even an inkling of these things. In fact he thinks it does have an inkling of them. We need Divine instruction about them *even though we do* have an inkling. This is one of those places where one might wish that St. Thomas's remarks had been less terse. He is counting on the reader to remember a number of matters concerning natural reason and the nature of faith that he has explained much earlier. Let us look into the matter more closely.

At the very beginning of the *Summa*, St. Thomas says that "To know that God exists in a general and confused way is implanted in us by nature, inasmuch as God is man's beatitude." What does this mean? We naturally long for beatitude, for that complete and utter happiness which would leave nothing further to be desired. Since nature makes nothing in vain, there must be Something which could satisfy this longing. So we naturally know God *as that Something*, as the supremely loveable object of the longing for beatitude.

Ah, but how far short of knowing what God is such knowledge falls! If we know God only as the object of the desire for beatitude, then if we suppose beatitude to lie in, say, pleasure, we will take pleasure as our "god."[5] So can we go further? Fortunately, yes, for experience shows that pleasure does leave something further to be desired – and that so do all natural things. It follows that if the object of the longing for beatitude is real, it must lie not within nature but beyond it.[6] If so, then to make idols of natural things is wrong. But will we persevere in reasoning long enough to reach this conclusion? Not many do. Failure to persevere may not be precisely a philosophical difficulty, but it is a grave one. Divine law helps.

---

[5] I, Q. 2, Art 1, ad 1.
[6] See the I-II, Q. 1–5. See also J. Budziszewski, *Commentary on Thomas Aquinas's Treatise on Law* (Cambridge: Cambridge University Press, 2014), section on question 90, article 2.

Do All Old Law Moral Precepts Coincide with Natural Law?

At other points St. Thomas explains that natural reason is able to know God "through His effects," meaning through his handiwork in Creation. Here St. Thomas invokes St. Paul, who wrote that "Ever since the creation of the world His invisible nature, namely, His eternal power and deity, has been clearly perceived in the things that have been made."[7] Now if God is the Creator, then He is distinct from everything in the created order. He cannot be identified with anything in the created world, whether riches, pleasures, or things in the earth, sky, or seas. So why can't natural reason recognize the wrong of idolatry? Just as before, it can, but just as before, we also run into a problem that is not purely philosophical. For there is a difference between what reason is able to know, and what it is willing to assent to. Again, Divine law helps.

St. Thomas alludes to a passage in the Old Testament book called Wisdom, which offers a poignant comment on this baffling obstacle:

> For from the greatness and beauty of created things comes a corresponding perception of their Creator. Yet these men [who are ignorant of God] are little to be blamed, for perhaps they go astray while seeking God and desiring to find him. For as they live among his works they keep searching, and they trust in what they see, because the things that are seen are beautiful. Yet again, not even they are to be excused; for if they had the power to know so much that they could investigate the world, how did they fail to find sooner the Lord of these things?[8]

As the passage suggests, from one point of view, these men are little to be blamed; yet from another point of view, they are greatly to be blamed. Since natural reason suffers from such infirmities even about things that in some way it is able to know, natural reason is plainly not enough. But if it is not enough, then it needs help.

The kind of help Divine law proposes is the help of faith – not of belief with no rationale, but of belief that finds its rationale in what God has revealed. St. Thomas holds that although natural reason perceives something of the invisible things of God, "In many respects faith perceives the invisible things of God *in a higher way* than natural reason does." Consequently, "It is necessary for man to accept by faith not only things which are above reason, *but also those which can* be known by reason."[9] For among other things, faith enables us to recognize and assent to moral truths which are obvious in themselves but not necessarily obvious *to us*. This is the meaning of a paradoxical remark St. Thomas makes a little later, that the rightness of loving God and neighbor is "self-evident to human reason, either through nature *or through faith*."[10]

So it is that we need Divine instruction about certain matters concerning our moral duty to God, not because natural reason is utterly unable to see what is

---

[7] Romans 1:20 (RSV-CE). For St. Thomas's use of the passage, see for example II-II, Q. 34, Art. 1.
[8] Wisdom 13:5–9 (RSV-CE); see II-II, Q. 94, Art. 4.
[9] II-II, Q. 2, Art. 3, ad 3; II-II, Q. 2, Art. 4; emphasis added.
[10] I-II, Q. 100, Art. 3, ad 1; compare Art. 4, ad 1.

right – in which case these matters really would lie outside natural law – but because natural reason needs corrective lenses. Or perhaps because it needs the reminder, "Stop turning your face aside – *look there.*"

This suffices for the Replies to the Objections.	How the Objections may be answered should now be clear.

What has been said suffices for the Reply to Objection 1, because natural knowledge is not inconsistent with the need for Divine instruction. Just as the point of human instruction in arithmetic is to bring the child to the point where he can say, "Now I see it – one, two, three, four – of *course* two and two make four," so the point of Divine instruction in morals is to bring us to the point where we can say, "Now I see it – the Creator is not something created – of *course* idolatry is wrong."

It suffices for the Reply to Objection 2, because although the Objector is right that Divine law adds moral precepts to natural law, he misunderstands what this means. Consider for example the saying "Rise in the presence of white hair, and honor the person of the aged man." This is really two precepts in one. The latter, veneration of the aged, belongs to natural law per se, but the former, rising in their presence, is something added, for natural law does not specify the manner in which respect is to be shown. Yet just because rising can be a *way* to show respect, we see that the thing that has been added is not completely unrelated to natural law, as the Objector seems to think; it is still rooted in it.

Finally, what has been said suffices for the Reply to Objection 3, because although the Objector is right that faith is a supernatural gift, he fails to distinguish between the ways in which faith works in doctrine and in morals. Yes, faith leads us to accept many things altogether beyond what natural reason could have found out by itself, such as the plan of salvation, of how to be *reconciled* to God, having cut ourselves off from Him. But our moral duties to God are not like that. Natural reason is quite able to recognize that there is a Creator and Divine Ruler to whom, in justice, we owe everything, and all our moral duties to God follow from this premise. The problem is not that natural reason cannot see this fact, but that it does not particularly want to. It is like an obstinate mule which is perfectly capable of walking, but sits on its haunches and refuses to go. Revelation, accepted through the Divine gift of faith, removes this balkiness, for faith joins together our knowledge and our assent.[11] We are able to grasp the moral truths concerning God more firmly, because we are no longer placing our hands over our eyes to keep them from seeing what is obvious.

---

[11] Concerning faith as the union of thought with assent, see II-II, Q. 2, Art. 1.

DISCUSSION

Does What Holds for the Old Law Hold for the New Law Too?

The topic of this Article has been whether the moral precepts of the Old Law belong to the natural law, and we find that they do. What about the moral precepts of the New Law? Although St. Thomas does not devote an entire Article to the question, he answers it in the course of other Articles. In a nutshell, the answer is yes.

"The precepts of the New Law," he explains, "are said to be greater than those of the Old Law, in the point of their being set forth explicitly. But as to the substance itself of the precepts of the New Testament, they are all contained in the Old." Since the precepts of the New Law are implicitly contained in the precepts of the Old Law, and since all the moral precepts of the Old Law belong to the natural law, it follows that all the moral precepts of the New Law also belong to the natural law. Still more clearly, St. Thomas writes that

Matters of faith are above human reason, and so we cannot attain to them except through grace ... On the other hand, it is through human reason that we are directed to works of virtue, for it is the rule of human action ... Wherefore in such matters as these there was no need for any [new] precepts to be given besides the moral precepts of the [Old] Law, which proceed from the dictate of reason.[12]

Collecting what St. Thomas says in these and other places, we find two main similarities and two main differences between the Old and New Law.

- The first similarity is that they are substantially identical in content; but the first difference, that the New Law is more explicit about the underlying principle of charity or love.
- The second similarity is that they have the same purpose, "namely, man's subjection to God"; but the second difference, that only the New Law carries with it the grace that makes it possible to obey.[13]

St. Thomas believes the relation among the three laws, natural, Old, and New, to have been well expressed by John Chrysostom's commentary on Mark 4:28, that God "brought forth first the blade, i.e. the Law of Nature; then the ear, i.e. the Law of Moses; lastly, the full corn, i.e. the Law of the Gospel." In other words, what is implicit in the natural law is made explicit in the Old Law and brought to glowing maturity in the New.[14] The practical implications of

---

[12] Q. 108, Art. 2 and ad 1.
[13] Quoting from Q. 107, Art. 1; alluding to Q. 106, Art. 1.
[14] Q. 107, Art. 3.

this blending of natural and Divine law are brought out in a strangely lovely way in St. Thomas's own commentary on Christ's remark, "But know this, that if the householder had known in what part of the night the thief was coming, he would have watched and would not have let his house be broken into" (Matthew 24:43):

> The house is the soul, in which man should be at rest. "*When I go into my house,*" that is, my conscience, "*I shall find rest with her* [that is, Wisdom]." The householder of the house is like the "*king who sits on the throne of judgment,*" who "winnows away all evil with his eyes." Sometimes the thief breaks into the house. The thief is any persuasive false doctrine or temptation ... Properly speaking, the door is natural knowledge, in other words, natural right. Therefore, anyone who enters through reason, enters through its door, but anyone enters through the door of concupiscence or irascibility or some such thing, is a thief. Thieves usually come at night. As Obadiah says, *If thieves came to you, if plunderers by night – how you have been destroyed!* So if they come in the day, do not fear. In other words, temptations do not come when a man is contemplating divine things; but when he relaxes, they come. For this reason, the prophet rightly says, *forsake me not when my strength is spent.*[15]

---

[15] Thomas Aquinas, *Lectures on Saint Matthew's Gospel*, chapter 24, lecture 4 (my translation). All scriptural quotations RSV-CE.

QUESTION 100, ARTICLE 5

Whether the Precepts of the Decalogue are Suitably Set Forth?

TEXT	PARAPHRASE
Whether the precepts of the Decalogue are suitably set forth?	Does the Decalogue include all of the commandments it ought to include?

It might be supposed that the moral precepts of Old Testament law would be of interest only to those who believe in Revelation, and even then only to Jews. Yet as we saw in Question 100, Article 1, St. Thomas holds that although the Old Law was taught by a revelation from God, its foundational moral precepts coincide with what the natural law teaches by means of reason. Just for this reason – though there are others – the Old Law moral precepts ought to interest everyone.

St. Thomas gives attention not only to the content but also to the structure of the Old Law moral precepts, for example how they are summarized and classified. This is not a dusty exercise in logic-chopping, but an investigation of the Divine pedagogy. For it calls attention to the fact that the Old Law was not just a set of rules, but a way of teaching and forming the Hebrew people. According to St. Thomas, however, the power of the Old Law was limited, for although, by itself, it could teach, demand, and arouse the longing for holiness, it could not actually *make* the people holy because the assistance of Divine grace is necessary to obey it. As we see when we reach Question 106, this limitation is addressed by the New Law.

In the present Article, we are concerned with the Decalogue, which is a summary of the Law. At first glance, what these Ten Commandments include and leave out might seem a bit quirky. For example, since we are forbidden *even to consider* possessing our neighbor's wives and husbands, why aren't we forbidden *even to consider* lying and murdering, acts that are also wrong? After compiling a thorough list of such puzzles, St. Thomas shows that far from being arbitrary or idiosyncratic, the Commandments are organized and systematic.

Objection 1. [1] It would seem that the precepts of the decalogue are unsuitably set forth. Because sin, as stated by Ambrose, is "a transgression of the Divine law and a disobedience to the commandments of heaven." [2] But sins are distinguished according as man sins against God, or his neighbor, or himself. [3] Since, then, the decalogue does not include any precepts directing man in his relations to himself, but only such as direct him in his relations to God and [his neighbor],[1] *it seems that the precepts of the decalogue are insufficiently enumerated.*

Objection 1. The Decalogue seems to have omitted some commandments that it ought to have contained. As St. Ambrose of Milan pointed out, sin is a breach of Divine law and a violation of heaven's precepts. Now we distinguish among sins against God, sins against neighbor, and sins against ourselves. However, although the Decalogue includes rules directing our relations with God and neighbor, it omits rules directing our relations with ourselves. These should have been included too.

[1] From one point of view, sin is whatever separates us from God. However, what separates us from God is precisely transgression, for His laws are not arbitrary whims but expressions of His eternal wisdom and of the requirements of life. Thus St. Ambrose of Milan writes,

What is sin, if not the violation of divine law and the disobedience to heavenly precepts? Not by the ear, but by the mind, do we form a judgment regarding injunction from above. But with the Word of God before us we are able to formulate opinions on what is good and what is evil. One of these we naturally understand should be, as evil, avoided, and the other we understand has been recommended to us as a good. In this respect we seem to be listening to the very voice of the Lord, whereby some things are forbidden and other things are advised. If a person does not comply with the injunctions which are believed to have been once ordained by God, he is considered to be liable to punishment. The commands of God are impressed in our hearts by the Spirit of the living God. We do not read these orders as if they were recorded in ink on a tablet of stone.[2] Hence, in our own thought we formulate a law: "For if the Gentiles who have no law do by nature what the law prescribes, those having no law of this kind are a law unto themselves. They show the work of the law written in their hearts."[3] There is something, therefore, like the Law of God which exists in the hearts of men.[4]

St. Ambrose is not arguing that God did *not* inscribe His commandments on the tablets of stone which Moses carried down to the people, but that when we

---

[1] Correcting the Blackfriars translation, which again has "himself."

[2] Alluding to 2 Corinthians 3:3, in which St. Paul writes "you show that you are a letter from Christ delivered by us, written not with ink but with the Spirit of the living God, not on tablets of stone but on tablets of human hearts."

[3] A quotation from Romans 2:14-15.

[4] Ambrose of Milan, *On Paradise*, chapter 8, section 39, in *Hexameron, Paradise, and Cain and Abel*, translated by John J. Savage (New York: Fathers of the Church, 1961), pp. 317-318, https://archive.org/stream/fathersofthechur02757 1mbp#page/n299.

Why Does the Old Law Contain Just These Moral Precepts?

receive them, they resonate in our hearts. In a deeper sense, then, we ourselves are the tablets on which He writes.

[2] Man owes God such things as reverence; because his neighbor is an image of God, he owes his neighbor such things as respect for his life and property; and because he himself is an image of God, he owes it to himself not to behave in such a way that this image is defaced.

[3] All sin defaces the image of God in us, and in this sense alienates us not only from God but from ourselves. However, not all sin is directly against God and neighbor. For instance, I sin against myself if I do not care enough to go to the trouble of seeking out the truth of things. Thus, the Objector thinks sins against ourselves should have been listed in the Decalogue too.

Objection 2. [1] *Further, just as the Sabbath-day observance pertained to the worship of God, so also did the observance of other solemnities, and the offering of sacrifices.* [2] *But the decalogue contains a precept about the Sabbath-day observance. Therefore it should contain others also, pertaining to the other solemnities, and to the sacrificial rite.*

Objection 2. Moreover, the Old Law addressed a number of matters concerning the worship of God, such as the Sabbath, matters of solemn ritual, and sacrifices. But although the Decalogue includes a rule about keeping the Sabbath holy, it does not include any rules about these other matters concerning God's worship. It should have.

---

[1] The Sabbath day commandment required laying down all servile toil on the seventh day, reserving it for worship and for rest. But many other requirements of the Law also concerned worship, for example keeping the Passover feast and making burnt offerings of animals for the atonement of sins. The former would count as a solemnity, the latter as a sacrifice.

[2] The Objector is puzzled as to why the Decalogue included only one precept pertaining to worship, seemingly treating the precepts regarding other aspects of worship as less important.

Objection 3. [1] *Further, as sins against God include the sin of perjury, so also do they include blasphemy, or other ways of lying against the teaching of God.* [2] *But there is a precept forbidding perjury, "Thou shalt not take the name of the Lord thy God in vain." Therefore there should be also a precept of the decalogue forbidding blasphemy and false doctrine.*

Objection 3. Moreover, sins against God include various matters such as false swearing, blasphemy, and other false speech against Divine teaching. But although the Decalogue includes a precept prohibiting false swearing – "Do not speak God's name in vain" – it contains no precepts about blasphemy and false teaching. Such precepts should have been included too.

---

[1] Speech is ordained to the communication of truth; all speech contrary to truth is sinful. For this reason, the Old Law prohibits swearing falsely in God's

name – taking God's name "in vain," that is, in a barren or manipulative way. But false swearing is not the only way to abuse the power of speech; it is not even the only way to abuse the power of speech with reference to God. All sacrilegious talk is sinful, along with false teaching about Him.

[2] For this reason the Objector holds that it was not enough for the Decalogue to prohibit false swearing; every form of light, careless, dishonest, contemptuous, hypocritical, or blasphemous speech about God should have been forbidden.

Objection 4. [1] *Further, just as man has a natural affection for his parents, so has he also for his children.* [2] *Moreover the commandment of charity extends to all our neighbors.* [3] *Now the precepts of the decalogue are ordained unto charity, according to 1 Tim. 1. "The end of the commandment is charity."* [4] *Therefore as there is a precept referring to parents, so should there have been some precepts referring to children and other neighbors.*	Objection 4. Moreover, man naturally loves not only his parents but also his children. Moreover, he is commanded to practice charity toward all his neighbors. (In fact, all of the commandments of the Decalogue direct us to charity, for as St. Timothy explains, charity is their purpose.) Now the Decalogue does include a rule about parents. Why then does it fail to include rules about children and other neighbors? Such precepts should not have been left out.

[1] Someone might suggest that the Decalogue commands everything in the natural law. But does it? Certainly it is a matter of natural law to honor one's mother and father; children naturally love their parents. But don't parents also naturally love their children? Of course they do.

[2] It might also be thought that the Decalogue commands everything pertaining to charity. Certainly it is a matter of charity to honor one's mother and father. But isn't it a matter of charity to love all our neighbors, including our children? Of course it is.

[3] Could it be, then, that the precepts of the Decalogue are *not* about charity? Certainly not, or St. Paul would not have written to his protégé Timothy as he did, criticizing useless speculations and emphasizing that charity is the very purpose of the Commandments:

As I desired you to remain at Ephesus when I went into Macedonia, that you might charge some not to teach otherwise, not to give heed to fables and endless genealogies: which furnish questions rather than the edification of God, which is in faith. Now the end of the commandment is charity, from a pure heart, and a good conscience, and an unfeigned faith.[5]

The expression "the commandment" is used metonymically to mean all of the commandments.

---

[5] 1 Timothy 1:3–5 (DRA), modernizing archaic language forms.

Why Does the Old Law Contain Just These Moral Precepts?

[4] Since both natural law and divinely infused charity direct not only the attentions of children to parents but also the attentions of parents to children, the Objector reasons that the Decalogue should have done so too.

Objection 5. [1] *Further, in every kind of sin, it is possible to sin in thought or in deed.* [2] *But in some kinds of sin, namely in theft and adultery, the prohibition of sins of deed, when it is said, "Thou shalt not commit adultery, Thou shalt not steal," is distinct from the prohibition of the sin of thought, when it is said, "Thou shalt not covet thy neighbor's goods," and, "Thou shalt not covet thy neighbor's wife."* [3] *Therefore the same should have been done in regard to the sins of homicide and false witness.*	Objection 5. Moreover, each kind of sin can be committed in two ways: by thought or by deed. Now in the cases of theft and adultery, the Decalogue prohibits sins of thought and deed separately: of deed, when it says "Do not steal" and "Do not commit adultery," and of thought, when it says "Do not cover your neighbor's goods" and "Do not covet your neighbor's wife." Therefore, it should have done the same thing in the cases of homicide and false testimony, but it does not.

[1] For example, I sin against my neighbor not only by murdering him but also by harboring murderous hatred against him in my heart, and not only by testifying falsely against him but also by desiring to do so.

[2] With regard to certain sins, the Decalogue does recognize this distinction: it prohibits not only taking one's neighbor's wealth and wife but also covetously desiring them.

[3] Therefore, the Objector reasons, the Decalogue should have recognized the same distinction with respect to other sins: it should have prohibited not only murder but also murderous hatred, and not only false accusations against one's neighbor but also the desire that false things be believed of him.

Apparently, murder and false witness are merely examples of a broader point, otherwise the Objector would have made the same complaint about the other sins mentioned in the Decalogue. For example, he might have said that the Decalogue should have not only commanded keeping the Sabbath holy but also forbidden wishing that one did not have to, and should have not only commanded honor to parents but also forbidden harboring mocking thoughts about them in one's heart.

Objection 6. [1] *Further, just as sin happens through disorder of the concupiscible faculty, so does it arise through disorder of the irascible part.* [2] *But some precepts forbid inordinate concupiscence, when it is said, "Thou shalt not covet."* [3] *Therefore the decalogue should have included some*	Objection 6. Besides, sin can occur through disorders of either the "concupiscible" or desiring power of the soul, or the "irascible" or ardent power of the soul. Now the Decalogue does include precepts against disordered concupiscence, for it prohibits coveting. Why, then, does it

precepts forbidding the disorders of the irascible faculty. Therefore it seems that the ten precepts of the decalogue are unfittingly enumerated.

not include any precepts against disordered irascibility? It seems that its ten commandments are badly composed.

[1] The soul's concupiscible power, or faculty, is its ability to be aroused to the pursuit of "delectable" goods, those we may simply enjoy. Although the soul's irascible power also concerns desires, it concerns desires of a different kind, for it is the ability to be aroused to the defense of "arduous" goods, those we must defend against threat. Thus hunger, which arouses us to seek something good, is a passion of the concupiscible power, but anger, which arouses us to defend something good, is a passion of the irascible power. Although the distinction between the concupiscible and irascible powers is plain, no English terms for these powers are really suitable, but I sometimes render concupiscibility as "desire" and irascibility as "ardor."

The point is that sin can happen through disorder of either of these powers. For example, my desire is disordered if I crave my neighbor's automobile for my own, and my impulse to defend is disordered if I am enraged at him for accidently stepping on my driveway.

[2] The Decalogue does include some rules that prohibit us from letting our concupiscence run riot, for it forbids improper desire for the wealth or wife of one's neighbor.

[3] The Objector reasons that therefore, the Decalogue should also have included some rules that prohibit his irascibility from running riot. He does not suggest examples, but his suggestion might cover any sort of improper fierceness, and we do find precepts against improper fierceness in the Old Law, though not in the Decalogue. The most famous is the *lex talionis*, or law of revenge:

If a malicious witness rises against any man to accuse him of wrongdoing, then both parties to the dispute shall appear before the Lord, before the priests and the judges who are in office in those days; the judges shall inquire diligently, and if the witness is a false witness and has accused his brother falsely, then you shall do to him as he had meant to do to his brother; so you shall purge the evil from the midst of you. And the rest shall hear, and fear, and shall never again commit any such evil among you. Your eye shall not pity; it shall be life for life, eye for eye, tooth for tooth, hand for hand, foot for foot.[6]

Notice that this precept is about civil punishment rather than private retaliation, and it is not just an authorization but also a limit, for although the authorities must punish, they may not take *more* than an eye for an eye, a tooth for a tooth, a hand for a hand, or a foot for a foot.

---

[6] Deuteronomy 19:16–21 (RSV-CE).

Why Does the Old Law Contain Just These Moral Precepts?

A final thought: In English, the word "inordinate" is normally used to mean excess. However, by the Latin word *inordinatione* St. Thomas means disorder of any kind: one may desire or defend something too much, too little, or in the wrong way. Thus, it might also have been open to the Objector to make another complaint: that the Decalogue should have included not only precepts against excess but also precepts against deficiency. For example, I should not desire my neighbor's wife, *but I ought to desire my own*, and I should not be fierce about a casual insult, *but I should be fierce to defend life against attack*. We return to this point in St. Thomas's Reply.

On the contrary, It is written (Dt. 4): "He shewed you His covenant, which He commanded you to do, and the ten words that He wrote in two tablets of stone."	On the other hand, there stands the authority of Divine revelation, for we read in the book of Deuteronomy that the covenant and the Decalogue come from God: He Himself revealed the Covenant to His people, commanded them to follow it, and wrote the Ten "words" or Commandments on two tablets of stone.

Restating the tradition, the *sed contra* maintains that the Objector's reasoning must be faulty, for the Ten "words" or Commandments were declared to the people by God Himself. For as we read in the book of Deuteronomy,

And you came near and stood at the foot of the mountain, while the mountain burned with fire to the heart of heaven, wrapped in darkness, cloud, and gloom. Then the Lord spoke to you out of the midst of the fire; you heard the sound of words, but saw no form; there was only a voice. *And he declared to you his covenant, which he commanded you to perform, that is, the ten commandments; and he wrote them upon two tables of stone.* And the Lord commanded me at that time to teach you statutes and ordinances, that you might do them in the land which you are going over to possess.[7]

However, the *sed contra* does not explain *how* the Objections are faulty. Someone who accepted them might even deny that the Commandments were declared by God. The task of showing how the Objector's reasoning falls short is reserved for the *respondeo*, to which we now turn.

I answer that, [1] *As stated above, just as the precepts of human law direct man in his relations to the human community, so the precepts of the Divine law direct man in his relations to a community or commonwealth of men under God.* [2] *Now in order that any man may dwell aright in a community, two things are*	Here is my response. We saw previously that both human and Divine law order man's relations with some community. The precepts of the former pertain to the human community per se, while the precepts of the latter pertain to a community or public association of men under

---

[7] Deuteronomy 4:11–14 (RSV-CE), emphasis added.

required: the first is that he behave well to the head of the community; the other is that he behave well to those who are his fellows and partners in the community. [3] It is therefore necessary that the Divine law should contain in the first place precepts ordering man in his relations to God; [4] and in the second place, other precepts ordering man in his relations to other men who are his neighbors and live with him under God.

God. But the same two things must abide[8] in any community, for a man must behave well first to him who presides over it,[9] and second to his comrades and partners in it. Thus it is fitting that the Divine law first lay down precepts which regulate his relations with God, and then others which do the same for his relations with his neighbors and consociates under God.

[1] At he mentions, St. Thomas has addressed this matter earlier:

Since the precepts of the Law are ordained to the common good ... the precepts of the Law must needs be diversified according to the various kinds of community ... Now human law is ordained for one kind of community, and the Divine law for another kind.

Because human law is ordained for the civil community, implying mutual duties of man and his fellows: and men are ordained to one another by outward acts, whereby men live in communion with one another. This life in common of man with man pertains to justice, whose proper function consists in directing the human community. Wherefore human law makes precepts only about acts of justice; and if it commands acts of other virtues, this is only insofar as they assume the nature of justice ...

But the community for which the Divine law is ordained, is that of men in relation to God, either in this life or in the life to come. And therefore the Divine law proposes precepts about all those matters whereby men are well ordered in their relations to God.[10]

The Blackfriars translation renders the Latin phrase *communitatem seu rempublicam* as "community or commonwealth." *Rempublicam* means literally "public thing," which I have paraphrased as "public association." This is the same word from which we derive the English term "republic," although St. Thomas is not using it in a narrowly political sense.

[2] We are social beings, so no one can live well without conducting himself fittingly toward others in the community. However, some of these others have authority, while others do not. Therefore, St. Thomas parses the idea of regulation. One must behave well both toward his neighbors and the ruler.

---

[8] *Bene commoretur*, literally "continue well."
[9] "Him who presides over [the community]" translates *eum qui praeest communitati*. Since *eum* can be plural, the phrase could also be rendered as "those who preside over the community." Here, though, we are to think of our ultimate head, who is God, so the singular is more appropriate.
[10] I-II, Q. 100, Art. 2.

[3] Since one must behave well toward the ruler, and since Divine law sets in order the community whose ruler is God, Divine law sets forth how to behave toward God.

The Blackfriars translation represents the phrase *oportet igitur quod* as meaning "It is therefore necessary that." However, we are speaking not of logical necessity but of the fitting, the proper, or what ought to be.

[4] In the Divine community, one's neighbors are not merely those with whom he lives, but those with whom he lives under God. In the Old Law, this community is the chosen nation, and it the New Law, it is the continuation of the chosen nation, which is the Church. St. Thomas calls a man's neighbors his *conviventes*. "[Those who] live together with him" is entirely correct; I have preferred "consociates" just because it is a single word.

[6] *Now man owes three things to the head of the community: first, fidelity; secondly, reverence; thirdly, service.* [7] *Fidelity to his master consists in his not giving sovereign honor to another: and this is the sense of the first commandment, in the words "Thou shalt not have strange gods."* [8] *Reverence to his master requires that he should do nothing injurious to him: and this is conveyed by the second commandment, "Thou shalt not take the name of the Lord thy God in vain."* [9] *Service is due to the master in return for the benefits which his subjects receive from him: and to this belongs the third commandment of the sanctification of the Sabbath in memory of the creation of all things.*	Man has three duties to the foremost man of the community: fidelity, reverence, and obedience or service. 1. Fidelity to his lord lies in not giving highest honors to anyone else. The First Commandment conveys this lesson by forbidding us to have "strange gods." 2. Reverence to him lies in doing nothing harmful to him. So the Second Commandment teaches by forbidding us to take the name of the Lord our God in vain. 3. The duty of service to him arises from the benefits due in recompense for the benefits the subjects receive from him. This is the teaching of the Third Commandment, to keep the Sabbath day holy in memory of the Creation.

[6] Duty to justly exercised authority is made clear in the New Testament too, this despite the fact that the rulers were hostile to the faith. For example, St. Peter writes,

Be subject for the Lord's sake to every human institution, whether it be to the emperor as supreme, or to governors as sent by him to punish those who do wrong and to praise those who do right. For it is God's will that by doing right you should put to silence the ignorance of foolish men. Live as free men, yet without using your freedom as a pretext for evil; but live as servants of God. Honor all men. Love the brotherhood. Fear God. Honor the emperor.[11]

---

[11] 1 Peter 2:13–17 (RSV-CE).

Notice that St. Thomas is *not* saying that tyrants should be given blind obedience. In fact, in I-II, Question 96, Article 4, "Whether human law binds a man in conscience?", he provides the first systematic analysis of cases in which civil disobedience is permissible and even obligatory. The Apostles practiced measured disobedience for the sake of God when they were unjustly commanded by the authorities in Jerusalem to stop preaching about Christ:

> And when they had brought them, they set them before the council. And the high priest questioned them, saying, "We strictly charged you not to teach in this name, yet here you have filled Jerusalem with your teaching and you intend to bring this man's blood upon us." But Peter and the apostles answered, "We must obey God rather than men."[12]

St. Thomas does not think that duties toward rulers are entirely erased even if the authorities are less than perfectly just. In the case of God, of course, the possibility of an unjust exercise of authority does not arise. Besides, at present we are not speaking of unjust laws or rulers.

[7] I am unfaithful to my ruler if I give to another ruler the homage due to my ruler alone. The homage due an earthly ruler is sharply limited, but the homage due our heavenly King is infinitely more than we can give Him; nothing should be treated as a matter of unconditional fealty but God Himself. The ancient Hebrews would have thought of this commandment as prohibiting the worship of carven idols. For us, a more likely form of idolatry is the worship of wealth, success, or some other stand-in for the Self.

[8] We can literally injure our earthly rulers. Although we are incapable of literal injury to God, we are certainly capable of belittling the respect which is due to His name, for example in making a false oath, or in punctuating our sentences with the careless phrase "O, my God" when we are not addressing Him.

[9] Service includes all other obedience and renunciation due to a ruler – due to him not because he has a big stick with which to threaten us, but because it is a return for his care for the community. Even in the case of earthly rulers, whose care for the community is all too flawed, this includes following just laws and paying taxes. In the case of God, who not only cares for us but brought us into being, it involves resting in Him and worshipping Him with all that is in us. The precept about keeping the seventh day holy symbolizes this rest and worship, because the people were commanded to withdraw themselves on the Sabbath from all servile toil and everyday concerns.

---

[12] Acts 5:27–29 (RSV-CE).

[10] *To his neighbors a man behaves himself well both in particular and in general. In particular, as to those to whom he is indebted, by paying his debts: and in this sense is to be taken the commandment about honoring one's parents.* [11] *In general, as to all men, by doing harm to none, either by deed, or by word, or by thought.* [12] *By deed, harm is done to one's neighbor—sometimes in his person, i.e. as to his personal existence; and this is forbidden by the words, "Thou shalt not kill":* [13] *sometimes in a person united to him, as to the propagation of offspring; and this is prohibited by the words, "Thou shalt not commit adultery":* [14] *sometimes in his possessions, which are directed to both the aforesaid; and with this regard to this it is said, "Thou shalt not steal."* [15] *Harm done by word is forbidden when it is said, "Thou shalt not bear false witness against thy neighbor": harm done by thought is forbidden in the words, "Thou shalt not covet."*

As to his neighbors in the community, man has duties both to particular men and to men in general. His duties to particular men are to those to whom he is indebted, so that good behavior lies in repayment. This lesson is represented by the commandment about the honor due to parents.

By contrast, his duties to men in general lie in committing no harm or nuisance to his neighbor in deed, in word, or in "heart" or thought. Concerning harm in deed, a further distinction is needed:

1. One might harm one's neighbor with respect to his own person, to his very existence. This is prohibited by the words "Do not murder."
2. One might harm him with respect to someone united with him in generating children. This is prohibited by the words "Do not commit adultery."
3. One might harm him with respect to his possessions, which are employed for his well-being in both of these two respects. This is prohibited by the words "Do not steal."

In turn, harm against one's neighbor by word is forbidden by the words "Do not testify falsely against your neighbor," and harm against him by thought is forbidden by the words "Do not covet."

---

[10] Duties to our neighbors may be divided into duties to particular neighbors and duties to all neighbors. The duty to honor one's mother and father is a duty of the former kind; I am not required to give the same special honor to my neighbor's parents, although, of course, I owe his parents the same things I owe all people.

My debt to my parents is my greatest earthly debt – so great, in fact, that I cannot fully repay it, so that justice toward them in the strictest sense is impossible. In this respect it is like my debt toward God.[13] Yet I am obviously indebted to other persons too. The commandment "Honor your father and

---

[13] Consequently, the virtues of filial piety and religion are not *species* of the virtue of justice, but virtues *related* to justice, which do not possess its full power. See II-II, Q. 80, Art. 1. I have

mother" seems to be a metonym, a part which represents a whole. Paying my most important earthly debt, so far as I can, is a placeholder for paying all my earthly debts, whatever I owe, to whomever I owe it.

[11] The contemporary slogan "It isn't wrong if it doesn't harm anyone" is very narrow, not only because it ignores our duties to God and our debts to particular neighbors but also because it is almost always expressed with a very limited notion of what counts as harm. Harm to which a person consents ought to be considered harm; so should seduction of another person to evil; so should having murderous or lustful thoughts toward someone. Commonly, though, these sorts of harms are viewed as though they were not harms at all. St. Thomas will have none of this careless attitude. Not only does he remember our duties to God and particular neighbors, but he also construes harm quite broadly, taking into account both harm done by outward deed, harm done by wicked speech, and harm done by disordered thoughts.

It may seem curious that by contrast with duties to specific neighbors, our duties to neighbors in general are negative (to do them no evil) rather than positive (to do them good). The reason our duties to neighbors in general are treated differently is that although we can always refrain from doing our neighbors in general any evil, we simply cannot do them every possible good: I cannot be obligated to feed everyone, heal everyone, or read stories to everyone's children, because doing so is impossible. I should, of course, have charity for all my neighbors, which is a firm and persistent commitment of the will to their true good, so that I should always be looking out for opportunities to serve them. As a matter of duty, however, I can only owe specific goods to specific persons.

[12] This is another metonym. It is not that I may not murder my neighbor, yet it is all right to knock out his tooth. Rather, the commandment uses the most conspicuous example of harm to the person of my neighbor to represent for the wrong of all harm to the person of my neighbor.

[13] Adultery is a metonymical placeholder for all wrong done to my neighbor with respect to his wife. Since husband and wife are united, harm to my neighbor's wife, or to the integrity of his relationship with his wife, is harm to my neighbor. The same goes for harm to my neighbor's husband, or to the integrity of her relationship with her husband.

Even in the case of ordinary friendship, St. Thomas remarks, "since he who loves another looks upon his friend as another self, he counts his friend's hurt as his own, so that he grieves for his friend's hurt as though he were hurt

discussed this point in *Commentary on Thomas Aquinas's Virtue Ethics* (Cambridge: Cambridge University Press, 2017).

himself."[14] The friendship of husband and wife is closer still, for they are joined in both body and mind: in body, by sexual intercourse, and in mind, by their shared purpose in children and a common family life.[15]

The story of the creation of the sexes describes the woman as having been formed from the very body of the man. After God makes her, the man says, "This at last is bone of my bones and flesh of my flesh; she shall be called Woman, because she was taken out of Man."[16] The passage concludes, "Therefore a man leaves his father and his mother and cleaves to his wife, and they become one flesh."

Jesus refers to this passage in declaring, "So they are no longer two but one. What therefore God has joined together, let not man put asunder."[17] St. Paul refers to it in exhorting, "Husbands should love their wives as their own bodies. He who loves his wife loves himself. For no man ever hates his own flesh, but nourishes and cherishes it."[18]

[14] Normally St. Thomas distinguishes between robbery (*rapina*), which is taking someone's property by violence, and theft (*furtum*), which is taking it by stealth. Here, though, he uses the term *furtum*, which we have rendered as "stealing," to cover both sins. Like murder and adultery, stealing is unjust. However, murder and adultery are against the person himself or against someone united with him, whereas stealing concerns only his possessions. St. Thomas writes, "for if a man takes what is another's not as a possession but as a part (for instance, if he amputates a limb), or as a person connected with him (for instance, if he carry off his daughter or his wife), it is not strictly speaking a case of theft" or of stealing.[19]

This point deserves emphasis for two reasons. The first is to refute the canard that St. Thomas's tradition views wives as property. On the contrary, he makes a clear distinction. I *own* my property, but I am not united with it; I am *united* with my wife, but I do not own her. "My property" expresses the "my" of possession, but "my wife" expresses the "my" of relationship.

The second reason is to point up the contrast between St. Thomas's view of property and certain modern theories. In his view, my property is distinct from my personality, but in their view, it is an extension of my personality. The latter

---

[14] II-II, Q. 30, Art. 2; compare I-II, Q. 77, Art. 4, ad 4. St. Thomas cites Aristotle, *Nicomachean Ethics*, book X, for philosophical authority.
[15] Supp., Q. 44, Art. 1.
[16] Genesis 2:23–24 (RSV-CE).
[17] Matthew 19:6 (RSV-CE).
[18] Ephesians 5:28–29a (RSV-CE). For discussion of St. Thomas's views of matrimony, see J. Budziszewski, "Thomas Aquinas on Marriage, Fruitfulness, and Faithful Love," in *Humanae Vitae 50 Years Later, Embracing God's Vision of Marriage, Love, and Life: A Compendium*, edited by Theresa Notare (Washington, DC: Catholic University of America Press, 2020).
[19] II-II, Q. 66, Art. 3.

outlook is especially widespread in European property law, but versions can be found in the Anglosphere too. Thus John Locke:

> Though the earth, and all inferior creatures, be common to all men, yet every man has a property in his own person: This no body has any right to but himself. The labor of his body, and the work of his hands, we may say, are properly his. Whatsoever then he removes out of the state that nature hath provided, and left it in, he hath mixed his labour with, and joined to it something that is his own, and thereby makes it his property.[20]

Frédéric Bastiat:

> For what are our faculties if not an extension of our personality, and what is property if not an extension of our faculties?[21]

G. W. F. Hegel:

> Since property is the means whereby I give my will an embodiment, property must also have the character of being "this" or "mine." ... Since property is the embodiment of personality, my inward idea and will that something is to be mine is not enough to make it my property; to secure this end occupancy is requisite. The embodiment which my willing thereby attains involves its recognisability by others.[22]

By contrast, for St. Thomas the natural basis of property is not the *individual* personality but the *common* good. Individual ownership of property has three advantages for everyone. First, each person takes better care of his own property than of what belongs to everyone at once. Second, it is easier to pinpoint responsibility if each person is charged with caring for particular things. Third, when goods are divided so that each person has something of his own, there are fewer quarrels. So even though some may have more or better property, the institution of private ownership makes everyone better off than if everything were owned in common.[23] Since St. Thomas's time, other advantages of private property have also been discovered, such as the fact that a collective economy – which is of necessity a planned economy – cannot allocate resources to their most efficient uses, as a healthy market does spontaneously.

The fact that even private property exists for the common good explains why it is wrong to withhold good from the poor, and why it is not stealing for those in desperate straits to take from those who have more than they need but who withhold it:

---

[20] John Locke, *Second Treatise of Government* (public domain), chapter 5, section 27.

[21] Frédéric Bastiat, *The Law*, translated by Jane Willems and Michel Willems, in Jacques de Guenin, gen. ed., *The Collected Works of Frédéric Bastiat*, volume II, *The Law, The State, and Other Political Writings, 1843–1850* (Indianapolis: Liberty Fund, 2012).

[22] G. W. F. Hegel, *Philosophy of Right*, translated by T. M. Knox (Oxford: Oxford University Press, 1952), sections 46A and 51.

[23] II-II, Q. 66, Art. 2.

Whatever certain people have in superabundance is due, by natural law, to the purpose of succoring the poor. For this reason Ambrose says, ... "It is the hungry man's bread that you withhold, the naked man's cloak that you store away, the money that you bury in the earth is the price of the poor man's ransom and freedom."

Since, however, there are many who are in need, while it is impossible for all to be succored by means of the same thing, each one is entrusted with the stewardship of his own things, so that out of them he may come to the aid of those who are in need. Nevertheless, if the need be so manifest and urgent, that it is evident that the present need must be remedied by whatever means be at hand (for instance when a person is in some imminent danger, and there is no other possible remedy), then it is lawful for a man to succor his own need by means of another's property, by taking it either openly or secretly: *nor is this properly speaking theft or robbery.*[24]

[15] Again, these precepts are metonyms. One may harm one's neighbor in word not only by giving false testimony but also, for example, by reviling or cursing him. One may harm him in thought not only by coveting his wife or wealth but also, for example, by envy or wrath. But false testimony stands for all sins of word against him, and coveting for all sins of thought.[25]

---

[17] *The three precepts that direct man in his behavior towards God may also be differentiated in this same way. For the first refers to deeds; wherefore it is said, "Thou shalt not make ... a graven thing":* [18] *the second, to words; wherefore it is said, "Thou shalt not take the name of the Lord thy God in vain":* [19] *the third, to thoughts; because the sanctification of the Sabbath, as the subject of a moral precept, requires repose of the heart in God.* [20] *Or, according to Augustine, by the first commandment we reverence the unity of the First Principle; by the second, the Divine truth; by the third, His goodness whereby we are sanctified, and wherein we rest as in our last end.*

The distinction among deeds, words, and thought which we have just made concerning man's relations with his neighbors also provides us with another way to consider his relations with God. For the First Commandment concerns deeds, in that it forbids making graven images; the Second concerns words, in that it forbids taking the name of the Lord our God in vain; and the Third concerns the heart or thoughts, because the moral precept to keep the Sabbath day holy demands that the heart rest in God.
Yet another way to view the matter is suggested by St. Augustine, who points out that by following the First Commandment we honor the *unity* of the First Beginning, by the Second we honor His Divine *truth*, and by the Third we honor His *goodness*, which makes us holy and in which we repose as our ultimate goal and purpose.

---

[24] II-II, Q. 66, Art. 7; compare Art. 2, emphasis added.
[25] For reviling and cursing, see II-II, QQ. 72 and 76; for backbiting, tale-bearing, and derision, II-II, QQ. 73–75; for envy, II-II, Q. 36; and for wrath, I-II, Q. 46, and II-II, Q. 158 (compare I-II, Q. 29, and II-II, Q. 34, on hatred).

[17] St. Thomas suggests that the prohibition of graven images complements the prohibition of having "strange gods" in God's place, because, taking the two precepts together, the worship of false deities is prohibited in both of its two forms – both with images and without them.[26] Interestingly, images which were *part* of the worship of the invisible God rather than in competition with it were omitted from the prohibition, for we find in the book of Exodus that two golden images of cherubim were commanded to be affixed to the mercy seat which covered the Ark of the Covenant.[27] The images of the cherubim, of course, were not images of God, but of His servants.

[18] The sin against God in word is offensive not only because it diminishes the honor due to God but also because it perverts words from their proper function of communicating truth. The latter reason is why lying is wrong even when it may seem to achieve a good result.

[19] One might have thought that the Sabbath commandment was about deeds, because it requires rest from labor. Outwardly, yes. Inwardly, however, the Sabbath rest is not truly observed only by physical rest. The heart must turn toward God and rest in Him.

[20] Here is what St. Augustine says:

These three commandments relate to the love of God: Reflect on His oneness, His truth, His desirability; for where there is a true Sabbath, a true rest, there is delight in the Lord. *Delight in the Lord, so it is said, and He will give thee the requests of thy heart.* Who can afford such delight as the Maker of all delights?[28]

Apart from this reference to the Commandments, Augustine speaks about the unity, truth, and goodness of God in many places. For example, he speaks of His unity here:

You are before all the past by the eminence of Your ever-present eternity: and You dominate all the future inasmuch as it is still to be: and once it has come it will be past: but Thou art always the Selfsame, and Thy years shall not fail.[29]

Of His goodness here:

This thing is good and that good, but take away this and that, and regard good itself if you can, so will you see God, not good by a good that is other than Himself, but the good of all good.[30]

---

[26] II-II, Q. 122, Art. 2, ad 2.
[27] Exodus 25:16–26.
[28] St. Augustine of Hippo, *Enarrations on the Psalms*, second discourse on Psalm 32, section 6, in *St. Augustine on the Psalms*, volume II (Psalms 30–37), translated by Scholastica Hebgin and Felicitas Corrigan (Westminster, MD: Newman Press, 1961), p. 108. The internal quotation is from Psalm 36:4, numbered in most contemporary translations as 37:4.
[29] *Confessions*, 2nd ed., translated by F. J. Sheed (Indianapolis: Hackett, 2006), book XI, chapter 13, p. 242.
[30] *On the Trinity*, book VIII, chapter 3, www.newadvent.org/fathers/1301.htm.

And of His truth here:

> The essence of body and soul is not the essence of the truth [reality] itself; as is the Trinity, one God, alone, great, true, truthful, the truth.[31]

Our freedom is this: To submit to this truth, which is our God Who set us free from death – that is, from the state of sin. Truth itself, speaking as a human being among others, said to those believing in Him: "If you continue in my word, you are truly my disciples; and you shall know the truth, and the truth shall set you free."[32]

God is true in a much deeper sense than a belief, a thought, or a proposition is true. Our thoughts are measured by reality; they are true if they correspond to it. But reality is measured by God's thoughts; it is what it is because He so conceives it and brings it into being:

> [T]he human intellect is measured by things, so that a human concept is not true by reason of itself, but by reason of its being consonant with things, since "an opinion is true or false according as it answers to the reality." But the Divine intellect is the measure of things: since each thing has so far truth in it, as it represents the Divine intellect.[33]

Reply to Objection 1. [1] *This objection may be answered in two ways. First, because the precepts of the decalogue can be reduced to the precepts of charity.* [2] *Now there was need for man to receive a precept about loving God and his neighbor, because in this respect the natural law had become obscured on account of sin:* [3] *but not about the duty of loving oneself, because in this respect the natural law retained its vigor:* [4] *or again, because love of oneself is contained in the love of God and of one's neighbor: since true self-love consists in directing oneself to God. And for this reason the decalogue includes those precepts only which refer to our neighbor and to God.*	**Reply to Objection 1.** The Objector had complained that the Decalogue does not include any precepts directing man in his relations to himself. Two answers may be given. The first answer: At bottom, every rule in the Decalogue is a rule of love. Precepts to love God and neighbor had to be given, because sin had obscured this aspect of natural law. Concerning the love of oneself, however, the natural law retained all its vigor and was not obscured. Besides, love of oneself is included in love of God and neighbor, for indeed, *true* self-love lies in turning oneself to Him. Thus, only precepts about loving God and neighbor are set forth in the Decalogue.

---

[31] Ibid., book VIII, chapter 2.
[32] *Augustine: On the Free Choice of the Will, On Grace and Free Choice, and Other Writings*, translated by Peter King (Cambridge: Cambridge University Press, 2010), book II, chapter 13, p. 59. The internal quotation is John 8:31–32.
[33] I-II, Q. 93, Art. 1, ad 3.

[1] Why doesn't the Decalogue include rules directing our relations with ourselves? St. Thomas's first answer is really two in one. Both answers depend on the fact that all of the precepts of the Decalogue concern love, whether for God, for neighbor, or for ourselves.

[2] The *duty* to follow natural law is based on *inclinations* which are built into our nature and direct us to our natural good. I spontaneously do love God, neighbor, and self. Unfortunately, because of the Fall, this natural inclination to love God and neighbor has been weakened.

[3] By contrast with my love for God and neighbor, my love for myself is as sharp as ever. Not even the Fall has weakened it. Thus, Divine law does not have to command me to love myself, because I do anyway. As St. Thomas points out in II-II, Question 44, Article 3, Reply to Objection 1, the needlessness of commanding us to love ourselves is also pointed out by St. Augustine, who writes in *On Christian Doctrine*,

> As, then, there are four kinds of things that are to be loved – first, that which is above us; second, ourselves; third, that which is on a level with us; fourth, that which is beneath us – no precepts need be given about the second and fourth of these. For, however far a man may fall away from the truth, he still continues to love himself, and to love his own body. The soul which flies away from the unchangeable Light, the Ruler of all things, does so that it may rule over itself and over its own body; and so it cannot but love both itself and its own body.[34]

What we *do* need to be reminded of is *how* to love ourselves, because we are often so drastically misled about our own true good. We follow as good for us ways of life that are dreadfully bad for us – as we see below.

[4] Besides, the precepts which instruct me in love of God *do* instruct me in love of myself, because I truly love myself only when I love Him. Though I am not God, I am a finite image of God and I am made for fellowship with Him. Therefore, even though God is a different Being than myself, the alternative "Self, or God?" is a false choice; to serve myself instead of Him is not really to serve myself.

---

[6] *Secondly, it may be answered that the precepts of the decalogue are those which the people received from God immediately;* [7] *wherefore it is written (Dt. 10): "He wrote in the tables, according as He had written before, the ten words, which the Lord spoke to you."* [8] *Hence the precepts of the decalogue need to be such as the people can understand at once.* [9] *Now a*

The other answer turns on the fact that the Decalogue contains the precepts which the people received directly from God, for as Moses tells them, "He wrote on the two tablets, just as He had done before, the ten commandments *which the Lord had spoken to you.*" And so these precepts needed to be so striking that they could immediately penetrate the minds of the people.

---

[34] *On Christian Doctrine*, chapter 23, section 22, www.newadvent.org/fathers/12021.htm.

precept implies the notion of duty. [10] *But it is easy for a man, especially for a believer, to understand that, of necessity, he owes certain duties to God and to his neighbor.* [11] *But that, in matters which regard himself and not another, man has, of necessity, certain duties to himself, is not so evident:* [12] *for, at the first glance, it seems that everyone is free in matters that concern himself.* [13] *And therefore the precepts which prohibit disorders of a man with regard to himself, reach the people through the instruction of men who are versed in such matters; and, consequently, they are not contained in the decalogue.*	Bear in mind that every precept expresses the idea of a debt or duty. The idea that he necessarily owes something to God and neighbor comes easily to man's mind, especially if he is a believer. But the idea that in personal affairs that concern no one else he necessarily owes something to *himself* is not at all obvious to him, because it seems at first glance that in these affairs he is free to do whatever he wishes. For this reason, the precepts that forbid the disordering of man's relations with himself are taught to the people not through the Decalogue but through the medium of the wise.

[6] This second answer to the Objection also depends on the natural law of love, but it is not so much about the *inclination* to love that is built into our nature as it is about the *intellectual understanding of the duty* that is based on this inclination. St. Thomas begins by pointing out that although the Hebrew people received many of the precepts of the Old Law from God through the intermediation of Moses, they received the Ten Commandments from God directly.

[7] The ten "words" are the Ten Commandments; the phrase "according as He had written before" refers to the fact that this was the second time God had written the Commandments on tablets of stone. The first time, Moses had destroyed the tablets in anger, because as he was coming down the mountain with them, he saw that instead of waiting patiently, the people had plunged themselves into idolatrous revels. In another translation, the passage from Deuteronomy from which St. Thomas is quoting reads as follows:

At that time the Lord said to me, "Hew two tables of stone like the first, and come up to me on the mountain, and make an ark of wood. And I will write on the tables the words that were on the first tables which you broke, and you shall put them in the ark." So I made an ark of acacia wood, and hewed two tables of stone like the first, and went up the mountain with the two tables in my hand. *And he wrote on the tables, as at the first writing, the ten commandments which the Lord had spoken to you on the mountain out of the midst of the fire on the day of the assembly; and the Lord gave them to me.*[35]

[8] These precepts, received immediately from God, were to be the *principles* or starting points of all the rest of the Law. Therefore, they had to be easily understandable, and they are.

---

[35] Deuteronomy 10:1–4 (RSV-CE), emphasis added.

Some of them have this character because they are obvious even without instruction, for as St. Thomas writes in I-II, Question 100, Article 1,

> there are certain things which the natural reason of every man, of its own accord and at once, judges to be done or not to be done: e.g. "Honor thy father and thy mother," and "Thou shalt not kill, Thou shalt not steal": and these belong to the law of nature absolutely.

Others have this character because once the mind is instructed, it immediately grasps the point:

> And there are some things, to judge of which, human reason needs Divine instruction, whereby we are taught about the things of God: e.g. "Thou shalt not make to thyself a graven thing, nor the likeness of anything; Thou shalt not take the name of the Lord thy God in vain."

Although those which may not be so obvious are still included in Divine law, they are not in the Decalogue itself:

> And there are certain things which, after a more careful consideration, wise men deem obligatory. Such belong to the law of nature, yet so that they need to be inculcated, the wiser teaching the less wise: e.g. "Rise up before the hoary head, and honor the person of the aged man," and the like.

A word on my paraphrase. The Blackfriars translation renders *oportet praecepta Decalogi talia esse* as "the precepts of the Decalogue need to be *such*," and represent *qiue statim in mente populi cadere possunt* as saying that they must be "as the people can *understand at once.*" Since *talia* can also mean *as great* as, and since *cadere* refers literally to the action of falling or sinking, I have preferred to render the former phrase by "needed to be *so striking*" and to render the latter phrase by "that they could immediately *penetrate* the minds of the people."

[9] The Latin term *debiti* refers to what is owed or due, to a debt, to a duty. A valid command implies that the action commanded is due from me.

[10] It would be difficult to find anyone who flatly denied that he should do unto others as he would have them do unto him. On the other hand, although believers more readily acknowledge their indebtedness to God, often even atheists agree that we should be grateful in some way for the blessings of life. It is revealing that they should do so, for gratitude implies the very thing that they deny: a giver to whom gratitude is due.

[11] St. Thomas could hardly be denying that man has a stronger tendency to love himself than to love God and neighbor, for he affirmed this point earlier in the Reply. What he does claim here is that man is more reluctant to admit that he has *duties* to himself than to admit that he has duties to God and neighbor. Paradoxically, the duty is not recognized as clearly as the inclination is felt.

[12] If I have duties to myself, then I may *not* do as I please, because I am not free to neglect my duties. However, just because they are *my* duties, it is easy not to recognize that they are duties at all. My first impulse may be to think "Since my life is my own, I may do as I please." For example, I may take the attitude that it is entirely up to me whether I ruin my mind and body with drugs. Just as some persons of St. Thomas's time conspicuously wasted their property, perhaps to demonstrate how rich they were,[36] some persons of our time conspicuously waste themselves, perhaps to demonstrate how autonomous they are.

[13] The argument works like this:

1. The Decalogue includes only precepts which can be easily understood.
2. Our duties to duties to ourselves are *not* easily understood. Rather they are among the aspects of Divine law which "need to be inculcated, the wiser teaching the less wise."
3. Therefore they are not included in the Decalogue itself.

Sapientes does not mean "men who are versed in such matters," which makes the knowledge of these duties seem to be merely a matter of book learning, but "the wise," which makes it a matter of intellectual virtue. We are to think not merely of the prudence that develops from experience, but of the deep understanding that develops from reflection on the highest things, aided by the Spirit of God.

Reply to Objection 2. [1] *All the solemnities of the Old Law were instituted in celebration of some Divine favor, either in memory of past favors, or in sign of some favor to come: in like manner all the sacrifices were offered up with the same purpose.* [2] *Now of all the Divine favors to be commemorated the chief was that of the Creation, which was called to mind by the sanctification of the Sabbath;* [3] *wherefore the reason for this precept is given in Ex. 20: "In six days the Lord made heaven and earth," etc.* [4] *And of all future blessings, the chief and final was the repose of the mind in God,* [5] *either, in the*

Reply to Objection 2. The Old Law established all of the solemn rituals – as well as all of the sacrifices – for the same reason: either to commemorate some past Divine blessing, or to foreshadow one expected in the future. The Sabbath day observance does both of these things.

As to commemoration: The first and greatest of God's past blessings was the gift of Creation. We know that one of the purposes of keeping the Sabbath day holy was to memorialize it, for in giving the reason for this precept, the book of Exodus speaks of God making the heavens and the earth in six days.

And as to foreshadowing: The greatest and last of God's blessings yet to come was the repose of the mind in God – whether in the

---

[36] I am thinking of Dante Alighieri's depiction of the Wasters in *Inferno*, canto 7.

present life, by grace, [6] or, in the future life, by glory; [7] which repose was also foreshadowed in the Sabbath-day observance: wherefore it is written (Is. 58): "If thou turn away thy foot from the Sabbath, from doing thy own will in My holy day, and call the Sabbath delightful, and the holy of the Lord glorious." [8] Because these favors first and chiefly are borne in mind by men, especially by the faithful. [9] But other solemnities were celebrated on account of certain particular favors temporal and transitory, [10] such as the celebration of the Passover in memory of the past favor of the delivery from Egypt, [11] and as a sign of the future Passion of Christ, which though temporal and transitory, brought us to the repose of the spiritual Sabbath. [12] Consequently, the Sabbath alone, and none of the other solemnities and sacrifices, is mentioned in the precepts of the decalogue.

present life by grace, or in the future life by glory. We know that one of the purposes of keeping the Sabbath day observance was to anticipate this rest, for the prophet Isaiah alludes to it in exhorting the people to regard the Sabbath day as holy ground and refrain from doing as they please on that day, calling it a delight and a glory.

These two Divine favors – Creation, and future rest in God – are first and foremost in men's minds, especially the minds of the faithful. But other solemn rituals were also observed because of certain temporal and transient blessings. For example, the Passover celebration both memorialized the past favor of liberation from Egypt and foreshadowed the future favor of the Passion of Christ which liberates from sin. Yet note that even though it was temporal and transient, it *brought us to* the eternal and enduring repose of the spiritual Sabbath.

All of these are reasons why, passing over any of the other solemn observances and sacrifices, the Decalogue calls to mind only the Sabbath.

---

[1] The Objector has protested that the Decalogue includes only one precept concerning worship, the commandment for Sabbath day observance. St. Thomas focuses our attention by pointing out that each precept concerning worship either expresses gratitude for something God has done, or foreshadows something He has promised that he will do.

[2] In an elegant *chiasmus* or reversed parallelism, St. Thomas calls Creation the "first and greatest" Divine favor commemorated (*primum et praecipuum*), and the future repose of the mind in God the "greatest and last" Divine favor anticipated (*praecipuum et finale*). This is overlooked in the Blackfriars translation, which reduces the first pair of adjectives to the single word "chief."

[3] The book of Exodus makes the connection between Creation and the Sabbath day clear:

Remember the sabbath day, to keep it holy. Six days you shall labor, and do all your work; but the seventh day is a sabbath to the Lord your God; in it you shall not do any work, you, or your son, or your daughter, your manservant, or your maidservant, or your cattle, or the sojourner who is within your gates; for in six days the Lord made heaven and earth, the sea, and all that is in them, and rested the seventh day; therefore the Lord blessed the sabbath day and hallowed it.[37]

As St. Augustine had remarked, "What kind of days these were it is extremely difficult, or perhaps impossible for us to conceive, and how much more to say!"[38] Most of St. Thomas's authorities thought of them as literal days, distinct periods of time, though Augustine himself viewed them instead as virtual days, phases or aspects of the work of Creation.[39] St. Thomas tries to be fair to both sides of the controversy, explaining the points of disagreement that can and cannot be harmonized in I, Question 74, Article 2, "Whether all these days are one day?"

[4] That for which man was made, and the very meaning of his fulfillment, is the rest of his mind in God, a consummation that the redeemed will possess when they enjoy the beatific vision, beholding with their minds the very Being of God, of what He is in Himself. St. Thomas develops the argument systematically in I-II, Questions 1-5, variously called the *Treatise on Happiness*, the *Treatise on Man's Last End*, and the *Treatise on Happiness and Ultimate Purpose*.[40]

[5] By their natural powers, in this life our minds are able to grasp only *that* God is, not *what* God is. They can know that God exists, and that He is good and so forth, but cannot grasp what He is in Himself; His uncreated Being and Goodness are far above our created minds. By the undeserved Divine favor called grace, however, our minds can catch glimpses or reflections of the glory which is to be revealed to them in the next, when the vision of God will leave nothing to be desired.

[6] "Or, in the future life, by glory": The contrast between grace in the present life, and glory in the next, is not meant to imply that to be shown God's glory is *not* a grace. Indeed, in the next life this grace will be complete, for by the power of God, the minds of the redeemed will be uplifted beyond their natural limits and confirmed in the vision of God.

[7] To us, the expression "turn your foot from the Sabbath" sounds as though it means dishonoring the Sabbath. Actually it means *honoring* the Sabbath. The seventh day of the week, which is reverenced by fearing to do servile toil upon it, is compared here to holy ground, which is reverenced by fearing to treat it like dirt by walking on it. The context of the passage St. Thomas is quoting from the book of the prophet Isaiah is a Divine promise:

---

[37] Exodus 20:8-11 (RSV-CE).
[38] St. Augustine of Hippo, *City of God against the Pagans*, book XI, chapter 6, www.newadvent.org/fathers/120111.htm.
[39] See especially St. Augustine of Hippo, *Confessions*, books XI and XII.
[40] See J. Budziszewski, *Commentary on Thomas Aquinas's Treatise on Happiness and Ultimate Purpose* (Cambridge: Cambridge University Press, 2020).

If you turn back your foot from the sabbath, from doing your pleasure on my holy day, and call the sabbath a delight and the holy day of the Lord honorable; if you honor it, not going your own ways, or seeking your own pleasure, or talking idly; then you shall take delight in the Lord, and I will make you ride upon the heights of the earth; I will feed you with the heritage of Jacob your father, for the mouth of the Lord has spoken.[41]

[8] "These favors" refers both to the great gift of Creation and the inconceivable boon of repose in glory. No created good can be greater than the gift of Creation itself. Rest in God, however, is a greater gift still, because He is the Infinite and Uncreated Good in which all created goods have their source.

[9] Just because Creation is the greatest of all boons in this life, the Decalogue uses gratitude for Creation to represent gratitude for all boons in this life. However, some of these temporal benefits are commemorated in other parts of the Divine law. Insofar as the Decalogue's provision for a Sabbath day of rest symbolizes not only of God's rest after Creation but also the spiritual Sabbath of eternal rest in God, this particular ordinance reminds us of both transitory *and* everlasting blessings, as we see again below.

[10] Especially prominent in the other parts of Divine law is the Passover feast, which commemorates the historical moment in which the angel of death struck the Egyptians but "passed over" God's people, so that they could depart from the land of their enslavers. The sign that they were to be spared was the smearing of lamb's blood on the doorposts and lintels of the doors of their houses. If any other sacred observance should have been mentioned in the Decalogue, this one should have been. As we are about to see, however, the symbolism of the Sabbath and the symbolism of the Passover are connected.

[11] St. Thomas argues that the feast of the Passover not only commemorated delivery from enslavement to the Egyptians but also foreshadowed a future delivery from enslavement to sin. Those who were under the sign of a lamb's blood were spared then; those who are under the sign of the blood of Christ, the Lamb of God, are spared now. As by the first great act of deliverance, the people were finally brought to a physical Promised Land, so by the second great act of deliverance, they are finally brought to a spiritual Promised Land. As the former land represented rest in the present life, so the latter land represents eternal rest in the next; and this is the spiritual Sabbath.

[12] Since the Sabbath observance both honors the greatest past blessing and foreshadows the greatest future blessing, no other sacred observance needs to be mentioned in the Decalogue. This one can stand for them all.

Reply to Objection 3. [1] As the Apostle says (Heb. 6), "men swear by one greater than

Reply to Objection 3. Two possible reasons might be given why the Decalogue prohibits false swearing but does not mention

---

[41] Isaiah 58:13–14 (RSV-CE).

themselves; and an oath for confirmation is the end of all their controversy." [2] Hence, since oaths are common to all, inordinate swearing is the matter of a special prohibition by a precept of the decalogue. [3] According to one interpretation, however, the words, "Thou shalt not take the name of the Lord thy God in vain," are a prohibition of false doctrine, [4] for one gloss expounds them thus: "Thou shalt not say that Christ is a creature."	blasphemy or false teaching. First, the unknown author of the letter to the Hebrews comments that men swear by what is greater than themselves, and use oaths to confirm that controversy has ended. Since oaths are so broadly used by everyone, there needs to be a special prohibition in the Decalogue to prohibit using oaths in a disordered way. Another possibility is that the prohibition of taking God's name in vain *is* a prohibition of false teaching. This is the implied opinion of a commentary which argues that it means "Do not say Christ is merely a created being."

[1] The Objector had complained that although the Decalogue includes a precept prohibiting false swearing, it contains no precepts about blasphemy and false teaching. St. Thomas begins his reply simply by pointing out what it means to swear an oath, quoting from the letter to the Hebrews:

For when God made a promise to Abraham, since he had no one greater by whom to swear, he swore by himself, saying, "Surely I will bless you and multiply you." And thus Abraham, having patiently endured, obtained the promise. *Men indeed swear by a greater than themselves, and in all their disputes an oath is final for confirmation.*[42]

So dependent are human beings on oaths that in in order to confirm His covenant with Abraham, God Himself swore an oath – an oath by Himself, since there was none higher.[43]

[2] Oaths are so important to the conduct of life that swearing falsely with the name of the very Source of Truth is profoundly wicked, and had to be forbidden.

[3] The Objector thought that the Decalogue should have forbidden not only false swearing but every form of light, careless, dishonest, contemptuous, hypocritical, or blasphemous speech about God. But now the suggestion is advanced that in an extended sense, the commandment against taking God's name "in vain" *does* forbid all such empty forms of speech about Him.

[4] Elsewhere, St. Thomas himself acknowledges that the literal meaning of the Second Commandment is to prohibit "swearing on that which is not" (*iurando pro re quae non est*); the gloss's suggestion that it means "Do not declare that Christ is merely a created being," he says, is "mystical," that is, symbolic.[44] Even

---

[42] Hebrews 6:13–16 (RSV-CE), emphasis added.
[43] "By myself I have sworn, says the Lord." Genesis 22:16a (RSV-CE).
[44] II-II, Q. 122, Art. 3, ad 1. "Swearing on that which is not" is St. Thomas's paraphrase of the language of the Vulgate, "tak[ing] His name upon a vain thing" (*super re vana nomen ejus assumpserit*).

so, the suggestion may at first seem bizarre. It makes sense, however if "Do not declare that Christ is merely a created being" is taken in the sense, "Do not speak falsely about God, *for example* by declaring that Christ is merely a created being." Taken this way, the gloss is using one metonym (in which a particular falsehood about God stands for all falsehoods about God) to explain another metonym (in which the prohibition of false swearing stands for all empty speech about God).

St. Thomas is very slightly paraphrasing a line in what the Ordinary Gloss says about the first three commandments, as they are given in Deuteronomy 5 (which parallels Exodus 20).[45] I render the Latin thus:

Do not take the name of God in vain, etc.

Taking the [first three] commandments in order, the first refers to the Father: *Hear, O Israel, the Lord is One* (Deut. 6);[46] So that one who hears may know with certainty that he is to worship one God, rather than upholding many gods.

The second refers to the Son, of whom it says, *You shall not take the name of thy God in vain*: that is, do not regard the Son of God as a created being. For every *creature is made subject to vanity*,[47] but you are to believe Him to be equal to the Father, God of gods, God with God, by whom all things were made.

The third refers to the Spirit, by whom is promised the gift of eternal rest, because the Holy Spirit, who is called sevenfold,[48] made holy the seventh day. No other days of the week are called holy, but only the Sabbath, on which God rested. Therefore this commandment refers rightly to the Spirit. And because making the day holy is mentioned, and eternal rest refers to the gift of the Holy Spirit, the commandment is expressed like this: *Remember that thou keep holy the Sabbath day: six days shalt thou labor*, etc. The six days of labor, etc. seem to symbolize a work of six thousand years,[49] with the seventh season being eternal rest, the promised eternal rest from good works. So then, whatever we do, if we do it for the sake of future rest, we are observing the Sabbath.[50]

---

[45] "Do not regard the Son of God as a creature" (*non aestimes creaturam esse Dei Filium*) becomes "Do not say Christ is a creature" (*non dices Christum esse creaturam*).

[46] Referring to verse 4.

[47] Alluding to Romans 8:20.

[48] Alluding to Apocalypse (Revelation) 1:4, 3:1, 4:5, and 5:6, which in turn alludes to Isaiah 11:2–3 (DRA), a messianic passage, which says of the promised Messiah, "And the spirit of the Lord shall rest upon him: the spirit of wisdom, and of understanding, the spirit of counsel, and of fortitude, the spirit of knowledge, and of godliness. And he shall be filled with the spirit of the fear of the Lord." From this passage is taken the tradition list of the seven gifts of the Holy Spirit as fear of the Lord, wisdom, understanding, counsel, fortitude, knowledge, and piety. These *uplift* the virtues – for example, the gift of fortitude uplifts the virtue of fortitude – by attuning us to the guidance of the Holy Spirit. They enable us to choose rightly even in matters in which ordinary virtue is out of its depth.

[49] The view that the interval is exactly 6,000 years is not critical to the interpretation; as the days are figurative, so the thousands of years are figurative.

[50] *Non usurpabis nomen Domini Dei frustra*, etc. *Primum mandatum ad Patrem pertinet quod dicitur in sequentibus: Audi, Israel, Dominus Deus tuus unus est (Deut. VI); ut hoc scilicet audiens, unum Deum Patrem colas, non multos deos suscipias. Secundum pertinet ad Filium, de quo hic dicitur: Non assumes nomen Dei tui in vanum, id est, non aestimes creaturam esse Dei*

Another way to view the gloss is to remember that if the essence of false swearing is to treat *that which is* as equivalent to *that which is not*, then among other things we must not *treat that which eternally exists in itself* as equivalent to *that which is caused to come into being at a certain point in time*. Whether or not St. Thomas himself had it in mind, perhaps some light can be shed on this point by a passage by Maximus the Confessor, in which he comments that Christ, the Son, is the Name of God, the Father. Maximus is commenting on the beginning of the Lord's Prayer, "Our Father, who art in heaven, hallowed be thy name. Thy kingdom come. Thy will be done, on earth as it is in heaven":[51]

At once, the Lord teaches those who pray that theology [literally, God-speech, whether speech about God, or, as in this case, speech to Him] fittingly begins with these [words], and initiates [his hearers] into the manner of existence of the Creative Cause of the things that are, being [Himself] by essence the Cause of the things that are. For what is said in prayer contains a manifestation of the Father, and of the Father's Name, and of the Father's Kingdom; a manifestation that serves to teach us to worship, invoke and adore the singleness of the Creator Trinity. *For the essentially subsisting Name of God the Father, is the only-begotten Son*; and the essentially subsisting Kingdom of God the Father, is the Holy Spirit ...

For the Father does not have a newly-acquired Name; nor do we at all think of [His] Kingdom as something He was found worthy of upon consideration. For He has not begun to exist, so that He might also begin to be Father or King; but as He exists eternally, so He is Father and King eternally, in no way having begun either to be or to be Father or King. Now if He eternally is, He is also eternally Father and King; therefore both the Son and the Holy Spirit have essentially subsisted *with* the Father eternally, and *not after* Him, being naturally from Him and in Him: ... but They did not come into existence afterwards by being caused.[52]

Reply to Objection 4. [1] *That a man should not do harm to anyone is an immediate dictate of his natural reason: and therefore the precepts that forbid the doing of harm are binding on all men.* [2] *But it is not an*	Reply to Objection 4. Since the wrong of doing harm follows immediately from man's natural reason, the prohibition of nuisance applies to everyone. By contrast, it does not follow

---

Filium. Omnis enim creatura subiecta est vanitati, sed credas eum aequalem Patri, Deum deorum, Deum apud Deum, per quem omnia facta sunt. Tertium ad Spiritum, cuius dono requies aeterna promittitur: quia enim Spiritus sanctus dicitur septiformis, ideo septimum diem sanctificavit Deus. In aliis enim diebus operum sanctificatio non nominatur, nisi in sabbato, in quo requievit Deus. Recte ergo hoc mandatum pertinet ad Spiritum: tum propter sanctificationis nomen; tum propter aeternam requiem, ad donum sancti Spiritus pertinentem. Dicitur enim sic: Memento ut diem sabbati sanctifices: sex diebus operaberis, etc. In opere sex dierum, etc. , videtur sex millium annorum operatio signari, in septimo tempus aeternae quietis, in quo post bona opera quies aeterna promittitur. Quidquid ergo agimus, si propter futuram requiem facimus, sabbatum observamus.

[51] Matthew 6:9–10 (RSV-CE).
[52] Maximus the Confessor, *Commentary on the Lord's Prayer*, unpublished translation by Richard Conrad, OP, who called the passage to my attention. Italics added; quoted by permission.

immediate dictate of natural reason that a man should do one thing in return for another, unless he happen to be indebted to someone. [3] *Now a son's debt to his father is so evident that one cannot get away from it by denying it: since the father is the principle of generation and being, and also of upbringing and teaching.* [4] *Wherefore the decalogue does not prescribe deeds of kindness or service to be done to anyone except to one's parents.* [5] *On the other hand parents do not seem to be indebted to their children for any favors received, but rather the reverse is the case.* [6] *Again, a child is a part of his father; and "parents love their children as being a part of themselves," as the Philosopher states (Ethic. viii).* [7] *Hence, just as the decalogue contains no ordinance as to man's behavior towards himself, so, for the same reason, it includes no precept about loving one's children.*

immediately from natural reason that something must be done for someone else, unless it is owed to him.

Now what a son owes to his father is so obvious that no evasion can negate it, for his father is the source of his birth and being, not to mention his rearing and teaching. For this reason, the Decalogue does not command kindness or service to anyone except parents. Parents do not seem to *owe* anything to their children because the children do good to them – quite the contrary.

Besides, as Aristotle reminds us, the child is a part of the father, and fathers love their children as parts of themselves. Viewing the matter from this perspective, the Decalogue omits any precept to love one's own children for the same reason that it declines to regulate one's relations toward himself.

---

[1] It may seem that doing no harm is *not* an immediate dictate of our natural reason, for isn't it right to harm wrongdoers by punishing them, and to harm those who have damaged us by requiring compensation? It is, but St. Thomas always uses the expression "do no harm" as shorthand for the more obvious principle "do no *undeserved* harm," for example when he writes, "The precepts of the second table contain the order of justice to be observed among men, that nothing *undue* be done to anyone, and that each one be given his due; for it is in this sense that we are to take the precepts of the decalogue."[53]

Later in this *Commentary* we return to the point at greater length.

[2] The appearance of tautology – I do not owe a return to someone unless I owe a return to him – is an artifact of the Blackfriars translation. In the Latin, St. Thomas does not speak of a man doing one thing *in return* for another, but simply of doing one thing for another (*pro alio*).

[3] The Objector had been puzzled by the fact that the Decalogue includes a rule about parents but no rules about children and other neighbors. Having laid the groundwork, St. Thomas now begins to reply. We recall from the reply to the first Objection that the precepts of the Decalogue needed to be easily understandable, and this precept fits that description; children owe so much to their parents that their debt is obvious.

---

[53] I-II, Q. 100, Art. 8, emphasis added.

Some readers may wonder why St. Thomas mentions only the father here, and not the mother. One possibility is that he is here speaking of the *principle of being* of the child, and medieval biology mistakenly believed that the active principle in generation – that which sets it in motion – is the father's semen. On the other hand, in other places he calls the parents *together* the child's principle of being – and in a broad sense, this description would be true even if medieval biology had *not* been mistaken about the function of paternal semen in generation, because the mother bears the child and participates fully in his upbringing. Consider for instance the following passage:

> Man becomes a debtor to other men in various ways, according to their various excellence and the various benefits received from them. On both counts God holds first place, for He is supremely excellent, and is for us the first principle of being and government. On the second place, the principles of our being and government are our parents and our country, that have given us birth and nourishment. Consequently man is debtor chiefly to his parents and his country, after God.[54]

For this reason, I think it is more likely that in his Reply to Objection 4 St. Thomas is using the term "father" not as a nod to medieval biology but as a metonym: He is simply using the more authoritative parent to represent both parents.

[4] Although we should repay the good done to us by others as well, such debts are not as obvious and undeniable as those to parents. Therefore, on the principle that the Decalogue includes only those obvious principles that explain all the others, only the debt to our parents needs to be mentioned. The most conspicuous of our debts stands for all of them. Notice that in passing, St. Thomas explains *what it means* to honor one's father and mother: to offer them kindness and service.

[5] Debts of parents to children are omitted from the Decalogue not only because they are not obvious but because they do not exist. Since what children do for parents is owed to them, no return is needed.

[6] Certainly parents ought to love their children, but because their natural inclination to love them is so powerful, there is no need for the Decalogue to put this in words. Parents who unnaturally lack affection for their children are universal objects of abhorrence.

As Aristotle writes in his *Nicomachean Ethics*, "Parents indeed love their children as part of themselves. But children love their parents as the authors of their existence."[55] St. Thomas explains in *Commentary* on the work,

> At "Parents indeed," [Aristotle] gives the reason for this friendship. He says that parents love their children as part of themselves; they are generated from the seed of their parents. Hence the son is a separated part of the father, so to speak. Consequently this

---

[54] II-II, Q. 101, Art. 1.
[55] Aristotle, *Nicomachean Ethics*, book VIII, chapter 12. I am following the wording in Thomas Aquinas, *Commentary on Aristotle's Nicomachean Ethics*, translated by C. I. Litzinger (Chicago: Regnery, 1964).

friendship is nearest to the love of a man for himself, from which all friendship is derived, as will be indicated in the ninth book (1797). With reason then paternal friendship is considered to be the starting point. But children love their parents as the source of their existence, much like a separated part would love the whole from which it is separated.[56]

The literal meaning of the phrase the Blackfriars translation renders as "is a part of," *est aliquid*, is "is something of." My child is not a part of me in the sense that my arm is a part of me, but in the sense that he cannot be understood except in relation to me. The very idea of my arm presupposes my body, and the very idea of the child presupposes his parents. It might also be added that I care for him as I care for my arm – in fact more so.

[7] We saw in the Reply to the first Objection that because one's natural inclination to love himself is so strong, there is no need to command him to love himself. The reason why there is no need to command parents to love their children is exactly the same.

Reply to Objection 5. [1] *The pleasure of adultery and the usefulness of wealth, insofar as they have the character of pleasurable or useful good, are of themselves, objects of appetite:* [2] *and for this reason they needed to be forbidden not only in the deed but also in the desire.* [3] *But murder and falsehood are, of themselves, objects of repulsion (since it is natural for man to love his neighbor and the truth):* [4] *and are desired only for the sake of something else.* [5] *Consequently with regard to sins of murder and false witness, it was necessary to proscribe, not sins of thought, but only sins of deed.*

Reply to Objection 5. Adultery is pleasurable; wealth is useful. The fact that these things hold forth the prospect of pleasure or use turns the appetite toward them. This is why sins concerning the wives and wealth of others had to be prohibited not only in deed but also in covetous desire.

Not so with murder and falsehood. In themselves, these are not attractive but horrible to us, because we naturally love our neighbors and the truth. For this reason, murder and falsehood are never desired except as means to other things. So concerning sins of murder and false testimony, there was no need to forbid sins of the heart, but only sins of deed.

---

[1] The Objector had complained that since the Decalogue prohibited not only certain sins of deed but also certain sins of thought, it should have followed through and forbidden *all* sins of thought – for example prohibiting not only the desire for one's neighbor's wife but also the desire to murder, and forbidding not only the desire for one's neighbor's wealth but also the desire to give false testimony. What are we to make of this argument?

St. Thomas begins his Reply by remarking that just because they seem good to us, we are attracted to adultery and wealth. The point is clear, although the

---

[56] Ibid., book VIII, lecture 12.

phrasing obscures it a bit because the desires for these two things are not parallel. We naturally desire those external goods that we need for the conduct of our lives; these goods are wealth. However, we do not naturally desire adultery per se. What we naturally desire is the union of the sexes, and just as covetousness is a *disordered* desire for wealth, adulterous lust is a *disordered* desire for the union of the sexes.

[2] *Just because* wealth and the union of the sexes are natural goods, we naturally desire them; *just because* we naturally desire them, we are easily tempted to desire them the wrong way; *just because* we are so easily tempted to do so, we must be commanded not to.

[3] I naturally desire wealth and sexual union *in themselves*, and this is why I can so easily be tempted to desire them in the wrong way. But I do not desire murder and false witness *in themselves*. On the contrary, my natural love is for my neighbor, not for his death, and my natural love is for the truth, not for its distortion.

Both love of my neighbor and love of the truth fall into what St. Thomas presents as the third category of natural inclinations. In the first category are inclinations which we share with all "substances" or essential natures, such as to preserve ourselves. In the second are those we share with all animals, such as to procreate, that is, to preserve not just ourselves but our kind. In the third, however, are those that are distinct to rational beings like ourselves. He mentions two – to know the truth (especially the truth about God), and to live in society.[57] These two are connected, because by society, he is not thinking of the instinct-driven togetherness of irrational creatures such as wolves; rather he has in mind a society which is *shaped* by our nature as truth-seekers. Except in community with the people with whom I live, I cannot flourish. Besides, God is my ultimate good, and my neighbors are made in His image.

To say that love of my neighbor and of the truth are built into me does not mean that these inclinations are as strong as they would have been without the Fall, or that I cannot act against them. What it does mean is that in order to act against them, *I need some obscuring temptation*, for I am certainly not naturally averse to them; by nature, I incline to them as the needle of the compass points north.

[4] We do not need *reasons* for external goods such as a roof to keep the rain off our heads, or the enjoyment of conjugal society with our spouses. They are, so to speak, their own reasons, because they are good in themselves. But just because murder and lying are *not* natural goods, we need reasons to lie and murder. The temptation to murder must offer me a strong enough inducement to overcome my natural inclination to love my neighbor, and the temptation to

---

[57] See I-II, Q. 94, Art. 2.

lie must offer a strong enough inducement to overcome my natural inclination to love the truth.

[5] The argument runs like this:

1. There is no need to forbid the desires to lie or murder for their own sakes, because no such desires exist; no one desires to lie or murder except for the sake of something else.
2. Therefore it was sufficient to forbid the acts of lying and murder.
3. By contrast, people can desire the wives and wealth of others for their own sakes.
4. Regarding these, then, the Decalogue needed to forbid not only the deed, but the desire as well.

Reply to Objection 6. [1] *As stated above, all the passions of the irascible faculty arise from the passions of the concupiscible part.* [2] *Hence, as the precepts of the decalogue are, as it were, the first elements of the Law,* [3] *there was no need for mention of the irascible passions, but only of the concupiscible passions.*

Reply to Objection 6. In arguing that Decalogue should have prohibited not only disorders of the soul's "concupiscible" or desiring power but also of its "irascible" or ardent power, the Objector overlooks the fact that all of the disorders of the latter *arise from* disorders of the former. So, bearing in mind that the Ten Commandments are but the first elements or starting points of the Law, it was sufficient to pass over the latter and address only the former.

---

[1] According to the Objector, since the Decalogue prohibits sins of disordered concupiscence, it should also have prohibited sins of disordered irascibility. First St. Thomas calls our attention to the fact that the passions of these two powers are related, since passions of the latter kind arise from passions of the former. Actually, they terminate in them too, although he is not pointing that out at present. First, perhaps, Stella desires tea. Then she becomes angry because Edgar stirred salt into it instead of sugar; had she not had the desire, she would not have had the anger. However, her anger arouses her to brew a new pot, and now she reposes in the pleasure of the hot cup. So the sequence of Stella's passions is desire, anger, repose; first her concupiscible power is aroused, then her irascible power is aroused, then her concupiscible power rests in the thing that it desired.

St. Thomas summarizes this point by saying, "the passions of the irascible faculty stand between those concupiscible passions that denote movement towards good or evil, and those concupiscible passions that denote rest in good or evil. And it is therefore evident that the irascible passions both arise from and terminate in the passions of the concupiscible faculty":

- They arise from them in the sense that "the passions of the irascible faculty add something to those of the concupiscible faculty; just as the object of the

irascible adds the aspect of arduousness or difficulty to the object of the concupiscible faculty. Thus hope adds to desire a certain effort, and a certain raising of the spirits to the realization of the arduous good. In like manner fear adds to aversion or detestation a certain lowness of spirits, on account of difficulty in shunning the evil."
- They terminate in them in the sense that "in the order of execution, the irascible passions take precedence of such like passions of the concupiscible faculty: thus hope precedes joy, and hence causes it."[58]

[2] We see later, in I-II, Question 105, Article 1, that the judicial precepts are the constitutional law of the Hebrew polity. However, the Decalogue constituted the *people* in a much more fundamental way. More than being their Magna Carta or their Articles of Confederation, they were the cornerstone of their entire way of life, and the basis of all the more detailed precepts, whether moral, judicial, or ceremonial.

[3] If the Decalogue had been concerned with every detail of the Law, then it would have forbidden disorders of both kind of passion. But since it is concerned only with the first elements of the Law, it rests with forbidding the passion in which both kinds of disorder begin – concupiscible passion. For example, anger and hope are irascible passions. But a man does not harbor disordered anger because he cannot have his neighbor's wife *unless he covets his neighbor's wife*, and he does not entertain disordered hope for his neighbor's cow *unless he covets his neighbor's cow*. So it is enough to command "Do not covet"; the rest is details.

One more point: When we first discussed the sixth Objection, we saw that it might also have been open to the Objector to suggest that the Decalogue should have included not only precepts against excess but also precepts against deficiency. For example, I should not desire my neighbor's wife, *but I ought to desire my own*, and I should not be fierce about a casual insult, *but I ought to be fierce to defend life from attack*. Although St. Thomas does not address this possible complaint, his Reply to the fifth Objection gives us a good idea of how he might have answered it. There, he suggested that because certain things are themselves natural objects of desire and certain other things are desired only for the sake of something else, it was more important for the Decalogue to forbid disordered desire for the former than for the latter. Here, he might suggest that just because we do naturally desire certain things, it was more important for the Decalogue to forbid the excess of such desire than its deficiency.

---

[58] I-II, Q. 25, Art. 1

DISCUSSION

The Moral Architecture of the Decalogue

The Old Law is the Divine law of the Old Testament. Leaving its ceremonial and judicial precepts aside, let us review the moral design of its foundation, the Decalogue, as viewed by St. Thomas.

All ten of the Commandments flow closely from love of God and neighbor, in such a way that even a person of slight wisdom can immediately recognize their truth. Each of the moral precepts is also a placeholder: That is, each of them symbolizes much more than it literally decrees. For instance, the fact that the Eighth Commandment mentions only bearing false witness – lying to get my neighbor in trouble, in the context of giving testimony – does not mean that other sorts of lies are all right. The worst sort of lie is used as a placeholder for every sort of lie.

Not everything in the Decalogue is a moral precept. For example, setting aside times and places for remittance from labor and worship of God is morally obligatory, but the specific requirement to do so on the seventh day belongs to the ceremonial rather than moral precepts. It is also an example of what St. Thomas calls a "determination" rather than what he calls a "conclusion from premises," for a different day than the seventh might have been designated, and indeed, after the Resurrection, a different day was.

A. First Tablet: Precepts ordering man in his relations to God as the Divine head of the community[59]

1. Fidelity (owed God in deeds)

First Commandment: I am the Lord your God, who brought you out of the land of Egypt, out of the house of bondage. You shall have no other gods before me. You shall not make for yourself a graven image, or any likeness of anything that is in heaven above, or that is on the earth beneath, or that is in the water under the earth; you shall not bow down to them or serve them; for I the Lord your God am a jealous God, visiting the iniquity of the fathers upon the children to the third and fourth generation of those who hate me, but showing steadfast love to thousands of those who love me and keep my commandments.

2. Reverence (owed God in words)

Second Commandment: You shall not take the name of the Lord your God in vain: for the Lord will not hold him guiltless who takes his name in vain.

3. Service (owed God in thoughts)

Third Commandment: Observe the sabbath day, to keep it holy, as the Lord your God commanded you. Six days you shall labor, and do all your work; but the seventh day is a sabbath to the Lord your God; in it you shall not do any work, you, or your son, or your

---

[59] Deuteronomy 5:6–15 (RSV-CE).

daughter, or your manservant, or your maidservant, or your ox, or your ass, or any of your cattle, or the sojourner who is within your gates, that your manservant and your maidservant may rest as well as you. You shall remember that you were a servant in the land of Egypt, and the Lord your God brought you out thence with a mighty hand and an outstretched arm; therefore the Lord your God commanded you to keep the sabbath day.

B. Second Tablet: Precepts ordering man in his relations to his neighbors, who live with him under God[60]
   1. Particular duties: Payment of debts to those to whom one is indebted
      Fourth Commandment: Honor your father and your mother, as the Lord your God commanded you; that your days may be prolonged, and that it may go well with you, in the land which the Lord your God gives you.[61]
   2. General duties: Doing no harm
   a. No harm by deed
      i. Concerning another's existence
         Fifth Commandment: You shall not kill.
      ii. Concerning unity with another for the propagation of offspring
         Sixth Commandment: Neither shall you commit adultery.
      iii. Concerning another's possessions
         Seventh Commandment: Neither shall you steal.
   b. No harm by word
         Eighth Commandment: Neither shall you bear false witness against your neighbor.
   c. No harm by thought
      i. Through the lust of the flesh
   Ninth Commandment: Neither shall you covet your neighbors wife;
      ii. Through the lust of the eyes
   Tenth Commandment: and you shall not desire your neighbor's house, his field, or his manservant, or his maidservant, his ox, or his ass, or anything that is your neighbors.

The Rest of the Moral Precepts

The other moral precepts of the Old Law – too numerous to list here – also flow from love of God and neighbor, but more remotely, so that if they had not been

---

[60] Deuteronomy 5:16–21 (RSV-CE).
[61] The commandment to honor parents may be viewed as a bridge between the First and Second Tablets, because the parents are not only ordinary neighbors but also the first representatives of God to the child. For this reason, some authorities – though not St. Thomas – place the Fourth Commandment in the First Tablet.

set down in writing, they might have been known only to the wise. Like the precepts of the Decalogue, some of them are probably placeholders. Some may also be determinations rather than conclusions from premises. For instance, a different mode of expressing respect for elders might have been designated in place of rising in their presence, but in any case, rising stands for all due expressions of respect.

QUESTION 100, ARTICLE 7

Whether the Precepts of the Decalogue are Suitably Formulated?

TEXT	PARAPHRASE
Whether the precepts of the Decalogue are suitably formulated?	Are the Ten Commandments well composed, taken not just individually, but as a set?

In this query we go beyond whether some things that should have been in the Decalogue were left out. Now, although what is included and omitted may still come up, we are considering principles of composition that apply with equal force to *each* of the Commandments. At stake is whether the Decalogue is just a collection of good ideas, haphazardly expressed, or a clear and systematic body of principles truly sufficient to serve as the foundation of the Old Law.

Objection 1. [1] *It would seem that the precepts of the decalogue are unsuitably formulated. Because the affirmative precepts direct man to acts of virtue, while the negative precepts withdraw him from acts of vice.* [2] *But in every matter there are virtues and vices opposed to one another.* [3] *Therefore in whatever matter there is an ordinance of a precept of the decalogue, there should have been an affirmative and a negative precept. Therefore it was unfitting that affirmative precepts should be framed in some matters, and negative precepts in others.*	Objection 1. The Ten Commandments appear to be poorly composed. Concerning some matters they provide affirmative rules, commanding acts of virtue, and concerning others they provide negative rules, forbidding acts of vice. But we find that virtues and vices oppose each other in *every* matter, not just some. Therefore, for every matter which the Decalogue addresses, there should have been both an affirmative and a negative precept. Since this is not the case, the framing of the Decalogue is defective.

[1] The affirmative precepts of the Decalogue are the third, about keeping the Sabbath day holy, and the fourth, about honoring parents: They command that something be *done*. All of the other precepts are negative, commanding that something *not* be done. Not having any other gods before God, not taking

His name in vain, not killing (in the sense of murdering), not committing adultery, not stealing, and not coveting either the wife or the wealth of one's neighbor.

[2] The Objector thinks the Decalogue is arbitrary in treating some matters, such as parents, solely as objects of commands to do something, but treating others, such as property, solely as objects of prohibition. Consider the affirmative precept to honor parents: Aren't there also things one should *not* do concerning parents? Or consider the negative precept concerning one's neighbor's property. Aren't there things one *should* do concerning one's neighbor's property.

[3] If the Objector's advice were taken, each of the ten items of the Decalogue would be a pair of commandments – one affirmative and one negative – rather than some of them being affirmative and others negative.

Objection 2. [1] *Further, Isidore says that every law is based on reason.* [2] *But all the precepts of the decalogue belong to the Divine law.* [3] *Therefore the reason should have been pointed out in each precept, and not only in the first and third.*

Objection 2. Moreover, as Isidore reminds us, all law depends on reason. But the rules of the Decalogue are law too – Divine law. Therefore, the reason for each precept should have been included. Unfortunately, although the reason is pointed out in the first precept, about having no gods before God, and in the third, about honoring the Sabbath day, it is not pointed out in any of the others.

---

[1] In English, the title of Isidore of Seville's enormously important *Etymologies* makes the work sound like a history of the origins of words. Although it contains a good deal of that, actually it is more a compendium of the sources of human knowledge. Thus its title is sometimes given as *Origins*. The observation about the relation between law and reason arises in Isidore's discussion of why not only written but also unwritten norms can count as true law. He says in book II,

Between law and custom there is this difference, that law is written, while custom is usage (*consuetudo*) tested and found good by its antiquity, or unwritten law ... Custom (*mos*) is longstanding usage, taken likewise from "moral habits" (*mores*, the plural of *mos*). "Customary law" (*consuetudo*) moreover is a certain system of justice (*ius*), established by moral habits, which is received as law when law is lacking; *nor does it seem to matter whether it exists in writing or in reason, seeing that reason commends a law.*

And again in book v,

"Customary law" (*consuetudo*) is a certain system of justice established by moral habits, which is taken as a law when law is lacking; *nor does it matter whether it exists in writing or reasoning, since reasoning also validates law. Furthermore, if law is based on reason, then law will be everything that is consistent with reason* – provided that it agrees with religion, accords with orderly conduct, and is conducive to well-being.[1]

In saying "if law is based on reason, then law will be everything that is consistent with reason," it may seem at first as though Isidore has made the same mistake as someone who says, "If a cat is something with four paws, then everything with four paws will be a cat." A dog has four paws but is not a cat; in the same way, a theorem in geometry is based on reason but is not a law. However, by "everything," Isidore does not mean literally everything, but *every norm of conduct*, provided that certain other conditions are met. Thus, he is really saying that if the term "law" refers to a norm of conduct based on reason, then every norm of conduct based on reason, provided that these other conditions are met, will be a law. This does not involve any fallacy.

St. Thomas agrees that reason pertains to the essence of law. He has argued earlier in the *Treatise on Law* that law is "a rule and measure of acts, whereby man is induced to act or is restrained from acting," but that since man is a rational being, the rule and measure of his acts has to be reason. As to the other conditions to be met, he holds that to be truly law, an enactment must be for the common good, made by competent public authority, and promulgated or made known.[2] So law is not merely the command of the sovereign, nor is it merely a system of conventional social rules, as maintained by the several varieties of legal positivists.[3]

[2] The Objector calls attention to the fact that the Ten Commandments are part of Divine law because Divine law is true law, and all law depends on reason. Consequently, the Ten Commandments must also depend on reason.

[3] The implied inference is that because the precepts of the Decalogue depend on reason, and because law, to be law, must be made known, the reason for each precept should also have been made known. For the First Commandment, the reason given in both Exodus and Deuteronomy is "for I the Lord your God am a jealous God."[4] For the Third Commandment, the reason given in Exodus is "for in six days the Lord made heaven and earth, the sea, and all that is in them, and rested the seventh day; therefore the Lord

---

[1] *The Etymologies of Isidore of Seville*, translated by Stephen A. Barney, W. J. Lewis, J. A. Beach, and Oliver Berghof (Cambridge: Cambridge University Press, 2006). I am quoting respectively from book II, chapter 10, p. 73, and book V, chapter 3, page 117, emphasis added in both cases.

[2] I-II, Q. 90; the quotation is from Art. 1. I discuss this in *Commentary on Thomas Aquinas's Treatise on Law* (Cambridge: Cambridge University Press, 2014).

[3] The version of positivism that holds that law is no more than the command of the sovereign is associated especially with Thomas Hobbes, *Leviathan* (1651), and John Austin, *The Province of Jurisprudence Determined* (1832). The version that holds that law is no more than a system of conventional social rules is associated especially with H. L. A. Hart., *The Concept of Law* (1961; Oxford: Oxford University Press, 1994). On the Continent, positivism is most often associated with Hans Kelsen, especially his *Pure Theory of Law* (1934).

[4] Exodus 20:5b, Deuteronomy 5:9b (RSV-CE).

blessed the sabbath day and hallowed it,"[5] and the reason given in Deuteronomy is "You shall remember that you were a servant in the land of Egypt, and the Lord your God brought you out thence with a mighty hand and an outstretched arm; therefore the Lord your God commanded you to keep the sabbath day."[6] These two reasons are not inconsistent, but complementary. Deuteronomy's reason makes it especially clear why servants should be included in the Sabbath rest too.

It may at first be surprising that the Second Commandment is not mentioned, because it seems to give a reason when it says "for the Lord will not hold him guiltless who takes His name in vain."[7] In Objection 4, however, St. Thomas has his Objector treat this not as a reason for the commandment, but as a threat of punishment for violating it.

| *Objection 3.* [1] *Further, by observing the precepts man deserves to be rewarded by God.* [2] *But the Divine promises concern the rewards of the precepts.* [3] *Therefore the promise should have been included in each precept, and not only in the second and fourth.* | Objection 3. Moreover, by obeying these commandments we merit God's reward. Since the rewards for obedience are specified in God's promises, each precept should have included a statement of the promise which corresponds to it. However, although the corresponding promise is included in the second rule, about not taking God's name in vain, and in the fourth, about honoring parents, it is omitted from each of the others. This is not fitting. |

[1] Holy Scripture is quite clear that God rewards good actions. Yet in view of other biblical teachings, the idea of Divine reward may seem strange. Since all of our ability to do good comes from God Himself, how can we deserve anything from Him? In one sense, we cannot, for what God gives is infinitely more than we can give back; what we do for Him is a drop in an infinite bucket, and even our ability to do anything at all for Him comes from Him. Yet in another sense, we can, for although our ability to do good works is a gift of loving grace, we freely choose whether to make a loving response to this gift; we are not marionettes on strings. Not because He is in debt to us, but of His own goodness, God condescends to recognize and honor this choice. In rewarding His children, God is not acting like an employer who pays the laborer a wage which makes the two parties square, for nothing can make us square with the infinitely bountiful God. As has often been observed, He is acting more like a mother who praises her obedient three-year-old child for "helping" her to make dinner.

---

[5] These need not be taken as literal days, and the reference to rest means that God desisted from further Creation – not that the Omnipotent was literally tired.
[6] Exodus 20:11, Deuteronomy 5:15: (RSV-CE).
[7] Exodus 20:7b, Deuteronomy 5:11b (RSV-CE).

But there is still more to the paradox. Because He bestows charity upon His people and guides them with His Holy Spirit, God Himself is the ultimate source even of our ability to perform truly good deeds. In the final analysis, then, His reward gives due credit *to the very gift of His grace!* One cannot help but think of a passage in the Apocalypse of John, in which certain elders, symbolically described as seated upon thrones and wreathed with golden crowns, fall prostrate before God in adoration. Casting their crowns at His feet, they sing, "Worthy art thou, our Lord and God, to receive glory and honor and power, for thou didst create all things, and by thy will they existed and were created."[8] God has condescended to honor them – yet they give the honor entirely back to Him.

[2] Not only does God reward obedience but He also *promises* reward for obedience.

[3] The implied argument here is similar to the one in the previous Objection: Since the promised reward concerns the law, and because law, to be law, must be made known, the reward for obedience should have been made known in each precept, not just the second and the fourth.

Explicitly, the Second Commandment states only a punishment for false swearing: "For the Lord will not hold him guiltless who takes His name in vain." Apparently the Objector is taking the reward for *not* swearing falsely to be simply that God then views us as innocent of doing so.

The reward for honoring parents, however, is explicit: Exodus says, "That your days may be long in the land which the Lord your God gives you." A little more fully, Deuteronomy says, "that your days may be prolonged, and that it may go well with you, in the land which the Lord your God gives you."[9]

Objection 4. [1] *Further, the Old Law is called "the law of fear," insofar as it induced men to observe the precepts, by means of the threat of punishments.* [2] *But all the precepts of the decalogue belong to the Old Law.* [3] *Therefore a threat of punishment should have been included in each, and not only in the first and second.*	Objection 4. Moreover, the Old Law has rightly been called a "law of fear" because it motivated men to obey its rules by threatening penalties for disobedience. Since all ten of the Commandments of the Decalogue are part of the Old Law, each one should have contained a statement of the associated punishment. This is done in the case of the first, about having no gods before God, and the second, about not taking His name in vain, but it is inappropriately omitted from the other eight.

---

[8] Apocalypse 4:11 (RSV-CE). The Apocalypse is also called the Revelation of John, or simply Revelations.
[9] Respectively Exodus 20:12b and Deuteronomy 5:16b (RSV-CE).

[1] In saying that the Old Law is called a law of fear, the Objector is no doubt thinking of St. Augustine of Hippo, who develops this theme in several passages. The first is from his book *Against Adimantus, a Disciple of Manichaeus*, where Augustine bends over backwards[10] to express the difference between the Old and New Law in a pun. In my own free paraphrase:

> So if even in New Testament times, when love [*caritas*] is most greatly commended, carnal fear is injected with the fear of visible Divine punishments – how much more, in the time of the Old Testament, should this be adapted to the understanding of people who were restrained by the fear of the Law, as a child is by his master? For the shortest and most obvious difference between the two Testaments is the difference between *timor* and *amor*, fear and love. The former pertains to the old man, the latter to the new man, yet by the most merciful dispensation of the One God, these were brought forth and conjoined.[11]

Another passage the Objector may have in mind is Augustine's explanation of Psalm 130,[12] which reads as follows:

> Out of the depths I cry to thee, O Lord! Lord, hear my voice! Let thy ears be attentive to the voice of my supplications! If thou, O Lord, shouldst mark iniquities, Lord, who could stand? *But there is forgiveness with thee, that thou mayest be feared.* I wait for the Lord, my soul waits, and in his word I hope; my soul waits for the Lord more than watchmen for the morning, more than watchmen for the morning. O Israel, hope in the Lord! For with the Lord there is steadfast love, and with him is plenteous redemption. And he will redeem Israel from all his iniquities.[13]

About the fourth verse, which I have italicized, Augustine says,

> A holy law was given to the Jews, a law that was just and good,[14] but all it could do was convict them. No law was given them that was *capable of giving life*,[15] only a law that revealed the sinner to himself. The sinner had forgotten himself and no longer kept his sins in view; he was therefore given a law to help him see himself. The law declared him guilty; only the lawgiver could set him free, for the lawgiver is the sovereign ruler of all.

---

[10] The bending over backwards lies in the shift from *caritas* to *amor*. The former word means love in the sense of charity. Though the latter word usually refers to the love between the sexes, here it too is used to mean charity. But perhaps the shift is not so forced, because Holy Scripture often compares the love of God for His people with the love of a husband for his betrothed.

[11] *Si ergo tempore Novi Testamenti, quo maxime caritas commendatur, de poenis visibilibus divinitus iniectus est carnalibus timor; quanto magis tempore Veteris Testamenti hoc congruisse illi populo intellegendum est, quem timor Legis tamquam paedagogi coercebat? Nam haec est brevissima et apertissima differentia duorum Testamentorum, timor et amor: illud ad veterem, hoc ad novum hominem pertinet; utrumque tamen unius Dei misericordissima dispensatione prolatum atque coniunctum.*

[12] Numbered 129 in the Vulgate.

[13] Psalm 130:1–8 (RSV-CE), emphasis added. "His," in the last sentence, refers to Israel; the male pronoun is used because the people Israel descends from the man Israel.

[14] See Romans 7:12.

[15] Galatians 3:21.

A law was given that can terrify us and lock us into our guilt; it does not free us but merely exposes our sins.

Perhaps it was someone bound by that law, and aware in his deep place how grievous were his transgressions of the law, who cried out in the psalm, *If you take account of our law-breaking, O Lord, Lord, who will stand?* Evidently, then, there is another law, a law of God's mercy, a law whereby God is propitiated. The old law dealt in fear; this new law is a law of charity. The law of charity grants pardon for sins, blots out the past, and cautions us with regard to the future. It keeps us company along the road and never deserts us; it makes itself our companion and leads us along the way.[16]

We saw earlier, in Question 91, Article 5, that St. Thomas endorses St. Augustine's contrast between the "law of fear" and the "law of love," for he mentions it to explain why the New Law was needed.[17] On the other hand, he thinks that the contrast needs to be qualified, for as he writes in another place,

There were some in the state of the Old Testament who, having charity and the grace of the Holy Ghost, looked chiefly to spiritual and eternal promises: and in this respect they belonged to the New Law. In like manner in the New Testament there are some carnal men who have not yet attained to the perfection of the New Law; and these it was necessary, even under the New Testament, to lead to virtuous action by the fear of punishment and by temporal promises. But although the Old Law contained precepts of charity, nevertheless it did not confer the Holy Ghost by Whom *charity ... is spread abroad in our hearts.*[18]

[2] If the Old Law was a law of fear, then the Ten Commandments, the very starting points of the Old Law, are precepts of fear. The Objector is not complaining about this fact, as many contemporary people would do – the "He's not the boss of me" syndrome. He is merely pointing it out. It is not that one could not obey the Commandments for the sheer love of God, but that at the time they were first given to the people, the sheer love of God was not what moved them. Obedience was encouraged by promises of temporal benefit, and enforced by threats of temporal harm.

[3] The Objector reasons that unfortunately, the thing threatened is identified only in the case of the first two precepts of the Decalogue.

As to the First Commandment, which prohibits idolatry, the threat is that "I the Lord your God am a jealous God, visiting the iniquity of the fathers upon the children to the third and fourth generation of those who hate me, but showing steadfast love to thousands of those who love me and keep

---

[16] St. Augustine of Hippo, "Exposition on Psalm 129," in *Expositions of the Psalms* (121–150), translated by Maria Boulding, volume v of *The Works of Saint Augustine: A Translation for the 21st Century* (Hyde Park, NY: New City Press, 2004), pp. 129–130, emphasis added. In another translation, www.newadvent.org/fathers/1801.html, the psalm is numbered 130.
[17] See I-II, Q. 91, Art. 5.
[18] I-II, Q. 107, Art. 1, ad 2. The internal quotation is from Romans 5:5.

my commandments." A little later, the thousands are represented as a thousand *generations*.[19]

As to the Second Commandment, which prohibits the false use of God's name, the threat is simply that "the Lord will not hold him guiltless who takes His name in vain."[20] Guilt and remorse are often confused. Remorse is the feeling or consciousness of guilt, but guilt itself is the objective condition of being in a culpable state of wrong which separates us from Him who is our Source and our Life. A person who knows that he is guilty *ought* to feel remorse, but not all persons do.

Two points concerning the First Commandment's threat require explanation. The first is God's description of himself as "jealous." This adjective does not refer to the human passion of jealousy, but to the fact that God utterly abominates the self-destructive adoration of what is false as though it were true. He made us rational beings; we are fashioned for truth. It would not increase our freedom to adore lies, but destroy it. Because of His inexorable love for us, He will not tolerate our doing so.

The second puzzling point is the warning about generational penalties. Because this requires lengthier treatment, we return to it in the Discussion at the end of this Article.

Objection 5. [1] Further, all the commandments of God should be retained in the memory: [2] for it is written (Prov. 3): "Write them in the tables of thy heart." [3] Therefore it was not fitting that mention of the memory should be made in the third commandment only. Consequently it seems that the precepts of the decalogue are unsuitably formulated.

Objection 5. Besides, each of God's Commandments should be preserved in memory. This is why the book of Proverbs instructs us to inscribe them on the tablets of our hearts. But although the Third Commandment, about honoring the Sabbath day, mentions memory, none of the others do. This omission was inappropriate.

---

[1] People strive to remember even such trivial things as the wording of their favorite jokes and limericks. Well, there is nothing wrong with that! But how much more should we remember the words of God Himself?

[2] The Objector is referring to these words of Proverbs 3:

My son, forget not my law, and let thy heart keep my commandments. For they shall add to thee length of days, and years of life and peace. Let not mercy and truth leave thee, put them about thy neck, and *write them in the tables of thy heart*: And thou shalt find grace and good understanding before God and men.[21]

---

[19] Exodus 20:5b–6, Deuteronomy 5:9b–10 (RSV-CE). The thousand generations are mentioned in Deuteronomy 7:9.
[20] Exodus 20:7b, Deuteronomy 5:11b (RSV-CE).
[21] Proverbs 3:1–4 (DRA), emphasis added.

Were the Old Law's Moral Precepts Appropriately Formulated?   159

He might also have referred to Proverbs 7:

My son, keep my words, and lay up my precepts with thee. Son, Keep my commandments, and thou shalt live: and my law as the apple of thy eye: Bind it upon thy fingers, *write it upon the tables of thy heart.* Say to wisdom: Thou art my sister: and call prudence thy friend.[22]

Here God *exhorts* the people to write the Law on the tablets of their hearts. Holy Scripture employs the image of writing on the heart in other contexts too, to which we return in the Discussion at the end of this Article.

[3] It might seem that either:

1. *All* of the Ten Commandments should include such an instruction, just because it is so important. Or else,
2. *None* of the Ten Commandments should include the instruction "Remember this," just because the importance of doing so goes without saying.

But no: The importance of remembering is not mentioned in any of the other commandments, but only in the Third Commandment. Its wording in Deuteronomy refers to memory explicitly: "You shall remember that you were a servant in the land of Egypt." Its wording in Exodus may be taken as referring to it implicitly, because it *reminds* the people that in six days God created and on the seventh day rested. Why should the Third Commandment be treated differently than all the others?

On the contrary, [1] *It is written (Wis. 11) that "God made all things, in measure, number and weight."* [2] *Much more therefore did He observe a suitable manner in formulating His Law.*	**On the other hand,** we read in the book of Wisdom that God made all things in measure, number, and weight. If all the rest of Creation was fashioned so well, how much more must His Law be formulated well!

[1] We read in the Old Testament book called the Wisdom of Solomon, "Even apart from [various possibilities of calamity], men could fall at a single breath when pursued by justice and scattered by the breath of thy power. *But thou hast arranged all things by measure and number and weight.* For it is always in thy power to show great strength, and who can withstand the might of thy arm?"[23]

Today we tend to take the double conjunction "measure and number and weight" as merely a sonorous phrase, as though it were no more than a poetical way of saying that God did a good job. Following St. Augustine, St. Thomas

---

[22] Proverbs 7:1–4 (DRA), emphasis added.
[23] Wisdom of Solomon 11:20–21 (RSV-CE), emphasis added. Wisdom of Solomon is not to be confused with Ecclesiastes, which is also traditionally attributed to Solomon.

takes it as saying a good deal more than that. For "in order for a thing to be perfect and good," he says, "it must have a form," but three different considerations precede and follow upon its form:

1. The *principles* of the form tell us the rule by which the thing operates and the yardstick by which it is measured.[24]
2. *What form the thing has* is determined by its species, meaning the genus to which it belongs along with its difference from other things in that genus.
3. The form in turn determines *the end toward which the thing tends*, and therefore indicates the order which it needs to acquire so that it can reach that end.

These three things are called by various equivalent expressions, including "mode" and "measure" for the first, "species" and "number" for the second, and "order" and "weight" for the third.[25] So in St. Thomas's reading, the passage which the Objector quotes from the Wisdom of Solomon commends God's work in a most precise and thorough manner. God has arranged how things work, how they are to be measured, what forms they have, to what purposes they tend, and what they need to get there.

[2] The *sed contra* asserts that if all the rest of Creation was fashioned so well, then much more must God's Law be formulated well. Why say *much more*? Why not say merely *to the same degree*? Because God's eternal law, which His Divine law reflects, is not just another created thing. It is the pattern in His uncreated mind by which He created and governs the universe. If we do admire the universe, then we should even more admire the principles on which it is based.[26]

I answer that, [1] *The highest wisdom is contained in the precepts of the Divine law:* [2] *wherefore it is written (Dt. 4):* "*This is your wisdom and understanding in the sight of nations.*" [3] *Now it belongs to wisdom to arrange all things in*	Here is my response. The precepts of Divine law express the pinnacle of wisdom. This is why the book of Deuteronomy tells the people that in the eyes of other peoples, their obedience to these precepts will be viewed as wisdom and understanding. But it behooves wisdom to dispose all things in

---

[24] St. Thomas derives from Aristotle's *Metaphysics*, book x (Iota) the argument that the principle in any genus is the rule and measure of that genus. He develops the argument most fully in connection with law, as a rule and measure of human acts based on reason, in I-II, Q. 90, Art. 1. I discuss this in *Commentary on Thomas Aquinas's Treatise on Law*.

[25] See I, Q. 5, Art. 5, which draws from a passage in Augustine's *On the Nature of the Good*, and Q. 45, Art. 7, which draws from a passage in Augustine's *On the Trinity*, book VI, chapter 10.

[26] On the eternal law as the pattern of God's creation and governance, see I-II, Q. 91, Art. 1, and Q. 93, Art. 1; on the natural law as the participation of the created rational mind in it, see I-II, Q. 91, Art. 2; and on the Divine law as its reflection in words, see I-II, Q. 91, Art. 4, and Q. 93, Art. 3.

due manner and order. [4]Therefore it must be evident that the precepts of the Law are suitably set forth.	the right manner and order. This fact should make it clear that the precepts of the law are well framed.

[1] The brevity of the *respondeo* is possible because in this particular instance St. Thomas merely amplifies the *sed contra*'s praise for the way Divine law is composed, fortifying it with an additional reference to Holy Scripture. Assuming that Divine revelation is true, we have good reason to believe that the Law is well framed. Even if the skeptic should scorn revelation as a dreaded "argument from authority," the burden lies upon him to show exactly how the Law is *not* well framed. This he has tried to do in the Objections – to which St. Thomas will turn next.

[2] The quotation given here comes from an address by Moses to the people of Israel before their entrance into the Promised Land, reminding them of God's providential care:

Behold, I have taught you statutes and ordinances, as the Lord my God commanded me, that you should do them in the land which you are entering to take possession of it. *Keep them and do them; for that will be your wisdom and your understanding in the sight of the peoples, who, when they hear all these statutes, will say, "Surely this great nation is a wise and understanding people."* For what great nation is there that has a god so near to it as the Lord our God is to us, whenever we call upon him? And what great nation is there, that has statutes and ordinances so righteous as all this law which I set before you this day?[27]

Although St. Thomas does not go into them here, this passage has interesting implications for natural law, to which we return in the Discussion at the end of this Article.

[3] The argument runs like this.

1. The other nations rightly admire the wisdom and understanding of the Israelites in keeping the Law.
2. If keeping the Law reflects wisdom, then the Law itself is a work of wisdom.
3. But if the Law is a work of wisdom, then it must deal with all things well.
4. If it deals with all things well, then its precepts must be well framed.

Reply to Objection 1. [1] *Affirmation of one thing always leads to the denial of its opposite: but the denial of one opposite does not always lead to the affirmation of the other.* [2] *For it follows that if a thing is white, it is not*	Reply to Objection 1. Although affirming P always entails denying not-P, denying that it is one kind of not-P does not entail affirming that it is P. For example, if something is white, then it is not black (which is a kind of nonwhite); yet if it is

---

[27] Deuteronomy 4:5–8 (RSV-CE), emphasis added. For "statutes and ordinances," DRA has "ceremonies, and just judgments, and all the law." As we saw in I-II, Q. 99, Art. 4, St. Thomas takes such expressions as referring to ceremonial, judicial, and moral precepts, respectively.

black: but it does not follow that if it is not black, it is white: because negation extends further than affirmation. [3] *And hence too, that one ought not to do harm to another, which pertains to the negative precepts, extends to more persons, as a primary dictate of reason, than that one ought to do someone a service or kindness.* [4] *Nevertheless it is a primary dictate of reason that man is a debtor in the point of rendering a service or kindness to those from whom he has received kindness, if he has not yet repaid the debt.* [5] *Now there are two whose favors no man can sufficiently repay, viz. God and man's father,* [6] *as stated in Ethic. viii.* [7] *Therefore it is that there are only two affirmative precepts; one about the honor due to parents, the other about the celebration of the Sabbath in memory of the Divine favor.*

not black, it is not necessarily white. The observation about white and black illustrates the fact that negation extends further than affirmation – for there are other kinds of not-black than white. And for the same reason, the negative precept "Do no harm" extends to more persons as a first dictate of reason than the positive precept "Do such and such a service or favor."

Therefore, the fact that a man owes a favor or service to anyone from whom he has received a favor is a first dictate of reason – provided that he has not already repaid him. But as Aristotle points out, he can never repay what God or his father have done for him. This is why the honor due to parents and the celebration of the Sabbath day to commemorate the Divine favor are the only two affirmative precepts.

[1] Objection 1 was that for every matter which the Decalogue addresses, there should have been both an affirmative and a negative precept. St. Thomas begins by making a logical point which the Objector has overlooked.

[2] The underlying point is that for any given thing there may be more than one contrary. Consider the following table.

Colors that are black	Colors that are not black
Black	White
	Red
	Yellow
	Blue
	Orange
	Green
	Purple
	And all other colors except black

If a thing is white, then it is not black. But if it is not black, although it *may* be white, it may instead be red, yellow, blue, or any of the other colors in the right-hand column – it doesn't have to be white. St. Thomas expresses the underlying principle by saying that "is not" extends further than "is": That negation extends further than affirmation.

[3] Another illustration of the principle that negation extends further than affirmation is that "I must not" extends further than "I must." Suppose that exactly one person, Mary, has done a favor for me. Then I owe the positive duty of repayment only to Mary, but my negative duties go much further.

I must	I must not
Do something for Mary in return for what she has done for me	Do undeserved harm to Mary Do undeserved harm to Samuel Do undeserved harm to Olivia Do undeserved harm to Logan Do undeserved harm to Mariana Do undeserved harm to Sebastian *Nor do undeserved harm to any other person, irrespective of what he has done or not done for me*

Another way to think of this is that I cannot be obligated to do more than I can actually do. Good is to be done, of course – but although I can be obligated to do specific good to specific persons, it would be impossible to do *every* good to *every* person, and so I cannot have a universal duty to do good. By contrast, nothing forces me to do *any* undeserved harm to *any* person, so I certainly can have a universal duty not to do so. So again we see that negation extends further than affirmation.

[4] Although I cannot have a universal duty to do all good to all persons, I am certainly obligated to do good to those who have done good to me, and the duty lasts until the debt is repaid. In calling this a primary dictate of reason, St. Thomas means it is one of those things which "the natural reason of every man, of its own accord and at once, judges to be done or not to be done."[28]

[5] God is the source of our very being. Our parents may also be called the source of our being, though in a qualified sense, because the powers to beget and bear children themselves come from God. Nothing *in* existence can repay the gift of existence itself. Notice, by the way, that although in the present sentence St. Thomas says "father," he is again using the term metonymically, for in the very next sentence he says "parents."

[6] God creates us, but, except for the soul, He does so through secondary causes, by making the sexual union of the parents fruitful. So just as in one sense we owe our entire lives to God, so in another sense, granted God's arrangements, we owe our entire lives to our parents. Not even the most devout

---

[28] His phrasing in I-II, Q. 100, Art. 1.

worship sufficiently adores God, and not even the most reverent honor sufficiently venerates parents. Aristotle had written:

Friendship indeed asks what is possible, not what is equal in value, for not all benefits can be repaid in honor as is evident in honors due to God and parents. No one can ever repay them what they deserve, although the man who serves them to the best of his ability appears to be virtuous.[29]

Just what is this virtue of the man who serves God and parents "to the best of his ability"? Certainly it resembles justice. However, it cannot precisely be justice, because justice is giving others what is due to them, and we cannot fully give God or our parents what is due to them. This is why St. Thomas gives the virtues of serving God and parents to the best of our ability different names than justice: the former he calls religion, and the latter he calls filial piety. We might say that although religion and filial piety are not justice, they partake of it. St. Thomas calls virtues of this sort – virtues which are connected with some principal virtue (such as justice) but which do not have its full power – "potential parts" of the principal virtue.[30]

[7] The precepts of the Decalogue bind us always, everywhere, and at every time. In general, the duties of repayment are not mentioned in the Decalogue because they are not of this kind; not only do they depend on whether we have received a favor but they pass out of existence once the favor is repaid. However, there are two exceptions, for there are two debts which *everyone* has and which *no one* can fully repay: our duties to honor God and our parents.

Now although the argument just given plainly explains the affirmative precept about honoring parents, it may not seem to explain the affirmative precept about keeping the Sabbath day holy. Isn't *each* of the first three commandments, not just the Sabbath day commandment, about reverencing God in some way? Yes, but only this one specifically commemorates a Divine favor: the gift of Creation.

| *Reply to Objection 2.* [1] *The reasons for the purely moral precepts are manifest; hence there was no need to add the reason.* [2] *But some of the precepts include ceremonial* | Reply to Objection 2. It would be fatuous to include the reasons for the purely moral rules, since they are obvious. With several of the precepts in the Decalogue, however, matters stand differently, either because they address not only moral but ceremonial points, or because |

---

[29] Aristotle, *Nicomachean Ethics*, book VIII, chapter 14. I am following the wording in Thomas Aquinas, *Commentary on Aristotle's Nicomachean Ethics*, translated by C. I. Litzinger (Chicago: Regnery, 1964).
[30] For discussion, including the distinction between potential, subjective, and integral parts, see J. Budziszewski, *Commentary on Thomas Aquinas's Virtue Ethics* (Cambridge: Cambridge University Press, 2017).

matter, [3] *or a determination of a general moral precept;* [4] *thus the first precept includes the determination, "Thou shalt not make a graven thing";* [5] *and in the third precept the Sabbath-day is fixed.* [6] *Consequently there was need to state the reason in each case.*	they "determine" or particularize the manner in which a more general moral rule is to be followed. The First Commandment particularizes the prohibition of idolatry by forbidding the making of carven images, and the Third Commandment particularizes the duty of worship by specifying the Sabbath as the day of worship. Therefore, there really was a need to include the reasons for these two commandments.

[1] The second Objection was that the reason for each precept should have been included in every precept, not just the first and third. St. Thomas maintains that in general, giving the reason for a precept is necessary only if otherwise the reason would have been obscure. The reason is not at all obscure in the case of the purely moral precepts; the rightness of such things as honoring parents, not murdering, and not stealing is immediately plain to every mind.

Everything, of course, can be denied. However, to deny is not the same thing as stating a cogent Objection. For example, someone might say, "It isn't plain to *me* that I should never deliberately take innocent life. Isn't it better to kill one innocent person and harvest his organs, if by doing so we can save four?" However, such objections are not evidence of real moral ignorance. The person who speaks in this way is shamming; he knows better.

[2] The point made just above concerns only precepts which are both *general* and *purely moral*. However, not all precepts in the Decalogue are purely moral: some are partly moral but also partly ceremonial. Even though the rightness of the moral part will be obvious, the reason for the ceremonial part will probably not be.

[3] Just as not every moral precept in the Decalogue is purely moral, not every one of its moral precepts is general. Some, after expressing a general duty, go on to specify the particular way in which it is to be obeyed.

[4] If the First Commandment did no more than forbid putting other gods in God's place, then it would be entirely general – and the reason for it would be clear. However, it goes on to specify that one of the ways in which the people are to honor the commandment is to forbear from making images. Although the general part of the precept is clear, this particularization of the precept requires explanation.

[5] If the Third Commandment did no more than command that times and places be set aside for rest and the worship of God, then it too would be entirely general. However, it goes on to specify that this should be done on the seventh day. Interestingly, in this case the "determination" of a general moral precept introduces *ceremonial* matter, so the need for explanation is doubled.

[6] As to the First Commandment, the reason given is that what is not God must not be worshipped as God; God will not tolerate the falsification of the very source of our being. As to the Third Commandment, reasons are given in both Exodus and Deuteronomy. In Exodus, the commandment reminds the people that on the seventh day, having finished the work of Creation, God set this work aside. By doing so, it emphasizes that one reason for honoring the Sabbath is to commemorate Creation itself. In Deuteronomy, the commandment reminds the people that God liberated them from slavery in Egypt. By doing so, it emphasizes that another reason for honoring the Sabbath is to commemorate their deliverance from bondage.

Reply to Objection 3. [1] *Generally speaking, men direct their actions to some point of utility.* [2] *Consequently in those precepts in which it seemed that there would be no useful result, or that some utility might be hindered, it was necessary to add a promise of reward.* [3] *And since parents are already on the way to depart from us, no benefit is expected from them: wherefore a promise of reward is added to the precept about honoring one's parents.* [4] *The same applies to the precept forbidding idolatry: since thereby it seemed that men were hindered from receiving the apparent benefit which they think they can get* [5] *by entering into a compact with the demons.*

Reply to Objection 3. Most men take something useful as the guide of their actions. Thus, in cases in which a Divine command seemed either useless or contrary to usefulness, it was necessary to promise a reward for obedience.

Why then is a promise attached to the commandment about honoring parents? Because since parents are already retiring from the scene, nothing useful is further expected from them, and the motive for honoring them is therefore weak. And why is one attached to the commandment prohibiting the worship of idols? Here the reason is much the same, for it would have seemed to men that the commandment prevented them from receiving the illusory benefit they expected to get by bargaining with these demons.

[1] Objection 3 was that the reward promised for obedience should have been identified in every precept, not just the second and the fourth. But since a reward provides a *motive* which might otherwise be lacking, St. Thomas begins by pointing out what the usual motive for doing anything is. In general, men do things because they expect some useful result. What he is about to do is show how this motive can go wrong, so that Divine law needs to straighten it out.

The Blackfriars translation of the Latin word *utilitas* by the English word "utility" is correct, but misleads some of my students into thinking that St. Thomas is somehow endorsing utilitarianism – a doctrine which he would abominate. St. Thomas insists that we must never do evil so that good will come;[31] by contrast, utilitarianism holds that a good enough result justifies

---

[31] See II-II, Q. 64, Art. 5, ad 3; III, Q. 68, Art. 11, ad 3.

doing anything whatsoever. There are many things wrong with utilitarianism, for example what it takes good results to be and its odd notions of how they are to be measured. Its gravest flaw, however, is that it does not recognize the possibility of an act which is *intrinsically* evil – an act which *by its nature* may not be done for the sake of any good result. For one who protests, "Not even for the sake of God?", the reply is that such acts are incapable of serving Him. One may not lie for God, steal for God, or murder for God – but one might certainly lie, steal, and murder for what the utilitarian calls utility! The best a utilitarian can offer in favor of doing the right thing is that *usually* it produces better results. Whenever, in his account book, it doesn't, he unhesitatingly suggests that the right thing to do is do wrong.

We see, then, that far from endorsing what we call utilitarianism in this passage, St. Thomas recognizes it as a permanent temptation.

[2] Just because human beings do keep their eye on usefulness, they are disinclined to do anything that seems to them to be useless or contrary to usefulness.

[3] With startling bluntness, St. Thomas points out that to many persons – at least many of those who lack the spiritual virtues – honoring parents seems useless, just because their parents will die soon. "I got a lot of good from them when I was growing up, but at their age I can't expect to get much more." Therefore it was necessary for God to motivate such people by some promise of temporal good. Some of those whom God is teaching are moral infants who cannot be expected to do what is right just because it is right.

[4] To understand the difficulty in prohibiting idolatry, we must ask why men do worship idols. The answer is that they expect to strike a bargain with these false gods, to do or give something so that they will get something in return. To people in this frame of mind, saying "Do not worship idols" seems like saying "Give up the prospect of advantages." All of these idols are still worshipped, though we no longer carve them in stone.[32] If we give up the worship of the sex god, we think, we might never have love; if we give up the worship of the god of wealth, we may end up poor. Consequently, to make up the loss of the imagined favors of false gods, the true God had to promise true favors.

St. Thomas's language bends over backwards to emphasize the fraud of idolatry. *Videbatur* refers to what *seemed* to men to be so. *Apparens* refers to the *apparent* benefit of serving false gods. *Credunt* refers to what they *think* they can get from them. All of this is illusion.

---

[32] "Put to death therefore what is earthly in you: fornication, impurity, passion, evil desire, and covetousness, *which is idolatry*." Colossians 3:55 (RSV-CE), emphasis added.

[5] Some places in Holy Scripture suggest that the false gods had no reality whatsoever. This view is made bitingly clear in Isaiah's satire of those who carve idols of them:

> The carpenter stretches a line, he marks it out with a pencil; he fashions it with planes, and marks it with a compass; he shapes it into the figure of a man, with the beauty of a man, to dwell in a house. He cuts down cedars; or he chooses a holm tree or an oak and lets it grow strong among the trees of the forest; he plants a cedar and the rain nourishes it. Then it becomes fuel for a man; he takes a part of it and warms himself, he kindles a fire and bakes bread; also he makes a god and worships it, he makes it a graven image and falls down before it. Half of it he burns in the fire; over the half he eats flesh, he roasts meat and is satisfied; also he warms himself and says, "Aha, I am warm, I have seen the fire!" And the rest of it he makes into a god, his idol; and falls down to it and worships it; he prays to it and says, "Deliver me, for thou art my god!" They know not, nor do they discern; for he has shut their eyes, so that they cannot see, and their minds, so that they cannot understand. No one considers, nor is there knowledge or discernment to say, "Half of it I burned in the fire, I also baked bread on its coals, I roasted flesh and have eaten; and shall I make the residue of it an abomination? Shall I fall down before a block of wood?" He feeds on ashes; a deluded mind has led him astray, and he cannot deliver himself or say, "Is there not a lie in my right hand?"[33]

However, other passages of Scripture suggest that the reality of idolatry is even worse, for whatever they may think they are doing, at least some of those who worship false gods are in fact adoring spirits of evil. Reminding the people of their former apostasy, Moses declares, "They stirred [God] to jealousy with strange gods; with abominable practices they provoked him to anger. They sacrificed to demons which were no gods, to gods they had never known, to new gods that had come in of late, whom your fathers had never dreaded."[34]

The New Testament agrees. Describing a future time of catastrophe, one apocalyptic passage declares, "The rest of mankind, who were not killed by these plagues, did not repent of the works of their hands nor give up worshipping demons and idols of gold and silver and bronze and stone and wood, which cannot either see or hear or walk; nor did they repent of their murders or their sorceries or their immorality or their thefts."[35]

Today, of course, it is considered knowing to scoff at the notion of demon worship, though in view of the revival of occultism and the widespread cultivation of disordered mental states, it may not be prudent.

Reply to Objection 4. [1] *Punishments are necessary against those who are prone to evil,* [2] *as stated in Ethic. x.* [3] *Wherefore a threat of punishment*

Reply to Objection 4. As Aristotle points out, punishments are especially necessary against those who are prone to evil. For this reason, threats were attached only to

---

[33] Isaiah 44:13–20 (RSV-CE).
[34] Deuteronomy 32:16–17 (RSV-CE).
[35] Apocalypse (Revelation) 9:20–21 (RSV-CE).

is only affixed to those precepts of the law which forbade evils to which men were prone. [4] Now men were prone to idolatry by reason of the general custom of the nations. [5] Likewise men are prone to perjury on account of the frequent use of oaths. [6] Hence it is that a threat is affixed to the first two precepts.	the rules which prohibited the evils which men were predisposed to commit. Men were apt to commit idolatry because it was the custom of all the nations. In much the same way, they are apt to lie under oath because oaths are so commonly taken. This is why threats were attached to these first two commandments.

[1] The Objector had protested that the punishment for disobedience should have been declared not just in the first and second precepts, but in each of them. St. Thomas wants the Objector to slow down – to ask himself why legislators employ punishments in the first place. They do so because people are prone to do wrong.

[2] In his *Nicomachean Ethics*, Aristotle explains the necessity of punishment by pointing out that the general run of people are moved more strongly by fear than by shame, and more strongly by the fear of punishment than the fear of disgrace:

Were persuasive words sufficient of themselves to make men virtuous, many great rewards would be due according to Theognis; and it would be necessary to give them to those who persuade. At present it seems that persuasive discourse can challenge and move youths of excellent character and can fill the lover of the good with virtue. But it cannot arouse the majority to virtue, for most people are not subject by nature to shame but to fear; nor do they refrain from evil because of disgrace but because of punishment. In fact, since they live by passion, they follow their own pleasures, by which the passions themselves are nourished, and avoid the contrary pains. They do not know what is truly good and pleasant, nor can they taste its delight. What words would reform people of this sort? It is impossible or at least difficult to change by argument what is held by inveterate habit.[36]

In his *Commentary* on the work, St. Thomas adds,

Something acceptable must be proposed to change a man by argument. Now, one who does not relish an honorable good but is inclined toward passion does not accept any reasoning that leads to virtue. Hence it is impossible, or at least difficult, for anyone to be able to change a man by argument from what he holds by inveterate usage. So also in speculative matters it is not possible to lead back to truth a man who firmly cleaves to the opposite of those principles to which goals are equivalent in practical matters.[37]

[3] Very well, punishment is needed because men are prone to do wrong. But are they equally prone to every sort of wrong? No, certain kinds of wrong attract them more strongly than others. Therefore, the reminder of punishment

---

[36] Aristotle *Nicomachean Ethics*, book x, chapter 9, following the wording of the text in Thomas Aquinas, *Commentary on Aristotle's Nicomachean Ethics*, trans. Litzinger.
[37] Ibid., book x, lecture 14.

for disobedience is not equally necessary in the case of every precept, as the Objector thought. The necessary for it arises only in the case of those precepts which men tend to resist.

[4] The people of the Old Testament were especially resistant to the prohibition of idolatry because monotheism was unique, idolatry was everywhere, and they expected to gain benefits from their false gods. The Old Testament history of the Chosen Nation is full of relapses into paganism, followed by calamity, followed at last by repentance and return to the true God.

Typically, each Near Eastern god was associated with a particular virtue, a particular aspect of nature, and a particular physical image, which was placed in a particular temple. The worship of the One God changed all this, and not just because He is only one. Rather than being associated with some aspect of nature, He is distinct from nature as its Creator. Rather than being associated with some virtue, He is the exemplar of all virtue. Although at certain periods He had a temple, in a deeper sense the entire universe was His temple. Rather than having man fashion images of Him, He Himself fashioned man as His image and placed this image in the temple of the universe.[38] As the book of Genesis reports, on the sixth day of Creation God declared,

> "Let us make man in our image, after our likeness; and let them have dominion over the fish of the sea, and over the birds of the air, and over the cattle, and over all the earth, and over every creeping thing that creeps upon the earth." So God created man in his own image, in the image of God he created him; male and female he created them.[39]

[5] People are also especially resistant to the prohibition of false swearing, just because the making of promises to seal agreements is so central a feature of everyday life, and false swearing seems therefore expedient. A true oath is more than saying "I promise," for one calls upon God to witness the promise. If there were no Divine punishment for invoking Him dishonestly, then it would be enormously tempting to say "So help me God, I will do this" even though one intended to do the opposite.

To this day, witnesses in criminal proceedings are sworn in. The English common law held that to be competent to give testimony, a person must believe in a God who punishes false swearing. In these supposedly enlightened times, the requirement has been dropped, on grounds that it unfairly impugns the virtue of atheists. But if it is true, as Aristotle thinks, that the general run of people are moved more strongly by fear than by shame, and more strongly by fear of punishment than by fear of disgrace, then the advisability of this development is questionable. After all, the very reason we seek testimony is to find out the truth. If the witnesses themselves are lying, then it is difficult to

---

[38] The illuminating observation about God placing His image, man, in the universe, as His temple, was first suggested to me in personal conversation with Professor Rikk Watts, presently of Alphacrucis College, Australia.

[39] Genesis 1:26–27 (RSV-CE).

Were the Old Law's Moral Precepts Appropriately Formulated? 171

detect their dishonesty and even harder to prove it. For this reason, fear of human punishment for false testimony is likely to be weak. Divine justice turns the tables, because God already knows the truth.

The argument is sometimes made that a person who is prone to lie will also lie about whether he believes in a God who punishes false swearing. This is true, and it may well pose a problem in an age in which infidelity is common but people conceal it. In an age in which infidelity is rare – or in an age like ours, in which it is common, but people are more likely to boast of it than conceal it – the objection does not seem to hold water.

[6] St. Thomas believes that the prohibitions of idolatry and false swearing are singled out for reminders of Divine punishment because these are the prohibitions men most strongly resist.

Reply to Objection 5. [1] *The commandment about the Sabbath was made in memory of a past blessing. Wherefore special mention of the memory is made therein.* [2] *Or again, the commandment about the Sabbath has a determination affixed to it that does not belong to the natural law, wherefore this precept needed a special admonition.*	Reply to Objection 5. Two reasons can be given for the fact that only the Sabbath precept refers to memory. One is that it memorialized a past favor. The other is that by specifying the day on which worship should take place, it went beyond the general duty to worship which is found in the natural law, so that it needed a special reminder.

[1] The fifth Objection was that the importance of memory should have been mentioned in every precept, not just the third. St. Thomas gives two reasons for treating the Third Commandment differently. The first is that among all the Ten Commandments, the third is the only one decreed specifically in commemoration of a Divine blessing – whether the blessing of Creation, as in the version given in Exodus, or the blessing of deliverance from slavery, as in the version given in Deuteronomy.

[2] The second reason for treating the Third Commandment differently is that although even the natural law prescribes rest and worship, and reflection is able to show how appropriate it is to set aside times and places for them, reason alone does not tell us why the designated time should be the seventh day. Thus, Exodus reminds the people that the seventh is the day on which God is said to have rested.

DISCUSSION

Sins of the Fathers

The First Commandment's prohibition of worshipping false gods concludes with the warning that God visits the iniquity of the fathers upon the children to the third and the fourth generation of those who hate Him. A little later than the Decalogue, Deuteronomy goes further, declaring that He "keeps covenant and steadfast love with those who love him and keep his commandments to a *thousand* generations."[40] However, generational consequences are often held to impugn His justice and deny the principle of responsibility, for they imply that in the case of this commandment, some will suffer for the sins of others.

But don't some always suffer for the sins of others? The natural consequence of sin is that damage ripples not only through me, the sinner, but outward in every direction. God could have made a world in which nothing had consequences, nothing had meaning: A world in which, among other things, children turned out the same no matter how their parents raised them. In that case, why should the parents care for them? Why bother with parents at all?

He bothers with parents because He chose to make a world in which finite rational creatures are given the astounding privilege of imitating His Fatherhood and participating in the Wisdom by which He governs the universe. "Among all others," St. Thomas writes, "the rational creature is subject to Divine providence in the most excellent way, insofar as it partakes of a share of providence, by being provident both for itself and for others. *Wherefore it has a share of the Eternal Reason.*"[41] By the fact that in raising my children, I am also helping raise my children's children and my children's children's children, this privilege is not taken away, but intensified.

With the privilege comes responsibility, for failure to live up to it causes real injury to others. The obverse of the power to do good is the power to do hurt. If I am a bad father, my children may find it more difficult to trust the Fatherhood of God. If I adore *that which is not*, I pave a path that they may walk on too. So the generational consequence is real – but it is the other side of a blessing: We are placed in a universe in which what we do matters.

Yet God's providential care may also mitigate some of the temporal consequences of forgiven sin. In view of the repeated sins of the people, Moses implores God,

And now, I pray thee, let the power of the Lord be great as thou hast promised, saying, "The Lord is slow to anger, and abounding in steadfast love, forgiving iniquity and transgression, but he will by no means clear the guilty, visiting the iniquity of fathers upon children, upon the third and upon the fourth generation." Pardon the iniquity of this people, I pray thee, according to the greatness of thy steadfast love, and according as thou hast forgiven this people, from Egypt even until now.[42]

God replies that although He will grant the pardon for which Moses has asked, there will still be a penalty for those who saw His glory and signs and yet despised Him. The generation of their children will enter into the Promised Land, but they will not.

---

[40] Deuteronomy 7:9 (RSV-CE), emphasis added.
[41] I-II, Q. 91, Art. 2.
[42] Numbers 14:17–19 (RSV-CE).

And would it have been better for them if they had been allowed to enter it along with their children? If it is true that temporal punishment is necessary for the correction of our souls, probably not! Besides, if they had they accompanied their children, would it have been better for their children?

Does the Old Law Recognize the Natural Law?

St. Thomas has argued in I-II, Question 100, Article 1 that the moral precepts of the Old Law *are in fact* precepts of natural law. Whether the Old Testament itself views them this way is another question. Indeed, some thinkers have claimed that the Old Testament has no concept of natural law, but only a concept of Divine positive law: "God commanded not murdering, so we had better not murder, but He could just as well have commanded murdering, and then we would have to murder."

Actually, the natural law is acknowledged even in the Old Testament's tributes to Divine law, although indirectly. Consider again Moses' address to the Israelites in Deuteronomy 4. The query "what great nation is there, that has statutes and ordinances so righteous as all this law which I set before you this day?" proposes a comparison. It presupposes their ability of the people to recognize the body of laws set before them as a more perfect expression of the principles of right and wrong, dimly known by everyone, than the laws of the other nations are.

Indeed the Old Testament contains many such indirect acknowledgements of natural law. For example, when God announces His intention to destroy the Cities of the Plain, Abraham protests in the name of God's own justice: "Far be it from thee to do such a thing, to slay the righteous with the wicked, so that the righteous fare as the wicked! Far be that from thee! Shall not the Judge of all the earth do right?"[43] Again, in the prologue to the Ten Commandments, God reminds the people of their indebtedness to Him: "And God spoke all these words, saying, "I am the Lord your God, who brought you out of the land of Egypt, out of the house of bondage. You shall have no other gods before me ..."[44]

How is it that Abraham knows something about God's justice before Torah has been given? How is it that the Israelites know the law of gratitude before the Law has been revealed to them? The answer is that His most fundamental moral requirements are already impressed upon the innermost design of the created moral intellect. We know a part of God's will for us through deep conscience, even before receiving it in words.

Utterly oblivious of this point, the political philosopher Leo Strauss argues that

---

[43] Genesis 18:23–25 (RSV).
[44] Exodus 20:1–3 (RSV).

> The idea of natural right must be unknown as long as the idea of nature is unknown. ... The Old Testament ... does not know "nature": the Hebrew term for "nature" is unknown in the Hebrew Bible. ... There is, then, no knowledge of natural right as such in the Old Testament. The discovery of nature necessarily precedes the discovery of natural right.[45]

This line of reasoning is exactly the reverse of what it should be. Conscience is the interior testimony to the fact that certain things are just and unjust not because we like or dislike them, not because some human government has commanded or prohibited them, but because *that is how things are*. We do not first develop the concept of conscience and then come to have what the concept describes; rather we discover that we have it, and then work out the concept "conscience." We do not first develop the concept of nature and then discover that things *are* a certain way; rather we discover that things *are* a certain way, and then work out the concept "nature." One would think from Strauss's statement that theory precedes facts. On the contrary, the recognition of facts provokes theory – yes, even conceding that a theory may call our attention to facts we had not noticed when we first developed it.

One of the inescapable features of the Old Testament is that God not only judges His own people but other nations as well, by a standard that can only be called natural law, since Divine law was not given to them. This fact is conspicuous at the beginning of the book of the prophet Amos, where more than a chapter is devoted to God's judgment upon the transgressions of the surrounding pagan peoples – Syrians, Moabites, Philistines, and others – before God even mentions the transgressions of Israel.

But the same fact can be seen throughout Torah. Otherwise what could it mean for God to say "Not because of your righteousness or the uprightness of your heart are you going in to possess their land; but because of the wickedness of these nations the Lord your God is driving them out from before you"?[46] Unless standards that distinguish righteousness from wickedness apply to all nations, the statement would be incoherent.

Besides, it is not at all true that the concept of nature is absent from the Old Testament. The only thing missing from it is a *word* which might be translated "nature." For the Old Testament attributes *how things are* to what God, in His goodness, has wrought. Not only has He created, but He has imparted to His Creation a certain integrity of its own. For He could have capriciously made this happen and then that, so that no regularity could be detected, but instead He has made a "covenant" with the day and with the night, as unbreakable as His literal covenant with David:

> The word of the Lord came to Jeremiah: "Thus says the Lord: If you can break my covenant with the day and my covenant with the night, so that day and night will not

---

[45] Leo Strauss, *Natural Right and History* (Chicago: University of Chicago Press, 1953), pp. 81–82.
[46] Deuteronomy 9:5a (RSV-CE). We have seen this verse before in another context.

come at their appointed time, then also my covenant with David my servant may be broken, so that he shall not have a son to reign on his throne, and my covenant with the Levitical priests my ministers. As the host of heaven cannot be numbered and the sands of the sea cannot be measured, so I will multiply the descendants of David my servant, and the Levitical priests who minister to me."[47]

The psalmist draws an elegant parallel between the celestial and moral aspects of the world that God has created:

The heavens are telling the glory of God; and the firmament proclaims his handiwork. Day to day pours forth speech, and night to night declares knowledge. There is no speech, nor are there words; their voice is not heard; yet their voice goes out through all the earth, and their words to the end of the world. In them he has set a tent for the sun, which comes forth like a bridegroom leaving his chamber, and like a strong man runs its course with joy. Its rising is from the end of the heavens, and its circuit to the end of them; and there is nothing hid from its heat.

The law of the Lord is perfect, reviving the soul; the testimony of the Lord is sure, making wise the simple; the precepts of the Lord are right, rejoicing the heart; the commandment of the Lord is pure, enlightening the eyes; the fear of the Lord is clean, enduring for ever; the ordinances of the Lord are true, and righteous altogether. More to be desired are they than gold, even much fine gold; sweeter also than honey and drippings of the honeycomb. Moreover by them is thy servant warned; in keeping them there is great reward.[48]

Lost in admiration of these graces, the inspired poet appeals to the Creator for purity:

But who can discern his errors? Clear thou me from hidden faults. Keep back thy servant also from presumptuous sins; let them not have dominion over me! Then I shall be blameless, and innocent of great transgression. Let the words of my mouth and the meditation of my heart be acceptable in thy sight, O Lord, my rock and my redeemer.[49]

---

[47] Jeremiah 33:19–22 (RSV-CE).
[48] Psalm 19:1–11 (in the Vulgate, numbered as 18:1–12). I quote this part of Psalm 18 a number of times in this *Commentary*, but it deserves the repeated mention.
[49] Ibid., verses 12–14 (in the Vulgate, numbered as 13–15).

QUESTION 100, ARTICLE 8

Whether the Precepts of the Decalogue are Dispensable?

TEXT	PARAPHRASE
Whether the precepts of the Decalogue are dispensable?	Can the precepts of the Decalogue ever be set aside, so that for certain people, or in certain cases, they need not be obeyed?

A precept is "dispensable" if the authority that issues it can allow an exception to the duty of obedience. Are the Ten Commandments dispensable? For example, could any person ever be allowed to dishonor his parents, be permitted to steal or murder, or be excused from being faithful to his wife?

Objection 1. It would seem that the precepts of the Decalogue are dispensable. For the precepts of the Decalogue belong to the natural law. But the natural law fails in some cases and is changeable, like human nature, as the Philosopher says (Ethic. v). Now the failure of law to apply in certain particular cases is a reason for dispensation, as stated above. Therefore a dispensation can be granted in the precepts of the Decalogue.	Objection 1. Apparently, the precepts of the Decalogue can indeed be set aside. True, they are precepts of natural justice, but in some cases precepts of natural justice fail to apply. As Aristotle points out, this is because even what exists by nature is subject to variation – so natural justice varies, just as human nature varies. Now we saw earlier in the *Treatise on Law* that an exception can be made whenever a precept fails to apply. So it follows that an exception can be made whenever a precept of the Decalogue fails to apply.

Aristotle's example of variation in nature is that even though by nature the right hand is stronger, some people are ambidextrous; something that holds *by nature* has failed to hold *for them*.[1] At present, of course, we are thinking not of exceptions to generalizations about the natural properties of the human body, but of exceptions to generalizations about the requirements of natural justice

---

[1] Aristotle, *Nicomachean Ethics*, book v, chapter 7.

expressed in the Ten Commandments. As we go along, we find that the hypothetical Objectors give several examples of the sorts of exceptions they think can be made.

The Objector reasons like this:

1. If anything that holds by nature can fail to hold, then any natural law can fail to hold.
2. Since the precepts of the Decalogue belong to the natural law – something we saw in Article 1 – then they too can fail to hold.
3. In every case in which a precept does fail to hold, a person can be excused from obedience.[2]
4. So whenever a precept of the Decalogue fails to hold, a person can be excused from obedience.

Notice, though, that premise 1 clouds an important distinction. To speak of the properties a thing has "by nature" is equivocal, for we may be speaking of either its essential properties or merely its statistical properties. Essential properties are those which *define* things of that kind; when we say that by nature man is a rational animal, we are speaking essentially. Statistical properties are merely those which things of that kind *usually* have; when we say that by nature man's right hand is strongest, we are speaking statistically. Aristotle is not saying that essential nature can vary, but only that statistical nature can vary. There are a few men who are ambidextrous, and they are still men. But there are no men who are not rational animals, and anything which is not by essence rational, or animal, or both – for example a cow, an angel, or a fungus – is not a man.

The Objector simply ignores this distinction, treating statistical nature as all there is. Many skeptics of our own day would approve. In their view, there are no such things as essential properties, definition is a mere convention, and "nature" is nothing but a generalization. For example, they say that obviously *not* all the beings whom essentialists call men are rational, for some are brain-damaged or immature. In their view, we should either stop saying that all men are rational, or else go ahead and say it but deny the brain-damaged and immature entrance to the human club.

But this sort of skeptic misunderstands the essentialist's point. To say that by nature all men are rational is not to say that in all men the potentiality for rational function is actualized, but to say that all men are *aimed* at rationality, so that an impairment of rational function really is an impairment. Brain damage is not a different kind of brain health; immaturity really does fall short of maturity. So the brain-damaged and the immature man are still men, but they are not fulfilled men. They are not flourishing.

---

[2] See I-II, Q. 97, Art. 4; compare Q. 96, Art. 6.

Objection 2. [1] *Further, man stands in the same relation to human law as God does to Divine law.* [2] *But man can dispense with the precepts of a law made by man. Therefore, since the precepts of the Decalogue are ordained by God, it seems that God can dispense with them.* [3] *Now our superiors are God's vicegerents[3] on earth;* [4] *for the Apostle says (2 Corinthians 2): "For what I have pardoned, if I have pardoned anything, for your sakes have I done it in the person of Christ." Therefore superiors can dispense with the precepts of the Decalogue.*	**Objection 2.** Moreover, man has the same relation to the laws man ordains as God has to the laws God ordains. It seems, then, that since man can authorize exceptions to the laws he ordains, God can authorize exceptions to the precepts He ordained in the Decalogue. In fact, not only may God do so, but so may those who are set over us [in the Church], because on earth, they stand in His place. St. Paul invokes this authority when he says to the Corinthians that if he has forgiven them anything, he has done "in the person of Christ," in His own place and authority.[4]

[1] The parallel proposed by the Objector is that just as God enacts Divine law, so man enacts human law. Therefore – he thinks – whatever is true of the relation between man and human law must also be true of the relation between God and Divine law. This argument blurs the difference between the sense in which God enacts and the sense in which man enacts. God is identical with the Eternal Wisdom by which His law is ordained; man is not identical with it, but only participates in it. The created intellect of man *follows and imitates* the standard; the uncreated Intellect of God *is* the standard.

[2] St. Thomas explained in Question 96, Article 6, and Question 97, Article 4, that human legislators can make exceptions to their laws whenever literal compliance would defeat the purposes for which they were enacted. The Objector reasons that if this is true, then the Divine legislator can make exceptions to *His* laws whenever literal compliance would defeat the purposes for which they were enacted. As we will see in the Reply, however, everything depends on the meaning of that "whenever."

[3] The participle translated "superiors" is *praelati*, literally "prelates," which St. Thomas normally employs to mean ecclesiastical rather than civil superiors. Almost certainly, the Objector too is thinking of ecclesiastical superiors.

---

[3] I have corrected the term used in the Blackfriars translation, substituting "vicegerent" (from *gerentis vicem*, one who carries on in place of another) for "viceregent," (one who assists a regent).

[4] As St. Thomas remarks in III, Q. 22, Art. 4, where he quotes the same statement of St. Paul, "Christ is the fountainhead of the entire priesthood: for the priest of the Old Law was a figure of Him; while the priest of the New Law works in His person." Pope Pius XII explains that by virtue of his consecration, the priest "is made like to [Christ] the High Priest and possesses the power of performing actions in virtue of Christ's very person." Pope Pius XII, encyclical *Mediator Dei* (1947), section 69.

[4] In his second letter to the Corinthians, referring to his previous letter, St. Paul says "For this is why I wrote, that I might test you and know whether you are obedient in everything. Any one whom you forgive, I also forgive. What I have forgiven, if I have forgiven anything, has been for your sake in the presence of Christ."[5] Apparently he means that he has excused certain Corinthians from the penalty for disobedience to his own previous instructions. The Objector, however, takes him to mean that he has released them from the very obligation to obey the precepts of the Decalogue. Further, the Objector reasons that if St. Paul can release them from Decalogical obligations, then so can our other superiors in the Church, because they act by the same Divine authority.

The Objector's use of 2 Corinthians 2:10 shows again that he is thinking of ecclesiastical rather than civil superiors. Had he been thinking of civil superiors as well, he might have cited Romans 13:2, "he who resists the authorities resists what God has appointed." Indeed, in II-II, Q. 105, Art. 1, citing the same passage in the letter to the Romans, St. Thomas treats obedience to ecclesiastical superiors as a special case of obedience to superiors in general. However, St. Thomas has made quite clear elsewhere that the authority of the state does not include declaring exemptions from the laws of God Himself.[6]

Objection 3. Further, among the precepts of the Decalogue is one forbidding murder. But it seems that a dispensation is given by men in this precept: for instance, when according to the prescription of human law, such as evildoers or enemies are lawfully slain. Therefore the precepts of the Decalogue are dispensable.	Objection 3. Still further, one of the precepts of the Decalogue forbids murder. But men seem to have authorized exceptions to this prohibition. For example, human statutes allow evildoers and enemies to be put to death by due process of law. This shows that the precepts of the Decalogue are dispensable.

The Objector takes murder in the sense prohibited by the Decalogue to mean any taking of human life whatsoever; he thinks all killing of humans is alike. In our day, this view of the commandment "You shall not kill" is sometimes called the "seamless garment" view. If it is true, then the Decalogue's prohibition of murder forbids even such things as capital punishment and just war. Yet human laws do allow such things as capital punishment and just war, and no one suggests that in doing so they exceed their authority. The Objector concludes that human authorities may suspend the precepts of the Decalogue.

---

[5] 2 Corinthians 2:9–10 (RSV-CE). The Blackfriars' text paraphrases the Vulgate rather than strictly quoting it, but the differences in wording are trivial.
[6] See for example Q. 96, Art. 4.

If the Objector is right, then it is hard to see how to escape the view expressed by Judge Richard A. Posner in a widely quoted address at Harvard University:

[M]orality is local. There are no interesting moral universals. There are tautological ones, such as "Murder is wrong," where murder means "wrongful killing," and there are a few rudimentary principles of social cooperation – such as "Don't lie all the time" or "Don't break promises without any reason" or "Don't kill your relatives or neighbors indiscriminately" – that may be common to all human societies. If one wants to call these rudimentary principles the universal moral law, fine; but as a practical matter, no moral code can be criticized by appealing to norms that are valid across cultures, norms to which the code of a particular culture is a better or worse approximation. Those norms, the rudimentary principles of social cooperation that I have mentioned, are too abstract to serve as standards for moral judgment. Any meaningful moral realism is therefore out, and moral relativism ... is in.[7]

Objection 4. Further, the observance of the Sabbath is ordained by a precept of the Decalogue. But a dispensation was granted in this precept; for it is written (1 Maccabees 2): "And they determined in that day, saying: Whosoever shall come up to fight against us on the Sabbath-day, we will fight against him." Therefore the precepts of the Decalogue are dispensable.	Objection 4. Besides, an exception was made to the precept of the Decalogue which requires Sabbath observance. As Scripture records, "So [the associates of Mattathias] made this decision that day: 'Let us fight against every man who comes to attack us on the Sabbath day; let us not all die as our brethren died in their hiding places.'"[8] Plainly then, exceptions can be made to the precepts of the Decalogue.

When the Greek, Antiochus Epiphanes became overlord of Israel, he desecrated the Temple and tried to impose pagan practices upon the people. After many faithful Jews retreated to the wilderness to escape his abominations, he ordered his forces into the wilderness to rout them. Because it was the Sabbath day, which the Decalogue reserves for rest and worship, the resistors refused to fight, and so, in consequence, they were massacred. When the friends and sons of Mattathias heard of the slaughter, they resolved that in the future, to escape death, they would fight even on the Sabbath. Thus began the Macabeean Revolt. The Objector regards the decision of the friends and sons of Mattathias to set aside Sabbath observance as a communal enactment bearing the authority of law, and so concludes that by human authority, the precepts of the Decalogue can be suspended.

---

[7] Richard A. Posner, "The Oliver Wendell Holmes Lectures: The Problematics of Moral and Legal Theory," *Harvard Law Review* 111 (1998), p. 1640.
[8] 1 Maccabees 2:41 (RSV-CE). The Blackfriars translators incorrectly cite verse 4.

Can Any Exceptions Be Made to the Old Law's Moral Precepts?

On the contrary, are the words of Isaiah 24:5, where some are reproved for that "they have changed the ordinance, they have broken the everlasting covenant"; which, seemingly, applies[9] principally to the precepts of the Decalogue. Therefore the precepts of the Decalogue cannot be changed by dispensation.

On the other hand, the prophet Isaiah rebukes those of his day who have violated the statutes and broken the everlasting covenant. Since he seems to be speaking mainly of the precepts of the Decalogue, it follows that exceptions must *not* be made to the Decalogical precepts.

The point, of course, is that those who claimed freedom from Divine law were condemned rather than approved for doing so. The context of the quotation makes this clear, for the prophet says *"The earth lies polluted under its inhabitants; for they have transgressed the laws, violated the statutes, broken the everlasting covenant."*[10]

I answer that, [1] As stated above, precepts admit of dispensation, when there occurs a particular case in which, if the letter of the law be observed, the intention of the lawgiver is frustrated. Now the intention of every lawgiver is directed first and chiefly to the common good; secondly, to the order of justice and virtue, whereby the common good is preserved and attained. [2] If therefore there be any precepts which contain the very preservation of the common good, or the very order of justice and virtue, such precepts contain the intention of the lawgiver, and therefore are indispensable. [3] For instance, if in some community a law were enacted, such as this – that no man should work for the destruction of the commonwealth, or betray the state to its enemies, or that no man should do anything unjust or evil, such precepts would not admit of dispensation. [4] But if other precepts were enacted, subordinate to the above, and determining certain special modes of procedure, these

Here is my response. I have explained previously that exceptions may be made to legal precepts in just those cases when following the literal instructions of the law would produce a result contrary to the intention of the lawmaker. First, and above all, the intention of the lawmaker is directed to the common good. Second, it is directed to justice and virtue, because these are the means by which the common good is brought about and preserved – to promote them *is* to promote the common good, because these are the things in which the common good consists.

It follows that whenever a legal precept embraces *the very idea* of the direction of affairs to the common good, or toward justice and virtue, then it is impossible to make an exception to it, because it *coincides* with the lawmaker's intention. For example, exceptions could never be authorized to such laws as "No one may tear down the commonwealth," "No one may betray the city to its enemies," or "No one may do what is intrinsically evil or unjust."

But matters stand differently with respect to subordinate legal precepts, which merely

---

[9] Correcting Blackfriars "apply."
[10] Isaiah 24:5 (RSV-CE).

latter precepts would admit of dispensation, insofar as the omission of these precepts in certain cases would not be prejudicial to the former precepts which contain the intention of the lawgiver. For instance if, for the safeguarding of the commonwealth, it were enacted in some city that from each ward some men should keep watch as sentries in case of siege, some might be dispensed from this on account of some greater utility.	specify the *ways* in which affairs are directed toward the great ends just mentioned. To such precepts, exceptions are allowable so long as they are not to the detriment of those precepts which do coincide with the lawmaker's intention. Suppose, for example, that a commonwealth established a law for its preservation, specifying that if the city is under siege, guards must be posted in each street. Certainly some persons might be exempted from guard duty if they could be used in a better way.

[1] Every true law is enacted for the sake of the common good. In turn, justice and virtue are the *chief elements* of the common good. They are means to its preservation and attainment, not in the sense that opening the curtains to let in the light is a means to the illumination of a room, but in the sense that light itself is a means to its illumination. A room can be made bright without opening the curtains – for example, by turning on a lamp or kindling a fire – but it cannot be illuminated without bringing in light. Therefore, to say "For the sake of the common good, one must sometimes commit acts of injustice or vice," makes no more sense than saying "For the sake of illumination, one must sometimes shut out light and make it dark."

[2] Suppose my supreme intention were to keep a certain room illuminated as brightly as possible. Then precepts such as "Do not block the light," "Do not destroy what is used to give light," and "Do nothing to diminish the light" could be said to "contain" the idea of illuminating the room and my intention that it be illuminated. It would be inconsistent with my supreme intention to authorize any exceptions to them. In just this way, certain precepts "contain" the idea of preserving the common good and the lawmaker's intention that it be preserved, and so they cannot be suspended.

[3] The third of these examples requires a bit of clarification, because someone might object that a law stating simply "No one should do anything unjust or evil" seems too vague to be considered genuinely promulgated, and St. Thomas holds that a law that is not promulgated is not a true law.[11] However, he is thinking not of those things that may or may not be unjust or evil, depending on the circumstances, but of those things that are *intrinsically* evil, such murdering, committing adultery, engaging in stealing, theft, or fraud, and lying to get someone in trouble. My paraphrase reflects this interpretation.

[4] There are no circumstances under which anyone could be allowed to act against the protection of the city, but many circumstances might be imagined

---

[11] See I-II, Q. 90, Art. 4.

under which someone could be exempted from a *particular way* of protecting the city, because he could be of greater use to the city in another capacity.

[1] *Now the precepts of the Decalogue contain the very intention of the lawgiver, who is God.* [2] *For the precepts of the first table, which direct us to God, contain the very order to the common and final good, which is God; while the precepts of the second table contain the order of justice to be observed among men, that nothing undue be done to anyone, and that each one be given his due; for it is in this sense that we are to take the precepts of the Decalogue.* [3] *Consequently the precepts of the Decalogue admit of no dispensation whatever.*	The precepts of the Decalogue do coincide with the intention of the lawgiver, who is God. For the precepts of the First Tablet, which direct us with reference to God, express the very idea of right relationship with the ultimate common good, which is God Himself. Moreover the precepts of the Second Tablet, which direct us with reference to our neighbors, in turn express the very idea of the order among men that is called justice, according to which each person is rendered everything that is due to him, and nothing is done to anyone that he does not deserve. This is how we should understand what the precepts of the Decalogue are about – and for this reason, no exceptions to them may be made whatsoever.

[1] God's commands are not arbitrary decrees; they are shaped by His purposes, purposes which cannot fail to be good, because He is Himself the ultimate Good on which all lesser goods depend.

[2] To say that the precepts of the First and Second Tablets "contain the very order" (*continent ipsum ordinem*) to God and to justice is to say that they express the very meaning of being rightly ordered to God and to our neighbors. As St. Thomas has already explained, the intention of every lawgiver, whether human or Divine, is directed first to the common good. But the common good to which the Old Law is directed includes not just the temporal common good, but the ultimate common good, which is God Himself, for "the community for which the Divine law is ordained, is that of men in relation to God, either in this life or in the life to come" (Article 2). So there need to be two classes of precepts. The point is further elaborated in Article 5:

[J]ust as the precepts of human law direct man in his relations to the human community, so the precepts of the Divine law direct man in his relations to a community or commonwealth of men under God. Now in order that any man may dwell aright in a community, two things are required: the first is that he behave well to the head of the community; the other is that he behave well to those who are his fellows and partners in the community. It is therefore necessary that the Divine law should contain in the first place precepts ordering man in his relations to God; and in the second place, other precepts ordering man in his relations to other men who are his neighbors and live with him under God.

[3] Just because these precepts do express the very meaning of being rightly ordered to God and to our neighbors, their violation is *intrinsically* wrong. No

good result of violating them could make violation right; no exception to them could ever be authorized. We may never take advantage of our neighbors, and we may never give ourselves to anything or anyone else in the same way that we should give ourselves to God.[12]

Reply to Objection 1. [1] *The Philosopher is not speaking of the natural law which contains the very order of justice: for it is a never-failing principle that "justice should be preserved."* [2] *But he is speaking in reference to certain fixed modes of observing justice, which fail to apply in certain cases.*	Reply to Objection 1. The venerable Aristotle is not speaking of those precepts of natural justice which embody the very idea of just social order, for the precept "Justice is to be protected" can never fail; it holds without exception. Rather he is speaking of certain specified *ways* of doing justice, to which there are, in some cases, exceptions.

[1] The expression "the natural law which contains the very order of justice" refers to those precepts that belong *intrinsically* to justice, requirements that cannot be distinguished from giving to each person what is due to him. For this reason, they must always be obeyed, without exception. Such are the precepts of the Decalogue. For example, the commandment "Do not steal" contains the very order of justice, and has no exceptions. By contrast, a rule like "Always return to another person upon his demand whatever property that he has left in your safekeeping" is merely a more detailed specification of what abstention from stealing *usually* requires, and does have exceptions. I should not return your hunting rifle if you demand it so that you can murder someone. In such a case, withholding the rifle would not count as stealing.

[2] Natural justice requires, for example, that persons accused of crimes be convicted only on a sufficient presentation of evidence, but it does not specify what counts as a sufficient presentation. Human law fills out the contours of natural justice by setting down rules of evidence, for example that hearsay is inadmissible. But there might arise a case in which the exclusion of hearsay would be unreasonable, and in such a case an exception might be made.[13]

Reply to Objection 2. [1] *As the Apostle says (2 Timothy 2), "God continueth faithful, He cannot deny Himself."* [2] *But He would deny*	Reply to Objection 2. We will be guarded against misinterpreting St. Paul's statement to the Corinthians if we reflect on something he said to Timothy – that God

---

[12] To the latter point it may be objected that in the Christian view, spouses are to give themselves to each other. This is true, but their mutual gift to each other is a *mode* in which they offer themselves mutually to the God who has joined them. They are not to set each other in the place of God, making idols of each other.

[13] For instance, US law permits various exceptions to the inadmissibility of hearsay evidence, including public records, learned treatises, and statements that a person made against his own interest.

Can Any Exceptions Be Made to the Old Law's Moral Precepts?

Himself if He were to do away with the very order of His own justice, since He is justice itself. [3] Wherefore God cannot dispense a man so that it be lawful for him not to direct himself to God, or not to be subject to His justice, even in those matters in which men are directed to one another.

remains faithful, for He cannot deny Himself. God *would* deny Himself if he were to cut off[14] the very order of His justice, since He is justice itself. Consequently, not even God can exempt anyone from directing himself to God or from submitting to His justice. This is true not only in our relations to God, but even in our relations, under God, with each other.

[1] The context of this quotation is an instruction of St. Paul to Timothy, in which he writes "The saying is sure: If we have died with him, we shall also live with him; if we endure, we shall also reign with him; if we deny him, he also will deny us; if we are faithless, he remains faithful – for he cannot deny himself."[15] "He" refers to Christ, who according to the later words of the Nicene Creed is "God from God, Light from Light, true God from true God."

[2] God's justice is not something He *has*, so that He could lose it and yet be Himself, as a man can lose his hair. It is something He *is*, inseparable from Him, just as He is inseparable from His wisdom, love, beauty, and other qualities. His qualities, by the way, are distinguishable only from our point of view, not in reality. His wisdom *is* His love, which *is* His beauty, which *is* Himself.

It is important to realize that St. Thomas is not saying that God is an abstract quality, justice, rather than a personal being. Rather he is saying that God is *Justice Himself, in person*. The finite, created relations we call justice, and which may seem like mere formulae to us, derive all of their reality and force from His infinite, uncreated, personal Being. At the heart of justice – as at the heart of wisdom, of love, of beauty, and of all other good things – we find not something but Someone. (Indeed we find a fiery unity of three Someones, the Father, Son and Holy Spirit, all of them the same one God.)

[3] God's omnipotence does not mean that He can be other than He is. He cannot release us from the requirement to direct ourselves to Him, because He *is* our end. But to direct ourselves to Him entails submitting to His justice, because He *is* His justice. So He cannot release us from submitting to His justice either.

Reply to Objection 3. [1] *The slaying of a man is forbidden in the Decalogue, insofar as it bears the character of something undue: for in this sense the precept contains the very essence of*

Reply to Objection 3. The Decalogue forbids killing anyone *to whom death is not due*. It is in this sense that the precept embodies the very idea of justice. Nor can human law concede that a man could ever

---

[14] *Auferret.*
[15] 2 Timothy 2:11–13 (RSV-CE).

justice. [2] Human law cannot make it lawful for a man to be slain unduly. But it is not undue for evildoers or foes of the common weal to be slain: hence this is not contrary to the precept of the Decalogue; and such a killing is no murder as forbidden by that precept, [3] as Augustine observes. [4] In like manner when a man's property is taken from him, if it be due that he should lose it, this is not theft or robbery as forbidden by the Decalogue.	be put to death if he did not deserve it. But the killing of evildoers or enemies of the commonwealth does not deprive them of anything due to them. Therefore it does not violate the precept of the Decalogue, nor does it constitute homicide in the sense forbidden by the Decalogue's prohibition – a point made by St. Augustine. Similarly, to confiscate property of which a man deserves to be deprived is not to commit theft or robbery in the sense the Decalogue forbids.

[1] St. Thomas has explained that the precepts of the Second Tablet coincide with the very meaning of justice. But justice is giving to each person what is due to him – punishment for doing wrong, honor for doing right. So if the commandment "You shall not kill" meant that one must not kill even those deserving of death, it would not be just; it would be just only if it forbade the killing of those *not* deserving of death. This is the sense in which the commandment "You shall not kill" it is to be taken.

[2] Since the commandment does not prohibit the slaying of those truly deserving of death, the Objector is mistaken in thinking that the authorization of such things as capital punishment and just war requires a dispensation from it. What the commandment prohibits is killing in the specific sense of *murder*.

To return to the Posnerian objection: Judge Posner is right to say that if murder means only the sort of killing we must not do, with no implicit specification, then the commandment "Do not murder" would be tautological; it would say nothing more than "You must not commit the sort of killing that you must not commit." But the commandment is not tautological because the meaning of murder can be specified in a universally valid way by specifying *when death is undue*. Murder is the killing of *innocent* human beings as well as the killing of the guilty without public authority, without adequate proof of guilt, or for offenses for which the punishment would be disproportionate to the guilt of their offense.

[3] Here is the context of the observation:

EVODIUS: If murder is killing a human being, it can sometimes happen without sin. For instance, a soldier kills an enemy;[16] a judge or his agent executes a convicted criminal;

---

[16] The reference is to the killing of an enemy in a just, not an unjust war. Augustine discusses just war in a number of places: *City of God against the Pagans*, book XIX, chapters 7, 12–13, and 15; "Reply to Faustus the Manichaean," book XXII, chapters 73–79; letter 139, "To Marcellinus," especially the discussion of whether good Christians are bad citizens; Letter 189, "To Boniface";

someone throws his weapon by chance imprudently and against his will. They do not seem to me to be sinning when they kill someone.

AUGUSTINE: I agree. But they are not usually called murderers, either.[17]

One might have left the matter here, but St. Thomas has more to say.

[4] Just as such things as capital punishment and just war are not the *kind* of killing – murder – forbidden by the commandment "Do not kill," so such things as just fines and taxes are not the *kind* of taking of property forbidden by the commandment "Do not steal." We must be careful to take each commandment of the Decalogue in the sense in which it is intended. In the cases we have just considered, the mistake lies in taking it too broadly, but error also lies in taking it too narrowly. For example, the fact that public authority may authorize putting criminals to death does not imply that it may authorize killing the old, the sick, the weak, or those not yet born; and the fact that it may authorize just fines and taxes does not mean that it may confiscate any property it pleases for any reason it wishes. In the sense of the respective commandments, the former is still murder, and the latter is still theft.

[5] *Consequently when the children of Israel, by God's command, took away the spoils of the Egyptians, this was not theft; since it was due to them by the sentence of God.* [6] *Likewise when Abraham consented to slay his son, he did not consent to murder, because his son was due to be slain by the command of God, Who is Lord of life and death: for He it is Who inflicts the punishment of death on all men, both godly and ungodly, on account of the sin of our first parent, and if a man be the executor of that sentence by Divine authority, he will be no murderer any more than God would be.* [7] *Again Osee, by taking unto himself a wife of fornications, or an adulterous woman, was not guilty either of adultery or of fornication: because he took unto*	And so when the children of Israel carried off plunder from the Egyptians at God's precept, they were not stealing, because by the divine verdict, the Egyptians deserved to give it up. Again, when Abraham agreed to kill his son at God's command, he was not agreeing to murder, because by the very fact that the boy's death was mandated by the Lord of life and death, death was due to him. Bear in mind that because of the sin of our first parents, God punishes all men with death, the just as well as the unjust, so if a man carries out the sentence by the authority of God Himself, he is no more a murderer than God is. Yet again, when Hosea married a "wife of fornications" – that is, an adulterous woman – he was committing neither

---

letter 229, "To Darius"; sermon 302, "On the Birthday of St. Lawrence" (not to be confused with Augustine's other sermons about St. Lawrence), sections 1–16, especially 15; and *Questions on the Heptateuch*, question 6, chapter 10.

[17] Augustine, *On Free Choice of the Will*, book 1, section 4, in *Augustine: On the Free Choice of the Will, On Grace and Free Choice, and Other Writings*, translated by Peter King (Cambridge: Cambridge University Press, 2010), p. 8.

himself one who was his by command of God, Who is the Author of the institution of marriage.	fornication nor adultery, because he married her by the mandate of the divine author of the institution of matrimony.

[5] This statement refers to an event in the release of the Israelites from bondage in Egypt. God says to Moses that He knows the king of Egypt will not willingly allow the slaves to leave, so He will compel him to release them by causing terrible calamities to befall the land. Moreover, the Israelites are to ask for precious things in parting, and the Egyptians will be glad to give them: "And I will give this people favor in the sight of the Egyptians; and when you go, you shall not go empty, but each woman shall ask of her neighbor, and of her who sojourns in her house, jewelry of silver and of gold, and clothing, and you shall put them on your sons and on your daughters; thus you shall despoil the Egyptians."[18] According to St. Thomas, in demanding these precious things from the Egyptians, the Israelites were not guilty of theft, because God, the always just Judge, had decreed these spoils as a punishment. The Egyptians deserved to give them up because of the wrong they had done to the Israelites.

[6] The argument is *not* that if God commands murder, it isn't murder. Nor has there been what Søren Kierkegaard called a "teleological suspension of the ethical."[19] God *is* the ethical; not even He can allow a man to kill another just because the man wishes to do so, because to allow it would be contrary to that justice which is Himself. There is no such thing as an act that is "ethically wrong but religiously right." Right is not divided, because God is not divided.

The argument works like this:

1. For their sin, God sentenced our first parents to the justly deserved penalty of eventual death.
2. Because of the community of human nature, all human beings share in the consequences of our first parents' rebellion, and so all are subject to the same penalty.
3. As Supreme Judge, God Himself decides for each human being when this sentence is to be carried out.
4. If a human being consents to carry out the sentence against someone, not to please himself, but by God's own command, then he is consenting not to be a murderer but to be a duly appointed executioner; he is not acting unjustly, but carrying out a decree of justice itself.[20]

---

[18] Exodus 3:21–22 (RSV-CE).
[19] The expression comes from the third chapter of Kierkegaard's work of 1843, *Fear and Trembling*, Problema 1, "Is there a Teleological Suspension of the Ethical?" Kierkegaard thought Abraham was guilty of murder (or would have been had the deed been carried out).
[20] Concerning the command to sacrifice Isaac, see also the commentary on Question 94, Article 5.

[7] The first three chapters of the book of Hosea relate that God commanded the prophet to marry first a whore, then an adulteress, as a shocking dramatization of Israel's shocking unfaithfulness to God. Someone might suppose that because adultery too is forbidden by a precept of the Decalogue, a dispensation must have been granted to Hosea, for God said "Go, take thee a wife of fornications," and again, "Go yet again, and love ... an adulteress." What St. Thomas is saying here is that no dispensation was necessary because the precept was not violated.

The idea of serving as an executioner of Divine justice does not come into the case of Hosea as it came into the case of Abraham, for although St. Thomas holds each human being to be under sentence of eventual death, he certainly does not suggest that any human being is under sentence of marrying badly! The key to the argument about Abraham is that God is the Divine judge, but the key to the argument about Hosea is that He is the Divine Author of marriage, the Creator who imbued it with order.

Then is St. Thomas saying that because God is the Author of marriage, he can violate the very order of marriage that He has ordained? No, not even God can permit a man to join sexually with a woman who is not his wife, for again, to deny the very order of His justice would be to deny Himself. But as St. Thomas explains in Question 94, Article 5, whenever a man and woman are joined by God – not just declared to be joined, *but joined in fact* – then she *is* his wife. So again, the question is not whether God can suspend the precepts of the Decalogue, but whether He can *apply* them, and of course He can.

[8] *Accordingly, therefore, the precepts of the Decalogue, as to the essence of justice which they contain, are unchangeable:* [9] *but as to any determination by application to individual actions – for instance, that this or that be murder, theft or adultery, or not – in this point they admit of change;* [10] *sometimes by Divine authority alone, namely, in such matters as are exclusively of Divine institution, as marriage and the like;* [11] *sometimes also by human authority, namely in such matters as are subject to human jurisdiction: for in this respect men stand in the place of God: and yet not in all respects.*

It all comes down to this: With respect to the very idea of justice which they embody, the precepts of the Decalogue cannot be changed. But with respect to the "determinations" by which these precepts are applied to particular acts – for instance that such and such an act *is* or *is not* a murder, a theft, or an adultery – they can be changed.

Sometimes – in things that have been instituted by God alone – the exception is declared by Divine authority alone. But at other times – in things God commits to human jurisdiction – the exception can be declared even by human authority. For although human authorities do not stand in God's place in all respects, in this respect they do.

[8] God cannot make it right to do any of the things the precepts of the Decalogue forbid, or to omit any of the things they require. For instance, He cannot make it right to murder, steal, or commit adultery.

[9] But the application of the precepts of the Decalogue *can* change. This does not mean that the precepts can reverse their meaning; it would not be a mere change in application for God to say, "In this case, unfaithfulness to your spouse is not adultery," or "In this case, killing a man who has not earned the penalty of death at your hands is not murder." But all sorts of more detailed secondary precepts inform how to apply these broad commandments, by telling me who is my spouse, and who does deserve the penalty of death at my hands. The broad commandments have no exceptions. Albeit rarely, however, such secondary precepts do have exceptions.

[10] In matters that God Himself has instituted, only He can authorize exceptions to the secondary precepts. St. Thomas mentions the institutions of marriage "and the like"; another example might be family. Marriage involves the relation of wife and husband with a view toward possible children; family involves the relation of the mother and father to their children. As God joined Hosea to a woman who would otherwise not have been accounted his wife, so we might say that He sometimes joins parents to children who would otherwise not have been accounted their sons and daughters. Our name for this dispensation is adoption.

[11] Just now we were speaking of matters that God Himself has instituted. But in rules that human authority has "added" to God's rules by way of determination, or in details of application that God does not specify, mere humans can authorize exceptions. In this way God has delegated to such rational creatures as ourselves a share in His Providence, though He remains the ultimate Governor of the universe.

Reply to Objection 4. [1] *This determination was an interpretation rather than a dispensation.* [2] *For a man is not taken to break the Sabbath, if he does something necessary for human welfare; as Our Lord proves (Matthew 12).*	Reply to Objection 4. This explanation is better viewed as an interpretation of the precept than as an exception to it. For as the Lord proves in the twelfth chapter of the Gospel of Matthew, doing something necessary for human well-being is not a violation of the Sabbath.

[1] "Determination" is a mistranslation. St. Thomas does not use the Latin term *determinatio*, which refers to a precept arrived at by specifying in which of the various ways a more general precept is to be followed. Instead he uses the term *excogitatio*, which means literally a thinking out, an explanation. So what he is saying here is that in the incident from the Maccabean revolt mentioned by the Objector, the friends and sons of Mattathias were working out what the Sabbath precept meant, not authorizing an exception to it. In ordaining a Sabbath rest, God had never intended that His people rest even from preserving their lives.

[2] To confirm that the friends and sons of Mattathias had interpreted the Sabbath rest correctly, St. Thomas refers to another incident, this one from the Gospels. Jesus and his disciples walked through a grainfield on the Sabbath. The disciples, who were hungry, picked and ate some of the grain, and were criticized by the Pharisees because Sabbath day labor is prohibited. Christ called their attention to two dispensations mentioned in Scripture, then remarked, "if you had known what this means, 'I desire mercy, and not sacrifice'" – an allusion to Hosea 6:6 – "you would not have condemned the guiltless." He concluded, "For the Son of Man is Lord of the Sabbath," implying His authority to interpret the Sabbath precept with finality and certainty.[21]

DISCUSSION

Difficulties with St. Thomas's treatment of the Divine command to Abraham to sacrifice Isaac, and the Divine commands to Hosea to marry a whore and an adulteress, fall into two categories, false and real. Let us consider each in turn.[22]

False Difficulties

1. *How can St. Thomas defend what Kierkegaard calls the "suspension of the ethical"?* He doesn't. In his view, no such suspension has taken place. If God commands marrying an adulterous woman, then He is not commanding adultery, for the marriage is real. If He commands taking property or life, he is not commanding theft or murder, for He owns everything. You would be stealing if you drove away my car to serve yourself, but not if you drove it away at my own request.

2. *How can St. Thomas expect human authorities to believe everyone who claims God has spoken to him?* He doesn't. Although God may dispense from the derivative and more detailed precepts of both natural and Divine law, the human authorities are not required to believe everyone who says "God gave me a dispensation from the Ten Commandments"; in fact, they are obligated *not* to believe him. In any case, *who to believe* is not the subject of this Article.

3. *How can St. Thomas require us to accept all seeming Divine communications as authentic?* He doesn't. Trusting God does not mean being credulous; elsewhere in the *Summa*, St. Thomas makes clear that there must be compelling evidence, such as miracles, for the Church to believe that a seeming communication really does come from God.[23]

---

[21] Matthew 12:1–8 (RSV-CE), quoting from the last two verses.
[22] The comments offered here may be considered together with my remarks on I-II, Q. 94, Art. 5 in *Commentary on Aquinas's Treatise on Law*.
[23] For example in II-II, Q. 1, Art. 4, ad 2, and III, Q. 43, Art. 4. Even so, not everyone presented with compelling evidence will accept it; faith is a gift. See II-II, Q. 6, Art. 1.

4. *How could God have approved child sacrifice?* He didn't. Since God intervened, the point of the story of the command to sacrifice Isaac is not that He wanted child sacrifice, but that Abraham needed to be trained in absolute trust. But this point is crucial: Absolute trust is not unthinking trust. St. Paul warns that not everything that presents itself as an inspiration from God is to be believed: "Do not quench the Spirit, do not despise prophesying, but test everything; hold fast what is good, abstain from every form of evil."[24] St. John says the same thing: "Beloved, do not believe every spirit, but test the spirits to see whether they are of God; for many false prophets have gone out into the world."[25] These statements, of course, are in the New Testament, but indeed, as we learn when the Divine law is given later in the Old Testament, God loathes child sacrifice.[26]

Perhaps Abraham himself was not fully clear in his mind about this point; in his day the sacrifice of children was common. True, the natural law itself testifies to the wrong of child sacrifice, and St. Thomas argues that the general principles of the natural law cannot be washed out of the human heart.[27] On the other hand, as we saw in the commentary on Question 102, Article 1, the Patristic writers held that before the giving of Divine law, conscience was coarsened and the awareness of these indelible principles was dimmed, even though not destroyed.[28] For Abraham, then, it is at least possible that the issue of trust arises not just because God has commanded something shocking, but because He has promised to make of Abraham's descendants a mighty nation – and yet now, in Abraham's extreme old age, He instructs him to slay his only descendant so far. By the way, it may be that not only Abraham's trust but also Isaac's trust is at stake. In a letter to the Christians at Corinth, St. Clement, one of the Patristic writers, maintains that "Isaac, with perfect confidence, *as if knowing what was to happen*, cheerfully yielded himself as a sacrifice."[29]

Real Difficulties

1. *Is greater precision possible?* St. Thomas holds that although God can dispense from the secondary moral precepts of Divine law, the primary moral precepts of Divine law hold without exception. He clears himself easily from the

---

[24] 1 Thessalonians 5:19–22 (RSV-CE).
[25] 1 John 4:1 (RSV-CE).
[26] See references in the commentary to Q. 94, Art. 5.
[27] I-II, Q. 94, Art. 6.
[28] Just how this dimming works is described by St. Thomas in I-II, q. 85, art. 2 and ad 3. I discuss this in "The Indestructibility of the Good of Nature," *Commentary on Thomas Aquinas's Treatise on Law*, pp. 132–135, www.cambridge.org/files/3614/2469/5786/9781107029392_-_Companion_to_the_Commentary.pdf.
[29] Clement I, *Letter to the Corinthians*, translated by John Keith, chapter 31 (public domain), emphasis added.

charge of tautology, for precepts like "Do not murder" and "Do not steal" mean something more specific than "You should not destroy life that you should not destroy" or "You should not take property that you should not take." For St. Thomas, the issue is not some vague, generic wrongness, but *injustice*. Justice requires giving everyone what is due to him. Murder is *undue* killing, taking the life of someone who does not deserve loss of life; stealing is *undue* appropriation, taking the property of someone who deserves to be allowed to hold onto it.

But even if the exceptionless precepts do have concrete meanings, are these meanings clear enough to do us any good? It may seem that even though we have been saved from tautology, we are still vulnerable to wild evasions and misinterpretations. Consider for example the precept against murder. "Commit no undue killing" is an improvement on "Commit no killing of the sort you ought not commit," but it would be good to know which killings *are* due and undue – who deserves loss of life and who doesn't. Can we achieve greater precision?

The answer is: With great effort, yes. Achieving greater precision is one of the great projects of the natural law tradition. Progress has been made in this task, but it has come slowly.

With murder the task has been pretty easy: leaving aside questions of authority, undue killing is deliberately or directly taking innocent human life. One may take the life only of someone who has committed grave wrong (and even then the sentence may be declared and carried out only by public authority). With theft the task is more difficult, but most casuists – specialists in the necessary moral distinctions – would now agree that undue taking is deliberately or directly taking what rightly belongs to another against his rational will. With lying the task is very hard indeed. What is the correct definition of lying, of that kind of falsehood which is always wrong?

St. Augustine and St. Thomas hold that lying is saying what one knows to be false with the intention of deceiving. This is also the view of the Catholic Church.[30] However, some natural law thinkers, both philosophers and theologians, think that one more qualifier is necessary: that lying is saying *to one who has a right to the truth* what one knows to be false with the intention of deceiving. In practice, the distance between the two positions is not as great as it may seem, because to one who does not have a right to the truth, one may equivocate without actually lying. Yet the two definitions are different in principle. How so? Whenever deliberate falsehood is practiced, two great problems arise. One is that it seems to pervert the human power of speech, which is naturally directed to truth; the other is that it may deprive someone of his right. The former definition of lying puts greater emphasis on the former problem, while the second puts greater emphasis on the latter. Unfortunately,

---

[30] St. Augustine, *On Lying*; St. Thomas, II-II, Q. 110, Art. 1; Catechism of the Catholic Church, sections 2481–2482.

these two problems are tightly bound, and it is not so obvious that they can be disentangled.

In the United States, the question "What is lying?" has become hot in recent years because of the strategy of a pro-life organization called Live Action. Live Action workers assume false identities to expose wicked and illegal acts; for example, a pair of activists may present themselves in a Planned Parenthood office as a pregnant young prostitute and her pimp, in order to expose the willingness of the staff to wink at the sexual exploitation of young women and to refer underage girls for abortions that are illegal even under our permissive laws. Are these activists heroes, promoting the cause of life? Or are they undermining the cause of life by "doing evil so that good will result"? The answer depends on which definition of lying is rationally correct.

2. *What about the natural consequences of dispensations?* If God dispenses from one of the secondary precepts of Divine law, then He does not hold the person using the dispensation *guilty* for not following the precept. But remember that the moral precepts of Divine law belong to natural law too. What then happens to the bad *natural* consequences of departing from them? For example, dispensation or no dispensation, one would expect Hosea's first wife to continue to play the harlot, and Hosea's children with her to suffer from having such an unsuitable mother. To expose the prophet to such fortune seems hard on him. Does God treat His prophets so badly?

To solve the problem, we must distinguish between two kinds of dispensations. One arises when for some unusual reason God *allows* an act contrary to virtue; the other arises when for some unusual reason He *commands* an act which would have been contrary to virtue had He not commanded it. We may call the former kind dispensation by permission, and the latter kind dispensation by command.[31]

The Old Law's provisions for divorce were a dispensation by permission. Christ said the Old Law permitted divorce only because of the hardness of the people's hearts; divorce was not God's intention in creating marriage.[32] According to an opinion of St. Chrysostom, what Christ meant by the hardness of the people's hearts was that if men had not been permitted to divorce their wives, they would have murdered them. St. Thomas considers two possible opinions about what to make of this. According to the opinion he considers more probable, although this dispensation freed men from "eternal punishment," that is, from the guilt of breaking up their marriages and the spiritual consequence of separation from God, it did *not* free them from "temporal

---

[31] These two kinds of dispensation should not be confused with the four kinds of permission St. Thomas distinguishes in Supp., Q. 67, Art. 3.

[32] Matthew 19:3–8 (RSV-CE); see also Supp. Q. 67, Art. 1.

punishment," from the natural consequences of doing so.³³ No doubt they suffered these direly.

On the other hand, God's instruction to Hosea to marry a whore was a dispensation by command. There is some reason to suppose that St. Thomas may have thought that God supernaturally deflected the natural consequences of the deed. In the first place, the argument is plausible within the terms of the allegory, for Hosea's marriage to a whore was symbolically intended to portray two things: not only Israel's unfaithfulness to her Divine lover and her adulterous relationship with the false gods called Baals but also *her ultimate redemption*. The book of Hosea represents God as saying of Israel,

> Therefore, behold, I will allure her, and bring her into the wilderness, and speak tenderly to her. And there I will give her vineyards, and make the Valley of Achor a door of hope. And there she shall answer as in the days of her youth, as at the time when she came out of the land of Egypt. And in that day, says the Lord, you will call me, "My husband," and no longer will you call me, "My Baal." For I will remove the names of the Baals from her mouth, and they shall be mentioned by name no more. ... And I will betroth you to me for ever; I will betroth you to me in righteousness and in justice, in steadfast love, and in mercy.³⁴

If Hosea's literal wife was an allegory for Israel, and if the allegory represented not only Israel's wretchedness but also her redemption, then for the allegory to be accurate, wouldn't Hosea's literal wife also have had to be redeemed? What other view is compatible with God's grace?

In the second place, St. Thomas's theory is compatible with this line of reasoning, for he agrees that in some cases God supernaturally alters nature's ordinary course:

> In the commandments, especially those which in some way are of natural law, a dispensation is like a change in the natural course of things: and this course is subject to a twofold change. First, by some natural cause whereby another natural cause is hindered from following its course: it is thus in all things that happen by chance less frequently in nature. In this way, however, there is no variation in the course of those natural things which happen always, but only in the course of those which happen frequently. Secondly, by a cause altogether supernatural, as in the case of miracles: and in this way there can be a variation in the course of nature, not only in the course which is appointed for the majority of cases, but also in the course which is appointed for all cases[.]³⁵

I suggest, then, that St. Thomas may view matters like this:

1. In the case of dispensation by permission, the person committing the act is spared only from its guilt, not from its bad natural consequences.

---

³³ Supp., Q. 67, Art. 3 and ad 5.
³⁴ Hosea 2:14–17, 19 (RSV-CE).
³⁵ Supp., Q. 67, Art. 2.

2. But in the case of dispensation by command, the person committing the act *may* be spared not only from its guilt but perhaps from some of its bad natural consequences too.

My suggestion is speculative, and should be taken with a grain of salt. From a logical point of view, it seems to provide a neat solution to the problem, and it may, in fact, be what St. Thomas believes. To develop it, however, I have expanded upon hints in the Supplement, which was drawn from St. Thomas's earlier writings and added to the *Summa* after his death. Between the earlier and later writings he has certainly changed his mind about certain applications of his analysis;[36] thus we cannot rule out the possibility that he has also changed his mind about the very principles of the analysis. If he has, then my suggestion is mistaken.

---

[36] For an illustration of such change, in Supp., Q. 67, Art. 2, which was written earlier, he holds that the command to sacrifice Isaac required a dispensation, while in I-II, Question 100, Article 8, which we have been studying, he holds that no dispensation was necessary because the act would not have been a murder.

QUESTION 100, ARTICLE 9

Whether the Mode of Virtue Falls Under the Precept of the Law?

TEXT	PARAPHRASE
Whether the mode of virtue falls under the precept of the Law?	When the Old Law commands a virtuous deed, does the precept simply require that it be done, or does it also require that it be done in a virtuous way – the way a virtuous person would do it?

The *mode of virtue* is the manner in which genuine virtue is exercised. Suppose I tell the cashier at the grocery store that he has given me too much change. Justice requires the deed; in that sense, it is just. But do I perform it as a just person would perform it – because it is ingrained in me to do the right thing the right way? Or do I perform it for some other reason, for instance because the person behind me in line is watching me? The query before us is whether the Old Law concerns itself only with the deed, or also with the manner in which I do it; to put it another way, whether it commands only the external deed of virtue, or also the interior act of doing it *because* of virtue.

Objection 1. [1] *It would seem that the mode of virtue falls under the precept of the law. For the mode of virtue is that deeds of justice should be done justly, that deeds of fortitude should be done bravely, and in like manner as to the other virtues.* [2] *But it is commanded (Dt. 16)[1] that "thou shalt follow justly after that which is just." Therefore the mode of virtue falls under the precept.*	Objection 1. Apparently, yes. A virtuous person performs what justice requires justly, what fortitude requires courageously, and so on. Concerning justice, this is exactly what Deuteronomy commands: The people are to follow the just, *because it is just*. So the precepts of the Old Law do require that what they prescribe be performed in a virtuous way.

[1] Persons who possess justice, fortitude, and the other virtues spontaneously perform the deeds which these virtues dictate. Such deeds are second

---

[1] Corrected. St. Thomas correctly refers to chapter 16; Blackfriars has chapter 26.

nature for them; in the truest sense they are *acts* – actualizations – of their moral excellences. By contrast, although an unjust man may still perform an act dictated by justice, and a coward (or a man not courageous but rash) may still perform a deed dictated by courage, he will perform it reluctantly, against inclination. Although sometimes, speaking loosely, we may call such deeds "acts" of virtue, they are not acts of virtue in the sense that they actualize virtues which those performing them really possess.

[2] The Objector's reasoning requires a little digression into the wording of the verse from which he is quoting. In context, it reads as follows:

Thou shalt appoint judges and magistrates in all thy gates, which the Lord thy God shall give thee, in all thy tribes: that they may judge the people with just judgment, and not go aside to either part. Thou shalt not accept person nor gifts: for gifts blind the eyes of the wise, and change the words of the just. Thou shalt follow *justly after that which is just*: that thou mayst live and possess the land, which the Lord thy God shall give thee.[2]

The Hebrew of the final verse uses the same word twice: "Justice, justice you shall follow." Translators have rendered this vivid language in a variety of different ways. For example, the KJV renders "justice, justice" as "that which is altogether just," while the RSV-CE renders it as "justice, and only justice." These two translations agree in taking the duplication of the noun for justice to mean something like pure justice, flawless justice, or justice without exception.

However, in the Vulgate, the Latin translation of the Bible which St. Thomas uses, a different approach is taken. Here "justice, justice" becomes *juste quod justum*. This takes the verse as meaning that one is to follow after what is just *justly*. In other words, one must not only do the right deed but also do it because it is right.

The Objector concludes that yes, the Old Law's requirement to do justice is not merely about doing the just thing but also about in doing it "in the mode of the virtue" – in the way a just person would do it.

Objection 2. [1] *Further, that which belongs to the intention of the lawgiver comes chiefly under the precept.* [2] *But the intention of the lawgiver is directed chiefly to make men virtuous,* [3] *as stated in Ethic. ii:* [4] *and it belongs to a virtuous man to act virtuously.* [5] *Therefore the mode of virtue falls under the precept.*	Objection 2. Moreover, what a legal precept requires depends mainly on the intention of the legislator. Aristotle points out that the primary intention of legislators is to make men virtuous. And virtuous men act virtuously. So yes, the precepts of the Old Law do intend that men act virtuously.

---

[1] As St. Thomas reminds us in I-II, Question 96, Article 6, St. Hilary of Poitiers argued in his work *On the Trinity* that the meaning of someone's

---

[2] Deuteronomy 16:18-20 (DRA), emphasis added.

statement must be gathered from what moved him to make it.³ If this view is correct, then we should pay attention to the intentions with which legislators make laws, not just the words they use in framing them. For instance, legislators would not intend the literal meaning of the words to be followed in circumstances in which doing so would cause obvious harm. In such cases, the guide is their intention, not their words.

For example, a fortified city might have a law directing that if the city is under siege, its gates must remain shut. Under most circumstances this rule promotes the common good, but does it always? Suppose the enemy is in hot pursuit of the city's own defenders. Wouldn't it greatly harm the city to obey the words of the law, deny the defenders entrance, and leave them at the mercy of the enemy? St. Thomas holds that in such a case, even though the words of the law say "Keep the gates shut," the gates should be opened just long enough to let the defenders back in. Otherwise, the intention of the legislators in making the law would be frustrated. One who keeps the gates closed might say "But I am following the law!" But if one understands the law in the light of the intentions of those who made it, he is really violating it.⁴

Obviously, the principle that laws must be interpreted according to their intention and not just their words can be abused. As a safeguard against abuse, St. Thomas emphasizes that in general, only the legislators themselves may authorize departing from the literal meaning of the law. However, in a genuine emergency, when there is no time to consult the legislators, a citizen may follow his own judgment.

[2] According to a very old view which Aristotle proposes and St. Thomas endorses, the purpose of law is not simply to make people do things, but to form virtuous habits in them so that the law itself will be less and less necessary. For example, laws that punish reckless driving have as their intention not just that reckless drivers will be intimidated into taking care, but that eventually taking care will become second nature to them.

[3] The point just made supposes that the way virtues are built up is by habituation – doing the right thing over and over until it does become second nature – and that well-framed laws can aid in this process by directing which acts are to be done repeatedly. Here is what Aristotle says about the matter in his *Nicomachean Ethics*:

[W]e become just by doing just actions, we become temperate by doing temperate actions, and we become courageous by doing courageous actions. Our contention is verified by what is done in the state, for legislators make men good in accordance with

---

³ For discussion see the corresponding section of my *Commentary on Thomas Aquinas's Treatise on Law* (Cambridge: Cambridge University Press, 2014).
⁴ The example is given in I-II, Q. 96, Art. 6. St. Hilary is cited in the *sed contra*.

political norms. Such is the aim of every legislator. In fact he who does not succeed in this fails in lawmaking. It is precisely in this way that a good constitution differs from a bad one.[5]

In his *Commentary* on the work, St. Thomas explains,

> Likewise men become temperate or courageous by doing just actions or temperate actions or courageous actions. Therefore, virtues of this kind are not in us by nature. Then ... he makes known what he had said, by a sign. He says the statement just made that by performing actions we become virtuous is verified by what is done in the state. Legislators make men virtuous by habituating them to virtuous works by means of statutes, rewards and punishment. Such ought to be the aim of every legislator – in fact he who does not succeed in this fails in lawmaking. It is precisely in this way that a good constitution differs from a bad one.[6]

A distinction is necessary, because strictly speaking, the claim that virtues are built up by habituation applies only to the "acquired" virtues such as everyday justice and temperance. Aristotle applies it to all virtues because the acquired virtues are the only ones he knows. According to St. Thomas, however, besides the acquired virtues there also exist "infused" virtues such as charity and faith, the attainment of which exceeds our natural powers so that they must be poured into us by the Holy Spirit. To be sure, even here the recipient is not passive, for the attainment of the infused virtues requires *cooperation* with this grace.

[4] But a virtuous man – one who *does* possess a virtuous disposition – acts *from this disposition*.

[5] The argument might be represented like this:

1. Ultimately, the meaning of a law is determined by the intention of the legislator.
2. But in every law, legislators intend that the people become virtuous.
3. A virtuous person not only does the right thing but does it because of his virtue.
4. Therefore, the law has in view not only what people do but also that they do it virtuously – "according to the mode of virtue."
5. This conclusion applies to all law whatsoever, so it must apply to Divine law too.

Objection 3. [1] *Further, the mode of virtue seems to consist properly in working willingly and with pleasure.*	Objection 3. Besides, doing the right thing virtuously seems to require doing it willingly and with pleasure. But Divine

---

[5] Aristotle, *Nicomachean Ethics*, book II, chapter 1. I am following the wording in Thomas Aquinas, *Commentary on Aristotle's Nicomachean Ethics*, translated by C. I. Litzinger (Chicago: Regnery, 1964).
[6] Thomas Aquinas, *Commentary on Aristotle's Nicomachean Ethics*, trans. Litzinger, book II, lecture 1.

[2] *But this falls under a precept of the Divine law, for it is written (Ps. 99):* "Serve ye the Lord with gladness"; [3] *and (2 Cor. 9):* "Not with sadness or necessity: for God loveth a cheerful giver"; [4] *whereupon the gloss says:* "Whatever ye do, do gladly; and then you will do it well; whereas if you do it sorrowfully, it is done in thee, not by thee." [5] *Therefore the mode of virtue falls under the precept of the law.*	law does require this, for a passage in the Psalms exhorts the people to serve the Lord *with gladness,* and St. Paul instructs the Christians at Corinth not to give sorrowfully or under compulsion, because God loves a cheerful giver. A commentary on the latter passage remarks "Whatever good you do, then, do with good cheer, and you do it well. If you do it glumly, the deed comes *from* you, but is not done *by* you." So the law does concern itself with the way in which things are done.

[1] A rebellious teenager may do his chores and fulfill his duties morosely and under protest. A mature adult does them without reluctance and with good cheer. Some acts of virtue are intrinsically satisfying; it is a pleasure to repay a favor or write a note of thanks to a friend. Others are not – there is no pleasure in carrying out the trash per se – yet even so, there is a certain pleasure just in the fact of doing a good activity (and as we see below, there is still another in doing it for the love of someone else).

[2] Divine law requires serving God, yet it expects Divine service to be offered with joy. One of the most beloved psalms exhorts,

> Make a joyful noise to the Lord, all the lands! Serve the Lord with gladness! Come into his presence with singing! Know that the Lord is God! It is he that made us, and we are his; we are his people, and the sheep of his pasture. Enter his gates with thanksgiving, and his courts with praise! Give thanks to him, bless his name! For the Lord is good; his steadfast love endures for ever, and his faithfulness to all generations.[7]

[3] St. Paul is writing to the Christians in Corinth about a collection which is being taken for the Christians in Jerusalem. He urges that it be prepared not as an onerous duty, but in the spirit of a gift,[8] and continues,

> The point is this: he who sows sparingly will also reap sparingly, and he who sows bountifully will also reap bountifully. Each one must do as he has made up his mind, not reluctantly or under compulsion, *for God loves a cheerful giver.* And God is able to provide you with every blessing in abundance, so that you may always have enough of everything and may provide in abundance for every good work. As it is written, "He scatters abroad, he gives to the poor; his righteousness endures for ever." He who supplies seed to the sower and bread for food will supply and multiply your resources and increase the harvest of your righteousness.[9]

---

[7] Psalm 100 (RSV-CE). In the Vulgate, this psalm is numbered 99.
[8] 2 Corinthians 9:5. Vulgate, *quasi benedictionem, non tamquam avaritiam;* DRA, "so as a blessing, not as covetousness"; RSV-CE, "not as an exaction but as a willing gift."
[9] 2 Corinthians 9:6–10 (RSV-CE), emphasis added.

Amusingly, comparison of chapters 8 and 9 shows that Paul has been using the example of the Corinthians to encourage the Macedonians, and the example of the Macedonians to spur the generosity of the Corinthians.[10]

[4] The Objector takes this reflection on 2 Corinthians 9:7 not from the *Glossa Ordinaria*, or Ordinary Gloss, as might be thought, but from an influential commentary on the letters of St. Paul, Peter Lombard's *Magna Glossatura*, or Great Gloss.[11] The idea is that if I do something with sorrowful reluctance, I am not *producing* the deed, but rather it is *pulled* from me.[12] Here is the whole passage:

> And so *everyone*, of course, should give, *as he has determined*, that is arranged, *in his heart*, that is, in the counsel of his mind. For if he gives against his will it is not beneficial; those who give against their will, driven by their present feelings, have no reward. And so whatever he gives from his heart, he wills to give, *not with sadness, or of necessity*, but of his own will. *A cheerful giver*, that is, one who gives willingly, *God loves*, that is, approves and rewards – not the sad and murmuring. For he who gives to free himself from the weariness of being pestered, rather than to relieve the bowels of the needy, destroys the deed and its merit. Whatever good you do, then, do with good cheer, and you do it well. If you do it glumly, the deed comes *from* you, but not *by* you.[13]

It might be held that Peter Lombard is exaggerating. In St. Thomas's book *On Evil*, another Objector uses the same quotation in an attempt to argue that *acedia* or sloth is not a sin, because things done with sorrowful reluctance are not one's own acts. But St. Thomas disagrees: "Acts done out of sadness or fear are mixtures of the voluntary and the involuntary, as the *Ethics* says, and *insofar as they are partially involuntary*, they are not attributable to us. But the very movement of sadness *is* attributable to ourselves."[14]

The place in Aristotle's *Nicomachean Ethics* which St. Thomas has in mind in that passage is book III, chapter 1, where the philosopher is distinguishing voluntary from involuntary actions. In his *Commentary* on the work, the

---

[10] To see this, compare chapters 8 and 9.
[11] Also known as his *Collectanea* (Collection, or Collections).
[12] *Si autem cum tristitia facis, fit de te, non tu facis.*
[13] *Et ideo* unusquisque, *scilicet det*, prout destinarit, is est praeordinavit, in corde suo, *id est in consilio rationis*, quia si invita darent non prodesset eis. Quia qui invitus dat propter praesentem pudorem, non habet mercedem, ed ideo quisque det, sicut proposuit in corde suo, se velle dare, non *det* ex tristitia, aut ex necessitate, *id est tristis vel coactus*, sed sponte. Hilarem enim datorem, *id est qui ex voluntate bona dat*, diligit Deus, *id est approbat et remunerat, non tristem et murmurantem*. Qui enim dat ut careat taedio interpellantis, non ut reficiat viscera indigentis, et rem et meritum perdit. Quidquid ergo boni facis cum hilaritate fac, et tunc benefacis, si autem cum tristitia facis, sit de te, non tu facis.
[14] Thomas Aquinas, *On Evil*, translated by Richard Regan (Oxford: Oxford University Press, 2003), Q. 11, Art. 1, Obj. 3 and ad 3, quoting from p. 363, emphasis added.

Angelic Doctor explains that according to Aristotle, actions done unwillingly may be viewed in two ways:

> One, absolutely and in general (involuntary); the other, in the particular circumstances occurring at the time the action is to be done (voluntary). But, since actions are concerned with particulars, the nature of the action must be judged rather according to the considerations of particulars than according to the consideration of what is general. This is what [Aristotle] means in his statement that these actions were done voluntarily at the time they were performed (i.e., after having considered all the particular circumstances then occurring), and the end and completion of the action conform to this particular time.[15]

St. Thomas seems to agree with Aristotle, then, that in one sense, the actions a person does unwillingly are voluntary, for he wills to do them – but that in another sense, they are involuntary, because he would rather not do them, and wills them only to avoid something else. In any case, the person is responsible *for his own unwillingness*.

But of course all three of these thinkers, St. Thomas, Peter Lombard, and the Objector, agree that no actions done unwillingly have merit.

[5] The argument runs like this:

1. The Old Law requires not merely serving God, but serving Him *with gladness*.
2. Similarly, in the New Law, we are exhorted not merely to give, but to give *cheerfully*.
3. Indeed, if someone gives only with glum reluctance, then in a certain sense he is not giving at all, but having something taken from him. If this is so, then to require him to give truly *just is* to require him to give cheerfully.
4. Each of these passages illustrates the same general point: that Divine law requires not simply that the right deeds be done, but that they be done in the way that a virtuous person would do them.

On the contrary, [1] *No man can act as a virtuous man acts unless he has the habit of virtue,* [2] *as the Philosopher explains (Ethic. ii, 4; v, 8).* [3] *Now whoever transgresses a precept of the law, deserves to be punished. Hence it would follow that a man who has not the habit of virtue, would deserve to be punished, whatever he does.* [4] *But this is contrary to the*	On the other hand, as Aristotle points out, no one can do anything as the virtuous do it unless he has a virtuous disposition. But anyone who violates the law deserves punishment. So if the law did require doing things virtuously, then a person who lacked a virtuous disposition would deserve punishment whether he did the right thing or the wrong one. This would be contrary to law's intention, which is to bring men to

---

[15] Thomas Aquinas, *Commentary on Aristotle's Nicomachean Ethics*, trans. Litzinger, book III, lecture 1.

| *intention of the law, which aims at leading man to virtue, by habituating him to good works.* [5] *Therefore the mode of virtue does not fall under the precept.* | virtue by getting them into the habit of doing good deeds. So the answer to the query is no: although the precepts of law mandate deeds, they do not require performing them virtuously. |

[1] When we consider whether a vase is a good vase, we ask questions only about the vase itself: Is it ugly or beautiful, leaky or watertight, flimsy or durable? If it has all the necessary qualities, then we do not care about the motivations of the glassblower. Perhaps he made the vase only to pay for his drug habit, or perhaps he was a poor glassblower and managed to make a good one only after twelve tries under close supervision. We do not care about that. All that matters is the vase.

By contrast, when we consider whether a deed is a virtuous deed, we do ask about the motivations of the doer. Suppose I am shopping for a necklace for my wife, and I pay the price owed instead of stealing it. Certainly the act has the outward qualities of justice; I give what was due to the person to whom payment is due. Yet we do not concede that the payment is given justly unless I give it *from justice*. Doing it because the store detective is standing behind me does not count.

[2] The *sed contra* seems to have in mind chiefly a passage in which Aristotle explains the difference between artisanship and virtue:

> [W]orks of art have their perfection in themselves. It is enough then that these be made with certain qualities. Yet works of virtue are not justly and temperately performed if they have certain qualities, but the agent performing them must fulfill the following conditions. (1) He must know what he is doing. (2) He must choose the virtuous works for their own sakes. (3) He must possess the disposition and operate according to it resolutely and with stability. Except for knowledge, these conditions are not required in the other arts. Mere knowledge, however, has little or no importance to the virtues but what occurs from the frequent performance of just and temperate actions is all important.[16]

We return to these three conditions in the *respondeo*.

[3] The argument contains a silent premise:

1. Explicit: Whoever transgresses a precept of the law deserves to be punished.
2. Tacit: If the precept required that the deeds they commanded be done from the habit of virtue, then then whoever did them without possessing the habit of virtue would transgress them.

---

[16] Aristotle, *Nicomachean Ethics*, book II, chapter 4. See also book V, chapter 8, where Aristotle emphasizes that an act is not called just unless it is done voluntarily: "If someone restores a deposit unwillingly and on account of fear his act is not said to be just, nor is it an act of justice except incidentally." I am following the wording given in Aquinas, *Commentary on Aristotle's Nicomachean Ethics*, trans. Litzinger.

3. Explicit: On this supposition, then, whoever does not have the habit of virtue would deserve to be punished whatever he does: for if he does not do what is commanded, he deserves punishment for not doing it, and if he does do what is commanded, he deserves punishment for not doing it because of virtue.

[4] The purpose of law is to lead men to virtue by habituating them to do the deeds that virtuous people do. By making the unjust do just deeds, it gradually makes them just; by making the cowardly (and the rash) do courageous deeds, it gradually makes them courageous; and so on. The way it habituates them is that it rewards them for doing the right things, and punishes them for doing the wrong things, even though they do not yet have virtue. If it punished them *for not* having virtue, it would defeat its purpose of leading them to it.

[5] Therefore, either the law can require men to do the right things *because they already have virtue*, or it can give up the purpose of leading them to virtue, but it cannot do both. If it truly aims at turning them into people who do what is right because it is right, it cannot punish them for not being that way already.

I answer that, [1] *As stated above (Question [90], Article [3], ad 2), a precept of law has compulsory power.* [2] *Hence that on which the compulsion of the law is brought to bear, falls directly under the precept of the law. Now the law compels through fear of punishment, as stated in Ethic. x, 9,* [3] *because that properly falls under the precept of the law, for which the penalty of the law is inflicted.* [4] *But Divine law and human law are differently situated as to the appointment of penalties; since the penalty of the law is inflicted only for those things which come under the judgment of the lawgiver; for the law punishes in accordance with the verdict given.* [5] *Now man, the framer of human law, is competent to judge only of outward acts; because "man seeth those things that appear,"* [6] *according to 1 [Samuel] 16.* [7] *while God alone, the framer of the Divine law, is competent to judge of the inward movements of wills,* [8] *according to Ps. 7, "The searcher of hearts and reins is God."*

Here is my response. We have seen previously that legal precepts have coercive power. Therefore, whatever the precept causes to happen by such coercion is included in its meaning. As Aristotle reminds us, law coerces by threatening punishment; so, that for the sake of which punishment is inflicted is also included in the meaning of the precept.

However, Divine and human law punish things differently, for punishment is decreed according to the judgment of the crime, and so law does not enact punishment except for things the legislator can judge.

Now human beings, who enact human law, can judge only outward acts; Only God, who enacts Divine law, can judge interior movements of the will. For as God declares to Samuel, man sees only outward appearances, but as the psalmist writes, God scrutinizes the heart and inward parts.

---

[1] St. Thomas has argued earlier that "the notion of law contains two things: first, that it is a rule of human acts; secondly, that it has coercive

power."[17] The reason law needs coercive power is that its purpose is to lead men to virtue, and without power to coerce, it cannot do so.[18] Concerning the latter point, he refers to an argument of Aristotle, which he summarizes as follows:

> [I]t is not enough for young men to be reared under good laws and to be well taken care of, but, even more, adults must discover honorable ways to act and become accustomed to them. For this reason we need laws not only in the beginning when someone is growing to manhood but generally throughout man's entire life. Many indeed there are who obey by necessity or force instead of persuasion; they pay more attention to deprivation, i.e., the hurt they receive from punishment than to what is honorable ... [T]he man who is going to become virtuous must have careful rearing and good customs; and afterwards he should live by a moral code so that he refrains from evil either by his own will or even by coercion contrary to his will. This is possible only when a man's life is directed by some intellect that has both the right order conducive to good and the firmness, i.e., the coercive power, to compel the unwilling.[19]

[2] If a precept of law employs coercion to make people do something, then the meaning of the precept is to do it, and if it employs coercion to make them forbear from doing it, then the meaning of the precept is to forbear from doing it.

[3] But the means by which law coerces are to threaten punishment. Therefore, we may reformulate the previous point by saying that if a precept of law *threatens punishment* to make people do something, then the meaning of the precept is to do it, and if it *threatens punishment* to make them forbear from doing it, then the meaning of the precept is to forbear from doing it.

[4] A person can be punished for violating the law only if it can be ascertained that he has violated it. The consequence of this fact is that human and Divine law cannot punish all the same things. We are about to see why.

[5] Human law can punish only outward acts, because humans can detect only outward acts. Thus, human law cannot punish invisible movements of the heart. It can punish murder, but not murderous anger; it can punish blasphemy, but not secret contempt and disbelief; in general, it can punish the acts of vice, but not the vices themselves.

[6] The historical narrative of the Old Testament recounts that when God rejected Saul as king over Israel, he instructed Samuel to select a new king from among the sons of the man Jesse. When Samuel saw Jesse's son Eliab, he was impressed by his bearing and aspect, and thought that surely this was the one

---

[17] I-II, Q. 96, Art. 5. See also Q. 90, Art. 3, ad 2, "A private person cannot lead another to virtue efficaciously: for he can only advise, and if his advice be not taken, it has no coercive power, such as the law should have, in order to prove an efficacious inducement to virtue."

[18] I-II, Q. 90, Art. 3, ad 2.

[19] Aristotle's argument is in his *Nicomachean Ethics*, book x, chapter 9. St. Thomas's summary is in *Commentary on Aristotle's Nicomachean Ethics*, trans. Litzinger, book x, lecture 14.

Were the Moral Precepts to Be Obeyed in a Certain Way?

God intended. But God said to Samuel, "Do not look on his appearance or on the height of his stature, because I have rejected him; for the Lord sees not as man sees; man looks on the outward appearance, but the Lord looks on the heart."[20]

[7] What is invisible to man is plain to God, who does not have to make dubious inferences about the states of our wills from our outward acts and facial expressions, for he perceives them directly.

[8] It may seem strange that St. Thomas thinks it necessary to add a second citation from Scripture, since in 1 Samuel 16 we have already seen that God looks on the heart. Presumably, the Angelic Doctor wants a passage which more clearly identifies God as the *only* one who looks on the heart. Psalm 7 serves that purpose: "The Lord judgeth the people. Judge me, O Lord, according to my justice, and according to my innocence in me. The wickedness of sinners shall be brought to nought: and thou shalt direct the just: *the searcher of hearts and reins is God.* Just is my help from the Lord: who saveth the upright of heart."[21]

Many passages of Scripture testify to God's knowledge of hidden things. A proverb declares, "The crucible is for silver, and the furnace is for gold, and the Lord tries hearts."[22] After the prophet Jeremiah cries in anguish, "The heart is deceitful above all things, and desperately corrupt; who can understand it?" he receives the reply, "I, the Lord, search the mind and try the heart, to give every man according to his ways, according to the fruit of his doings."[23] Reflecting on God's knowledge of the heart, the psalmist is staggered:

O Lord, thou hast searched me and known me! Thou knowest when I sit down and when I rise up; thou discernest my thoughts from afar. Thou searchest out my path and my lying down, and art acquainted with all my ways. Even before a word is on my tongue, lo, O Lord, thou knowest it altogether. Thou dost beset me behind and before, and layest thy hand upon me. Such knowledge is too wonderful for me; it is high, I cannot attain it.[24]

---

[9] *Accordingly, therefore, we must say that the mode of virtue is in some sort regarded both by human and by Divine law; in some respect it is*	The preceding facts will enable us to show: 1. That in one way both human and Divine law take account of how a deed is done;

---

[20] 1 Samuel 16:1–7 (RSV-CE). St. Thomas numbers 1 Samuel as 1 Kings; what are now called 1 and 2 Kings he numbers as 3 and 4 Kings.

[21] Psalms 7:9–11 (DRA), emphasis added; most contemporary translations number these verses as 7:8–10. The heart is here viewed as the seat of the will, and the "reins," or kidneys, as the seat of the feelings. Thus the verse means that God's vision penetrates to our inmost depths.

[22] Proverbs 17:3 (RSV-CE).

[23] Jeremiah 17:9–10 (RSV-CE), punctuation added.

[24] Psalm 139:1–6 (RSV-CE). In the Vulgate, this psalm is numbered as 138.

regarded by the Divine, but not by the human law; and in another way, it is regarded neither by the human nor by the Divine law. [10] Now the mode of virtue consists in three things, as the Philosopher states in Ethic. ii. [11] The first is that man should act "knowingly": and this is subject to the judgment of both Divine and human law; because what a man does in ignorance, he does accidentally. [12] Hence according to both human and Divine law, certain things are judged in respect of ignorance to be punishable or pardonable.	2. That in another way Divine law takes account of it, but not human; 3. And that in still another way, neither takes account of it. To see why, remember that as Aristotle remarks, human virtue lies in three things: The first is that virtuous deeds are done *knowingly*. Both human and Divine law take account of this aspect of how a deed is done, because if a person does not know what he is doing, he is doing it in a manner extraneous to his will. Thus, his deed may be judged as culpable or pardonable depending on whether he knew.

[9] This statement reads like a summary of what the previous section of argument has already shown. Actually, St. Thomas is stating what he is now *prepared* to show – and it will take some time for him to show it.

[10] The way in which a virtuous person performs a virtuous deed satisfies three conditions which we have already seen in the discussion of the *sed contra*: he does the deed knowingly, for its own sake, and with consistency. We have already encountered these conditions in the *sed contra*. In his *Commentary on Aristotle's Nicomachean Ethics*, St. Thomas explains the conditions and parses them a little further:

- Doing the deed knowingly pertains to the *intellect or reason*.
- Doing it for its own sake pertains to the *faculty of appetite*, or power of desire. This implies two further points: (a) that the action is not done because of some passion, such as fear, and (b) that it is not done for the sake of something else, such as money or vainglory.
- Doing it consistently and unshakably pertains to the *nature of a habitual disposition*.[25]

We see, then, that Aristotle's three conditions are not listed haphazardly but according to the properties of virtue itself, for a virtue *simply is* a habitual disposition to act according to reason, not because of passion but for the true good. It is important to avoid a certain Stoic misunderstanding of not being driven by passion, because virtue does not require *not having* any passions; what it requires is that reason governs and moderates them, rather than them governing reason.

We now consider these conditions in their relation to law, beginning with the first.

---

[25] Aquinas, *Commentary on Aristotle's Nicomachean Ethics*, trans. Litzinger, book ii, lecture 4.

[11] The first element in how a virtuous man does a virtuous deed is that he knows what he is doing. Neither Divine nor human law punishes a man for what he does in ignorance. Suppose the doctor has prescribed the wrong medicine for the patient's condition, and the patient dies from it. The pharmacist who filled the prescription is not to blame; so far as he could know, he was doing the right thing. What happened, happened, not because of his will, but for reasons extraneous to his will – in the philosophical sense, it is "accidentally" rather than essentially related to his will.

[12] So in this respect – whether the deed is done (or not done) knowingly – both Divine and human law pay attention to the way in which a deed is done.

| [13] *The second point is that a man should act "deliberately," i.e. "from choice, choosing that particular action for its own sake"*; [14] *wherein a twofold internal movement is implied, of volition and of intention, about which we have spoken above:* [15] *and concerning these two, Divine law alone, and not human law, is competent to judge.* [16] *For human law does not punish the man who wishes to slay, and slays not:* [17] *whereas the Divine law does, according to Mt. 5, "Whosoever is angry with his brother, shall be in danger of the judgment."* | The second is that virtuous deeds are done *willingly*, from choice and choice alone. As we have seen previously, this involves a double interior movement, both volition and intention. Only Divine, not human, law can judge such acts of the will. For this reason, human law does not punish a man who wishes to murder but for some reason does not. However, Divine law does: as Christ says in the Gospel of Matthew, "everyone who is angry with his brother shall be liable to judgment." |

[13] The second element in how a virtuous person performs a virtuous act is that he does it of his own will. St. Thomas explains that this means *eligens et propter hoc eligens* – literally, "choosing and because of this choosing." The Blackfriars translators' expression "for its own sake" and my paraphrase "from choice and choice alone" reflect attempts to translate into English an idea that Latin expresses differently.

[14] In colloquial English, the terms "volition," "choice," and "intention" are often treated as though they mean the same thing. St. Thomas distinguishes them. We *have volition* for the end;[26] we *choose* the means to reach it; and we *intend* the end *as acquired by* the means.[27] Viewed in themselves, the will's movements to the means and to the end are different acts. However, viewing the means as chosen *for the sake* of the end, the will's movement to the end and to the means are the same act viewed from different angles.[28]

---

[26] I-II, Q. 8, Art. 1, ad 1, and Art. 2.
[27] I-II, Q. 8, Art. 4, ad 3.
[28] I-II, Q. 12, Art. 4.

[15] Whether we are speaking of volition or intention, however, we are speaking of the interior movements of the heart, which are known to God but hidden from human beings.

[16] In speaking of someone who "wishes to slay, and slays not," St. Thomas is not thinking of someone who wills the death of another but then changes his mind, but of someone who continues to have this will *yet does not carry through*. Perhaps the opportunity does not arise, the deed would be too difficult, or he is afraid of getting caught.

Human law does not punish the *will* for the other man to die, because the human legislator cannot detect it. Divine law does punish such a will, because the Divine legislator can detect it. So in this second respect – whether the deed is done (or not done) willingly – Divine law pays attention, but human law does not.

[17] St. Thomas is quoting from Jesus' Sermon on the Mount:

You have heard that it was said to the men of old, "You shall not kill; and whoever kills shall be liable to judgment." But I say to you that *every one who is angry with his brother shall be liable to judgment*; whoever insults his brother shall be liable to the council, and whoever says, 'You fool!' shall be liable to the hell of fire. So if you are offering your gift at the altar, and there remember that your brother has something against you, leave your gift there before the altar and go; first be reconciled to your brother, and then come and offer your gift.[29]

[18] *The third point is that he should "act from a firm and immovable principle": which firmness belongs properly to a habit, and implies that the action proceeds from a rooted habit.* [19] *In this respect, the mode of virtue does not fall under the precept either of Divine or of human law, since neither by man nor by God is he punished as breaking the law, who gives due honor to his parents and yet has not the habit of filial piety.*	The third is that his act should proceed from a *staunch and unwavering* disposition. Such firmness is ingrained – it arises from a habit with deep roots. Neither Divine nor human law takes account of this aspect of how an act is done. For example, if a person lacks the firm disposition to give his parents the honor they deserve, but treats them with honor anyway, neither man nor God punishes him for violating the precept.

[18] In English we tend to confine the word "habit" to things that we do without thinking, like popping chewing gum, scratching the chin, or whistling while others are working. This is not what St. Thomas has in mind, for a *habitus* can be any kind of settled disposition; it can even be a settled *way* of thinking. Moral virtues and vices are settled dispositions to *choose* in certain ways. For example, the courses of action habitually chosen by a courageous man avoid both cowardice and rashness.

---

[29] Matthew 5:21–24 (RSV-CE), emphasis added.

[19] If I always treat my parents with honor, neither Divine nor human law punishes me, *even if I do not inwardly honor them* – for example, even if I find treating them this way wearisome and unpleasant. If the law *did* punish me for not having the underlying virtue, then it could never move me to acquire it by habituating me to the act. So in this respect – whether the deed is done (or not done) from a staunch and unwavering disposition – neither human *nor* Divine law commands doing the deed in the way a virtuous person does it. Moreover, the way that I acquire the virtue of justice is to keep on performing just acts until just acts become second nature to me; so if I had to be just already in order to perform a just act, I never could acquire the virtue of justice.

Whether treating my parents with respect even without inwardly honoring them deserves *eternal reward*, however, is not at all the same thing as whether the law punishes me for not doing so. Ultimately, only acts done with charity are meritorious, and charity requires the gift of Divine grace. We return to this matter in the Discussion at the end of the Article.

Reply to Objection 1. The mode of doing acts of justice, which falls under the precept, is that they be done in accordance with right; but not that they be done from the habit of justice.	Reply to Objection 1. When the precepts of the Old Law command acts of justice, they do require that the acts correspond to justice, but they do not require that they arise from a disposition to do justice.

The Objector had pointed out that according to the Old Testament book of Deuteronomy, the people are to follow the just, *because it is just*. According to St. Thomas, this shows that just deeds must be done as the just do them in one respect, but it does not show that they must be done as the just do them in all respects. I must do the act *that justice requires* must be done – for example, I must pay my debts. But the law does not command that I do so because I am a just person, because it does not suppose that I have already been made altogether just.

Reply to Objection 2. [1] *The intention of the lawgiver is twofold.* [2] *His aim, in the first place, is to lead men to something by the precepts of the law: and this is virtue.* [3] *Secondly, his intention is brought to bear on the matter itself of the precept: and this is something leading or disposing to virtue, viz. an act of virtue.* [4] *For the end of the precept and the matter of the precept are not the same: just as neither in other things is the end the same as that which conduces to the end.*	Reply to Objection 2. The legislator's intention is not single but double. 1. He intends by his law to *bring* men to something – that is, to *virtue* itself. 2. But he intends to do this by means of something which *disposes* them to virtue – that is, an *act* of virtue. For the purpose of the rule is not the same as its subject matter. In other things too, the end that is sought differs from the means of achieving it.

[1] The Objector had argued that since legislators intend that men become virtuous, and the virtuous act virtuously, the precepts of the Old Law do intend that they act virtuously. St. Thomas counters that legislators have not one but two intentions, and this changes the picture. Yes, they intend an end, but they intend it *as acquired by the means*. So we must consider both the end at which they aim, and the means by which they intend it.

[2] The end at which law aims is that men *become* virtuous.

[3] The means by which law aims to make men virtuous is that even though they are not yet virtuous, they repeatedly perform *acts* of virtue.

[4] The Objector's mistake was to think that because the law aims at virtue, *therefore it commands virtue*. But no: Generally speaking, the end which we seek and the means by which we seek it are not the same thing. That is certainly true here, for the purpose of the precept is not the same thing as what the precept commands in order to attain its purpose (what the Blackfriars translation calls its matter).

Reply to Objection 3. [1] *That works of virtue should be done without sadness, falls under the precept of the Divine law; for whoever works with sadness works unwillingly.* [2] *But to work with pleasure, i.e. joyfully or cheerfully, in one respect falls under the precept, viz. insofar as pleasure ensues from the love of God and one's neighbor (which love falls under the precept), and love causes pleasure:* [3] *and in another respect does not fall under the precept, insofar as pleasure ensues from a habit;* [4] *for "pleasure taken in a work proves the existence of a habit," as stated in Ethic. ii, 3.* [5] *For an act may give pleasure either on account of its end, or through its proceeding from a becoming habit.*

Reply to Objection 3. The precepts of the Old Law do require that the virtuous deeds they require be done *without sadness*, because to do something glumly is to do it unwillingly. But concerning whether the precepts require that these deeds be done *with pleasure* – gladly and with good cheer – we must make a distinction. For a deed may be pleasurable in either of two ways: because of the purpose for which it is performed, or because of the sheer enjoyment of exercising a habit (in this case the habit of virtue).

The kind of pleasure which Divine law requires is the former. One ought to have that pleasure which arises from the purpose, which is love of God and neighbor, for this love is included in the rule, and from it, pleasure arises.

But the precept does not require the latter kind of pleasure, which arises from sheer habit – the sort which Aristotle has in mind when he comments that the pleasure which is taken in doing something is a sign of the disposition which generates the deed.

---

[1] The Objector holds that doing the right thing as a virtuous person would it lies in doing it willingly. This in turn means doing it with pleasure and without sadness. But Divine law does require doing it that way, so apparently, it requires doing it as a virtuous person would do it. In St. Thomas's view, however, this argument overlooks important distinctions. In the first place,

although it is true that virtue involves doing the right thing willingly, that is not all virtue involves. In the second place, the question of how doing a thing virtuously is related to doing it *without sadness* is not the same as the question of how doing it virtuously is related to doing it *with pleasure.*

Doing it virtuously, he says, does involve doing it without sadness. *This aspect* of doing it virtuously really is required by the Divine law, just because Divine law requires doing it willingly. So *in this respect* the Objector is right.

[2] As to the matter of acting with pleasure, matters are more complicated. Doing the right thing just the way a virtuous person would do it generates two kinds of pleasure, not one. The first kind of pleasure arises from doing it for the love of God and neighbor, and in fact, the law does require doing it for the love of God and neighbor. As to the love of God:

Hear, O Israel: The Lord our God, the Lord is One; and you shall love the Lord your God with all your heart, and with all your soul, and with all your might.[30]

As to the love of neighbor:

You shall not hate your brother in your heart, but you shall reason with your neighbor, lest you bear sin because of him. You shall not take vengeance or bear any grudge against the sons of your own people, but you shall love your neighbor as yourself: I am the Lord.[31]

Of course these great commandments of the Old Law are repeated and highlighted in the New Law:

And one of [those who were listening to Him], a lawyer, asked [Jesus] a question, to test him. "Teacher, which is the great commandment in the law?" And he said to him, "You shall love the Lord your God with all your heart, and with all your soul, and with all your mind. This is the great and first commandment. And a second is like it, You shall love your neighbor as yourself. On these two commandments depend all the law and the prophets."[32]

[3] In view of its subtlety, perhaps the Objector may be excused for overlooking the distinction that St. Thomas makes. St. Thomas is calling our attention to the fact that there is a difference between the pleasure of doing something, and the pleasure of doing it *as an exercise of the associated virtue.* For example, the pleasure of giving a gift is one thing, but the pleasure of giving it *as an exercise of friendship* is another. More to the present point is that *even if I possess charity*, which is the virtue of loving God and of loving neighbor for the sake of God, there is a difference between the pleasure which arises *from love* in an act of love, and the pleasure which arises *from the fact that this love*

---

[30] Deuteronomy 6:4–5 (RSV-CE), substituting "The Lord our God, the Lord is One" for the RSV-CE's "The Lord our God is one Lord."

[31] Leviticus 19:17–18 (RSV-CE).

[32] Matthew 22:35–40 (RSV-CE).

is a firm and constant disposition in me. According to St. Thomas, the sort of pleasure which the precepts of Divine law have in mind when they say we should act cheerfully is the former, not the latter.

[4] The "habits" of the infused virtues were unknown to Aristotle. However, Aristotle did know that the exercise of virtue produces a certain kind of pleasure which cannot arise otherwise – so that the experience of this kind of pleasure proves that the person has the virtue. Here is what Aristotle says in his *Nicomachean Ethics*:

> We may understand pleasure or sorrow that follows activity as an indication of the habits that are present. Indeed the man who avoids bodily pleasures is temperate if he is glad about it; intemperate, if sad about it. Likewise, the man who encounters dangers is brave if he rejoices or is not sad, but cowardly if he is saddened. Moral virtue then is concerned with pleasure and sorrows.[33]

In his *Commentary* on the work, book II, lecture 3, St. Thomas explains like this:

> When virtue produces actions similar to the actions that formed it, ... the performance of this action differs before and after virtue. Before virtue man does a kind of violence to himself in operating this way. Such actions, therefore, have some admixture of sorrow. But after the habit of virtue has been formed, these actions are done with pleasure. The explanation is that a habit exists as a sort of nature, and that is pleasurable which agrees with a thing according to nature.
>
> [Aristotle] says that an indication that habits, good or bad, have already been formed is given by the pleasure or sorrow that follows the operations. He illustrates this by examples. The man who is glad that he has avoided bodily pleasures is temperate because he performs an action in keeping with the habit. Likewise, he who encounters dangers with pleasure, or at least without sorrow, is brave. Particularly in the act of fortitude it is enough not to have sorrow, as will be explained in the third book. One who faces dangers with sorrow is cowardly. He then assigns the reason for what he has said from the fact that every moral virtue is concerned with pleasures and sorrows.[34]

[5] For example, a father may enjoy reading to his little girl because it gives her delight (an end), or because reading aloud to her has become second nature to him (a habit). Or a scholar may enjoy writing a book about Thomas Aquinas because it gives him knowledge and edifies others (an end), or because the writing of books is ingrained in him (a habit). Of course it is possible to have both pleasures in the same act – but they are different pleasures!

In the case of activities which are undertaken for their own sake, a related distinction is sometimes made between goods internal and external to a habit. Concerning the habit of sportsmanship, for instance, an athlete may enjoy

---

[33] Aristotle, *Nicomachean Ethics*, book II, chapter 6. I am following the wording in Aquinas, *Commentary on Aristotle's Nicomachean Ethics*, trans. Litzinger.
[34] Ibid., book II, lecture 3.

baseball because it enables him to make money through endorsements, or to meet women impressed by his abilities (these are goods external to the habit), or because he delights in his skill, or in the intensity of its exercise in competition (and these are goods internal to the habit).[35]

For the Reply to the Third Objection, the bottom line is that although the Objector is right about some things, his observations about the scriptural exhortations to do the right things cheerfully, not sorrowfully, fail to show that the Old Law requires doing them *in every way* as a virtuous person would do them. In some ways, it does; in other ways, it doesn't.

DISCUSSION

Do Legislators Really Aim at Making Men Virtuous? Should They?

As we have seen, St. Thomas agrees with the second Objector that the purpose of law is to make men virtuous; he merely thinks the Objector has misunderstood it. Law does not command "Be virtuous." Rather it commands certain acts and forbids certain others *so that* men will become virtuous.

Today, the idea that the purpose of law is to make men virtuous is widely ridiculed as "enforcing morality." But what else does law enforce, if not some kind of moral conduct? Its whole point is to induce citizens to perform certain kinds of acts and not to perform others. The reason it commands the former is that its deems them good in some way; the reason it forbids the latter is that it deems them bad in some way. What else is morality but the principles of character and conduct which help us to attain the good and avoid the bad? And what does law do but enforce them?

Rather than complaining that law induces us to perform some acts and avoid others, we ought to make sure that it is inducing us to perform good acts rather than bad ones, and to avoid bad ones rather than good ones. Someone who says "But who is to judge?" is either ducking responsibility, because law always judges,[36] or else he is dishonest, using the mantra "Don't make moral judgments" as a way to suppress the other person's moral judgments while enforcing his own. Nonjudgmentalism is always, without exception, a smokescreen.

Even a wicked regime aims at making men good in a relative sense. While legislators in a free republic aim at inducing citizens to behave in a way that is good for the republic, legislators in a tyranny aim at inducing citizens to behave

---

[35] This distinction is elaborated by Alasdair MacIntyre, *After Virtue*, 3rd ed. (Notre Dame, IN: Notre Dame University Press, 2007).

[36] Read in context, Christ's oft-quoted warning "Judge not, that you be not judged" forbids only hypocritical judgment. Indeed, in another place he commands "Do not judge by appearances, but judge with right judgment." See respectively Matthew 7:1-5 and John 7:25 (RSV-CE), emphasis added.

in a way that is good for the tyranny. Saying this does not commit us to relativism, because there is a profound difference between a good and bad regime. The crucial thing is to understand the difference between "good" and "good for." What is good for a bad regime *is not good simply*; what is good for a good regime *is*. We might say that a good regime is one in which the good man and the good citizen are identical.

The proposition that law aims at making men virtuous does not imply that it must aim at this end by any means available. The fallacy that law must not "enforce morality" seems to arise from thinking that if law does aim at making men virtuous, then it must aim at every kind of virtue by every possible means. But this is not true at all. In the first place, it cannot aim at every kind of virtue, and in the second place, some means are inappropriate.

As to why it cannot aim at every kind of virtue:

- The chief reason is that as we have seen repeatedly, it simply cannot impart infused virtue, for that depends on the grace of God. One can engender an acquired virtue, say, temperance, by getting people into the habit of temperate acts, but one cannot engender, say, faith, by getting them into the habit of faithful acts. Until one has faith, not a single act of faith is possible. (Although the law can be friendly and cooperative toward the Church, in which the means of grace are made available.)
- An argument might also be made that by itself, law cannot impart the prudence to *make* good laws, because greater virtue is required to make them than just to obey them. Moreover, the development of so-called political prudence requires broader experience than ordinary prudence. (Though it might be suggested that laws providing for public deliberation do provide something of the experience that inculcates prudence.)

As to why it must not employ every means of inculcating virtue that come to hand:

- Law must not try to command the interior movements of the heart – for example, it cannot command "Be thankful to God" or "Admire those who have sacrificed for others." For even apart from other considerations, how can it enforce what it cannot see?[37] The attempt to *command* thankfulness or admiration would produce not thankful people but hypocrites. By various indirect means, interior movements of the heart can certainly be encouraged; for example, trust in God is encouraged by setting aside days for it, and admiration of those who have sacrificed for others is encouraged by publicly giving them honors. Commanding them is quite another kettle of fish.
- Law must not attempt to suppress every vice, but only the gravest, because in the attempt to do so it may make men burst out into even greater evils.[38] For

---

[37] I-II, Q. 91, Art. 4.
[38] I-II, Q. 96, Art. 2.

example, the attempt to forbid all drinking of alcohol – which in moderation is not wrong anyway – may impart glamor to being drunk.
- Since law is concerned with the common rather than the private good, it must not command every act of virtue, but only those that are crucial to the good of others. For example, witnesses in court should be commanded to speak the truth, but teenagers who stretch the truth in their diaries should be left alone.[39]
- Some acts are intrinsically evil; they are never to be done for the sake of any result, no matter how good, even the good of virtue itself. So we must not punish innocent persons for, say, having red hair, even if a statistical correlation could be shown between having red hair and committing felonies. The term "evil" applies here to moral evil – to sin or "evil of fault," such as injustice. One may of course do such things as vaccinate children against chickenpox and punish criminals as they deserve, and the pain of the needle and the sorrow of imprisonment are certainly evils of a sort, but they are not evils of fault, for we do not violate the moral law by inflicting them.[40]

These qualifications to the purpose of making men virtuous do not arise from the liberal ideology of making laws morally neutral; to be a law is already to be other than neutral. Rather they arise from realistic consideration of virtue itself, and of what law can and cannot contribute toward its achievement.

---

[39] I-II, Q. 96, Art. 3.
[40] St. Paul, commenting that some people have slanderously charged him with teaching that evil may be done so that good will ensue, says that they are justly condemned (Romans 3:8). St. Thomas cites the implied principle, that we must not do evil so that good will ensue, in many places, especially III, Q. 79, Art. 4, ad 4, and II-II, Q. 64, Art. 5, ad 3.

QUESTION 100, ARTICLE 10

Whether the Mode of Charity Falls Under the Precept of the Divine Law?

TEXT	PARAPHRASE
Whether the mode of charity falls under the precept of the Divine law?	Do the precepts of the law require doing the deeds that they command from charity – because they spring from the love of God?

We have already considered whether the precepts of Divine law require doing the deeds that they perform as a virtuous person would perform them – for example, honoring my father because honor is due to him, not just because I don't want to be disinherited. However, the complete development of the virtues lies in that loving friendship between man and God which is called charity. In fact, without charity, even the ordinary moral excellences are virtues only "in a restricted sense," because although they direct us to good purposes, they do not have the power to place these purposes in right relationship to our ultimate purpose, which is God. For the same reason, St. Thomas argues that no matter how good our deeds may be in themselves, no deed merits Divine reward unless it arises from charity.[1]

These facts force us to broaden our inquiry. If even acts of virtue are not all that they should be unless motivated by charity, then do the precepts of Divine law require acting *from this motive*?

Complicating the question is the fact that charity is an infused virtue; it is not built up in us in the same way as an acquired virtue such as justice. We can work ourselves into the virtue of justice by repeatedly performing the deeds which a just person would perform, and this is exactly why the discipline of obedience to law is so helpful: it enforces that repetition. However, it is impossible to work ourselves into the virtue of charity by repeatedly performing the deeds which a charitable person would perform; in fact it is impossible to work ourselves into it at all. The reason is that even a single act of charity exceeds our

---

[1] Charity is the friendship of man with God: II-II, Q. 23, Art. 1. The moral virtues are not complete without charity: I-II, Q. 65, Art. 2. For reasons explained below, charity is necessary for a deed to merit Divine reward: Q. 114, Art. 4.

natural powers. It requires a literally supernatural transformation of motive. Although by my natural powers, and for ordinary motives, I might have goodwill or affection for my neighbor, to love Him for the sake of God is quite another thing. The love of God for Himself, and the love of my neighbor for God's sake, can be attained only by the gift of Divine grace – by the influx of God's own love, uplifting me beyond what my natural powers can achieve.[2]

This is not to say that the natural virtues do not *anticipate* the supernatural virtues; they do. Of itself, nature cannot reach heaven, but nature has a face, and it looks up. For example, the more a husband and wife love each other, the more they feel the longing for 'something more' that transcends their love and wants to take it up into itself. This is the love of God.

Objection 1. [1] *It would seem that the mode of charity falls under the precept of the Divine law. For it is written (Mt. 19):* "*If thou wilt enter into life, keep the commandments*": [2] *whence it seems to follow that the observance of the commandments suffices for entrance into life.* [3] *But good works do not suffice for entrance into life, except they be done from charity:* [4] *for it is written (1 Cor. 13):* "*If I should distribute all my goods to feed the poor, and if I should deliver my body to be burned, and have not charity, it profiteth me nothing.*" [5] *Therefore the mode of charity is included in the commandment.*

Objection 1. Apparently the answer to the question is yes. In the Gospel of Matthew, Christ tells a young man that if he wishes to enter into life, he must keep the Commandments. This seems to imply that keeping them is sufficient to bring the young man into life. But good deeds are not sufficient to bring a person into life *unless they are done from charity*. This is why St. Paul writes to the Corinthians that even if he gave all that he had to feed the poor, and offered his body to be burned, it would do him no good unless he had charity. From this it follows that the precepts of law do require acting from charity.

---

[1] This statement is quoted from a conversation between Jesus and a conscientious young man of wealth. Notice that although the conversation is recounted in the New Testament, it bears closely on the meaning of the Old Law:

And behold, one came up to him, saying, "Teacher, what good deed must I do, to have eternal life?" And he said to him, "Why do you ask me about what is good? One there is who is good. If you would enter life, keep the commandments." He said to him, "Which?" And Jesus said, "You shall not kill, You shall not commit adultery, You shall not steal, You shall not bear false witness, Honor your father and mother, and, You

---

[2] Unlike the acquired virtues, the virtue of charity is caused not by preceding works but by the infusion of Divine grace: II-II, Q. 24, Art. 2. Although charity surpasses the natural power of the will, our nature is so fashioned as to anticipate grace: II-II, Q. 23, Art. 2. Each act of cooperation with the grace of charity makes us readier to cooperate with it again, and that each act of resistance to it makes us less: II-II, Q. 24, Art. 6.

shall love your neighbor as yourself." The young man said to him, "All these I have observed; what do I still lack?" Jesus said to him, "If you would be perfect, go, sell what you possess and give to the poor, and you will have treasure in heaven; and come, follow me." When the young man heard this he went away sorrowful; for he had great possessions.[3]

Along with certain other texts, this passage presents a distinction between precepts, the standard which is obligatory for everyone, and what are called "counsels," a higher standard offered to those few who are called to a more perfect way of life. The sorrow of the story arises from the fact that the wealthy young man recognizes his call, but declines it.

Here, six commandments are mentioned, along with just one counsel, poverty. We know, of course, that there are other commandments, and from other passages, other counsels can be gleaned, such as perpetual virginity, or celibacy.[4] We return to the distinction between counsels and precepts in Question 108, Article 4.

[2] Fulfilling the counsels is not necessary to receive eternal life with God; however, Jesus treats fulfilling the Commandments as not only necessary, but sufficient. The question – to which we are about to turn – is what fulfilling the Commandments means.

[3] The Objector argues that a merely external observance of the Commandments is not sufficient, for Holy Scripture also makes clear that no deeds merit eternal life, however good they may be in themselves, unless they spring from charity.

[4] In support of his point, the Objector quotes briefly from a magnificent passage of St. Paul's first letter to the young church at Corinth. It seems that the Corinthians have been putting on airs because they have received such Divine gifts as prophecies, speaking in tongues, and spiritual knowledge, but Paul teaches them that without love, these things count for nothing:

If I speak in the tongues of men and of angels, but have not love, I am a noisy gong or a clanging cymbal. And if I have prophetic powers, and understand all mysteries and all knowledge, and if I have all faith, so as to remove mountains, but have not love, I am nothing. If I give away all I have, and if I deliver my body to be burned, but have not love, I gain nothing. ... Love never ends; as for prophecies, they will pass away; as for tongues, they will cease; as for knowledge, it will pass away. For our knowledge is imperfect and our prophecy is imperfect; but when the perfect comes, the imperfect will pass away. ... So faith, hope, love abide, these three; but the greatest of these is love.[5]

---

[3] Matthew 19:16–22 (RSV-CE).
[4] See Matthew 19:9–12.
[5] 1 Corinthians 13:1–3, 8–10, 13 (RSV-CE).

[5] As in other places, "the commandment" is a metonymical expression for all of the Commandments. The argument works like this:

1. Keeping the Commandments suffices for entrance into eternal life.
2. Yet nothing suffices for entrance into eternal life except charity.
3. Therefore the meaning of keeping the Commandments includes not only doing the right deeds, but doing them from charity.

Objection 2. [1] *Further, the mode of charity consists properly speaking in doing all things for God.* [2] *But this falls under the precept; for the Apostle says (1 Cor. 10): "Do all to the glory of God." Therefore the mode of charity falls under the precept.*	Objection 2. Moreover, the meaning of acting from charity is to do everything for God. But the precepts of the law do require this, as we see from St. Paul's exhortation to the Corinthians to do everything for God's glory. So the precepts require acting in this way.

[1] We saw above that charity is friendship between man and God. However, it is not everyday friendship. Our ultimate purpose and fulfillment lies in God; it does not lie in our earthly friends. Therefore, although Lucy's friendship for Ethel does not involve doing everything she does for Ethel's sake, charity does involve doing everything we do for God's sake.

The contrast should not be misunderstood, because ordinary friendship can be supernaturally elevated by friendship with God. In Lucy's case, this would mean exercising even her friendship with Ethel for God's sake, recognizing in Ethel God's image.

[2] The Objector argues that doing everything for the sake of God *does* come under the Commandments, because we are *commanded to* do everything for the sake of God. To support his point, he quotes from St. Paul's discussion, in 1 Corinthians 10, of whether Christians may eat meat that has been sacrificed to idols.

In itself, the question Paul addresses may seem narrow, but larger issues are at stake; besides, for his readers, the question is urgent. Why? Because on the one hand, idolatry is absolutely forbidden, but on the other hand, many of them are poor, and meat which has been offered in pagan temples is sometimes sold in butcher's shops at a lower price. Paul argues that although the followers of Christ may not participate in idolatrous sacrificial feasts (verses 14–22), they are free to eat what they find in the butcher shop or what nonbelievers offer them at dinner without worrying about its origin (verses 25–27) – except that one should not eat it if doing so would cause misunderstanding among those who do not understand these things (verses 28–29).

Paul concludes that whether we eat or drink, we should do all to the glory of God. Although the context of the statement is eating and drinking, the statement has always been taken as meaning not merely that we should enjoy the blessings of food and drink for the glory of God, but that we should do everything whatsoever for His glory. That is certainly how the Objector views the passage. He might also have cited another passage of Paul. The Apostle – who in one letter had urged bond servants, "if you can gain your freedom, avail yourself of the opportunity"[6] – in another letter encourages those who have no choice but to remain in servile roles, "Whatever your task, work heartily, as serving the Lord and not men, knowing that from the Lord you will receive the inheritance as your reward; you are serving the Lord Christ."[7]

Objection 3. [1] *Further, if the mode of charity does not fall under the precept, it follows that one can fulfill the precepts of the law without having charity.* [2] *Now what can be done without charity can be done without grace, which is always united to charity. Therefore one can fulfill the precepts of the law without grace.* [3] *But this is the error of Pelagius, as Augustine declares (De Haeres. lxxxviii).* [4] *Therefore the mode of charity is included in the commandment.*

Objection 3. Besides, suppose the precepts did not require acting from charity. In this case, one would be able to fulfill the precepts without having it. But charity is always joined with grace – so whatever can be done without charity can be done without grace. It would follow that one could fulfill the rules without grace. But this is not true; as St. Augustine points out, it was the error of Pelagius. So yes, the precepts do require acting from charity.

---

[1] The Objector proposes a *reductio ad absurdum*: He seeks to show that if the precepts of Divine law do *not* require acting from charity, then an unacceptable conclusion follows; therefore they do require acting from charity. The first step in the argument is obvious: If they do not require charity, then charity is not needed to obey them.

[2] Where there is grace, there is charity; therefore, whoever lacks charity, lacks grace. This being the case, whatever can be done by a person who lacks charity can be done by a person who lacks grace. So if a person can obey the Commandments without charity, he can obey them without grace.

[3] In his book *On Heresy, to Quodvultdeus*, St. Augustine identifies the error in question, attributes it to Pelagius, and tells what is wrong with it:

At the present time, the newest of all heresies is that of the Pelagians, founded by the monk Pelagius. Caelestius followed this master to such a degree that their adherents are also called the Celestines.

These heretics are so opposed to the grace of God by which we are predestined to adoption as His sons through Jesus Christ, and by which we are rescued from the power of darkness that we may believe in him and be transferred into His kingdom; wherefore He says, "No one can come to me, unless He is enabled to do so by my Father," and by

---

[6] 1 Corinthians 7:21b (RSV-CE).
[7] Colossians 3:23–24 (RSV-CE).

which charity is poured forth into our hearts, that faith may work through charity; they are so opposed to this grace, I say, that they believe that man can fulfill all the commandments of God without it. But, if this were true, in vain would it seem that the Lord said, "Without me, you can do nothing."[8]

[4] The argument runs like this:

1. If the precepts did not require acting from charity, then the precepts could be fulfilled without charity.
2. But in this case, since charity and grace presuppose each other, it would also be true that the precepts could be obeyed without grace.
3. This conclusion is inadmissible, for the precepts cannot be obeyed without grace.
4. To avoid the inadmissible conclusion, at least one of the premises which lead to it must be false: either the precepts do require acting from charity, or charity and grace do not presuppose each other.
5. But charity and grace do presuppose each other.
6. Therefore, the precepts do require acting from charity.

On the contrary, [1] *Whoever breaks a commandment sins mortally.* [2] *If therefore the mode of charity falls under the precept, it follows that whoever acts otherwise than from charity sins mortally.* [3] *But whoever has not charity, acts otherwise than from charity.* [4] *Therefore it follows that whoever has not charity, sins mortally in whatever he does, however good this may be in itself:* [5] *which is absurd.*	On the other hand, anyone who fails to keep a precept of the law has committed mortal sin. So, if the precept really did require acting from charity, then anyone who acted from a motive other than charity would have sinned mortally. But those who lack charity do act from motives other than charity. From all this it would follow that anyone who lacked charity would commit mortal sin, no matter what he did, even if what he did is something generically good.[9] But this conclusion is inadmissible. So the precepts of the law do *not* command that the acts they require be done from charity.

[1] In the *sed contra* we find another *reductio ad absurdum,* this one supporting the opposite view. Its first step involves the distinction between mortal and venial sin.

The cause of the soul's order is the direction of everything to our ultimate good, who is God. This is charity, the friendship which unites us with Him. We easily understand that there are two levels of danger in physical disease: In one,

---

[8] St. Augustine of Hippo, *The de Haeresibus of Saint Augustine,* translated by Liguori G. Müller, *Patristic Studies,* vol. XC (Washington, DC: Catholic University of America Press, 1956), book LXXXVIII, section 1, p. 123.

[9] *De genere bonorum,* literally "of the genus of good." See also below, in the *respondeo.*

the body is disordered but still lives, but in the other, it loses the very cause of order and dies. In the same way, there are two levels of danger in sin: In one, the soul does something wrong but does not turn away from God, so that the charity which is the cause of the its order is damaged but not destroyed, but in the other, the soul does turn away from God, and charity is destroyed. Although the soul continues in existence, this is spiritual death.[10]

Although the distinction between mortal and venial sin puzzles some readers and is rejected out of hand by others, the underlying idea is simply that some wrongs are worse than others and do greater damage to our relationship with God. A helpful analogy has been offered by Richard Conrad, OP. Consider a husband who is determined to love his wife and stay married to her, but is "silent at the breakfast table, lazy about the house, critical and bad-tempered." His faults do not show a loss of faithfulness to his wife, but they prevent his love from growing and from penetrating more and more into his behavior. At the other extreme, he may abandon his wife, seek a divorce, live separately, and even marry someone else. This deliberately breaks his relation with his wife in such a way that although reconciliation may still be possible, it would be very difficult. The former sort of fault is analogous to venial sin in our relationship with God, because it impedes love even though it does not destroy it. The latter sort is analogous to mortal sin, because it tends to close us off to that love.[11]

Now to the point:
1. Charity is that by which we love God and neighbor.
2. Loving God requires obeying His commandments.
3. So to disobey the Commandments knowingly and deliberately is to act against charity.
4. But to act against charity is mortal sin.
5. Therefore, to disobey the Commandments knowingly and deliberately is to commit mortal sin.[12]

As St. Thomas writes, it is essential to charity

that man should so love God as to wish to submit to Him in all things, and always to follow the rule of His commandments; since whatever is contrary to His commandments is manifestly contrary to charity, and therefore by its very nature is capable of destroying charity ... through every mortal sin which is contrary to God's commandments, an obstacle is placed to the outpouring of charity, since from the very fact that a man chooses to prefer sin to God's friendship, which requires that we should obey His will, it follows that the habit of charity is lost at once through *one mortal sin*.[13]

---

[10] I-II.72.5, I-II.88.1
[11] Richard Conrad, OP, *Liturgy and Sacraments: A Course-Book for the M.A. in R.E. and Catechesis* (Birmingham, UK: Maryvale Institute, 2006), appendix 3B.
[12] II-II.105.1.
[13] II-II.24.12, emphasis added.

Were the Moral Precepts to Be Obeyed According to Charity?   225

Why through even one? Shouldn't it take an entire series of mortal sins to destroy charity? St. Thomas explains that if the "habit" or disposition of charity were acquired – built up by repeated acts which are in our own power – then a single act of disobedience to the Commandments would not necessarily destroy it, because a habit is not destroyed by one deed. However, charity is not acquired; it is infused virtue. It depends not on our own power but on the inpouring of grace by God Himself. To disobey one of His commandments is to refuse this inflow, just as though an object were interposed between earth and the sun so that earth was plunged into darkness.[14]

If genuinely repented, through the grace of Christ, even a mortal sin can be forgiven. However, forgiveness of a mortal sin is less like the cure of a disease than like the resuscitation of the dead. It is a spiritual miracle. In the life of the faithful, it may be a frequent miracle; nevertheless it is something miraculous.

[2] If the precepts of Divine law do require acting from charity, then mortal sin includes not only doing gravely wrong things but also doing the right things from a disposition other than love. Consider the following cases:

1. I may fail to treat my parents with respect.
2. I may treat my parents with respect merely because they control my trust fund.
3. I may treat them with respect because they deserve respect.
4. I may treat them with respect, *for the love of God and neighbor*, because they deserve respect.

Suppose the precepts of Divine law require merely outward observance; then conduct of types 2, 3, and 4 fulfills them. Suppose they require obeying them "in the mode" of virtue; then only conduct of types 3 and 4 fulfills them. This was the query in Article 9. But suppose they require obeying "in the mode" of that perfected virtue which is charity; then only conduct of type 4 fulfills them.

[3] It is impossible to act from the love of God and neighbor *unless one loves God and neighbor*.

[4] So if the precepts require charity, then a person who lacks charity sins whether he fails to treat his parents with respect, treats them with respect because of something other than virtue, or *even treats them with respect because of virtue*.

[5] According to the *sed contra*, this conclusion is ridiculous. Although it is not logically impossible, it is *inconveniens*, which means unfitting. It *just isn't right* that things should stand this way. But since the conclusion is unfitting, at

---

[14] Ibid.

least one of the premises which lead to it must be wrong – and given everything else we know about grace, the only premise that might be wrong is the one under examination – the one that states that the precepts of Divine law require acting from charity. From this the *sed contra* concludes that the precepts of Divine law must *not* require acting from charity.

I answer that, [1] *Opinions have been contrary on this question.* [2] *For some have said absolutely that the mode of charity comes under the precept;* [3] *and yet that it is possible for one not having charity to fulfill this precept: because he can dispose himself to receive charity from God.* [4] *Nor (say they) does it follow that a man not having charity sins mortally whenever he does something good of its kind: because it is an affirmative precept that binds one to act from charity, and is binding not for all time, but only for such time as one is in a state of charity.* [5] *On the other hand, some have said that the mode of charity is altogether outside the precept.*	Here is my response. Those who have written about this puzzle have disagreed. Some have taken the absolute position that the precepts of Divine law *do* require acting from charity. Yet they argue that even a person who lacks charity can obey the precept, because he can put himself in such a condition that God can pour charity *into* him. They also *deny* that the requirement of charity implies that a person who lacks charity commits mortal sin even if he does something generically good,[15] for the commandment to act from charity is "affirmative" – it binds a person not always to do a given act, but to do it only at the time when it is actually applicable to him.[16] But others have held that acting from charity is entirely beyond what the precepts require.

[1] Sometimes those who hold diverse opinions agree about the right answer but give different reasons for it. Sometimes they give different answers but each of them is wrong. Sometimes they give different answers and just one of them is right. But sometimes each is right in some respect but not in others, and St. Thomas thinks that is what we find here.

[2] One set of thinkers replies yes to the point at issue: Obedience to the precepts of Divine law requires not just doing what the precepts command, but doing them from charity.

[3] These thinkers *deny* the claim of the *sed contra* that no one who lacks charity can obey the Commandments. They point out that even if someone lacks charity, and even though it is impossible for him to work himself into a state of charity, and even though charity must be poured into him by God – still, he can be willing to *cooperate* with God's grace. And if God does pour charity into him, then he can obey the Commandments.

---

[15] As in the *sed contra*, the Latin is *de genere bonorum*, literally "of the genus of good."
[16] At this point in the paraphrase I have had to take liberties. The Latin is *sed pro tempore illo quo aliquis habet caritatem.*

St. Thomas is not suggesting that by his own natural power, a person can *merit* the inflow of grace. Grace is an undeserved gift; God must help us even to receive His own help. Yet we are not passive in this process. As he writes in another place, "Infused virtue is caused in us by God without any action on our part, *but not without our consent* ... As to those things which are done by us, God causes them in us, *yet not without action on our part*, for He works in every will and in every nature."[17]

[4] These thinkers also deny the *sed contra*'s claim that to affirm the necessity of charity entails that a person who lacks charity commits mortal sin even when he does something good. The reason is that the commandment to love God is affirmative rather than negative: it commands doing something rather than forbidding doing something. Why should this matter? Because no affirmative precept can bind us to do something *all the time*. I must never treat my parents with disrespect, but I have the opportunity to treat them with respect only when I am dealing with them, not when I am washing the car. I must never act contrary to the love of God, but it would be impossible to perform every act of charity at every time; for example, I cannot teach class for the love of God when class is not in session.

The principle, then, is that although a negative precept must always be obeyed – I must *never* commit an act of stealing, *never* commit an act of murder, and so forth – an affirmative precept requires me to do something only at certain times and under certain conditions. St. Thomas writes elsewhere, "The sin of omission is contrary to an affirmative precept which binds *semper, sed non pro semper* – always, but not for always. Hence, by omitting to act, a man sins *only for the time at which the affirmative precept binds him to act*."[18]

The fact that affirmative precepts bind *semper, sed non pro semper* also sheds light on the quotation from St. Paul, "do all to the glory of God," which was quoted in Objection 2. For since this precept is affirmative, it does not require one to *always be doing everything that glorifies God* – that would be impossible. It is enough that when we *actually do some particular thing*, we do it for God's glory, and that we possess the *settled disposition* of acting in this way.[19]

[5] St. Thomas has presented such a convincing case for the first of the two contrary opinions that one might expect him to simply make it his own. But no: For some have *denied* that the precepts of Divine law require acting from charity, and as he is about to explain, there is something to be said for their view too.

---

[17] I-II, Q. 55, Art. 4, ad 6, emphasis added. I discuss this passage in *Commentary on Thomas Aquinas's Virtue Ethics* (Cambridge: Cambridge University Press, 2017).
[18] I-II, Q. 71, Art. 5, ad 3, emphasis added.
[19] See I-II, Q. 88, Art. 1, ad 2.

[6] *Both these opinions are true up to a certain point. Because the act of charity can be considered in two ways.* [7] *First, as an act by itself: and thus it falls under the precept of the law which specially prescribes it, viz. "Thou shalt love the Lord thy God," and "Thou shalt love thy neighbor."* [8] *In this sense, the first opinion is true. Because it is not impossible to observe this precept which regards the act of charity;* [9] *since man can dispose himself to possess charity, and when he possesses it, he can use it.* [10] *Secondly, the act of charity can be considered as being the mode of the acts of the other virtues, i.e. inasmuch as the acts of the other virtues are ordained to charity,* [11] *which is "the end of the commandment," as stated in 1 Tim. i.* [12] *for it has been said above (Question [12], Article [4]) that the intention of the end is a formal mode of the act ordained to that end.* [13] *In this sense the second opinion is true in saying that the mode of charity does not fall under the precept, that is to say that this commandment, "Honor thy father," does not mean that a man must honor his father from charity, but merely that he must honor him.* [14] *Wherefore he that honors his father, yet has not charity, does not break this precept: although he does break the precept concerning the act of charity, for which reason he deserves to be punished.*

Each position is partly true, because the act of charity can be viewed in two ways. First, the act can be viewed according to what it is in itself. Considering it this way, certain precepts of Divine law do require it – the ones which specifically command it: "You shall love the Lord your God" and "You shall love your neighbor." Taken this first way, the first opinion is true – because these precepts do require acting from charity, and this is not impossible. Why isn't it? Because although a man cannot *work himself into* charity, he *can* put himself in readiness to receive charity, and he *can* exercise it when he has it.

Second, the act of charity can be viewed as the way that the other virtues act, since the other virtues are directed to it – for as St. Paul writes to St. Timothy, charity is the purpose of the Commandments. For as we saw earlier in the *Summa*, one of the formal aspects of an act directed to a purpose is intending the achievement of that purpose. Taken this second way, the second opinion is true – that is, the precepts do *not* require acting from charity. For example, the commandment to honor one's father does not mean that one must honor him because of charity, but only that one must honor him. So a person who honors his father even though he lacks charity has not violated the commandment to honor his father. On the other hand, he *has* violated the commandment to love his neighbor – so even though not for the former reason, he does deserve punishment.

[6] The act of charity – the deed in which charity is actualized – may be viewed either with reference to the virtue of charity itself, or with reference to the relation of this virtue to the other virtues. Viewing it in the first way, the first opinion is true: the precepts of Divine law do require acting from charity. Viewing it in the second way, the second opinion is true: they don't. St. Thomas views the act from each of these two perspectives in turn.

[7] If we take the question "Do the precepts of Divine law require acting from charity?" as meaning "Do any of them *command the act of charity*

itself?" then the answer is yes. Not only does Divine law explicitly command the love of God, it explicitly commands the love of neighbor, who is made in God's image.

[8] Since it is impossible to require the impossible, we must also ask whether the precepts to love God and neighbor can actually be obeyed. At first it might seem that obedience is impossible, for as we have seen, no one can work himself up into charity by his own powers. Of course, with the acquired virtues, matters stand differently. A person who lacks the virtue of friendliness might, with difficulty, perform one friendly act, then another, then another, until eventually he is habituated to friendliness, and its performance has become second nature. But a person who lacks the virtue of charity cannot perform even that first act of charity, much less repeat it, so repetition cannot bring the virtue into existence. The only way to love God *is to have the love of God*, and this cannot occur unless God pours it into us. Despite this fact, St. Thomas says that the precepts to love God and neighbor *can* be obeyed.

[9] The reason the precepts to love God and neighbor can be obeyed is that even though I cannot produce charity in myself, I can make myself available to God, who can produce it in me. If I oppose God's grace, He will not force it on me. But if I cooperate with the grace that He offers, I can receive it, and if I receive it, I can exercise it.

[10] To view the act of charity as "the mode of the other virtues" means to view charity as their fulfillment, as the full development of the theme at which each one hints. For as we saw earlier,

- Acquired prudence guides us in making good decisions for the sake of earthly life, but prudence enlightened by infused charity guides us in making good decisions for the sake of eternal life with God.
- Acquired justice prompts us to give each person what is due to him in the light of ordinary reason, but justice illuminated by infused charity helps us to see what is due to him in the light of his being made in God's image.
- Acquired fortitude helps us to face frightening things to attain the goods of this life or resist what endangers them, but fortitude ennobled by infused charity helps us to face frightening things for the sake of the kingdom of heaven.
- Acquired temperance helps us to moderate our desires for the sake of earthly goods like health, but temperance strengthened by infused charity helps us to cleanse our desires of whatever makes us unfit to see God.

Acts motivated by the acquired virtues alone are virtuous only in a qualified sense. Acts motivated by the infused virtues – or, perhaps, by the acquired virtues when they are *penetrated and elevated* by infused charity[20] – are virtuous in an unqualified sense.

---

[20] "Since there is no merit without charity, the act of acquired virtue cannot be meritorious without charity. But other virtues are infused along with charity; hence, the act of acquired virtue can

[11] As we saw in Article 5, this quotation comes from a passage from a letter of St. Paul to St. Timothy. After urging his protégé to discourage the Christians in Ephesus from wasting their attention on fables and genealogies which do nothing to edify them, he concludes that the end or purpose of the commandment is "charity, from a pure heart, and a good conscience, and an unfeigned faith."[21]

The word which the DRA and other translations render as "commandment"[22] comes originally from the Greek word *parangelias*, which has a range of meanings including not only commandment but also instruction and charge. In choosing the first of these meanings, these translations take it as a reference to all of the Divine commandments, using the figure of speech in which a part represents a whole. However, some contemporary translations render the word as "our charge," which takes it as a reference to Paul's commission to serve as an apostle, mentioned in verse 1. But the latter way of taking it does not make good sense of the context. In verse 5, Paul does not seem to be speaking of his own authority, but criticizing the obsession of the Ephesians with matters which have nothing to do with how God wants them to live.

[12] As we saw in Article 9, whenever we will something for the sake of something else, the will operates in several different modes. Here, St. Thomas is merely calling attention to the fact that we intend the end *as acquired* by the means.

[13] If we take "the mode of charity" in the sense of intending the end as acquired by the means, then to ask whether the precepts of Divine law require acting in the mode of charity means to ask, "In doing the things which the precepts command, must one do them *as means* to charity – *for the sake* of the love of God and neighbor?" Taking the question this way, St. Thomas says the answer is no. True, certain precepts do command us to love God and neighbor, as we saw above. But not all of them do. Consider for example the commandment to treat one's parents with respect. *In itself* this precept can be fulfilled merely by treating them with respect; *in itself* it does not mean that one must do so for the sake of the love of God and neighbor.

[14] Suppose, then, that someone treats his father with respect. But suppose he is not doing it because he has charity. Is he obeying Divine law? St. Thomas concludes that

---

only be meritorious by the mediation of infused virtue. For the virtue ordered to an inferior end does not produce an act ordered to the superior end without the mediation of the superior virtue. Just as courage, which is a virtue of man as man, does not order its act to the political good except by the mediation of the courage, which is the virtue of man insofar as he is a citizen." Thomas Aquinas, *Disputed Question on the Virtues in General* [*De virtutibus in communi*], Q. 10, ad 4, in *Disputed Questions on Virtue*, translated by Ralph McInerny (South Bend, IN: St. Augustine's Press, 1999), p. 69.

[21] 1 Timothy 1:5 (DRA).
[22] Vulgate, *praecepti*.

Were the Moral Precepts to Be Obeyed According to Charity? 231

1. He *is* obeying the Divine commandment to honor his parents.
2. But he is *not* obeying the Divine commandment to love God and neighbor – for this commandment requires doing *all that we do* for the sake of the love of God and neighbor, a point explained more fully in the Reply to Objection 2.

The upshot of the *respondeo* is that Divine law as a whole requires charity, but that not every precept of Divine law *in itself* requires charity.

Reply to Objection 1. Our Lord did not say, "If thou wilt enter into life, keep one commandment"; but "keep" all "the commandments": among which is included the commandment concerning the love of God and our neighbor.

Reply to Objection 1. In speaking to the young man, Our Lord did not say that if he wished to enter into life, he must keep *one* commandment, but that he must *keep the commandments* – that is, keep all of them. Among these commandments are the precepts requiring love of God and neighbor.

St. Thomas agrees with the Objector that good deeds are not sufficient to bring a person into life unless they are done with charity, and he agrees that Divine law requires charity. However, he does *not* agree that each of the Commandments prescribes charity *in itself*.

In themselves, only the Commandments to love God and neighbor prescribe charity. However, they prescribe it in everything that we do. So if the question is "Must I obey each of the Commandments from charity?" then the answer is yes, but if the question is "Does each of the Commandments *in itself* require that the act it commands be done from charity?" then the answer is no.

Reply to Objection 2. [1] *The precept of charity contains the injunction that God should be loved from our whole heart, which means that all things would be referred to God.* [2] *Consequently man cannot fulfill the precept of charity, unless he also refer all things to God.* [3] *Wherefore he that honors his father and mother, is bound to honor them from charity, not in virtue of the precept, "Honor thy father and mother," but in virtue of the precept, "Thou shalt love the Lord thy God with thy whole heart."* [4] *And since these are two affirmative precepts, not binding for all times,* [5] *they can be binding, each one at a different time: so that it may happen*

Reply to Objection 2. The commandment to love God includes that He be loved *from our whole heart*. This means that *all* things he does must be done for His sake. Thus, no one can keep the commandment to love God unless he does do all things for His sake.

So a person who honors his father and mother *is* obligated to honor them from charity – but why? Because of the precept "Honor your father and mother?" No, because of the precept "you shall love the Lord your God with all your heart, and with all your soul, and with all your might."

And because these two precepts are "affirmative" – because they do not always bind one to a specific act – they

that a man fulfills the precept of honoring his father and mother, without at the same time breaking the precept concerning the omission of the mode of charity.	might be binding at different times. At a particular time, then, a man might obey the commandment to honor his father and mother *without* violating the commandment not to fail in charity.

[1] The Objector had argued that the precepts of Divine law do require doing everything for God, claiming proof in St. Paul's command to the Corinthians, "Do all to the glory of God." St. Thomas agrees that charity requires doing everything for God, and gives an even better proof, for the commandment which begins "Hear, O Israel: The Lord our God, the Lord is One;[23] and you shall love the Lord your God" continues with the description "with all your heart, and with all your soul, and with all your might." To love God with *all* my heart – with my *whole* heart – means not only loving Him without any division in the will but also loving Him in everything that I do. If I serve him in worship but not in paying my bills, taking care of my family, and pursuing my livelihood, then I am not truly serving Him. St. Thomas might also have cited the words of Christ in the Gospel of Matthew, "No one can serve two masters; for either he will hate the one and love the other, or he will be devoted to the one and despise the other."[24]

St. Thomas argues in another part of the *Summa* that everyone already does everything for the sake of his ultimate fulfillment. However, not everyone knows that this perfect consummation lies nowhere else but in God. The commandment in question directs us to recognize and love God Himself as the final end for which everything is to be done.[25]

[2] An explicit commandment requires that we practice charity; charity involves doing everything we do for God; therefore this commandment requires that we do everything we do for God.

[3] St. Thomas treats the Commandments to love God and to love neighbor as two branches of a single precept of charity. Now the Commandment to honor one's father and mother requires only treating them with respect. But the Commandment to practice charity requires doing *everything* for charity, including giving them respect. The requirement to have charity for them arises from the latter Commandment, not the former. We have seen almost the same point, with the same example, at the end of the *respondeo*, except that there the

---

[23] Substituting "The Lord our God, the Lord is One" for the RSV-CE's "The Lord our God is one Lord."
[24] Matthew 6:24 (RSV-CE).
[25] I-II, Q. 1, Art. 6, "Does man ordain all to the last end?"; I-II, Q. 5, Art. 8, "Does every man desire happiness?" For detailed discussion, see J. Budziszewski, *Commentary on Thomas Aquinas's Treatise on Happiness and Ultimate Purpose* (Cambridge: Cambridge University Press, 2020).

point was made with respect to disobedience, and here it is made with respect to obedience.

[4] The precepts to honor parents and to love God and neighbor are affirmative. As we saw before, affirmative precepts bind us *semper, sed non pro semper* – always, but not for always.

- The *always* part of the formula applies to the disposition: thus I should always be in readiness for an act of respect to my parents, and I should always be in readiness for an act of love, and I must never do anything contrary to this respect or to this love.
- The *but not for always* part of the formula applies to the act: thus I am not at all times and under all conditions required to perform a *particular act* of respect or of love.

[5] Let us call the time at which I am required to perform a *particular act* of respect to my parents time P, and the time at which I am required to perform a *particular act* of love of God and neighbor time Q. What St. Thomas suggests here is that times P and Q might be different. Should this be the case, then if I honor my parents at time P, but honor them for a motive different from love, I have not necessarily violated the precept to act from love.

At first the argument seems quite strange. To make it clear, we must bring in in the distinction among *levels* of charity. One might wish that St. Thomas had mentioned it here, but he does not develop it explicitly until much later in the *Summa*.[26] We find there that we can consider the fullness or perfection of charity in several ways:

1. The highest perfection of charity is to love God (and for His sake, neighbor) *as much as He is lovable*. Only God Himself can do this. He is not just the best among all good things, but Goodness Himself, in person – the infinite source of the goodness of everything else that is good. Finite creatures cannot fully grasp how good – and so lovable – He is.
2. The highest perfection *possible to us* is to love God *as much as we can*. No one in this life loves God as much as he can, but the blessed will be able to do this in heaven. By grace they will receive the power to love Him, not as much as He is lovable, but according to their uttermost uplifted capacity.
3. The highest perfection possible to us *in this life* is simply to remove all the *obstacles* to the movement of love toward God. But now another distinction is needed.
    a. Its first stage of development – we might call it the first perfection, attainable even by those who are just beginning to walk with God – is to remove everything which *opposes* turning to Him, such as mortal sin.

---

[26] II-II, Q. 184, Art. 2.

b. Its second stage of development – we might call it the second perfection, attained by those more advanced in walking with God – is to remove whatever hinders the mind from turning *more readily* to Him.

Since we are not at the moment speaking of the life to come, the only levels of perfection which concern us are 3.a and 3.b – the beginning and advanced stages of charity in this life. Both stages deserve to be viewed as obedience to charity. Yet as we see, for beginners this obedience takes the lower form of doing everything we do *in a way which does not destroy* charity, but for the advanced it takes the higher form of doing everything we do *in a way which furthers* charity.

Both forms of obedience concern everything we do – they "refer everything to God" – but the former is about avoiding roadblocks while the latter is about speeding ahead on the road that has been cleared. Neither kind of obedience can be accomplished without grace – both are infused – but the former is much easier and the latter is much better. Both kinds of obedience are about friendship with God, but the former is about the minimal requirements of such friendship, while the latter is about entering into it more fully and richly. As we will see in Question 108, Article 4, much the same distinction is involved in the contrast between precepts and counsels that we saw earlier in the discussion of Objection 1: For in one sense the young man who consults Jesus has been obeying the precepts, yet Christ says to him that *if he would be perfect* there is something more he must do.

Now if St. Thomas were thinking of an *advanced* person's obedience to the Commandment of charity, then it would make no sense at all to say that a person who honors his parents for a motive other than charity is acting in obedience to charity. The solution is that St. Thomas is thinking of a *beginner's* obedience to the Commandment of charity. In this sense, a person who honors his parents for a motive other than charity can be said to be acting in obedience to charity so long as he does nothing contrary to it.

Reply to Objection 3. [1] *Man cannot fulfill all the precepts of the law, unless he fulfill the precept of charity, which is impossible without charity.* [2] *Consequently it is not possible, as Pelagius maintained, for man to fulfill the law without grace.*

Reply to Objection 3. No one can obey *all* of the commands of Divine law unless he obeys the command to love God – and this is impossible without charity, [which in turn requires grace]. Therefore, Pelagius was mistaken in thinking that man can obey the Divine law without grace.

---

[1] Since Divine law includes an explicit Commandment to love God, no one can fulfill *all* of the Commandments unless he fulfills this one too. But to fulfill this one too means loving God, and no one can love God *unless, in fact, he has the supernaturally infused virtue of loving God.* The silent premise, which I have added to the paraphrase in square brackets – silent only because

St. Thomas considers it too obvious to need repeating – is that no one can possess this virtue without grace.

[2] Pelagius had held that man could fulfill the Divine law by his own powers alone, without superadded grace. As we see now, St. Thomas in no way accepts such a view. Because the law includes the precept of charity, he agrees that no one can fulfill *the Law* – the whole law – without the grace of charity. He merely points out that one can fulfill *certain* precepts of the law without the grace of charity. For example, one who treats his parents with honor, though without charity, has fulfilled the Commandment to treat them with honor; in this respect, he has not committed mortal sin. But he has violated the Commandment of charity itself; in this respect, he *has* committed mortal sin.

In the final analysis, to fail in charity is to fail to be directed to God. He is our ultimate purpose. How can we expect to reach our ultimate purpose if we are not even directed to it? An act such as honoring parents really is good taken in itself, and doing it without charity does not change that fact. The problem is that apart from the love of God, the act misses the point. It does not even grasp why human persons, such as parents, are *capable* of having anything owed to them – what gives them value as images of God – why they are not just *stuff*. God is the Author and Purpose of life; He is what life is about.

DISCUSSION

Love is Complicated

One might think that all acts are either required, forbidden, or indifferent. As we have found in our examination of the relation of the moral precepts to charity, matters are a good deal more complex.

Negative precepts concern acts we are commanded to omit and condemned for performing. These are forbidden at all times and under all conditions. They include venial sins, which injure the love of God and neighbor, as well as mortal sins, which destroy it.

Affirmative precepts concern acts we are commanded to perform and condemned for omitting, such as treating parents with respect. Although these are always to be kept in mind, they bind a person to do certain things only at certain times and under certain conditions. It is possible to honor parents from love, but it is possible to honor them from other motives as well. Honoring them from these other motives fulfills the commandment to honor them, but not the commandment of love.

Counsels concern acts we are urged to perform but not condemned for omitting, such as vowing perpetual virginity, or celibacy. These lift a person above bare adherence to the precepts. As we have seen, it is one thing merely to avoid what destroys love, and another to enter into it more deeply by removing everything which distracts from it.

It may seem that all these distinctions are splitting hairs. Isn't love supposed to be easy? One of the hits of my own generation said so. It's a golden song for singing in the shower. The singer croons that he "don't know much" about history, biology, "a science book," or "the French I took" –

> But I do know that I love you
> And I know that if you love me too
> What a wonderful world this would be.[27]

There you have it. The liberal arts, languages, and the natural sciences are hard, but love is simple, and it makes everything all right.

The illusion of thinking that love is simple arises mostly from considering it a feeling – in the case of the song, an erotic feeling – although no doubt it underestimates the complexity of the feelings too. Certainly love involves feelings, but in essence it is not a feeling at all, but a commitment of the will. If it were just a feeling, then it would be absurd for a bride and groom to vow to love each other, for one cannot promise to have a feeling.

What one can promise is whatever lies in the power of the will. One of the difficulties is that our wills are fallen. But if the will is uplifted by grace, and if it persists in cooperation with this grace, then it lies in the power of the will to do everything for the sake of God, and, for His sake, always to act for the true good of our neighbor.

---

[27] Sam Cooke, "Wonderful World" (1960).

QUESTION 100, ARTICLE 11

Whether it is Right to Distinguish Other Moral Precepts of the Law Besides the Decalogue?

TEXT	PARAPHRASE
Whether it is right to distinguish other moral precepts of the law besides the Decalogue?	Is it appropriate that the Old Law includes additional moral precepts, distinct from the Ten Commandments?

Besides the Ten Commandments, the Old Testament contains a host of other moral precepts. Were they really needed? Why isn't the Decalogue enough? Unlike the previous two Articles, which focus on the manner in which the Law must be followed, this one focuses on its architecture: on the relation among (1) the two precepts of love of God and neighbor, (2) the Decalogue itself, and (3) all the other Old Law moral rules.

Objection 1. [1] *It would seem that it is wrong to distinguish other moral precepts of the law besides the decalogue. Because, as Our Lord declared (Mt. 22), "on these two commandments" of charity "dependeth the whole law and the prophets."* [2] *But these two commandments are explained by the ten commandments of the decalogue. Therefore there is no need for other moral precepts.*	Objection 1. It seems that it isn't. Christ, Our Lord, says in the Gospel of Matthew that the entire content of the Law and the entire teaching of the Prophets depend on the two commandments of love of God and neighbor. But these two commandments are sufficiently unfolded and set forth in the ten precepts of the Decalogue, so no other moral precepts are required.

[1] When asked which commandment in the Old Law is the greatest, Christ replied with two which are closely connected. Interestingly, they are greatest commandments not just in the sense that they are most important, but in the sense that in some way the others hinge upon them:

When the Pharisees heard that he had silenced the Sadducees, they came together. And one of them, a lawyer, asked him a question, to test him. "Teacher, which is the great commandment in the law?" And he said to him, "You shall love the Lord your God with all your heart, and with all your soul, and with all your mind. This is the great and first commandment. And a second is like it, You shall love your neighbor as yourself. *On these two commandments depend all the law and the prophets."*[1]

We see something like this in the case of the virtues too: Although there are many acquired virtues, all of them hinge upon justice, fortitude, temperance, and prudence, and although there are many infused virtues, all of them hinge upon faith, hope, and charity or love.

[2] The idea is that although the two commandments of charity provide the *basis* for the law, their implications need to be worked out in greater detail. The Two provide the purpose of the Ten; the Ten explain the ramifications of the Two. The Objector suggests that there would be a good reason for additional moral precepts if the Ten did not fully explicate the Two, but they do, so these others are unnecessary.

Objection 2. [1] *Further, the moral precepts are distinct from the judicial and ceremonial precepts, as stated above.* [2] *But the determinations of the general moral precepts belong to the judicial and ceremonial precepts:* [3] *and the general moral precepts are contained in the decalogue, or are even presupposed to the decalogue,* [4] *as stated above.* [5] *Therefore it was unsuitable to lay down other moral precepts besides the decalogue.*	Objection 2. Moreover, we have already seen that the moral precepts differ from the judicial and ceremonial. Further, we have seen that the *general* moral rules are included in or presupposed by the Decalogue, and the more detailed *determinations* of these general moral rules are contained in the judicial and ceremonial rules. So it was inappropriate to set forth still further moral rules.

---

[1] As we have seen, the moral precepts are general principles of conduct, but the judicial and ceremonial precepts "determine" them – they set forth in detail the manner in which these general principles are to be followed.

[2] St. Thomas explains the point in the following passage from I-II, Question 99, Article 4, which we have already covered in this commentary.

It belongs to the Divine law to direct men to one another and to God. Now each of these belongs in the abstract to the dictates of the natural law, to which dictates the moral precepts are to be referred: yet each of them has to be determined by Divine or human law, because naturally known principles are universal, both in speculative and in practical matters. Accordingly just as the determination of the universal principle about Divine worship is effected by the ceremonial precepts, so the determination of the general precepts of that justice which is to be observed among men is effected by the judicial precepts.

---

[1] Matthew 22:34-40 (RSV-CE), emphasis added.

We must therefore distinguish three kinds of precept in the Old Law; viz. "moral" precepts, which are dictated by the natural law; "ceremonial" precepts, which are determinations of the Divine worship; and "judicial" precepts, which are determinations of the justice to be maintained among men.

[3] For example, the Decalogue *contains* the general moral precept that we should honor parents, and *presupposes* that we should be grateful to them for bringing us into the world and caring for us.

[4] The matter is explained in some detail in I-II, Question 100, Article 3, which we will examine in chunks. Here is the first chunk:

> The decalogue includes those precepts the knowledge of which man has immediately from God. Such are those which with but slight reflection can be gathered at once from the first general principles: and those also which become known to man immediately through divinely infused faith.

The most general of the "first general principles" are love of God and neighbor. The Decalogue contains their immediate implications. All of these implications are obvious – but to whom? Some of them are obvious to everyone, others are obvious only to those who have faith. It would have been helpful if St. Thomas had told us which precepts belong in each category. Some would place the precepts in the Second Tablet, concerning our duties to neighbor, in the category "obvious to everyone," while placing those in the First Tablet, concerning our duties to God, in the category "obvious only to those who have faith." I have suggested in the commentary on I-II, Question 100, Article 1, that the matter is more complex. If natural reason were utterly unable to grasp the wrong of worshipping idols or speaking irreverently of God – if all such knowledge depended entirely on faith – then St. Thomas could not claim, as he does, that such precepts belong to natural law. In fact, we need Divine instruction about them even though we do have an inkling of them. Under the conditions of the Fall, natural reason tends to squint and requires corrective lenses. Thus the passage in Q. 100, Article 3, continues,

> Consequently two kinds of precepts are not reckoned among the precepts of the decalogue: viz. first general principles, for they need no further promulgation after being once imprinted on the natural reason to which they are self-evident; as, for instance, that one should do evil to no man, and other similar principles: and again those which the careful reflection of wise men shows to be in accord with reason; since the people receive these principles from God, through being taught by wise men.

Although reason is not entirely without a clue about certain things, the teaching of wise and faithful persons makes them explicit; this is how reason's squint is corrected. Finally, the passage goes on,

> Nevertheless both kinds of precepts are contained in the precepts of the decalogue; yet in different ways. For the first general principles are contained in them, as principles in their proximate conclusions; while those which are known through wise men are contained, conversely, as conclusions in their principles.

Here the Objector argues that matters can be silently "contained" in the Decalogue even if they are not stated in it explicitly. It might at first seem that matters stand as follows:

- The prohibition of murder is contained in the Decalogue.
- The prohibition of doing evil to others, which is a general principle of practical reason, is not contained in the Decalogue.
- The prohibition of murderous hatred, which is found in Leviticus 19:17, is not contained in the Decalogue.

But according to the Objector, that way of thinking is incorrect. Actually,

- The prohibition of murder is explicitly contained in the Decalogue.
- The prohibition of doing evil to others is contained in the Decalogue as a *presupposition* of the prohibition of murder – for principles are implicitly contained in whatever follows from them.
- The prohibition of murderous hatred is contained in the Decalogue as an *implication* of the prohibition of murder – for conclusions are implicitly contained in the principles from which they follow.

[5] The Objector does not say exactly how this conclusion follows from his premises; he expects us to see it for ourselves. The inference works like this:

1. The first principles of moral reasoning did not need to be stated in the Old Law, because the Decalogue presupposes them.
2. The additional moral precepts did not need to be stated in the Old Law, because the Decalogue implies them.
3. Therefore the Decalogue is sufficient. There was no need for the Old Law to include any other moral precepts.

The Objector's premises do not seem to contain anything to which St. Thomas must object. But does his conclusion follow? For this we await St. Thomas's Reply.

Objection 3. [1] *Further, the moral precepts are about the acts of all the virtues, as stated above.* [2] *Therefore, as the Law contains, besides the decalogue, moral precepts pertaining to religion, liberality, mercy, and chastity;* [3] *so there should have been added some precepts pertaining to the other virtues, for instance, fortitude, sobriety, and so forth. And yet such is not the case. It is therefore unbecoming to distinguish other moral precepts in the Law besides those of the decalogue.*

Objection 3. Besides, we have shown that the moral precepts propose acts of *all* of the virtues. Now in addition to the Decalogue, the Old Law includes rules which address acts of *some* of the virtues – religion, liberality, mercy and chastity. So by this standard, it should also have included rules which address acts of the *rest* of the virtues, such as fortitude and soberness. Since it doesn't include the latter, it shouldn't have included the former; it should have stopped with the Decalogue.

[1] In the second Article of this Question, St. Thomas reminds his readers of his previous argument that the purpose of law is to promote the common good of the community. As he wrote in the second Article of I-II, Question 90, "Since the law is chiefly ordained to the common good, any other precept in regard to some individual work, must needs be devoid of the nature of a law, save insofar as it regards the common good."[2]

However, the meaning of promoting the common good depends on which community we have in mind. For the civil community, it means regulating the relations among the citizens, that is, upholding public justice. Although human law may address acts of other virtues besides justice, it does so "only insofar as they assume the nature of justice." For example, it may command speaking the truth when giving testimony, but only because this particular act of truthfulness is due, in justice, to the community.

By contrast, Divine law is made for a community under God. For two reasons, here the common good acquires a broader meaning. The first is that the people must be directed not only in relation to each other, but in relation to God; the second that they must be directed not only with a view to this life but with a view to the life to come. Now since the aspect of man by which he bears God's image is his mind, it is through his mind that he is joined in friendship with God. Therefore, Divine law seeks to set his mind in proper order. This task has two aspects: First, reason in itself must be set in order. Second, reason must be enabled to regulate his actions and passions. The former aspect of the task is accomplished by the intellectual virtues, and the latter by the moral virtues. Thus, Divine law concerns itself not only with acts of justice, but with acts of *all* the virtues, just as the Objector says, and it concerns itself with them not only when they "assume the nature of justice," but in all sorts of cases.

Just one qualification is needed, for as we saw in the previous Article, in the story of the wealthy young man who questioned Jesus about what he must do to have eternal life, some acts of virtue are addressed by precepts, which command, while others are addressed by counsels, which urge without commanding. Which are which? St. Thomas's answer is that "certain matters, without which the order of virtue, which is the order of reason, cannot even exist, come under an obligation of precept; while other matters, which pertain to the well-being of *perfect* [complete] virtue, come under an admonition of counsel."[3]

[2] The term "religion" refers not to the social institution of religion but to the virtue which disposes us to render to God the fidelity we owe Him in deeds, the reverence we owe Him in words, and the service we owe Him in thoughts – not that we can ever fully repay Him for what He has given us. The term "liberality" refers to generosity in small matters, as distinguished from

---

[2] I-II, Q. 90, Art. 2.
[3] I-II, Q. 100, Art. 2, emphasis added.

generosity in large matters, which is traditionally called "magnanimity." "Mercy" is the virtue which directs the compassion for another's misery which impels us to offer succor. "Chastity" is the branch of the virtue of temperance which regulates us with respect to sexual pleasures.

Old Law precepts that supplement the Decalogue concerning religion include, for example, rules for the annual Day of Atonement.[4] Those concerning liberality include requirements about leaving some of the harvest to be gleaned by the poor.[5] Those concerning mercy include provisions for Cities of Refuge to which those who have killed accidentally can flee to escape from revenge.[6] Those concerning chastity include prohibitions of sexual intercourse among unmarried persons and close relations.[7]

[3] The Objector has already made it impossible to claim that like human law, Divine law is concerned *only* with justice. It seems, then, that Divine law might have taken either of two approaches:

- It might have stopped with the Decalogue, omitting *all* additional moral precepts (which seems to be what the Objector would prefer), or
- It might have included additional moral precepts about *each* of the moral virtues.

However, he says, it does neither of these things. Instead, while commanding acts of some of the virtues besides justice, it ignores the rest of them. Such inconsistency, he thinks, is unbefitting.

On the contrary, [1] *It is written (Ps. 18): "The law of the Lord is unspotted, converting souls."* [2] *But man is preserved from the stain of sin, and his soul is converted to God by other moral precepts besides those of the decalogue. Therefore it was right for the Law to include other moral precepts.*

On the other hand, we read in the Psalms that the law of the Lord is untainted[8] and converts souls. But is it only by the Ten Commandments that man is kept from the taint[9] of sin and his soul is converted to God? No, the observance of other moral rules does this too. Therefore it was fitting for the Law to include them.

---

[1] The *sed contra* is quoting from a passage in the book of Psalms, which reads in the DRA as follows:

The law of the Lord is unspotted, converting souls: the testimony of the Lord is faithful, giving wisdom to little ones. The justices of the Lord are right, rejoicing

---

[4] Leviticus 16, 23:26–32.
[5] Leviticus 19:9–10, Leviticus 23:22; Deuteronomy 24:19–22, Numbers 29:7–11.
[6] Exodus 21:12–14, Numbers 35:9–34, Deuteronomy 19:1–13; compare Joshua 20.
[7] Leviticus 18:6–18, 20:11–21; Deuteronomy 22:30, 27:20, 22–23.
[8] *Immaculata.*
[9] *Macula.*

hearts: the commandment of the Lord is lightsome, enlightening the eyes. The fear of the Lord is holy, enduring for ever and ever: the judgments of the Lord are true, justified in themselves. More to be desired than gold and many precious stones: and sweeter than honey and the honeycomb. For thy servant keepeth them, and in keeping them there is a great reward.[10]

The psalmist calls the Law spotless because it *makes the soul* spotless, using a figure of speech in which the effect of a thing is attributed to the thing itself (a variety of metalepsis). To be converted (*convertens*) means to be *turned around* – reoriented toward God – and so transformed.

[2] The argument works like this:

1. Divine law is a body of precepts that preserve man from the stain of sin and turn his soul to God.
2. Therefore, it is fitting that whatever precepts do these things be included in Divine law.
3. But the moral precepts of Divine law that are not listed in the Decalogue do these things.
4. Therefore, it is fitting for these moral precepts not listed in the Decalogue to be included in Divine law.

I answer that, [1] *As is evident from what has been stated, the judicial and ceremonial precepts derive their force from their institution alone: since before they were instituted, it seemed of no consequence whether things were done in this or that way.* [2] *But the moral precepts derive their efficacy from the very dictate of natural reason, even if they were never included in the Law.* [3] *Now of these there are three grades: for some are most certain, and so evident as to need no promulgation; such as the commandments of the love of God and our neighbor, and others like these,* [4] *as stated above,* [5] *which are, as it were, the ends of the commandments;* [6] *wherefore no man can have an erroneous judgment about them.* [7] *Some precepts are more*

Here is my response. From our previous arguments it follows that the judicial and ceremonial precepts are binding just because they were commanded, for before that, it seemed to make no difference which way things were done. But with the moral precepts, matters stand otherwise: their authority arises from the dictate of natural reason, and would be binding even if the law had never proposed them.

Among the latter, we find three levels:

1. Some are so certain and so obvious that they do not need to be declared. As we have seen, these include the commandments to love God and neighbor, as well as others of the sort. They may be viewed as the purposes for which all other precepts are made. Therefore, no one's rational judgment about them can go astray.
2. Other precepts pin down in greater detail the manner in which these

---

[10] Psalm 18:8–12 (DRA). In most contemporary translations this passage is numbered 19:7–11.

detailed, the reason of which even an uneducated man can easily grasp; and yet they need to be promulgated, because human judgment, in a few instances, happens to be led astray concerning them: these are the precepts of the decalogue. [8] Again, there are some precepts the reason of which is not so evident to everyone, but only the wise; these are moral precepts added to the decalogue, and given to the people by God through Moses and Aaron.	obvious precepts are to be followed. Even an ordinary person can immediately see the reason for them. And yet, because in a few cases a man's judgment about them may be perverted, they do need to be declared. These are the Ten Commandments. 3. For still other precepts, however, the reason is not equally obvious to everyone, but only to those who have wisdom. These are the rules superadded to the Ten Commandments, given to the people by God through Moses and Aaron.

[1] Both in human and Divine law, the very fact of enactment, or institution, can generate a new obligation. Suppose there were no traffic laws; then although drivers would be obligated to take care for the safety of others, they would not be obligated to drive on the right side of the road. It would make just as much sense to drive on the left (though driving on either side would be dangerous!). But now suppose a traffic law has been enacted, designating the right side of the road as the one drivers should use. Then a new obligation, "Drive on the right," would have come into being from institution alone. So it is with all of the precepts called "determinations." By enactment, or institution, they pin down how to follow a general precept when, prior to enactment, a number of ways would remained open, but when not all of these ways can be followed – or safely followed – at once.

Determination differs from the other way of deriving detailed precepts from general ones, called "conclusion" or "conclusion from premises." From the general precept "Do not murder," the detailed precept "Do not murder by poisoning" is derived by conclusion; it is a strict logical inference. But the detailed precept "Punish murder by imprisonment" is derived by determination; it is not a logical inference, but a choice among various possible punishments.

The point made here is that the ceremonial and judicial precepts of Divine law are derived from its general moral precepts by determination, not conclusion, so that their authority rests not on sheer inference, but on enactment. As to the ceremonial precepts, it is one thing for God to say that one should worship God, but it is another thing for Him to specify that He be worshipped with particular sacrifices and offerings. As to the judicial precepts, it is one thing for Him to say that one should be just to others, for example by not committing adultery, but it is another thing for Him to arrange the details of who may marry and how adulterers should be treated.[11]

---

[11] Concerning ceremonial precepts, see I-II, Q. 99, Art. 3, ad 2; concerning judicial, see Q. 99, Art. 4.

The Decalogue's Moral Precepts in Relation to Others

Although we are developing this point in the context of Divine law, it also applies to Divine "right" or justice. What is right, or due, or owed, to someone depends in part on natural justice but also in part on institution or enactment. It is naturally right that those who do good are honored; concerning *how* they are to be honored, something more is needed.[12]

[2] By contrast, the moral precepts are conclusions rather than determinations. Unlike determinations, they do not derive their authority just from enactment. Rather they express rules, or principles from which rules spring, which could not reasonably be other than they are.

[3] The mind spontaneously recognizes a number of truths. In the realm of theoretical reason – reasoning about *what is* – these include the principle of noncontradiction, the principle that a whole is greater than its proper part, and the principle that things equal to a third thing are equal to each other. In the realm of practical reason – reasoning about *what is to be done* – the most important is the principle of love of God and neighbor; the "others like these" which St. Thomas mentions are such principles as that good is to be done and evil is to be avoided, and that no one do undeserved harm to anyone else. The legislator does not need to announce such things because they are obvious.

[4] In an earlier passage, St. Thomas called these truths the "first general principles" which "need no further promulgation after being once imprinted on the natural reason to which they are self-evident."[13] It may be puzzling that here he says they need no promulgation, but there he said they need no *further* promulgation. The explanation of the puzzle is that they do not need to be made known *in words* because they are already so plainly made known *through the design of the created intellect*. Natural law is an imprint, or a reflection, of the eternal law; it is how the finite rational mind shares in the infinite wisdom by which God created and governs the universe.[14] Moreover, as we saw above, such truths are contained *in a sense* in the Decalogue even though they are not stated there explicitly, because they are presupposed by the ones that are stated there explicitly.

[5] These general principles are the purposes for which all other rules are given. It is *for the sake* of the love of God that we are commanded to worship Him, keep the Sabbath, and speak reverently of Him; it is *for the sake* of the love of neighbor that we are commanded to honor our parents, and not murder, commit adultery, steal, bear false witness, or crave what is not ours.

[6] The rightness of loving God and neighbor is obvious to everyone. If someone says "It isn't obvious to *me* that I should love God and neighbor," he is not being honest with himself. He may not love God and neighbor, and he

---

[12] See II-II, Q. 57, Art. 2.
[13] I-II, Q. 100, Art. 3.
[14] See I-II, Q. 91, Art. 2; Q. 93, Art. 2; and Q. 94, entire.

may not feel bad about not loving them, but at some level he knows that he should love them. These are things we *can't not know*.

[7] St. Thomas does not speak of an "uneducated man" but of a *popularis*, an ordinary member of the community. The term translated mildly as "led astray" is *perverti*, which carries the strong meaning of subversion or corruption. There is a certain tension between the claim that an ordinary person "can easily" grasp the truth of the precepts of the Decalogue, and his claim that nevertheless human judgment about them is sometimes subverted. The crucial point seems to be what kind of subversion this is. Many readers, perhaps most, leap to the conclusion that the way reason is perverted is that we *might not even know* that these precepts are true – that we may be wholly ignorant of the right of honoring parents, the wrong of murder, the wrong of theft, and so on. However, it is impossible for this to be what St. Thomas means. As we saw in the first Article of the present Question, he writes, "there are certain things which the natural reason of *every* man, of its own accord and at once, judges to be done or not to be done: e.g. 'Honor thy father and thy mother,' and 'Thou shalt not kill, Thou shalt not steal': and these belong to the law of nature absolutely."[15]

Plainly, if all men judge that these precepts should be observed, *and yet* in some cases their judgment about them is subverted, then the subversion of judgment *cannot* mean that they do not know they should be observed. What then does it mean? The solution is found in another place, where St. Thomas remarks that although broad rules like this cannot be completely erased from the mind, they can be blotted out "in the case of a particular action, insofar as reason is hindered from applying the general principle to a particular point of practice."[16] So it isn't that I haven't an inkling of the wrong of murder, theft, or dishonor to parents, for I do. But perhaps I am so full of passion that I do not allow myself to dwell upon the reality of what I am doing. Or perhaps I am so determined to commit the deed that I lie to myself about the reality – I say "But *this* isn't *that* sort of thing!" And yet it is – and in fact, I know better.[17]

For example, St. Thomas points out that the ancient German tribes did not consider raiding other tribes as wrong.[18] Unfortunately, the Blackfriars translation of the passage in which he says this – "thus formerly, theft, although it is expressly contrary to the natural law, was not considered wrong among the Germans, as Julius Caesar relates" – is dreadfully misleading, and misinterpretations of the passage have given rise to endless confusion. Actually, the passage

---

[15] I-II, Q. 100, Art. 1, emphasis added.
[16] I-II, Q. 94, Art. 6.
[17] I present a complete development of this theme in "'The Same as to Knowledge,'" in Christopher Wolfe and Steven Brust, eds., *Natural Law Today: The Present State of the Perennial Philosophy* (Lanham, MD: Lexington Books, 2018).
[18] I-II, Q. 94, Art. 4.

has nothing to do with theft in general. *Latrocinium*, the word mistranslated "theft," actually means banditry, or plundering. It is a *particular form* of robbery, or taking by force, which, like Roman law, St. Thomas distinguishes from theft, or taking by stealth. The ancient Germans knew very well that banditry is wrong, for as we find in the source which St. Thomas cites, the sixth book of Julius Caesar's *Commentaries on the Gallic Wars*, they punished it severely. The problem, then, is they cut themselves an exception; they refused to admit to themselves that raiding other tribes was banditry.[19]

Such distortions of moral thought are common in every age. In ours, for instance, people of various persuasions admit that murder is wrong but try to convince themselves that honor killing, abortion, or the deliberate bombing of noncombatants isn't murder. The function of the Ten Commandments, then, seems to be not to tell the people something they might not otherwise know, but to confront them with it by putting it in words: to hold it before their minds, so that evasions are more difficult.

[8] This completes the gradation of Old Law precepts:

- The first level includes the principles which *underlie* the Decalogue. These are the starting points of all moral reasoning; we use them at all times, even without realizing that we are doing so. They are so obvious that they don't need to be listed in the Decalogue explicitly. Although the Scriptures mention them too, the primary manner in which they are promulgated is the way that God fashioned our minds; they are written on the tablets of the heart.[20]
- The second level includes the Ten Commandments themselves. These are immediate implications of the first principles. Although they are obvious enough for everyone to recognize their truth, they are not so obvious that no one is ever tempted to twist them or play games with his own moral knowledge. The Decalogue is a constant reminder of them. God Himself inscribed these Commandments on tablets of stone.
- The third level includes all the rest of the moral precepts. As St. Thomas is about to explain, these are derived from the Ten Commandments – we might say they are derived *from what is derived* from the first principles. Although they are clear enough when explained by those who have wisdom, people do not necessarily grasp them without help. We know these not because God wrote them on the tablets of the heart, and not because he wrote them on tablets of stone, but because he announced them through the intermediation of His servants Moses and Aaron.

---

[19] I make the same point in *Commentary on Aquinas's Treatise on Law* and take it up at full length in the *Companion to the Commentary* (both Cambridge: Cambridge University Press, 2014). The *Companion* is available at www.cambridge.org/files/3614/2469/5786/9781107029392_-_Companion_to_the_Commentary.pdf.
[20] The expression is from Romans 2:14-16.

[9] But since the things that are evident are the principles whereby we know those that are not evident, [10] these other moral precepts added to the decalogue are reducible to the precepts of the decalogue, as so many corollaries. [11] Thus the first commandment of the decalogue forbids the worship of strange gods: and to this are added other precepts forbidding things relating to worship of idols: thus it is written (Dt. 18): "Neither let there be found among you anyone that shall expiate his son or daughter, making them to pass through the fire: ... neither let there be any wizard nor charmer, nor anyone that consulteth pythonic spirits,[21] or fortune-tellers, or that seeketh the truth from the dead." [12] The second commandment forbids perjury. To this is added the prohibition of blasphemy (Lev. 24) and the prohibition of false doctrine (Dt. 13). [13] To the third commandment are added all the ceremonial precepts. [14] To the fourth commandment prescribing the honor due to parents, is added the precept about honoring the aged, according to Lev. 19. "Rise up before the hoary head, and honor the person of the aged man"; and likewise all the precepts prescribing the reverence to be observed towards our betters, or kindliness towards our equals or inferiors. [15] To the fifth commandment, which forbids murder, is added the prohibition of hatred and of any kind of violence inflicted on our neighbor, according to Lev. 19, "Thou shalt not stand against the blood of thy neighbor": likewise the prohibition against hating one's brother (Lev. 19): "Thou shalt not hate thy brother in thy heart." [16] To the sixth commandment which forbids adultery, is added the prohibition about whoredom, according

But we come to know things that are *not* obvious from principles or starting points that *are* obvious. For this reason, the extra moral precepts – the ones in the third category – are, so to speak, superadded to the Ten Commandments, and can be traced back to them. Let us see how:

- The First Commandment prohibits the worship of gods other than God – and additional precepts forbid things pertaining to idolatry. For example, no one is to "pass his children through the fire" (that is, make sacrifices of them), no one is to deal in black magic or enchantments, and no one is to consult demons, "gods," or the spirits of the dead.
- The Second Commandment prohibits perjury – and additional precepts forbid blasphemy and false doctrine.
- The Third Commandment commands keeping the Sabbath – and the entire set of ceremonial precepts is added.
- The Fourth Commandment commands giving honor to parents – and additional precepts require honor to the old, such as "rise up in the presence of a gray head, and honor the face of the aged." To much the same effect are all the precepts about giving reverence to our superiors – or, for that matter, doing good to our equals or inferiors.
- The Fifth Commandment prohibits murder – and additional precepts forbid hatred and every sort of violation of our neighbor. Examples include "Do not stand up against your neighbor's life" and "Do not hate your brother in your heart."

---

[21] A spirit of divination, one consulted for knowledge of the future or of things which are obscure.

to Dt. 23, "There shall be no whore among the daughters of Israel, nor whoremonger among the sons of Israel"; and the prohibition against unnatural sins, according to Lev. 28. "Thou shalt not lie with mankind ... thou shalt not copulate with any beast." [17] To the seventh commandment which prohibits theft, is added the precept forbidding usury, according to Dt. 23. "Thou shalt not lend to thy brother money to usury"; and the prohibition against fraud, according to Dt. 25. "Thou shalt not have divers weights in thy bag"; and universally all prohibitions relating to peculations and larceny. [18] To the eighth commandment, forbidding false testimony, is added the prohibition against false judgment, according to Ex. 23. "Neither shalt thou yield in judgment, to the opinion of the most part, to stray from the truth"; and the prohibition against lying: "Thou shalt fly lying," and the prohibition against detraction, according to Lev. 19. "Thou shalt not be a detractor, nor a whisperer among the people." [19] To the other two commandments no further precepts are added, because thereby are forbidden all kinds of evil desires.

- The Sixth Commandment prohibits adultery – and additional precepts forbid prostitution ("There shall be no whore among Israel's daughters, nor pursuer of whores among Israel's sons") as well as sins against the sexual pattern of our nature ("Do not join sexually with another man," "do not copulate with a beast").
- The Seventh Commandment forbids theft – and to it are conjoined not only the prohibitions of usury ("Do not lend your brother at interest") and fraud ("You shall not carry two standards of weight in your bag"), but in general all the prohibitions of financial subterfuge and plundering.
- The Eight Commandment bans false testimony – and additional precepts forbid false judgment ("In judgment, do not acquiesce to the majority and so deviate from the truth") lying ("fly from lying"), and slander ("Do not be a denouncer or a whisperer among the people").

Though no precepts are added to the Ninth and Tenth Commandments, none are needed, since they forbid every sort of wicked desire.

---

[9] We learn a theorem, which at first is not obviously true, by working forward from the axioms, which are obviously true. We discern the solution to a puzzle, which is not clear, from piecing together the clues, which are clear. We acquire calculus, which we do not possess, by making use of arithmetic, algebra, and trigonometry, which we do possess. We perceive the shape of the face in the darkened room, which is obscure, by considering the variations in hue and shadow, which are not so obscure. In all knowledge we make progress by moving from what is more plain to what is less plain.

[10] St. Thomas says these superadded moral precepts can be traced back to the Ten Commandments as "certain additions" to them (*cuiusdam additionis*). Although the term *additionis* was sometimes used in mathematics, in this context the mathematical term "corollaries" is a little misleading, because a corollary is derived from a principle by way of conclusion – by strict inference. As we have seen, however, not all of the additional precepts are derived in this way, for some of them are derived by way of determination. St. Thomas is

simply saying that in the same way we grasp other difficult things by reasoning from things that are less difficult, we grasp the goodness of the additional moral precepts of the Old Law from the moral precepts of the Decalogue.

[11] The First Commandment prohibits not only the worship of false gods, but everything which is connected with it or that smacks of it. Thus the Old Law commands:

> When you come into the land which the Lord your God gives you, you shall not learn to follow the abominable practices of those nations. There shall not be found among you any one who burns his son or his daughter as an offering, anyone who practices divination, a soothsayer, or an augur, or a sorcerer, or a charmer, or a medium, or a wizard, or a necromancer. For whoever does these things is an abomination to the Lord; and because of these abominable practices the Lord your God is driving them out before you.[22]

It would be unwise to consider ourselves above all that weirdness. Although we no longer sacrifice our sons and daughters by fire to the gods of fertility, we sacrifice them by knives to the gods of sterility. As to the rest of the practices mentioned, it is immaterial to the validity of the prohibitions whether people can really tell the future, speak to the dead, or cast evil spells. Those who think they can – both practitioners and clients – do a great deal of harm even in the present life. Moreover, they are ruining not only their own souls but also those of others, by promulgating false beliefs such as the omnipotence of fate and the associated denial of personal responsibility. Their purpose is to gain favors, or attain mastery, by placating false gods, conniving with evil powers, or perverting the course of nature.

Does this claim seem exaggerated? Curiously, the high-tech forms that charms and wizardry sometimes take today are not usually recognized for what they are. A person who ingests hallucinogens because they make him feel divine, more than human, or in touch with another world, is really practicing what used to be called mediumistic sorcery. Similarly, a man who uses the "date rape" drug Rohypnol to induce a woman's sexual compliance is employing what used to be called a love philtre. The authentic means of contacting divinity are to pray and to practice charity, and the authentic means of cultivating love are to be kind and chaste.

[12] The Second Commandment forbids taking God's name in vain, and by extension condemns all empty forms of speech about Him. Thus, the Old Law forbids blasphemy not only by Hebrews but also by resident aliens: "And say to the people of Israel, Whoever curses his God shall bear his sin. He who blasphemes the name of the Lord shall be put to death; all the congregation shall stone him; the sojourner as well as the native, when he blasphemes the

---

[22] Deuteronomy 18:9-12 (RSV-CE), substituting "anyone" for "any one."

Name, shall be put to death."²³ It forbids the teaching of false prophecy and doctrine like this:

If a prophet arises among you, or a dreamer of dreams, and gives you a sign or a wonder, and the sign or wonder which he tells you comes to pass, and if he says, "Let us go after other gods," which you have not known, "and let us serve them," you shall not listen to the words of that prophet or to that dreamer of dreams; for the Lord your God is testing you, to know whether you love the Lord your God with all your heart and with all your soul. You shall walk after the Lord your God and fear him, and keep his commandments and obey his voice, and you shall serve him and cleave to him.²⁴

Up to this point the passage merely admonishes the people not to listen to such false teachers. It goes on, however, to declare the penalty for them, which raises questions about the proper range of religious toleration. We return to these questions in the Discussion at the end of the Article.

[13] Although previously St. Thomas has explained that moral and ceremonial precepts are different, here he is treating the ceremonial precepts, such as the rules about sacrifices, as belonging to the additional *moral* precepts. He calls them moral because they are *determinations of* those moral precepts which have to do with the worship of God. Chiefly they extend the idea behind the commandment to honor the Sabbath.

[14] A student studying Thomas Aquinas once asked me why the Angelic Doctor should have included "Rise up before the hoary head, and honor the person of the aged man"²⁵ among the precepts that need to be inculcated by the wise. For haven't almost all men in almost all times and places venerated persons of advanced years? Why do they need the wise to teach them this? Perhaps the reason almost all men in almost all times and places have venerated persons of advanced years is exactly that the wise *have* taught them this. For unfortunately, not all people find the rightness of honoring the aged as obvious as my former student did. In some traditional societies, the old were abandoned or killed. With modifications, the same irreverent impulse lives on in youth-worshipping, change-craving societies like ours, which lay scant value on either age or wisdom. Though people may see dimly that those of advanced years deserve respect, most are more struck by their infirmities. Their dominant reaction is not to venerate, but to pity, or even to hold in contempt. Many physicians have come to think of euthanasia as though it were a kind of medical treatment.

[15] If murder is wrong, things that partake of the spirit of murder are also wrong. Both of St. Thomas's quotations are taken from the following passage of Leviticus:

---

²³ Leviticus 24:15–16 (RSV-CE).
²⁴ Deuteronomy 13:1–4 (RSV-CE).
²⁵ Leviticus 19:32 (DRA).

You shall not go up and down as a slanderer among your people, and you shall not stand forth against the life of your neighbor: I am the Lord. You shall not hate your brother in your heart, but you shall reason with your neighbor, lest you bear sin because of him. You shall not take vengeance or bear any grudge against the sons of your own people, but you shall love your neighbor as yourself: I am the Lord.[26]

Jesus drew out the implications of the Fifth Commandment in much the same fashion:

You have heard that it was said to the men of old, "You shall not kill; and whoever kills shall be liable to judgment." But I say to you that everyone who is angry with his brother shall be liable to judgment; whoever insults his brother shall be liable to the council, and whoever says, "You fool!" shall be liable to the hell of fire. So if you are offering your gift at the altar, and there remember that your brother has something against you, leave your gift there before the altar and go; first be reconciled to your brother, and then come and offer your gift.[27]

The word here translated "fool" is the word *raca*, which maligns not just a person's intellect but his moral character. We might say, "You worthless reprobate!" Christ is saying that although for insult a man suffers the civic punishment of the Sanhedrin or Jewish council, for contemptuous anger he suffers the eternal punishment of God Himself.

[16] Like each of the Ten Commandments, the Sixth Commandment is a metonym. Since among all of the various kinds of sexual impurity, the one involving the greatest injustice is unfaithfulness to wife or husband, the commandment uses this kind as a placeholder for all kinds. The DRA takes the first passage cited by St. Thomas as a reference to prostitutes and those who consort with them, although most recent translations take it as a reference to female and male pagan temple prostitutes. Thus in one recent translation the passage reads like this:

There shall be no cult prostitute of the daughters of Israel, neither shall there be a cult prostitute of the sons of Israel. You shall not bring the hire of a harlot, or the wages of a dog [a sodomitical prostitute], into the house of the Lord your God in payment for any vow; for both of these are an abomination to the Lord your God.[28]

The second passage he cites refers to "unnatural" sins, a term which needs explanation. As St. Thomas explains elsewhere,[29] when we speak of human nature, we may have in mind either the aspects of nature that belong specifically to man or the aspects of nature that man shares with other animals. If our nature is taken in the former sense, then any sin may be called unnatural, because all sins are against reason. But if our nature is taken in the latter sense, then only certain kinds of sins are called unnatural. The sexual conjunction of

---

[26] Leviticus 19:16–18 (RSV-CE).
[27] Matthew 5:21–24 (RSV-CE), substituting "everyone" for "every one."
[28] Deuteronomy 23:17–18 (RSV-CE).
[29] See I-II, Q. 94, Art. 3, ad 2, in the context of Q. 94, Art. 2.

persons of the same sex is called unnatural because the aspects of nature that we share with other animals direct males to seek union with females of the same species and direct females to seek union with males of the same species. Why? Because the sexual powers have as their inbuilt purpose the procreation of the young and the loving union of the procreative partners, who are their parents. Here is the context of the passage from which St. Thomas is quoting:

> You shall not lie with a male as with a woman; it is an abomination. And you shall not lie with any beast and defile yourself with it, neither shall any woman give herself to a beast to lie with it: it is perversion. Do not defile yourselves by any of these things, for by all these the nations I am casting out before you defiled themselves; and the land became defiled, so that I punished its iniquity, and the land vomited out its inhabitants.[30]

Sometimes readers think that because the passage speaks only of a man having intercourse with a man, it allows a woman to have intercourse with a woman. This is like thinking that just because it mentions only coupling with a beast, it allows coupling with a fish – or, as in politically correct editing practices, thinking that since the English term "mankind" begins with the term "man," it includes only people with Y chromosomes. Traditionally, precepts framed with reference to the man have been taken as referring to both men and women unless there are special reasons to think that men only are intended. There are no such reasons here.

[17] Over the course of Church history, Deuteronomy 23:19 has often been taken as forbidding all charging of interest to fellow members of the community: "You shall not lend upon interest to your brother, interest on money, interest on victuals, interest on anything that is lent for interest."

However, this interpretation *may* miss the point. We can distinguish between loaning to someone because he is in want, and loaning to him because he wants to invest the money in an enterprise and make a profit. If "your brother" means *your fellow who is in want*, then the passage prohibits exploiting the poor: after lending them what they desperately need, one may not then demand that they give back even more. But if "your brother" means *all* of your fellows, then it prohibits *all* charging of interest to those who belongs to the nation of Israel.

Scripture often praises lending to the poor, and two other passages of the Law which condemn taking interest do make clear that the context of the prohibition is loans to the poor:

- If you lend money to any of my people with you who is poor, you shall not be to him as a creditor, and you shall not exact interest from him. If ever you take your neighbor's garment in pledge, you shall restore it to him before the sun goes down; for that is his only covering, it is his mantle for his body; in

---

[30] Leviticus 18:22–25 (RSV-CE). The Blackfriars translation mistakenly gives the chapter as 28.

what else shall he sleep? And if he cries to me, I will hear, for I am compassionate.[31]

- And if your brother becomes poor, and cannot maintain himself with you, you shall maintain him; as a stranger and a sojourner he shall live with you. Take no interest from him or increase, but fear your God; that your brother may live beside you. You shall not lend him your money at interest, nor give him your food for profit.[32]

Taken in this way, the prohibition of usury forbids taking unfair advantage of those who are vulnerable, and this makes it a natural extension of the commandment against stealing, because stealing is another kind of injustice with respect to property. The prohibition of using one standard of measure for buying and another standard of measure for selling, which is a form of fraud, is another such extension:

You shall not have in your bag two kinds of weights, a large and a small. You shall not have in your house two kinds of measures, a large and a small. A full and just weight you shall have, a full and just measure you shall have; that your days may be prolonged in the land which the Lord your God gives you. For all who do such things, all who act dishonestly, are an abomination to the Lord your God.[33]

The question may arise, "If the idea is to forbid financial subterfuge and plundering, then why not simply declare 'Commit no financial subterfuge or plundering'?" Because although that is a good moral principle, it does not have enough precision for the regulation of a community. The very purpose of the additional precepts is to provide the necessary exactness.

[18] Following the Vulgate, the DRA renders the verses from which St. Thomas is quoting like this: "Thou shalt not receive the voice of a lie: neither shalt thou join thy hand to bear false witness for a wicked person. Thou shalt not follow the multitude to do evil: neither shalt thou yield in judgment, to the opinion of the most part, to stray from the truth."[34]

In this translation, the second verse seems to mean that *judges* are not to give in to the multitude. Most contemporary translations understand it a little differently, so that it means that *witnesses* are not to give in to the multitude. Plainly, though, the two verses together extend the meaning of the Eighth Commandment to cover not only lying testimony but lying in general. By forbidding lying accusations and slanders, the other two verses St. Thomas quotes make this extension even clearer:

---

[31] Exodus 22:25–27 (RSV-CE).
[32] Leviticus 25:35–37 (RSV-CE).
[33] Deuteronomy 25:13–16 (RSV-CE).
[34] Exodus 23:1–2 (DRA).

- Thou shalt fly lying. The innocent and just person thou shalt not put to death: because I abhor the wicked.[35]
- Thou shalt not be a detractor nor a whisperer among the people. Thou shalt not stand against the blood of thy neighbor. I am the Lord.[36]

[19] The Ninth Commandment forbids wanting to have one's neighbor's wife as one's own; the Tenth forbids craving to take over his material possessions. Since these two precepts take in all forms of coveting, no further precepts about coveting are needed to explicate them, and since they are framed not in terms of evil acts but in terms of the evil desires which give rise to them, no further precepts about acts are needed either.

It might be objected that these two precepts do *not* take in all forms of coveting. Besides my neighbor's wife and wealth, might I not also covet, for example, his friends or his honors? In defense of St. Thomas, I think we might reply that coveting one's neighbor's wife is a good placeholder for all coveting any of his personal relationships, and that coveting his material possessions is a good placeholder for all coveting any of his possessions. Taken in this way, the Ninth and Tenth Commandments do forbid all sorts of coveting.

Reply to Objection 1. The precepts of the decalogue are ordained to the love of God and our neighbor as pertaining evidently to our duty towards them; but the other precepts are so ordained as pertaining thereto less evidently.	Reply to Objection 1. Indeed, the Ten Commandments guide us to love of God and neighbor, and the duties they express are obvious. However, the other precepts also guide us to love of God and neighbor, though more obscurely.

The Objector had argued that since the implications of the love of God and neighbor and Christ are sufficiently explained in the Ten Commandments, no other precepts are needed. St. Thomas agrees that the Ten Commandments explain the proximate and clear implications of the love of God and neighbor, but he points out that additional rules are needed to explicate their remote and obscure implications.

Reply to Objection 2. It is in virtue of their institution that the ceremonial and judicial precepts "are determinations of the precepts of the decalogue," not by reason of a natural instinct, as in the case of the superadded moral precepts.	Reply to Objection 2. The ceremonial and judicial precepts are *determinations* of the precepts of the Decalogue – they pin down in greater detail how they are to be followed. Thus they owe their authority not just to the movement of natural reason (as in the case of the additional *moral* precepts), but to the sheer fact that they were enacted.

---

[35] Exodus 23:7 (DRA). The Hebrew word translated "lying," *seqer*, seems to mean any kind of falsehood. Because of the context, some translations render the term as "false charge."
[36] Leviticus 19:16 (DRA).

According to the Objector, since the general moral rules are included in or presupposed by the Decalogue, and the more detailed determinations of these general moral rules are contained in the judicial and ceremonial rules, there was no need for yet more moral rules. However, this argument blurs the distinction between the two ways of deriving something from a general principle, conclusion and determination. True, some additional precepts might be said to be "contained" or included in the Decalogue just in the sense that they are implied by it. But it would have been impossible to work out *all* of the additional precepts by this means, because reason alone would have allowed them to be fulfilled by more than one course of action, and not all of these courses could be followed at once. By means of institution, the judicial and ceremonial precepts indicate which courses of action are to be followed. Should a certain ritual require the sacrifice of a lamb, a goat, or a dove? Should a certain crime be punished by a fine, by penal servitude, or by death? Should one rise up before the hoary head, sit at the venerable feet, or simply listen respectfully to the aged and experienced voice? It depends on what has been enacted about the matter.

Much the same thing is true of our own law. From love of neighbor alone, we know we should drive carefully, but not everyone is a good judge of how fast to drive, and besides, for different vehicles to drive at different speeds would invite accident. Therefore, laws are enacted setting speed limits applicable to all.

Reply to Objection 3. [1] *The precepts of a law are ordained for the common good, as stated above.* [2] *And since those virtues which direct our conduct towards others pertain directly to the common good, as also does the virtue of chastity, insofar as the generative act conduces to the common good of the species; hence precepts bearing directly on these virtues are given, both in the decalogue and in addition thereto.* [3] *As to the act of fortitude there are the orders to be given by the commanders in the war, which is undertaken for the common good: as is clear from Dt. 20, where the priest is commanded (to speak thus): "Be not afraid, do not give back."* [4] *In like manner the prohibition of acts of gluttony is left to paternal admonition, since it is contrary to*

Reply to Objection 3. We have seen previously that precepts of law are directed to the common good. The virtues which direct our relations with others especially concern the common good. So does the virtue of chastity, because the act by which children are generated serves the common good of the species. For this reason, precepts directly referring to these virtues are provided both in the Decalogue and in additional precepts.

But to return to the Objector's complaint, what about fortitude and soberness? The direction of acts of fortitude is left to the exhortations given by way of the commands of superiors in wars for the common good. Deuteronomy makes this clear when it commands the priests to say to the army, "Have no fear, do not withdraw."

Similarly, the prohibition of acts of gluttony is left to the warnings of fathers, because it is contrary chiefly to the good of the

the good of the household; hence it is said (Dt. 21) in the person of parents: "He slighteth hearing our admonitions, he giveth himself to revelling, and to debauchery and banquetings."	household. This is why the book of Deuteronomy represents parents as complaining to the elders of the city that their son despises their admonitions, for he has abandoned himself to carousing, extravagance, and partying.

[1] As we saw in examining the third Objection, law is directed to the well-being of the community. For the sake of the temporal common good, even human law *can* address acts of all the virtues, though only when they "assume the nature of justice," that is, when they concern our relations with other people. For the sake of the eternal common good, Divine law has even stronger reasons to address all the virtues, because it concerns not only our relations with other people but also our relations with God, both here and hereafter.

It is not surprising that St. Thomas agrees with all this, because it was from his own statements that the Objector took it. However, the Objector complained that the additional precepts of the Old Law address only some of the virtues, such as religion, liberality, mercy, and chastity. Why didn't some of them address the other virtues, such as fortitude and soberness? It seemed to him that the entire policy of including additional precepts is undermined by its inconsistency.

[2] We have also seen that Divine law addresses not only our relations with God but also our relations with others in a community of faith under Him. Now the virtue which epitomizes the right ordering of our relations with others is justice, but any virtue may "assume the nature of justice" in some cases. For example, telling a joke is an act of the virtue of wittiness, but it is unjust to make a joke by slandering another person, because it denies him the respect which in justice is due to his character.

St. Thomas takes for granted that we will see how the virtues of religion, liberality, and mercy affect others. It may be surprising that he gives no special attention to the virtue of religion. However, he does not expect us to need help to see that the faithlessness of one person may drag others down with him. Besides, Divine law is ordained not just for any community but for the community of faith.

He does give special attention to chastity, and this may surprise us too. Some may prefer to view the precepts concerning sex as merely ceremonial taboos, like not eating without first washing hands or not wearing clothing that mingles wool and linen. St. Thomas obviously considers them moral precepts, belonging to the natural law. According to the mores of our own day, this is strange, because who we sleep with is not supposed to affect other people at all – as the contemporary mantra goes, "It doesn't hurt anyone."

There are two difficulties here. First, the notion that any conduct whatsoever is morally acceptable so long as it doesn't hurt anyone is crude and selfish. What should we think of a husband who never treated his wife with consideration, but bragged that he had never beaten her? Of a man who failed to sound the fire alarm, but boasted that he hadn't set the fire? How about a teacher who had never taught his students a single truth, but preened himself on the fact that he had never taught them a lie?

The second problem is that unchaste behavior does hurt others, if we consider them not just as fellow members of the civil community at a single point in time, but as fellow members of the community of human nature as it continues from age to age. If I am unfaithful to my wife, I am unjust to her. Because my unfaithfulness to her undermines the common good of my family, I am unjust to my children. Because the good order of the family is the bedrock of good order in the broader community, and because damaged families must be cared for by everyone else, I am unjust to everyone. Sexual intercourse outside marriage spreads the damage even further, because among other things it means that my children and I might not know each other, that I cannot be counted on to help bring them up, and that even if I do play some part in their nurture, I cannot provide them with the security of being married to their mother. Technology does not provide a fix. Indeed the rate of births outside wedlock did not diminish with the advent of widespread contraception, but soared.

[3] The Objector's first alleged example of a virtue the Old Law overlooks is the virtue of fortitude, but St. Thomas points out that it is not overlooked at all. The exercise of fortitude is displayed especially in the face of fear of death, and we must confront and overcome our fear of death especially when the community is at war. Notice, though, that St. Thomas does not speak of any war, but of a war undertaken for the common good. Since justice is crucial to both the temporal and eternal well-being of the people, no unjust war can truly serve the common good. One of the principal contributors to the Just War tradition, he sketches some of the criteria for just war later in the *Summa*.[37]

Here is the context of the Old Law precept he quotes, commanding priests to encourage soldiers to fight without fearing or drawing back:

When you go forth to war against your enemies, and see horses and chariots and an army larger than your own, you shall not be afraid of them; for the Lord your God is with you, who brought you up out of the land of Egypt. And when you draw near to the battle, the priest shall come forward and speak to the people, and shall say to them, "Hear, O Israel, you draw near this day to battle against your enemies: let not your heart

---

[37] See II-II, Q. 40, Art. 1. St. Thomas lists only three criteria: just cause, rightful intention, and competent public authority. In the spirit of his analysis, later just war thinkers have expanded his list.

The Decalogue's Moral Precepts in Relation to Others

faint; do not fear, or tremble, or be in dread of them; for the Lord your God is he that goes with you, to fight for you against your enemies, to give you the victory."[38]

[4] The Objector's second alleged example of an overlooked virtue is soberness, which opposes the capital vice of gluttony. But the Old Law does address this virtue; it merely does so indirectly. For although it does not include any precept warning of excess in the pleasures of food and drink, it plainly expects parents to supply the warning. St. Thomas does not mean that the parents are the last resort, for if offspring hold their parents in contempt, the civil authorities are commanded to take this lapse very seriously indeed. As usual, St. Thomas quotes only a fragment of the passage he has in mind. Here is the rest of it:

If a man has a stubborn and rebellious son, who will not obey the voice of his father or the voice of his mother, and, though they chastise him, will not give heed to them, then his father and his mother shall take hold of him and bring him out to the elders of his city at the gate of the place where he lives, and they shall say to the elders of his city, "This our son is stubborn and rebellious, he will not obey our voice; he is a glutton and a drunkard." Then all the men of the city shall stone him to death with stones; so you shall purge the evil from your midst; and all Israel shall hear, and fear.[39]

Those who think the Old Law is ridiculous sometimes portray this passage as demanding the stoning of naughty little boys and girls. We ought to know better, for we have our own troubles with juvenile delinquency. This is about young people who have become too wild and lawless for their parents to control.

But we were speaking of gluttony. Although the books of the Law themselves leave the correction of this vice to parental admonition, the Wisdom books are full of admonitions against it. The problem lies not in eating and drinking, for wine is praised: "Thou dost cause the grass to grow for the cattle, and plants for man to cultivate, that he may bring forth food from the earth, and wine to gladden the heart of man, oil to make his face shine, and bread to strengthen man's heart."[40] Rather it lies in excess, for drunkards are mocked:

Who has woe? Who has sorrow? Who has strife? Who has complaining? Who has wounds without cause? Who has redness of eyes? Those who tarry long over wine, those who go to try mixed wine. Do not look at wine when it is red, when it sparkles in the cup and goes down smoothly. At the last it bites like a serpent, and stings like an adder. Your eyes will see strange things, and your mind utter perverse things. You will be like one who lies down in the midst of the sea, like one who lies on the top of a mast. "They struck me," you will say, "but I was not hurt; they beat me, but I did not feel it. When shall I awake? I will seek another drink."[41]

---

[38] Deuteronomy 20:1–4 (RSV-CE).
[39] Deuteronomy 21:18–21 (RSV-CE).
[40] Psalm 104:14–15 (RSV-CE); in the DRA this psalm is numbered 103. Compare Deuteronomy 14:23–26.
[41] Proverbs 23:29–35 (RSV-CE).

Perhaps it is no accident that another warning against excess is followed immediately by an admonition to listen to one's parents:

Hear, my son, and be wise, and direct your mind in the way. Be not among winebibbers, or among gluttonous eaters of meat; for the drunkard and the glutton will come to poverty, and drowsiness will clothe a man with rags. Hearken to your father who begot you, and do not despise your mother when she is old.[42]

A question arises here, because the Objector had not merely claimed that the Old Law ignored fortitude and soberness. In fact he had claimed that that it overlooked a number of virtues, with fortitude and soberness mere examples. We have seen that these examples are faulty, since the Law does address fortitude and soberness. However, St. Thomas makes no effort to prove that it addresses every other virtue too. This could have been done, for although there are a quite a few virtues, their number is finite. Later on in the *Summa*,[43] he even classifies them.

The explanation of why he does not do so is no doubt that there are so many of them; to provide examples of how the Old Law addresses each and every one could have been done but would have taken far too long, and would have been superfluous. His tacit argument seems to be, "Just as I have shown that the Old Law addresses fortitude and soberness, so any careful reader of Holy Scripture can discern that it addresses the other virtues too. It is not necessary to go into each one in turn."

DISCUSSION

Is "Determination" Arbitrary?

St. Thomas's statement that determinations of general principles derive their authority not from reason but from institution can easily be misunderstood, since reason operates in various modes, and when he says they do not derive their authority from reason, he is speaking of only one of these modes. For example, one cannot tell just from the prohibition of adultery whether divorce should be permitted – in that sense, the fact that the Old Law permitted it does not depend on reason. But on the other hand, as the Patristic writers pointed out, if the men of that time had not been permitted to divorce their wives, *they would have killed them* – and in that sense the fact that the Old Law permitted divorce does depend on reason.

---

[42] Proverbs 23:10–22 (RSV-CE). Compare Proverbs 20:1, "Wine is a mocker, strong drink a brawler; and whoever is led astray by it is not wise," and Sirach 31:29–30, ""Wine drunk to excess is bitterness of soul, with provocation and stumbling. Drunkenness increases the anger of a fool to his injury, reducing his strength and adding wounds." Both quotations RSV-CE. Sirach is also known as Ecclesiasticus, not to be confused with Ecclesiastes.

[43] In II-II, QQ. 1–170.

So in saying that such details do not derive their authority from reason, St. Thomas does not mean that they do not require wise judgment; in fact he means that they *do* require it, because they cannot be pinned down by sheer logical inference.

To pin down the details of a general principle in a fitting manner, one must always consider the circumstances. Viewing the Old Law from the perspective of our own narrow slice of time, it is easy to overlook this fact. Consider, for example, its provision that if a man seizes an unmarried woman to have sexual intercourse with her, then he must marry her for life:

> If a man meets a virgin who is not betrothed, and seizes her and lies with her, and they are found, then the man who lay with her shall give to the father of the young woman fifty shekels of silver, and she shall be his wife, because he has violated her; he may not put her away all his days.[44]

Today we think "How brutal is this so-called Law of God! The poor young woman is forced to marry her rapist!" This law may have been about seduction rather than rape, but even apart from that possibility, the complaint misses the point very badly. It was the times that were brutal, not the law, and the nation was only one step removed from paganism. In the only way reasonably possible, the law was gradually humanizing it. Women had low status, and marriage was protection. An unmarried young woman who had been violated or seduced would have been held in shame. Had it not been for the rule, no one would have been willing to marry her, and even if her father had felt sorry for her, he would have resented having to provide for her, because there would be no one to pay him a bridal gift.

The right way to think of the precept, then, is not that it forces the young woman to marry the man, but that it spares her the shame of having been his unmarried sexual plaything. It is he who is forced, not her, because to compensate for what he has done to her he must shelter her for the rest of his days, treating her not as a concubine but as a true wife, never being able to divorce her or cast her off.

False Teachers

We saw before that one of the additional precepts instructs the people not to listen to false prophets and teachers of false doctrine. Rather than ending with this warning, it goes on to state penalties:

> But that prophet or that dreamer of dreams shall be put to death, because he has taught rebellion against the Lord your God, who brought you out of the land of Egypt and redeemed you out of the house of bondage, to make you leave the way in which the Lord your God commanded you to walk. So you shall purge the evil from the midst of you.[45]

---

[44] Deuteronomy 22:28–29 (RSV-CE).
[45] Deuteronomy 13:5 (RSV-CE).

The chapter continues in this uncompromising vein to prescribe penalties for other instances of false teaching. For one who accepts the authenticity of Divine revelation, this raises a question. Is religious toleration in the modern state wrong?

In the first place one must recognize that Old Testament law was adapted to the circumstances and calling of the Hebrew people, and the status of ancient Israel was unique. No other nation was chosen to be the birthplace of the Messiah and a light to the Gentiles; no other nation enjoyed a divinely ordained code of laws intended to prepare it for this role. Moreover Israel was surrounded by pagan nations, the grotesquely evil cults of which presented a continuing temptation to relapse. The biblical description of them as "abominations" is in no way excessive.

By contrast, the Church is commanded not to set itself up as an enclave, but to go into all nations to spread the Gospel. Its doctrine distinguishes between the proper work of the Church and of the state, for the care of souls is entrusted to the former, not the latter. The teachers and doctors of the Church have always held that although the fundamentals of Old Testament moral teaching are true, the way in which they were applied to Israel does not provide a universal blueprint for all nations. Consider for example the following incident from the giving of the Law, immediately before Moses was called up Mount Sinai to receive the Ten Commandments:

And the Lord said to Moses, "Go to the people and consecrate them today and tomorrow, and let them wash their garments, and be ready by the third day; for on the third day the Lord will come down upon Mount Sinai in the sight of all the people. And you shall set bounds for the people round about, saying, 'Take heed that you do not go up into the mountain or touch the border of it; *whoever touches the mountain shall be put to death; no hand shall touch him, but he shall be stoned or shot; whether beast or man, he shall not live.*' When the trumpet sounds a long blast, they shall come up to the mountain."[46]

St. Gregory of Nazianzus explains that in the age of the Church, this commandment is to be taken in its spiritual rather than literal meaning. For us, he says, to be "stoned" does not mean to be struck by rocks, but to suffer the refutation of one's arguments by means of better ones:

But if any is an evil and savage beast, and altogether incapable to taking in the subject matter of contemplation and theology, let him not hurtfully and malignantly lurk in his den among the woods, to catch hold of some dogma or saying by a sudden spring, and to tear sound doctrine to pieces by his misrepresentations, but let him stand yet afar off and withdraw from the Mount, or he shall be stoned and crushed, and shall perish miserably in his wickedness. *For to those who are like wild beasts true and sound discourses are stones.*[47]

---

[46] Exodus 19:10–13 (RSV-CE), emphasis added.
[47] St. Gregory of Nazianzus, *Second Theological Oration* (Oration 28), emphasis added, www.newadvent.org/fathers/310228.htm.

For such reasons, among others, St. Thomas explicitly forbids compelling nonbelievers to accept the faith, "because to believe depends on the will."[48] He says the Church "has not the right to exercise spiritual judgment over them";[49] and he prohibits baptizing children against the will of nonbelieving parents, which he declares "against natural justice" because a child is "enfolded in the care of its parents, which is like a spiritual womb."[50]

He does hold that in some cases civil penalties may be applied to the teachers of false doctrines. However, he makes distinctions:

- Jews, he says, must not in any way be hindered from practicing their rites and beliefs. He argues that the observance of Jewish worship is a good even from a Christian point of view, because it was the precursor of the Gospel and foreshadowed what was to come. It indirectly witnesses to the truth of the Christian faith, even if its adherents intend no such thing.
- Pagans, along with those who have at one time accepted Christian faith but now oppose it, present an altogether different situation. St. Thomas views their rites and beliefs as not only false, and therefore inimical to spiritual good, but also "unprofitable," or inimical to the temporal common good. However, although pagan rites have no unconditional right to toleration, he does think that depending on circumstances, some of them may be tolerated to prevent some greater evil – for example, if forbidding them would produce confusion or disorder, cause others to stumble morally, or stand in the way of the conversion of those who might otherwise be attracted to the faith. For this reason, he thinks, the case for toleration of pagans is strongest when they make up a large part of the community.[51]

Such views are considered unenlightened today: we tend to take the virtue of toleration to mean not tolerating what ought to be tolerated, but tolerating indiscriminately. If we care to remember what pagan practices have historically included – cult prostitution and sodomy, widow burning, child sacrifice, and so on – the view that they should *all* be tolerated is difficult to maintain.

Indeed, no one believes, and no one could believe, that *everything* should be tolerated. The way that the ideology of nonjudgmentalism actually functions is to suppress one set of judgments for the sake of other judgments that the so-called nonjudgmentalists prefer. For example, public universities often try to force Christian student associations to allow persons who reject Christian doctrine and morals to serve as officers. Although such policies are defended in the name of not discriminating, they are, of course, attempts to suppress Christianity – and nothing analogous to this is forced upon campus atheist clubs.

---

[48] II-II, Q. 10, Art. 8.
[49] Ibid., Art. 9.
[50] Ibid., Art. 12.
[51] Ibid., Art. 11.

Today we sometimes try to avoid questions about authentic religious toleration by saying "I just believe in separation of Church and state," but the term "separation" is used in so many inconsistent ways that it only provokes further questions:

- Does it mean that citizens should not consider their faith when they vote? Since there is no such thing as neutrality, this would amount to substituting false worldly ideologies *for* the faith. Surely separation in this sense would be bad.
- Does it mean that the state should not subject candidates for public office to an official religious test? It would seem better for the citizens themselves to judge the faith of the candidates than for the government to do it. So separation in this sense would be good.
- Does it mean that firemen may not put out fires in Church buildings or schools? This would be wicked and absurd.
- Does it mean that the state may not tell the Church what to teach? Good.
- Does it mean that priests are not magistrates? Good.
- Does it mean that magistrates are not priests? Also good.
- Does it mean that the Church may not condemn unjust and evil laws? Bad.

These hardly exhaust the questions to be asked, much less the things to be said about them. This sort of discussion can go on for a long, long time.

QUESTION 100, ARTICLE 12

Whether the Moral Precepts of the Old Law Justified Man?

TEXT	PARAPHRASE
Whether the moral precepts of the Old Law justified man?	Did fulfilling the moral precepts of Old Testament law make the people entirely just in the sight of God, and so acceptable to Him?

How we can be justified – how we can be made just in God's sight and acceptable to Him – is one of the great doctrines of Christianity, and was also one of the great fault lines during the Protestant Reformation. Since at the time St. Thomas is writing, the Reformers have not yet come onto the scene, it would be anachronistic to suppose that he is replying to them. On the other hand, his views and theirs can be fruitfully compared. A brief explanation of the differences is included in the Discussion at the end of this Article.

The question of this Article is whether a person can earn his way into God's approval by doing the sorts of good "works" or deeds which were commanded by the Old Law. One of the difficulties the theologians of justification confront is that some New Testament passages seem to suggest that obedience to the Law's moral precepts does have the power to justify, but others seem to suggest that it does not.

One cannot help but wonder whether the term "justification" is being used in the same sense in all of these passages. The Reformers tended to write as though it had to be. St. Thomas is convinced that it isn't. As we will see, this Article is one of the finest exhibitions of the art of *distinctio* in the *Summa*. At every step the argument proceeds by disentangling the various senses of things which we are prone to entwine and confuse.

Objection 1. [1] *It would seem that the moral precepts of the Old Law justified man. Because the Apostle says (Rm. 2): "For not the hearers of the Law are justified before God, but the doers of the Law shall be justified."* [2] *But the doers of the Law are those who fulfill the precepts of the Law.*	Objection 1. The answer to the question is yes. St. Paul writes to the young Church at Rome that those who are justified are not those who hear the Law, but those who do it. Those who do it are those who satisfy its precepts.

265

Therefore the fulfilling of the precepts of the Law was a cause of justification.	So the moral precepts of the Law do justify those who follow them.

[1] Speaking of final judgment, which is the ultimate measure of justification, St. Paul says in the passage quoted that the situations of Jews, who have been given the Old Law, and of Gentiles, to whom it has not been given, are not as different as one might think:

For God shows no partiality. All who have sinned without the law will also perish without the law, and all who have sinned under the law will be judged by the law. For it is not the hearers of the law who are righteous before God, but the doers of the law who will be justified. When Gentiles who have not the law do by nature what the law requires, they are a law to themselves, even though they do not have the law. They show that what the law requires is written on their hearts, while their conscience also bears witness and their conflicting thoughts accuse or perhaps excuse them on that day when, according to my gospel, God judges the secrets of men by Christ Jesus.[1]

The Jewish people were certainly blessed with far more precise instruction. However, as we learned in I-II, Question 100, Article 1, the moral precepts of the Old Law are precepts of natural law. Since these precepts are written on the heart, no one can plead genuine ignorance, and everyone must follow them.

[2] The Objector concludes that since those who "do" the Law – who obey its moral precepts – are approved by God, obedience to these precepts justifies us.

Objection 2. [1] *Further, it is written (Lev. 18): "Keep My laws and My judgments, which if a man do, he shall live in them."* [2] *But the spiritual life of man is through justice. Therefore the fulfilling of the precepts of the Law was a cause of justification.*	Objection 2. Moreover, in the book of Leviticus, where God commands taking heed of His laws and judgments, he describes them as enabling whoever obeys them to live in them. This refers to *spiritual* life, showing that what makes us live spiritually is justice. So again we see that obedience to the moral precepts of the Law had the effect of justifying.

[1] The Objector is quoting from the following passage in the book of Leviticus:

And the Lord said to Moses, "Say to the people of Israel, I am the Lord your God. You shall not do as they do in the land of Egypt, where you dwelt, and you shall not do as they do in the land of Canaan, to which I am bringing you. You shall not walk in their statutes. You shall do my ordinances and keep my statutes and walk in them. I am the

---

[1] Romans 2:11–16 (RSV-CE).

Lord your God. You shall therefore keep my statutes and my ordinances, *by doing which a man shall live*: I am the Lord."[2]

The prophet Ezekiel emphasizes the idea by referring to life three times in the same passage, representing God speaking as follows:

> I gave them my statutes and showed them my ordinances, *by whose observance man shall live* ... But the house of Israel rebelled against me in the wilderness; they did not walk in my statutes but rejected my ordinances, *by whose observance man shall live*; and my sabbaths they greatly profaned ... Nevertheless my eye spared them, and I did not destroy them or make a full end of them in the wilderness ... But the children [descendants] rebelled against me; they did not walk in my statutes, and were not careful to observe my ordinances, *by whose observance man shall live*; they profaned my sabbaths.[3]

The book of Proverbs endorses the idea:

> He who keeps the commandment keeps his life; he who despises the word will die.[4]

And Christ Himself endorses it, at least with reference to the precept of loving God:

> And behold, a lawyer stood up to put him to the test, saying, "Teacher, what shall I do to inherit eternal life?" He said to him, "What is written in the law? How do you read?" And he answered, "You shall love the Lord your God with all your heart, and with all your soul, and with all your strength, and with all your mind; and your neighbor as yourself." And he said to him, "You have answered right; *do this, and you will live*."[5]

[2] The argument works like this:

1. Scripture says that whoever obeys the moral precepts of the Old Law will live.
2. This means that whoever obeys them will live *spiritually*.
3. But we live *spiritually* through becoming wholly just; in other words, through being justified.
4. Therefore whoever obeys the moral precepts of the old law is justified.

Objection 3. [1] *Further, the Divine law is more efficacious than human law.* [2] *But human law justifies man; since there is a kind of justice consisting in fulfilling the precepts of law. Therefore the precepts of the Law justified man.*	Objection 3. Besides, Divine law has greater power to bring about its effects than human law does. But even human law justifies, for a certain justice lies in obeying it. Certainly, then, obeying Divine law must justify!

---

[2] Leviticus 18:1–5 (RSV-CE), emphasis added.
[3] Ezekiel 20:11, 13, 17, 21 (RSV-CE), emphasis added.
[4] Proverbs 19:16 (RSV-CE).
[5] Luke 10:25–28 (RSV-CE), emphasis added. The expert in the Law has quoted Deuteronomy 6:5.

[1] St. Thomas argues in I-II, Question 92, Article 1, that

> [E]very law aims at being obeyed by those who are subject to it. Consequently it is evident that the proper effect of law is to lead its subjects to their proper virtue: and since virtue is "that which makes its subject good," it follows that the proper effect of law is to make those to whom it is given, good, either simply or in some particular respect.

But he makes a distinction:

> For if the intention of the lawgiver is fixed on true good, which is the common good regulated according to Divine justice, it follows that the effect of the law is to make men good simply. If, however, the intention of the lawgiver is fixed on that which is not simply good, but useful or pleasurable to himself, or in opposition to Divine justice; then the law does not make men good simply, but in respect to that particular government. In this way good is found even in things that are bad of themselves: thus a man is called a good robber, because he works in a way that is adapted to his end.

So the effect of Divine law is to make men *truly* good. Human law also aims at making men good, but because legislators do not always aim at what they should, the effect of human law may be merely to make them good in a relative sense – good for the purposes of that regime.

[2] We may call a person just in several senses. If we are thinking of justice as one kind of virtue among others ("special justice"), then when we say "He is a just man" we mean that the man doesn't cheat. If we are thinking of justice as all-around virtue ("general justice"), then when we say "He is a just man" we mean that he is a person of fully developed moral character – the sort of person who used to be called "righteous." But since in our conduct toward others, the law commands the acts of all the virtues, when we call a man just in the latter sense we may also be approving him for following the law. The Objector is calling attention to the latter sense of justice, for it is in this sense that we are justified, or made just, by following good laws. The Objector reasons that since even following human law justifies us in this sense, certainly following Divine law must justify us too.

On the contrary, [1] *The Apostle says (2 Cor. 3): "The letter killeth":* [2] *which, according to Augustine (De Spir. et Lit.), refers even to the moral precepts.* [3] *Therefore the moral precepts did not cause justice.*

On the other hand, St. Paul writes to the Christians in the city of Corinth that the "letter" of the law kills. According to St. Augustine, Paul is speaking even of the moral precepts of the law. It follows that obeying the moral precepts does *not* justify.

---

[1] Having had to correct certain tendencies among the Corinthians, St. Paul affirms his authority and that of the other Apostles to do so but also tenderly reassures them. In the course of these remarks, he comments on the difference between the Old Law and the New:

Did the Moral Precepts Make Men Just in God's Sight?

For we are not, like so many, peddlers of God's word; but as men of sincerity, as commissioned by God, in the sight of God we speak in Christ. Are we beginning to commend ourselves again? Or do we need, as some do, letters of recommendation to you, or from you? You yourselves are our letter of recommendation, written on your hearts, to be known and read by all men; and you show that you are a letter from Christ delivered by us, written not with ink but with the Spirit of the living God, not on tablets of stone but on tablets of human hearts. Such is the confidence that we have through Christ toward God. Not that we are competent of ourselves to claim anything as coming from us; our competence is from God, who has made us competent to be ministers of a new covenant, not in [the letter] but in the Spirit; *for [the letter] kills, but the Spirit gives life.*[6]

The "letter" of the Law is the literal meaning of its written precepts. To say that the letter kills is a hyperbolic way of denying that it is capable of giving life.

[2] St. Augustine is alluding to the following passage in St. Paul's epistle to the Romans:

What then shall we say? That the law is sin? By no means! Yet, if it had not been for the law, I should not have known sin. I should not have known what it is to covet if the law had not said, "You shall not covet." But sin, finding opportunity in the commandment, wrought in me all kinds of covetousness. Apart from the law sin lies dead. I was once alive apart from the law, but when the commandment came, sin revived and I died; the very commandment which promised life proved to be death to me. For sin, finding opportunity in the commandment, deceived me and by it killed me.[7]

Paul is often taken to be making the *psychological* observation that the more he is told not to do something, the more he wants to do it – and that may be part of his meaning. In context, however, it is more likely that he is making the *legal* observation that the more he is told not to do it, the guiltier he is when he does it anyway. In this sense, it kills.

But the prohibition of coveting is a *moral* precept. Thus, St. Augustine concludes that St. Paul's reference to the letter that kills refers not only to the ceremonial precepts, but to the moral precepts too:

Is it possible to contend that it is not the law which was written on those two tables that the apostle describes as "the letter that kills," but the law of circumcision and the other sacred rites which are now abolished? But then how can we think so, when in the law occurs this precept, "You shall not covet," by which very commandment, notwithstanding its being holy, just, and good, "sin," says the apostle, "deceived me, and by it slew me?" What else can this be than "the letter" that "kills"?[8]

---

[6] 2 Corinthians 2:17–3:6 (RSV-CE), emphasis added. Where the RSV-CE has "written code," I have substituted "letter," which more literally translates *grammatos*, in the original Greek, and *littera*, in the Latin of the Vulgate, and which corresponds with how the term is given in both St. Thomas, here, and St. Augustine, below.

[7] Romans 7:7–11 (RSV-CE).

[8] St. Augustine of Hippo, *On the Spirit and the Letter*, chapter 14, section 23, www.newadvent.org/fathers/1502.htm. We have considered this passage at greater length in connection with Question 99, Article 2.

[3] The argument of the *sed contra* works as follows.

1. The letter of the Old Law is so far from giving life that St. Paul says it kills.
2. To say that the letter of the Old Law kills is to deny that obedience to it is capable of justifying us, of making us wholly just and acceptable to God.
3. But the letter of the Old Law includes not just its ceremonial but also its moral precepts.
4. Therefore, obedience *even to the moral* precepts of the Old Law is incapable of justifying.

I answer that, [1] *Just as "healthy" is said properly and first of that which is possessed of health,* [2] *and secondarily of that which is a sign or a safeguard of health;* [3] *so justification means first and properly the causing of justice;* [4] *while secondarily and improperly, as it were, it may denote a sign of justice or a disposition thereto.* [5] *If justice be taken in the last two ways, it is evident that it was conferred by the precepts of the Law; insofar, to wit, as they disposed men to the justifying grace of Christ, which they also signified,* [6] *because as Augustine says (Contra Faust.), "even the life of that people foretold and foreshadowed Christ."*

Here is my response. The word "healthy" is rightly applied in a primary sense to something that has health, and only in a secondary sense to something that signifies or preserves health. Analogously, the term "justification" is rightly applied in in a primary sense to something that makes us just, and only in a secondary, and so to speak improper, sense, either to something that symbolizes or signifies justice, or to something that prepares us for justice or predisposes us to acquiesce to it without actually producing it in us.

Taking it in the two secondary and nonliteral senses – signifying justification or preparing us for it – it is clear that in these ways the precepts of law did justify:[9]

1. They predisposed men to acquiesce to the justifying grace of Christ; and
2. They symbolized it, for as St. Augustine writes, even the life of the people of Israel was prophetic, a foreshadowing of the coming Messiah.

---

[1] When the doctor tells Irving that he is healthy, he means that Irving possesses health. This is the primary and literal meaning of "healthy."

[2] By contrast, when the doctor tells Irving that he has a healthy heartbeat, he does not mean literally that the heartbeat possesses health, but that the heartbeat shows that Irving himself possesses it. Similarly, when he tells Irving to eat a healthy diet, he does not mean literally that such a diet possesses health,

---

[9] *Quibus duobus modis manifestum est quod praecepta legis iustificabant.* St. Thomas is speaking of two ways in which law justifies; since to justify is to make just, the Blackfriars translators rephrase the idea in terms of two ways in which justice is conferred by it. Though my paraphrase is in this case more literal, the two renderings are entirely equivalent.

but that it predisposes Irving to health. These figures of speech belong to the category called *transferred meaning*.

[3] The primary and literal meaning of justifying something is *making* it just, in the same way that fossilizing something means making it into a fossil, and sterilizing something means making it sterile.

[4] But just as the word "healthy" can be applied not only to what has health but also to what predisposes us to health, so also in a secondary way the word "justifies" can be applied not only to what makes us just but also to what signifies justice or leads us to acquiesce to it. Similar extended senses of the term turn up in nontheological contexts. For example, when we say "Lawrence *justified* himself by pleading that he acted in self-defense," we do not mean that he was *making* himself just, but that he was trying to *signify or show* that he was just.

[5] Taking justification in the primary and literal sense of *making* us just, only the grace of Christ justifies us – as we see more fully below. Following the precepts of the Old Law had no power to do that. However, following the precepts of the Old Law did justify the Hebrew people in the two figurative senses, for it prepared them for the coming of the justifying grace of Christ, and it also symbolized or foreshadowed it.

St. Thomas does *not* here explain how observance of the Law prepared the Hebrew people to acquiesce to the grace of Christ. However, the point can be illustrated by a passage from St. Paul's letter to the Galatians, to which St. Thomas often returns. We have already seen the passage in I-II, Question 91, Article 5, and Question 99, Article 6:[10]

Now before faith came, we were confined under the law, kept under restraint until faith should be revealed. So that the law was our custodian until Christ came, that we might be justified by faith. But now that faith has come, we are no longer under a custodian; for in Christ Jesus you are all sons of God, through faith.[11]

According to St. Paul, in the same way that the *paidagogos* or child-leader escorted the children to school and kept watch over them on the way so that they got there safely, the Old Law escorted or predisposed the Hebrew people to the justifying grace of Christ who was to come. Though in and of itself it could not impart the power to be truly just or righteous, it formed in them a clear idea of what justice or righteousness means.

St. Thomas *does* explain how the observance of the Law *symbolized or foreshadowed* the grace of Christ. We have already seen something of how this works in I-II, Question 100, Article 5. For instance, the Sabbath day observance, which recalled the blessing of Creation, foreshadowed the eternal

---

[10] See I-II, Q. 98, Art. 2, cor., ad 1, ad 2; Q. 104, Art. 3; Q. 106, Art. 3; Q. 107, Art. 1; and II-II, Q. 1, Art. 7, ad 2.
[11] Galatians 3:23–26 (RSV-CE).

Sabbath of the repose of the mind in God, and the Passover celebration, which recalled liberation from slavery, foreshadowed the Passion of Christ, which liberates from sin. To the same effect, he goes on to quote St. Augustine.

[6] Not only did following the precepts of the Old Law prepare the people for the justifying grace of Christ who was to come, it also symbolized it. Augustine develops the point as follows:

> Truly these men were prophetic, not only in speech but in life. The whole kingdom of the Hebrew people was like a great prophet, suggesting the great one who was prophesied. We discover in those Hebrews who whose hearts became erudite in the wisdom of God a prophecy of Christ and the Church, not only in what they said but in what they did. God brought about the same thing in the whole nation at once. "All these things," the Apostle says, "are our examples."[12]

[7] *But if we speak of justification properly so called, then we must notice that it can be considered as in the habit or as in the act: so that accordingly justification may be taken in two ways.* [8] *First, according as man is made just, by becoming possessed of the habit of justice: secondly, according as he does works of justice, so that in this sense justification is nothing else than the execution of justice.* [9] *Now justice, like the other virtues, may denote either the acquired or the infused virtue, as is clear from what has been stated.* [10] *The acquired virtue is caused by works; but the infused virtue is caused by God Himself through His grace.* [11] *The latter is true*

However, taking justification in the primary and proper sense as that which *causes* justice, we may view justice, the thing that is caused, either as a settled disposition to act in a certain way, or as the just act itself. This gives two senses of justification:

1. From the perspective of the disposition, justification means that man *comes to have* justice.
2. From the perspective of execution, it means simply that he *does* justice.

We will consider both of these senses of justification in turn. However, before we consider the former – coming to have the disposition of justice – we must make one more distinction. Just as in speaking of the other virtues, when we speak of the disposition of justice we may have in mind either the acquired or the infused virtue of justice. The acquired virtue is developed in us through the discipline of repeating just deeds, but the infused virtue is brought about by God Himself, through His grace.

---

[12] *Illorum hominum non tantum linguam, verum etiam vitam fuisse propheticam; totumque illud regnum gentis Hebraeorum, magnum quemdam, quia et magni cuiusdam, fuisse prophetam. Quocirca quod ad eos quidem attinet, qui illic erant eruditi corde in sapientia Dei, non solum in iis quae dicebant, sed etiam in iis quae faciebant; quod autem ad caeteros ac simul omnes illius gentis homines, in iis quae in illis vel de illis divinitus fiebant, prophetia venturi Christi et Ecclesiae perscrutanda est. Omnia enim illa, sicut dicit Apostolus: Figurae nostrae fuerunt.* St. Augustine of Hippo, *Against Faustus, the Manichean*, book XXII, chapter 24, my rendering. For another translation see www.newadvent.org/fathers/1406.htm. The internal reference is to 1 Corinthians 10:11.

justice, of which we are speaking now, and in this respect of which a man is said to be just before God, [12] according to Rm. 4. "If Abraham were justified by works, he hath whereof to glory, but not before God." [13] Hence this justice could not be caused by moral precepts, which are about human actions: wherefore the moral precepts could not justify man by causing justice.	So when we speak of coming to have the disposition of justice, of which of these two virtues should we be thinking? Of the infused virtue. Only this disposition is *true* justice, and it is only by having *this* justice that a man is just in the sight of God. *This* is the justice of which St. Paul is speaking when he writes that Abraham would have glory if he were justified by his deeds – *but not before God!* We see then that *this* justice could never be brought about by obeying the moral precepts, that is, by the repetition of human acts. So in *this* sense – causing infused justice – obeying the moral precepts of the Old Law cannot justify anyone.

[7] In turning from the secondary, figurative meanings of justification to its primary, literal meaning, we discover that here to a distinction must be made, because even the primary meaning can be taken in two senses.

[8] Literally becoming just may mean coming to have the virtue of justice – the "habit" or dispositional tendency that leads us to do just deeds. But it may also mean simply the *exercise* of such deeds – the carrying out of justice. We begin by considering literal justification in the first way.

[9] It may seem that if justification is taken in the sense of coming to have the virtue of justice, then the answer to the question "Does obeying the precepts of the Old Law justify us?" is obvious: sure it does. Not so fast, says St. Thomas. As we have seen earlier in this *Commentary*,[13] virtue comes in two varieties, acquired and infused. Here, St. Thomas makes the further claim that this distinction applies not only to the other virtues but also to justice. So whether we have in mind acquired or infused justice will make a difference to our answer to the question.

In I-II, Question 63, Article 4, St. Thomas illustrates the difference between acquired and infused virtue by means of the virtue of temperance. Acquired temperance follows the rule of natural reason: We should not eat so much, or so little, that we harm our health or hinder our use of reason. Infused temperance agrees, but follows a higher rule: We must discipline our bodies and bring them into subjection so that we are prepared to be fully obedient to God.

In that passage, he does not say specifically, as he does here, that the distinction between acquired and infused virtue applies to justice. However, he has made this claim in other places. For example, in his *Commentary on the Sentences* he writes that "Justice can be taken in two senses: civil justice or

---

[13] See the discussion of I-II, Q. 99, Art. 2.

infused justice. Civil justice can be brought about without superadded grace; infused justice, not so."[14] Throughout the *Summa*, one must pay close attention to context to know when he is speaking of acquired justice, and when of infused.

[10] Acquired justice helps a person to do the right thing toward his neighbors as an ordinary citizen, guided by the light of reason. It is developed by doing the right thing over and over until it becomes habitual. By contrast, infused justice helps him to do the right thing as a member of the household of God, guided by the additional light of charity or supernatural love. It is not developed by our own acts, but poured into us by the Holy Spirit.

Later in the *Summa*, St. Thomas explains that grace is "a gratuitous strength superadded to natural strength" so that we can act well. Even if we had not fallen, we would need the inpouring of this grace "to do and wish supernatural good." However, because we have fallen, we need it not only to perform such deeds of supernatural virtue but also "in order to be healed."[15]

[11] Ordinary justice may give my fellow citizens in the earthly commonwealth nothing to sue me for and no reason to put me in prison, but it is far short of making me acceptable in the sight of God. The only justice fully deserving the name "justice" is the one that is inseparably connected with love of God and neighbor, and so makes me a fit citizen of the commonwealth of heaven.

[12] In context, this quotation from St. Paul's letter to the Romans reads: "What then shall we say about Abraham, our forefather according to the flesh? For if Abraham was justified by works, he has something to boast about, but not before God. For what does the scripture say? 'Abraham believed God, and it was reckoned to him as righteousness.'"[16]

In the view of the Protestant Reformers, the statement that Abraham's belief was reckoned as or reputed to him as justice means that because Abraham trusted in God, God *regarded him as just, even though he wasn't*. In St. Thomas's interpretation, the statement means that because Abraham trusted in God, *God, through this faith, made him just*. For faith – the yes! of assent to God – is the gateway to hope and love as well, and these transform us.

---

[14] *Aliquis potest dici iustus dupliciter: vel iustitia civili, vel iustita infusa. Iustitia autem civili potest aliquis iustus effici sine aliqua gratia naturalibus superaddita; non autem iustitia infusa.* Thomas Aquinas, *Commentary on the Sentences of Peter Lombard*, II, dist. 28, q. 1, art. 1, reply to objection 4.

[15] I-II, Q. 109, Art. 2.

[16] Romans 4:1–3 (RSV-CE), emphasis added. The internal quotation is from Genesis 15:6.

Since St. Thomas has placed so much emphasis on charity or love, why is faith the gateway? Why shouldn't it have been said that because Abraham *loved* God, it was reckoned to him as righteousness – or perhaps that because he *hoped* in God, it was reckoned to him as righteousness?

Although St. Thomas does not pose this question in so many words, an answer to it can be found earlier in the *Summa*. He writes that the supernatural virtues "are all infused together" – faith, hope, and love are poured into us not one at a time, but all at once. Yet in another sense, he says, faith is the first step, for it is presupposed by hope and love. By faith in God, we grasp what it is that we have to hope for in Him; by hoping for it, we love Him; and loving Him changes everything.[17] So yes, Abraham's justification depended on his faith.

We might dare a comparison with the way it is between husband and wife. The rules, such as not committing adultery, are true, important, and inviolable. However, mere obedience to the rules is not what makes their marriage live. As the vitality of their marriage flows from their belief in each other, from their confidence in their future together, and from their conjugal love, so life with God flows from faith, hope, and charity.

[13] The argument works like this:

1. The only kind of justice that can be produced in us by repeated "works" or deeds is acquired justice.
2. But the only kind of justice fully and truly deserving of the name "justice" is infused justice.
3. Therefore, taking justification in the sense of being made just, and taking being made just in the sense of having infused justice, we cannot be justified merely by consistently observing the moral precepts of the Old Law.

---

[14] *If, on the other hand, by justification we understand the execution of justice, thus all the precepts of the Law justified man, but in various ways.* [15] *Because the ceremonial precepts taken as a whole contained something just in itself, insofar as they aimed at offering worship to God;* [16] *whereas taken individually they contained that which is just, not in itself, but by being a determination of the Divine law.*

Now we turn to the latter sense – justification not as coming to have the virtue of justice, but simply as executing it. Viewing it this way, all of the precepts of Divine law justify those who follow them, but not all in the same way.

Taken as a group, the ceremonial precepts contained an element of what is just in itself, insofar as they expressed the worship of God. Taken individually, although none of them contained what justice demands in itself, each one did contain an element of justice insofar as it was a determination of Divine law. This is why we say of these precepts that they justified

---

[17] I-II, Q. 62, Arts. 3-4; the quotation is from Art. 4.

> [17] Hence it is said of these precepts that they did not justify man save through the devotion and obedience of those who complied with them. [18] On the other hand the moral and judicial precepts, either in general or also in particular, contained that which is just in itself: [19] but the moral precepts contained that which is just in itself according to that "general justice" which is "every virtue" [20] according to Ethic. v. [21] whereas the judicial precepts belonged to "special justice," which is about contracts connected with the human mode of life, between one man and another.

> man, not in themselves, but only through the devotion and obedience with which they were obeyed.
> The moral and judicial precepts present a different picture. They do contain elements of what is just in itself, taken either generally or individually. However, moral precepts and judicial precepts do this in different ways.
> 1. Moral precepts contain what is just in itself, insofar as they concern *general* justice. As we recall from Aristotle's *Nicomachean Ethics*, justice in the general sense is another term for all of the virtues together.
> 2. Judicial precepts, however, concern *special* justice. Justice in the special sense is a *particular* virtue distinct from the others – the one connected with fairness in the agreements between one man and another that are so much a part of how human beings live.

[14] We saw above that in the primary and literal sense, justification, or becoming just, may refer to either coming to have the virtue of justice, or coming to be a "doer" of justice. Having considered whether obeying the precepts of the Old Law makes men just in the former sense, we now turn to whether it does so in the latter sense. At once we see that in this way, obeying the precepts of the Old Law *does* justify us, but again St. Thomas slows us down, for the ceremonial, moral, and judicial precepts do so in different ways.

[15] To be doers of the Old Law makes us doers of justice if and only if the Old Law *contains* justice. Well, it does, but different parts contain justice in different ways. One way to consider the ceremonial precepts is to consider them, not one at a time, but as a group. Now justice is giving to each person what is due to him, so to ask how the ceremonial precepts contain justice as a group is to ask "Taken as a set, how do they give what is due?" The answer is that taken as a set, they give God the worship due to God. Giving God the worship due to Him is not a "determination" of justice, but just in itself. That is, it would have been just even if there never had been any ceremonial precepts pinning down the manner in which worship were to be done.

[16] Taken one at a time, however, the ceremonial precepts *are* determinations. Each one settles *some particular detail* of how God is to be worshipped. For giving God what is due to Him does not *in itself* require worshipping on this day or in that manner. Rather the rules about worshipping on this day or in that manner specify or determine *how* God is to be given what is due to Him.

[17] Setting apart the Sabbath day or offering a particular kind of sacrifice does not make a man a doer of justice in the sense that justice itself requires setting apart the Sabbath day or offering a particular kind of sacrifice. Rather it

makes a man a doer of justice *insofar as his intention is to give God what is due to Him* by doing these things – insofar as he does them in devotion to God and because he wants to obey Him.

[18] We have just seen that the ceremonial precepts contain justice as such when taken as a whole, but contain only determinations of justice when taken one by one. One might expect St. Thomas to say the same thing about the moral and judicial precepts – that they contain justice as such *either* taken generally *or* taken individually – a somewhat vague formulation, which would seem to mean that we can find elements of justice in itself (rather than merely determinations of justice) not only in moral and judicial precepts taken as a whole but also in some of the individual precepts. This would probably mean some of the individual *moral* precepts; the requirement to give parents the honor due them, for example, is a moral precept that contains justice in itself, not just a determination of justice. He is about to add, however, that although moral and judicial precepts taken as groups *do* contain justice in itself, they contain different *kinds* of justice in itself.

[19] General justice is whatever is right, no matter what virtue calls for it. We might paraphrase it as *righteousness.* So another way of saying that the moral precepts direct us in acts of every virtue is to say that they direct us in general justice, or that they direct us in righteousness.

[20] The distinction between general justice and special justice – between justice in the sense of all-around good conduct toward others, which we might call righteousness, and justice in the sense of a particular aspect of good conduct toward others, which we might call fairness – comes from Aristotle. The pagan sage had remarked that "general justice touches upon everything by reason of which a man can be called virtuous," so in this sense a courageous act can be called just, a temperate act can be called just, and a wise act can be called just. But "if a person makes an exorbitant profit, it is not reduced to any other vice but only to injustice. Hence it is clear that over and above general justice, there is a particular justice."[18]

[21] As we have just seen, special justice is a *particular* virtue, not a term for virtue in general; it is the virtue which disposes us to give others what is due to them. It is a little odd that St. Thomas gives special place here to contracts. In the first place, he knows that the fulfillment of contracts is not the only context in which we give others what is due to them; for example, the Decalogue commands us to give due honor to parents and due worship to God. In the second place, he knows that the fulfillment of contracts is not the only matter treated by the judicial precepts; for example, as we see later, they lay out details of government. However, the fulfillment of contracts is the most distinctive and

---

[18] Aristotle, *Nicomachean Ethics*, book v, chapter 1. I am following the wording in Thomas Aquinas, *Commentary on Aristotle's Nicomachean Ethics*, translated by C. I. Litzinger (Chicago: Regnery, 1964).

explicit context in which one person gives another what is due to him, and so it is the one St. Thomas mentions here.

To summarize this last, complex part of the *respondeo*:

- The ceremonial precepts, taken as a group, contain justice as such, because they concern the worship justly due to God. As St. Thomas reminds us a few lines later, the kind of justice as such that they contain is *special* justice. However, taken individually these precepts contain not special justice as such, but determinations of it.
- The judicial precepts, taken as a group, also contain special justice as such, because they too concern giving each person what is due to him.
- The moral precepts, taken as a group, contain not special but *general* justice as such, because they concern the acts of all the virtues.
- Even taken individually, the broadest of the moral precepts – those in the Decalogue – concern justice as such; for example, giving parents the honor justly due them.
- Taken individually, however, the "additional" moral precepts, as well as the judicial precepts, contain not justice as such, but determinations of justice.

Thus, here we may summarize the finding of the entire *respondeo*. The upshot is that the precepts of the Old Law justify us in certain senses but not in others:

1. In the *primary and literal* sense, justification is *causing* justice in us – either the virtue of justice, or the execution of it.
    a. Observance of the Old Law precepts does *not* cause us to have the virtue of justice in the sense of infused justice, which is the only kind that can make us truly just and acceptable to God. We are not fully just and acceptable unless we are inwardly transformed by His grace. So observance of the Old Law precepts does not justify us in this sense in and of itself.
    b. The observance of these precepts certainly does cause us to *do* just things – although some cause us to do one kind of justice, some another. It does make us behave. So in this sense it does justify.
2. In the *secondary and figurative* sense, justification is *signifying or preparing* someone to be justified in sense 1.a, above.
    a. Observance of the Old Law precepts did prepare the Hebrew people for the advent of justifying grace. So in this sense it did justify. They awaited the Messiah; the Law was like the servant who got the children ready and led them to school, where their true education would begin.
    b. Their observance also signified the grace which was to come. So in this sense it did justify. In various ways it was a symbol, foreshadowing it.

Reply to Objection 1. The Apostle takes justification for the execution of justice.	Reply to Objection 1. When St. Paul writes that we are justified not by hearing the law but by doing it, he is using the term "justification" in the sense of doing just things, not in the sense of becoming a just person.

We have seen that the term "justification" is used in a number of different senses. One of them is simply that one comes to do just things, and it is in this sense that St. Paul is speaking. The one who does just things will certainly not be condemned for not doing them. It is quite another question whether the sort of obedience he can muster up by his own powers apart from grace can renew his inward self and make him acceptable to God; it can't.

Reply to Objection 2. [1] The man who fulfilled the precepts of the Law is said to live in them, because he did not incur the penalty of death, which the Law inflicted on its transgressors: [2] in this sense the Apostle quotes this passage (Gal. 3).	Reply to Objection 2. When God declares that a man who keeps His precepts "lives in them," he means simply that the man is not put to death, as the Law prescribes for transgression. This is the sense in which St. Paul quotes the passage in his letter to the Christians of Galatea. He does not mean that the man who keeps these precepts has *spiritual* life.

[1] The Objector had held that the passage about man "living in" the precepts of the law was about spiritual life. St. Thomas responds that the Law was speaking much more literally, of physical life, for if a man kept them, then he would not suffer capital punishment. The Objector had also held that what gives us spiritual life is justice. Whether this is true depends on the sort of justice that is meant. The Objector is thinking of acquired justice – the ordinary kind of justice which is developed in us by habitually conducting ourselves with propriety toward our fellow citizens. This does make us able to participate in the life of the earthly commonwealth. However, it is not sufficient to enable us to participate in the life of the commonwealth of heaven. The kind of justice or righteousness which we need for that must be infused by the grace of God Himself.

[2] St. Thomas points out that in St. Paul's letter to the Galatians, Paul takes the statement in Leviticus about "living in" God's laws in the same way that St. Thomas has just done. Here is the passage:

For all who rely on works of the law are under a curse; for it is written, "Cursed be everyone who does not abide by all things written in the book of the law, and do them." Now it is evident that no man is justified before God by the law; for "He who through faith is righteous shall live"; but the law does not rest on faith, for "He who does them shall live by them."[19]

---

[19] Galatians 3:10–12 (RSV-CE), changing "every one" to "everyone."

Paul's argument is extremely condensed, and the brevity of St. Thomas's quotation does not help us much. The argument contains three allusions to the Old Testament. The statement, "Cursed be everyone who does not abide by all things written in the book of the law, and do them" is from Deuteronomy 27:26, Deuteronomy being a book of the Law. The statement "He who through faith is righteous" is from Habakkuk 2:4, Habakkuk being one of the prophets. The statement "He who does them shall live by them" is the passage from Leviticus 18:5 which we have already seen in Objection 2.

Thus St. Thomas thinks that St. Paul's argument works like this:

1. We see from Deuteronomy that whoever does not do everything the law requires is condemned to death.
2. Thus, when Leviticus says that whoever *does* do these things will live, it means merely that he will not suffer capital punishment.
3. But the prophet Habakkuk says that he who is righteous *through faith* will live.
4. Plainly, then, the prophet is speaking of life in a different sense: he means not mere exemption from capital punishment, but spiritual life.
5. Since spiritual life comes not by the righteousness of following the law, but by the righteousness which comes through faith, we are *justified* not by the righteousness of following the law, but by the righteousness which comes through faith.

We may draw the further inferences that since such righteousness does not come through following the law, it is not acquired justice – rather, since it comes through the grace of faith, which is the gateway to all the infused virtues, it is infused justice.

Reply to Objection 3. [1] *The precepts of human law justify man by acquired justice:* [2] *it is not about this that we are inquiring now, but only about that justice which is before God.*

Reply to Objection 3. Obeying the precepts of human law does justify men in the sense that it causes the acquired virtue of justice. At present, however, we are asking about the justice which makes men acceptable to God, which is infused justice.

The Objector had pointed out that at least in one sense, even human law justifies us – it brings about the justice which lies simply in obeying it. If even human law can bring about the justice of obedience, then surely Divine law can do so.

St. Thomas replies that yes, Divine law can bring about the justice of obedience – it can cause us to become executors of the law. And this is one of the senses in which the term "justification" can be taken. The problem is that for present purposes, it is the *wrong* sense of justification. Certainly God expects obedience, but merely doing what He tells us to do is not the kind of righteousness which makes us acceptable in His sight. That is merely acquired justice. What makes us acceptable is infused justice.

DISCUSSION

St. Thomas and the Reformers

How does St. Thomas's view of justification compare with that of the Protestant Reformers? We have seen that the Angelic Doctor distinguishes two senses of justification, each of which is divided again to make four. In only one of these four senses does justification make us wholly acceptable to God, fully members of His kingdom – and this sense, of course, is most important. The justification which makes us acceptable to God is *becoming* just by the grace of Christ poured into our hearts, becoming people who possess the virtue of that justice which is illuminated by charity. Thus, the redeemed person is not only forgiven but also healed: although his free will does make it possible to fall into sin again, he actually becomes righteous, and if all goes well he matures in this righteousness.

The writers of the Protestant Reformation did not accept this view of justification. Typically, they held that we become acceptable to God not because we *become* just, but because God *declares* us to be just. God does not declare us just because we really have become just, but simply because He chooses to do so in view of our faith. A motto widely (though apparently incorrectly) attributed to Martin Luther sums up the idea in its most radical form by declaring that saved souls are heaps of dung covered with white snow. The dung in this picture is the reality of our hearts, while the snow is the righteousness of Christ. We see then why the Reformers thought it wrong to view justification as being made fully just and acceptable to God. For being declared acceptable to God is one thing; that, they said, is justification. But becoming just or holy is quite another; that, they said, is sanctification. If justification really is only a matter of God's declaration, then it has nothing to do with our obedience, which depends on our natural powers. Rather it depends solely on our faith, which depends solely on God's grace. This way of thinking makes justification an event rather than a process, for it happens at a point in time – the first moment of faith, when God declares us just. After that it cannot be undone. As a widely quoted aphorism puts it, "Once saved, always saved."

For St. Thomas, since justification is not just being declared just but actually being made just,[20] when God declares us just, He is commenting on His own

---

[20] I-II, Q. 113, Art. 1.

work. From this point of view, justification (becoming acceptable to God) and sanctification (becoming holy) are not radically different things, but different aspects of the same thing. Certainly justification depends on grace rather than human power;[21] he would have said that the Reformers were right about that. However, St. Thomas views our dependence on grace differently than they were later to view it. How so?

- In the first place, although God does demand obedience, St. Thomas does not view the obedience that fully pleases God as referring to things that we do by our natural powers apart from grace. Why not? Because obedience itself depends on grace,[22] and because nothing we can do without grace merits receiving it.[23]
- In the second place, St. Thomas would consider it wrong to think of faith and obedience as diametrically opposed, for faith itself is a form of obedience.[24] As St. Paul wrote, we are justified by faith *working in love*.[25]
- And in the third place, although justification does take place at a point in time[26] – when a sinful person turns in faith to God, it is like light entering a darkened room – yet justification must also continue and deepen, because it can subsequently be lost through sin.[27]

The query in the present Article is the role of moral observance in justification, and the form the query takes is to ask whether the Old Testament people were justified by fulfilling the precepts of the Old Law. Although the New Testament states at several points that we cannot be made fully just and acceptable to God by "the works of the law," St. Thomas follows Augustine in taking these statements to mean not that it makes no difference whether we do the right things, but that we cannot do the right things in a truly acceptable way unless we do the all-important right thing of loving God and neighbor, which requires the grace of Christ.

Since during Old Testament times, Christ had not yet come, were the Old Testament saints cut off from grace? No, for according to St. Thomas, they were justified by faith in the Messiah whose coming had been promised to them.[28] Yet it does make a difference when Christ comes, because after the

---

[21] I-II, Q. 113, Art. 2.
[22] I-II, Q. 109, Art. 4.
[23] I-II, Q. 109, Art. 6–7; Q. 112, Art. 2; and Q. 114, Art. 5.
[24] III, Q. 7, Art. 3, ad 2.
[25] Galatians 5:6.
[26] I-II, Q. 113, Art. 7.
[27] I-II, Q. 109, Art. 8; II-II, Q. 137, Art. 4.
[28] See for example I-II, Q. 106, Art. 1, ad 3, which I will discuss later.

Cross, the Resurrection, and the advent of the Holy Spirit, grace is poured out so much more freely.

At several points in this Article, St. Thomas has hinted at what happens when the Gospel of grace, the New Law, comes into the picture. As we will see, later on he takes up this matter more fully, beginning with Question 106.

QUESTION 102, ARTICLE 1

Whether there was any Cause for the Ceremonial Precepts?

TEXT	PARAPHRASE
Whether there was any cause for the ceremonial precepts?	Can explanations be given for the various ceremonial precepts, or were they arbitrary?

As we find in the Discussion at the end of this Article, there is still a good deal to be learned from the ceremonial precepts. However, since they are abolished by the New Law, they are much less important than formerly, for although their power to teach us something persists, their power to command does not. For this reason, the present Article is the only one we devote to them. The previous Question, 101, which is not covered in this book, concerns the nature, characteristics, number, and kinds of the ceremonial precepts. The next Question, 103, also omitted here, concerns their duration (in particular, whether they passed away when Christ came). Question 102, to which the present Article is the introduction, presents a detailed examination of the reasons for them. This is the aspect of the topic which has the most enduring interest, even to the present day.

The ceremonial precepts are *determinations* of the first three of the Ten Commandments, which concern the worship of God. As we saw discovered during the discussion of I-II, Question 100, Article 11, they do not depend on "the very dictate of reason," because although it could not be other than right to worship God, He might have enacted other modes of worshipping Him instead. But this fact does not imply that there were *no reasons* for enacting these modes rather than others. Were there such reasons? Or did the Divine legislator flip a coin?

Suppose Martian legal scholars, observing earth with telescopes and radio receivers, make an effort to understand human traffic regulations. This is a puzzling matter for Martians, because they have no traffic; they teleport. Evidently, the mere need to prevent collisions makes it sensible for humans to drive on only one side of the road; that is clear enough. However, it does not dictate on which side of the road they should drive. How, then, did the humans in some places decide that drivers should keep to the right? And how did they decide in other places that they should keep to the left? Can no further reason be given for these rules than "this is what they are"?

Were the Ceremonial Precepts Arbitrary or Reasonable? 285

But the Martians come to realize that there may have been further reasons after all. One of them points out that human traffic regulations might have descended from the days before automobiles, when humans travelled by horse and on foot. Bearing in mind that most humans are right-handed – another odd fact, because Martians are ambidextrous – he speculates that humans driving teams of horses on highly traveled roads would have preferred to keep to the right, so that the right hand, which was the whip hand, faced away from other traffic. Yet it would not necessarily have been unreasonable for the opposite custom to develop in other places, because humans traveling on foot, especially through dangerous country, might have preferred to keep to the left, so that the right hand, which was the sword hand, faced toward passersby. Perhaps this is the solution to the puzzle! Reasons can be given for driving on a particular side of the road, *even though the other side might also have been chosen*. The humans were not so much flipping a coin irrespective of reasons as *choosing among reasons*.

Although St. Thomas has much more information than the Martians, although he is studying his own species rather than another, and although he is considering Divine legislation rather than human, even so he is trying to solve a similar problem. God might have enacted different ceremonial precepts for the Hebrew people than He actually did. For example, He might have required different sacrifices, or He might not have required sacrifices at all. Was the fact that just these precepts and not others were enacted wholly unaccountable, or can we infer reasons for the choices?

The brevity of the present Article results partly from the fact that it is elliptical: some parts of the argument are tacit. Rather than elaborating each of his points fully, the Angelic Doctor depends on what he has said earlier in the *Summa*, what he says later in the *Summa*, and what he trusts us to figure out for ourselves. Let us try to put all this together.

Objection 1. [1] *It would seem that there was no cause for the ceremonial precepts. Because on Eph. 2, "Making void the law of the commandments,"* [2] *the gloss says, (i.e.) "making void the Old Law as to the carnal observances, by substituting decrees, i.e. evangelical precepts, which are based on reason."* [3] *But if the observances of the Old Law were based on reason, it would have been useless to void them by the reasonable decrees of the New Law. Therefore there was no reason for the ceremonial observances of the Old Law.*

Objection 1. Apparently the ceremonial precepts were arbitrary. Consider St. Paul's remark that in his flesh, Christ emptied the law of commandments, reducing it to nothing. A commentary on the passage explains that He did this by replacing them with evangelical precepts, which originate in reason. Now if the ceremonial observances of the Old Law themselves originated in reason, there would have been no reason to replace them with decrees of the New Law, which do originate in it. But since they *were* replaced, it follows that the ceremonial observances of the Old Law did *not* originate in reason.

---

[1] The Scholastic habit of quoting only a few words of a passage is convenient for people who have read all the same works and need only a cue in order to bring the whole passage into memory – but it is frustrating for most of us, who may not have read all the same works and certainly do not have such highly trained memories. St. Thomas is thinking of the following passage from the letter of St. Paul to the Christians in the city of Ephesus. Paul argues that although, for good reasons, the Old Law kept the Chosen People from mingling with other nations, the time for that has now ended. In Christ, Jew, and Gentile can be reconciled and united. Here I give the passage in the words of the RSV-CE, which uses the word "abolishing" where the Vulgate says *evacuans* and the DRA says "making void."

For [Christ] is our peace, who has made us both one, and has broken down the dividing wall of hostility, by abolishing in his flesh the law of commandments and ordinances, that he might create in himself one new man in place of the two, so making peace, and might reconcile us both to God in one body through the cross, thereby bringing the hostility to an end.[1]

What interests the Objector about this passage is what it says about abolishing the Old Law, and he now turns to what one of the commentaries says about that.

[2] The Objector is abbreviating an explanation of the Ephesians passage found in Peter Lombard's *Great Gloss*, according to which, when St. Paul writes the quoted words to the Ephesians,

He explains the wall separating the Jews as though to say that [Christ] Himself, *abolishing the commandments of the Law* – that is, abolishing the Old Law with respect to the things it commanded, with respect to its bodily observances, though not with respect to the truth which they foreshadowed – abolishing, I say, *the decrees*, by the Evangelical precepts, which are based on reason – abolishes the law's division of the two peoples, *reconciling [them] in Himself*, that is, joining them to Himself in faith.[2]

For the Objector's purposes, these three points in the passage are important:

1. The moral precepts of the Old Law were not abolished, only its "carnal observances" were – that is, its ceremonial precepts, called "carnal" because they concerned physical acts.
2. They were replaced by the Evangelical precepts – the precepts of the Gospel.
3. The Evangelical precepts are based on reason – once God has revealed them, the mind can see that they are good.

---

[1] Ephesians 2:14–15 (RSV-CE).
[2] My rendering. The Latin is *Hic exponit parietem quantum ad partem Judaeorum; quasi dicat: Ipse dico, evacuans legem mandatorum, idest evacuans legem veterem, quantum ad ea quae mandabat, idest ad carnales observantias, non quantum ad veritatem quam praesignabat. Evacuans dico, decretis, idest praeceptis Evangelii quae ex ratione sunt, idio evacuavit ut duos populos prius divisos per legem, condat in semetipso, idest conjungat in fide ejus.*

Were the Ceremonial Precepts Arbitrary or Reasonable?

[3] The argument works like this:

1. The ceremonial precepts were replaced by the Evangelical precepts because the Evangelical precepts are based on reason.
2. Had the ceremonial precepts been based on reason, their replacement with precepts based on reason would have been pointless.
3. But God does nothing pointlessly (tacit premise).
4. Therefore, the ceremonial precepts were not based on reason.

Objection 2. [1] *Further, the Old Law succeeded the law of nature.* [2] *But in the law of nature there was a precept for which there was no reason save that man's obedience might be tested;* [3] *as Augustine says (Gen. ad lit. viii), concerning the prohibition about the tree of life.* [4] *Therefore in the Old Law there should have been some precepts for the purpose of testing man's obedience, having no reason in themselves.*

Objection 2. Moreover, the Old Law took the place of the natural law. But as St. Augustine points out, the natural law included a precept, the prohibition of eating from the tree of life, which had no other purpose than to test man's obedience. It follows that the Old Law should also have included precepts that were arbitrary in the sense that they had no other purpose than to test man's obedience – precepts for which no cause could be found in the thing commanded or prohibited. In the ceremonial precepts, we do find such precepts.

---

[1] Although we cannot fail to know the general precepts of natural law, such as the duty of honoring our parents, it is all too easy for us to misapply them – and the knowledge of their remote implications can be entirely obliterated.[3] Before the days of the Patriarchs, all such matters had become dreadfully obscured by sin. God gave the Divine law as medicine. It "succeeded" the natural law, not in the sense that it nullified it, but in the sense that it restated it more forcefully, repromulgating it in words. Paradoxically, for some people one of the strongest motives for *not* believing in Divine law is just that it *does* make the natural law more clear. Having just enough left of the tooth of conscience to feel its bite, one may not want that tooth further sharpened. This makes the Divine pedagogy a formidable task, which may be why God began with a single nation, radiating His truth outward from there.

---

[3] "There belong to the natural law, first, certain most general precepts, that are known to all; and secondly, certain secondary and more detailed precepts, which are, as it were, conclusions following closely from first principles. As to those general principles, the natural law, in the abstract, can nowise be blotted out from men's hearts. But it is blotted out in the case of a particular action, insofar as reason is hindered from applying the general principle to a particular point of practice, on account of concupiscence or some other passion, as stated above. But as to the other, i.e. the secondary precepts, the natural law can be blotted out from the human heart, either by evil persuasions ... or by vicious customs and corrupt habits." I-II, Q. 94, Art. 6.

The idea that the Old Law clarified the natural law and confirmed its authority was well known to the Fathers of the Church. St. Jerome discusses the Old Law as a supplement to the natural law in two places, one of them his *Commentary on Isaiah*, where he pithily remarks, "The law was given by Moses because the first law was squandered."[4]

The other, a bit longer, is in his *Commentary on the Letter to the Galatians*:

> Cornelius[5] received the Spirit by believing what he had heard and by obeying the natural law, which speaks in our hearts and directs us to do good and to shun evil … This natural law can then be augmented by observance of the Law and the righteousness that comes from the Law – not the fleshy Law, which has passed away, but the spiritual Law, for the Law is spiritual.[6]

Ambrosiaster, also known as Pseudo-Ambrosius – a writer once confused with St. Ambrose of Milan because of the excellence of his commentaries – writes as follows in his *Commentary on the Letter to the Romans*:

> Indeed, law is triple. The first part, concerning the sacraments, pertains to the divinity of God; the second corresponds to natural law, which reveals sin; and the third concerns such things as the Sabbath, New Moons, and circumcision. This, then, is the natural law, in part restored by Moses, and in part, by his authority, confirmed in prohibiting vices and making sin known.[7]

The real St. Ambrose writes to much the same effect, but at greater length:

> Here is one reason the Law on the one hand was superfluous and yet became necessary. It was superfluous herein, that it would not have been needed could we have kept the natural Law, but as we kept it not, the law of Moses became needful for us, to the intent that it might teach us obedience and loose that knot of Adam's transgression which has fettered his whole posterity. Guilt indeed was increased by the Law, but pride, the author of this guilt, was overthrown by it, and this was profitable to me, for pride discovered the guilt, and this guilt brought grace.

---

[4] My rendering. The Latin is *postea lex data sit per Moysen, quia prima lex dissipata est*. St. Jerome, *Commentary on Isaiah*, on Isaiah 24:6.

[5] Cornelius, a Roman centurion who was directed by an angel to receive the Apostles into his house and hear their teaching, is described to St. Peter in Acts 10:22 (RSV-CE) as an "upright and God-fearing man, who is well spoken of by the whole Jewish nation." The "God-fearers" were Gentiles who believed in the God of Israel and practiced Jewish worship but were not circumcised and assimilated into the Jewish nation. We consider their status later on, in Q. 105, Art. 3. Here Jerome's point is that although Cornelius did not obey the ceremonial precepts of the Old Law, he did obey the natural law, which the Old Law's moral precepts amplified.

[6] St. Jerome, *Commentary on the Letter to the Galatians*, translated by Andrew Cain (Washington, DC: Catholic University of America Press, 2010), p. 121, on Galatians 3:2. The remark that the law is spiritual alludes to Romans 7:14.

[7] My rendering. The Latin is *Triplex quidem lex est; ita ut prima pars de sacramento divinitatis sit Dei: secunda autem quae congruit legi naturali, quae indicit peccatum: tertia vero factorum, id est, Sabbati, neomeniae, circumcisionis, etc. Haec est ergo lex naturalis, quae per Moysen partim reformata, partim auctoritatas ejus firmata in vitiis cohibendis, cognitum fecit peccatum.* Ambrosiaster is commenting on Romans 3:20.

Were the Ceremonial Precepts Arbitrary or Reasonable? 289

Hear another reason. At first [before the Fall], Moses' Law was not needed; it was introduced subsequently, and this appears to intimate that this introduction was in a sense clandestine and not of an ordinary kind, seeing that it succeeded in the place of the natural Law. Had this maintained its place, the written Law would never have entered in; but the natural Law being excluded by transgression and almost blotted out of the human breast, pride reigned, and disobedience spread itself; and then this Law succeeded, that by its written precepts it might cite us before it, and every mouth be stopped, and all the world become guilty before God.[8]

[2] True, the natural law directs us to nothing but our good. But as we asked in this book's introduction, is it possible that part of what makes it good for us lies in doing it just because God commands it? If so, then such obedience is good even apart from the goodness of the thing commanded. Invoking St. Augustine to back him up, the Objector reasons that it was important for this fact to be demonstrated. Thus, God commanded our first parents not to eat of the fruit of the tree, even though nothing about the fruit itself made such an act wrong.

It is curious that the Objector calls the prohibition of eating the fruit a *natural* law, because natural laws can be discerned by reason alone, and reason alone would not have instructed our first parents not to eat the fruit. On the other hand, reason alone would certainly have instructed them *that they ought to obey God, even if they could not see the reason for His commandment*. So perhaps this is the natural law principle to which the Objector is referring. Another possibility is that the prohibition of eating the fruit is called a natural law because it was promulgated while our nature was still in the condition of its original integrity, before the Fall.

[3] Actually, there are two trees in the story, the tree of life and the tree of knowledge of good and evil, and the prohibited tree is the latter – not, as the Objector states, the former.[9] This is a mere slip, and is immaterial to the Objector's argument. It is an easy slip to make, because *after* our first parents violated the prohibition of eating from the tree of knowledge of good and evil, *then* they were also prevented from eating from the tree of life. At any rate, in his Reply to Objection 2, St. Thomas identifies the forbidden tree correctly.

To support his claim that the prohibition had no other reason but to test man's obedience, the Objector calls on St. Augustine, who explains: "The tree was called 'the knowledge to discern good from evil' not because it was evil, but

---

[8] St. Ambrose, *The Letters of Ambrose, Bishop of Milan*, translated by H. Walford (public domain), letter 73, sections 9–10.

[9] "And out of the ground the Lord God made to grow every tree that is pleasant to the sight and good for food, the tree of life also in the midst of the garden, and the tree of the knowledge of good and evil." Genesis 2:9. "And the Lord God commanded the man, saying, 'You may freely eat of every tree of the garden; but of the tree of the knowledge of good and evil you shall not eat, for in the day that you eat of it you shall die.'" Genesis 2:16–17. Both quotations RSV-CE.

because if man ate from it after being forbidden to do so, his transgression taught him a lesson. Just by experiencing the penalty, the difference between the good of obedience and the evil of disobedience became clear to him."[10]

The penalty of which Augustine speaks is the rupture of the integrity of man's relationship with God, along with the resulting rupture of his internal integrity. Since man's mind has rebelled against God, his passions and appetites also rebel against his mind. As a consequence, man also becomes subject to physical death. A little later, St. Augustine adds,

> The tree is not prohibited because it is evil, but because the very act of keeping the precept is good, and its transgression evil.[11]

Still later,

> Why is it prohibited, unless to demonstrate the good of obedience itself, and the evil of disobedience itself?[12]

[4] The omniscient God "tests" man's obedience not in the sense that He needs to find out something about man, but in the sense that man needs to find out something about himself. If man obeys the prohibition, then he will discover the good of obedience by experiencing its delight. If he disobeys, then he will discover the good of obedience by experiencing the deadly consequences of rebellion, for it is no small thing to break away from the very wellspring of our life and being.

The Objector does not merely claim that one purpose of the prohibition was to test man's obedience. He goes further, claiming that it had *no other* purpose. The specific thing prohibited is in this view irrelevant. God might have accomplished the same test, say, by forbidding man from setting foot in a certain rivulet of water. Because such a prohibition would have accomplished the same test as the prohibition which was actually given, this stream might then have been called "the rivulet of the knowledge of good and evil."

Objection 3. [1] Further, man's works are called moral according	Objection 3. Besides, the reason that man's deeds are called "moral" is that there are

---

[10] My rendering. The Latin is *Arbor itaque illa non erat mala, sed appellata est scientiae dignoscendi bonum et malum, quia si post prohibitionem ex illa homo ederet, in illa erat praecepti futura transgressio, in qua homo per experimentum poenae disceret, quid interesset inter obedientiae bonum, et inobedientiae malum.* St. Augustine of Hippo, *The Literal Meaning of Genesis*, book VIII, chapter 6, section 12.

[11] My rendering. The Latin is *Ab eo ligno quod malum non erat prohibitus est, ut ipsa per se praecepti conservatio bonum illi esset, et transgressio malum.* Ibid., book VIII, chapter 13, section 28.

[12] My rendering. The Latin is *Quare prohibitum est, nisi ut ipsius per se bonum obedientiae, et ipsius per se malum inobedientiae monstraretur?* Ibid., book VIII, chapter 13, section 29.

as they proceed from reason. [2] If therefore there is any reason for the ceremonial precepts, they would not differ from the moral precepts. It seems therefore that there was no cause for the ceremonial precepts: [3] *for the reason of a precept is taken from some cause.*	reasons for them. So if there were reasons for the ceremonial precepts, then they too would be moral precepts; and since they are *not* moral precepts, there must *not* be any reason for them. Apparently, then, no explanations can be given for the ceremonial precepts, because a precept has an explanation only if the mind can grasp the *why* of it.

[1] The expression "moral acts" does not mean morally good acts, but acts capable of being judged morally good or bad. Only man can be said to perform genuinely moral acts, because moral action is based on reason, and only man is rational.[13]

St. Thomas credits the identification of moral acts with human acts to St. Ambrose of Milan.[14] Borrowing from "the philosophers of this world," Ambrose distinguishes three aspects of wisdom – the natural, moral, and rational – which in his view correspond to the historical, moral, and allegorical aspects of the gospels. In a famous passage, he says that the Gospel of Matthew excels in the moral aspect of wisdom because it emphasizes Christ's precepts, and "it is well that such an opinion not be passed over," he says, for "morality is properly called human."[15]

[2] The argument works like this:

1. Morality is based on reason.
2. So moral precepts are those for which there is a reason.
3. So if there were reasons for the ceremonial precepts, then they too would be moral precepts.
4. But this is not the case; the ceremonial precepts are not moral precepts.
5. Therefore there were no reasons for them.

The argument is a little odd because the original reason for placing the ceremonial precepts in a different category than the moral precepts was not that there was no reason for them, but that the moral precepts declared general principles while the ceremonial precepts determined them. They pinned down the details of how these general principles were to be observed.

---

[13] I-II, Q. 18, Art. 8.
[14] I-II, Q. 1, Art. 3.
[15] Although Ambrose is speaking about the Gospel of Matthew, these remarks appear in his exposition of the Gospel of Luke. For an English translation, see St. Ambrose of Milan, *Commentary on the Gospel According to St. Luke*, Prologue, sections 2, 3, and 7, in Boniface Ramsey, OP, trans., *Ambrose* (London: Routledge, 1997). For the Latin text see http://monumenta.ch/latein.

[3] In many places, the term "cause" can be paraphrased "reason," but here such a paraphrase would fail because the statement "the reason of a precept is taken from some cause" would then become "the reason of a precept is taken from some reason," which says exactly nothing. We can climb out of this terminological difficulty by recalling that in the broadest sense, by the "cause" of a thing St. Thomas means its *explanation* – why it is what it is instead of something else. Since there are four aspects of explaining a thing – what it is made of, what is its pattern, what brought it into being, and what it is for – St. Thomas follows Aristotle in calling these the four causes. These considerations enable us to paraphrase "the reason of a precept is taken from some cause" as "the explanation of a precept provides the reason for it," or "a precept has an explanation only if the mind can grasp the *why* of it."

On the contrary, [1] *It is written (Ps. 18): "The commandment of the Lord is lightsome, enlightening the eyes."* [2] *But the ceremonial precepts are commandments of God. Therefore they are lightsome:* [3] *and yet they would not be so, if they had no reasonable cause. Therefore the ceremonial precepts have a reasonable cause.*	**On the other hand,** the inspired poet of the Psalms writes that God's precepts are clear and bright, giving light to the eyes. Since the ceremonial observances are included in His precepts, they too are clear and bright. Yet if they had no reasonable cause, they would not be. It follows that they do have a reasonable cause.

[1] Here is the context of the quotation, which is taken from the Psalms:

The law of the Lord is perfect, reviving the soul; the testimony of the Lord is sure, making wise the simple; the precepts of the Lord are right, rejoicing the heart; *the commandment of the Lord is pure, enlightening the eyes*; the fear of the Lord is clean, enduring forever; the ordinances of the Lord are true, and righteous altogether. More to be desired are they than gold, even much fine gold; sweeter also than honey and drippings of the honeycomb.[16]

The Universal Doctor often describes the light of God as illuminating our minds. One of his favorite passages of Scripture is Psalm 4:6 (DRA),[17] "The light of Thy countenance, O Lord, is signed upon us," which he takes to mean that the light of natural reason which enables us to distinguish good from evil is nothing other than an impression of the Divine light upon us.[18]

---

[16] Psalm 19:7–10 (RSV-CE), emphasis added. In the DRA, this passage is numbered as Psalm 18:8–11.
[17] In most contemporary translations this verse is numbered 4:7.
[18] See especially I-II, Q. 91, Art. 2.

Of course here the expression "light" does not refer to physical light, nor does the expression "eyes" refer to bodily eyes. Yet in St. Thomas's view, the expressions are much more than a metaphor, for the analogy between physical and intellectual light is precise. Just as things become visible to our bodily eyes only to the degree that they are illuminated by the physical light of the sun, so things become intelligible to our minds only to the degree that they are illuminated by the intellectual light of Divine reason. Even the animal "sees" a thing, because of physical light that illuminates its eyes, but only a rational being knows what it is seeing, because of the intellectual light that illuminates its mind.

In this life we cannot perceive God in Himself – just we cannot gaze directly at the sun – but the problem is not that the light is not bright enough, but that it is too bright to take in. Among the redeemed souls in heaven, this limitation is removed, because God supernaturally uplifts their intellects in order to perceive Him as He is in His essence. Yet even in this life, just as the sun's light makes it possible for other things to be seen, so the Divine light makes it possible for other things to be understood.

[2] Since all of God's commandments impart understanding to our minds, *ipso facto* His ceremonial commandments impart understanding to our minds.

[3] But how could they impart understanding to our minds if there was nothing in them which touched the rational nature of our minds? There must be something in them which does so; therefore, the *sed contra* concludes, they are not arbitrary, but have reasons.

I answer that, [1] *Since, according to the Philosopher (Metaph. i), it is the function of a "wise man to do everything in order,"* [2] *those things which proceed from the Divine wisdom must needs be well ordered,* [3] *as the Apostle states (Rom. 13).* [4] *Now there are two conditions required for things to be well ordered. First, that they be ordained to their due end, which is the principle of the whole order in matters of action:* [5] *since those things that happen by chance outside the intention of the end, or which are not done seriously but for fun, are said to be inordinate.* [6] *Secondly, that which is done in view of the end should be proportionate to the end.* [7] *From this it follows that the reason for whatever*

Here is my response. Since even among humans, the wise set things in order (as Aristotle says), certainly the all-wise God must set in order the things that proceed from His wisdom (as St. Paul says). However, order has two requirements:

1. *The things that are done must be directed to their end or purpose,* because this is the foundation of all order in action. Indeed, things that turn out differently than intended, or that are done not in earnest but as a tease or a frolic, are called irregular rather than orderly.
2. *Since they are directed to their end, these things must also accord with their end.* This is why the reason for doing something is drawn from the purpose to which it is directed. For example, as Aristotle says, the saw is

conduces to the end is taken from the end: [8] *thus the reason for the disposition of a saw is taken from cutting, which is its end, as stated in* Phys. ii. *[9] Now it is evident that the ceremonial precepts, like all the other precepts of the Law, were institutions of Divine wisdom: [10] hence it is written (Dt. 4): "This is your wisdom and understanding in the sight of nations." [11] Consequently we must needs say that the ceremonial precepts were ordained to a certain end, wherefrom their reasonable causes can be gathered.*

shaped and handled in a certain way so that it will be able to cut.

Plainly, the ceremonial precepts were framed by Divine wisdom, just like all the other precepts of Divine law. This is why, as recorded in Deuteronomy, Moses told the people that other nations would view their obedience to them as their wisdom and understanding.

Taken together, these considerations drive us necessarily to the conclusion that the ceremonial precepts were indeed directed to some end or purpose – and that from it, we can work out the reasons for them.

---

[1] Aristotle writes in his *Metaphysics*,

And we think that a superior science which is rather the more basic comes nearer to wisdom than a subordinate science. For a wise man must not be directed but must direct, and he must not obey another but must be obeyed by one who is less wise. Such then and so many are the opinions which we have about the wise and about wisdom. Now [the attribute of] knowing all things necessarily belongs to him who has universal knowledge in the highest degree, because he knows in which are subordinate.[19]

St. Thomas explains in book 1, lecture 1 of his *Commentary* on the work,

[I]n the opinion of all it is not fitting that a wise man should be directed by someone else, but that he should direct others. The second is that inferior artists are induced to act by superior artists inasmuch as they rely upon superior artists for the things which they must do or make. Thus the shipbuilder relies upon the instructions of the navigator for the kind of form which a ship ought to have. However, it does not befit a wise man that he should be induced to act by someone else, but that he should use his knowledge to induce others to act.

These, then, are the kind of opinions which men have of wisdom and the wise; and from all of these a description of wisdom can be formulated, so that the wise man is described as one who knows all, even difficult matters, with certitude and through their cause; who seeks this knowledge for its own sake; and who directs others and induces them to act ...

Whoever knows universals knows in some respect the things which are subordinate to universals, because he knows the universal in them. But all things are subordinate to

---

[19] Aristotle, *Metaphysics*, book 1, chapter 2. I am following the wording of Thomas Aquinas, *Commentary on Aristotle's Metaphysics*, translated by John P. Rowan (Chicago: Regnery, 1961).

those which are most universal. Therefore the one who knows the most universal things, knows in a sense all things.[20]

He speaks of the same passage of the *Metaphysics* in his *Commentary on Aristotle's Nicomachean Ethics*, where he writes in book 1, lecture 1,

> As the Philosopher says in the beginning of the *Metaphysics*, it is the business of the wise man to order. The reason for this is that wisdom is the most powerful perfection of reason whose characteristic is to know order. Even if the sensitive powers know some things absolutely, nevertheless to know the order of one thing to another is exclusively the work of intellect or reason.
>
> Now a twofold order is found in things. One kind is that of parts of a totality, that is, a group, among themselves, as the parts of a house are mutually ordered to each other. The second order is that of things to an end. This order is of greater importance than the first. For, as the Philosopher says in the eleventh book of the Metaphysics, the order of the parts of an army among themselves exists because of the order of the whole army to the commander.
>
> Now order is related to reason in a fourfold way. There is one order that reason does not establish but only beholds, such is the order of things in nature. There is a second order that reason establishes in its own act of consideration, for example, when it arranges its concepts among themselves, and the signs of concept as well, because words express the meanings of the concepts. There is a third order that reason in deliberating establishes in the operations of the will. There is a fourth order that reason in planning establishes in the external things which it causes, such as a chest and a house.[21]

[2] St. Thomas quotes frequently from the Wisdom books of the Old Testament. One of his favorite passages personifies the Wisdom by which God Created, saying that "she reacheth from end to end mightily, and ordereth all things sweetly."[22] He also quotes often from the eighth chapter of Proverbs, where personified Wisdom declares,

> I, Wisdom, dwell in prudence, and I find knowledge and discretion ... By me kings reign, and rulers decree what is just; by me princes rule, and nobles govern the earth ... The Lord created me at the beginning of his work, the first of his acts of old. Ages ago I was set up, at the first, before the beginning of the earth. When there were no depths I was brought forth, when there were no springs abounding with water ... then I was beside him, like a master workman; and I was daily his delight, rejoicing before him always, rejoicing in his inhabited world and delighting in the sons of men.[23]

[3] Throughout the *Summa*, St. Thomas paraphrases St. Paul's remark in Romans 13:1 that "those [powers] that are, are ordained [or ordered] by God" as "whatever is of God is well ordered" (*quae autem sunt, a Deo ordinatae*

---

[20] Ibid., book 1, lesson 2.
[21] Thomas Aquinas, *Commentary on Aristotle's Nicomachean Ethics*, trans. Litzinger.
[22] Wisdom of Solomon 8:1 (DRA). This single verse is quoted eight times in the *Summa* alone.
[23] Proverbs 8:12, 15–16, 30–31 (RSV-CE). The *Summa* alone includes thirteen quotations from this chapter.

becomes *quae a Deo sunt, ordinata sunt*).²⁴ However, the use of this passage may seem a stretch, because St. Paul is speaking only of earthly authorities, but St. Thomas is speaking more generally. The passage from the Wisdom of Solomon that we saw just above would support his claim more convincingly.

[4] The process of preparing a meal would hardly be well ordered if the cook spent most of his time juggling teacups and did not watch the sauce pot.

[5] In everyday English, we tend to use the word "inordinate," from *inordinata*, to mean "excessive." Its original meaning, in both English and Latin, was rather that something is not well ordered to, or not well directed to, a serious purpose.

St. Thomas is not, by the way, suggesting that *everything* must be done for a serious purpose. In fact, he seriously suggests that there is a time for not being serious. For joking and frolic are themselves directed to a purpose, though a light one. We return to this point in the Discussion at the end of the Article.

[6] To be "proportionate" to something means to correspond to it, to be fittingly related to it, to be congruent with it, to accord with it. Even if the cook does everything for the sake of the meal, his actions are not proportionate to the end if he melts the ice cream, puts salt in the coffee, or serves the omelette raw.

[7] The fitness of the act depends on what we are doing it for. If there is to be a house, we must gather bricks and stones; but the bricks and stones are for the sake of the house, not the house for the sake of the bricks and stones. First-time readers sometimes ask whether this implies that "the ends justify the means." No, not in the sense the questioner intends. Even if the assassin's knife and garrote are well proportioned to his end, we must not approve murder. However, the reason is not that the ends and means are unrelated. Rather it is that the act of murder is intrinsically incapable of being offered to our *ultimate* end, who is God.

[8] The "disposition" of a saw is its suitability for the use to which we put it. Speaking in his *Physics* of the relationship of means to ends, Aristotle asks,

For instance, why is a saw such as it is? To effect so-and-so and for the sake of so-and-so. This end, however, cannot be realized unless the saw is made of iron. It is, therefore, necessary for it to be of iron, it we are to have a saw and perform the operation of sawing. What is necessary then, is necessary on a hypothesis; it is not a result necessarily determined by antecedents. Necessity is in the matter [it is necessary that we use iron], while "that for the sake of which" is in the definition [of what we are doing].²⁵

---

²⁴ See I, Q. 22, Art. 2; I, Q. 96, 3, *sed contra*; I-II, Q. 100, Art. 6, *sed contra*; I-II, Q. 111, Art. 1; II-II, Q. 172, Art. 2; III, Q. 30, Art. 4, *sed contra*; III, Q. 36, Art. 2; III, Q. 42, Art. 1; III, Q. 55, Art. 2; and III, Q. 69, Art. 2, Obj. 1.

²⁵ Aristotle, *Physics*, book II, chapter 9. I am following the wording of Thomas Aquinas, *Commentary on Aristotle's Physics*, translated by Richard J. Blackwell, Richard J. Spath, and W. Edmund Thirlkel (New Haven, CT: Yale University Press, 1963).

Were the Ceremonial Precepts Arbitrary or Reasonable? 297

One might wonder what a discussion of the purposes of saws is doing in Aristotle's book on physics. Its context is a discussion of how things (such as saws, bodies, and houses) come to be what they are, and of the absurdity of materialistic thinking, which tries to reduce the *purpose for which* a thing exists to the *stuff of which* it consists. In his *Commentary* on the work, St. Thomas explains as follows:

> He says that some are of the opinion that the generation of natural things arises from an absolute necessity of matter. For example, one might say that a wall or a house is such as it is by the necessity of matter because heavy things are disposed to move downward and light things to rise above. And because of this the heavy and hard stones remain in the foundation, while earth being lighter rises above the stones, as is clear in walls constructed of tiles which are made of earth. But the timbers which are the lightest are placed at the highest point, i.e., at the roof. Thus they thought that the dispositions of natural things have come to be such as they are from the necessity of matter. For example, it might be said that a man has feet below and hands above because of the heaviness or lightness of [bodily fluids] . . .
>
> He says, therefore, first that granting that it seems absurd to say that there is such a disposition in natural things because of the matter, it also appears absurd to say that this is true of artificial things . . . However, such a disposition [to the end] is not produced in natural things and in artificial things unless the material principles have an aptitude for such a disposition. For a house would not stand well unless the heavier materials were placed in the foundation and the lighter materials above . . .
>
> [T]he parts of a house are so disposed for the sake of an end, which is to shelter and protect men from the heat and the rain. And just as it is with a house, so it is with all other things in which something happens to act for the sake of something. For in all things of this sort the dispositions of what is generated or made do not follow without material principles, which have a necessary matter by which they are apt to be so disposed.[26]

[9] A traditional quotation in praise of the Divine Wisdom was provided in the *sed contra*, but the idea of this Wisdom pervades Holy Scripture. In the following passage the psalmist speaks of how the study and observance of its commandments has made him wise as well:

> O how have I loved thy law, O Lord! it is my meditation all the day. Through thy commandment, thou hast made me wiser than my enemies: for it is ever with me. I have understood more than all my teachers: because thy testimonies are my meditation. I have had understanding above ancients: because I have sought thy commandments. . . . By thy commandments I have had understanding: therefore have I hated every way of iniquity.[27]

[10] We have seen this passage once before in the context of Question 100, Article 7. Before their entrance into the Promised Land, Moses reminds the

---

[26] Aquinas, *Commentary on Aristotle's Physics*, trans. Blackwell, Spath, and Thirlkel, book II, lecture 15.
[27] Psalm 118:97–100, 103–104 (DRA).

people of God's care and urges them to keep His commandments, which are so wisely framed that because of them even other nations will regard the nation as wise:

> And you shall observe, and fulfill them in practice. For this is your wisdom, and understanding in the sight of nations, that hearing all these precepts, they may say: Behold a wise and understanding people, a great nation ... For what other nation is there so renowned that hath ceremonies, and just judgments, and all the law, which I will set forth this day before your eyes?[28]

[11] In the passage just quoted, Moses commends not only the wisdom of the moral precepts but also the wisdom of the ceremonial and judicial precepts. Assuming the truth of Holy Scripture, this makes it impossible to suggest that the ceremonial precepts were arbitrary. If we know their end, or purpose, we can work out the reason for each one of them.

What then is their purpose? To direct the people to the worship of God, yes, but this purpose is very general. By itself, it would not show why the people were directed to worship God in these particular ways rather than in others. So there must be more to it than that – and as we are about to see in the Reply to Objection 1, there is.

| *Reply to Objection 1.* [1] *It may be said there was no reason for the observances of the Old Law, in the sense that there was no reason in the very nature of the thing done: for instance that a garment should not be made of wool and linen.* [2] *But there could be a reason for them in relation to something else: namely, insofar as something was signified or excluded thereby.* [3] *On the other hand, the decrees of the New Law, which refer chiefly to faith and the love of God, are reasonable from the very nature of the act.* | Reply to Objection 1. In one respect, the Objector is right: We may say that there was no reason for the ceremonial observances of the Old Law in the sense that there was no reason *in the nature* of each thing that was prescribed – say, not wearing a single garment of both wool and linen.

But in another respect, we can indeed speak of a reason for these precepts. For each thing that was done either symbolized some other thing, or established a barrier keeping some other thing away.

The reasons for the precepts of the New Law are different. Since they mainly concern faith and love of God, the acts they prescribe are reasonable in their own nature. |

---

[1] The Objector had argued that since the ceremonial observances of the Old Law were *replaced* by the reasonable precepts of the Gospel, they must not themselves have been reasonable; otherwise, why replace them? The essence of St. Thomas's reply is that although they were not based on reason in the same

---

[28] Deuteronomy 4:6,8 (DRA). In Q. 100, Art. 7 the RSV-CE was used.

way as the moral precepts and the precepts of the Gospel were (that is what he concedes here), they are certainly based on reason in another sense (that is what he will argue next).

The Old Law contained a number of precepts directing that certain kinds of things be kept apart. For instance, an ox and an ass were not to be yoked together, two different kinds of seed were not to be sown in the same field, and, as he here points out, a garment should not be made of both wool and linen.[29] In the case of the moral precepts, the reason can always be found in the nature of the thing which is prohibited. For example, dishonoring our parents and craving our neighbor's goods are intrinsically wrong – wrong just because of what they are. Yet there seems to be nothing intrinsically wrong with wearing two kinds of fiber or fabric together. In fact, the Old Law *requires* the use of both wool and linen in the various garments to be worn by the priests.[30] Had there been something intrinsically wrong with combining them, surely this would have been forbidden to the priests too.

[2] As we have already seen, the general purpose of the ceremonial precepts was to direct the people to the worship of God. However, this general purpose does not explain why they were required to worship Him in one way rather than another. Here St. Thomas states two specific purposes, for in each case, the particular ways of worship that were commanded either symbolized some other thing, excluded some other thing, or both. We can illustrate with the required animal sacrifices, for all at the same time they *represented* the offering of the mind to God, *separated* the people from the worship of the idols to which they had formerly offered sacrifice, *represented* atonement for sins, and *foreshadowed* the "one individual and paramount sacrifice" of Christ, which not only symbolized the taking away of sins, but actually took sins away.

Oddly, St. Thomas does not take the opportunity here to explain *just what was* symbolized or excluded by the prohibition of wearing garments containing both linen and wool; he saves that for later. We return to the puzzle about not mingling linen with wool, and elaborate his argument with additional examples, in the Discussion at the end of this Article.

[3] It would be easy to misunderstand this point. St. Thomas certainly believes that the New Law prescribes certain external observances, such as the sacrament of baptism. He certainly believes that these are determinations,

---

[29] See for example Leviticus 19:19 (RSV-CE): "You shall keep my statutes. You shall not let your cattle breed with a different kind; you shall not sow your field with two kinds of seed; nor shall there come upon you a garment of cloth made of two kinds of stuff." Compare Leviticus 22:9–11.

[30] See Exodus 28. The "stuff" of various colors is understood to be wool.

for God might have prescribed something else. Even so, he says the reason for the sacrament lies in the nature of the act. Why does he say this? Isn't baptism a mere symbol of something else, just as animal sacrifice was a symbol of something else? No. A sacrament is certainly a symbol, but it is not a symbol of *something else*, for it actually brings about the New Birth that it symbolizes.

For example, not only does baptism signify a certain grace, it is the very means by which God has chosen to impart that grace. Baptism is every bit as much a channel of the Second Birth as the mother's birth canal is a channel of the First.[31] In the same way, the elements of Holy Communion are not mere bread and wine which symbolize the presence of Christ; they are Christ Himself, made present in all His Divinity. The bread is transformed into His Body, the wine is transformed into His Blood. These are literal sacraments. By contrast, the sacraments of the Old Law, such as circumcision, were sacraments only in an analogical sense, because though they foreshadowed the sacraments of the New Law, which have power to confer grace, they had no such power in themselves.[32]

Summing up, the Reply to Objection 1 works as follows.

1. Conceded: The precepts of the Gospel are reasonable from the very nature of the things commanded and forbidden.
2. But although the ceremonial precepts were not reasonable in this sense, they did have reasons in the sense that each one symbolized or excluded something.
3. Therefore, although the precepts of the Gospel did replace the ceremonial precepts, there is no need to think that the ceremonial precepts were replaced *because they were unreasonable*.

Why then *were* the ceremonial precepts replaced? Because those things which they had symbolized had now been fulfilled by Christ.

Reply to Objection 2. [1] *The reason for the prohibition concerning the tree of knowledge of good and evil was not that this tree was naturally evil:* [2] *and yet this prohibition was*	Reply to Objection 2. No reason for the prohibition of eating from the tree of knowledge of good and evil could be found in the nature of the tree, for it was not evil in itself. Nevertheless, there was a

---

[31] In fact, for all we know, procreation itself might have been arranged differently. Instead of creating human beings whose females bear young from their wombs, God could have created rational animals that budded or underwent division. Creation was a free choice; though it was directed by His eternal wisdom, this wisdom neither required Him to create, nor required that everything in His Creation be arranged exactly as it was.

[32] "Nevertheless the Fathers of old were justified by faith in Christ's Passion, just as we are. And the sacraments of the old Law were a kind of protestation of that faith, inasmuch as they signified Christ's Passion and its effects. It is therefore manifest that the sacraments of the Old Law were not endowed with any power by which they conduced to the bestowal of justifying grace: and they merely signified faith by which men were justified." III, Q. 62, Art. 6.

reasonable in its relation to something else, inasmuch as it signified something. [3] And so also the ceremonial precepts of the Old Law were reasonable on account of their relation to something else.	reason for the prohibition, for the tree symbolized something else. In the same way – that is, because of its relations with another thing – each of the other ceremonial precepts was also reasonable.

[1] The Objector was right to think that the tree was not naturally evil. However, he was mistaken to think that the prohibition must therefore have been arbitrary – that there could not have been any reason why God tested man's obedience by forbidding him to eat from a certain tree, rather than, say, by forbidding him to hop on one foot. We are about to see why.

[2] If the prohibition of eating from the tree was reasonable because it was a symbol of something other than the tree, then what did it symbolize? Although St. Thomas gives the answer, again he does not give the answer *here*. He has given part of it much earlier in the *Summa*, where after agreeing with St. Augustine's opinion about why the tree was called "the knowledge of good and evil," he says that one of the things it may symbolize is free will: "[T]he tree of the knowledge of good and evil was ... so called in view of future events; because, after eating of it, man was to learn, by experience of the consequent punishment, the difference between the good of obedience and the evil of rebellion. It may also be said to signify spiritually the free-will as some say."[33]

In the remark "as some say," he may be thinking of Augustine, who argued that although the Garden was a literal place, the things in it can also be taken allegorically. As Augustine writes:

No one, then, denies that Paradise may signify the life of the blessed; its four rivers, the four virtues ... ; its trees, all useful knowledge; its fruits, the customs of the godly; its tree of life, wisdom herself, the mother of all good; *and the tree of the knowledge of good and evil, the experience of a broken commandment* ...

These things can also and more profitably be understood of the Church, so that they become prophetic foreshadowings of things to come. Thus Paradise is the Church ... ; the four rivers of Paradise are the four gospels; the fruit-trees the saints, and the fruit their works; the tree of life is the holy of holies, Christ; *the tree of the knowledge of good and evil, the will's free choice*.[34]

But this cannot be the whole story because any matter of choice might symbolize free will and the question is why *this particular* choice was set before man. Indeed there is more, for another part of the reason is a *reciprocal* symbolism, the typological relationship between the tree and the Cross – the former foreshadowing the latter and the latter restoring what was lost by the former:

---

[33] I, Q. 102, Art. 1, ad 4.
[34] St. Augustine of Hippo, *City of God against the Pagans*, book XIII, chapter 21, emphasis added, www.newadvent.org/fathers/1201.htm.

It was most fitting that Christ should suffer the death of the cross ... [T]his kind of death was especially suitable in order to atone for the sin of our first parent, which was the plucking of the apple from the forbidden tree against God's command. And so, to atone for that sin, it was fitting that Christ should suffer by being fastened to a tree, as if restoring what Adam had purloined; according to Psalm 68:5:[35] "Then did I pay that which I took not away." Hence Augustine says in a sermon on the Passion: "Adam despised the command, plucking the [fruit][36] from the tree: but all that Adam lost, Christ found upon the cross."[37]

Still later, St. Thomas deepens the explanation of this symbolism in the context of his discussion of how the suffering of Christ is fulfilling all its precepts of the Old Law and thereby brought them to an end. It fulfilled the *moral* precepts, which are founded on charity, because he suffered for the love of the Father and of neighbor. It fulfilled the *judicial* precepts, which concern paying the penalty for injury to others, because he "paid that which [He] took not away," allowing Himself to be hung from a figurative tree in recompense for the sin of eating from the original tree against the command of God. And it fulfilled the *ceremonial* precepts – this is the point which most concerns us here – which are mostly about sacrifices and offerings, "insofar as all the ancient sacrifices were figures of that true sacrifice which the dying Christ offered for us."[38]

[3] Just as the prohibition of eating from the tree of knowledge of good and evil symbolized something else (perhaps more than one "something else"), so each of the ceremonial precepts of the Old Law either symbolizes something else, pushes out and excludes something else, or both.

| *Reply to Objection 3. The moral precepts in their very nature have reasonable causes: as for instance, "Thou shalt not kill, Thou shalt not steal." But the ceremonial precepts have a reasonable cause in their relation to something else, as stated above.* | Reply to Objection 3. There are reasons for both the moral and ceremonial precepts, though not in the same sense. The reason for a moral precept lies in its own nature, as we see in the case of the prohibitions of murdering and stealing. But as we have also seen, the reason for a ceremonial precept lies in its connection with something else. |

The Objector had argued that there must not be any reasons for the ceremonial precepts, because if there were, they would be moral precepts, and they

---

[35] In most contemporary translations this psalm is numbered 69.
[36] The Blackfriars translation has "apple." However, St. Thomas does not use the word *mālum*, which refers especially to apple-like fruits, but the word *pomum*, which can refer to any kind of fruit. The book of Genesis does not specify the type of fruit. A common Latin pun connects *malum*, evil, with *mālum*, apple.
[37] III, Q. 46, Art. 4.
[38] III, Q. 47, Art. 2, ad 1.

aren't. By now it is easy to anticipate the saint's reply. Moral precepts express general duties which are right in themselves. Among these is the duty of worship. Ceremonial precepts are determinations; they specify the details of how to worship. Though not right in themselves – God could have required the people to worship in some other way – it does not follow that the way God chose was arbitrary. For as we have seen, a reason for each ceremonial precept can be found either in what it symbolizes, what it keeps us away from, or both.

DISCUSSION

So What Was the Problem with Mixing Linen with Wool?

Although St. Thomas argues that reasons for the ceremonial precepts can be found in the things they symbolized or excluded, he gives no examples (though he does elsewhere in the *Summa*), and he does not even slow down to show how his point applies to the puzzling precept he mentions: What exactly is symbolized or excluded by the prohibition of wearing garments made from both linen and wool?

He explains the symbolism a little later. By contemporary standards, the way it works is bizarrely elaborate. What we must remember is that if this seems strange, artificial, or burdensome to us, the oddity is on our part. For although at the present moment in history, our culture does not employ elaborate symbolism, *most cultures have*, and have enjoyed it. The ways in which we represent what is important to us would very likely seem crude, flat, and unserious to them.

In Question 102, Article 6, the sixth Objection suggests that it was inappropriate to forbid certain kinds of garments, because "clothing is something extraneous to man's body." St. Thomas begins his reply with a reference to Sirach, where we read, "A man is known by his look, and a wise man, when thou meetest him, is known by his countenance. The attire of the body, and the laughter of the teeth, and the gait of the man, shew what he is."[39] "Hence," he writes, "the Lord wished His people to be distinguished from other nations, not only by the sign of the circumcision, which was in the flesh, but also by a certain difference of attire." The prohibition on combining linen with wool served three purposes. (1) It discouraged idolatry, because the pagans used such garments in their rites. (2) It signified the wrong of lust, because the casual combination of fibers was a symbol for disorderly sexual union. (3) It encouraged holiness, because the simplicity of innocence (represented by wool) must not be joined with the duplicity of malice (represented by wool). Probably, wool symbolizes innocence because it comes from sheep, long associated with gentleness and innocence not only because of their natures but also because an

---

[39] Sirach 19:26–27 (DRA); in most modern translations these verses are numbered 29–30. Sirach is also known as Ecclesiasticus, not to be confused with Ecclesiastes.

unblemished lamb was offered in sacrifices. Linen itself can also symbolize holiness – but not here, because here the point is its difference from wool. Indeed, wool and linen shrink differently when washed, so that a garment that blended them would eventually fall apart. The same thing would happen to a people blended of innocence and malice.

On the other hand, we have seen that although garments that mixed linen with wool were forbidden to the people, they were actually required for the priests; though the priestly garments did not interweave the two fibers, some parts were made of one fabric, and others of the other. Additional insight might be derived, then, from considering why, though they were prohibited to the people, they were required for the priests. St. Thomas writes that precepts about such things as clothing "pertain to a certain preparation of the ministers, with the view of fitting them for the Divine worship: just as those who administer to a king make use of certain special observances."[40] So the reason for having priests wear special garments is that they *solemnize* the act of ministering to God in public prayer, sacrifice, and praise. "It behooved special times, a special abode, special vessels, and special ministers to be appointed for the divine worship," he writes, "so that thereby the soul of man might be brought to greater reverence for God."[41]

The purpose of priestly garments, then, is to exclude something – it keeps the people from bringing profane and careless attitudes into the joyful noises and holy silences of worship.[42] To be sure, all of life belongs to God, not just the life of worship. In that sense, every occasion is sacred. But if we simply said "Everything is sacred," without setting aside special times, places, words, gestures, and clothing for worship, the result would not be that we always thought of God, but that we never thought of Him.

If this is why such garments were required for the priests, then they may also have been forbidden to the people *just because* they were required for the priests. For if the sorts of garments used by priests were meant to solemnize public worship, then their use had to be separated from everyday life.

In fact – though I speculate – there may be even more to the matter than that. For why not just prescribe that *everyone*, both priests and worshippers, wear one kind of garment during worship, but another kind the rest of the time? Indeed, some regulations concerning clothing did apply all of the time. For instance, the people were required to wear tassels in the corners of their garments *precisely* to sanctify ordinary life, because whenever they saw the tassels, they would be reminded of God's commandments.[43]

---

[40] I-II, Q. 101, Art. 1, ad 1.
[41] I-II, Q. 102, Art. 4.
[42] "Make a joyful noise to the Lord, all the lands!" Psalm 100:1. "Be still, and know that I am God." Psalm 46:10. Both translations RSV-CE. In the DRA, these passages are numbered respectively 99:1 and 45:11.
[43] "Speak to the people of Israel, and bid them to make tassels on the corners of their garments throughout their generations, and to put upon the tassel of each corner a cord of blue; and it

But forbidding the people to wear priestly clothing had the further effect of preventing them from impersonating priests, or pretending that they could do the same things that priests did. This would have been terribly important, because to the surrounding pagan nations, worship was something like magic, a way to make the gods do things. One can easily imagine people thinking, "If only I wear priestly garments, I will be able to compel God Himself to do things" – an attitude which practitioners of forbidden rites hold to this day.

If so, then this provides a second purpose for the prohibition, and this one too is exclusionary. As we saw before, forbidding the people from wearing priestly garments solemnized the occasions of worship at which the priests presided; it kept out the casualness of everyday life. But as we see now, forbidding them from wearing such garments also discouraged them from playing priest; it kept out the magical aims and attitudes of the surrounding pagan peoples. We are not to suppose that God can be compelled.

Any of these matters could have been arranged differently. The point of explaining "reasons" for them is not to suggest that they had to be this way, but to show that their arrangement was not capricious.

Another Example: Avoiding Blood

Another illuminating example of a ceremonial precept is the prohibition of consuming blood – whether by consuming the blood of the sacrifices themselves, or eating meat with the blood still in it. Other ceremonial precepts also concerned blood. Granted that the general purpose of the ceremonial precepts is worship, what has not consuming blood to do with worship? In itself, nothing – but indirectly, a great deal. St. Thomas lists four reasons for forbidding the consumption of blood:[44]

- *To keep the people from idolatry*, "because idolaters used to drink the blood and eat the fat of the victims." This was an exclusionary purpose. It separated them from the practices of the pagan nations.
- *To lead them to the right way to live*, "for they were forbidden the use of the blood that they might abhor the shedding of human blood." This too was an exclusionary purpose. By associating blood with holy fear, it separated them from the love of bloodshed.
- *To inculcate reverence for God*, because blood represents the Divine gift of life. This was a symbolic purpose. God declares in the book of Leviticus,

---

shall be to you a tassel to look upon and remember all the commandments of the Lord, to do them, not to follow after your own heart and your own eyes, which you are inclined to go after wantonly." Leviticus 15:38–39 (RSV-CE); compare 22:12.

[44] I-II, Q. 102, Art. 3, ad 8.

"For the life of the flesh is in the blood; and I have given it for you upon the altar to make atonement for your souls."[45]

- *To foreshadow the shedding of the blood of Christ*, by reserving the use of blood for the sacrifice. This too was a symbolic purpose. The sacrifice of animals anticipated the sacrifice of Christ for our sins.

Granted, the fact that the prohibition has exclusionary and symbolic purposes does not convert "determination of generalities" into "conclusion from premises." For instance, so far as we know, God might have prescribed some other means of keeping the people from idolatry, of imparting to their minds a horror of bloodshed, or of inculcating reverence for the Author of Life (though it is not easy to imagine another way of foreshadowing the sacrifice of Christ). Yet even so, the prohibition of consuming blood is not arbitrary. To the question "What has that got to do with worship?" we can give an answer.

Can Anything Still Be Learned from the Ceremonial Precepts?

It might be thought that since the Old Law has been fulfilled, there is nothing further to learn from its precepts. This is far from being true, even in the case of the ceremonial observances. Consider the prohibition of consuming blood. Although this rule is no longer binding, the purposes for which it was once made binding are far from obsolete. As we have just seen, St. Thomas lists them as keeping the people from idolatry, introducing a horror of shedding innocent blood, inculcating reverence for the Divine gift of life, and foreshadowing the sacrifice of Christ. But although the foreshadowing of Christ's sacrifice has now been fulfilled, shouldn't we still detest idolatry, abhor bloodshed, and revere the sanctity of life?

For alongside the ancient idolatries such as the worship of the Baals, we may now list the perennial ones such as the worship of the Self: that which once was covert is now professed openly; once condemned, it is now taken for common sense. And alongside the ancient forms of bloodshed and irreverence for life such as killing with the sword, we have added novel ones such as killing with poison gas and injecting mothers' wombs with saline solution. The ancients held life so cheap they thought little of killing prisoners, but we hold it so cheap that we compliment ourselves for our humanity in doing away with the laws that protect the very young, the very old, the weak, the sick, and the unwanted. Neopaganism not only recapitulates paganism, but exceeds it. Even the ancient practice of infanticide no longer stirs us to revulsion as once it did.

As to the fourth purpose, it is true that we no longer need to look forward to the sacrifice of Christ, because it has already taken place. All the more reason to pray for the grace to be conformed to Him, through being united with His suffering on the Cross.

---

[45] Leviticus 17:11a (RSV-CE).

Or consider the provision of the Old Law which forbids allowing two different kinds of animals to mate. St. Thomas gives three reasons for this prohibition: (1) To show abhorrence for idolatry, for the Egyptians did combine various kinds of animals (as well as various kinds of other things) in order to represent the various conjunctions of the stars; (2) To express loathing for unnatural sins;[46] (3) To remove occasions of lust, because animals of different kinds do not easily breed unless human beings put them up to it for their own lascivious amusement. No more need be said about this first reason, because we have already discussed the need to build a wall against idolatry. As to the second and third reasons, if today such cautions provoke rolling of eyes, the reason is that unnatural practices have gone so thoroughly mainstream that persons are considered dirty-minded for seeing anything problematic in them.[47] Disgust is viewed as something to repress, or even as an insult to the dignity of those who behave disgustingly.

But the importance of honoring natural boundaries and not transgressing them goes far beyond questions of sex. Consider the biologists of our own day who seek to make human animal *chimaeras*. In their view, there could be nothing wrong with this because nature is meaningless stuff that we are free to manipulate as we please. In fact, horror about mixing the human and animal genomes seems ridiculous to them, a "yuck factor" to be laughingly dismissed. It might be wiser to reflect on the intuitions which give rise to such horror in the first place.[48]

---

[46] I-II, Q. 102, Art. 6, ad 8. As we saw in I-II, Q. 100, Art. 11, every sin is unnatural in the sense of being contrary to our rational nature, but the term "sin against nature" is more often used for actions that are contrary to those aspects of our nature which we share even with the animals. The sexual conjunction of persons of the same sex is called unnatural because the aspects of nature that we share with other animals direct us to seek union with persons of the same species but of opposite sex, for the sake of the procreation of children and the union of the procreative partners.

[47] We are told that there are "fifty shades of gray." A popular movie website maintains a page about the "Top 10 Alien Seductions in Movie History." Same-sex couplings have been redefined as marriages. Peter Singer, Ira B. DeCamp Professor of Bioethics at the University Center for Human Values, Princeton University, touted by the *New Yorker* as "the most influential living philosopher" and by former Princeton president Harold T. Shapiro, chairman of the National Bioethics Advisory Commission under former President William Jefferson Clinton, as "the most influential ethicist alive," explicitly defends bestiality. By his theory, a human being may have sex with a calf, but only so long as both enjoy it, but a human being should not have sex with a chicken, because it usually kills the chicken. (Professor Shapiro was quoting a letter to the *Wall Street Journal* by New York University philosophy professor Peter Unger. Professor Singer's defense of bestiality appeared in "Heavy Petting", a review of Midge Dekkers, trans. Paul Vincent, *Dearest Pet: On Bestiality*, in the 1 March 2001 edition of defunct journal *Nerve*. The text of the article may still be found at philpapers.org/rec/SINHP.)

[48] Besides, such research is strongly motivated. One might seek to produce creatures that would have human biochemistry so that drugs could be tested on them, but which would not be protected by the laws which limit research on human beings. One might hope to produce creatures that would have *impaired* human function in order to find out more about the requirements for human development. Finally, one might wish to produce creatures intelligent enough to be useful as slaves, but that would not be protected by the laws which prohibit reducing human beings to chattel.

Does God Have a Sense of Humor?

We saw earlier that St. Thomas thinks God's wisdom "ordereth all things sweetly," and that to be sweetly ordered is to be well directed to His purposes. On the other hand, St. Thomas does not suggest that for things to be ordered sweetly, everything must be done seriously and without humor. In fact, he *seriously* suggests that at least among humans, there is a time for *not* being serious, for joking and frolic are themselves directed to a purpose, though a light one: "[M]an's mind would break if its tension were never relaxed. Now such like words or deeds wherein nothing further is sought than the soul's delight, are called playful or humorous. Hence it is necessary at times to make use of them, in order to give rest, as it were, to the soul."[49]

Considered from this perspective, a human act of playfulness may itself be either ordinate or inordinate, either well or poorly ordered. Three points need special care:

> The first and chief is that the pleasure in question should not be sought in indecent or injurious deeds or words ... Another thing to be observed is that one lose not the balance of one's mind altogether ... Thirdly, we must be careful, as in all other human actions, to conform ourselves to persons, time, and place, and take due account of other circumstances, so that our fun "befit the hour and the man."[50]

It turns out that wittiness is a real moral virtue. Like all moral virtues, it lies in a mean. Never to have fun is contrary to reason, but so is finding fun in cruelty, indecency, buffoonery, discourtesy, or incivility.

Of course God Himself does not need to frolic, because His mind is in no danger of breaking from tension. His "rest" after the metaphorical six days of Creation was not a literal rest, as though He were tired.

On the other hand, it is not impossible that some things in Creation were arranged in the way that they were to give diversion *to us*. If one of the reasons for making ants was to reprove sluggards with the spectacle of diligence,[51] and one of the reasons for making stars was to fill our minds with awe for the Divine power and artistry,[52] then is it too much to suggest that one of the reasons for making monkeys might have been to humble and amuse us?

Does St. Thomas Have a Sense of Humor?

St. Thomas does have sense of humor, and it is thoroughly deadpan. In one place in the *Summa* he quips that "the proof from authority is the weakest –

---

[49] II-II, Q. 168, Art. 2.
[50] Ibid.
[51] "Go to the ant, O sluggard; consider her ways, and be wise" Proverbs 6:6 (RSV-CE).
[52] "When I look at thy heavens, the work of thy fingers, the moon and the stars which thou hast established; what is man that thou art mindful of him, and the son of man that thou dost care for him?" Psalm 8:3–4 (RSV-CE).

according to Boethius."⁵³ On another occasion he has a little fun by giving a logically sophisticated reply to a riddle that was no doubt meant in jest.

The riddle is from the Greek version of the book of Ezra, sometimes called Eszra or Esdras – a book which is read and respected but not accepted as canonical. It seems that the Persian king, Darius, had encouraged three young men of his noble bodyguard to compete over who could give the best answer to the question, "Which one thing is strongest?" The first said wine is the strongest; the second, flatteringly, that the king is the strongest; the third that women are the strongest, but that truth conquers everything. By the way, the third fellow wasn't cheating by giving two answers. He was punning on the Old Testament personification of Divine Wisdom as a woman. Anyway, after each of the young men had presented his arguments, Darius delightedly declared in favor of the third, urging him to ask for whatever he wished. Seizing the moment, the young man asked Darius to remember the vow he had once made to rebuild Jerusalem. True to his word, the king set the project in motion, whereupon the three young men broke out into thanks to God.

St. Thomas reconsiders the young man's answer to the riddle in *Quaestiones Quodlibitales* ("questions about whatever you want"). In his day, philosophy and theology professors the University of Paris had to appear in public twice a year to answer questions anyone could pose on any subject, so presumably someone really asked him this question. The fun of it was that the answer, which was made up on the spot, was expected to make sense – and surprisingly, it does. According to a recent translation, here is what the Angelic Doctor says.⁵⁴

Is truth stronger than wine, kings, and women?

> Objection 1. Wine seems strongest, since it affects people the most.
> Objection 2. Kings seem strongest, since they make people do the most difficult things, viz. risk their lives.
> Objection 3. Women seem strongest, since they even control kings.

On the contrary, Esdras says that truth is strongest.

Here is my response. This is the question debated by the young men in Esdras. Now, if we consider these four things in themselves – wine, kings, women, and truth – they are not comparable, since they are not things of the same kind. But considered in relation to a certain effect, they are the same, and can be compared accordingly. The effect they share, on which they can be compared, is their effect on the human heart. Hence, we should see which one of them affects the human heart the most.

Now, human beings can be affected either in body or in soul, and then either through their senses or their intellect, which is either practical or speculative. So, of all the things

---

⁵³ I, Q. 1, Art. 8, Obj. 2: *Locus ab auctoritate est infirmissimus, secundum Boetium.* The phrase "according to Boethius" has somehow disappeared from the Blackfriars translation.
⁵⁴ I have slightly adapted the language of the passage as given in *Thomas Aquinas's Quodlibetal Questions*, translated by Turner Nevitt and Brian Davies (Oxford: Oxford University Press), XII, Q. 13, Art. 1, p. 446.

that can naturally affect the state of the body, the greatest is wine, "which makes everyone talk too much." Of all that can affect the sense-appetites, the greatest is pleasure, especially sexual pleasure, and thus women are strongest. In practical matters and things that human beings can do, kings have the most power. But in speculative matters, the greatest and most powerful thing is truth. Now, the body's powers are below those of the soul, and [among the powers of the soul] the powers of sense are below those of the intellect, and [among the powers of the intellect] the practical intellect is below the speculative. Absolutely speaking, therefore, truth is the best, greatest, and strongest.

Funny – and philosophically elegant.

QUESTION 105, ARTICLE 1

Whether the Old Law Enjoined Fitting Precepts Concerning Rulers?

TEXT	PARAPHRASE
Whether the Old Law enjoined fitting precepts concerning rulers?	Did the Old Law make appropriate arrangements concerning ruling and those who would rule?

As we have seen, although the ceremonial precepts passed away with the coming of Christ, their underlying rationale continues to have much to teach us. This is even more true of the judicial precepts, which were the civil law of the ancient Jewish people, a commonwealth of human beings united under God. For this reason, although we examined only one Article concerning the ceremonial precepts, concerning the judicial precepts we examine three. For context: The previous Question, which is not covered in this book, investigated the nature of the judicial precepts, whether they were literal or figurative, for what period of time they were in force, and their varieties. The present Question investigates the reasons for them: Article 1, concerning the rules about rulers and governance; Article 2, concerning the rules about relations among citizens; Article 3, concerning the rules about relations with foreigners; Article 4, omitted here, concerning relations among members of the household.

The expression "precepts concerning rulers" is almost equivalent to the expression "constitutional laws." It includes such things as how many rulers there are, how and from whom they are chosen, and how they exercise their authority. These are part of the judicial precepts, because they are *determinations* of those moral precepts which concern our relations to our neighbors, especially those with whom we are united in a community. The Israelite community had the special characteristic of being united in subjection to God – as all communities *ought* to be – but most of what we find here has implications for any community whatsoever.

Objection 1. [1] *It would seem that the Old Law made unfitting precepts concerning rulers. Because, as the Philosopher says (Polit. iii), "the ordering of the people depends mostly*	Objection 1. Apparently, the Old Law made inappropriate arrangements for human government. Aristotle rightly observes that how the people are governed depends above all on the

on the chief ruler." But the Law contains no precept relating to the institution of the chief ruler; [2] and yet we find therein prescriptions concerning the inferior rulers: firstly (Exodus 18): "Provide out of all the people wise [Vulgate: 'able'] men," etc.; again (Numbers 11): "Gather unto Me seventy men of the ancients of Israel"; and again (Deuteronomy 1): "Let Me have from among you wise and understanding men," etc. Therefore the Law provided insufficiently in regard to the rulers of the people.

highest ruler, but we find nothing in the Old Law about how the highest ruler should be chosen. All we find are instructions about subordinate rulers. First Jethro advises Moses to select wise men to assist him, then God commands Moses to choose seventy such men from the elders, and subsequently Moses instructs the tribes to send him wise, understanding, and experienced men whom he would appoint to the office. So the law of old did not provide adequate instructions concerning rulers.

[1] Aristotle writes in his *Politics*,

A constitution is the arrangement of magistracies in a state, especially of the highest of all. The government is everywhere sovereign in the state, and the constitution is in fact the government. For example, in democracies the people are supreme, but in oligarchies, the few; and, therefore, we say that these two forms of government also are different: and so in other cases.[1]

A "precept relating to the institution of the chief ruler" could be any instruction which pertains to the chief ruler in any way – whether there is to be a chief ruler, what qualifications he must have, how far his authority extends, and so on.

"Chief ruler" translates the phrase *supremus princeps*. Earlier in the *Treatise*, the Blackfriars translation has rendered the term *princeps* by such words as "prince" or "sovereign," and I have preferred to render it more literally as "foremost man" because that was the original meaning of the Latin term, which originated during the era of the republic. Here, though, the term "ruler" is better, because it more easily accommodates itself to St. Thomas's distinction among higher and lower *principes*.

[2] Jethro, Moses' father-in-law, advises him, "Moreover choose able men from all the people, such as fear God, men who are trustworthy and who hate a bribe; and place such men over the people as rulers of thousands, of hundreds, of fifties, and of tens. And let them judge the people at all times; every great matter they shall bring to you, but any small matter they shall decide themselves; so it will be easier for you, and they will bear the burden with you."

---

[1] Aristotle, *Politics*, trans. Benjamin Jowett, book III, chapter 6 (public domain). The Blackfriars translators suggest, however, that St. Thomas is referring to chapter 4.

Later, when Moses complains to God of the burden of ruling the people alone, God replies, "Gather for me seventy men of the elders of Israel, whom you know to be the elders of the people and officers over them; and bring them to the tent of meeting, and let them take their stand there with you. And I will come down and talk with you there; and I will take some of the spirit which is upon you and put it upon them; and they shall bear the burden of the people with you, that you may not bear it yourself alone."

Much later, reflecting on the past, Moses reminds the people that he instructed them, "Choose wise, understanding, and experienced men, according to your tribes, and I will appoint them as your heads," and that with their agreement, "I took the heads of your tribes, wise and experienced men, and set them as heads over you, commanders of thousands, commanders of hundreds, commanders of fifties, commanders of tens, and officers, throughout your tribes."[2]

| *Objection 2.* [1] *Further, "The best gives of the best," as Plato states (Tim. ii). Now the best ordering of a state or of any nation is to be ruled by a king: because this kind of government approaches nearest in resemblance to the Divine government,* [2] *whereby God rules the world from the beginning. Therefore the Law should have set a king over the people, and they should not have been allowed a choice in the matter,* [3] *as indeed they were allowed (Deuteronomy 17): "When thou ... shalt say: I will set a king over me ... thou shalt set him," etc.* | Objection 2. Moreover, as Plato remarks, the best gives rise to the best. Then what is the best arrangement for a city or a people? To be ruled by a king, because this kind of rule fully reflects the best rule of all, the Divine rule in which one God governs the world. So the Old Law should have set up a king over the people from the beginning; it should not have left the matter to their own decision, as in Deuteronomy 17, where Moses provides instructions to be followed when the people ask for a king. |

[1] Today Plato's best-known work is the *Republic*. In the Middle Ages, however, the *Timaeus* was unquestionably best known. The Objector is probably thinking of the remark of the character after whom the dialogue is named, that "God desired that all things should be good and nothing bad, so far as this was attainable.... Now the deeds of the best could never be or have been other than the fairest."[3] The Objector draws the conclusion that God's rule is the ground of all human rule, and that the best human government is shaped by imitation of His.

Although St. Thomas qualifies the claim, as we will see below, he agrees with the Objector that one person must be set over the whole commonwealth, just as one God is set over the whole universe. As he argues in his treatise *On Kingship*,

---

[2] Exodus 18:21–22, Numbers 11:16–17, Deuteronomy 1:13, 15 (RSV-CE).
[3] Plato, *Timaeus*, trans. Benjamin Jowett, 30a (public domain).

[E]very natural governance is governance by one. In the multitude of bodily members there is one which is the principal mover ... and among the powers of the soul one power presides as chief, namely, the reason. Among bees there is one king[4] bee, and in the whole universe there is One God, Maker and Ruler of all things. And there is a reason for this. Every multitude is derived from unity. Wherefore, if artificial things are an imitation of natural things, and a work of art is better according as it attains a closer likeness to what is in nature, it follows that it is best for a human multitude to be ruled by one person.

This is also evident from experience. For provinces or cities which are not ruled by one person are torn with dissensions and tossed about without peace, so that the complaint seems to be fulfilled which the Lord uttered through the Prophet: "Many pastors have destroyed my vineyard." On the other hand, provinces and cities which are ruled under one king enjoy peace, flourish in justice, and delight in prosperity. Hence, the Lord by His prophets promises to His people as a great reward that He will give them one head and that "one Prince will be in the midst of them."[5]

[2] The translation here is misleading, for in the actual text of Objection 2, the phrase "from the beginning" belongs to the sentence about how the Old Law should have set things up, not to the sentence about how God rules the world.[6] However, this makes little difference to the Objector's point. What he means is that just as God ruled over the human race from the moment they were formed into a species, without their choice, so a king should have been set over the Hebrew people from the moment they were formed into a nation, without their choice.

[3] The Objector protests that the people *were* allowed a choice, for as Moses said to them, "When you come to the land which the Lord your God gives you, and you possess it and dwell in it, and then say, 'I will set a king over me, like all the nations that are round about me'; [then] you may indeed set [him] as king over you."[7] According to the Objector, this is to be read as meaning that until the people asked to have a king, they did not have one.

---

[4] St. Thomas is following Aristotle. In words which date back to St. Ambrose of Milan, the *Exsultet* or Easter proclamation of the Church praises the "mother bee" who brings forth wax which melts to feed the precious light of the Paschal candle: *Alitur enim liquantibus ceris, quas in substantiam pretiosae hujus lampadis apis mater eduxit.* However, European biologists did not finally realize that the monarch of the bees was female until the seventeenth century.

[5] Thomas Aquinas, *De Regno: On Kingship, to the King of Cyprus*, translated by Gerald B. Phelan, revised by Thomas Eschmann, reedited by Joseph Kenny (Toronto: Pontifical Institute of Mediaeval Studies, 1949), chapter 3, sections 19–20. The internal references are to Jeremiah 12:10, Ezekiel 34:24, and Jeremiah 30:21 respectively.

[6] *A principio igitur lex debuit regem populo instituere; et non permittere hoc eorum arbitrio, sicut permittitur Deut. XVII, cum dixeris, constituam super me regem, eum constitues, et cetera.*

[7] Deuteronomy 17:14–15a (RSV-CE).

Reasons for Judicial Precepts between Citizens and Rulers 315

Objection 3. [1] Further, according to Matthew 12: "*Every kingdom divided against itself shall be made desolate*": [2] *a saying which was verified in the Jewish people, whose destruction was brought about by the division of the kingdom.* [3] *But the Law should aim chiefly at things pertaining to the general well-being of the people. Therefore it should have forbidden the kingdom to be divided under two kings:* [4] *nor should this have been introduced even by Divine authority; as we read of its being introduced by the authority of the prophet Ahias the Silonite* (1 Kings 11).[9]	Objection 3. Further, as Christ says in Matthew 12, "every kingdom divided against itself is laid waste."[8] In the case of the Israelites, this became clear through experiment, for the division of their kingdom led to its destruction. Since the guiding intention of law is the people's common good, the Old Law should have forbidden dividing the kingdom under two kings. Not even by Divine authority should such a change have been brought in, as we read that it was brought in through a prophet, Ahijah the Shilonite.

[1] After Jesus heals a certain man who is blind, unable to speak, and oppressed by an evil spirit, the Pharisees make the accusation that He is able to cast out demons only by the power of the prince of demons. Jesus replies, "Every kingdom divided against itself is laid waste, and no city or house divided against itself will stand; and if Satan casts out Satan, he is divided against himself; how then will his kingdom stand?"[10]

[2] In the Objector's view, the disunity brought about by division into a northern kingdom and a southern kingdom was ultimately responsible for the defeat and exile of the people of both kingdoms. (In several waves, some of the exiles eventually returned and rebuilt their national culture, but that is not pertinent here.)

[3] The Old Law in no way commanded that the kingdom be cut in two. But since such division was contrary to the common good, the Objector thinks the Old Law should have anticipated the possibility and forbidden it.

[4] The division of the kingdom seemed to have been authorized by the authority of the prophet Ahijah, or Ahiah, the Shilonite, and whatever a true prophet did by the authority of his office was done by the authority of God. The story begins with King Solomon, during his later life, turning aside from the wisdom for which he had previously been celebrated in order to practice idolatry under the influence of his many pagan wives. Coming across Jeroboam, one of Solomon's high officials, Ahijah symbolically tears the new garment he is wearing into twelve pieces to represent the twelve tribes of Israel.

---

[8] Called by St. Thomas 3 Kings 11; his 1 and 2 Kings correspond to what most contemporary translations call 1 and 2 Samuel, and his 3 and 4 Kings to what most contemporary translations call 1 and 2 Kings.
[9] Matthew 12:25 (RSV-CE).
[10] Matthew 12:25b–26 (RSV-CE).

Giving ten of the pieces to Jeroboam, he declares "thus says the Lord, the God of Israel, 'Behold, I am about to tear the kingdom from the hand of Solomon, and will give you ten tribes." God says He is doing this "because he has forsaken me ... and has not walked in my ways, doing what is right in my sight and keeping my statutes and my ordinances, as David his father did."[11] After Solomon's death, the ten northern tribes revolt against his son and heir, Rehoboam, taking as their king Jeroboam, who had been an official under Solomon, and who promptly leads them into further idolatry. This leaves only two tribes to Rehoboam in the south, who, once his reign is secured, also apostasizes. The northern kingdom continues to be called Israel; the southern kingdom comes to be called Judah, because at first only the tribe of Judah remains loyal to Rehoboam (later joined by the tribe of Benjamin).

| *Objection 4.* [1] *Further, just as priests are instituted for the benefit of the people in things concerning God, as stated in Hebrews 5; so are rulers set up for the benefit of the people in human affairs.* [2] *But certain things were allotted as a means of livelihood for the priests and Levites of the Law: such as the tithes and first-fruits, and many like things. Therefore in like manner certain things should have been determined for the livelihood of the rulers of the people:* [3] *the more that they were forbidden to accept presents,* [4] *as is clearly stated in Exodus 23: "You shall not [Vulgate: 'Neither shalt thou'] take bribes, which even blind the wise, and pervert the words of the just."* | Objection 4. Still further, just as priests are established for the people's good in Divine affairs (as emphasized in Hebrews 5), so rulers are established for the people's good in human affairs. The Old Law set aside many things for the living of priests and Levites, such as tenths and first fruits of the harvest. However, similar arrangements should have been made to sustain the people's rulers. This was especially necessary because Exodus 23 forbade them from taking bribes: "You shall not take bribes, which blind even the prudent, and undermine the judgments of the just." |

[1] In the passage cited by the Objector, the unknown author of the letter to the Hebrews (that is, to the Jewish converts to faith in Christ) is beginning a long passage suggesting that the institution of the high priest, under the Old Law, foreshadowed the coming of Christ, under the New: "For every high priest chosen from among men is appointed to act on behalf of men in relation to God, to offer gifts and sacrifices for sins."[12] The Objector draws a parallel, arguing that just as priests were designated to care for the people's Divine good, so earthly rulers are designated to care for their temporal good.

---

[11] 1 Kings 11:31, 33 (RSV-CE). See note above about numbering differences between the books of Kings and the books of Samuel.
[12] Hebrew 5:1 (RSV-CE).

[2] Levites were members of the tribe of Levi who assisted the priests and fulfilled lesser sacred duties. Extending his previous parallel, the Objector reasons that since the Old Law made provision for the support of priests and Levites, it should have made provision for the support of governmental rulers too, but it did not.

[3] The word translated "presents," which can mean gifts, offerings, and tributes of all sorts, is a form of the word used below for "bribes." The Objector is not approving bribery; he is merely observing that had the rulers been allowed to accept such offerings, they would have had less need for other income. How to support public officials is a perennial dilemma of government, for the payment of salary to each and every one of them is an expensive luxury which most states throughout history have been unable to afford. Among the other things that have been tried are giving them some of the king's land, restricting choice to those who have wealth of their own, letting them take a cut of the taxes and fees they collect, and, what is almost the same thing, letting them take bribes. This is why, over most of the world, bribery is so deeply entrenched.

[4] In the Vulgate for Exodus 23:8, "The words of the just," *verba iustorum*, is a figurative expression for the judgments of those set in authority.

Objection 5. [1] Further, as a kingdom is the best form of government, so is tyranny the most corrupt. [2] But when the Lord appointed the king, He established a tyrannical law; for it is written (1 [Samuel] 8): "This will be the right of the king, that shall reign over you: He will take your sons," etc. Therefore the Law made unfitting provision with regard to the institution of rulers.	Objection 5. Still further, just as kingship is the best government, so tyranny is its most thoroughly debased corruption. But when the Lord instituted a king, He instituted a tyrant. For as the prophetic words of Samuel declare, "This shall be the right of the king that shall reign over you: He will take your sons," and so on. So when the Old Law set up arrangements for rule, it did so poorly.

[1] As Aristotle writes in his comparison of political regimes, "That which is the perversion of the first and most divine is necessarily the worst."[13] The Latin adage, *corruptio optimi pessima est*, "the corruption of the best is the worst," would have been ringing in the ears of St. Thomas's readers.

[2] If tyranny is worst, then it should have been prohibited; yet, claims the Objector, tyranny was not only permitted, but commanded. For when the people of Israel asked through their elders for a king, the prophet Samuel, speaking with Divine authority, told them, "These will be the ways of the king who will reign over you: he will take your sons and appoint them to his chariots and to be his horsemen, and to run before his chariots; and he will appoint for

---

[13] Aristotle, *Politics*, trans. Jowett, book IV, chapter 2.

himself commanders of thousands and commanders of fifties, and some to plow his ground and to reap his harvest, and to make his implements of war and the equipment of his chariots."[14] The full chapter is reproduced in the Discussion at the end of this Article.

On the contrary, [1] *The people of Israel is commended for the beauty of its order (Numbers 24): "How beautiful are thy tabernacles, O Jacob, and thy tents."* [2] *But the beautiful ordering of a people depends on the right establishment of its rulers. Therefore the Law made right provision for the people with regard to its rulers.*

On the other hand, in the book of Numbers the prophet Balaam extols the people of Israel because they are so beautifully set in order: "How fair are your tabernacles,[15] O Jacob, and your tents, Israel!" But how beautifully a people is set in order depends on how well their rulers are set up. From this it follows that the Old Law *must* have set up good arrangements for rule.

---

[1] These are the first words of an inspired blessing pronounced by the non-Israelite seer, Balaam, which concludes, "Blessed be everyone who blesses you, and cursed be everyone who curses you."[16] His blessing of Israel is even more impressive because he speaks it against his will, having been offered money by Balak, the Moabite king, to curse them.

[2] The orderly beauty of Israel's tents and encampments in the wilderness expresses the orderly beauty of its life under God. But how could it have enjoyed such beauty, if God's law had made inadequate provision to preserve it?

I answer that, [1] *Two points are to be observed concerning the right ordering of rulers in a state or nation. One is that all should take some share in the government: for this form of constitution ensures peace among the people, commends itself to all, and is most enduring, as stated in Polit. ii.* [2] *The other point is to be observed in respect of the kinds of government, or the different ways in which the constitutions are established. For whereas these differ in kind, as the Philosopher states (Polit. iii), nevertheless the first place is held by the "kingdom," where the power of government is vested in one; and "aristocracy," which signifies*

Here is my response. Concerning sound ruling arrangements in a city or people, two things must be kept in mind: One is that everyone should have some share in ruling. As Aristotle points out, such an arrangement keeps the people at peace, and everyone loves and protects it.
The other concerns the *species* of governments, the ways in which they are organized. Aristotle explains that even though these species are diverse, two of them come first: (1) Kingship, in which one governs according to virtue; (2) aristocracy, or rule of the best, in which a small number govern according to virtue.

---

[14] 1 Samuel 8:11–12 (RSV-CE). St. Thomas calls 1 Samuel "1 Kings."
[15] Tabernacles are light or temporary constructions, suitable to a nomadic people; the term refers especially to the tent which housed the Ark of the Covenant.
[16] Numbers 24:5–9 (RSV-CE), quoting verse 9.

government by the best, where the power of government is vested in a few. [3] *Accordingly, the best form of government is in a state or kingdom, where one is given the power to preside over all; while under him are others having governing powers: and yet a government of this kind is shared by all, both because all are eligible to govern, and because the rulers are chosen by all.* [4] *For this is the best form of polity, being partly kingdom, since there is one at the head of all; partly aristocracy, insofar as a number of persons are set in authority; partly democracy, i.e. government by the people, insofar as the rulers can be chosen from the people, and the people have the right to choose their rulers.*

So the best form of government in a city or kingdom is as follows. One is put in charge according to virtue, and presides over everyone. Under him are a number of others who also govern according to virtue. Yet all this is done in such a way that the government involves everyone, for anyone may be chosen to rule, and everyone shares in the choice.

This then is the best constitutional mixture, a blend of three elements: kingdom, since one presides; aristocracy, since a number rule according to virtue; and democracy, or rule of the people, since not only are the rulers chosen from the people, but it is up to the people to choose them.

[1] St. Thomas's interpretation of Aristotle actually pulls together reflections from a number of places in the *Politics*. The philosopher states as a universal principle, common to all forms of rule, that "the portion of the state which desires the permanence of the constitution ought to be stronger than that which desires the reverse." At another point, he defines citizens as those who have some share in both deliberation and the administration of justice, though not necessarily an equal share, because this must depend on their ability. The manner in which they share in these offices may take many different forms. For example, they may meet as a body or hold offices in rotation, and they may deliberate on all things, on some things, or on who should be chosen to deliberate on all things. Ideally, each citizen has the qualities of prudence and virtue necessary both "to be governed and to govern with a view to the life of virtue." If perfect virtue is difficult to attain, "we need only suppose that the majority are good men and good citizens, and ask which will be the more incorruptible, the one good ruler, or the many who are all good? Will not the many?" Besides, if not every citizen shares fully in these qualities, nevertheless some understand one thing and some understand another, so that taken together they are a better judge than any one man. "There is still a danger in allowing them to share the great offices of state," he cautions, "for their folly will lead them into error, and their dishonesty into crime. But there is a danger also in not letting them share, for a state in which many poor men are excluded from office will necessarily be full of enemies. The only way of escape is to assign to them some deliberative and judicial functions."[17]

---

[17] The quotations are from Aristotle, *Politics*, trans. Jowett, book III, chapters 11, 13, and 15, and book IV, chapter 12, though not in this order.

[2] Though St. Thomas refers to Aristotle's *Politics*, book III, as usual he does not actually specify a chapter. The Blackfriars translators suggest that he is referring to chapter 5. I consider a more likely source to be chapter 7, where the philosopher writes as follows:

> The true forms of government, therefore, are those in which the one, or the few, or the many, govern with a view to the common interest; but governments which rule with a view to the private interest, whether of the one or of the few, or of the many, are perversions. For the members of a state, if they are truly citizens, ought to participate in its advantages. Of forms of government in which one rules, we call that which regards the common interests, kingship or royalty; that in which more than one, but not many, rule, aristocracy [*aristos*, best, plus *kratia*, rule]; and it is so called, either because the rulers are the best men, or because they have at heart the best interests of the state and of the citizens. But when the citizens at large administer the state for the common interest, the government is called by the generic name – a constitution (*politeia*).[18]

St. Thomas says that in kingship and aristocracy, one or a few "rule according to virtue" (*principatur secundum virtutem*). The Blackfriars translation renders the passage differently, saying that in kingship and aristocracy, the "power of government is vested" in one or a few, probably because the term *virtus* can sometimes be translated "strength" or "power" rather than "virtue." In this context, however, that way of taking the term is not the best. Virtue in the moral sense is precisely what distinguishes kingship from tyranny, and aristocracy from oligarchy.

[3] Again, St. Thomas does not say that under the king others "have governing powers," but that under him there are others "who rule according to virtue" (*principantes secundum virtutem*). Interestingly, for what the king does he uses a weaker verb: the king "presides." Apparently, though a good king orchestrates, he does not play all the instruments himself. The sort of order that we now call "subsidiarity," according to which the lower levels are permitted to do what they can do without being absorbed into the highest level, exists even among the levels of the government itself.[19]

Interestingly, St. Paul also seems to distinguish between different modes of exercising authority, although the context of his remarks is the household rather than the polity. For the sort of authority that the husband exercises, Paul uses the Greek verb *proistemi*, which means to "preside" or "stand before," and which has overtones of protecting, superintending, maintaining, helping, and acting as patron.[20] By contrast, for the kind of authority which is found in the wife, he uses the noun *oidodespotes*, which means literally the

---

[18] Ibid., book III, chapter 7.
[19] I discuss subsidiarity at greater length in *Commentary on Aquinas's Treatise on Law*, in the section on I-II, Q. 96, Art. 5.
[20] 1 Timothy 3:4, 5, 12.

Reasons for Judicial Precepts between Citizens and Rulers 321

"despot" or ruler of the household.[21] It seems that the husband is more like the chairman of the board, and the wife is more like the chief executive officer.

At first, to think of kingly rule as "presiding" seems utterly at odds with the view expressed by Objector 2 that the best human government imitates the Divine government. St. Thomas does not mean to contrast Divine and human rule quite so sharply, for as we saw above, in his work *On Kingship* he too expresses the analogy between Divine and human government. Unlike Objector 2, however, he qualifies the comparison. One qualification is expressed in his Reply, below: Fallen men suffer the temptation to become tyrants. Another qualification may be drawn from how he describes the Divine government in I-II, Question 91, Article 2. For as we see there, God prefers to govern rational beings not by jerking them around, or pulling their strings, but by drawing them into His own providential care of things, by enabling them to share in it; that is the whole point of implanting the natural law on their hearts. If even the omnipotent King of the Universe chooses so to govern, how much more should finite human kings?

[4] The term translated "polity" is *politia*. This Latin word, like the corresponding Greek word, *politeia*, has both a broad and a narrow meaning: it can refer to constitutional government in general, or to the particular kind of constitution formed by mixing and balancing the elements of other kinds of government.

---

[5] *Such was the form of government established by the Divine law. For Moses and his successors governed the people in such a way that each of them was ruler over all; so that there was a kind of kingdom.* [6] *Moreover, seventy-two men were chosen, who were elders in virtue: for it is written (Deuteronomy 1): "I took out of your tribes wise and honorable, and appointed them rulers": so that there was an element of aristocracy.* [7] *But it was a democratical government insofar as the rulers were chosen from all the people; for it is written (Exodus 18): "Provide out of all the people wise [Vulgate: 'able'] men," etc.;* [8] *and, again, insofar as they were chosen by the people; wherefore it is written*

And that is precisely what the Old Divine Law established. For here is what we find:

1. Moses and his successors governed the people in such a way that each of them ruled over everyone – that was a species of kingship.
2. Seventy-two elders were chosen according to their virtue, for as Deuteronomy says, "From your tribes I selected wise and worthy men, and made them rulers" – that was aristocracy.
3. Yet it was democratic that these men were selected both *from* all the people and *by* all the people. In support of the first point is Jethro's suggestion to Moses to choose wise men from among the people (Exodus 18), and of the second, Moses' command to

---

[21] 1 Timothy 5:14.

(Deuteronomy 1): "Let me have from among you wise [Vulgate: 'able'] men," etc. [9] Consequently it is evident that the ordering of the rulers was well provided for by the Law.	the people themselves to provide these wise men (Deuteronomy 1). Obviously, then, the Old Law did make sound provision concerning rulers.

[5] We see already that according to St. Thomas, but contrary to the view of Objector 2, Israel did have "a kind of" kingdom from the beginning – though the Judges who exercised authority between the times of Joshua and of Saul were certainly not human kings in the conventional sense, and were not called kings. Some led Israel in battle, some were prophets, some only adjudicated cases brought to them by the tribes. Besides being "raised up by God," the only element they shared was that each of them held authority over all the tribes in common. Precisely because they did, however, St. Thomas considers them "a kind of" kings.

[6] St. Thomas views this small number of men, esteemed for their character and wisdom, as an aristocratic element in the constitution. At first, the number seventy-two here in Deuteronomy 1:15 seems to be incorrect, for as St. Thomas's previous citation of the passage in Numbers 11:16 makes clear, only seventy elders were chosen to assist Moses. The seventy-two cannot refer to the seventy plus Moses and Aaron, because Moses is distinguished from them; they were chosen to assist him. Probably St. Thomas is thinking of Exodus 24:1, where God instructs Moses to come and worship him at a distance, "you and Aaron, Nadab, and Abihu, and seventy of the elders of Israel." Seventy plus Nadab and Abihu make seventy-two. We learn from Exodus 6:23 that Nadab and Abihu were sons of Aaron. Aaron himself has a higher position than these elders and counselors because he is Moses' brother and spokesman.

[7] The government was democratic in part because the elders were selected from all the people, rather than only from the rich or well born. The context of the quotation is the advice given Moses by Jethro, his father-in-law:

Moses' father-in-law said to him, "What you are doing is not good. You and the people with you will wear yourselves out, for the thing is too heavy for you; you are not able to perform it alone. Listen now to my voice; I will give you counsel, and God be with you! You shall represent the people before God, and bring their cases to God; and you shall teach them the statutes and the decisions, and make them know the way in which they must walk and what they must do. *Moreover choose able men from all the people*, such as fear God, men who are trustworthy and who hate a bribe; and place such men over the people as rulers of thousands, of hundreds, of fifties, and of tens. And let them judge the people at all times; every great matter they shall bring to you, but any small matter they shall decide themselves; so it will be easier for you, and they will bear the burden with you. If you do this, and God so commands you, then you will be able to endure, and all this people also will go to their place in peace." So Moses gave heed to the voice of his father-in-law and did all that he had said.[22]

---

[22] Exodus 18:17–24 (RSV-CE), emphasis added.

In a slight departure from the language of the Vulgate, St. Thomas describes these "able men" (*viros potentes*) as "wise men" (*viros sapientes*). This would seem natural to him because their ability lies precisely in their wisdom.

[8] The government was also democratic because the people themselves decided which persons from among them should be chosen for this role.

[9] And so finite human wisdom is able to discern the lineaments of Divine wisdom in this matter after all.

Reply to Objection 1. [1] *This people was governed under the special care of God: wherefore it is written (Deuteronomy 7): "The Lord thy God hath chosen thee to be His peculiar people": and this is why the Lord reserved to Himself the institution of the chief ruler.* [2] *For this too did Moses pray (Numbers 27): "May the Lord the God of the spirits of all the flesh provide a man, that may be over this multitude." Thus by God's orders Josue was set at the head in place of Moses;* [3] *and we read about each of the judges who succeeded Josue that God "raised ... up a saviour" for the people, and that "the spirit of the Lord was" in them (Judges 3).* [4] *Hence the Lord did not leave the choice of a king to the people; but reserved this to Himself, as appears from Deuteronomy 17:15: "Thou shalt set him whom the Lord thy God shall choose."*

Reply to Objection 1. The people of Israel were ruled by God in a particular way. As He says to them in the book of Deuteronomy, "the Lord, your God, has chosen you to be a people for his own possession." For this reason, He reserved the choice of the highest ruler to Himself. We read in the book of Numbers that Moses prayed for this very thing, asking the Lord, the God of the spirits of all flesh, to appoint someone over the great throng of people. God responded by setting Joshua in place as Moses' successor, and we read in Scripture that in turn, each of the Judges who succeeded Joshua was raised over the people as their preserver by God Himself, and was filled with His Spirit.

The Objector, then, has missed the point: The reason God did not set out rules for the choice of a king is that He Himself chose the king. Deuteronomy makes this clear where it says, "you may indeed set as king over you him whom the Lord your God will choose."

---

[1] St. Thomas is quoting from the following passage of Deuteronomy:

[T]hou art a holy people to the Lord thy God. The Lord thy God hath chosen thee, to be his peculiar people of all peoples that are upon the earth. Not because you surpass all nations in number, is the Lord joined unto you, and hath chosen you, for you are the fewest of any people: But because the Lord hath loved you, and hath kept his oath, which he swore to your fathers: and hath brought you out with a strong hand, and redeemed you from the house of bondage, out of the hand of Pharaoh the king of Egypt.[23]

---

[23] Deuteronomy 7:6–8 (DRA).

The word "peculiar," from Latin *peculiaris*, should be taken not in its contemporary English sense of "strange," but in the sense "unique, set apart as God's own." So although God Himself chose the king, this must not be taken as a blueprint for other nations, because He had chosen Israel for a special role in the history of redemption.

[2] Concerned about who will care for Israel after him, Moses prays for a successor. In response, God first appoints Joshua to succeed him:

> Moses said to the Lord, "Let the Lord, the God of the spirits of all flesh, appoint a man over the congregation, who shall go out before them and come in before them, who shall lead them out and bring them in; that the congregation of the Lord may not be as sheep which have no shepherd." And the Lord said to Moses, "Take Joshua the son of Nun, a man in whom is the spirit, and lay your hand upon him; cause him to stand before Eleazar the priest and all the congregation, and you shall commission him in their sight. You shall invest him with some of your authority, that all the congregation of the people of Israel may obey."[24]

[3] In the subsequent history of the people, God "raises up" a series of judges and military deliverers, whom St. Thomas considers equivalent to kings insofar as they preside over the whole nation. Several of these, Othoniel and Ehud, are called in the Vulgate "saviors" (*salvatorem*), not in the spiritual sense that they saved the people from their sins, but in the military sense that they delivered the people from their enemies.[25]

[4] Concerning what to do after he is gone, Moses instructs the people, "When you come to the land which the Lord your God gives you, and you possess it and dwell in it, and then say, 'I will set a king over me, like all the nations that are round about me'; you may indeed set as king over you him whom the Lord your God will choose."[26]

At first it may seem that in giving this instruction, Moses is anticipating the incident in 1 Samuel 8, when the people demand a king "like all the nations" because they are dissatisfied with the Judges. However, that cannot be the case, because in 1 Samuel 8, the people are not acting in obedience but in rebellion. For this reason, St. Thomas takes a different view. According to St. Thomas, the words of Moses actually look forward to the rule of Joshua and the Judges. Certainly Joshua and the Judges were not kings of the kind which was wrongly demanded by the elders in 1 Samuel 8 – strongmen who rule for their personal aggrandizement. Yet he calls them "a kind of" kings, just in the sense that they were set over all the people for the common good. Moreover, they fulfilled Moses' instructions concerning kings, because God chose them and the people

---

[24] Numbers 27:15–20 (RSV-CE).
[25] Judges 3:9–10, 15.
[26] Deuteronomy 17:14–15 (RSV-CE).

accepted God's choice. Since the Old Law provided instructions concerning kings after all – and we see more such instructions below – Objection 1 fails.

Reply to Objection 2. [1] *A kingdom is the best form of government of the people, so long as it is not corrupt. But since the power granted to a king is so great, it easily degenerates into tyranny, unless he to whom this power is given be a very virtuous man:* [2] *for it is only the virtuous man that conducts himself well in the midst of prosperity, as the Philosopher observes (Ethic. iv).* [3] *Now perfect virtue is to be found in few: and especially were the Jews inclined to cruelty and avarice, which vices above all turn men into tyrants.* [4] *Hence from the very first the Lord did not set up the kingly authority with full power, but gave them judges and governors to rule them.* [5] *But afterwards when the people asked Him to do so, being indignant with them, so to speak,* [6] *He granted them a king, as is clear from His words to Samuel: "They have not rejected thee, but Me, that I should not reign over them."*

Reply to Objection 2. The best government is the rule of a king, provided that it is not corrupt. But just because such broad authority is relinquished to him, if his virtue is less than complete the regime easily slips into tyranny. Just as Aristotle says, none but the virtuous bear good fortune well.

Unfortunately, few pass the test of complete virtue. Now the particular moral weaknesses of the Israelites were hardheartedness and desire for gain, and these, even more than other vices, make men into tyrants. This is why the Lord did not give them a king with full authority from the beginning, but rather judges and governors to restrain them. Later, when the people petitioned Him for a king, he conceded – but as though He were angry with them. This is shown by His words to the prophet Samuel: "They have not rejected you, but they have rejected me from being king over them."[27]

---

[1] In thinking that the best form of government places all power in the hands of one man, the Objector had overlooked the peril of corruption. Considering this danger, kingship is good only when blended with elements of aristocracy and democracy.

[2] Aristotle is speaking of the man of crowning virtue, who among other things "will also bear himself with moderation towards wealth and power and all good or evil fortune, whatever may befall him, and will be neither over-joyed by good fortune nor over-pained by evil." Compare St. Paul: "I have learned, in whatever state I am, to be content. I know how to be abased, and I know how to abound; in any and all circumstances I have learned the secret of facing plenty and hunger, abundance and want."[28]

[3] This is not a racial characterization of the Jewish people, but a portrait of the moral and cultural condition of the ancient Israelites. St. Thomas's words are harsh, but Old Testament history is harsh too. Notice that he does not say

---

[27] 1 Samuel 8:7 (RSV-CE).
[28] Aristotle, *Nicomachean Ethics*, translated by W. D. Ross, book IV, chapter 3 (public domain); Philippians 4:11a–12 (RSV-CE).

that the Israelites were less virtuous than other nations of that era. Through the Law, they enjoyed moral training superior to that of neighbors. But just as certain vices tempt men to bow their necks to tyrants, others tempt them to become tyrants themselves. And as each people has its own besetting vices, so he thinks the Israelites had these two moral flaws.

It is likely that the prophets and holy men of ancient Israel would have agreed with him, for Hebrew Scripture is rich in incidents of blood and greed which it frankly records without approving. Concerning these vices, Deuteronomy warns, "Cursed be he who perverts the justice due to the sojourner, the fatherless, and the widow," and the Proverbs wisely counsel, "A ruler who lacks understanding is a cruel oppressor; but he who hates unjust gain will prolong his days."[29] All of the classical historians emphasized that the education of a people must be fashioned with a view to its own moral character, uprooting what is evil, strengthening what is good. According to St. Thomas, this is exactly what the Old Law did. For a chilling exercise, the reader may consider what the besetting vices of his own nation may be.

[4] Although from the beginning Israel had "a kind of" kingship, the judges and governors who first succeeded Moses were far from having full regal authority, for they did not exercise rule over everything.

[5] "So to speak" (*quasi*): Since God is not subject to emotional changes as we are, He cannot be literally indignant. The point is that God disapproved.

[6] Though deploring their rejection of His personal guidance through the Judges, God granted the Israelites' foolish demand for a human king who, though inevitably flawed, had full regal authority. The story is recounted in full in the Discussion at the end of this Article.

---

[7] *Nevertheless, as regards the appointment of a king, He did establish the manner of election from the very beginning (Deuteronomy 17):* [8] *and then He determined two points: first, that in choosing a king they should wait for the Lord's decision;* [9] *and that they should not make a man of another nation king, because such kings are wont to take little interest in the people they are set over, and consequently to have no care for their welfare:* [10] *secondly, He prescribed how the king after his appointment should behave, in regard to himself; namely, that he should not accumulate chariots and horses, nor wives,*

Yet from the beginning, the Lord did determine two points concerning the selection of the king. First, to wait for His own choice; second, never to make a man from another nation their king, because such kings are usually but little moved by the people over whom they are placed, so that they fail to look after them.

The Lord also provided instructions for how kings should bear themselves toward themselves, toward Himself, and toward their subjects. Toward themselves: They

---

[29] Deuteronomy 27:19, Proverbs 28:16 (RSV-CE).

nor immense wealth: because through craving for such things princes become tyrants and forsake justice. [11] He also appointed the manner in which they were to conduct themselves towards God: namely, that they should continually read and ponder on God's Law, and should ever fear and obey God. [12] Moreover, He decided how they should behave towards their subjects: namely, that they should not proudly despise them, or ill-treat them, and that they should not depart from the paths of justice.	should amass neither chariots and horses, nor wives, nor immense riches, because by coveting these things rulers decay into tyrants, abandoning justice. Toward God: They should always read and reflect upon His Law, in constant fear and obedience to Him. Toward their subjects: Never to hold them in proud contempt or oppress them, and never to stoop to injustice.

[7] When the Objector quoted from the Deuteronomy 17, he quoted selectively, as though God had said only that the people could have a king when they wanted one. St. Thomas points out that actually the passage says a good deal more – as we are about to see.

[8] Verse 15 says "you may indeed set as king over you him *whom the Lord your God will choose.*"[30]

[9] The same verse continues, "One from among your brethren you shall set as king over you; you may not put a foreigner over you, who is not your brother."

[10] Verses 16–17 instruct, "Only he must not multiply horses for himself, or cause the people to return to Egypt in order to multiply horses, since the Lord has said to you, 'You shall never return that way again.' And he shall not multiply wives for himself, lest his heart turn away; nor shall he greatly multiply for himself silver and gold." Needless to say, these instructions were often disregarded, but the point in question is whether they were given, not whether they were always followed.

[11] We read in verses 18–19, "And when he sits on the throne of his kingdom, he shall write for himself in a book a copy of this law, from that which is in the charge of the Levitical priests; and it shall be with him, and he shall read in it all the days of his life, that he may learn to fear the Lord his God, by keeping all the words of this law and these statutes, and doing them."

The commands to read, ponder, and obey are clear enough, but contemporary readers often trip over the word "fear." Even a good king will suffer dreadful retribution for sin, as when the great David yielded to the temptation to commit adultery with Bathsheba and murder her husband Uriah.[31] Yet the

---

[30] Emphasis added. This and subsequent quotations from Deuteronomy 17 are from the RSV-CE.
[31] 2 Samuel 11:2–5, David commits adultery with Bathsheba; 11:6–25, he deliberately brings about the death of Bathsheba's husband; 11:26–27, he takes Bathsheba in marriage; 12:1–10, the prophet Nathan confronts him about his sin; 12:11–12, God, through Nathan, decrees David's

admonition does not mean that God should be dreaded as though He were a tyrant Himself. Rather He should be approached with the awed reverence of a child for his father, who chastises him when he does wrong because he loves him. The book of Proverbs teaches, "The fear of the Lord is the beginning of knowledge; fools despise wisdom and instruction." But it later exhorts, "My son, do not despise the Lord's discipline or be weary of his reproof, for the Lord reproves him whom he loves, as a father the son in whom he delights."[32]

[12] The king should study God's law not only that he may fear God but also (verse 20) "that his heart may not be lifted up above his brethren, and that he may not turn aside from the commandment, either to the right hand or to the left; so that he may continue long in his kingdom, he and his children, in Israel."

Reply to Objection 3. [1] The division of the kingdom, and a number of kings, was rather a punishment inflicted on that people for their many dissensions, [2] specially against the just rule of David, than a benefit conferred on them for their profit. [3] Hence it is written (Hosea 13:11): "I will give thee a king in My wrath"; [4] and (Hosea 8:4): "They have reigned, but not by Me: they have been princes, and I knew not."

Reply to Objection 3. In view of their many quarrels, especially against the justice of David's rule, the division of the kingdom and the multiplication of kings were given to the people more for their punishment than for their advantage. This is why God says through the prophet Hosea that He will give them a king "in my anger," and that "They made kings, but not through me; they set up princes, but without my knowledge."

---

[1] The Objector had complained that the division of the kingdom was contrary to the common good. But if it was a just punishment, intended to bring the people back from their wayward paths, then it was for the common good after all. St. Thomas calls punishment of this kind medicine: "The punishments of this life are medicinal rather than retributive. For retribution is reserved to the Divine judgment which is pronounced against sinners 'according to the truth.'"[33]

---

punishment; 12:13a, David repents (see also Psalm 51); 12:13b–18a, God spares David from death but not from other punishments, including the death by illness of the son who resulted from his adultery.

[32] Proverbs 1:7, 3:11–12 (RSV-CE); see also Hebrews 12:5–6 and Apocalypse (Revelation) 3:19. The discussion of the difference between servile and filial fear, in the section of this commentary dealing with Q. 99, Art. 6, is also very much to the point.

[33] II-II, Q. 66, Art. 6, ad 2; the internal quotation is from Romans 2:2. St. Thomas speaks of the medicinal quality of punishment in several places, especially I-II, Q. 87, Art. 3, ad 2, where he explains that punishment "is not always intended as a medicine for the one who is punished, but sometimes only for others: thus when a thief is hanged, this is not for his own amendment, but for the sake of others, that at least they may be deterred from crime through fear of the punishment, according to Proverbs 19:25: 'The wicked man being scourged, the fool shall be wiser.'" The medicinal theory of punishment was known to the pagans too, for instance Socrates as portrayed in Plato's dialogue *Gorgias*. "*Socrates*: And was not punishment said by us to be a

[2] Though David sinned spectacularly in the incident with Bathsheba, he profoundly repented, and was viewed as a superior king. It may be added that David did, in fact, experience severe medicinal punishment for his sin.[34]

[3] In its entirety, the verse reads, "I will give thee a king in my wrath, and will take him away in my indignation."[35] Usually it is viewed as a reference to the events following the incident in 1 Samuel 8, discussed above and recounted at greater length in the Discussion – for after the people rebelliously demanded a king, God, through Samuel, appointed Saul, but later deprived him of the kingship for disobedience. St. Thomas seems to view the verse differently, taking "I will give you a king in my wrath" to mean "I will give you *another* king in my wrath," or perhaps "I will give you *yet more* kings in my wrath," so that it refers to division of the kingdom. His case for this reading may be strengthened by the fact that according to some translators, the word "kings" in the verse should be plural: in the RSV-CE, for example, the verse reads "I have given you *kings* in my anger, and I have taken *them* away in my wrath" (emphasis added).

[4] "They have reigned," God says, "but not by me: they have been princes, and I knew not: of their silver, and their gold they have made idols to themselves, that they might perish."[36] Since God is omniscient, the expression "and I knew not" is to be taken not in the literal but in the figurative sense, meaning that God was not consulted. During the period of the divided kingdom, the biblical narrative portrays most of the kings of Judah, and all of the kings of Israel, as disloyal to God and bringing destruction upon themselves.

Reply to Objection 4. [1] *The priestly office was bequeathed by succession from father to son: and this, in order that it might be held in greater respect, if not any man from the people could become a priest: since honor was given to them out of reverence for the divine worship.* [2] *Hence it was necessary to put aside certain things for them both as to tithes and as to first-fruits, and, again, as to oblations and sacrifices, that they might be afforded a means of livelihood.* [3] *On the other hand, the rulers, as stated above, were chosen from the whole people; wherefore they*

Reply to Objection 4. Men were assigned to the duties of the priesthood by inheritance from their fathers, because that way the priests would be more greatly honored for their role in divine worship than if the office had been open to everyone. For this reason, it was necessary that special things be set aside for the priests' living: tenths and first fruits of the harvest, offerings, and sacrifices.

But as we have seen, rulers were accepted from the whole people. This made a difference, because, for their living, they already had certain possessions of their

---

deliverance from the greatest of evils, which is vice? *Polus*: True. *Socrates*: And justice punishes us, and makes us more just, and is the medicine of our vice?" I am following the public domain translation of Benjamin Jowett.

[34] See 2 Samuel 12:1–23.
[35] Hosea 13:11 (DRA).
[36] Hosea 8:4 (DRA).

had their own possessions, from which to derive a living: [4] *and so much the more, since the Lord forbade even a king to have superabundant wealth to make too much show of magnificence: both because he could scarcely avoid the excesses of pride and tyranny, arising from such things,* [5] *and because, if the rulers were not very rich, and if their office involved much work and anxiety, it would not tempt the ambition of the common people; and would not become an occasion of sedition.*

own. The reasons for treating them differently are even more compelling in view of the fact that the Lord forbade them extravagant wealth and splendid pomp. He did this not only because arrogance and tyranny are so difficult to resist in the face of such enticements but also because, if the rulers were not very rich but were weighed down with labor and solicitude, their countrymen would not burn so strongly with envy, and the fuel of sedition would be taken away.

[1] St. Thomas is giving his opinion as to why priesthood was a hereditary office among the Israelites. Perhaps there would have been no other way to insure that the people would have due reverence for the priest's divine duties. However, he is not suggesting that the same arrangement would be best under all circumstances. Indeed, under the New Law the Church forbids priests to marry partly to *prevent* the priesthood from being a matter of inheritance.

[2] St. Thomas reasons that because serving in Divine worship was the family business, so to speak, the priests would have no other business from which they might make a living (such as farming).

[3] In St. Thomas's era, as in most eras, political power is tied to ownership of land, so it is natural for him to think that rulers who are chosen from the people would have means of livelihood already. Where political power is not tied to ownership of land, this might not be the case. Such rulers as the seventy elders, chosen from the people to assist Moses, would certainly have had means of livelihood already. True, one can hardly regard the kings from Saul onward as "chosen from the people," because the office quickly came to be viewed as hereditary, like the priesthood. However, St. Thomas is not considering what actually happened, but what the Old Law directed, and the Old Law did not direct that the office be hereditary.

[4] There was no danger that the kings would have insufficient possessions; the real danger was that the pride of wealth, and the greed for yet more of it, would turn them into oppressors.

[5] Though St. Thomas insists that the reason for law *as such* is to uphold the common good, we must not think he is naïve. As this remark shows, he is quite aware that men generally seek high public office to serve themselves.

Reply to Objection 5. [1] *That right was not given to the king by Divine institution: rather was it foretold that kings would usurp that right, by framing unjust laws, and by*

Reply to Objection 5. This right was not given over to the king by God's enactment. Rather God was warning, through Samuel, that the kings would take to themselves a right that was not theirs, decreeing injustice

| *degenerating into tyrants who preyed on their subjects.* [2] *This is clear from the context that follows: "And you shall be his slaves": which is significative of tyranny, since a tyrant rules his subjects as though they were his slaves.* [3] *Hence Samuel spoke these words to deter them from asking for a king; since the narrative continues: "But the people would not hear the voice of Samuel."* [4] *It may happen, however, that even a good king, without being a tyrant, may take away the sons, and make them tribunes and centurions; and may take many things from his subjects in order to secure the common weal.* | and plundering their subjects. The concluding words of His announcement make this obvious: "Then you shall be his slaves." This is the characteristic mark of tyranny, for tyrants do rule their subjects as slaves. Samuel spoke as he did in an unsuccessful attempt to discourage the people from asking for a king, for the passage goes on, "But the people refused to listen to the voice of Samuel." Yet we should not misunderstand, for circumstances can arise in which even a good king, who is not at all a tyrant, takes away the people's sons to make them "captains of thousands and of hundreds." Indeed, in order to look after the common good, he may have to take many things from his subjects. |

[1] Misreading the passage and forgetting that not everything recorded in Scripture is approved by Scripture, the Objector has mistaken the Divine warning in 1 Samuel 8 as a Divine instruction. The same misinterpretation was famously made later by the early modern political thinker Thomas Hobbes.[37]

[2] The word *servi*, in verse 17 of the Vulgate, can mean either "servants" or "slaves." The DRA renders the word as "servants," but contemporary Bible translations, as well as the Blackfriars text, render it as "slaves," which is surely the intended meaning in this context. Just as the aim of tyranny is the private interest of the ruler, so the mode in which the tyrant operates is to treat all the subjects as his tools. St. Thomas explains elsewhere, "a power is called despotic whereby a man rules his slaves, who have not the right to resist in any way the orders of the one that commands them, since they have nothing of their own. But that power is called politic and royal by which a man rules over free subjects, who, though subject to the government of the ruler, have nevertheless something of their own, by reason of which they can resist the orders of him who commands."[38]

[3] In verse 19, "Would not hear him" means "would not heed him."

[4] "And make them tribunes and centurions" refers to the warning, "and he will appoint for himself commanders of thousands and commanders of fifties."

---

[37] "Concerning the right of kings, God Himself by the mouth of Samuel, saith, "This shall be the right of the king you will have to reign over you ... This is absolute power, and summed up in the last words, you shall be his servants." Thomas Hobbes, *Leviathan*, chapter 20, www.gutenberg.org.

[38] I, Q. 81, Art. 3, ad 2.

St. Thomas reminds us that a tyrant will need commanders in unjust wars, but even a good king will need commanders – and many other things besides – in just wars.

DISCUSSION

What St. Thomas Really Means by Kingship

St. Thomas's recommendation of a certain mixed form of government as the best kind of "kingship" or "kingdom" forcefully reminds us of the need to be sure of what he means when he uses these words. He is not thinking of one man who wields all of the power unchecked. Sometimes he even uses the term "kingdom" as a metonym for *any* rightful form of government, whether or not it is literally a kingdom, for he agrees with Aristotle that each thing is most truly identified with the element that is most eminent or authoritative in it.[39] We easily overlook this way of speaking, because although we too use metonymy, the figure of speech in which a thing is called by the name of something associated with it, we do not often use the particular metonymy of calling the good by the name of the best. But St. Thomas does, and he tells us outright that he does:

A kingdom is the best of all governments, as stated in Ethic. viii: wherefore the species of prudence should be denominated rather from a kingdom, yet so as to comprehend under regnative [*regnative*, "royal"] all other rightful forms of government, but not perverse forms which are opposed to virtue, and which, accordingly, do not pertain to prudence.[40]

In this sense, a monarchy, an aristocracy, a democracy, or any of their composites may be called a kingdom, and the foremost man in any of them may be called a king. The only forms of government that would not be called kingdoms, or whose foremost men would not be called kings, are the pure and composite varieties of tyranny, oligarchy, and oligocracy – the "perverted" forms.

Of course St. Thomas is not always speaking metonymically. When he says that a kingdom is the *best* of all governments, as he does, for instance, in his work *On Kingship*, he is *distinguishing* kingdoms from the other good forms, so in this case he is using the term literally. Even so, we should not leap to the conclusion that the best kingdom in the literal sense is a *pure* or unmixed kingdom. It may be a composite of several forms of government. St. Thomas normally calls any composite form a kingdom, so long as one man is foremost – even if he shares

---

[39] Aristotle offers this remark in *Nicomachean Ethics*, book ix, chapter 8; St. Thomas discusses it in Question 106, Article 1.
[40] II-II, Q. 50, Art. 1, ad 2.

power with others, even if he holds his office only for a fixed period of time, and even if he does not inherit it.

So when St. Thomas says a kingdom is the best of all governments, alert readers will ask, "Which kind of kingdom do you mean?" We saw his answer above: A thoroughly blended form of government, borrowing and balancing elements of pure monarchy, pure aristocracy, and pure democracy:

> For this is the best form of polity, being partly kingdom, since there is one at the head of all; partly aristocracy, insofar as a number of persons are set in authority; partly democracy, i.e. government by the people, insofar as the rulers can be chosen from the people, and the people have the right to choose their rulers.

Because of our own inherited distaste for monarchies and aristocracies, we would probably call this sort of mixed regime a mixed or constitutional republic instead of a mixed monarchy. However, any such comparison would have to be qualified in two ways.

First, for St. Thomas, although the king or presider is not higher than the constitution, he is the highest authority within the constitution. For contemporary republics, this is not the case. In the American system, for example, the three branches are supposed to be distinct and coequal, so that the president heads only the executive branch. (At least so it is in theory. In practice, of course, Americans commonly despise their legislators, and call the president not the head of the executive branch but the "leader of the country." Moreover, our constitutional system exhibits strong drifts toward both kritarchy, as the judiciary takes on legislative functions, monarchy, as the executive takes on both legislative and judicial functions, and autonomous magistracy, as subordinate bureaucrats escape the control of the chief executive.)

The second difference is that for St. Thomas (as for ancient and medieval writers in general), the king is not the "leader" of the country but its *ruler*. To us, the word "ruler" smacks of tyranny, but to him, tyranny is not true rule at all, but the perversion of rule. Ruling is caring for the common good, for what St. Augustine called *tranquillitas ordinis*, which is rightly ordered peace.[41] Leading, by contrast, is taking the nation somewhere, going on a journey, recasting its pattern of life. For the ruler, laws are instruments of justice; for the leader, they are instruments of change. To be sure, a certain kind of change can take place under the older conception too, for right must be encouraged and injustice must be suppressed. But the notion of leading suggests a social revolution in which even the most fundamental norms of justice may be set aside or replaced for the sake of "progress" toward an undefined end.[42]

---

[41] Augustine, *City of God against the Pagans*, book XIX, chapter 13.
[42] As C. S. Lewis remarks, "In all previous ages that I can think of the principal aim of rulers, except at rare and short intervals, was to keep their subjects quiet, to forestall or extinguish widespread excitement and persuade people to attend quietly to their several occupations. And on the whole their subjects agreed with them. They even prayed (in words that sound curiously

The Peril of Tyranny

Good as St. Thomas thinks kingship is, he thinks *unmixed* kingship is perilous. To fully understand his argument – especially his dispute with Objectors 2 and 5 – the bleak, ominous, and pivotal incident in which the people of Israel implore Samuel to appoint a king should be read in its entirety.

When Samuel became old, he made his sons judges over Israel. The name of his firstborn son was Joel, and the name of his second, Abijah;[43] they were judges in Beersheba. Yet his sons did not walk in his ways, but turned aside after gain; they took bribes and perverted justice. Then all the elders of Israel gathered together and came to Samuel at Ramah, and said to him, "Behold, you are old and your sons do not walk in your ways; now appoint for us a king to govern us like all the nations."

But the thing displeased Samuel when they said, "Give us a king to govern us." And Samuel prayed to the Lord. And the Lord said to Samuel, "Hearken to the voice of the people in all that they say to you; for they have not rejected you, but they have rejected me from being king over them. According to all the deeds which they have done to me, from the day I brought them up out of Egypt even to this day, forsaking me and serving other gods, so they are also doing to you. Now then, hearken to their voice; only, you shall solemnly warn them, and show them the ways of the king who shall reign over them."

So Samuel told all the words of the Lord to the people who were asking a king from him. He said, "These will be the ways of the king who will reign over you: he will take your sons and appoint them to his chariots and to be his horsemen, and to run before his chariots; and he will appoint for himself commanders of thousands and commanders of fifties, and some to plow his ground and to reap his harvest, and to make his implements of war and the equipment of his chariots. He will take your daughters to be perfumers and cooks and bakers. He will take the best of your fields and vineyards and olive orchards and give them to his servants. He will take the tenth of your grain and of your vineyards and give it to his officers and to his servants. He will take your menservants and maidservants, and the best of your cattle and your asses, and put them to his work. He will take the tenth of your flocks, and you shall be his slaves. And in that day you will cry out because of your king, whom you have chosen for yourselves; but the Lord will not answer you in that day."

---

old fashioned) to be able to live 'a peaceable life in all godliness and honesty' and 'pass their time in rest and quietness.' But now the organization of mass excitement seems to be almost the normal organ of political power. We live in an age of 'appeal,' 'drives,' and 'campaigns.' Our rulers have become like schoolmasters ... And you notice that I am guilty of a slight archaism in calling them 'rulers.' 'Leaders' is the modern word ... this is a deeply significant change of vocabulary. Our demand upon them has changed no less than theirs on us. For of a ruler one asks justice, incorruption, diligence, perhaps clemency; of a leader, dash, initiative, and (I suppose) what people call 'magnetism' or 'personality.'" C. S. Lewis, "*De Descriptione Temporum*," Inaugural Lecture from the Chair of Mediaeval and Renaissance Literature at Cambridge University, 1954, in C. S. Lewis, *They Asked for a Paper: Papers and Addresses* (London: Geoffrey Bles, 1962), pp. 17–18.

[43] Not to be confused with Ahijah, the later prophet of Shiloh.

But the people refused to listen to the voice of Samuel; and they said, "No! but we will have a king over us, that we also may be like all the nations, and that our king may govern us and go out before us and fight our battles." And when Samuel had heard all the words of the people, he repeated them in the ears of the Lord. And the Lord said to Samuel, "Hearken to their voice, and make them a king."[44]

After concluding the assembly and sending the elders back to their cities, Samuel takes steps to appoint a king, and all the things he had warned about come to pass.

---

[44] 1 Samuel 8:1–22a (RSV-CE).

QUESTION 105, ARTICLE 2

Whether the Judicial Precepts were Suitably Framed as to the Relations of One Man with Another?

TEXT	PARAPHRASE
Whether the judicial precepts were suitably framed as to the relations of one man with another?	Were the judicial precepts appropriately adapted to the regulation of relations among members of the community?

In Article 2, we are still dealing with the reasons for the judicial precepts, but having in the previous Article considered the structure of governance, St. Thomas now turns to the relations among citizens. Afterward, in Article 3, he takes up relations between citizens and noncitizens – the "strangers" among them.

A different procedure must be followed in the present Article than all the others covered in this book. Although the Article cannot reasonably be omitted, it is extremely long, and my object is to fit everything essential to the topic between the covers of a single book. Fortunately, although Article 2 includes twelve detailed Objections and Replies, the general idea behind each Objection is much simpler than is usually the case, and can be summarized in a sentence. Although the Replies are a little more complex, they also lend themselves to summary, although for them I must use full paragraphs. Consequently, the only parts of this Article to which I have found it necessary to devote the usual line-by-line commentary are the *sed contra* and *respondeo*.

SUMMARY OF THE OBJECTIONS

Summary of Objection 1 The judicial precepts inappropriately endangered peace by allowing persons to eat grapes from the vineyards of others. (Deuteronomy 23:24.)

Summary of Objection 2 They inappropriately allowed women to hold property, which, as Aristotle points out, has often led to the downfall of states because there were too few men who could afford families and so fight for the country. (In most contemporary translations, Numbers 27:8–11; in the DRA, verses 7–11.)

Summary of Objection 3 They voided the force of sales by requiring the return of sold property every fiftieth year. This regulation was also inconsistent with others, because houses in towns could be sold in perpetuity. (Leviticus 25:25–28.)

Summary of Objection 4 In various ways, they inappropriately discouraged lending: By not allowing lenders to demand the return of borrowed property during the seventh year; by not allowing them to demand restitution for the death of borrowed animals; by forbidding lenders to enter the houses of borrowers to confiscate pledges; and by requiring that confiscated pledges must be returned overnight. (Deuteronomy 15:1–15, Exodus 22:14–15, Deuteronomy 24:10–13.)

Summary of Objection 5 They failed to provide sufficient security for goods held in trust by another person, because the owner was not compensated if the goods were lost. (2 Maccabees 3:14–15, Exodus 22:10–11.)

Summary of Objection 6 They were excessively stringent in requiring that workmen be paid every day, and also inconsistent because the rent of such possessions as houses did not have to be paid every day. (Leviticus 19:13.)

Summary of Objection 7 They made it difficult for aggrieved persons to appeal for justice, because judges were required to exercise their office only in fixed places. (Deuteronomy 17:8–11.)

Summary of Objection 8 By requiring only two or three witnesses, they made it too easy for the witnesses to conspire to give false testimony. (Deuteronomy 19:15.)

Summary of Objection 9 They prescribed unequally severe punishments for equally grave wrongs (such as the theft of an ox and a sheep), and excessive ones for certain minor wrongs (such as gathering sticks on the Sabbath, or being an unruly son given to revelry and drunkenness). (Exodus 22:1–2, Numbers 15:32–36, Deuteronomy 21:18–21.)

Summary of Objection 10 Of the eight forms of punishment recognized by Marcus Tullius Cicero, they employed only six – fines, chains, whipping, compensation in kind, loss of status, and death – inappropriately neglecting slavery and exile. (Numerous passages.) I add that although this list of punishments seems archaic, perhaps it shouldn't, because their use is not an entirely dead issue, even in the United States. Compelling a person to perform labor in prison is a form of involuntary servitude. Even in recent times there have been a few controversial cases of banishment or exile, albeit not from the country but from a single state or from the District of Columbia.[1] Although it may also seem strange to us that imprisonment without chains is not mentioned, the building and staffing of permanent prisons, and their routine use for a variety of crimes, requires a much larger bureaucracy with much more formidable resources than most ancient governments would have had.

---

[1] For a brief discussion see Brian Palmer, "Can States Exile People?", *Slate*, 24 January 2013, https://slate.com/news-and-politics/2013/01/banishment-as-punishment-is-it-constitutional-for-states-to-exile-criminals.html.

Summary of Objection 11 They inappropriately prescribed certain punishments for brute animals that had killed someone, or with which someone had committed bestiality, but this is inappropriate because a beast cannot be guilty of a fault. (Exodus 21:28–29, Leviticus 20:15–16.)

Summary of Objection 12 They prescribed that when a body was discovered but the murderer was unknown, the elders of the nearest city should bring a calf into an uncultivated valley, ceremonially cut off its head, and leave it there to rot – inappropriately treating the life of a brute animal as equal in value to the life of a human being. (Deuteronomy 21:1–9.)

On the contrary, It is recalled as a special blessing (Ps. 147) that "He hath not done in like manner to every nation; and His judgments He hath not made manifest to them."	On the other hand, the psalmist reminds the Chosen People that God's "judgments" – his judicial precepts – were a particular blessing to them, one which He had not given to other peoples.

The *sed contra* is quoting from these words of the psalmist:

Praise the Lord, O Jerusalem! Praise your God, O Zion! For he strengthens the bars of your gates; he blesses your sons within you. He makes peace in your borders; he fills you with the finest of the wheat ... He declares his word to Jacob, his statutes and ordinances to Israel. He has not dealt thus with any other nation; they do not know his ordinances. Praise the Lord![2]

Jacob, later called Israel, was the remote ancestor of the people; Jerusalem is their capital; Zion the hill on which the city stands. Thus, all of these are figurative terms for the nation itself. From earliest times, then, God had expressly taught the various aspects of His law to the Hebrew people alone. How great and wise a blessing, this instruction! But if it was so great and wise, the *sed contra* reflects, then how can it be said that it was framed ineptly?

I answer that, [1] As Augustine says (De Civ. Dei ii), quoting Tully, "a [people][3] is a body of men united together by consent to [justice][4] and by community of welfare." [2]	Here is my response. Quoting a remark the statesman Marcus Tullius Cicero puts in the mouth of his hero Scipio, St. Augustine writes that a people is not any multitude joined together, but a multitude joined

---

[2] Psalm 147:12–14, 19–20 (RSV-CE).
[3] The Blackfriars translation renders the term *populus* as "nation," which is commonly used to refer to a community of common descent. I have substituted the literal meaning of the term, which is "people." St. Augustine is not thinking of a community of common descent, but a community possessing other sorts of commonality – what Marcus Tullius Cicero had called a commonwealth. Actually, as we see below, St. Augustine criticizes Scipio's (Cicero's) definition of a commonwealth.
[4] The term *iuris* can refer to the laws, or to justice and what is right. The Blackfriars translation renders the word as "the laws." I have substituted "justice" because it must be taken in that sense for St. Augustine's critique of Cicero's definition to make sense. According to Augustine, the

Consequently it is of the essence of a [people] that the mutual relations of the citizens[5] be ordered by just laws. [3] Now the relations of one man with another are twofold: some are effected under the guidance of those in authority: others are effected by the will of private individuals. [4] And since whatever is subject to the power of an individual can be disposed of according to his will, [5] hence it is that the decision of matters between one man and another, and the punishment of evildoers, depend on the direction of those in authority, to whom men are subject. [6] On the other hand, the power of private persons is exercised over the things they possess: and consequently their dealings with one another, as regards such things, depend on their own will, for instance in buying, selling, giving, and so forth. [7] Now the Law provided sufficiently in respect of each of these relations between one man and another. For it established judges, as is clearly indicated in Dt. 16, "Thou shalt appoint judges and magistrates in all its [Vulg.: 'thy'] gates ... that they may judge the people with just judgment." [8] It also directed the manner of pronouncing just judgments, according to Dt. 1, "Judge that which is just, whether he be one of your own country or a stranger: there shall be no difference of persons." [9] It also removed an occasion of pronouncing unjust judgment, by forbidding judges to accept bribes.

together by agreement with justice and united by a community of well-being.[6] From this we see that the direction of the mutual relationships of the citizens by just precepts is part of the very meaning of a people.

But these mutual relationships have two aspects, for some are brought about by the authority of the foremost men, but others by the individual will of private persons. And since each person is competent to arrange those matters which are subject to his own will, it is fitting that the authority of the foremost men should exercise judgment among those who are subject to them, and inflict punishment on wrongdoers. However, the power of private persons extends over the things they possess. And so they can arrange things among themselves, by their own will rather than at the direction of the foremost men, concerning such things as buying, selling, and giving their possessions.

But the law made adequate provision for both of these aspects of relationships among the citizens.

Concerning the relations among the people and those in authority:

- It instituted judges, as we see in the instruction to appoint judges and magistrates to judge justly.
- It directed how judges should execute judgment, as we see in the instruction to judge according to justice, regardless of whether the person being judged is a citizen or an alien.
- It removed a temptation to judge unjustly, by forbidding judges to accept gifts or favors.

---

problem is not that no earthly commonwealth has had laws, but that no earthly commonwealth has really been united in agreement with justice.

[5] The Latin is *hominum*, "men." However, the context indicates that these are not any men, but members of the same community, hence "citizens."

[6] Or "by the common good." The Latin is *utilitatis communione sociatus*, but *utilitatis* is not to be understood in the sense of contemporary utilitarianism.

[10] *It prescribed the number of witnesses, viz. two or three:* [11] *and it appointed certain punishments to certain crimes, as we shall state farther on.*	• It specified that there must be at least two or three witnesses for conviction of crimes. • As we will see later, for various offenses it specified particular punishments.

[1] In this quotation from St. Augustine's *City of God against the Pagans*, Augustine is referring to Marcus Tullius Cicero's criterion of the commonwealth. However, St. Thomas's appeal to Augustine is surprising. From it, one would get the impression that Augustine approves Cicero's definition. He does not seem to object to it as describing what a commonwealth *should* be, and that, after all, is what St. Thomas has in mind. However, Augustine argues that no earthly commonwealth has ever fulfilled Cicero's criterion, and so – not for ideal but for practical purposes – he proposes a different one: that what we call commonwealths are merely bodies of rational beings united by whatever they happen to love. During the republican period, for example, the Roman political class was united by the love of glory.[7]

This is not the only place in the *Summa* at which St. Thomas uses Augustine to advance a somewhat more favorable view of the earthly commonwealth than Augustine actually held. For instance in I-II, Question 96, Article 1, he says "the community of the state is composed of many persons; and its good is procured by many actions; nor is it established to endure for only a short time, but to last for all time by the citizens succeeding one another, as Augustine says."[8] Augustine would certainly agree that legislators should take the long view, and after all, that is the main point of St. Thomas's allusion. But Augustine's own purpose is quite different: to show that the only commonwealth that really lasts "for all time" is the commonwealth of heaven, and that the succession of generations in the City of Man is but a pallid reflection of what is promised to the City of God. While St. Thomas emphasizes that even though our earthly commonwealths are not eternal, we should build them to last, Augustine emphasizes that even though we should build our earthly commonwealths to last, they are not eternal.

We return to these issues in the Discussion at the end of this Article.

[2] If it belongs to the definition of a true commonwealth that the citizens are united in agreement with justice, then the relations among them must be directed by just laws.

---

[7] St. Augustine of Hippo, *City of God against the Pagans*, book v, chapters 12–21.
[8] For discussion, see the corresponding section of my *Commentary on Thomas Aquinas's Treatise on Law* (Cambridge: Cambridge University Press, 2014).

[3] Public authority directs me concerning such things as giving testimony when called upon in criminal cases. However, public authority does not direct me concerning such things as whether to rent a house; that depends on my own will.

[4] It is a bit difficult to find a nontautological way to explain the meaning of the statement "whatever is subject to the power of an individual can be disposed of according to his will," for being subject to an individual's power seems to *mean* being subject to the disposition of his will. I take what is *subject* to the individual's power to mean what it is *fitting* for him to arrange, and what *can* be disposed of according to his will to mean what he is *capable* of arranging. On these assumptions, St. Thomas is saying that all those things it is right for individuals to arrange are also within their ability to arrange. These would be matters which pertain to their own good but which do not significantly affect the common good – for example, whether someone rents or purchases a house. After all, one of the pivotal elements in the definition of law is that it is for the common good, and St. Thomas explicitly denies that law may command the performance of those acts of virtue which do not affect the common good.[9]

[5] Some matters are beyond the ability of individuals to arrange because they concern the common good rather than the individual good, *and therefore* lie beyond their right to try to arrange, because such matters are reserved for public authority. St. Thomas does not make the premises in this argument fully explicit, probably because he has stated them earlier. I-II, Question 90, Article 2 shows that genuine law is made for the common good, and Article 3 shows that it can be made only by competent public authority.[10] It follows that the individual may not personally do such things as punish thieves or settle disputes between his neighbors about their possessions. For these things, judges must be established.

[6] Normally, private persons are well able to look after their individual good, the paramount example of which is looking after their possessions. Ordinarily, then, it falls within the rightful scope of their will to make their own decisions about the transference of their possessions, such as whether to buy a house, sell a barn, or give a gift. St. Thomas does not intend this statement to be taken as absolute, for some decisions concerning possessions exceed the scope of personal decision because they impinge on the good of others. For example, as we have just seen, *disputes* about possessions (and about other things) must be settled by public authority – a matter to which we are about to return. We meet another example a little further on in the *respondeo*, for the judicial precepts require that certain possessions be relinquished for the use of the poor.

---

[9] I-II, Q. 90, Art. 2, and Q. 96, Art. 3.
[10] The other two elements in the definition are that law is an ordinance of reason (Art. 1) and that it must be promulgated or made known (Art. 4).

[7] In the DRA, the full text of the verse St. Thomas quotes is "Thou shalt appoint judges and magistrates in all thy gates, which the Lord thy God shall give thee, in all thy tribes: that they may judge the people with just judgment." Markets for such things as produce, animals, and fuel were located outside the gates of the walled cities, and this was where justice was administered too. So the expression "in all your gates" means, in effect, "in the place where you administer justice in all your cities."[11]

[8] Moses is reminding the people that judges are to administer justice impartially between citizen and citizen, between citizen and alien, and between the powerful and the weak:

And I charged your judges at that time, "Hear the cases between your brethren, and judge righteously between a man and his brother or the alien that is with him. You shall not be partial in judgment; you shall hear the small and the great alike; you shall not be afraid of the face of man, for the judgment is God's; and the case that is too hard for you, you shall bring to me, and I will hear it."[12]

In remembrance of these instructions, Psalm 82 represents God as warning unjust judges that they are inviting His own judgment against them:

God has taken his place in the divine council; in the midst of the gods he holds judgment: "How long will you judge unjustly and show partiality to the wicked? Give justice to the weak and the fatherless; maintain the right of the afflicted and the destitute. Rescue the weak and the needy; deliver them from the hand of the wicked." They have neither knowledge nor understanding, they walk about in darkness; all the foundations of the earth are shaken. I say, "You are 'gods,' sons of the Most High, all of you; nevertheless, you shall die like men, and fall like any prince." Arise, O God, judge the earth; for to thee belong all the nations![13]

[9] As we saw in the previous Article, states have commonly attempted to solve the problem of supporting judges and other public officials by allowing them to accept "gifts," or bribes, as though they were fees. This practice obviously invites corrupt judgment, and the Old Law sternly forbids it. Among other prohibitions, the Book of Exodus declares, "Neither shalt thou take bribes, which even blind the wise, and pervert the words of the just." In similar language, immediately after the statement in Deuteronomy that judges are to judge with just judgment, the words are added, "And not go aside to

---

[11] Deuteronomy 16:18 (DRA).
[12] Deuteronomy 1:16–17 (RSV-CE). This refers to previous declarations in Exodus 23:6 and Leviticus 19:15.
[13] Psalm 82:1–8 (RSV-CE). In the Vulgate, this psalm is numbered 81. The word "gods," which was apparently used for powerful individuals, is here intended figuratively (for yes, like the rest of us, the authorities are made in God's image, and God has ordained that there be human government) and sarcastically (for no matter how full of themselves the powerful become, they are under God's judgment). Because the use of the term is often misunderstood, I have enclosed it in warning quotes.

either part. Thou shalt not accept person [show partiality] nor gifts: for gifts blind the eyes of the wise, and change the words of the just."[14]

[10] Here, St. Thomas simply commends the law for specifying how many witnesses are necessary to settle an accusation or dispute. However, he returns to the matter in the Reply to Objection 8. In our own day, for certain kinds of offenses, such as sexual harassment, some people consider the requirement for corroborating testimony from two or three other persons too stringent, claiming that accusers *never* lie about such matters. Needless to say, witnesses sometimes do lie, and about all sorts of things. Indeed, the eighth Objector makes the opposite complaint: that the requirement for two or three witnesses is not stringent *enough*. Not only do accusers sometimes lie, he says, but they sometimes conspire to lie. As we will see, St. Thomas's Reply relies on prudential considerations. The question is just how easy conspiracy to give false testimony really is – not how easy it is in the abstract, but how easy it remains *provided* that suitable things have been done *both* to discourage it *and* to make it more difficult to get away with. In our day, under the benign name of "opposition research," partisan conspiracies to encourage public accusations against political enemies have come to seem almost routine, and persons who maliciously make accusations they know to be false are rarely held accountable.

[11] Whether the law prescribed punishments is not really in dispute; the real issue is whether it provided *appropriate* punishments. However, St. Thomas is not ducking the question, for he returns to it in the replies to several of the Objections – especially number 9, where he takes up the whole question of what makes a punishment fitting.

---

[12] *But with regard to possessions, it is a very good thing, says the Philosopher (Polit. ii) that the things possessed should be distinct, and the use thereof should be partly common, and partly granted to others by the will of the possessors.* [13] *These three points were provided for by the Law. Because, in the first place, the possessions themselves were divided among individuals:* [14] *for it is written (Num. 33): "I have given you" the land "for a possession: and you shall divide it among you by lot."* [15] *And since many states have been ruined through want of regulations in the matter of possessions, as the Philosopher*

Now concerning possessions – that is, concerning those matters the people could settle among themselves – Aristotle makes three salient points: (1) each person's possessions should be distinct; (2) in certain respects, what each person possesses should be available for the use of others; and (3) in other respects, each person should decide for himself whether his possessions may be used by others. But the law provides for these three points too. Let us see how.

As to Aristotle's first point, the need for distinct possessions:

- Possessions were divided into separate allotments rather than remaining in

---

[14] Respectively Exodus 23:8 and Deuteronomy 16:19 (DRA). See also the previous remarks on Deuteronomy 16:20 offered in the commentary on I-II, Q. 100, Art. 9.

observes (Polit. ii); [16] *therefore the Law provided a threefold remedy against the [ir]regularity of possessions.*[15] [17] *The first was that they should be divided equally,* [18] *wherefore it is written (Num. 33):* "*To the more you shall give a larger part, and to the fewer, a lesser.*" [19] *A second remedy was that possessions could not be alienated for ever, but after a certain lapse of time should return to their former owner, so as to avoid confusion of possessions (cf. ad 3).* [20] *The third remedy aimed at the removal of this confusion, and provided that the dead should be succeeded by their next of kin: in the first place, the son; secondly, the daughter; thirdly, the brother; fourthly, the father's brother; fifthly, any other next of kin.* [21] *Furthermore, in order to preserve the distinction of property, the Law enacted that heiresses should marry within their own tribe, as recorded in Num. 36.*

common, as we see in the Divine instruction to divide the Promised Land among families by lot.

- Moreover, because (as Aristotle also remarks) irregularity of possessions has led many states to their downfall, the law guarded against this eventuality in three ways. (a) The initial allocation of possessions among tribes was to be equal in the sense that the larger tribes received more, and the smaller tribes less. (b) So that the initial allotment would not become disordered, possessions could not be alienated forever, but were to return to their owners after a certain amount of time. (c) For the same reason, the property of those who died was to pass on to other members of the family according to the degree of kinship.
- The law went still further to keep the allotment among families and tribes intact, providing that women who inherited should marry within their own tribe.

[12] Aristotle finds fault with both completely *private* and completely *common* ownership and use of things. His ideal is private ownership, but with some of the things that are privately owned available for common use:

Property should be in a certain sense common, but, as a general rule, private; for, when everyone has a distinct interest, men will not complain of one another, and they will make more progress, because every one will be attending to his own business. And yet by reason of goodness, and in respect of use, "Friends," as the proverb says, "will have all things common." Even now there are traces of such a principle, showing that it is not impracticable, but, in well-ordered states, exists already to a certain extent and may be carried further. For, although every man has his own property, some things he will place at the disposal of his friends, while of others he shares the use with them ... It is clearly better that property should be private, but the use of it common; and the special business of the legislator is to create in men this benevolent disposition. Again, how immeasurably greater is the pleasure, when a man feels a thing to be his own; for surely the love of self is a feeling implanted by nature and not given in vain, although selfishness is rightly censured; this, however, is not the mere love of self, but the love of self in excess, like the miser's love of money; for all, or almost all, men love money and other such objects in a measure. And further, there is the greatest pleasure in doing a

---

[15] Corrected: See commentary below.

kindness or service to friends or guests or companions, which can only be rendered when a man has private property. These advantages are lost by excessive unification of the state.[16]

As we saw earlier, St. Thomas thinks the very reason for private ownership is that it serves the common good. First, each person takes better care of his own property than of what belongs to everyone at once. Second, it is easier to pinpoint responsibility if each person is charged with caring for particular things. Third, when goods are divided so that each person has something of his own, there are fewer quarrels. So even though some may have more or better property, the institution of private ownership makes everyone better off than if everything were owned in common.[17] Since St. Thomas's time, other advantages of private property have also been discovered, such as the fact that a collective economy – which is of necessity a planned economy – cannot allocate resources to their most efficient uses, as a market does spontaneously. (This is not to say that what economists call efficiency is, or should be, the only consideration!)[18]

In this view, since the rationale for private ownership is the common good, the common good shapes the contours of the right to private property. This is equally far from socialism (which resists the very idea of private property) and from laissez-faire (which resists any consideration of the common good). Yet it is not the same as the "third way" some social democrats champion either, for that term usually refers to an administrative state with some private property but the state in ultimate control. Rather it is a fourth way, for in general, property is private yet its owners are generous in allowing its use by neighbors – and the law encourages them, in small but important ways, to take a broad view of just who their "neighbors" are.

We are about to see how St. Thomas thinks this worked under the judicial precepts. Obviously, their provisions would not accomplish the same ends in an industrial society like ours that they would have in the agricultural society for which they were designed. But what provisions *would or might* accomplish such ends in an industrial society like ours is very much worth considering.

[13] After taking possession of the Promised Land, the Israelites divided the territory among the twelve tribes by lot, according to their families. Most economic functions were carried out by families, and various restrictions on

---

[16] Aristotle, *Politics*, translated by Benjamin Jowett (public domain), book II, chapter 5, http://classics.mit.edu/Aristotle/politics.html. The Blackfriars translators suggest that St. Thomas is referring to chapter 2, which seems incorrect.
[17] II-II, Q. 66, Arts. 1–2.
[18] Economists call an allocation of resources "efficient" if and only if when it cannot be changed without making anyone worse off in his own judgment. Markets incline toward such outcomes because they depend on voluntary exchange, and no party to an exchange will agree to it if it does make him worse off in his own judgment.

transfer of possessions helped to insure that the families and tribes did not lose their property and die out. Although our economy is no longer primarily agricultural, the Old Law's concern for the economic integrity of the family is far from irrelevant today.

The Levites, who were the priestly tribe, did not receive a territory of their own because "the Lord God of Israel is their inheritance."[19] They received tithes and offerings from the people, and they were given towns and adjoining pastures from among the territories of the other tribes.[20]

[14] The full text of the partially quoted passage is as follows:

[Y]ou shall take possession of the land and settle in it, for I have given the land to you to possess it. You shall inherit the land by lot according to your families; to a large tribe you shall give a large inheritance, and to a small tribe you shall give a small inheritance; wherever the lot falls to any man, that shall be his; according to the tribes of your fathers you shall inherit.[21]

[15] St. Thomas refers only to Aristotle's *Politics*, book II. The Blackfriars translators suggest that he is thinking of chapter 6, but although Aristotle discusses various matters concerning property in chapter 6, it is more likely that St. Thomas is thinking of chapter 8, where in his *Commentary* on Aristotle's work he explains that according to the philosopher, "it seemed to some lawmakers most necessary that there is a right order about property (i.e. the private property of citizens), since property most causes all the rebellions in political communities, which lawmakers strive chiefly to avoid." A little later St. Thomas remarks,

Then Aristotle approves ... some limit on property ... for two reasons. First, he approves it on the authority of ancient lawmakers, saying that some of them seem to have recognized that equalizing the property of the citizens has great power to preserve the well-being of the political community ... there are laws in some political communities that prohibit citizens from selling their property ... Similarly, there are laws ordaining that the ancient lots of citizens are preserved intact. And all these things belong to equalizing the property of citizens. Second, Aristotle shows the same thing by the unsuitable consequences.[22]

Aristotle is not commending *absolute equality* of property, but rather *limits on inequality* of property, so that families do not lose what they have and become poor or die out. That is what St. Thomas has in mind too – not only for fear of rebellion, however, but also (and even more) for love of neighbor.

---

[19] Joshua 13:33 (RSV-CE).
[20] Numbers 35:1–8 (RSV-CE).
[21] Numbers 33:53–54 (RSV-CE).
[22] Thomas Aquinas, *Commentary on Aristotle's Politics*, translated by Richard J. Regan (Indianapolis: Hackett, 2007), book II, chapter 8, pp. 123–125.

[16] The Blackfriars translation, "therefore the Law provided a threefold remedy against the regularity of possessions,"[23] cannot be right. *Regulandas* refers to regulation, not regularity, and St. Thomas has just spoken in favor of regularity of possessions, not against it. In the Blackfriars text, I have therefore corrected "regularity" to "irregularity." The sentence might have been rendered, "Therefore, *for the regulation* of possessions, the law brought in a triple remedy," or, as in the Freddoso translation, "the Law applied a threefold remedy *for regulating* possessions."[24] My own paraphrase is a little more free.

[17] This statement refers to proportionate rather than arithmetic equality. It was not the case that each tribe received the same amount of land. However, each tribe received land *in the same proportion to its size*.

[18] "To the more" means "to the larger tribe," and "to the fewer" means "to the smaller tribe." The tribe of Manasseh received the most territory, the tribe of Dan the least. Lots were cast to determine which families received which tracts of land as their inheritance.

[19] "Possessions" refers not to every kind of possession but to such possessions as land, which were meant to remain in families. Such things could be sold for only fifty years, after which they would revert to the original owner. The effect of this law was very much like a requirement that land and houses could not be sold in perpetuity, but only leased for a fixed period of time, so that inheritances were not destroyed.

[20] The line of succession is defined in Numbers 27:8–11. Its purpose, like that of various other regulations we have seen, was to preserve the allotment of property among families, lest some accumulate vast amounts of property and others be extinguished or thrown into poverty. Although in some of our own jurisdictions the laws of inheritance incorporate similar restrictions, ours are far weaker; for example, they may merely prohibit the disinheritance of spouses or dependent children.

[21] In some of our own jurisdictions, a testator may specify that the inheritance of certain property depends on the heir marrying before a certain age, or marrying within the testator's religion. This is something like that, but the Old Law judicial precepts did not leave such matters to the testators, and the purpose was different. By requiring women who inherited to marry within the tribe, these precepts insured that initial allotments of territory among the tribes remained intact. This is spelled out in the book of Numbers, where we read that the heads of certain families brought a dispute about inheritance to Moses:

They said, "The Lord commanded my lord to give the land for inheritance by lot to the people of Israel; and my lord was commanded by the Lord to give the inheritance of

---

[23] Latin, *Ideo circa possessiones regulandas triplex remedium lex adhibuit*.
[24] Alfred J. Freddoso, trans., *Treatise on Law: The Complete Text* (South Bend, IN: St. Augustine's Press, 2009).

Zelophehad our brother to his daughters. But if they are married to any of the sons of the other tribes of the people of Israel then their inheritance will be taken from the inheritance of our fathers, and added to the inheritance of the tribe to which they belong; so it will be taken away from the lot of our inheritance."[25]

Moses replies:

"The tribe of the sons of Joseph is right. This is what the Lord commands concerning the daughters of Zelophehad, 'Let them marry whom they think best; only, they shall marry within the family of the tribe of their father. The inheritance of the people of Israel shall not be transferred from one tribe to another; for every one of the people of Israel shall cleave to the inheritance of the tribe of his fathers. And every daughter who possesses an inheritance in any tribe of the people of Israel shall be wife to one of the family of the tribe of her father, so that every one of the people of Israel may possess the inheritance of his fathers. So no inheritance shall be transferred from one tribe to another; for each of the tribes of the people of Israel shall cleave to its own inheritance.'"[26]

---

[22] Secondly, the Law commanded that, in some respects, the use of things should belong to all in common. Firstly, as regards the care of them; for it was prescribed (Dt. 22): "Thou shalt not pass by, if thou seest thy brother's ox or his sheep go astray; but thou shalt bring them back to thy brother," and in like manner as to other things. [23] Secondly, as regards fruits. For all alike were allowed on entering a friend's vineyard to eat of the fruit, but not to take any away. [24] And, specially, with respect to the poor, it was prescribed that the forgotten sheaves, and the bunches of grapes and fruit, should be left behind for them (Lev. 19; Dt. 24). [25] Moreover, whatever grew in the seventh year was common property, as stated in Ex. 23 and Lev. 25.

As to Aristotle's second point, concerning the need for what is privately owned to be used [or cared for] by all in certain respects:

- Anyone who saw that his fellow citizen's domestic animal or other property had gone astray was required to return it.
- Anyone could enter a friend's vineyard to eat its fruit (though not to carry it away).
- The sheaves and bunches of fruit which were overlooked during the harvest were to be left for the poor to gather.
- Every seven years, whatever grew belonged to everyone.

---

[22] One sense of the common use of possessions is common *care* for them. Suppose that when I enter a classroom to teach, I find that someone has left his laptop computer behind. Rather than leaving it there to be stolen, I should arrange for its return to him, or, if I do not know who he is, turn it in to the lost property office. In much the same spirit, the book of Deuteronomy instructs,

---

[25] Numbers 36:2–3 (RSV-CE).
[26] Ibid., verses 5b–9.

Reasons for Old Law Judicial Precepts Among Citizens

You shall not see your brother's ox or his sheep go astray, and withhold your help from them; you shall take them back to your brother. And if he is not near you, or if you do not know him, you shall bring it home to your house, and it shall be with you until your brother seeks it; then you shall restore it to him. And so you shall do with his ass; so you shall do with his garment; so you shall do with any lost thing of your brothers, which he loses and you find; you may not withhold your help. You shall not see your brother's ass or his ox fallen down by the way, and withhold your help from them; you shall help him to lift them up again.[27]

The care of possessions is not *entirely* in common, for each person continues to keep his own ox, sheep, ass, garments, and so on. When objects have been lost, however, we need to help each other out.

[23] The other sense of the common use of possessions is common *enjoyment* of them.

When you go into your neighbor's vineyard, you may eat your fill of grapes, as many as you wish, but you shall not put any in your vessel. When you go into your neighbor's standing grain, you may pluck the ears with your hand, but you shall not put a sickle to your neighbor's standing grain.[28]

If enjoyment were entirely common, then it would be impossible to distinguish common use from common ownership. Thus, although the owner's neighbors are permitted to sample one's grapes and ears of grain while passing over his land, they are not permitted to harvest them. A famous instance of this practice is recounted in the gospel of Matthew. Jesus and His disciples passed through some grainfields on the Sabbath day, and the disciples, who were hungry, plucked some of the heads of grain to eat. Although the disciples were criticized by nearby Pharisees, they were not accused of trespass and theft, as they might have been today, for taking the grain was allowed. Rather they were accused of performing labor on the Sabbath.[29]

[24] The provisions for common enjoyment were especially solicitous of the needy:

When you reap your harvest in your field, and have forgotten a sheaf in the field, you shall not go back to get it; it shall be for the sojourner, the fatherless, and the widow; that the Lord your God may bless you in all the work of your hands. When you beat your olive trees, you shall not go over the boughs again; it shall be for the sojourner, the fatherless, and the widow. When you gather the grapes of your vineyard, you shall not glean it afterward; it shall be for the sojourner, the fatherless, and the widow. You shall remember that you were a slave in the land of Egypt; therefore I command you to do this.[30]

---

[27] Deuteronomy 22:1-4 (RSV-CE).
[28] Deuteronomy 23:24-25 (RSV-CE).
[29] For the incident, including Christ's reply, see Matthew 12:1-6.
[30] Deuteronomy 24:19-22 (RSV-CE); compare Leviticus 19:9-10.

How this worked in practice is illustrated by Ruth, one of the ancestresses of Christ, who had been a gleaner in the field of Boaz.[31] We return to her story in the next Article.

[25] This provision is briefly stated in Exodus but restated more fully in Leviticus:

> Say to the people of Israel, When you come into the land which I give you, the land shall keep a Sabbath to the Lord. Six years you shall sow your field, and six years you shall prune your vineyard, and gather in its fruits; but in the seventh year there shall be a Sabbath of solemn rest for the land, a Sabbath to the Lord; you shall not sow your field or prune your vineyard. What grows of itself in your harvest you shall not reap, and the grapes of your undressed vine you shall not gather; it shall be a year of solemn rest for the land. The Sabbath of the land shall provide food for you, for yourself and for your male and female slaves and for your hired servant and the sojourner who lives with you; for your cattle also and for the beasts that are in your land all its yield shall be for food.[32]

This is a rather difficult observance, but the people are assured that God will provide:

> The land will yield its fruit, and you will eat your fill, and dwell in it securely. And if you say, "What shall we eat in the seventh year, if we may not sow or gather in our crop?" I will command my blessing upon you in the sixth year, so that it will bring forth fruit for three years. When you sow in the eighth year, you will be eating old produce; until the ninth year, when its produce comes in, you shall eat the old.[33]

When at a certain point in their history, because of grave sins, God brings the people to their senses by allowing them to be taken into exile for seventy years, the territory is described as enjoying the "Sabbaths of the land" that had apparently been neglected:

> All the leading priests and the people likewise were exceedingly unfaithful, following all the abominations of the nations; and they polluted the house of the Lord which he had hallowed in Jerusalem. The Lord, the God of their fathers, sent persistently to them by his messengers, because he had compassion on his people and on his dwelling place; but they kept mocking the messengers of God, despising his words, and scoffing at his prophets, till the wrath of the Lord rose against his people, till there was no remedy ... [The king of the Chaldeans] took into exile in Babylon those who had escaped from the sword, and they became servants to him and to his sons until the establishment of the kingdom of Persia, to fulfil the word of the Lord by the mouth of Jeremiah, until the land had enjoyed its Sabbaths. All the days that it lay desolate it kept Sabbath, to fulfil seventy years.[34]

---

[31] See the book of Ruth, especially chapter 2.
[32] Leviticus 25:2–7 (RSV-CE).
[33] Ibid., verses 19–22.
[34] 2 Chronicles 36:14–16, 20–21. The internal reference is to Jeremiah 25:11, "This whole land shall become a ruin and a waste, and these nations shall serve the king of Babylon seventy years,"

[26] Thirdly, the law recognized the transference of goods by the owner. There was a purely gratuitous transfer: thus it is written (Dt. 14): "The third day thou shalt separate another tithe ... and the Levite ... and the stranger, and the fatherless, and the widow ... shall come and shall eat and be filled." [27] And there was a transfer for a consideration, for instance, by selling and buying, by letting out and hiring, by loan and also by deposit, concerning all of which we find that the Law made ample provision. [28] Consequently it is clear that the Old Law provided sufficiently concerning the mutual relations of one man with another.	Finally, as to Aristotle's third point – the need for what is privately owned to be under the control of the owner in other respects – the law provided that by the owner's act, goods could be transferred. • It provided for gratuitous transfer, that is, for gift, as we see in the instructions concerning the tithe set apart for Levites, aliens, the fatherless, and widows. • It provided for transfer in return for something given, such as buying and selling, renting out and renting, loaning and depositing. From all this we see that the judicial precepts of the Old Law did give sufficient direction to the relations among the people.

[26] The gifts mentioned here are not discretionary gifts, but obligatory gifts, mandated in sheer recognition of need – in the case of members of the Levitical or priestly tribe, because its families had not been included from the initial distribution of land, and in the case of foreigners, widows, and orphans, because they were poor or vulnerable:

At the end of every three years you shall bring forth all the tithe of your produce in the same year, and lay it up within your towns; and the Levite, because he has no portion or inheritance with you, and the sojourner, the fatherless, and the widow, who are within your towns, shall come and eat and be filled; that the Lord your God may bless you in all the work of your hands that you do.[35]

[27] The rules concerning such transfers as buying and selling, renting out and renting, loaning and depositing are too numerous to be listed here, but we have seen several of them already.

[28] In sum, the judicial precepts did all of these things:

- They provided judges, gave instruction as to how judgment should be executed, removed temptations to judge unjustly, specified the requisite number of witnesses, and specified punishments.
- They provided for a just initial distribution of property in the Promised Land among families and tribes, and ensured that the allotments should remain intact.

---

and 29:10, "For thus says the Lord: When seventy years are completed for Babylon, I will visit you, and I will fulfil to you my promise and bring you back to this place." All quotations RSV-CE.
[35] Deuteronomy 14:28–29 (RSV-CE).

- They provided that although property was owned privately, even so, in certain respects, it would be used in common, partly to build bonds of friendship and mutual assistance, and partly to succor the poor and weak.
- Finally, they made provision for the transfer of possessions – both through gifts, such as the tithe for Levites and for the poor, and through voluntary exchanges of goods and services.

St. Thomas concludes that the Law made fitting arrangements not only for relations between the people and those in authority but also for what might be called the "public" relations among the people themselves.[36]

SUMMARY OF THE REPLIES TO THE OBJECTIONS

Summary of the Reply to Objection 1 All of the precepts, especially those concerning our neighbors, aim at encouraging men to love each other. An effect of love is to give willingly to others, especially those in need. Besides, one who does not give willingly to others will be disposed to harm anyone who does take some little thing from him. Consequently, the Objector has it exactly backwards. Rather than endangering peace, the regulation allowing persons to eat grapes from the vineyards of others encouraged the peace of friendship.

Summary of the Reply to Objection 2 For two reasons, the evil of which Aristotle warned did not take place. In the first place, women inherited only if there were no male descendants, so that the family land would not pass to strangers. In the second place, women who did inherit were required to marry within their own tribe, to prevent disturbance of the allotment of property among families.

Summary of the Reply to Objection 3 The Objector is right to warn of indiscriminate sale of possessions, because it may cause possessions to become concentrated in just a few hands. However, by allowing sales of property to hold good only for a certain time, the Old Law protected against this danger, and at the same time allowed persons to help themselves in case of need. It was entirely reasonable that houses in walled towns (just like houses in Levite towns) were exempt from this rule (even though houses in unwalled towns near family estates were subject to it), because the number of houses in a walled town could be increased.

Summary of the Reply to Objection 4 These and other regulations concerning lending were aimed at habituating men to be ready to assist their neighbors (which is a great incentive to friendship), as well as to be patient with those in need. As to the remission of debts during the seventh year, it is unlikely that those who really could pay their debts before the seventh year would defraud their lenders by failing to do so; remission of their debts was for the sake of

---

[36] He discusses the Old Law's arrangements for their domestic relations in Article 4, which is omitted from this commentary.

love. As to not requiring restitution for the death of borrowed animals, the law made appropriate distinctions according to whether the animals had been properly cared for, and whether they had been rented or freely loaned.

Summary of the Reply to Objection 5 True, in some cases the duty to return loans was stricter than the duty to return goods held in trust. However, this was reasonable in view of the fact that in the case of loans, goods are transferred for the benefit of the borrower, but in the case of goods held in trust, they are transferred for the benefit of the depositor. The law did make appropriate distinctions according to whether the goods held in trust had been lost unavoidably or through negligence.

Summary of the Reply to Objection 6 Workmen who offer their labor for hire are poor, and must be paid each day so that they can eat. There is no inconsistency in not requiring the daily payment of rent, because those who offer other things for hire than just their labor, such as houses, tend to be wealthy.

Reply to Objection 7 Simple people could easily appeal for justice in ordinary cases, because judges and magistrates were appointed for this purpose in each tribe. Only those rare cases which were doubtful even among ordinary judges were referred to higher authorities who were further away.

Summary of the Reply to Objection 8 Demonstrative certainty is impossible in matters in which testimony must be taken, and we must be satisfied with conjectural probability. True, two or three witnesses might conspire to lie, yet it would be difficult for them to get away with it because (1) the Law required that they be carefully examined, (2) they were to be trusted only if they gave their testimony unwaveringly and were not otherwise suspect, and (3) the penalty for perjury was severe. In view of certain comments in the Gospel of John,[37] St. Augustine suggests that we may also recognize symbolic value in the fact that the law specified two or three witnesses, because the Divine Persons are sometimes described as three (since they are Father, Son, and Holy Spirit), and sometimes as two (since the Holy Spirit is the bond between the Father and the Son).

Summary of the Reply to Objection 9 Other things being equal, yes, a graver wrong deserves a graver punishment. However, this is not the only consideration in punishment. Graver punishments should be inflicted if the wrong is habitual, or if there is great pleasure in committing it, because otherwise it will not be cured. Moreover, greater ones should be inflicted if the wrong is easy to

---

[37] See John 8:13–18 (RSV-CE): "The Pharisees then said to [Jesus], 'You are bearing witness to yourself; your testimony is not true.' Jesus answered, 'Even if I do bear witness to myself, my testimony is true, for I know whence I have come and whither I am going, but you do not know whence I come or whither I am going. You judge according to the flesh, I judge no one. Yet even if I do judge, my judgment is true, for it is not I alone that judge, but I and He who sent me. In your law it is written that the testimony of two men is true; I bear witness to myself, and the Father who sent me bears witness to me.'"

commit and to hide, because otherwise people will not be sufficiently deterred from committing it. Even considering just the gravity of the wrong itself, we must make distinctions. One who does wrong involuntarily should not be punished at all. All other things being equal, one who does wrong voluntarily, but through weakness, should receive diminished punishment. One who does wrong in ignorance of relevant facts should be punished only for negligence in finding out about them. One who does wrong from pride – through deliberate malice – should be punished according to the gravity of the sin. But one who does wrong done in impudent recklessness or stubborn defiance should be completely cut off from the people by death as a destroyer of the Law itself. Thus, with certain exceptions for special reasons, the judicial precepts inflicted double compensation for the theft of most things, quadruple compensation for the theft of sheep (which are difficult to guard), and quintuple compensation for the theft of oxen (which are still harder to guard).[38] The man who gathered sticks on the Sabbath was punished for defiance of the faith, and the unruly son was punished severely, not for reveling and drunkenness, but for contumacy and rebellion, like any rebel.

Summary of the Reply to Objection 10 Actually slavery *was* prescribed by the Law, but only if a bond servant was unwilling to be freed in the seventh year, or if a thief was unable to make restitution. The Law did not prescribe absolute exile because the exiled person would have been in danger of falling into idolatry, since no other nation worshipped God. However, there was a limited sort of exile, because persons who had committed involuntary manslaughter and were in danger of revenge could flee to a City of Refuge until the death of the current high priest.

Summary of the Reply to Objection 11 The purpose of killing animals that had killed, or that had been used for bestiality, was not to punish the beasts themselves. One reason was to punish the owners, who had not prevented these things from happening. Another possible reason was to express loathing for what was done, and to spare people the horror of having to see the beasts that had been involved.

Summary of the Reply to Objection 12 In case of a murder by a person unknown, a calf was slain not because the life of a calf and a human being were equal in value, but for other reasons both literal and symbolic. Rabbi Moses (Maimonides) explains that the literal reason was to encourage the giving of evidence, because to avoid having to compensate the owner of the calf, and to avoid the loss of the tract of land (which was to remain forever uncultivated), the men of the city would willingly tell what they knew of the murder. Another reason might have been to inculcate the fear of committing murder, for to slay such a strong and useful animal, by such a method, and to leave it to rot,

---

[38] Citing a commentary, St. Thomas says another possible reason for the difference in punishment is that a cow is useful in five ways (for ploughing, sacrifice, meat, milk, and its hide), but that a sheep is useful in four ways (for sacrifice, meat, milk, and its wool.).

dramatized the fact that even a strong and useful man who murders must suffer a harsh death and be cut off from the fellowship of the living. Symbolically, various details about the slaying of the heifer foreshadow the death of Christ.

DISCUSSION

Commonwealths Considered Ideally and Considered as They Are in Real Life

As we saw earlier, St. Augustine rejects Marcus Tullius Cicero's definition of a commonwealth – a multitude joined together by consent to justice and united by a community of interest, that is, by the common good – on the grounds that no earthly community has ever fulfilled it. Augustine proposes that we would do better to regard a commonwealth as a body of rational beings united by *the objects of their love*.

The Ciceronian definition which Augustine is quoting and criticizing comes from a dialogue called *De Re Publica*, written in imitation of Plato's *Republic*. Cicero puts the definition in the mouth of the great Roman statesman of the past, Scipio Africanus. This part of *De Re Publica*[39] has been lost; we know the passage only from quotations by other ancient writers, especially Augustine himself. St. Augustine warns,

> For I mean in its own place to show that – according to the definitions in which Cicero himself, using Scipio as his mouthpiece, briefly propounded what a republic [or commonwealth][40] is, and what a people is, and according to many testimonies, both of his own lips and of those who took part in that same debate – Rome never was a republic, because true justice had never a place in it. But accepting the more feasible definitions of a republic, I grant there was a republic of a certain kind, and certainly much better administered by the more ancient Romans than by their modern representatives. But the fact is, true justice has no existence save in that republic whose founder and ruler is Christ, if at least any choose to call this a republic; and indeed we cannot deny that it is the people's good.[41]

Much later in *The City of God*, he returns to the theme:

> If we are to accept the definitions laid down by Scipio in Cicero's *De Republica*, there never was a Roman republic; for he briefly defines a republic as the good of the people. And if this definition be true, there never was a Roman republic, for the people's good was never attained among the Romans. For the people, according to his definition, is an assemblage associated by a common acknowledgment of right and by a community of interests. And what he means by a common acknowledgment of right he explains at

---

[39] Book I, section 39.
[40] The literal meaning of *res publica*, from which we derive the word "republic," is "public thing"; thus the word "commonwealth."
[41] St. Augustine of Hippo, *The City of God*, book II, chapter 21 (public domain), www.newadvent.org/fathers/1201.htm.

large, showing that a republic cannot be administered without justice ... Thus, where there is not true justice there can be no assemblage of men associated by a common acknowledgment of right, and therefore there can be no people, as defined by Scipio or Cicero; and if no people, then no good of the people, but only of some promiscuous multitude unworthy of the name of people.[42]

He says again that in this world, what we call commonwealths are united not by agreement with justice but by agreement on the objects of their love:

> But if we discard this definition of a people, and, assuming another, say that a people is an assemblage of reasonable beings bound together by a common agreement as to the objects of their love, then, in order to discover the character of any people, we have only to observe what they love. Yet whatever it loves, if only it is an assemblage of reasonable beings and not of beasts, and is bound together by an agreement as to the objects of love, it is reasonably called a people; and it will be a superior people in proportion as it is bound together by higher interests, inferior in proportion as it is bound together by lower. According to this definition of ours, the Roman people is a people, and its good is without doubt a commonwealth or republic. But what its tastes were in its early and subsequent days, and how it declined into sanguinary seditions and then to social and civil wars, and so burst asunder or rotted off the bond of concord in which the health of a people consists, history shows, and in the preceding books I have related at large. And yet I would not on this account say either that it was not a people, or that its administration was not a republic, so long as there remains an assemblage of reasonable beings bound together by a common agreement as to the objects of love. But what I say of this people and of this republic I must be understood to think and say of the Athenians or any Greek state, of the Egyptians, of the early Assyrian Babylon, and of every other nation, great or small, which had a public government. For, in general, the city of the ungodly, which did not obey the command of God that it should offer no sacrifice save to Him alone, and which, therefore, could not give to the soul its proper command over the body, nor to the reason its just authority over the vices, is void of true justice.[43]

On Whether the Lower Is Really More Solid

The usual approach to political classification is to compare forms of *government*, for example monarchy, aristocracy, democracy, along with all their relatives and blends. But Augustine's argument against Cicero's definition of the commonwealth suggests a different approach to classification. For we might also compare kinds of *political society*, or perhaps kinds of *political classes*, focusing on the objects of their shared love.

Augustine's approach also promises insights into how political societies change over time. According to Augustine, the Romans (or at least their political classes) were first united in the love of freedom in the sense of self-rule, then

---

[42] Ibid., book XIX, chapter 21.
[43] Ibid., book XIX, chapter 24.

united by the love of glory in the sense of the admiration of others, and finally united in the love of wealth and power. Interestingly, during the republican period – the period in which they were united by the love of glory – they believed themselves to be highly virtuous. What made this self-deception possible, Augustine thinks, was that the love of glory *imitates* virtue: although in reality it is a grievous vice, it can motivate persons to suppress their lesser vices in order to gain the admiration of others by performing deeds that benefit the commonwealth.[44] Our own political and economic arrangements attempt a similar imitation of virtue, for we count on the love of power and the jealousy of the power of others to maintain the system of checks and balances, and we count on the love of money and empire to maintain the system of competitive private enterprise.

From an Augustinian perspective, the problem is that no such arrangement can be stable. Attempts to uphold the common good without virtue succeed only to the degree that at least *some* real virtue is present after all. For in practice, we find that:

- Apart from the motive of true virtue, reliance on love of glory provokes deeds of benefit to the commonwealth only so long as one gains more admiration from this sort of deeds than from corrupt ones. (This was Augustine's insight about the collapse of the republic.)
- Apart from the motive of true virtue, reliance on the love of power and the jealousy of the power of others provokes the proper use of checks and balances only so long as one can be more secure in one's power by making use of the constitutional system than by subverting it.
- Apart from the motive of true virtue, reliance on love of money and empire provokes people to better their products and services only so long as they cannot gain even more money and empire by colluding with the government for private subsidies and privileges.

We need not be cynical. The lesson is *not* that even in a fallen world, in which virtue is in short supply, such attempts to minimize reliance on virtue have no use at all. Rather the lesson is that they cannot serve the common good unless *there is some virtue too*. They are not like meat, but like the popular brand of meat extender called Hamburger Helper. They do not replace virtue, but only make it "stretch." They prompt imperfectly virtuous people do some of the things which greater virtue might have motivated them to do, but not if the virtue of these people is *too* imperfect.

A dangerous hallmark of modern political thought is the view that reliance on virtue is impractical and unrealistic, because vice is more dependable. As Leo Strauss famously wrote, "By building civil society on the 'low but solid ground' of selfishness or of certain 'private vices,' one will achieve much greater 'public

---

[44] St. Augustine of Hippo, *City of God against the Pagans*, book v, chapters 12–21.

benefits' than by futilely appealing to virtue."[45] But if St. Augustine is right, the lower ground is not more solid; the higher ground is. True, it really would be impractical and unrealistic to expect people to be perfectly virtuous. But to expect that we can do without virtue and rely on our favorite vices to promote the common good is more than unrealistic. It is deluded.

---

[45] Leo Strauss, *Natural Right and History* (Chicago: University of Chicago Press, 1953), p. 247.

QUESTION 105, ARTICLE 3

Whether the Judicial Precepts Regarding Foreigners were Framed in a Suitable Manner?

TEXT	PARAPHRASE
Whether the judicial precepts regarding foreigners were framed in a suitable manner?	Did the Old Law appropriately frame the regulations about persons who were not members of the nation?

Besides addressing relations among persons of the Chosen Nation, the Old Law also addressed their relations with foreigners, or "strangers," both inside and outside their borders. Some of these aliens were friendly, others hostile. Some lived in the cities and towns of other lands, some were sojourners passing through the land, and some, though not Israelites, were residents of the land.

Objection 1. [1] *It would seem that the judicial precepts regarding foreigners were not suitably framed. For Peter said (Acts 10): "In very deed I perceive that God is not a respecter of persons, but in every nation, he that feareth Him and worketh justice is acceptable to Him."* [2] *But those who are acceptable to God should not be excluded from the Church of God.* [3] *Therefore it is unsuitably commanded (Dt. 23) that "the Ammonite and the Moabite, even after the tenth generation, shall not enter into the church of the Lord for ever":* [4] *whereas, on the other hand, it is prescribed to be observed with regard to certain other nations: "Thou shalt not abhor the Edomite, because he is thy brother; nor the Egyptian because thou wast a stranger in his land."*	Objection 1. Apparently at least some of the Old Testament regulations concerning aliens were badly composed. Later, in the New Testament, the book of Acts reports St. Peter as having said that God shows no partiality, but accepts anyone of any nation who fears Him and acts righteously. Surely, then, those from every nation whom God accepts should be accepted into the assembly of God's people, but the Old Law rejected them, for it entirely excluded members of the Ammonite and Moabite nations. And yet, inconsistently, it prohibited contempt for members of certain other nations: for Edomites, because of their ancestral relations with the Israelites, and for Egyptians, because the Israelites themselves had once been strangers in Egypt.

[1] The statement quoted here alludes to an epochal event in the life of the early Church. St. Peter, having been convinced by a vision that he should accept an invitation from a Gentile to speak to his household, addresses them as follows:

You yourselves know how unlawful it is for a Jew to associate with or to visit any one of another nation; but God has shown me that I should not call any man common or unclean. So when I was sent for, I came without objection ... Truly I perceive that God shows no partiality, but in every nation anyone who fears him and does what is right is acceptable to him.

While Peter is still explaining the Gospel of Jesus Christ to them, the Gentiles who are present begin to show signs that the Holy Spirit has come upon them, and Peter asks the Jewish Christians present, "Can any one forbid water for baptizing these people who have received the Holy Spirit just as we have?"[1]

[2] St. Thomas speaks of the *Ecclesia* of God. Although this is the term used for the Church, its more general meaning is an assembly, as he himself points out later. The term can refer to either the congregation of worship or to the group of those eligible to take part in public affairs, and St. Thomas distinguishes between these two bodies. Since both were under Divine protection, both were in this sense "of God." So despite the wording of the Blackfriars translation, St. Thomas is probably not calling the *Ecclesia* of Israel "the Church"; on the other hand, he certainly views the Old Testament community of faith as foreshadowing the Church, so the translation is not impossible.

[3] Members of certain nations were perpetually excluded from the deliberative assembly (although, according to St. Thomas, not from the assembly of worship). In context, the quoted passage reads,

No Ammonite or Moabite shall enter the assembly of the Lord; even to the tenth generation none belonging to them shall enter the assembly of the Lord for ever; because they did not meet you with bread and with water on the way, when you came forth out of Egypt, and because they hired against you Balaam the son of Beor from Pethor of Mesopotamia, to curse you.[2]

The allusion to Balaam the son of Beor refers to an incident that is recounted in Numbers 22–24. Balak, the king of Moab, sends messengers to Balaam, who, though not an Israelite, is believed to be a prophet. They offer divination fees to Balaam if he will come and curse the Israelites, because "he whom you bless is blessed, and he whom you curse is cursed."[3] Although Balaam is not unwilling to accept the commission, God intervenes to prevent Balaam from cursing the Israelites, revealing that in fact, they have His favor. Thus, Balaam

---

[1] Acts 10:28–29, 34b–35, 47 (RSV-CE), changing "any one" to "anyone."
[2] Deuteronomy 23:3–4 (RSV-CE).
[3] Numbers 22:6 (RSV-CE).

Reasons for Old Law Judicial Precepts About Noncitizens 361

does the opposite of what Balak has charged him to do. Furious, Balak says, "What have you done to me? I took you to curse my enemies, and behold, you have done nothing but bless them." Balaam replies, "Must I not take heed to speak what the Lord puts in my mouth? Behold, I received a command to bless: he has blessed, and I cannot revoke it."[4] Hoping to cut his losses, Balak demands that Balaam neither curse *nor* bless them, but Balaam refuses: "Did I not tell you, 'All that the Lord says, that I must do'?"[5] Relations between Balak and Balaam go from bad to worse, and eventually Balaam returns to his home.

[4] The members of certain other nations were treated differently than the Ammonites and Moabites. In full, the passage quoted reads,

You shall not abhor an Edomite, for he is your brother; you shall not abhor an Egyptian, because you were a sojourner in his land. The children of the third generation that are born to them may enter the assembly of the Lord.[6]

The Israelites regarded Edomites as kin because of shared ancestry. God had made a covenant with Abraham to make of his descendants a mighty nation. Abraham's son was Isaac; Isaac in turn had twin sons, Jacob and Esau. Though Esau was the firstborn, Jacob took advantage of Esau's impulsiveness and poor judgment to have the birthright and associated blessings transferred to himself. Jacob, who is later named Israel, becomes the father of the Israelites; Esau, in turn, becomes the father of the Edomites, who are also called Idumaeans.

Although the Egyptians are not regarded as kin, and although before the Exodus the Israelites had been cruelly oppressed by the Egyptian pharaoh, or king, nevertheless there was a certain affinity between the Israelites and the Egyptians because the Israelites had dwelt in Egypt as resident aliens for so many years.

| *Objection 2.* [1] *Further, we do not deserve to be punished for those things which are not in our power.* [2] *But it is not in man's power to be an eunuch, or born of a prostitute.* [3] *Therefore it is unsuitably commanded (Dt. 23) that "an eunuch and one born of a prostitute shalt not enter into the church of the Lord."* | Objection 2. Consider too that punishment is not deserved for things we cannot help. Among the things a man cannot help are having his testicles crushed, having his male member severed, or being of illegitimate birth. Therefore, it was wrong for the Old Law to forbid those suffering these misfortunes from entering the sacred assembly. |

---

[4] Numbers 23:11–12, 20 (RSV-CE).
[5] Numbers 23:25 (RSV-CE). For irony, compare Balaam's blessing in 24:9b with Balak's flattery in 22:6b.
[6] Deuteronomy 23:7–8 (RSV-CE).

[1] We are responsible only for what is within our power to do, not do, or prevent. No one can be commanded to do what is impossible; no one can be blamed for failing to do it.

[2] The term translated "eunuch" probably refers to a person with injured genitals, and the term translated "born of a prostitute" is usually translated "bastard." A person may wish that his crushed or severed genitals were intact, or that his birth had been legitimate, but as the common saying has it, wishing doesn't make it so; the facts are not in his power.

[3] In another translation, and in context, the quoted passage reads,

> He whose testicles are crushed or whose male member is cut off shall not enter the assembly of the Lord. No bastard shall enter the assembly of the Lord; even to the tenth generation none of his descendants shall enter the assembly of the Lord.[7]

The Objector, viewing this exclusion as a punishment, considers it unjust. He does not consider the possibility that punishment may not been its rationale.

Objection 3. [1] *Further, the Old Law mercifully forbade strangers to be molested: for it is written (Ex. 22):* "*Thou shalt not molest a stranger, nor afflict him; for yourselves also were strangers in the land of Egypt*": *and (Ex. 23):* "*Thou shalt not molest a stranger, for you know the hearts of strangers, for you also were strangers in the land of Egypt.*" [2] *But it is an affliction to be burdened with usury.* [3] *Therefore the Law unsuitably permitted them (Dt. 23) to lend money to the stranger for usury.*

Objection 3. Moreover, as we find in the book of Exodus, the Old Law compassionately prohibited afflicting resident aliens or holding them down. "You shall not wrong a stranger or oppress him, for you were strangers in the land of Egypt," it warns, and again, "You shall not oppress a stranger; you know the heart of a stranger, for you were strangers in the land of Egypt." Yet the Law was inconsistent in this matter, for it did allow lending money at interest to aliens, and it is certainly an affliction to be loaded down by interest charges.

---

[1] The Latin terms used by the Vulgate in Exodus 22:21 and 23:9 forbid every sort of torment, maltreatment, or oppression of resident aliens. *Contristabis* means to sadden, depress, discourage, or afflict; *affliges* means to strike, afflict, humble, or overthrow; and *molestus* means to be a worry, trouble, nuisance, or source of grief. The words of the original Hebrew text contain a similar range of meanings.

[2] Various nations, philosophers, and religions have prohibited charging interest on loans, considering it the taking of unfair advantage. From the perspective of the demand theory of value widely held today, this is difficult to understand; it seems absurd to view charging interest as unfair, because a

---

[7] Deuteronomy 23:1-2 (RSV-CE).

thing (in this case the use of borrowed money) is deemed to be worth whatever price people are willing to pay for it (in this case interest). However, for people who are borrowing not to expand their business but to eat, and who might starve if they do not borrow, this way of thinking seems harsh.

Another reason for holding the charging of interest in suspicion is that unlike someone who invests his money in a productive activity such as a farm, the lender seems to get something for nothing. That is Aristotle's view:

> There are two sorts of wealth-getting, as I have said; one is a part of household management, the other is retail trade: the former necessary and honorable, while that which consists in exchange is justly censured; for it is unnatural, and a mode by which men gain from one another. The most hated sort, and with the greatest reason, is usury, which makes a gain out of money itself, and not from the natural object of it. For money was intended to be used in exchange, but not to increase at interest. And this term interest, which means the birth of money from money, is applied to the breeding of money because the offspring resembles the parent. Wherefore of all modes of getting wealth this is the most unnatural.[8]

On the other hand, if the charging of interest is prohibited, then why would anyone loan money at all? Certainly not as a shrewd business practice. He would have to be motivated by love of neighbor. In this case lending money becomes a form of friendship or aid to the poor.

Some, seeking to harmonize the ancient suspicion of interest with modern banking practice, suggest that although perhaps some charging of interest is getting something for nothing, not all of it is. After all, the lender is giving up the use of money which he *might otherwise* have put to productive use, and so, they say, it is not unreasonable to compensate him for his loss. From this point of view, the crime of usury should be viewed not as charging interest per se, but as charging interest in excess of the lender's opportunity cost. This is a plausible objection to Aristotle's economic argument against charging interest. However, it is not a sufficient objection to the charitable argument – that one should lend money not to make money, but to help one's brother, especially if he is in need. From this point of view, one might say that modern banking practice presupposes that *nobody counts as one's brother.*

[3] The Old Law prohibited charging interest on loans to fellow Israelites, but it allowed charging interest on loans to outsiders:

> You shall not lend upon interest to your brother, interest on money, interest on victuals, interest on anything that is lent for interest. To a foreigner you may lend upon interest, but to your brother you shall not lend upon interest; that the Lord your God may bless you in all that you undertake in the land which you are entering to take possession of it.[9]

---

[8] Aristotle, *Politics*, translated by Benjamin Jowett, book 1, chapter 10 (public domain).
[9] Deuteronomy 23:19–20 (RSV-CE).

The Objector approves of the former prohibition, but thinks it should have applied to loans to foreigners too.

Objection 4. *[1] Further, men are much more akin to us than trees. [2] But we should show greater care and love for these things that are nearest to us, according to Ecclus. 13, "Every beast loveth its like: so also every man him that is nearest to himself." [3] Therefore the Lord unsuitably commanded (Dt. 20) that all the inhabitants of a captured hostile city were to be slain, but that the fruit-trees should not be cut down.*	Objection 4. Moreover, we should have greater concern, and exercise greater care, for things that are more like us. This is why the book of Sirach observes that even beasts love those who are like them, and that in the same way men love those most akin. Yet we find in the Old Law a requirement that when an enemy city is conquered, the captives should be put to death – and yet that the fruit trees should be left alone! Surely other men are far more closely related to us than trees!

[1] All human beings are of the same species, sharing in the same community of nature. But not only are trees of a different species, they are not even of the same genus. We are rational animals, but they are neither rational nor animal.

[2] Although in Question 99, Article 2, St. Thomas takes the same meaning from the quoted passage that the Objector takes from it here, the interpretation is a little puzzling, because, read in its context, the quoted passage is not so much about what people *should* do as about what they *actually* do – something the prudent man is advised to keep in mind. It merely observes that creatures in general do prefer creatures like themselves:

Every creature loves its like, and every person his neighbor; all living beings associate by species, and a man clings to one like himself. What fellowship has a wolf with a lamb? No more has a sinner with a godly man. What peace is there between a hyena and a dog? And what peace between a rich man and a poor man? Wild asses in the wilderness are the prey of lions; likewise the poor are pastures for the rich. Humility is an abomination to a proud man; likewise a poor man is an abomination to a rich one.[10]

And so yes, men do love other men more than trees – but as the passage bitterly points out, rich men are more likely to have contempt for the needy than to love them, since the poor are not "their kind of people." Read this way, the passage is a warning. Just as the sinner seeks to prey on the godly man, and the lion seeks to prey on the ass, so the rich seek to prey on the poor. Not much fellow feeling there.

But even if the interpretation of the passage shared by St. Thomas and the Objector is questionable, the Objector has a point. Even if the passage is not really *about* how we should love foreigners better than trees, nevertheless *we should* love foreigners better than we love trees. Much later in sacred

---
[10] Sirach 13:15–20 (RSV-CE). Sirach, also known as Ecclesiasticus, is not be confused with Ecclesiastes.

history, Christ taught the Jews that even the despised Samaritans were their neighbors.[11]

[3] When hostile cities are captured, the fruit trees are to be left alone:

When you besiege a city for a long time, making war against it in order to take it, you shall not destroy its trees by wielding an axe against them; for you may eat of them, but you shall not cut them down. Are the trees in the field men that they should be besieged by you? Only the trees which you know are not trees for food you may destroy and cut down that you may build siegeworks against the city that makes war with you, until it falls.[12]

So rather than pointing out that trees are less akin than hostile foreigners (which is true), the passage points out that trees are not dangerous like hostile foreigners (which is also true).

Women and children are to be spared in captured hostile cities which are far away. However, in captured hostile cities within the Promised Land, everyone is to be slain:

But in the cities of these peoples that the Lord your God gives you for an inheritance, you shall save alive nothing that breathes, but you shall utterly destroy them, the Hittites and the Amorites, the Canaanites and the Perizzites, the Hivites and the Jebusites, as the Lord your God has commanded; that they may not teach you to do according to all their abominable practices which they have done in the service of their gods, and so to sin against the Lord your God.[13]

The abominable practices of these cities to which the passage refers included such things as ritual obscenity, temple prostitution, and the sacrifice of children to their gods. Just as the passage suggests, the Hebrew people, themselves escapees from paganism, were always in danger of learning these practices from their enemies (or of relearning them). One such crisis occurs sometime after the Exodus, when the Hebrews are encamped in the trans-Jordanian valley before crossing the River Jordan into the Promised Land. According to the scriptural account, so many of the Israelite men have become sexually involved with the women of the pagan Moabites, participating into the ritual obscenities involved in initiation into the cult of the Baal of Mt. Peor, that Moses commands the judges of Israel to execute all those who have done so. At the height of the crisis, Zimri, the son of Salu, defies the ban by openly entangling himself with a pagan woman, Cozbi, the daughter of Zur, a ruler of the Midianites, with whom the Moabites had close relations. From the way the story is told, it seems that Zimri is having ritual intercourse with her publicly, in the very sight of the people who are weeping about the nation's sins in the tent of meeting and worship. Phinehas responds by impaling both

---

[11] See again the parable of the Good Samaritan, cited above.
[12] Deuteronomy 20:19–20 (RSV-CE).
[13] Deuteronomy 20:16–18 (RSV-CE).

Zimri and Cozbi with a single thrust of his spear, apparently catching them *in flagrante delicto*.[14]

Objection 5. [1] *Further, every one should prefer the common good of virtue to the good of the individual.* [2] *But the common good is sought in a war which men fight against their enemies.* [3] *Therefore it is unsuitably commanded (Dt. 20) that certain men should be sent home, for instance a man that had built a new house, or who had planted a vineyard, or who had married a wife.*

Objection 5. Moreover, the common good, pursued according to the individual's power, is more important than the individual's private good. But the purpose of fighting enemies in war is the common good. Thus, it was wrong for the Old Law to command that that when battle is imminent, certain men should be released to go back home – if they had just built a new house, planted a new vine, or entered into marriage with a woman.

---

[1] The Blackfriars translation renders *bonum commune secundum virtutem* as "the common good of virtue," which makes sense in the abstract – since virtue is one of the chief elements of the common good – but does not make sense in this context. However, *virtutem* can also refer to strength or power. For this reason, I take the expression as comparing the pursuit of one's own private good with his pursuit of the common good *according to his power or means*. The Vulgate uses the phrase *secundum virtutem* in this sense in 2 Corinthians 8:3, where St. Paul praises the Macedonian Christians for giving "according to their power ... and beyond their power" (*secundum virtutem ... et supra virtutem*) for the relief of the needy Christians of Jerusalem.

[2] St. Thomas does not mean any war, but a just war (about which, more later). It is not to be supposed that God would command injustice.

[3] The passage to which the Objector alludes reads as follows:

Then the officers shall speak to the people, saying, "What man is there that has built a new house and has not dedicated it? Let him go back to his house, lest he die in the battle and another man dedicate it. And what man is there that has planted a vineyard and has not enjoyed its fruit? Let him go back to his house, lest he die in the battle and another man enjoy its fruit. And what man is there that has betrothed a wife and has not taken her? Let him go back to his house, lest he die in the battle and another man take her."[15]

The Objector's argument works like this:

1. If there is a conflict between pursuing one's private good and pursuing the common good according to one's ability, then one should pursue the common good.

---

[14] Numbers 25:1–8.
[15] Deuteronomy 20:5–7 (RSV-CE).

2. There is certainly such a conflict if a man wishes to enjoy his new house, vineyard, or wife, but is needed to fight in in the nation's just war. Applying the principle just stated, therefore, he ought to fight.
3. However, the Old Law supposes that such a man ought to go home. This would make sense only on the incorrect principle that the private good should be preferred to the common.

Objection 6. [1] *Further, no man should profit by his own fault.* [2] *But it is a man's fault if he be timid or faint-hearted: since this is contrary to the virtue of fortitude.* [3] *Therefore the timid and faint-hearted are unfittingly excused from the toil of battle (Dt. 20).*	Objection 6. Besides, no one should have an advantage because of his faults. Surely, though, a man is at fault for a terrified and fearful heart, for cowardice is a vice: it is opposed to the virtue of courage. For this reason, it was inappropriate for the Old Law to excuse the terrified and fearful-hearted from the labor and hardship of battle.

[1] The maxim that no one may gain advantage from his own fault is also well entrenched in Anglo-American law, and in words almost identical to St. Thomas's: *Commodum ex injuria sua nemo habere debet.*[16] For example, someone who gains property by murdering its owner must not be allowed to keep it.[17]

[2] Two opposite vices cause one to miss the mark of true courage or fortitude. The one the Objector blames here is cowardice, which is a defect of deficiency. The other is rashness, which is a defect of excess.

[3] The passage quoted in the previous Objection continues, "And the officers shall speak further to the people, and say, 'What man is there that is fearful and fainthearted? Let him go back to his house, lest the heart of his fellows melt as his heart.'"[18]

Thus it seems to the Objector that under the Old Law, cowards do gain advantage from their own fault, for they do not have to fight. This seems to him intolerable.

---

[16] The maxim is phrased in a variety of ways. St. Thomas's own wording is *ex culpa non debet quis commodum reportare.*
[17] As one jurist remarks, "To permit the murderer to retain title to the property acquired by his crime as permitted in some states is abhorrent to even the most rudimentary sense of justice. It violates the policy of the common law that no one shall be allowed to profit by his own wrong: *nullus commodum capere potest de injuria sua propria.* This doctrine ... 'so essential to the observance of morality and justice, has been universally recognized in the laws of civilized communities for centuries and is as old as equity. Its sentiment is ageless.'" Justice C. J. Vanderbilt, delivering the opinion of the New Jersey Supreme Court in *Neiman v. Hurff*, 93 A. 2d 345 (1952).
[18] Deuteronomy 20:8 (RSV-CE).

On the contrary, Divine Wisdom declares (Prov. 8): *"All my words are just, there is nothing wicked nor perverse in them."*	**On the other hand,** the book or Proverbs represents Lady Wisdom as saying that all of her teaching is right and straight, not a bit of it crooked or twisted.

Lady Wisdom is a poetic personification of the Wisdom of God. Praising her own teaching, she offers it free of charge to any who will but hear it:

Does not Wisdom call, does not Understanding raise her voice? On the heights beside the way, in the paths she takes her stand; beside the gates in front of the town, at the entrance of the portals she cries aloud: "To you, O men, I call, and my cry is to the sons of men. O simple ones, learn prudence; O foolish men, pay attention. Hear, for I will speak noble things, and from my lips will come what is right; for my mouth will utter truth; wickedness is an abomination to my lips. *All the words of my mouth are righteous; there is nothing twisted or crooked in them.* They are all straight to him who understands and right to those who find knowledge."[19]

The *sed contra*'s implied argument works like this:

1. All the works of Divine wisdom are flawless.
2. But Divine law is the work of Divine wisdom.
3. Therefore Divine law is also flawless.

Needless to say, this will not persuade someone who doubts that Divine law really is the work of Divine wisdom, but St. Thomas now goes on to defend it.

I answer that, [1] *Man's relations with foreigners are twofold: peaceful, and hostile: and in directing both kinds of relation the Law contained suitable precepts.* [2] *For the Jews were offered three opportunities of peaceful relations with foreigners. First, when foreigners passed through their land as travelers.* [3] *Secondly, when they came to dwell in their land as newcomers.* [4] *And in both these respects the Law made kind provision in its precepts: for it is written (Ex. 22):* "Thou shalt not molest a stranger [advenam]"; *and again (Ex. 23):*[20] *"Thou shalt not*	**Here is my response.** Relations with resident aliens may be either peaceful and hostile, and the Old Law appropriately regulated both kinds of relations. Let us take them in turn. As to the first category of relations, the Jews were presented with three occasions for peaceful dealings with outsiders: 1. When such outsiders passed through their land temporarily, as sojourners or migrants. 2. When they came into their land to live in it, as resident aliens. 3. When they wished to be taken completely into their community and rituals, as proselytes or converts.

---

[19] Proverbs 8:1–9 (RSV-CE), emphasis added, capitalizing Wisdom and Understanding because the passage personifies them.
[20] Corrected: The Blackfriars translation mistakenly refers to Exodus 22.

molest a stranger [peregrino]." [5] Thirdly, when any foreigners wished to be admitted entirely to their fellowship and mode of worship. [6] With regard to these a certain order was observed. For they were not at once admitted to citizenship: [7] just as it was law with some nations that no one was deemed a citizen except after two or three generations, as the Philosopher says (Polit. iii). [8] The reason for this was that if foreigners were allowed to meddle with the affairs of a nation as soon as they settled down in its midst, many dangers might occur, since the foreigners not yet having the common good firmly at heart might attempt something hurtful to the people. [9] Hence it was that the Law prescribed in respect of certain nations that had close relations with the Jews (viz., the Egyptians among whom they were born and educated, and the Idumeans, the children of Esau, Jacob's brother), that they should be admitted to the fellowship of the people after the third generation; [10] whereas others (with whom their relations had been hostile, such as the Ammonites and Moabites) were never to be admitted to citizenship; [11] while the Amalekites, who were yet more hostile to them, and had no fellowship of kindred with them, were to be held as foes in perpetuity: for it is written (Ex. 17): "The war of the Lord shall be against Amalec from generation to generation."

The Old Law made compassionate provision for the first two cases by commanding "Do not discourage or afflict an outsider" and "Do not make trouble for a foreigner."

The third case required that a certain procedure be followed. No one was accepted into citizenship immediately. We read something similar in Aristotle, who remarks that some nations regarded persons as citizens only after their families had been present in the land for several generations. The reason for such a rule is that if newly arrived foreigners were immediately allowed to take a hand in the people's affairs, many dangers might result. Some of these newcomers, not yet confirmed in love for the people's good, might try to harm them.

In view of this danger, the law distinguished between outsiders from nations that had some affinity with the Jews, and outsiders from nations that had been hostile to them.

In the category of those having affinity with them were the Egyptians, among whom they had been born and raised, and the Idumaeans or Edomites, who were descended from Jacob's brother Esau. These were to be allowed into the fellowship of the people after the third generation.

In the category of those who had been hostile to them were the Ammonites and Moabites, who were never to be allowed into their fellowship, and the Amelikites, who had no blood relationship with the community and had been so hostile that they were to be regarded as perpetual enemies. This is why the book of Exodus warns that the Lord will always be at war with Amalek, generation after generation.

---

[1] The distinction between peaceful and hostile relations with foreigners may seem obvious, but in our own political debate nothing is easier than to find persons who think either that all such relations must be amicable or that all such relations must be hostile. In fact, though peaceful relations are preferable, they are not always possible.

[2] In the first category of peaceful relations, we are to think of foreigners who have no intention of settling down, but come into the land temporarily.

[3] In the second category we are to think of foreigners whose aim is to settle down and live in the community.

[4] We have already seen these admonitions in the context of Objection 3. Both admonitions give the same reason for treating aliens compassionately: For many years, the Israelites themselves had been aliens in the land of Egypt. Therefore, as the second admonition goes on to say, they *know the souls* of strangers – as we would put the idea (and as most translations render it), "you know their hearts." The fact that they had been so sorely oppressed by the pharaoh toward the end of their time in Egypt encouraged an even greater sense of identification with all who are outsiders, poor, and vulnerable.

Recent scholarship perceives internal development in the Old Law, distinguishing among the Book of the Covenant (Exodus 20:22–23:33), the Book of the Law (Deuteronomy 12–26), and the Holiness Code (Leviticus 17–26).[21] Considered from this point of view, the note of compassion for the weak and vulnerable seems to become more prominent as time goes on. Although St. Thomas himself treats the Old Law as a unit, there is every reason to think that he would welcome the evidence that the Old Law developed. Such a possibility would not at all imply that the Old Law was not really the work of God. In fact, its development over time would strengthen St. Thomas's argument that it was an exercise in Divine pedagogy. For if God is a good teacher, then the moral condition of the people should become better over time, but when it does become better, then they will be able to receive better laws.

Because the development of law can easily be misunderstood, a caveat must be added. In the view of St. Thomas, neither the natural nor the Divine law can change *in their essence*. Why? Because neither God Himself, nor the creational design of human nature, can change in their essence, and because changes in what God reveals to us about His will are not changes in His will. So the differences between the Old and New Divine Law do not mean that God changed His mind, or changed His plan, concerning us, and the fact that the understanding of Adam, Noah, Abraham, and Moses concerning what we call the natural law *may* have changed, as some say, does not mean – as some would say – that the natural law itself changed.

[5] In the third category we are to think of aliens who desire to become completely assimilated into the Israelite nation and converted to its worship of

---

[21] I am grateful to Richard Conrad, OP, director of the Aquinas Institute, Oxford, for calling my attention to this fact. See his article "The Tasks of Human Lawgivers: The Torah as Exemplar," *Law & Justice* 183 (2019), pp. 62–82, originally presented at the 2018 Aquinas colloquium, "Aquinas and the Development of Law," held at Blackfriars, Oxford. For a broader review of the state of the literature, see Frank Crüsemann, *The Torah: Theology and Social History of Old Testament Law* (Edinburgh: T&T Clark, 1996).

the true God. Probably, some aliens closed only part of this gap, taking up belief in the true God and the practice of Jewish worship but not becoming circumcised and assimilated. However, only those who went all the way are meant here.

The status of the others, sometimes called "God-fearers," was a topic not only in rabbinical writing but also, many centuries later, in the New Testament. At a certain point in the book of Acts, which recounts the history of the early Church, St. Paul, invited to address the synagogue in Antioch, explicitly addresses his words about Christ not only to "men of Israel," whom he calls "brothers" and "sons of the family of Abraham," but also to "those among you that fear God."[22]

[6] The Old Law welcomes those who seek full assimilation into the nation, but it is also cautious. As St. Thomas argues later, such persons were admitted into worship. But as we see here, they were not immediately admitted into full citizenship – that is, into participation in the affairs of the community. St. Thomas accepts the definition of full citizenship worked out in Aristotle's *Politics* (to which we will return): "When anyone has the power to share in deliberative and judicial powers, we say that he is a citizen of that political community, and that a political community consists of enough such citizens for a self-sufficient life, absolutely speaking."[23]

Certainly the civil law of ancient Israel was also a religious law, and certainly it demanded adherence to the true God. However, the distinction between the assembly of deliberation and the assembly of worship refutes the common view that the nation entirely fused civil with religious functions.

[7] In the same place in the *Politics*, Aristotle points out that the idea of delaying full citizenship to the members of a family until it had lived in a country for several generations is commonly held: "People also define *citizen* in a practical way as one descended from citizen parents on both sides, not only from one citizen parent (i.e., a father or mother). And others require descent from citizens for more generations (e.g., two, three, or more)."[24]

Though Aristotle has no objection to this restriction on citizenship, he points out that descent from citizens on both sides cannot be the *definition* of citizenship, because it would produce a difficulty concerning the first people of the community. As St. Thomas remarks in his *Commentary* on the work, it would produce an endless regress, for "it would follow that the original

---

[22] Acts 13:16, 26 (RSV-CE).
[23] Aristotle, *Politics*, book III, chapter 1. The wording is taken from Thomas Aquinas, *Commentary on Aristotle's Politics*, translated by Richard J. Regan (Indianapolis: Hackett, 2007), p. 180.
[24] Ibid.

people were not citizens, and so none of the others descended from them were. And this is odd."[25]

[8] Allowing outsiders who desire assimilation to share in deliberative and judicial powers right away would invite subversion, because they might not yet identify with the community and so might not regard its good as their own. Making them wait for a few generations is a precept of prudence.

[9] As we saw in the context of Objection 1, the Israelites regarded the Edomites as kin because of shared ancestry, and recognized a certain affinity with the Egyptians because the Israelites had dwelt for so long in Egypt. Thus, Egyptian and Edomite families who desired assimilation into the Israelite community were accepted – but only guardedly, after a probation of several generations.

[10] We have seen some of the reasons for extreme distrust of the Ammonite and Moabite peoples in the context of Objections 1 and 4, and will return to them in the Replies to these Objections.

[11] The memory of the Amalekites was especially bitter because of their attempt to destroy the Israelites while they were still in the wilderness before crossing over into the Promised Land, the very time when they were most vulnerable:

Then came Amalek and fought with Israel at Rephidim ... And Joshua mowed down Amalek and his people with the edge of the sword. And the Lord said to Moses, "Write this as a memorial in a book and recite it in the ears of Joshua, that I will utterly blot out the remembrance of Amalek from under heaven." And Moses built an altar and called the name of it, *The Lord is my banner*, saying, "A hand upon the banner of the Lord! The Lord will have war with Amalek from generation to generation."[26]

---

[12] *In like manner with regard to hostile relations with foreigners, the Law contained suitable precepts.* [13] *For, in the first place, it commanded that war should be declared* [14] *for a just cause:* [15] *thus it is commanded (Dt. 20) that when they advanced to besiege a city, they should at first make an offer of peace.* [16] *Secondly, it enjoined that when once they had entered on a war they should undauntedly persevere in it, putting their trust in God.* [17] *And in order that they might be the more heedful of this command, it ordered that on the approach of battle the priest should hearten them by promising them God's aid.* [18] *Thirdly, it prescribed*	As to the second category of relations, the Old Law also contained appropriate regulations for relations with enemies. 1. War was to be undertaken only for a just cause. This is why Deuteronomy commanded that when the people approached a city to lay siege to it, they should first offer peace. 2. Having embarked upon a war, the people were to persist in it bravely, trusting in God. To encourage obedience to this command, a priest was to encourage those fighting by promising them God's help.

---

[25] Ibid., pp. 184–185.
[26] Exodus 17:8, 13–16 (RSV-CE).

the removal of whatever might prove an obstacle to the fight, and that certain men, who might be in the way, should be sent home. [19] *Fourthly, it enjoined that they should use moderation in pursuing the advantage of victory, by sparing women and children, and by not cutting down fruit-trees of that country.*	3. Whatever might hinder the fight was to be removed. Thus, men who might hinder their fellows were to be sent home. 4. Victory was not to be pressed too hard. Not only were women and children to be spared, but even nearby fruit trees should be left to grow.

[12] Just by considering those who did *not* present opportunities for friendly relations – the Ammonites, Moabites, and Amalekites – we have already touched on the Old Law's provisions for relations with hostile foreigners. Now St. Thomas takes up the topic of relations with hostiles more systematically than before.

[13] St. Thomas refers only to *embarking* upon war (*iniretur*). The reference in the Blackfriars translation to *declaring* war is slightly anachronistic, since the idea that war must be formally declared does not arise until much later in the development of just war theory.

[14] St. Thomas almost certainly intends the expression "for a just cause" as a metonym – as a figurative reference to all of the criteria related to just cause. He discusses these criteria more fully later on in the *Summa,* in II-II, Question 40, Article 1:

In order for a war to be just, three things are necessary. First, the authority of the sovereign by whose command the war is to be waged. For it is not the business of a private individual to declare war, because he can seek for redress of his rights from the tribunal of his superior ... And as the care of the common weal is committed to those who are in authority, it is their business to watch over the common weal of the city, kingdom or province subject to them.

Secondly, a just cause is required, namely that those who are attacked, should be attacked because they deserve it on account of some fault ...

Thirdly, it is necessary that the belligerents should have a rightful intention, so that they intend the advancement of good, or the avoidance of evil ... For it may happen that the war is declared by the legitimate authority, and for a just cause, and yet be rendered unlawful through a wicked intention.

Since St. Thomas's time, just war thinkers have articulated further desiderata to be satisfied for embarking on a war to be right. For example, it must be reasonable to think that the wrong to be cured cannot be redressed by means short of war, and that less harm will be brought about by going to war than by neglecting to do so. Such further desiderata are already implicit in St. Thomas's own thinking; for example, unless he agreed that war is just only if lesser means to redress a wrong do not suffice, he would not say that the enemy city must first be offered the possibility of surrendering (see below, concerning line 15).

We might add that although most nations regard their wars as just, few actually follow the desiderata of just war doctrine. Nevertheless, the doctrine has had a significant humanizing influence. Certainly this influence has been gradual. The United States government has committed itself to the observance of the principles of just war only since the first of the two wars in the Persian Gulf.

[15] Deuteronomy 20:10 mandates that the enemy city is not to be attacked if it is willing to lay down hostilities.

[16] St. Thomas is thinking of the following passage from Deuteronomy: "When you go forth to war against your enemies, and see horses and chariots and an army larger than your own, you shall not be afraid of them; for the Lord your God is with you, who brought you up out of the land of Egypt."[27]

[17] Immediately after the verse quoted just above, the book of Deuteronomy continues,

And when you draw near to the battle, the priest shall come forward and speak to the people, and shall say to them, "Hear, O Israel, you draw near this day to battle against your enemies: let not your heart faint; do not fear, or tremble, or be in dread of them; for the Lord your God is he that goes with you, to fight for you against your enemies, to give you the victory."[28]

[18] St. Thomas is thinking of the very men whose dismissal from battle was protested in Objections 5 and 6 – those who had built a new house, planted a new vineyard, or married a new wife, and those who were incapacitated by the terror of impending battle. His description of them as "in the way" gives us a hint of how he will argue in his Replies: Such men are sent home not for their private advantage, but for the good of their fellow soldiers and the rest of the nation.

[19] We saw the passage about sparing fruit trees in Objection 4. The passage about sparing women and children is a continuation of the passage we read earlier requiring that an enemy city first be offered peace:

And if its answer to you is peace and it opens to you, then all the people who are found in it shall do forced labor for you and shall serve you. But if it makes no peace with you, but makes war against you, then you shall besiege it; and when the Lord your God gives it into your hand you shall put all its males to the sword, *but the women and the little ones, the cattle, and everything else in the city, all its spoil, you shall take as booty for yourselves*; and you shall enjoy the spoil of your enemies, which the Lord your God has given you. Thus you shall do to all the cities which are very far from you, which are not cities of the nations here.[29]

---

[27] Deuteronomy 20:1 (RSV-CE).
[28] Ibid., verses 2–5.
[29] Deuteronomy 20:11–14 (RSV-CE), emphasis added.

Hostile writers assume that taking the marriageable women as plunder means taking them as sex slaves. This is false; there was no such thing as sex slavery in the Old Testament. What the passage means is that the captured women would have entered the pool of women available for marriage to Hebrew men. Upon marriage, they would have been assimilated into the Hebrew nation. The expectation would be that they would give up their pagan practices and adopt the religion of their husbands (although, as we saw in the context of Objection 4, sometimes the influence of wives from pagan nations went in the other direction – something that would be most unlikely if they really were merely sex slaves).

Reply to Objection 1. [1] *The Law excluded the men of no nation from the worship of God and from things pertaining to the welfare of the soul:* [2] *for it is written (Ex. 12): "If any stranger be willing to dwell among you, and to keep the Phase of the Lord; all his males shall first be circumcised, and then shall he celebrate it according to the manner, and he shall be as that which is born in the land."* [3] *But in temporal matters concerning the public life of the people, admission was not granted to everyone at once, for the reason given above: but to some, i.e. the Egyptians and Idumeans, in the third generation; while others were excluded in perpetuity, in detestation of their past offense, i.e. the peoples of Moab, Ammon, and Amalec.* [4] *For just as one man is punished for a sin committed by him, in order that others seeing this may be deterred and refrain from sinning; so too may one nation or city be punished for a crime, that others may refrain from similar crimes.*

Reply to Objection 1. The law did not exclude those of any nation from worshipping God or caring for the health of their souls. This is why the book of Exodus declared that if any aliens were willing to cross over into Hebrew land and keep the Passover of the Lord, then so long as their males were first circumcised, they were to be permitted to celebrate the rite in the proper way and be accepted alongside those native to the land.

Concerning temporal matters pertaining to the fellowship of the people, however, matters stood differently. For as explained above, not everyone was accepted into the community at once.

The Egyptians and the Idumaeans, or Edomites, were accepted in the third generation. But in utter rejection of their past wrongs, the Moabites, Ammonites, and Amalekites were excluded forever. For just as one man is punished for his sins, so that others, seeing what happens to him, may desist from sin for dread of its happening to them – in just the same way, a few peoples or cities are punished for their sins so that others will hold back from similar offenses.

[1] The first Objector had complained that the perpetual exclusion of certain categories of foreigners from the assembly contradicts the principle that all who fear God and act righteously are acceptable to Him. However, there is a difference between exclusion from public deliberation and exclusion from participation in worship. Certainly many foreigners were excluded from the former, some for three generations, others in perpetuity. Quoting Exodus

12:48, however, St. Thomas argues that no foreigners at all were excluded from the latter.

[2] After the Old Law gives instructions for the feast of the Passover,[30] which commemorates how the angel of the Lord "passed over" the Hebrews, sparing them but striking down the firstborn of the Egyptians, the following command is given:

> And when a stranger shall sojourn with you and would keep the passover to the Lord, let all his males be circumcised, then he may come near and keep it; he shall be as a native of the land. But no uncircumcised person shall eat of it. There shall be one law for the native and for the stranger who sojourns among you.[31]

In Latin, the wording contains a little pun, for those willing to *pass over* into the land (*transire*) and live in it were to be permitted to celebrate the rite which commemorated how the angel of death *passed over* the people of Israel.[32]

[3] As St. Thomas reads these passages, no one who was willing to dwell in the community and be circumcised could be excluded from the celebration of the Passover. Public affairs were a different matter, because they needed to be protected from subversion. From these, Egyptians and Edomites were excluded for three generations, and Moabites, Ammonites, and Amalekites forever.

[4] The perpetual exclusion of the Moabites, Ammonites, and Amalekites from full citizenship may seem harsh. Can't there ever be forgiveness? But in the first place, as St. Thomas points out, the Law distinguished between those who could worship God and those who could take a hand in the temporal decisions of the people. In the second place, the Moabites, Ammonites, and Amalekite nations *were in fact* perpetual enemies of the people of Israel, and the peoples of that age had long memories. And in the third place, it was of overpowering importance that the surrounding nations be taught a lesson which could not be forgotten about the consequences of oppressing the Jews. For this was the Chosen Nation, the covenant community, the people through whom a light was one day to break out, not only among the Hebrew people but among all peoples.[33]

---

[30] Curiously, the DRA translation of the Vulgate retains the Latin word, *Phase*, rather than using its English equivalent, *Passover*.

[31] Exodus 12:48–49 (RSV-CE).

[32] For the same verb used in relation to the action of the angel of death, see for example Exodus 12:13, *Erit autem sanguis vobis in signum in aedibus in quibus eritis: et videbo sanguinem, et transibo vos: nec erit in vobis plaga disperdens quando percussero terram Aegypti* (RSV-CE, "The blood shall be a sign for you, upon the houses where you are; and when I see the blood, I will *pass over* you, and no plague shall fall upon you to destroy you, when I smite the land of Egypt.")

[33] Isaiah 42:6: "I am the Lord, I have called you in righteousness, I have taken you by the hand and kept you; I have given you as a covenant to the people, a light to the nations, to open the eyes that are blind, to bring out the prisoners from the dungeon, from the prison those who sit in darkness." Isaiah 52:10: "The Lord has bared his holy arm before the eyes of all the nations; and all the ends of the earth shall see the salvation of our God." Isaiah 60:2b–3: "The Lord will arise

Therefore, although God also punishes Israel for its sins, sometimes even using other nations to do so,[34] nevertheless He blesses the nations that bless Israel, and punishes the nations that curse Israel:

- Isaac speaking to Jacob, and through him to his future descendants: "Cursed be everyone who curses you, and blessed be everyone who blesses you!"
- Balaam, speaking apostrophically to Israel, despite his commission to say the opposite: "Blessed be everyone who blesses you, and cursed be everyone who curses you."
- The prophet Zechariah, also addressing Israel apostrophically: "He who touches you touches the apple of [God's] eye."
- God, through Zechariah, speaking of the day of deliverance: "And on that day I will seek to destroy all the nations that come against Jerusalem."[35]

And yet the coming Messiah, the "Servant of the Lord," is represented centuries later, in the prophet Isaiah, as speaking as follows:

And now the Lord says, who formed me from the womb to be his servant, to bring Jacob back to him, and that Israel might be gathered to him, for I am honored in the eyes of the Lord, and my God has become my strength – he says: "It is too light a thing that you should be my servant to raise up the tribes of Jacob and to restore the preserved of Israel; I will give you as a light to the nations, that my salvation may reach to the end of the earth."[36]

So the hostile nations were perpetually excluded from Israel's councils for the sake of Israel's preservation, and those who persist in oppression will be destroyed. Even so, Israel was preserved for the salvation for all nations – even those who in the time of the Old Law were still excluded.

[5] *Nevertheless it was possible by dispensation for a man to be admitted to citizenship on account of some act of virtue:* [6] *thus it is*	Even so, it was possible for an exception to be made to this rule, for a man could be admitted into the brotherhood of the people because of an act of virtue. We learn this

---

upon you, and his glory will be seen upon you. And nations shall come to your light, and kings to the brightness of your rising." See also Isaiah 49:5–6, quoted below, and compare the New Testament, as follows. John 8:12: "Again Jesus spoke to them, saying, 'I am the light of the world; he who follows me will not walk in darkness, but will have the light of life.'" Acts 13:47 (Sts. Paul and Barnabas speaking): "For so the Lord has commanded us, saying, 'I have set you to be a light for the Gentiles, that you may bring salvation to the uttermost parts of the earth.'" Acts 26:22–23 (St. Paul speaking): "To this day I have had the help that comes from God, and so I stand here testifying both to small and great, saying nothing but what the prophets and Moses said would come to pass: that the Christ must suffer, and that, by being the first to rise from the dead, he would proclaim light both to the people and to the Gentiles." All quotations RSV-CE.

[34] See the Discussion at the end of this Article.
[35] Respectively Genesis 27:29, Numbers 24:9b, Zechariah 2:8, and Zechariah 12:9. All quotations RSV-CE.
[36] Isaiah 49:5–6 (RSV-CE).

related *(Judith 14)* that Achior, the captain of the children of Ammon, *"was joined to the people of Israel, with all the succession of his kindred."* [7] The same applies to Ruth the Moabite who was *"a virtuous woman"* (the book of *Ruth)*: [8] *although it may be said that this prohibition regarded men and not women, who are not competent to be citizens absolutely speaking.*

from the book of Judith, which relates how Achior, the commander of the Ammonites – and not only he but also his family for all generations – were joined to the people of Israel. We see much the same thing from the story of Ruth, a Moabite whom Boaz whom Boaz praises for her reputation as a woman of virtue – although it might be argued that the exclusion from citizenship did not apply to women, because the women of Israel were not citizens in an unqualified sense (a fact that is about to be explained).

[5] As we saw in Question 100, Article 8, no exceptions can be made to precepts which embody the very idea of the direction of affairs to the common good, or more particularly toward justice and virtue – for example the precepts of the Decalogue. However, exceptions can certainly be made to the subordinate precepts which merely specify the *ways* in which affairs are directed toward these great aims. Such exceptions are allowable so long as they are not to the detriment of those precepts which do coincide with the lawmaker's intention. Certainly the prohibition of admitting the members of hostile nations to full citizenship serves the common good. However, there is no harm to the common good if an exception is made for someone of outstanding virtue who is friendly rather than hostile.

[6] St. Thomas's first example is Achior, the chief man of the Ammonites, who advises Holofernes, the general of the Assyrian forces, not to make war against the Hebrews because they are protected by their God. Holofernes is so infuriated that he commands that Achior be handed over to the enemy. The Israelites find him tied up and abandoned outside the gates of one of their cities. They untie him, learn what has transpired, and commend and console him. Later, accompanied by her maidservant, Judith enters the Assyrian encampment, pretending to be a deserter and informant. After several days, leading Holofernes to believe that he can ravish her, she is admitted to his tent, where he lies in a drunken stupor, and kills him in his sleep. As proof of the deed, she takes her maidservant and returns with his head to her people, telling them that now they will be able to rout the Assyrian forces. "And when Achior saw all that the God of Israel had done, he believed firmly in God, and was circumcised, and joined the house of Israel, remaining so to this day." The Vulgate adds that Achior joined "with all the succession of his kindred".[37]

[7] St. Thomas's second example is Ruth, a Moabite woman, the widow of a Hebrew man who had been living in Moab. When her Hebrew mother-in-law, Naomi, prepares to return to Judah, her homeland, where she has heard that

---

[37] Judith 14:10 (RSV-CE), corresponding to 14:6 in the DRA.

there is more food, she urges her two daughters-in-law to return to their mothers' houses and remarry, and prays that the Lord will deal kindly with them, "as you have dealt with the dead and with me."[38] However, Ruth insists on going with her, saying "Entreat me not to leave you or to return from following you; for where you go I will go, and where you lodge I will lodge; your people shall be my people, and your God my God; where you die I will die, and there will I be buried. May the Lord do so to me and more also if even death parts me from you."[39] Back in Judah, Ruth uses the privilege of the poor to glean from the fields of Boaz, who is one of Naomi's kinsmen. Boaz, impressed with her beauty and virtue,[40] shows kindness to her. Eventually she asks him to exercise the duty of the next of kin to marry the widow so that the dead man's line will not die out. After everything is arranged with a still closer kinsman, who would normally have exercised the duty, Boaz announces to the elders and people of the village his intention to marry Ruth, and they declare,

> We are witnesses. May the Lord make the woman, who is coming into your house, like Rachel and Leah, who together built up the house of Israel. May you prosper in Ephrathah and be renowned in Bethlehem; and may your house be like the house of Perez, whom Tamar bore to Judah, because of the children that the Lord will give you by this young woman.[41]

The story of Ruth is particularly important to Christians because she is one of the remote ancestresses of Jesus.[42] The startling fact that Christ's lineage includes an assimilated Moabite foreshadows the opening of the people of God to the Gentiles. Thus, St. Peter declares that all followers of Christ, Jews and Gentiles alike, regardless of earthly race and nation, are members of the one chosen people:

But you are a chosen race, a royal priesthood, a holy nation, God's own people, that you may declare the wonderful deeds of him who called you out of darkness into his marvelous light. Once you were no people but now you are God's people; once you had not received mercy but now you have received mercy.[43]

They are "aliens and exiles," Peter says, not *from* God's people but *because they belong* to God's people, a nation on pilgrimage through the present life on the way to their true commonwealth in heaven.[44]

---

[38] Ruth 1:8–9 (RSV-CE).
[39] Ibid., 1:16–17.
[40] Ibid., 3:11.
[41] Ibid., 4:11–12.
[42] See Matthew 1:5.
[43] 1 Peter 2:9–10 (RSV-CE).
[44] Ibid., verse 11. Compare Philippians 3:20, Hebrews 11:13–16, and Romans 11, entire.

[8] St. Thomas acknowledges in passing that someone might protest his use of Ruth as an example of a Moabite admitted to citizenship, because, since women were ordinarily excluded from participation in deliberative and judicial powers, she would never have been a citizen in the full sense.

The implied distinction between different senses of citizenship is more fully explained in the next Reply. Before turning to it, however, we should take note that some women of Israel did exert significant influence in its counsels. Before the Hebrew people were ruled by kings in the ordinary sense, the woman Deborah, one in the line of heads who were called judges, led her nation to a great victory over the Canaanite oppressors, ushering in a time of peace.[45] After the people were ruled by kings in the ordinary sense, queens consort and queen mothers could also wield significant influence, as we see in the following anecdote from the reign of King Solomon. To understand the incident we must bear in mind that Adonijah, Solomon's half-brother, considers himself the legitimate heir of their father King David, and has already tried once to usurp power:

So Solomon sat upon the throne of David his father; and his kingdom was firmly established. Then Adonijah the son of Haggith came to Bathsheba the mother of Solomon. And she said, "Do you come peaceably?" He said, "Peaceably." Then he said, "I have something to say to you." She said, "Say on." He said, "You know that the kingdom was mine, and that all Israel fully expected me to reign; however the kingdom has turned about and become my brother's, for it was his from the Lord. And now I have one request to make of you; do not refuse me." She said to him, "Say on." And he said, "Pray ask King Solomon – he will not refuse you – to give me Abishag the Shunammite as my wife." Bathsheba said, "Very well; I will speak for you to the king." So Bathsheba went to King Solomon, to speak to him on behalf of Adonijah. And the king rose to meet her, and bowed down to her; then he sat on his throne, and had a seat brought for the king's mother; and she sat on his right. Then she said, "I have one small request to make of you; do not refuse me." And the king said to her, "Make your request, my mother; for I will not refuse you." She said, "Let Abishag the Shunammite be given to Adonijah your brother as his wife."[46]

Plainly, before hearing his mother Bathsheba's request, Solomon expects that he will be able to comply with it. As matters turn out, he does not, for Abishag had been King David's last concubine, and marrying her would have been a way for Adonijah to declare himself king. Since this is Adonijah's second attempt at the throne, Solomon has him put to death. However, nothing in the story suggests that the counsels of Bathsheba do not continue to be held in honor afterward.

---

[45] See Judges 4–5.
[46] 1 Kings 2:12–21 (RSV-CE).

Reasons for Old Law Judicial Precepts About Noncitizens

Reply to Objection 2. [1] *As the Philosopher says (Polit. iii), a man is said to be a citizen in two ways: first, simply; secondly, in a restricted sense. A man is a citizen simply if he has all the rights of citizenship, for instance, the right of debating or voting in the popular assembly.* [2] *On the other hand, any man may be called citizen, only in a restricted sense, if he dwells within the state, even common people or children or old men, who are not fit to enjoy power in matters pertaining to the common weal.* [3] *For this reason bastards, by reason of their base origin, were excluded from the "ecclesia," i.e. from the popular assembly, down to the tenth generation.* [4] *The same applies to eunuchs, who were not competent to receive the honor due to a father,* [5] *especially among the Jews, where the divine worship was continued through carnal generation:* [6] *for even among the heathens, those who had many children were marked with special honor, as the Philosopher remarks (Polit. ii).* [7] *Nevertheless, in matters pertaining to the grace of God, eunuchs were not discriminated from others, as neither were strangers, as already stated: for it is written (Is. 56): "Let not the son of the stranger that adhereth to the Lord speak, saying: The Lord will divide and separate me from His people. And let not the eunuch say: Behold I am a dry tree."*

Reply to Objection 2. Aristotle points out that one may be a citizen either in an unqualified or a qualified sense. Someone is a citizen in the former sense if he can do all of the things that citizens do, such as giving counsel or judgment in the assembly of the people. But anyone may be called a citizen in the latter sense, just because he lives in the community. This is true even of commoners, children, and aged men, who have no authority in public matters.

Bastards were omitted from the deliberative assembly down to the tenth generation because they were of illegitimate descent. Similarly, eunuchs were excluded because they could never earn the honor due to fathers. This point was especially important among the Jews, because the worship of God was preserved by teaching it to one's children. But as we learn from Aristotle, even among other nations, those who had many children were awarded a mark of honor.

Even so, in matters pertaining to the grace of God, eunuchs were not distinguished from others – and as we saw earlier, neither were foreigners. The prophet Isaiah represents God as declaring that no son of a foreigner who has joined himself to the Lord should say, "The Lord will divide and separate me from His people," and no eunuch who has done so should mourn, "Behold, I am a dry tree."

[1] The Objector had protested the exclusion from the assembly of men whose genitals were damaged or who were of illegitimate birth. St. Thomas begins his Reply by reminding us of the Aristotelian definition of full citizenship: having the power to share in judicial and executive powers.[47]

[2] Here we are to think of a typical commonwealth in which public affairs are managed by adult males of good lineage who have not yet retired from public life. Since the children, commoners, and elderly men do not participate in

---

[47] Aristotle, *Politics*, book III, chapters 1–2. The Blackfriars translators suggest chapter 3.

judicial or deliberate functions, in Aristotle's sense they are not citizens. Yet we do consider them citizens, even if only in a qualified sense, just because they are part of the community. So if we are to speak of people being excluded from citizenship, we must make clear in what sense they are excluded.

[3] St. Thomas might have given a more complete explanation of the point he makes here. To be a full member of the community, a native-born person had to be of recognized descent from full members of the community on both sides. Even in our own very different sort of country, the residents of close-knit communities marked by deep family ties and strong memories of their ancestors find it difficult to know what to make of persons to whom they are unrelated. I speak from personal experience, since I spend a certain amount of time each year in a small community in the mountains of eastern Kentucky, where although no one would think of "molesting or afflicting" me, I too am a "stranger" in the biblical sense of the term because my forbears are unknown. The puzzled question is often posed to me, "Who are your people?" I am accepted by the community not because my forbears are known, but because my wife's are.

The difficulty for bastards is that their descent is more radically uncertain, and so in a community which is held together by kinship they cannot be quite trusted. What would have been even more important is that illegitimacy confused the lines of inheritance, which, as we have seen, were zealously guarded so that the tribes and the family would not lose their property and die out. Moreover, accepting persons of illegitimate birth into the public councils would have seemed to treat the integrity of the family as an unimportant thing, something to be regarded lightly. Consequently, although bastards were members of the Old Testament community in the weak sense, they were not citizens in the strong sense. Not until the tenth generation, when they would have generated their own lineages, could their descendants be accepted into the deliberative assembly.

However, these matters were handled practically. Jephthah, the ninth judge of Israel, during a violent period when apparently the Law is not well followed, is the offspring of a liaison between his father and a prostitute. When his half-brothers are grown, they thrust him from the family home, saying "You shall not inherit in our father's house; for you are the son of another woman."[48] Jephthah moves to a nearby territory and becomes a raider. After the Ammonites begin a war against Israel, Israel's elders approach Jephthah to lead them in battle and be their head – a prudent choice, under the circumstances, for he obviously knows how to command men of arms.

[4] Any sane society holds parents in honor, not only because each child owes so much to his own parents, but because the society as a whole (indeed, the human race) owes its continuation to the generation of children. Although

---

[48] Judges 11:2 (RSV-CE).

through no fault of their own, men who are unable to sire children cannot share in this necessary honor, unless, perhaps, by adoption. So important was the lineage that in some societies, even adult adoption has been practiced.

[5] Fatherhood was yet more important among the Hebrew people than it was among other nations, because in this case the question was not merely the perpetuation of an earthly society but the perpetuation of the worship of the true God. As St. Thomas points out, "the worship of God was spread and safeguarded by a carnal propagation." Not until Christ came was it "spread abroad among all nations by a spiritual propagation" – by preaching the Gospel and making disciples.[49] Even now, "The chief good of marriage is the offspring to be brought up to the worship of God." St. Thomas explains that this is the reason why disparity of worship – the unbelief of one of the parties – is an obstacle to their marriage.[50] We return to the question of having children and passing on the faith in the Discussion at the end of this Article.

[6] Aristotle remarks that in Sparta, "the father of three sons is exempt from military service, and the father of four from taxes."[51]

[7] St. Thomas insists that although men with crushed testicles, or with their male members cut off, were not able to participate in the deliberative assembly, they were welcome to keep the Sabbath and worship God. Like others, they were to look forward to the messianic age, when they would be consoled with another kind of inheritance, different from biological sons and daughters. For as the prophet Isaiah writes,

> Thus says the Lord: "Keep justice, and do righteousness, for soon my salvation will come, and my deliverance be revealed. Blessed is the man who does this, and the son of man who holds it fast, who keeps the sabbath, not profaning it, and keeps his hand from doing any evil." Let not the foreigner who has joined himself to the Lord say, "The Lord will surely separate me from his people"; and let not the eunuch say, "Behold, I am a dry tree." For thus says the Lord: "To the eunuchs who keep my sabbaths, who choose the things that please me and hold fast my covenant, I will give in my house and within my walls a monument and a name better than sons and daughters; I will give them an everlasting name which shall not be cut off. And the foreigners who join themselves to the Lord, to minister to him, to love the name of the Lord, and to be his servants, every one who keeps the sabbath, and does not profane it, and holds fast my covenant – these I will bring to my holy mountain, and make them joyful in my house of prayer; their burnt offerings and their sacrifices will be accepted on my altar; for my house shall be called a house of prayer for all peoples. Thus says the Lord GOD, who gathers the outcasts of Israel, I will gather yet others to him besides those already gathered."[52]

---

[49] Supp., Q. 65, Art. 2, ad 4.
[50] Supp., Q. 59, Art. 1. See also I-II, Q. 106, Art. 1, Discussion.
[51] Aristotle, *Politics*, book II, chapter 13. The wording is taken from Thomas Aquinas, *Commentary on Aristotle's Politics*, trans. Regan, p. 146. Some editions of the *Politics* list this as chapter 9. The Blackfriars translators suggest that St. Thomas is referring to chapter 6.
[52] Isaiah 56:1–8 (RSV-CE).

Reply to Objection 3. [1] *It was not the intention of the Law to sanction the acceptance of usury from strangers, but only to tolerate it* [2] *on account of the proneness of the Jews to avarice; and in order to promote an amicable feeling towards those out of whom they made a profit.*	Reply to Objection 3. The law did not *intend* that the Israelites take interest on loans to aliens, but only *tolerated* the practice. The people were prone to an excessive desire for wealth, and would be more peaceful toward aliens if they were able to earn something through their dealings with them.

[1] The Objector had protested the provision of the Old Law forbidding interest to be charged on loans to aliens but allowing it on loans to Hebrews. His argument was that since the Law also forbade afflicting foreigners, and since the charging of interest is an affliction, the rules for loans to foreigners should have been the same as those on loans to Hebrews. St. Thomas agrees with the Objector's underlying idea: If only you can get people to consider foreigners as neighbors, then you can get them to lend without expectation of interest to foreigners too. As the Old Law declares, "You shall not hate your brother in your heart, but you shall reason with your neighbor, lest you bear sin because of him. You shall not take vengeance or bear any grudge against the sons of your own people, but you shall love your neighbor as yourself: I am the Lord."[53]

What the Objector overlooks is that it is much easier to get people to view "the sons of their own people" as neighbors than to view members of other nations as neighbors. Not until much later, in the teachings of Christ, is the circle of the neighbor expanded to take in non-Jews.[54] In the meantime, St. Thomas thinks, the law did not *approve* the charging of interest to foreigners, but only put up with the practice as one that it was not yet feasible to reform.

[2] If St. Thomas is right, then permitting the charging of interest to foreigners is but one of the Old Law's various accommodations of the moral and spiritual immaturity of the people at that time. It is analogous to the law of revenge, the purpose of which was not to require taking an eye for an eye and a tooth for a tooth, but to limit retaliation to taking *no more than* an eye for an eye and *no more than* a tooth for a tooth. This was a first step toward abolishing revenge altogether.[55]

---

[53] Leviticus 19:17–18 (RSV-CE), repeated in the Gospels in Matthew 22:35–40, Mark 12:28–31, and Luke 10:25–28.
[54] In the parable of the Good Samaritan, Luke 10:25–37.
[55] Compare Exodus 21:23b–25, "you shall give life for life, eye for eye, tooth for tooth, hand for hand, foot for foot, burn for burn, wound for wound, stripe for stripe," with Matthew 5:38–41, where Christ says "You have heard that it was said, 'An eye for an eye and a tooth for a tooth.' But I say to you, Do not resist one who is evil. But if any one strikes you on the right cheek, turn to him the other also; and if any one would sue you and take your coat, let him have your cloak as well; and if any one forces you to go one mile, go with him two miles." Both quotations RSV-CE.

Reasons for Old Law Judicial Precepts About Noncitizens

Reply to Objection 4. [1] A distinction was observed with regard to hostile cities. [2] For some of them were far distant, and were not among those which had been promised to them. When they had taken these cities, they killed all the men who had fought against God's people; whereas the women and children were spared. [3] But in the neighboring cities which had been promised to them, all were ordered to be slain, on account of their former crimes, to punish which God sent the Israelites as executor of Divine justice: for it is written (Dt. 9) "because they have done wickedly, they are destroyed at thy coming in." [4] The fruit-trees were commanded to be left untouched, for the use of the people themselves, to whom the city with its territory was destined to be subjected.

Reply to Objection 4. The Old Law distinguished among hostile cities. In one category were those that were remote and not part of the Promised Land. When cities of this sort were subdued, the fighters put to death the men who had battled against God's people, but spared the women and children.
In the other category were nearby cities that were part of the land promised to them. In these cities, all were to be killed because of their prior iniquities; the Lord sent the people of Israel to punish these offenses as executors of Divine justice. As we read in Deuteronomy, "because of the wickedness of these nations, the Lord your God is driving them out from before you."
Yes, they were instructed to leave fruit trees alone, not out of pity for the trees, but for the use of the Israelites themselves, to whom these cities and their territories were to be subjected.

[1] The Objector had protested that although in certain cases everyone in hostile cities was to be put to death, fruit trees were not to be wantonly destroyed. It seemed to him that this implied a closer kinship between the Hebrew people and trees than between the Hebrew people and their enemies. St. Thomas begins his reply by pointing out that just as there is a distinction between peaceful and hostile relations with foreigners, so there is a distinction between hostile cities distant from the Promised Land and hostile cities within it.

[2] The chief problem with distant hostile cities is simply that they are hostile. Therefore, only the enemy soldiers are killed, and no one else.

[3] By contrast, hostile cities within the Promised Land present a number of problems. First, like the distant ones, they are enemies; second, through their hostility they prevent the settlement of the land God has promised; third, they commit abominations which reek to heaven, which is why God has appointed Israel to drive them out; and fourth, since they dwell in the same country, the risk is ever present that they may teach the same abominations to the Israelites. Consequently, they must be treated differently than hostile cities far away.

Hear, O Israel; you are to pass over the Jordan this day, to go in to dispossess nations greater and mightier than yourselves, cities great and fortified up to heaven, a people great and tall, the sons of the Anakim, whom you know, and of whom you have heard it said, "Who can stand before the sons of Anak?" Know therefore this day that he who goes over before you as a devouring fire is the Lord your God; he will destroy them and subdue them before you; so you shall drive them out, and make them perish quickly, as the Lord has promised you. Do not say in your heart, after the Lord your God has thrust them out before you, "It is because of my righteousness that the Lord has brought me in to possess this land"; *whereas it is because of the wickedness of these nations that the Lord is driving them out before you.* Not because of your righteousness or the uprightness of your heart are you going in to possess their land; but because of the wickedness of these nations the Lord your God is driving them out from before you, and that he may confirm the word which the Lord swore to your fathers, to Abraham, to Isaac, and to Jacob. Know therefore, that the Lord your God is not giving you this good land to possess because of your righteousness; for you are a stubborn people.[56]

As we have just seen, Israel is to drive out the nations occupying the Promised Land not because Israel is so righteous, but because the nations to be driven out are so wicked. The following passage builds on this idea by emphasizing that Israel is all too vulnerable to their bad influence:

But in the cities of these peoples that the Lord your God gives you for an inheritance, you shall save alive nothing that breathes, but you shall utterly destroy them, the Hittites and the Amorites, the Canaanites and the Perizzites, the Hivites and the Jebusites, as the Lord your God has commanded; *that they may not teach you to do according to all their abominable practices which they have done in the service of their gods, and so to sin against the Lord your God.*[57]

Again it should be emphasized that although God appoints the Israelites to execute His justice against the pagan nations occupying the Promised Land, at times God uses the pagan nations surrounding the Promised Land to execute His justice against the Israelites themselves. The fact that God has chosen the Israelites does not mean that everything they did was right, or that He would overlook their faults. He did not choose them for leniency, but to be made holy and righteous all through.

[4] The reason for leaving the fruit trees alone is not that trees are more akin to the Israelites than the people of the conquered cities are, as the Objector ridiculously supposes. Rather the reason is that there is no need to cut them down (for they are not dangerous), and there is good reason to leave them standing (for their fruit is good for food).

| *Reply to Objection 5.* [1] *The builder of a new house, the planter of a vineyard, the newly married husband, were excluded from fighting, for two reasons.* [2] *First, because man is wont to give all his affection to those things which he has lately acquired, or is on* | Reply to Objection 5. Those who had just built houses, planted vineyards, or married wives were released from fighting for two reasons. First, men tend to lavish greater love on things they have just acquired or |

---

[56] Deuteronomy 9:1–6 (RSV-CE), emphasis added.
[57] Deuteronomy 20:16–18 (RSV-CE).

the point of having, and consequently he is apt to dread the loss of these above other things. [3] *Wherefore it was likely enough that on account of this affection they would fear death all the more, and be so much the less brave in battle.* [4] *Secondly, because, as the Philosopher says (Phys. ii), "it is a misfortune for a man if he is prevented from obtaining something good when it is within his grasp."* [5] *And so lest the surviving relations should be the more grieved at the death of these men who had not entered into the possession of the good things prepared for them;* [6] *and also lest the people should be horror-stricken at the sight of their misfortune:* [7] *these men were taken away from the danger of death by being removed from the battle.*

are about to acquire, and to fear their loss more keenly. Such feelings would probably make them fear death all the more, so that they would be less courageous in fighting. Second, as Aristotle remarks, it seems dreadful when someone who is just about to attain a good is deprived of it. Thus, if a man dies at the very point of gaining something all ready for him, his death may plunge his relatives into even greater grief, and other people who see what has happened to him may be horrified. Consequently, men who were on the point of receiving such goods were separated from the danger of death by being excused from the battle.

[1] The Objector had argued that to excuse a man from fighting so that he can go back to his new house, vineyard, or wife, is to prefer the private good even to the detriment of the common good. St. Thomas points out two reasons for thinking that sending him home does benefit the common good. Any benefit to the private good is incidental; it is not the reason for the law.

[2] Both reasons turn on psychological observations. The first one, presented here, concerns the psychology of the man himself. All death severs us from earthly blessings. However, it is much easier to face the prospect of losing blessings we have enjoyed for a long time than that of losing blessings we have just attained or are about to attain. It is grievous to bid farewell to a wife of many years, but if I must go and die when I have hardly begun to enjoy her, the sorrow of parting may be insupportable. I may seem to be taunted, as in the Greek myth of Tantalus, from whom fruit was withdrawn just as he was about to grasp it, and water was withdrawn just as he was about to drink.

[3] But why should it matter to the Law that some soldiers fear the possibility of losing their worldly blessings through death more than others do? The Law takes account of their fear not for their own sake, but for the sake of their fellows. If a soldier's dread overmasters him, he may become unfit to fight so that he endangers the rest of the army.

[4] St. Thomas's second psychological observation concerns the emotions not of the man himself, but of those who see what has happened to him. For they too think it makes a difference whether death cuts him off from blessings he has long enjoyed or from blessings he has not yet had time to savor. Here is what Aristotle says about the matter in his *Physics*, where he is discussing things that happen by chance:

Chance or fortune is called "good" when the result is good, "evil" when it is evil. The terms "good fortune" and "ill fortune" are used when either result is of considerable magnitude. Thus one who comes within an ace of some great evil or great good is said to be fortunate or unfortunate. The mind affirms the essence of the attribute, ignoring the hair's breadth of difference. Further, it is with reason that good fortune is regarded as unstable; for chance is unstable, as none of the things which result from it can be invariable or normal.[58]

Although St. Thomas gives credit to Aristotle, it seems that St. Thomas's own view is more subtle. For Aristotle says that a person is considered *equally* unfortunate whether he loses something he has already attained or is merely on the point of attaining. By contrast, St. Thomas uses Aristotle's statement as a springboard for the much more interesting idea that a person is considered *more* unfortunate when he loses something he is on the point of attaining, or has only just attained, than something he has long possessed.[59]

[5] Just as man fears death all the more if it severs him from his newest blessings, so his relatives sorrow all the more if he suffers that kind of death. "Poor Zeke! He never even tasted the grapes from his new vineyard, and now it passes on to someone else! Poor Ike! Killed so young, just when he was just about to get married to that sweet girl!" The Law fears this eventuality.

[6] Not only are the relatives plunged more deeply into sorrow by this kind of death; the neighbors are also more stricken with dread, and the Law fears this eventuality too.

[7] Even though any death may weaken morale, deaths of this kind pose the much greater risk of destroying it. Such deaths must be prevented, for otherwise the nation may lack the spirit to go on fighting. *This* is why the Old Law provides that men in such circumstances should be sent home to live.

Reply to Objection 6. The timid were sent back home, not that they might be the gainers thereby; but lest the people might be the losers by their presence, since their timidity and flight might cause others to be afraid and run away.	Reply to Objection 6. Those who lacked courage were sent home not so that they would gain from being cowards, but to protect others from being harmed through association with them. Their own fear and flight might have caused others to fear and flee.

---

[58] Aristotle, *Physics*, book II, chapter 5. I am following the wording of Thomas Aquinas, *Commentary on Aristotle's Physics*, translated by Richard J. Blackwell, Richard J. Spath, and W. Edmund Thirlkel (New Haven, CT: Yale University Press, 1963).

[59] Interestingly, the Angelic Doctor does *not* read this more subtle idea into Aristotle's statement when he analyzes it in *Commentary on Aristotle's Physics*, book II, lecture 9. There he simply says that according to Aristotle, "the intellect takes that which is only a little removed as if it were not removed at all, but already possessed" – which is exactly what Aristotle says.

The Objector had protested sending the terror-stricken back home because it seemed to reward them for their fault. Actually, they are sent back home because terror is contagious. Seeing a few soldiers flee, the others may be filled with blind panic, so that the victory is turned into a rout.

DISCUSSION

Building Families and Transmitting Faith

As we have seen in this Article, St. Thomas makes no secret of the fact that he shares the Old Law's view about having children. Not only is it good to build families, but the chief good of marriage itself is passing the faith on to one's offspring.[60] The contrast to the attitude of our own time could hardly be sharper, and this fact is worth pondering.

Even in our day of plummeting birth rates, children may still be desired, although adults tend more and more to view them as a lifestyle enhancement, something like a home entertainment center, but more expensive. Having a few children may still be viewed favorably, but having more than a few is commonly looked upon as strange, for children consume resources, use up disposable income, and require a great deal of care. Increasing these costs is the fact that although parents may not think that they owe it to their offspring to stay together or to guard and nourish the children's virtues, they probably do think that they owe them entertainment. They may decline to have a second child if it would prevent the family trip to Disney World. Many couples decline to have any children at all, considering what is sometimes called the "child-free" lifestyle superior because it leaves them more at liberty to engage in activities they consider more worthwhile. A writer who is not quite so extreme as to condemn all childbearing, but who nevertheless views it as a puzzle, writes in unwitting self-satire that "I don't have the answer to the origin of the longing for children that many experience. It's almost certainly due to a complex mixture of biological and social factors. It might even be an evolutionary trick."[61]

As to the propagation of the faith, a good many parents decline to give their children any religious instruction at all, saying they think it is better to "let them make up their own minds". But declining to teach is itself a way of teaching,

---

[60] The remarks in this section of the Discussion are adapted from my article "Thomas Aquinas on Marriage, Faithful Love, and Fruitfulness," in *Humanae Vitae 50 Years Later, Embracing God's Vision of Marriage, Love, and Life: A Compendium*, edited by Theresa Notare (Washington, DC: Catholic University of America Press, 2020), and from chapter 8, "Eclipse," of my book *What We Can't Not Know: A Guide* (San Francisco: Ignatius Press, 2011). See also I-II, Q. 105, Art. 3, ad 2.

[61] Bernadette Young, "Parenthood and Effective Altruism," *Effective Altruism Forum* 14 (April 2014), http://effective-altruism.com/ea/66/parenthood_and_effective_altruism.

and a very effective one, for it teaches children a very definite creed with eight articles:

1. It is not important for children to know anything about God.
2. The questions that children naturally ask about Him require no answers.
3. Parents know nothing about Him worth passing on.
4. To think about Him adequately, no preparation is needed.
5. What adults think about Him makes no difference.
6. By implication, He does not make any difference either; God is not to be treated as God.
7. If anything is to be treated as God, it will have to be something other than He.
8. This is the true creed, and all other creeds are false.

One may dispute whether biblical faith is true. In general, however, a person who has been raised in a living tradition is far better prepared to change his mind, should his beliefs prove faulty in some particular respect, than a person who has been raised to "make up his own mind" about them. The former has at least acquired some equipment – the habit of taking important things seriously, and a body of inherited reflections about what some of these things are. By contrast, the latter is weighed down with different baggage: the habit of *not* taking important things seriously, the habit of considering the way things really are as less important than how he feels about them at the moment, and the habit of viewing beliefs about God as nothing more than lifestyle choices.

Harm to Innocents

Earlier we saw that according to Thomas Aquinas, certain criteria must be fulfilled for embarking on war to be right. Although he does not address them in the *Summa*, just war doctrine includes also not only criteria for entrance upon war (*ius ad bellum*), for example defense and the correction of evils, but also criteria for how war must be waged (*ius in bello*). The most important of the latter criteria is that one must not deliberately target innocent bystanders. This presents a difficulty in the case of those wars in which the Israelites killed not only the enemy combatants but also the rest of the enemy population.

Some common responses to the difficulty are unsatisfying. For example, the response that the ancient Hebrew people didn't know any better – that although they believed God had commanded them, He hadn't – might be satisfactory to nonbelievers, who simply do not see a problem, but the cost of this response is to deny Divine revelation. Another common response, that God merely tolerated rather than intended the extermination of these cities, is a little better, but not very. One advantage is that it takes the claim of Divine revelation seriously. Another advantage is that it allows for Divine pedagogy – for God's slowly reforming the moral understanding of the people. But it does not explain enough. It is one thing to view the dictum "you shall give life for life, eye for eye, tooth for tooth" in the sense that "you shall give *no more than* life for life, eye for eye, tooth for tooth," as the first step of Divine pedagogy, because this maxim *limits* the practice of unlimited retaliation that would otherwise have prevailed. But the wording of the passage, "You shall save alive nothing that breathes, but you shall utterly destroy them, the Hittites and the Amorites, the Canaanites and the Perizzites, the Hivites and the Jebusites, as the Lord your God has commanded," seems to preclude that sort of interpretation. It does not limit.

The Old Testament book of Wisdom reflects awareness of the difficulty, and addresses it as follows:

Those who dwelt of old in thy holy land thou didst hate for their detestable practices, their works of sorcery and unholy rites, their merciless slaughter of children, and their sacrificial feasting on human flesh and blood. These initiates from the midst of a heathen cult, these parents who murder helpless lives, thou didst will to destroy by the hands of our fathers, that the land most precious of all to thee might receive a worthy colony of the servants of God. But even these thou didst spare, since they were but men ... But judging them little by little thou gavest them a chance to repent, though thou wast not unaware that their origin was evil and their wickedness inborn, and that their way of thinking would never change.[62]

Speaking of the total destruction of Sodom and Gomorrah by fire from heaven, St. Thomas writes as follows:

To understand why one person is punished on account of the sins of another, we must realize that a punishment has two aspects: it is an injury and a remedy. Sometimes a part of the body is cut off to save the entire body. And a punishment of this kind causes an injury insofar as a part is cut off, but it is a remedy insofar as it saves the body itself. Still, a doctor never cuts off a superior member to save one which is inferior, but the other way around. Now in human matters, the soul is superior to the body, and the body is superior to external possessions. And so it never happens that someone is punished in his soul for the sake of his body, but rather he is punished in his body as a curing remedy for his soul. Therefore, God sometimes imposes physical punishments, or difficulties in external concerns, as a beneficial remedy for the soul. And then punishments of this kind are not given just as injuries, but as healing remedies.

Thus, the killing of the children of Sodom was for the good of their souls: *not because they deserved it, but so they would not be punished more severely for increasing their sins in a life spent in imitating their parents*. And in this way some are often punished for the sins of their parents.[63]

In his view, then, the question presented by these violent incidents of Old Testament history is not what human beings may do on their own initiative, but what God Himself may do. Even death is a blessing to a person if it keeps him from going on to commit dreadfully wicked acts without repenting. We have

---

[62] Wisdom of Solomon 12:3–8,10 (RSV-CE).
[63] Thomas Aquinas, *Commentary on the Gospel of John*, translated by Fabian R. Larcher (Albany, NY: Magi Books, 1998), emphasis added.

neither the wisdom nor the holiness to make such judgments about others. It would be what we call playing God, usurping the deity's own prerogatives. But God does not have to play God; He is God. All human beings are under His judgment, and if the Divine Judge chooses to appoint some nation as the executor of His justice rather than executing it Himself, He may do so with no wrong.

In the cases considered here, the executor of Divine justice is Israel. Yet at certain times in Old Testament history, God is represented as employing other nations to bring Israel itself to its senses. For example, we read in the prophet Habakkuk that because "the law is slacked and justice never goes forth," and because "the wicked surround the righteous, so justice goes forth perverted," God is stirring up an unjust nation to punish His people for their own unrighteousness:

> Look among the nations, and see; wonder and be astounded. For I am doing a work in your days that you would not believe if told. For lo, I am rousing the Chaldeans, that bitter and hasty nation, who march through the breadth of the earth, to seize habitations not their own.[64]

These may seem harsh means of discipline, but "the Lord reproves him whom he loves, as a father the son in whom he delights."[65] His love is inexorable. It will not be satisfied until His people are made pure and whole, for the stakes are eternal.

---

[64] Habakkuk 1:4–5 (RSV-CE).
[65] Proverbs 3:12 (RSV-CE), repeated in the New Testament in Hebrews 12:5–13 and Apocalypse (Revelation) 3:19.

III

THE NEW DIVINE LAW, OR LAW OF THE GOSPEL

QUESTION 106, ARTICLE 1

Whether the New Law is a Written Law?

TEXT	PARAPHRASE
Whether the New Law is a written law?	Is the New Law a written law, or is it implanted in us?

The *utrum* or "whether" is usually posed in such a way that the traditional answer is yes. It seems at first that this is one of the few cases in which St. Thomas departs from that procedure, because the query is phrased *Utrum lex nova sit lex scripta?* – "Whether the New Law is a written law?" But in the Prologue to Question 106 it is phrased a bit differently, *Utrum scilicet scripta vel indita?* – "Whether the New Law is a written law, *or is introduced inwardly*?" Latin has three words for "or." *Vel*, the one used here, is the inclusive "or," allowing the possibility that both of the alternatives are correct. This turns out to be just what St. Thomas thinks, for he argues that in one sense the New Law is a written law, but in another sense it is not, and he explains which sense is primary.

Objection 1. [1] *It would seem that the New Law is a written law. For the New Law is just the same as the Gospel. But the Gospel is set forth in writing, according to John 20: "But these are written that you may believe." Therefore the New Law is a written law.*	Objection 1. Apparently, the New Law is written, because the New Law is the Gospel itself, and the Gospel is written. For John 20 describes the Gospel by saying that "These things are *written* that you may believe." We conclude that the New Law is a written law.

Near the conclusion of St. John's Gospel, the author remarks, "Now Jesus did many other signs in the presence of the disciples, which are not written in this book; but these are written that you may believe that Jesus is the Christ, the Son of God, and that believing you may have life in his name."[1] To "do a sign" was to not to proclaim a precept, but to perform a miraculous deed which

---

[1] John 20:30–31 (RSV-CE).

signified and confirmed Jesus' identity as the promised Messiah. However, there is no reason to think that the Objector is confused about this. He is merely saying that the Gospel – which records not only signs but also precepts – is a written document.

| *Objection 2.* [1] *Further, the law that is instilled in the heart is the natural law,* [2] *according to Romans 2: "(The Gentiles) do by nature those things that are of the law ... who have [Vulgate: 'show'] the work of the law written in their hearts."* [3] *If therefore the law of the Gospel were instilled in our hearts, it would not be distinct from the law of nature.* | Objection 2. Moreover, although there really is a law that is implanted in us rather than written, this law is the natural law. We derive this inference from St. Paul's remark that the Gentiles "do by nature what the law requires" and "show that what the law requires is written on their hearts."[2] It follows that if the law of the Gospel really were implanted in us rather than written, it would be no different than natural law; yet it is. |

[1] The Latin word *indita* means "put into," which may be rendered by a variety of words. The English translators prefer the term "instilled," which in English suggests the introduction of something into us drop by drop. I have preferred the term "implanted," which in English suggests rooting something deeply in our soil.

[2] St. Thomas certainly thinks Scripture attests to the reality of natural law, although, throughout the *Summa*, the Objections and *sed contras* tend to show a greater fondness for Romans 2:14–15 as a proof text than St. Thomas does himself – probably because there is some question about whether the text in Romans is speaking of Gentiles in general, or only about regenerate Gentiles.[3] He tends to find a clearer testimony to the natural law in other passages of Scripture, especially Psalm 4:7, which reads in the DRA, "The light of thy countenance, O Lord, is signed upon us."[4] In his reading, this verse speaks of the fact that our minds are imprinted by the Divine light so that they receive the reflection of the Wisdom by which He created and governs the universe. As he writes in I-II, Question 91, Article 2, "this participation of the eternal law in the rational creature is called the natural law."[5]

---

[2] Romans 2:14–15 (RSV-CE).
[3] A question I have discussed at greater length in *Commentary on Thomas Aquinas's Treatise on Law* (Cambridge: Cambridge University Press, 2014), in connection with I-II, q. 91, art. 2, *sed contra*.
[4] In most modern translations the verse is numbered 6. Usually it is also rendered in the imperative rather than the indicative mood – God is *implored* to lift up the light of his countenance. However, as we saw in connection with I-II, Q. 100, Art. 7, there are ample scriptural grounds besides this verse to believe that God *actually has* imparted a natural law to us.
[5] In the *Summa*, St. Thomas cites the passage about the light of God's countenance five times, always in the *respondeo*, the presentation of his own view. Although the passage about the law written on the heart comes up just as frequently, he never brings it up in the *respondeo*, instead

Is the New Law a Written Law, or Is It Poured Into Us?

[3] The Objector and St. Thomas agree that in some sense the natural law is put into our hearts. But in this case, the Objector protests, the New Law could not be put into our hearts, because that would make the New Law and the natural law the same thing, and we know that they aren't. The argument that this would make them the same thing depends on a curious tacit premise that St. Thomas later calls into question.

Objection 3. [1] *Further, the law of the Gospel is proper to those who are in the state of the New Testament. But the law that is instilled in the heart is common to those who are in the New Testament and to those who are in the Old Testament:* [2] *for it is written (Wisdom 7) that Divine Wisdom "through nations conveyeth herself into holy souls, she maketh the friends of God and prophets." Therefore the New Law is not instilled in our hearts.*	Objection 3. Still further, the law of the Gospel, strictly speaking, is the law of those who are under the New Testament, not of those who are under the Old Testament. But the law implanted in those who are under these two Testaments is exactly the same. For as the book of Wisdom teaches, "in every generation [Divine Wisdom] passes into holy souls and makes them friends of God, and prophets." It follows that this inward law that "passes into" us, that is imparted without words, is not the New Law, but something else.

---

[1] The terms "Old Testament" and "New Testament" are used here not for the two parts of the Christian Bible, but for the two covenantal relationships or "testaments" between God and His people that they describe: The first covenant, between God and a single nation, the Jews, and the second covenant, between God and all who put their trust in the Messiah, or Christ, who was promised *through* the Jews. To be "in" the New Testament, then, is to have been drawn into the new covenantal relationship.

The Objector points out that God speaks of putting his law into the hearts of the people not only in the context of the Old Testament but also in the context of the New. If a law is implanted into us under *both* covenantal relationships, then how could it be the Law of the *new* covenantal relationship?

[2] We read in the book of Wisdom,

For Wisdom is more mobile than any motion; because of her pureness she pervades and penetrates all things. For she is a breath of the power of God, and a pure emanation of the glory of the Almighty; therefore nothing defiled gains entrance into her. For she is a reflection of eternal light, a spotless mirror of the working of God, and an image of his goodness. Though she is but one, she can do all things, and while remaining in herself, she renews all things; *in every generation she passes into holy souls and makes them*

---

leaving it to the *sed contra* (where it appears twice) or the objections (where it appears three times). I discuss the reasons for this preference in *Commentary on Aquinas's Treatise on Law* in connection with I-II, q. 91, art. 2, *sed contra.*

friends of God, and prophets; for God loves nothing so much as the man who lives with Wisdom.[6]

What makes it possible for the Objector to use this quotation is that although it is found in the scriptures of the old covenant, it does not make explicit reference to either of the covenants; therefore it seems to apply to the new covenant too.

| On the contrary, [1] The New Law is the law of the New Testament. [2] But the law of the New Testament is instilled in our hearts. For the Apostle, quoting the authority of Jeremiah 31: "Behold the days shall come, saith the Lord; and I will perfect unto the house of Israel, and unto the house of Judah, a new testament," says, explaining what this statement is (Hebrews 8:8-10): "For this is the testament which I will make to the house of Israel ... by giving [Vulgate: 'I will give'] My laws into their mind, and in their heart will I write them." Therefore the New Law is instilled in our hearts. | On the other hand, the New Law is the law of the New Testament, and the law of the New Testament is implanted in the heart. We see this from Hebrews 8, where the Apostle, quoting the authority of Jeremiah 31, writes "The days will come, says the Lord, when I will establish a new covenant with the house of Israel and with the house of Judah." He then explains this new covenant, representing God as saying that He will bring about the new covenant by putting His laws into the people's minds and writing them in their hearts. It follows that the New Law and this implanted law are the very same thing. |

[1] Protestant readers may find it strange to call the Gospel a new *law*, because they view the Gospel as a matter of grace, which they contrast with law. As we will see, however, St. Thomas does not deny that the Gospel is grace; he merely denies that law and grace are utterly antithetical. Unlike the Old Law, the New Law not only commands the deeds of love (and so is true law), but makes us able to do them (and so is true grace).

[2] The unknown author of the letter to the Hebrews, which belongs to the New Testament, is quoting the book of the prophet Jeremiah, which belongs to the Old Testament. In context, the Jeremiah passage reads:

Behold, the days are coming, says the Lord, when I will make a new covenant with the house of Israel and the house of Judah, not like the covenant which I made with their fathers when I took them by the hand to bring them out of the land of Egypt, my covenant which they broke, though I was their husband, says the Lord. But this is the covenant which I will make with the house of Israel after those days, says the Lord: I will put my law within them, and I will write it upon their hearts; and I will be their God, and they shall be my people.[7]

---

[6] Wisdom of Solomon 7:24-28 (RSV-CE), emphasis added, capitalizing Wisdom.
[7] Jeremiah 31:31-33 (RSV-CE).

Is the New Law a Written Law, or Is It Poured Into Us?

What exactly is the unknown author of the letter to the Hebrews trying to show by quoting this passage? According to Jeremiah, God *will* put his law into the hearts of His people, but at the time Jeremiah writes, God has not yet done so. This prophecy, made under the Old Covenant, is to be fulfilled only under the New. But according to the author of the letter to the Hebrews, the prophecy has finally come to pass; the Old Covenant has been *fulfilled* by the new. So God does place His law into the hearts of His people – and the law that He implants in them is the same as the New Law, the law of the Gospel.

I answer that, [1] *"Each thing appears to be that which preponderates in it,"* as the Philosopher states (Ethic. ix). [2] *Now that which is preponderant in the law of the New Testament, and whereon all its efficacy is based, is the grace of the Holy Ghost, which is given through faith in Christ. Consequently the New Law is chiefly the grace itself of the Holy Ghost, which is given to those who believe in Christ.* [3] *This is manifestly stated by the Apostle who says (Romans 3): "Where is ... thy boasting? It is excluded. By what law? Of works? No, but by the law of faith": for he calls the grace itself of faith "a law."* [4] *And still more clearly it is written (Romans 8): "The law of the spirit of life, in Christ Jesus, hath delivered me from the law of sin and of death."* [5] *Hence Augustine says (De Spir. et Lit.) that "as the law of deeds was written on tables of stone, so is the law of faith inscribed on the hearts of the faithful":* [6] *and elsewhere, in the same book: "What else are the Divine laws written by God Himself on our hearts, but the very presence of His Holy Spirit?"*

Here is my response. As Aristotle writes in the *Nicomachean Ethics*, each thing is most truly identified with the element that is most eminent in it. Now the element which is most eminent in the law of the New Testament – the very thing in which all its power and excellence consists – is the grace of the Holy Spirit, bestowed on us by faith in Christ. In the first place, then, the New Law is the grace of the Holy Spirit itself, bestowed upon the Christian faithful.

This fact is clearly shown in St. Paul's remark in Romans 3, "What becomes of your glorious boasting? It is shut out. By what law? Your own 'works' or accomplishments? No, by the law of faith." For notice that he calls the grace of faith itself a "law." His meaning is elaborated in Romans 8, where he says "the law of the Spirit of life in Christ Jesus has set me free from the law of sin and death."

In the same vein, St. Augustine writes in *The Spirit and the Letter* that just as the law of "works" or deeds was written on tablets of stone, so the law of faith is written in the hearts of the faithful. He asks elsewhere in the book, "What are God's laws, written in hearts by God Himself, but the very presence of the Holy Spirit?"

[1] The term "preponderates" (*potissimum*) should be taken here in the sense of the highest or most eminent, not in the sense of the biggest or most conspicuous, for St. Thomas is quoting Aristotle to make the point that everything should be understood in terms of the most authoritative element in its nature. Aristotle himself develops the point in the context of a discussion of which persons are most accurately called "lovers of self." Although most people apply

the term "lovers of self" to those who seek to grab as much wealth, honor, and bodily pleasure as they can, Aristotle thinks that such persons are not really loving themselves, because the gratifications of wealth, honor, and bodily pleasure are not what is highest and best about them. Rather Aristotle thinks the term "lovers of self" ought to be applied to those who seek to act virtuously, because only they obey the noblest and most authoritative element that their "selves" naturally contain. Aristotle concludes, "As a state, or any other society, seems to be identical with the most dominant element in it, so too does a man. Consequently, a person who loves and yields to this part will be a lover of self in a marked degree."[8]

Elaborating on the passage in his *Commentary on Aristotle's Ethics*, St. Thomas writes "In the state it is the most authoritative part that especially seems to be the state," so that "what the rulers of a state do is said to be done by the whole state." In the same way, "in man it is his reason or intellect, his principal element, that especially seems to be man,"[9] so that what a man's mind decides is said to be done by the whole man. I do not say that my eyes read a book, but that I read a book, because this act was directed by my mind. By contrast, I do not say that I beat my heart, but that my heart beat, because this act was not directed by my mind.

[2] We have just seen that each thing is most truly identified with its most eminent element. Applying this principle, St. Thomas says that since the highest element in the New Law is the grace of the Holy Spirit, in the most important sense the New Law *simply is* the grace of the Holy Spirit. This equation of the New Law with grace may disconcert those who view law and grace as opposites!

The word translated "efficacy" is *virtus*, from which we derive "virtue." Both the Latin and the English word have two meanings, power and excellence. The Dominican Fathers translation, "efficacy," chooses the former meaning; my paraphrase, "power and excellence," seeks to preserve both meanings.

[3] In Romans 3:27, St. Paul is arguing that it would be ridiculous for the faithful to take pride in their salvation, as though they had won high scores by performing the deeds required by the Old Law. On the contrary, salvation is a gift of grace, made possible through trust in the Redeemer, Jesus Christ. Paradoxically, this does not make deeds unimportant, for the very life of faith is to practice the law of love. The difference is that now one is empowered to do so by the inward renewal that grace brings about.

---

[8] Aristotle, *Nicomachean Ethics*, book IX, chapter 8. The wording is taken from Thomas Aquinas, *Commentary on Aristotle's Nicomachean Ethics*, translated by C. J. Litzinger, OP, revised edition (Notre Dame, IN: Dumb Ox Books, 1993), p. 566.

[9] Ibid., book IX, lecture 9.

Is the New Law a Written Law, or Is It Poured Into Us?

[4] The context of this quotation from Romans 8:2 is St. Paul's discussion of the fact that although the Old Law was good, it did not have the power to liberate us from the power of sin. It indicated what should be done, but did not make it possible to do it. This should not be misunderstood; certainly moral discipline makes a difference. Yet even the most virtuous and godly persons find, when they examine themselves honestly, that their motives are mixed, their virtues are full of holes, and their hearts are divided against themselves. The deeper the Old Law's instruction, the clearer this fact became, for as Jeremiah wrote, "The heart is deceitful above all things, and desperately corrupt; who can understand it?"[10] St. Augustine reflected long afterward, in his *Commentary* on St. Paul's letter to the Galatians, that God "had given a just law to unjust men to reveal their sin, not remove it."[11]

St. Thomas has discussed the terrible and continuing tendency to do wrong even though knowing what is right in several places, especially Question 91, Article 6. Here, his point is that there is a solution: the New Law of grace. To be sure, inward renewal is not often – if ever – completed in this life. But now it can begin.

[5] St. Thomas is paraphrasing a longer statement, in which St. Augustine writes,

As then the law of works, which was written on the tables of stone, and its reward, the land of promise, which the house of the carnal Israel after their liberation from Egypt received, belonged to the Old Testament; so the law of faith, written on the heart, and its reward, the beatific vision which the house of the spiritual Israel, when delivered from the present world, shall perceive, belong to the New Testament.[12]

To parse this complex statement:

- The Old Law was a law of external deeds, but the New Law is a law of faith (which is in turn a law of love, as we see below);
- The Old Law was written in literal words, on stone tablets, but the New Law is "written on" or implanted in the heart;
- The reward for following the Old Law was a physical county, but the reward for following the New Law is a heavenly country – that is, to see God;
- And the people of literal Israel received their reward in the present life, but the people of the "spiritual Israel" will receive theirs in the next life.

---

[10] Jeremiah 17:9 (RSV-CE).
[11] *Iustam scilicet legem iniustis hominibus dando ad demonstranda peccata eorum non auferenda.* St. Augustine of Hippo, *Commentary on the Letter to the Galatians*, preface, p. 2.
[12] St. Augustine of Hippo, *On the Spirit and the Letter* (public domain), chapter 41, www.newadvent.org/fathers/1502.htm. I have changed a comma to a semicolon to distinguish the two main clauses of the sentence more clearly.

To be sure, members of the literal Israel can also be members of the spiritual Israel, for as we have seen, St. Thomas teaches that the Old Testament faithful were reconciled with God through faith in the Christ *who was to come*.

[6] Again St. Thomas is paraphrasing. St. Augustine writes, "What then is God's law written by God Himself in the hearts of men, but the very presence of the Holy Spirit, who is 'the finger of God,' and by whose presence is shed abroad in our hearts the love which is the fulfilling of the law, and the end of the commandment?"[13]

---

[7] *Nevertheless the New Law contains certain things that dispose us to receive the grace of the Holy Ghost, and pertaining to the use of that grace: such things are of secondary importance, so to speak, in the New Law;* [8] *and the faithful need to be instructed concerning them, both by word and writing,* [9] *both as to what they should believe* [10] *and as to what they should do.* [11] *Consequently we must say that the New Law is in the first place a law that is inscribed on our hearts, but that secondarily it is a written law.*

Even so, the New Law includes things which prepare us to receive the grace of the Holy Spirit and show us how to enjoy its benefits. These things may be considered secondary to the New Law. Even so, believers need to be taught about them, both by spoken and written word, concerning both what is to be believed and what is to be done. For this reason, we conclude that the New Law is first and foremost an implanted law, but in a secondary sense a written law.

---

[7] This statement does not mean that *without grace*, one can prepare oneself to receive grace; the ability to prepare for further grace is itself a gift of grace, one which, in this case, is helped along by explicit Divine instruction.

[8] "By word": That is, by spoken word. "By writing": That is, by written word.

[9] "As to what they should believe": Today it is fashionable to consider it more humble and holy *not* to believe; "Who are we," we ask, "to know what is true?" St. Thomas considers it more humble and holy *to believe*: Who are we to reject what God has offered to our minds? Another fashionable view has it that truth is found in relationships, not propositions. St. Thomas agrees that we must be in right relationship with God, who is Himself the living Truth. But unless we know certain things about who He is, how can we be in right relationship with Him? Fred cannot even be in right relationship with his wife Audrey unless he can distinguish her from the lady next door.

[10] "As to ... what they should do": We cannot receive the grace of the God, whose very Being is love, unless we are willing to conform ourselves to that love, both inwardly and in our deeds.

---

[13] Ibid., chapter 36, section 21.

[11] The root of the law of the Gospel is something implanted in our hearts by grace, but utterly indispensable instructions about receiving and using this grace have been set down in the Gospel writings.

Reply to Objection 1. [1] *The Gospel writings contain only such things as pertain to the grace of the Holy Ghost, either by disposing us thereto, or by directing us to the use thereof.* [2] *Thus with regard to the intellect, the Gospel contains certain matters pertaining to the manifestation of Christ's Godhead or humanity, which dispose us by means of faith through which we receive the grace of the Holy Ghost:* [3] *and with regard to the affections,* [4] *it contains matters touching the contempt of the world, whereby man is rendered fit to receive the grace of the Holy Ghost:* [5] *for "the world," i.e. worldly men, "cannot receive" the Holy Ghost (John 14).* [6] *As to the use of spiritual grace, this consists in works of virtue to which the writings of the New Testament exhort men in divers ways.*

Reply to Objection 1. The Gospel *books* do not contain the Gospel *itself*, the grace of the Holy Spirit. Rather they contain instructions concerning this grace. Some of these instructions help make us ready to receive it, while others direct us in cooperating with it.

As to how the grace of the Holy Spirit is received, the things contained in the Gospel affect us in two ways, one concerning the intellect, the other the feelings. Concerning the intellect, the Gospel contains teachings about the manifestation of the divinity and humanity of Christ. These teachings dispose the mind to receive the grace of the Holy Spirit, which is given to us through faith. Concerning the feelings, it contains teachings which influence us to hold worldly things in contempt. This contempt in turn makes man fit to receive the Holy Spirit's grace. The latter point is explained by Christ in John 14, where He says that "the world" – meaning those who love the world – "cannot receive" the Holy Spirit.

As to cooperation with spiritual grace, this lies in virtuous deeds, to which men are urged by a multitude of New Testament scriptures.

---

[1] As the Objector insists, the Gospel certainly sets things in writing, so in a secondary sense, yes, the New Law is a written law. However, all of these written things pertain to the grace of the Holy Spirit, implanted in our hearts, and that is the primary sense in which the expression "New Law" is to be taken. (I take this opportunity to point out that my paraphrase of the present Reply is much freer than usual, because the Latin phrasing is so different from how such thoughts are most naturally expressed in English.)

[2] In English, the "or" in the statement "the Gospel contains certain matters pertaining to the manifestation of Christ's divinity *or* humanity" seems a little strange. St. Thomas is using the inclusive "or," which is *vel*. His meaning is simply that some passages testify to Christ's divinity, others to His humanity, and others, perhaps, to both at once. But the Gospel instructs us in many matters. Why then does St. Thomas single out this one? Probably because unless we grasp the unity of Christ's Divine and human natures, we will find

it difficult or impossible to see how He can be bridge the gap between man and God, how he can heal our age-old breach with God as our mediator and advocate.

[3] The Latin word translated "affections" is *affectum*, meaning feelings or emotional dispositions.

[4] The expression "the world" does not refer to creation as such, but to creation in alienation from its Creator. After all, God Himself called His what He had made "very good"![14] But one must resolutely bear in mind that the visible beauties of this life are valuable to us only insofar as we see in them the reflection of the invisible glory of the God who made them. To have contempt for "the world," then, is not to hate or reject creation, which witnesses to the glory of the Creator, but to hate and reject the wrong attitude to creation, which glorifies the Creation in place of the Creator. One who has contempt for the world regards it not as worthless per se, but as worthless *apart from, or in preference to, Him*. The reference to contempt is hyperbolic.

This rhetorical device, hyperbole, would have been most familiar to St. Thomas, not least from his study of the New Testament. For example, when Christ says "If any one comes to me and does not hate his own father and mother and wife and children and brothers and sisters, yes, and even his own life, he cannot be my disciple," He is not urging literal hatred, but dramatizing a difference in *degree* of love. Likewise, when St. Paul writes that for the sake of Christ he has suffered the loss of all things and counts them as *skubala*, that is, garbage or excrement – in the Latin translation, *stercora* or dung – he does not literally mean that such things as love for his friends are no better than what is kept in the cesspool or thrown to the dogs, but that all else is worth losing for Christ.[15]

[5] St. Thomas does not say precisely "worldly men," but "those who love the world." To love the world is to have an undue attachment to it, to place one's ultimate trust in it, to seek in it that fulfillment which is to be found only in God Himself. In the passage from which St. Thomas is alluding, Christ says to His disciples, "If you love me, you will keep my commandments. And I will pray the Father, and he will give you another Counselor, to be with you for ever, even the Spirit of truth, whom the world cannot receive, because it neither sees him nor knows him; you know him, for he dwells with you, and will be in you."[16]

[6] Grace is not given to us pointlessly, but for a reason: to make us imitators of Christ. To suppose that we could be conformed to the God of love without actually practicing the love of God would be absurd.

---

[14] Genesis 1:31.
[15] Luke 14:26 (RSV-CE); Philippians 3:8.
[16] John 14:15–17 (RSV-CE).

Reply to Objection 2. [1] *There are two ways in which a thing may be instilled into man. First, through being part of his nature, and thus the natural law is instilled into man. Secondly, a thing is instilled into man by being, as it were, added on to his nature by a gift of grace.* [2] *In this way the New Law is instilled into man, not only by indicating to him what he should do, but also by helping him to accomplish it.*

Reply to Objection 2. There are two ways in which something may be implanted in man. One way is to put it into his very nature: That is how natural law is implanted in us. The other way is to graft it onto his nature as something extra, a gift of grace: That is how the New Law is implanted into us. Rather than merely showing which deeds must be done, it also helps us to fulfill them.

[1] Objector 2 had argued "If therefore the law of the Gospel were instilled in our hearts, it would not be distinct from the law of nature," which is also instilled in our hearts. The tacit premise, which St. Thomas here refutes, is that if both are instilled in our hearts, they must be instilled in the same way. Actually they are *not* instilled in the same way, so there is no reason whatsoever to think that they are the same thing. One is instilled in us through the nature that God gave us; the other is instilled in us through how God crowns that nature with superadded grace.

[2] The New Law is an implanted law in the latter sense. Just because grace is added to our nature, it heals our nature, lifts our nature above itself, and enables us to do what we cannot do by our natural powers alone.

Reply to Objection 3. [1] *No man ever had the grace of the Holy Ghost except through faith in Christ either explicit or implicit:* [2] *and by faith in Christ man belongs to the New Testament.* [3] *Consequently whoever had the law of grace instilled into them belonged to the New Testament.*

Reply to Objection 3. No one at any time has had the grace of the Holy Spirit, except through explicit or implicit faith in Christ. Faith in Christ, in turn, is how man comes under the New Testament. Therefore, anyone who has had this law of grace implanted in him has by this very fact come under the New Testament.

[1] The Old Testament saints had *implicit* faith in Christ: they looked forward to the promised coming of the Messiah, putting their trust in the one who was to come. The New Testament saints have *explicit* faith in Christ: they look back upon the fulfillment of the promise, putting their trust in the one who has now come. So both the faithful before Christ and the faithful after Christ are saved through Christ.

[2] Although the holy Jews of old lived during the time of the Old Covenant, they were already essentially under the New Covenant by anticipating God's promise of a Redeemer.

[3] From what was said above, it follows that the law implanted in the hearts of the Old Testament saints, through anticipation of the New Covenant, *was*

the law of the New Covenant. So the Objector is mistaken in thinking that the New Law is something different than the law that was implanted in their hearts.

The upshot of the Article is that grace does not destroy nature but heals and uplifts it. Readers interested in the implications of the relations among sin, grace, natural law, and the New Law for public life may pursue the following Discussion.

DISCUSSION

The Relevance of the Gospel to Philosophy

Obviously, the Gospel keenly matters to Christians and to those inquiring into Christianity. However, it should also be interesting from the perspective of sheer ethical and legal philosophy. It would be irresponsible not to consider what the New Law is and why it exists at all.

Natural law philosophers should find St. Thomas's discussion particularly intriguing, because it shows why it makes a difference whether we view human nature as timeless, or instead view it in the context of the three phases of salvation history, Creation, Fall, and Redemption. It is true that our nature *as such* is unchangeable, or it would not truly be our nature. But its *condition* can change, and in the Christian view, if we ignore or deny this fact, we run a double risk.

One risk is to mistakenly incorporate the afflictions of our nature into our conception of what our nature is in itself, so that we think that they cannot be overcome. This error encourages despair, cynicism, and abandonment to injustice.

The other risk is to mistakenly believe that we can overcome the afflictions of our nature by means of our own natural powers, without the help of grace, as though a surgeon could sew his own severed hands back on. During my freshman year of college I attended a lecture by the well-known democratic socialist Michael Harrington, one of the great influences on President Lyndon Johnson's "War on Poverty." A questioner put to Harrington the objection that socialism could never work because of human selfishness. Harrington replied that people are selfish only because of the scarcity of goods; that goods are scarce only because of capitalism; that socialism would put an end to scarcity; and therefore, that under socialism, there would be a "psychic mutation" of human character such that people would no longer be selfish. Such notions encourage utopian fantasies which not only inevitably fail, but fail bloodily.

The Relation between Nature and Grace

Grace does not destroy nature, but presupposes and uplifts it. In particular, although faith, hope, and love do not replace temperance, courage, justice, and practical wisdom, they do two other things. For in the first place, they purify them, something they need because they have been weakened and stained by the Fall; and in the second place, they give them a new orientation, not just to their natural but to their supernatural end. If all this is true, then to fully understand even natural law, one must understand how grace was lost, and how it is heightened and regained.

The Old Law, offered to a single nation, was the first stage of redemption. It reaffirmed the moral precepts of the natural law, so badly blurred by sin, as well as directing us to God. In this way it began drawing the Chosen People into grace. The New Law, St. Thomas writes, is that grace itself, offered to the entire human race by the atoning work of Christ and through the community of faith which He founded. Because, in itself, grace is no more written down than the natural law is, it seems strange to call it a law at all. But as human nature has operating principles, so has grace, and these operating principles may certainly be written down – though God's grace is not limited to what He has told us about grace.

Since grace is a gift, one might wonder why it should have operating principles at all. The question might be put as an objection: Isn't grace like the food put into baby birds by their parents? Aren't their parents doing all the work? Yes, in a way. But we must be taught to open our beaks to accept it; and even that is a gift of grace.

QUESTION 106, ARTICLE 2

Whether the New Law Justifies?

TEXT	PARAPHRASE
Whether the New Law justifies?	Does the New Testament law make us entirely just in the sight of God, and so acceptable to Him?

This Article should be read together with Question 100, Article 12. Notice that the *whethers* of the two questions are not exactly parallel. In the former Article the query was whether the *moral precepts of the Old Law* justified man,[1] but in the present Article it is not whether the moral precepts of the New Law justify man, but whether *the New Law itself justi*fies man.[2] This small difference is important, because although the New Law does contain precepts, and St. Thomas holds that they are crucial, he also insists that the principal element in the New Law is the grace of the Holy Spirit, without which the precepts merely condemn us because we cannot fulfill them.

Historically, most Protestants have rejected St. Thomas's view of justification – treating God's declaration that His followers are have been "justified" or made just as a sort of legal fiction, a claim which is at variance with their actual condition. For being made actually just, they use a different term, "sanctification." However, during the last generation this objection has begun to fade as a result of renewed investigation into the New Testament texts by Protestant interpreters, and the Catholic and Protestant sides are becoming closer. The eminent Protestant scholar N. T. Wright comments, "it seems that there has been a massive conspiracy of silence [among Protestants] on something which was quite clear for Paul (as indeed for Jesus). Paul, in company with mainstream Second Temple Judaism, affirms that God's final judgment will be in accordance with the entirety of a life led – in accordance, in other words, with works."[3]

---

[1] *Utrum praecepta moralia veteris legis iustificarent.*
[2] *Utrum lex nova iustificet.*
[3] He adds that Paul "says this clearly and unambiguously in Romans 14:10–12 and 2 Corinthians 5:10." N. T. Wright, *Pauline Perspectives: Essays on Paul, 1978–2013* (Minneapolis: Fortress Press, 2013), p. 281. The cited passage from Romans 14 reads, "Why do you pass judgment on

Does the New Law Make Men Just and Accepted in God's Sight? 409

Indeed, in some places the New Testament plainly speaks of justification as the beginning of the process of becoming just;[4] in other places as its continuation, lest it be lost;[5] and in still other places as its fulfillment.[6] Not only does the God of Truth declare His followers just but also, through the perfect integrity of the Savior with whom He joins them, He makes them just. St. Thomas considers Objections from various points of view, exploring how this could be.

Objection 1. [1] *It would seem that the New Law does not justify. For no man is justified unless he obeys God's law,* [2] *according to Heb. 5, "He," i.e. Christ, "became to all that obey Him the cause of eternal salvation."* [3] *But the Gospel does not always cause men to believe in it:* [4] *for it is written (Rm. 10): "All do not obey the Gospel." Therefore the New Law does not justify.*	**Objection 1.** Apparently the question should be answered no, for nobody becomes just in the sight of God except by obeying God's law. This is why the unknown author of the letter to the Hebrews writes that Christ became the cause of salvation *to all who obey Him*. But the New Law, or Gospel, cannot be the cause of obedience to Christ, because it does not always cause us to believe in it! For if it did, then all men *would* believe in it – and as St. Paul reminds us, not all men do.

[1] Two very different questions are often confused:

1. Does God require us to obey His law?
2. Suppose we do obey His law, merely in the sense that we do the right things. Is this enough to make us just and acceptable in His sight?

---

your brother? Or you, why do you despise your brother? For we shall all stand before the judgment seat of God; for it is written, 'As I live, says the Lord, every knee shall bow to me, and every tongue shall give praise to God.' So each of us shall give account of himself to God." The cited passage from 2 Corinthians reads, "For we must all appear before the judgment seat of Christ, so that each one may receive good or evil, according to what he has done in the body."

[4] Romans 5:1: "Therefore, since we are justified by faith, we have peace with God through our Lord Jesus Christ." 1 Corinthians 6:11: "You were washed, you were sanctified, you were justified in the name of the Lord Jesus Christ and in the Spirit of our God." Both quotations RSV-CE.

[5] Acts 13:42: "Continue in the grace of God." 2 Corinthians 6:1: "Working together with Him then, we entreat you not to accept the grace of God in vain." Both quotations RSV-CE.

[6] Matthew 12:36–37: "I tell you, on the day of judgment men will render account for every careless word they utter; for by your words you will be justified, and by your words you will be condemned." Galatians 5:6: "For through the Spirit, by faith, we wait for the hope of righteousness." Romans 8:24–25: "For in this hope we were saved. Now hope that is seen is not hope. For who hopes for what he sees? But if we hope for what we do not see, we wait for it with patience." Romans 2:13,16: "For it is not the hearers of the law who are righteous before God, but the doers of the law who will be justified ... on that day when, according to my gospel, God judges the secrets of men by Christ Jesus." All quotations RSV-CE.

To put the two in another way:

1. Is obedience to God's law a *necessary* condition for becoming acceptable to God?
2. Is such obedience *enough* to make us acceptable to God?

It is not clear whether the Objector is taking a position on the latter question. However, he is certainly taking a position on the former question: God *requires* obedience, so that if we do not obey Him, we cannot please Him. With this point, at least, St. Thomas agrees, though as we will see, he does not agree with where the Objector goes with it.

[2] In the letter to the Hebrews – to certain Jews who had accepted the Gospel – we read as follows:

In the days of his flesh, Jesus offered up prayers and supplications, with loud cries and tears, to him who was able to save him from death, and he was heard for his godly fear. Although he was a Son, *he learned obedience* through what he suffered; and being made perfect he became the source of eternal salvation *to all who obey him*.[7]

There are a number of things the Objector might have found interesting about the passage, but he calls attention to it for one reason only: it emphasizes the importance of obedience.

[3] Having called attention to the importance of obedience, the Objector reasons that the Gospel cannot *make* us just and acceptable in the sight of God unless the mere hearing of the Gospel *makes* us believe (and so obey) it. Here, "believing" the Gospel means not just intellectually recognizing that it is true, but assenting to it with heart and will, for in the sense of mere intellectual recognition, St. James writes, "Even the demons believe – and shudder. Do you want to be shown, you shallow man, that faith apart from works is barren?"[8]

[4] The Objector's statement that one can hear the Gospel without believing it may seem so obviously true as to need no confirmation from Scripture. Just for good measure, however, he does provide confirmation. The passage from St. Paul's letter to the Romans emphasizes *both* the necessity of hearing the Gospel *and* the fact that not everyone who hears it believes it:

But how are men to call upon him in whom they have not believed? And how are they to believe in him of whom they have never heard? And how are they to hear without a preacher? And how can men preach unless they are sent? As it is written, "How beautiful are the feet of those who preach good news!" *But they have not all obeyed the gospel*; for Isaiah says, "Lord, who has believed what he has heard from us?"[9]

---

[7] Hebrews 5:7–9 (RSV-CE), emphasis added.
[8] James 2:19b–20 (RSV-CE).
[9] Romans 10:14–16, emphasis added. The internal quotations are from Isaiah 52:7, "How beautiful upon the mountains are the feet of him who brings good tidings, who publishes peace, who brings good tidings of good, who publishes salvation, who says to Zion, 'Your God reigns,'" and Isaiah 53:1, "Who has believed what we have heard? And to whom has the arm of the Lord been revealed?" St.

Does the New Law Make Men Just and Accepted in God's Sight? 411

Perhaps the reason the Objector seeks scriptural confirmation for the claim that the Gospel does not compel is that careless readers sometimes think that it *does* compel. After all, doesn't the letter to the Hebrews state that "the word of God is living and active, sharper than any two-edged sword"? Here is the passage:

[T]hose who formerly received the good news failed to enter [God's rest] because of disobedience ... Let us therefore strive to enter that rest, that no one fall by the same sort of disobedience. *For the word of God is living and active, sharper than any two-edged sword*, piercing to the division of soul and spirit, of joints and marrow, and discerning the thoughts and intentions of the heart. And before him no creature is hidden, but all are open and laid bare to the eyes of him with whom we have to do.[10]

However, taken in context the statement about the Word of God being living and active does not imply that no one who hears it can resist believing in it and following it, but rather that no one can escape detection for setting himself against it. It isn't about whether we believe, but about whether God discerns what is in the depths of our hearts. So it is hard to quarrel with the Objector's argument that not everyone who hears believes.

Objection 2. [1] *Further, the Apostle proves in his epistle to the Romans that the Old Law did not justify, because transgression increased at its advent:* [2] *for it is stated (Rm. 4): "The Law worketh wrath: for where there is no law, neither is there transgression."* [3] *But much more did the New Law increase transgression: since he who sins after the giving of the New Law deserves greater punishment,* [4] *according to Heb. 10. "A man making void the Law of Moses dieth without any mercy under two or three witnesses. How much more, do you think, he deserveth worse punishments, who hath trodden underfoot the Son of God," etc.? Therefore the New Law, like the Old Law, does not justify.*

Objection 2. Moreover, consider what St. Paul says in his letter to the Christians at Rome. He shows that the Old Law did not make us just in the sight of God, for on the contrary, it exposed us to God's wrath. If there had been no Law, no one could have transgressed it. Surely, though, the New Law increased transgression much more, for those who continue to sin even after the New Law has been given are even more worthy of punishment. The letter to the Hebrews makes this point by reminding its readers that those who trample on the law of Moses are put to death on the testimony of two or three witnesses, then asking how much more a man deserves punishment if he tramples on the Son of God. The conclusion is plain: The New Law does not make us just in God's sight any more than the Old Law did.

[1] The Objector works his way up to the New Law, beginning with an observation about the Old Law. He reasons that the Old Law could not make

---

Paul applies these verses to the Gospel because they occur in the middle of messianic prophecies, and he recognizes Jesus as the Christ, the Messiah. All quotations RSV-CE.
[10] Hebrews 4:6b, 11–13 (RSV-CE).

us just and acceptable to God, because becoming just requires obedience, and yet the Old Law *increased disobedience*.

[2] In another translation, Romans 4:15 reads, "For the law brings wrath, but where there is no law there is no transgression."[11] The point of the statement that there is no sin where there is no law is that nobody can be blamed for violating a precept that has not been made known to him. Thus, the more precepts God gave, the more possibilities for sin there were.

True, even before God gave the Old Law in words, he had already imparted its moral precepts to us in another way, through the natural law. Although the natural awareness of the moral basics had been dimmed by sin, it had not been obliterated. However, only in the Old Law itself did God give the more detailed *determinations* of the moral precepts which make up the ceremonial and judicial precepts.

It is fascinating how devious St. Thomas allows his imaginary Objectors to be. Had the Objector quoted a little more of the passage from which this quotation is taken, one might have drawn the lesson that although external observance of the Old Law did not justify, *the transformation brought about through faith in the New Law does* – a conclusion the Objector is trying hard not to reach:

For the law brings wrath, but where there is no law there is no transgression. That is why it depends on faith, in order that the promise may rest on grace and be guaranteed to all his descendants – not only to the adherents of the law but also to those who share the faith of Abraham, for he is the father of us all.[12]

[3] Ignoring the possibility just described, the Objector argues that if the Old Law could not make us just, because it increased transgression, then the New Law certainly cannot make us just, because it increases transgression even more. How so? Because if we continue to disobey God *even after* hearing the New Law, the guilt of our transgression is deeper.

[4] To back up his claim that the giving of the New Law makes transgression even worse, the Objector quotes a passage from the letter to the Hebrews, which in turn alludes to Deuteronomy 17:1–7, a provision of the Old Law which prescribed that anyone found to have worshipped false gods was to be put to death. Why such a severe punishment? Because, as the wording of Deuteronomy suggests, to repudiate the true God was to repudiate His entire covenant, to reject the Law of Moses as a whole:

If there is found among you, within any of your towns which the Lord your God gives you, a man or woman who does what is evil in the sight of the Lord your God, in transgressing his covenant, and has gone and served other gods and worshiped them, or the sun or the moon or any of the host of heaven, which I have forbidden, and it is told

---

[11] RSV-CE.
[12] Romans 4:15–16 (RSV-CE).

Does the New Law Make Men Just and Accepted in God's Sight? 413

you and you hear of it; then you shall inquire diligently, and if it is true and certain that such an abominable thing has been done in Israel, then you shall bring forth to your gates that man or woman who has done this evil thing, and you shall stone that man or woman to death with stones. On the evidence of two witnesses or of three witnesses he that is to die shall be put to death; a person shall not be put to death on the evidence of one witness. The hand of the witnesses shall be first against him to put him to death, and afterward the hand of all the people. So you shall purge the evil from the midst of you.[13]

As the unknown author of the letter to the Hebrews points out, if it is so dreadful a transgression to repudiate the Old Covenant which was given by God through Moses, then how much more dreadful it is to repudiate the New Covenant which is given by God in Person!

The issue here is the depth of the transgression, not what penalties are to be meted out for it by the civil authorities. The Old Testament's whole system of penalties has been ended, because unlike the Old Law, the New Law is not also a civil code. Rather it is the law of grace, and the executor of justice against those who spurn grace is the Spirit of Grace Himself.[14] "It is a fearful thing to fall into the hands of the living God."[15]

Objection 3. [1] *Further, justification is an effect proper to God,* [2] *according to Rm. 8,"God that justifieth."* [3] *But the Old Law was from God just as the New Law. Therefore the New Law does not justify any more than the Old Law.*	Objection 3. Besides, only God Himself can make us just. This is why St. Paul refers to Him as "God who justifies." But the Old Law that merely *comes from* God was not enough to make us just, and for the same reason, the New Law that merely *comes from* God is not enough to make us just either.

[1] An "effect proper to God" is a result that God and only God brings about. Thus, to say that justification is an effect proper to God is to say that only God Himself can make us just and acceptable in His sight.

[2] In support of the teaching that only God Himself can make us just and acceptable in His sight, the Objector quotes from a famous passage in St. Paul's letter to the Christians in Rome, which reads as follows:

If God is for us, who is against us? He who did not spare his own Son but gave him up for us all, will he not also give us all things with him? Who shall bring any charge against God's elect? *It is God who justifies*; who is to condemn? Is it Christ Jesus, who died, yes, who was raised from the dead, who is at the right hand of God, who indeed intercedes for us? Who shall separate us from the love of Christ? Shall tribulation, or distress, or persecution, or famine, or nakedness, or peril, or sword? As it is written, "For thy sake we are being killed all the day long; we are regarded as sheep to be slaughtered." No, in

---

[13] Deuteronomy 2:1–7 (RSV-CE).
[14] Hebrews 10:29.
[15] Hebrews 10:31 (RSV-CE).

all these things we are more than conquerors through him who loved us. For I am sure that neither death, nor life, nor angels, nor principalities, nor things present, nor things to come, nor powers, nor height, nor depth, nor anything else in all creation, will be able to separate us from the love of God in Christ Jesus our Lord.[16]

[3] The implied contrast is between God Himself, and something merely *from* God. The Objector reasons that although God can make us just, it does not follow that something merely from God – whether the Old Law or the New Law – can make us just.

| *On the contrary,* [1] *The Apostle says (Rm. 1): "I am not ashamed of the Gospel: for it is in the power of God unto salvation to everyone that believeth."* [2] *But there is no salvation but to those who are justified. Therefore the Law of the Gospel justifies.* | **On the other hand,** St. Paul writes to the Christians in Rome that he is not ashamed of the Gospel because it is the power by which God gives salvation to all believers. But no one has salvation unless he is just in God's sight, so the New Law – the Law of the Gospel – *does* make us just in God's sight. |

[1] The Objectors have been arguing that the Gospel, or New Law, does *not* justify, yet St. Paul says that it does. Contrary to Objector Three, who distinguishes the power of the New Law from the power of God, St. Paul says the power of the New Law is the *same thing* as the power of God:

I am under obligation both to Greeks and to barbarians, both to the wise and to the foolish: so I am eager to preach the gospel to you also who are in Rome. *For I am not ashamed of the gospel: it is the power of God for salvation to everyone who has faith*, to the Jew first and also to the Greek. For in it the righteousness of God is revealed through faith for faith; as it is written, "He who through faith is righteous shall live."[17]

"The Greek" is a metonymical expression not just for all Greeks but for all Gentiles or non-Jews.

[2] St. Paul had said that the Gospel is the power of God *for salvation* for those who have faith. Salvation – rescue – *simply is* becoming justified, becoming just and acceptable to God and so reconciled with Him. Therefore, the *sed contra* concludes that the New Law, or the Law of the Gospel, does justify.

---

[16] Romans 8:31b–39 (RSV-CE), emphasis added. The internal quotation is from Psalm 44:11, numbered 43:12 in the Latin translation of the Bible.
[17] Romans 1:14–17 (RSV-CE), changing "every one" to "everyone" and adding emphasis. The internal quotation is a passage from one of the Old Testament prophetic books, Habakkuk 2:2–4: "And the Lord answered me: 'Write the vision; make it plain upon tablets, so he may run who reads it. For still the vision awaits its time; it hastens to the end – it will not lie. If it seem slow, wait for it; it will surely come, it will not delay. Behold, he whose soul is not upright in him shall fail, but the righteous shall live by his faith.'"

Does the New Law Make Men Just and Accepted in God's Sight?

I answer that, [1] *As stated above, there is a twofold element in the Law of the Gospel.* [2] *There is the chief element, viz. the grace of the Holy Ghost bestowed inwardly. And as to this, the New Law justifies.* [3] *Hence Augustine says (De Spir. et Lit.): "There," i.e. in the Old Testament, "the Law was set forth in an outward fashion, that the ungodly might be afraid"; "here," i.e. in the New Testament, "it is given in an inward manner, that they may be justified."* [4] *The other element of the Evangelical Law is secondary: namely, the teachings of faith, and those commandments which direct human affections and human actions. And as to this, the New Law does not justify.* [5] *Hence the Apostle says (2 Cor. 3) "The letter killeth, but the spirit quickeneth":* [6] *and Augustine explains this (De Spir. et Lit. xiv, xvii) by saying that the letter denotes any writing external to man, even that of the moral precepts such as are contained in the Gospel.* [7] *Wherefore the letter, even of the Gospel would kill, unless there were the inward presence of the healing grace of faith.*

Here is my response. The question requires a double answer, because as I explained in the previous Article, the New Law – the Law of the Gospel – has both a main element and a secondary one.

The main element is the grace of the Holy Spirit that is poured into us. This aspect of the New Law *does* make us just and acceptable in God's sight. This is why St. Augustine writes that the Law of the Old Testament was given outwardly, so that the unjust might be *terrified*, but that the Law of the New Testament was given inwardly, so that the unjust might be *justified*.

The secondary element is the teachings of faith and the precepts that direct our feelings and acts. This aspect of the New Law does *not* justify us, and that is why St. Paul contrasts the letter of the law, which brings death, with the Spirit, which gives life. In his book *On the Spirit and the Letter*, St. Augustine explains that "the letter" means any writing external to us, even the moral precepts written in the Gospel. For apart from the grace of faith, which heals us, even these would bring death.

[1] We recall that Article 1 asked whether the New Law is a written law. There, St. Thomas argued that the preeminent element in the New Law is not written but implanted in the heart: the grace of the Holy Spirit, bestowed on us through Jesus Christ. However, there is also a secondary element, which instructs us by spoken and written word concerning what is to be believed and done *so that we can* receive the Holy Spirit's full grace and enjoy its benefits.

[2] The chief element – the grace of the Holy Spirit – makes us just and acceptable to God because it transforms us inwardly.

[3] Neither St. Augustine nor St. Thomas says "that the *ungodly* might be afraid," as the Blackfriars translation has it. Rather they say "that the *unjust* (*iniusti*) might be afraid." Now it is true that the ungodly and the unjust are the same people. However, rendering the term as "ungodly" blurs the contrast Augustine is drawing. For as we see below, where I quote the passage at some length, the Old Law terrifies the unjust, but the New Law *makes them just*. The former pours fear into their hearts, but the latter converts their hearts.

Here is what Augustine says in *On the Spirit and the Letter*:[18]

Now, amidst this admirable correspondence [between the Old Law and the New], there is at least this very considerable diversity in the cases, in that the people in the earlier instance[19] were deterred by a horrible dread from approaching the place where the law was given;[20] whereas in the other case the Holy Ghost came upon them who were gathered together in expectation of His promised gift.[21] There it was on tables of stone that the finger of God operated; here it was on the hearts of men. There the law was given outwardly, so that the unrighteous might be terrified; here it was given inwardly, so that they might be justified.[22] For this, "You shall not commit adultery, You shall not kill, You shall not covet; and if there be any other commandment," – such, of course, as was written on those tables – "it is briefly comprehended," says he, "in this saying, namely, You shall love your neighbor as yourself. Love works no ill to his neighbor: therefore love is the fulfilling of the law."[23] Now this was not written on the tables of stone, but "is shed abroad in our hearts by the Holy Ghost, which is given unto us."[24] God's law, therefore, is love. "To it the carnal mind is not subject, neither indeed can be";[25] but when the works of love are written on tables to alarm the carnal mind, there arises the law of works and "the letter which kills" the transgressor; but when love itself is shed abroad in the hearts of believers, then we have the law of faith, and the spirit which gives life to him that loves.

[4] The secondary element of the Gospel is spoken and written instructions as to what to believe, how to order our feelings, and how to direct our actions. These are crucial because they guide us *toward* the grace of the Holy Spirit,

---

[18] St. Augustine of Hippo, *On the Spirit and the Letter*, chapter 17, section 29, www.newadvent.org/fathers/1502.htm. The Latin may be found at www.augustinus.it/latino/spirito_lettera/index.htm.

[19] That is, the Hebrews.

[20] That is, the mountain on which Moses received the tablets of the Law: "Now when all the people perceived the thunderings and the lightnings and the sound of the trumpet and the mountain smoking, the people were afraid and trembled; and they stood afar off, and said to Moses, 'You speak to us, and we will hear; but let not God speak to us, lest we die.' And Moses said to the people, 'Do not fear; for God has come to prove you, and that the fear of him may be before your eyes, that you may not sin.' And the people stood afar off, while Moses drew near to the thick darkness where God was." Exodus 20:18–21 (RSV-CE).

[21] That is, the house in which the Apostles were gathered on the day of Pentecost: "When the day of Pentecost had come, they were all together in one place. And suddenly a sound came from heaven like the rush of a mighty wind, and it filled all the house where they were sitting. And there appeared to them tongues as of fire, distributed and resting on each one of them. And they were all filled with the Holy Spirit and began to speak in other tongues, as the Spirit gave them utterance." Acts 2:1–4 (RSV-CE).

[22] *Ibi ergo lex extrinsecus posita est, qua iniusti terrerentur, hic intrinsecus data est, qua iustificarentur.*

[23] Quoting Romans 13:9–10. Although St. Paul is focusing on our duties toward our neighbors, he is not deprecating our duties toward God.

[24] Quoting Romans 5:5.

[25] Quoting Romans 8:7. The expression "flesh" refers not to our body and nature per se, but to our *fallen* body and nature.

which justifies us. *In themselves*, though, they do not justify us because they are not the same as that grace.

This is the point which Objector Three missed. He grasped that there is a difference between God and what comes from God, and that only God justifies us. However, he did not grasp that references to the Gospel are intended to mean *both* that which merely comes from God *and* that which is the very power of God – for they refer to *both* the Gospel's teachings in words *and* the grace of the Holy Spirit which is at its heart.

[5] We have considered this passage before. As St. Paul writes, "Not that we are competent of ourselves to claim anything as coming from us; our competence is from God, who has made us competent to be ministers of a new covenant, not in a written code but in the Spirit; for the written code kills, but the Spirit gives life."[26]

As a guide to cooperating with the Spirit who pours grace into our hearts, the spoken and written instructions are good – they are not the life of grace itself, but they tell us about that life. Taken by themselves, though, apart from that grace, they are deadly, because they merely increase the depth of our transgression in turning away from the Spirit from whom all grace comes.

[6] A widely held view in Augustine's time and in ours holds that the expression "the letter that kills" refers only to the ceremonial precepts, not to the moral precepts. St. Augustine emphasizes that this is not true. Even though God expects us to obey His moral precepts, the expression "the letter that kills" refers to them too. Here is what Augustine writes a few chapters earlier in the work quoted above:[27]

Although, therefore, the apostle seems to reprove and correct those who were being persuaded to be circumcised, in such terms as to designate by the word "law" circumcision itself and other similar legal observances, which are now rejected as shadows of a future substance by Christians who yet hold what those shadows figuratively promised; he at the same time nevertheless would have it to be clearly understood that the law, by which he says no man is justified, lies not merely in those sacramental institutions which contained promissory figures, but also in those works by which whosoever has done them lives in a holy way, and among which occurs this prohibition: "You shall not covet."

Now, to make our statement all the clearer, let us look at the Decalogue itself. It is certain, then, that Moses on the mount received the law, that he might deliver it to the people, written on tables of stone by the finger of God. It is summed up in these ten commandments, in which there is no precept about circumcision, nor anything concerning those animal sacrifices which have ceased to be offered by Christians. Well, now, I should like to be told what there is in these ten commandments, except the observance

---

[26] 2 Corinthians 3:5–6 (RSV-CE).
[27] St. Augustine of Hippo, *On the Spirit and the Letter*, chapter 14, section 23, changing "holily" to "in a holy way" and "any one" to "anyone."

of the Sabbath, which ought not to be kept by a Christian – whether it prohibit the making and worshipping of idols and of any other gods than the one true God, or the taking of God's name in vain; or prescribe honor to parents; or give warning against fornication, murder, theft, false witness, adultery, or coveting other men's property? Which of these commandments would anyone say that the Christian ought not to keep?

Augustine poses a rhetorical question, just in case someone might think that "the letter that kills" refers only to the letter of the ceremonial precepts, which no longer bind us, and not to the letter of the moral precepts too:

> Is it possible to contend that it is not the law which was written on those two tables that the apostle describes as "the letter that kills," but the law of circumcision and the other sacred rites which are now abolished?

But he answers his question no, for it refers to both:

> But then how can we think so, when in the law occurs this precept, "You shall not covet," by which very commandment, notwithstanding its being holy, just, and good, "sin," says the apostle, "deceived me, and by it slew me?" What else can this be than "the letter" that "kills"?

So the terrible warning "the letter kills" does not mean that the Commandments are bad or unnecessary, or that because of grace I am free to disobey them. I *must* obey them: I must not murder, I must be faithful to my wife, and so forth. But on the other hand, if I obey the Commandments to the letter *without opening myself to the grace of God to which they are intended to direct me*, then they are deadly to me, because my failure to open myself to that grace will make my sin all the more terrible. Certainly I must follow the rules to be saved, but I am not saved by the rules; I am saved by God who gave me the rules and who gives me the power to follow them.

[7] The statement that even the words of the Gospel might "kill" is truly shocking. One might think that what St. Augustine has been saying applies only to the Old Law: that the letter of the Old Law kills, but that the letter of the New Law gives life. St. Thomas says "No, that is not how it is." Certainly the precepts of the Gospel are about the life of grace – they are about how those who do receive that grace. Yet these very same Gospel precepts would be useless and deadly to us *apart from* that healing grace itself.

For example, Christ says "This is my commandment, that you love one another as I have loved you. Greater love has no man than this, that a man lay down his life for his friends."[28] But suppose someone lays down his life for his friends without such love. What then? In a well-known passage in his first letter to the Corinthians, St. Paul answers the question. He writes that even if he gives away all he has, and even if he gives up his body to be burned (that is, even if he submits to martyrdom) –

---

[28] John 15:12–13 (RSV-CE).

if he does so without love, he gains nothing. This love, the very mark and the very effect of grace – this love, which is patient and kind, neither jealous, boastful, arrogant, rude, selfish, irritable, resentful, nor malicious – this love, which bears, believes, endures, and hopes for all things for the sake of God[29] – is not something that I can do or develop or "work up" in myself in order to deserve grace. If I imagine that, I am on the way not to life, but to destruction. No, this love is something that springs up in me *because* of grace.

The written and spoken teachings about this love are good because they tell us how those who do have it live, and they invite us into the grace that makes it possible to live this way through faith in Christ. But living in imitation of love, without love, is but an imitation of life, without life.

So does the New Law justify? Its words must be followed; they direct us to the grace of God which is expressed in the New Law, and that grace justifies. But following the words without the grace of which they speak does not justify. Put another way, the main element of the New Law justifies, but its secondary element does not.

Reply to Objection 1. This argument holds true of the New Law, not as to its principal, but as to its secondary element: i.e. as to the dogmas and precepts outwardly put before man either in words or in writing.

Reply to Objection 1. The Objection makes a valid point about the secondary element in the New Law – that is, about the teachings and precepts it sets forth before man externally, whether in words or in writing. However, the point it makes does not apply to the main element in the New Law.

The Objector had argued that the New Law cannot justify us unless it makes us adhere to it and follow it – and it doesn't. St. Thomas retorts: By the New Law, do you mean its chief part, the grace of the Holy Spirit, or its secondary part, the instructions which tell us how to cooperate with that grace? The Objector is certainly right that the words by themselves do not make us just and acceptable to God. But the grace of the Holy Spirit does.

Reply to Objection 2. [1] Although the grace of the New Testament helps man to avoid sin, yet it does not so confirm man in good that he cannot sin: [2] for this belongs to the state of glory. [3] Hence if a man sin after receiving the grace of the New Testament, he deserves greater punishment, as being ungrateful for greater benefits, and as not using the help given to him.

Reply to Objection 2. Certainly the grace of the New Testament helps us not to sin. However, it does not root us so firmly in good that we cannot sin at all. That will not happen until we are in glory.
So it is true that someone who persists in sin after accepting the grace of the New Testament deserves greater punishment. For although he received greater help, he was not grateful for it and did not make use of it. And this is why, although St. Paul says that the

---

[29] 1 Corinthians 13:1–7 (RSV-CE).

> [4] *And this is why the New Law is not said to "work wrath": because as far as it is concerned it gives man sufficient help to avoid sin.*

Old Law brings about wrath, he does not say that the New Law does so. For the help it provides us is sufficient to avoid sin, if only we do use it.

[1] According to the Objector, rather than helping us avoid sin and so become just in the sight of God, the New Law merely brings about greater wrath when we do sin. St. Thomas begins by pointing out that it *does* help us to avoid sin. The help that it gives should not be deprecated just because it does not make it *impossible* to sin.

[2] Sin really is impossible for the redeemed souls in heaven. Since they see the glory of God face to face, His supreme, uncreated goodness so fills their minds that no lesser, created good could possibly tempt them away from him. But here, where we do not see God face to face, sin is always possible.

[3] So yes, it is true that the gravity of sin is even greater for someone who has received the grace of the New Law – but what makes this true is not that he hasn't received help to avoid sin, *but that he has.*

[4] So the sense in which the New Law brings wrath is not that it makes the punishment for sin worse without giving us help to avoid it, but that just because it *has* given us help to avoid it, it increases sin's punishment. Insofar as it does give us that help, then so long as we continue to accept that help, it does make us just and acceptable to God.

Reply to Objection 3. [1] *The same God gave both the New and the Old Law, but in different ways.* [2] *For He gave the Old Law written on tables of stone: whereas He gave the New Law written "in the fleshly tables of the heart," as the Apostle expresses it (2 Cor. 3).* [3] *Wherefore, as Augustine says (De Spir. et Lit.), "the Apostle calls this letter which is written outside man, a ministration of death and a ministration of condemnation: whereas he calls the other letter, i.e. the Law of the New Testament, the ministration of the spirit and the ministration of justice: because through the gift of the Spirit we work justice, and are delivered from the condemnation due to transgression."*

Reply to Objection 3. The God who imparted the New Law to us is the same as the God who imparted the New, but He gave the two laws in different ways. He gave the Old Law written on stone tablets, but as St. Paul puts it, he gave the New Law written on the tablets of the heart.

That is why St. Augustine explains in *On the Spirit and the Letter* that Paul calls the "letter" of the Old Testament, written outside us, a servant of death and of damnation, but calls the "letter" of the New Testament, written inside us, a servant of the Spirit and of justice. For through the Holy Spirit's gift, we do justice and we are set free from the damnation of sin.

---

[1] The Objector had distinguished between God Himself and what God gives us, His gifts including both the Old Law and the New. Only God Himself

Does the New Law Make Men Just and Accepted in God's Sight?

can make us just, for as we see from the Old Law, what God merely gives us cannot. St. Thomas begins by pointing out that although both the Old and New Law are given to us, they are not given to us in the same sense, and the failure to recognize this fact unravels the Objector's argument. He is about to explain how.

Notice too St. Thomas's insistence that *the same God* gave both the Old and New Law. This shows his utter rejection of heterodox doctrine called Marcionism (after Marcion of Sinope), according to which the supreme beings of the Old and New Testaments are actually two different gods, the former wicked, cruel, and ignorant, the latter good, loving, and wise. Viewing the two Testaments this way has been a persistent temptation throughout the history of Christianity. Although those who tend in this Marcionite direction may not literally believe that the Old and New Testaments are about different Gods, they often speak as though at some point the God of the Old Testament "got religion" and was reformed. This unfortunate theological tendency takes various forms. The radical antithesis some people propose between Law (which they associate exclusively with the Old Testament) and Grace (which they associate exclusively with the New) is but one of them.

By contrast, St. Thomas thinks all such ways of thinking completely wrongheaded. True, God employed different methods to guide the people in the Old Testament than the people of the New. However, He did this in view of the condition of the people He was dealing with, for it was *because* of how He gave spiritual nourishment to the Old Testament people that He was able to give better food to the New Testament people. Indeed the Old Law anticipated the New, and was a drawn-out preparation for receiving it. As St. Paul says, it was a servant leading the children to the true teacher, who is Christ.[30]

[2] St. Paul says to the Corinthian converts, "you show that you are a letter from Christ delivered by us, written not with ink but with the Spirit of the living God, not on tablets of stone but on tablets of human hearts."[31] How does this statement figure into St. Thomas's argument? Recall the Objector's argument that although God Himself can make us just, nothing merely *from* God can make us just, whether it is the Old Law or the New Law. The Objector's distinction makes sense in the context of the Old Law, written on tablets of stone, for in that case God did give the people something different than Himself. However, the distinction does not make sense in the context of the New Law, written on the heart by the inflowing grace of the Holy Spirit, because in that case what God gives is His very self.

This language of writing on the heart alludes to a number of other passages of Holy Scripture. As Paul says in his letter to the Romans, in the sense of

---

[30] Galatians 3:24.
[31] 2 Corinthians 3:1–3 (RSV-CE).

conscience the law is *already* written on our hearts: "When Gentiles who have not the law do by nature what the law requires, they are a law to themselves, even though they do not have the law. They show that what the law requires is written on their hearts, while their conscience also bears witness and their conflicting thoughts accuse or perhaps excuse them."[32]

Because this natural law does not sufficiently restrain us, God gives the Old Law and *exhorts* the people to write it on their hearts:

You shall therefore lay up these words of mine in your heart and in your soul; and you shall bind them as a sign upon your hand, and they shall be as frontlets between your eyes. And you shall teach them to your children, talking of them when you are sitting in your house, and when you are walking by the way, and when you lie down, and when you rise. And you shall write them upon the doorposts of your house and upon your gates, that your days and the days of your children may be multiplied in the land which the Lord swore to your fathers to give them, as long as the heavens are above the earth.[33]

Since we continue to disobey, the Old Testament prophet Jeremiah says that the *sins* of the people are written on their hearts: "The sin of Judah is written with a pen of iron; with a point of diamond it is engraved on the tablet of their heart, and on the horns of their altars."[34]

Yet God *promises* that one day He Himself will write His *law* on their hearts. For Jeremiah also says:

"Behold, the days are coming," says the Lord, "when I will make a new covenant with the house of Israel and the house of Judah, not like the covenant which I made with their fathers when I took them by the hand to bring them out of the land of Egypt, my covenant which they broke, though I was their husband," says the Lord. "But this is the covenant which I will make with the house of Israel after those days," says the Lord: "I will put my law within them, *and I will write it upon their hearts*; and I will be their God, and they shall be my people. And no longer shall each man teach his neighbor and each his brother, saying, 'Know the Lord,' for they shall all know me, from the least of them to the greatest," says the Lord; "for I will forgive their iniquity, and I will remember their sin no more."[35]

Finally, in the passage from the second letter to the Corinthians with which we began, St. Paul claims that this messianic promise has finally come to pass.

---

[32] Romans 2:14–15 (RSV-CE). As we have seen before, in some interpretations, this passage is not about all persons, but only about redeemed persons. If so, then it is not so much about what is written on the heart by creation, but about what is subsequently written on the heart by grace. In his *Commentary on St. Paul's Letter to the Romans*, St. Thomas considers this interpretation possible. However, although no other passage of Scripture uses the image of writing on the heart *for* natural law, other passages of Scripture do testify to natural law.

[33] Deuteronomy 11:18–21 (RSV-CE), emphasis added. Compare Proverbs 3:3 and 7:3.

[34] Jeremiah 17:1 (RSV-CE).

[35] Jeremiah 31:31–34 (RSV-CE), emphasis added. This passage is quoted in Hebrews 8:8–13. Compare Ezekiel 11:17–20 and 36:22–27 (RSV-CE).

Does the New Law Make Men Just and Accepted in God's Sight? 423

[3] The "letter which is written outside man" – the mere verbal teaching of the Law, external to our hearts, whether the words of the Old Law or New – merely increases the sinfulness of our sins. But "the other letter" – not just the words but the *grace* of the New Law – frees us from sinfulness and so makes us just and acceptable in the sight of God. Here is the passage in St. Augustine from which St. Thomas is quoting:[36]

Now, since, as [St. Paul] says in another passage, "the law was added because of transgression,"[37] meaning the law which is written externally to man, he therefore designates it both as "the ministration of death,"[38] and "the ministration of condemnation."[39]

But the other, that is, the law of the New Testament, he calls "the ministration of the Spirit"[40] and "the ministration of righteousness,"[41] *because through the Spirit we work righteousness, and are delivered from the condemnation due to transgression.*

The one, therefore, vanishes away, the other abides; for the terrifying schoolmaster will be dispensed with, when love has succeeded to fear.

DISCUSSION

The Letter that Kills

It is one thing to say that apart from the grace of God, the letter of the law is useless. It is another thing to say that it kills. Yet Thomas Aquinas agrees with the New Testament that it does kill. Thinking that we can be holy by ourselves, without the help of God, is more deadly than swallowing arsenic.

How is this to be understood? C. S. Lewis made an interesting, if slightly flawed, suggestion: "Morality is indispensable," he writes,

But the Divine Life, which gives itself to us and which calls us to be gods, intends for us something in which morality will be swallowed up. We are to be re-made. The idea of reaching "a good life" without Christ is based on a double error. Firstly, we cannot do it; and secondly, in setting up "a good life" as our final goal, we have missed the very point of our existence. Morality is a mountain which we cannot climb by our own efforts; and if we could we should only perish in the ice and unbreathable air of the summit, lacking those wings with which the rest of the journey has to be accomplished. For it is from there that the real ascent begins. The ropes and axes are "done away" and the rest is a matter of flying.[42]

---

[36] Augustine, , *On the Spirit and the Letter*, chapter 18, section 31, with modified punctuation and with emphasis and paragraph breaks added.
[37] Galatians 3:19.
[38] 2 Corinthians 3:7.
[39] 2 Corinthians 3:9.
[40] 2 Corinthians 3:8.
[41] 2 Corinthians 3:9 again.
[42] C. S. Lewis, "Man or Rabbit?", in *God in the Dock* (Grand Rapids, IN: Eerdmans, 1970), pp. 111–112.

St. Thomas could agree with much of this statement. Certainly he agrees that supreme happiness is not just following rules, but beholding the goodness and beauty of God as He is in Himself. On the other hand, he reminds us that only the pure in heart will see God, and the pure in heart are obedient. Certainly St. Thomas agrees that we do all sin. On the other hand, he reminds us that when we do sin we must repent, be renewed, and start ascending again. And certainly St. Thomas agrees that we cannot climb the mountain of the Commandments by our own efforts. But he reminds us that we *can* climb this mountain by the grace of God – a point which perhaps Lewis does not make clear enough. We are not justified even though we unjust. Rather we are justified because God *makes us just*.

So grace is not a permission slip for transgression. Although our sins can be forgiven, they can never be simply excused. Whatever it takes, however long it takes, we must be made holy. Indeed, it is always open to us to obey our present duty, and God helps us to do so. Moreover He prevents us from being tempted beyond our ability to resist, for as St. Paul writes to the Christians of Corinth, "Therefore let any one who thinks that he stands take heed lest he fall. No temptation has overtaken you that is not common to man. God is faithful, and he will not let you be tempted beyond your strength, but with the temptation will also provide the way of escape, that you may be able to endure it."[43]

I think St. Thomas would also point to another reason why the letter kills (one which Lewis also overlooks), for the Angelic Doctor's portrait of moral character highlights the *interconnectedness* of the moral virtues.[44] It is no use saying "I lie constantly, but I am not unjust," for to fail in truthfulness is to fail in justice too. Nor is it any use saying "I may be a disloyal friend, but I am a good statesman," for if I cannot keep faith even with those whom I supposedly love, it is hard to see why I will keep faith with strangers. Without temperance, I will lack patience; without patience, prudence; without prudence, fortitude. In fact, if I am damaged in any virtue, I am impaired in all of them.

Why is this important? Consider a man who is overly impressed with his own virtue, and who does delude himself that he flawlessly conforms to the Law. Although there is no merit in denying that we possess virtue that we do possess, no one is really faultless. If the man falsely thinks that he is, he is grossly deficient in humility. But humility is one of the virtues, and not least among them. Since the virtues are interconnected, this vice – this lack of humility – will beget a host of other vices. The worms of proud self-deception will eat through all his moral woodwork. So although we might be tempted to say of such a man "He has all of the moral virtues except humility," the true state of affairs is that because he lacks humility, he is radically impaired in all the other virtues too.

---

[43] 1 Corinthians 10:12–13 (RSV-CE).
[44] See I-II, Q. 65, especially Art. 1, which I discuss at some length in *Commentary on Thomas Aquinas's Virtue Ethics* (Cambridge: Cambridge University Press, 2017).

The Scandal of This Teaching

What makes the teaching of the Gospel unique is not that it proposes a lofty and difficult view of moral purity (although it does). Rather its uniqueness lies in the facts, first, that even as it declares the absolute necessity of this holiness, it asserts our utter inability to achieve holiness by our own power – and second, that as the solution to this paradox, it proposes a person, Jesus Christ, who suffered a bloody execution for our sins. So it is that although Thomas Aquinas vigorously defends the urgency of following the Gospel's moral precepts, he at the same time insists that the chief element of the Gospel is not the precepts themselves, but the grace of the Holy Spirit. This grace, which indwelt Christ, can indwell us, if only we allow His life, death, and resurrection to be appropriated to us.

These distinctive elements of the Gospel also make it scandalous to us. St. Paul writes,

> For since, in the wisdom of God, the world did not know God through wisdom, it pleased God through the folly of what we preach to save those who believe. For Jews demand signs and Greeks seek wisdom, but we preach Christ crucified, a stumbling block to Jews and folly to Gentiles, but to those who are called, both Jews and Greeks, Christ the power of God and the wisdom of God.[45]

First the Gospel tramples and wounds our religious sensibilities by speaking of the Almighty making Himself weak and vulnerable and dying like a common criminal, then it rubs salt into the wounds by saying that He did this to take upon Himself the death we deserved ourselves. How insulting. It goes on to insult our philosophical sensibilities because it both *testifies* to things we could never have figured out for ourselves, and *does* things we could never have done for ourselves. No, the Crucifixion and Resurrection are not just another miracle, and the Gospel is not just another moral philosophy. They are as far from being that as God is from being a mongoose.

All those things of which the Gospel speaks were done to justify sinful men, to make them good and holy. As we have seen, it is sometimes held that God does not actually make the convert just, but merely declares him just. Certainly God does declare him just, but in the view of Thomas Aquinas, the declaration is no legal fiction. It is not as though there were no real change in the sinner, and yet God lied and pretended that there were. Rather the God of Truth, who cannot lie, declares the sinner just because by the grace of the Holy Spirit He has actually made him just. Something has changed in the very condition of the man's nature.

I have just said that God "has actually made him just," but if we wish to be precise, we need all three verb tenses: God *has made*, He *is making*, and He *will make* him just. The sinner has already been justified, in the sense that at the

---

[45] 1 Corinthians 1:21-24 (RSV-CE).

moment of his baptism into the community of faith, an ontological change was brought about within him – something he could never have deserved or accomplished by his own efforts. He is being justified, in the sense that with his cooperation, God's grace is confirming and consolidating this change, for otherwise he might relapse. And he will be justified, in the sense that at the conclusion of the Divine surgery, when he is admitted into glory, he will have been entirely cleansed, not only of the guilt of his former sin (which has already been forgiven), but even of its stains. Then at last he will see his Redeemer.

QUESTION 108, ARTICLE 4

Whether Certain Definite Counsels are Fittingly Proposed in the New Law?

TEXT	PARAPHRASE
Whether certain definite counsels are fittingly proposed in the New Law?	According to the Tradition, the New Law contains not only precepts, obedience to which is commanded, but also clearly defined counsels, which are urged but not commanded. Is the provision of these counsels appropriate?

St. Thomas has already established that the most important element in the New Law is the grace of the Holy Spirit. In order to cooperate with that grace, following the Commandments is also necessary. Thus, when a certain young man approaches Christ to ask what he must do to have eternal life, Christ tells him "If you would enter life, keep the Commandments." When the young man asks "Which?", Christ alludes to the Ten Commandments by quoting several of its precepts, then adds the commandment to love our neighbors as ourselves. Even after this, the young man seems to think that his approach to God is missing something. "All these I have observed," he says; "what do I still lack?" Christ answers, "If you would be perfect, go, sell what you possess and give to the poor, and you will have treasure in heaven; and come, follow me."[1]

Christ had already said that so far as behavior is concerned, following the Commandments is sufficient to enter into life. Thus it would be unreasonable for His final remark to be taken as meaning, "I was mistaken. There is one more precept that you must also observe." Evidently, this further exhortation is not just another commandment. Why then does He offer it at all? What He actually says is that for the young man to give up all his wealth to the poor and follow Him is not a necessary condition of salvation, but an aid to becoming *perfect*. In the Greek of the New Testament, the word we render "perfect" is *teleios*; the Latin of St. Thomas's translation uses the close equivalent *perfectus*. These words refer to something which is complete or mature, something which has

---

[1] The incident, with the ensuing discussion among Jesus and the disciples, is recorded in Matthew 19:16–30. My quotations are from the RSV-CE.

attained its full development, and here, of course, we are speaking of spiritual development.

For such reasons as this, the Tradition has always distinguished between *precepts* and *evangelical counsels*. The precepts are utterly necessary for entering into redeemed life, and so they bind everyone. These are the moral commands of the Decalogue, interpreted in the light of the New Testament, especially its teaching about love. By contrast, the counsels are not commands, but directions for those who wish to progress even more swiftly and with a minimum of distractions to the fullness of that life. According to the Tradition, chief among these directions are perpetual poverty, perpetual virginity, and obedience. The best example of someone following them is a person in a religious order, who has given up personal wealth, relinquished the option of marrying, and placed himself under authority delegated by God, laying aside his self-will and craving for recognition. It is not that the enjoyment of property, of sexual relations within marriage, and of the direction of one's own life are sinful and prevent the attainment of eternal life with God; that is not at all the case. But for those who are called to relinquish these things, poverty, virginity, and obedience remove difficulties and distractions from the path of faith so that it can be traveled more swiftly, freely, and easily. They are *helps* – but not everyone can follow them, nor is everyone specially called or invited to do so.

The distinction between precepts and counsels has historically been disputed by most Protestants, on grounds that if something is good then it *must* be required, and so neglecting it must be a sin. Anticipating this objection, St. Thomas replies that the New Law makes some things a matter of counsel rather than obligation precisely because it is a law of liberty rather than bondage. The precepts concern things without which we cannot achieve eternal beatitude with God at all, while the counsels concern things that help us to reach this end in a better way, unencumbered by the things that weigh us down.

To an age like ours, all three evangelical counsels are baffling. Perpetual poverty puzzles us because we crave gain; perpetual virginity, because although we greatly misunderstand love, we are obsessed with sex; and obedience, because we although we are quite willing to obey authorities whom we do not recognize as authorities – such as public opinion, or the approval of our friends or professional milieu – we *think* that we cherish independence from authority.[2] From a Thomistic point of view, the very fact that the evangelical counsels seem unthinkable to us is a sign of how much we need them.

Perhaps the most misunderstood of these counsels is the third, evangelical obedience. Secular persons sometimes even think that having to obey is somehow totalitarian. The scandal is partly dispelled by the fact that obedience is not

---

[2] Interesting reflections on the first and third points may be found in Alexis de Tocqueville, *Democracy in America* (public domain), volume II, part 1, chapters 10 and 1, respectively, "Of the Taste for Material Well-Being in America" and "Of the Philosophical Method of the Americans."

Did the New Law Really Need both Precepts and Counsels? 429

the same as *blind* obedience. In fact, evangelical obedience is limited in a variety of ways. For example, no superior may command anything contrary to the rule of his order; even a licit command does not bind the conscience of the person to whom it is given unless the superior makes clear his intention that it should do so; and in any case, no command to do what is morally wrong may be obeyed. The highest obedience of every human being is to God, not to man – which is infinitely greater protection than human regimes and ideologies give.

Yet even so, much of the scandal remains, for obedience yokes the will, and we tend to think nothing so important as "autonomy." St. Thomas thinks this attitude is simply mistaken. In his view, our problem is not that we cannot always do as we please, but that we make an idol of doing as we please. Submitting to a human authority delegated by God may be an antidote to this spiritual illness.

Objection 1. [1] *It would seem that certain definite counsels are not fittingly proposed in the New Law. For counsels are given about that which is expedient for an end, as we stated above, when treating of counsel.* [2] *But the same things are not expedient for all. Therefore certain definite counsels should not be proposed to all.*	Objection 1. These counsels seem to have been badly framed and given. Earlier in this *Summa*, we have discussed counsels in general, finding that a counsel concerns the means to be followed for some end. Now that which helps one person to attain a given end may not be helpful to another. Nevertheless, the New Law recommends the same fixed counsels to everyone. Plainly this is unfitting.

[1] This remark refers to a series of discussions in the section on the nature of human acts, earlier in the *Summa*. Some acts concern ends while others concern the means employed to reach them. The act of *counsel*, deliberation as to the best means to reach an end, falls into the latter category; for example, reason may offer me the counsel, "on sunny days, the best way to light up the room is to open the curtains so that the sun shines in." The evangelical counsels tell us the best way to attain our final end, or ultimate purpose, which is perfect fellowship with God.

[2] Both Felicity and Perpetua need to eat wholesome food; this is a necessity of health for everyone. However, it so happens that Felicity has an iron deficiency. She will attain health more easily if she eats foods rich in iron, supplemented with vitamin C because it helps in iron's absorption. By contrast, Perpetua is prone to iron overload. She will attain health more easily if she *avoids* eating such foods. Therefore, even granted that the two women must both eat wholesome food, the most expeditious path to health is somewhat different for each of them.

The Objector reasons that just as wholesome food is a universal necessity for bodily health, keeping the Commandments is a universal necessity for spiritual health – yet just as the most expeditious path to bodily health may vary somewhat among individuals, so the most expeditious path to spiritual health may vary somewhat among them. It would be just as inappropriate to offer the same evangelical counsels to everyone, he thinks, as to offer the same advice about iron-rich foods and vitamin C supplements to both Felicity and Perpetua.

Objection 2. [1] *Further, counsels regard a greater good.* [2] *But there are no definite degrees to the greater good. Therefore definite counsels should not be given.*

Objection 2. Moreover, a counsel directs us to a *better* good. But which goods are better and worse varies according to the individual. Therefore, the New Law should not have given fixed counsels at all.

---

[1] Whoever says "The best thing to do is P" means "P is the best thing to do *in order to attain some greater end*, Q." In our previous example, Felicity eats foods rich in iron, along with vitamin C, because this is the best way to attain the greater good of bodily health.

[2] Objector 1 had argued that the best *means* to the end vary among individuals, but Objector 2 argues that the best *ends* vary among individuals. Perhaps the best lives for Sophia and Matthew lie in being married to each other, but the best lives for Scolie and Ben lie in entering the consecrated religious life and being friends. Since we do vary in such ways, says the Objector, then how can it be fitting to offer the same counsels to everyone?

Objection 3. [1] *Further, counsels pertain to the life of perfection.* [2] *But obedience pertains to the life of perfection. Therefore it was unfitting that no counsel of obedience should be contained in the Gospel.*

Objection 3. Moreover, counsels concern the *perfect* life – the life that is mature and complete in every respect. But although one of the things such a life requires is obedience, the Gospel lacks a counsel of obedience. Whatever may be said about the other counsels, surely the omission of this one is a defect.

---

[1] In his final remark to the young man who has approached Him, Jesus speaks of *perfection*: not of the bare necessities for the attainment of blessed unity with God, but of the higher standard of conduct for the life that leads there most swiftly and effectively. According to the Tradition, just as it is with the counsels offered to the young man, so it is with the other evangelical counsels.

[2] "I do find the counsel of perpetual poverty in the Gospels," the Objector says – "it's right there in Christ's advice to the young man. And I find the counsel of perpetual virginity in the Gospels too, for Christ figuratively describes celibate persons as 'eunuchs for the kingdom of heaven' and recommends this state of life to those who can follow it. But why isn't there a counsel of obedience? Yes, we must obey the Commandments, but over and above that, there ought to be a counsel worded something like 'Commit yourself to accept direction from others,' and I don't see one."

The Objector is well aware of the fact that every Christian is called to obey Christ's commands; he is not complaining that believers are given no precepts that they must obey. Rather he is complaining that there is no invitation to freely give up the personal direction of one's life and place oneself under the direction of spiritual authorities whom God appoints. The difference between obeying God's laws and placing myself under the authority of my religious superiors in a religious order is something like the difference between obeying human laws and joining the military.

Objection 4. [1] *Further, many matters pertaining to the life of perfection are found among the commandments, as, for instance, "Love your enemies" (Mt. 5),* [2] *and those precepts which Our Lord gave His apostles (Mt. 10).* [3] *Therefore the counsels are unfittingly given in the New Law: both because they are not all mentioned; and because they are not distinguished from the commandments.*	Objection 4. Besides, the Gospel addresses numerous aspects of the perfect life by giving commands rather than counsels. For example, Christ commands all persons to love their enemies in Matthew 5, and gives additional commands just to His Apostles in Matthew 10. From this fact we see two more things wrong with the traditional enumeration of three evangelical counsels. First, these three do not include *everything* pertaining to the perfect life, and second, the New Law sets out some of the things pertaining to the perfect life in the form of commands.

[1] The Old Law already contains the germ of Christ's teaching about the love of enemies, for it clearly recognizes hatred of enemies as a sin. For example, in a poignant passage of the book of Job, when this righteous but suffering man is pleading his innocence before God, he includes hatred of enemies in his long list of sins he has not committed. Acknowledging that he would deserve punishment "If I have rejoiced at the ruin of him that hated me, or exulted when evil overtook him," he protests that "I have not let my mouth sin by asking for his life with a curse."[3]

On the other hand, the wording of the Old Law's command of love seems to suggest that the "neighbors" whom one must love are limited to the members of the chosen nation: "You shall not take vengeance or bear any grudge against the sons of your own people, but you shall love your neighbor as yourself." Moreover, although hatred of enemies was certainly not commended, even so it was common. Consider for example this heartbreaking psalm of the captives, along with its chilling conclusion:

By the waters of Babylon, there we sat down and wept, when we remembered Zion. On the willows there we hung up our lyres. For there our captors required of us songs, and our tormentors, mirth, saying, "Sing us one of the songs of Zion!" How shall we sing the

---

[3] Job 31:29-30 (RSV-CE).

Lord's song in a foreign land? If I forget you, O Jerusalem, let my right hand wither! Let my tongue cleave to the roof of my mouth, if I do not remember you, if I do not set Jerusalem above my highest joy! Remember, O Lord, against the Edomites the day of Jerusalem, how they said, "Raze it, raze it! Down to its foundations!" O daughter of Babylon, you devastator! Happy shall he be who requites you with what you have done to us! Happy shall he be who takes your little ones and dashes them against the rock![4]

Granted, not every attitude recorded in the Scriptures is approved by the Scriptures. Even so, considering the fact that this piteous cry for vengeance is recorded in the Psalms, Christ's followers must have been shocked when He challenged the attitude expressed in its last verse:

You have heard that it was said, "You shall love your neighbor and hate your enemy." But I say to you, Love your enemies and pray for those who persecute you, so that you may be sons of your Father who is in heaven; for he makes his sun rise on the evil and on the good, and sends rain on the just and on the unjust. For if you love those who love you, what reward have you? Do not even the tax collectors do the same? And if you salute only your brethren, what more are you doing than others? Do not even the Gentiles do the same? You, therefore, must be perfect, as your heavenly Father is perfect.[5]

To return to the Objector's argument: Christ's statement "I say to you, love your enemies" is plainly worded as a command, but His statement "you, therefore, must be perfect" tells us that the purpose of this command is perfection. So even though the Tradition associates the life of perfection not with commands but with counsels, here, the Objector says, we have commands *about perfection* – and he considers this inappropriate. As he points out, the Gospel includes many other commands about perfection too, such as "Be merciful, even as your Father is merciful," "Give, and it will be given to you," and "Forgive, and you will be forgiven."[6]

[2] The Objector thinks that the instructions Christ gives to His disciples as they are about to go out to the towns to preach the Kingdom of God fall into the same category – the category of *commands* rather than *counsels* of perfection: "You received without paying, give without pay. Take no gold, nor silver, nor copper in your belts, no bag for your journey, nor two tunics, nor sandals, nor a staff; for the laborer deserves his food. And whatever town or village you enter, find out who is worthy in it, and stay with him until you depart."[7]

[3] In the Objector's view, his examples demonstrate two things:

1. That the traditional listing of evangelical counsels – perpetual poverty, perpetual virginity, and obedience – fails to include all of the instructions

---

[4] Psalm 137 (RSV-CE), numbered in the Vulgate as 136, changing the archaic "rase" to "raze."
[5] Matthew 5:43–48 (RSV-CE).
[6] These are from Luke 6:36–38, but the chapter includes many other examples.
[7] Matthew 10:8b–11 (RSV-CE). See also Luke 9–10.

Did the New Law Really Need both Precepts and Counsels? 433

proposed in the Gospels about perfection, because some of these instructions are commands.
2. That none of the Gospel's instructions about perfection should have been framed as commands anyway.

| *On the contrary,* [1] *the counsels of a wise friend are of great use, according to Prov. 27: "Ointment and perfumes rejoice the heart: and the good counsels of a friend rejoice the soul."* [2] *But Christ is our wisest and greatest friend. Therefore His counsels are supremely useful and becoming.* | On the other hand, there is great benefit in the counsel of a wise friend. An Old Testament proverb reminds us vividly of this fact by saying that just as sweet-smelling ointments and perfumes delight the heart, so a friend's good counsels waft sweetness to the soul. But our wisest and greatest friend is Christ, so whose counsels could more helpful and fitting than His? |

[1] The value of a wise friend's counsel is obvious to any person of good will. Just for good measure, the *sed contra* offers confirmation from Proverbs 27:9. Unfortunately, translators disagree about the proper rendering of this proverb. Some take it the way the *sed contra* does, comparing the goodness of a friend's counsel with the sweetness of a pleasant scent:

- DRA: Ointment and perfumes rejoice the heart: and the good counsels of a friend are sweet to the soul.
- ESV: Oil and perfume make the heart glad, and the sweetness of a friend comes from his earnest counsel.

But according to other translations, like the following, the passage contrasts sweet scents with sorrow, making no reference at all to a friend's counsel:

- RSV-CE: Oil and perfume make the heart glad, but the soul is torn by trouble.
- NABRE: Perfume and incense bring joy to the heart, but by grief the soul is torn asunder.

Fortunately, even if we deny the *sed contra* the use of this particular proverb, others proverbs, which do not vary across translations, confirm the *sed contra*'s point:

- Where there is no guidance, a people falls; but in an abundance of counselors there is safety.[8]
- Without counsel plans go wrong, but with many advisers they succeed.[9]

---

[8] Proverbs 11:14 (RSV-CE). DRA has, "Where there is no governor, the people shall fall: but there is safety where there is much counsel."
[9] Proverbs 15:22 (RSV-CE). DRA has, "Designs are brought to nothing where there is no counsel: but where there are many counsellors, they are established."

If the "wounds of a friend" are wise counsels that bring us pain, then we may include this one too:

- Better is open rebuke than hidden love. Faithful are the wounds of a friend; profuse are the kisses of an enemy.[10]

[2] The traditional understanding that Christ is our wisest and greatest friend is an obvious inference from such passages as the following. In the first, Christ is speaking to the disciples at the Last Supper. The other three are from letters written by the Apostles.

- This is my commandment, that you love one another as I have loved you. Greater love has no man than this, that a man lay down his life for his friends. You are my friends if you do what I command you. No longer do I call you servants, for the servant does not know what his master is doing; but I have called you friends, for all that I have heard from my Father I have made known to you.[11]
- Why, one will hardly die for a righteous man – though perhaps for a good man one will dare even to die. But God shows his love for us in that while we were yet sinners Christ died for us.[12]
- For we have not a high priest who is unable to sympathize with our weaknesses, but one who in every respect has been tempted as we are, yet without sin.[13]
- See what love the Father has given us, that we should be called children of God; and so we are.[14]

Although the *sed contra* gives good reasons to trust Christ's counsels, it does not entirely remove the difficulties posed by the Objectors, especially concerning the distinction between counsels and commands. To respond to these, a deeper analysis is needed, which St. Thomas is about to provide.

I answer that, [1] *the difference between a counsel and a commandment is that a commandment implies obligation, whereas a counsel is left to the option of the one to whom it is given.* [2] *Consequently in the New Law, which is the law of liberty, counsels are added to the commandments, and not in the Old*	**Here is my response.** This is the difference between precept and counsel: A precept conveys the necessity of obedience, but a counsel is left to the choice of the person who receives it. Thus, the New Law adds counsels to precepts because it is the law of freedom, but the Old Law

---

[10] Proverbs 27:5–6. DRA has, "Open rebuke is better than hidden love. Better are the wounds of a friend, than the deceitful kisses of an enemy."
[11] John 15:12–15 (RSV-CE).
[12] Romans 5:7–8 (RSV-CE).
[13] Hebrews 4:15 (RSV-CE).
[14] 1 John 3:1 (RSV-CE).

Law, which is the law of bondage. [3] We must therefore understand the commandments of the New Law to have been given about matters that are necessary to gain the end of eternal bliss, to which end the New Law brings us forthwith: but that the counsels are about matters that render the gaining of this end more assured and expeditious.	includes *only* precepts because it is the law of servitude. Thus, we must see that the New Law provides *precepts* about things that are *necessary* to attain the goal of eternal happiness to which it is the entrance, but it provides *counsels* about things which lead us to this goal *more readily and swiftly*.

[1] By confirming the traditional use of these two terms, St. Thomas signals that he considers the distinction between them justified.

[2] Christ declares, "If you continue in my word ... you will know the truth, and the truth will make you free," explaining that "everyone who commits sin is a slave to sin."[15] In various passages of the New Testament, the freedom of which Christ speaks is called the "law of liberty," and explained as keeping the moral precepts in the spirit of love. Thus St. James writes,

If you really fulfil the royal law, according to the scripture, "You shall love your neighbor as yourself," you do well. But if you show partiality, you commit sin, and are convicted by the law as transgressors. For whoever keeps the whole law but fails in one point has become guilty of all of it. For he who said, "Do not commit adultery," said also, "Do not kill." If you do not commit adultery but do kill, you have become a transgressor of the law. So speak and so act as those who are to be judged under the law of liberty.[16]

This liberty is contrasted with the bondage of the ceremonial precepts. Thus St. Paul writes, "For freedom Christ has set us free; stand fast therefore, and do not submit again to a yoke of slavery ... For in Christ Jesus neither circumcision nor uncircumcision is of any avail, but faith working through love."[17] It is not that the ceremonial precepts were bad, but that for the followers of Christ to relapse into the minute supervision of the Old Law would be like a person who had reached the age of mature instruction returning to the tutelage of his childhood guardian.[18]

---

[15] John 8:31–34, 36 (RSV-CE).
[16] James 1:8–12. Compare James 1:25, "he who looks into the perfect law, the law of liberty, and perseveres, being no hearer that forgets but a doer that acts, he shall be blessed in his doing"; and 1 Peter 2:15–16, "For it is God's will that by doing right you should put to silence the ignorance of foolish men. Live as free men, yet without using your freedom as a pretext for evil; but live as servants of God." All translations RSV-CE.
[17] Galatians 5:1, 6 (RSV-CE).
[18] We have discussed this image from St. Paul before: "Now before faith came, we were confined under the law, kept under restraint until faith should be revealed. So that the law was our custodian until Christ came, that we might be justified by faith. But now that faith has come, we are no longer under a custodian; for in Christ Jesus you are all sons of God, through faith." Galatians 3:24–26 (RSV-CE).

Today we tend to find the notion of a "law of liberty" perplexing, because we think of liberty and law as opposites. The reason for our confusion is that we think of liberty as having no government. However, for the classical writers, including the authors of Holy Scripture, liberty did not signify *lack* of government but *self*-government. Thus a free city has liberty because it rules itself rather than being under a tyrant; a freedman has liberty because he directs his own life rather than being enslaved by a master; and a person obedient to God has liberty because his mind freely accepts God's direction and is fulfilled by it. Moreover, rather than merely being jerked around by God's providence, the person who is obedient to Him actually shares in His providence, through caring for himself and for others.[19]

[3] So, as befitted the spiritual condition of the people, the Old Law made everything a matter of commandment. The contrasting liberty of the New Law lies in two things: As to the primary element in the New Law, the grace of the Holy Spirit, it lies in the liberating grace of love. As to its secondary element, its actual verbal instructions, its freedom lies in the fact that it gives commandments only about the absolute necessities for salvation, leaving the individual free concerning those counsels which are helpful to the life of faith, but not absolutely necessary. The person who is *most* free is the person who does choose to follow these counsels.

[4] *Now man is placed between the things of this world, and spiritual goods wherein eternal happiness consists:* [5] *so that the more he cleaves to the one, the more he withdraws from the other, and conversely.* [6] *Wherefore he that cleaves wholly to the things of this world, so as to make them his end, and to look upon them as the reason and rule of all he does, falls away altogether from spiritual goods.* [7] *Hence this disorder is removed by the commandments.* [8] *Nevertheless, for man to gain the end aforesaid, he does not need to renounce the things of the world altogether: since he can, while using the things of this world, attain to*	Now man is made in such a way that he stands midway between the things of this world and the spiritual goods in which eternal happiness lies. For this reason, the more he clings to either one, the more he lets go of the other. So anyone who clings entirely to the things of this world, taking them as his purpose in life and viewing them as the rule and guide of everything he does, utterly destroys his spiritual good. The Commandments are directed to the cure of this disorder. On the other hand, for man to reach this spiritual goal, he need not *completely* give up the things of this world. Provided that he does not take them as

---

[19] See I-II, Q. 91, Art. 2: "Now among all others, the rational creature is subject to Divine providence in the most excellent way, insofar as it partakes of a share of providence, by being provident both for itself and for others. Wherefore it has a share of the Eternal Reason, whereby it has a natural inclination to its proper act and end: and this participation of the eternal law in the rational creature is called the natural law."

eternal happiness, provided he does not place his end in them: [9] *but he will attain more speedily thereto by giving up the goods of this world entirely: wherefore the evangelical counsels are given for this purpose.*	his purpose in life, he can engage them and still reach eternal happiness. Still, he will reach it *more swiftly* if he gives them up completely, and this is why the evangelical counsels are provided.

[4] St. Thomas says man is "constituted" between the things of this world and the things in which spiritual good lies. The Latin verb *constitutus* can mean either how something is positioned or how it is made. In this case, I think, it means both: man's very nature positions him between mundane and spiritual goods, because he has both a body and a rational soul. A dog, which is animal but not rational, would not be attracted to eternal life. An angel, which is intellectual but not animal, would not be attracted to material things.

The fact that we are both rational and animal is not a flaw in our nature, because our bodies were *made to obey* our rational souls. In our fallen condition, however, our composite nature opens the possibility that we will suffer divided hearts, pulled on one side toward worldly things, and on the other side toward spiritual.

[5] The more tightly we grasp the goods of this world, the looser becomes our grasp on the goods of the spirit. The more firmly we place our hope in the goods of the spirit, the less important the goods of this world seem to us.

[6] Of course we should not *ignore* our bodies and imagine that we have no worldly needs; this is the heresy of angelism. But if we build our aspirations on worldly goods, as though wealth, bodily satisfactions, and doing as we please were the meaning of happiness, we will utterly miss the target of our happiness – for worldly goods inevitably let us down, and we can be perfectly satisfied only in God.[20]

[7] In various ways, the Commandments restrain us from entirely indulging our love of worldly goods. They hold us back from headlong pursuit of riches by forbidding both theft and avarice. They keep us from abandoning ourselves to bodily pleasure by condemning impurity and lust. They bridle our self-will and craving for recognition by instructing us about how to live. However, St. Thomas does not mean that mere external observance of the Commandments cures us from excessive attachment to the goods of this world. Again we must remember his emphasis on the grace of love, poured into us by God Himself.

[8] My salvation is not endangered by the fact that I save money for the care of my children, so long as I do not place my ultimate hope and trust in my

---

[20] See the parable of the Rich Fool, along with Christ's explanation, in Luke 12:16–31.

wealth. A faithful marital partnership is an excellent and holy thing, so long as wives and husbands encourage each other in the adoration of God rather than making idols of each other in His place. It is quite all right to direct my life, so long as I do not become intoxicated with the exercise of my will and the approval of others.

[9] The dangers of the goods of this world, then, are not that they are bad when well used, but that they tempt me to use them badly, and distract me from goods that are greater. Therefore, a way of life that so far as possible eliminates these distractions and temptations is even better. This is the liberating possibility to which the evangelical counsels are directed. They describe the shape of a way of life which not only expresses God's grace but also makes us readier to receive it.

---

[10] *Now the goods of this world which come into use in human life, consist in three things: viz. in external wealth pertaining to the "concupiscence of the eyes"; carnal pleasures pertaining to the "concupiscence of the flesh"; and honors, which pertain to the "pride of life," according to 1 Jn. 2.* [11] *and it is in renouncing these altogether, as far as possible, that the evangelical counsels consist.* [12] *Moreover, every form of the religious life that professes the state of perfection is based on these three: since riches are renounced by poverty; carnal pleasures by perpetual chastity; and the pride of life by the bondage of obedience.*

There are two ways in which all of the various particular counsels may be boiled down to three general and perfect counsels of perpetual poverty, virginity, and obedience.

To understand the first of these ways, reflect that the worldly goods we use in human life lie in three things: wealth, bodily pleasures, and honors. The first of these tempts us to what St. John called the lust of the eyes, the second, to what he called the lust of the flesh, and the third, to what he called the pride of life. Now the evangelical counsels propose that as much as possible, we forsake these things. Every form of consecrated religious life that teaches and aims at the state of perfection is founded on them, for wealth is set aside by the discipline of poverty, of giving up personal possession; bodily pleasures are set aside by the discipline of perpetual virginity; and the pride of life, by the discipline of obedience.

---

[10] St. John famously suggests a threefold classification of confused or deranged passions, each of them involving the excessive desire for something that *in itself* can be good. Here is what he says:

Do not love the world or the things in the world. If anyone loves the world, love for the Father is not in him. For all that is in the world, the lust of the flesh and the lust of the eyes and the pride of life, is not of the Father but is of the world. And the world passes away, and the lust of it; but he who does the will of God abides for ever.[21]

---

[21] 1 John 2:15–17 (RSV-CE).

Did the New Law Really Need both *Precepts* and *Counsels?* 439

In teaching, I find that many students take "lust" as a synonym for "desire," and think that it has to be about sex. No, lust is desire which is *disordered* in some way – desire which is not directed by reason. Thus:

- "Lust of the flesh" means the disordered craving for bodily pleasure, for example desiring sexual intercourse without consideration for my wife, or desiring it with someone who is not my wife. It can also include disordered cravings for other bodily pleasures, as in gluttony, but as St. Thomas often remarks, the greatest bodily pleasures are the pleasures of touch, especially sexual touch. Therefore, these pleasures are the most important to keep in check.
- "Lust of the eyes" means the disordered craving for wealth. The image evokes the fact that whatever fine thing the avaricious man sees, he wants for himself.
- "Pride of life" means the disordered craving to have my way with others and gain their admiration. Notice that St. Thomas associates these two lusts. However, moderate satisfaction in the fact that one has done something well, or in being commended by a friend, is not pride in this sense.

[11] The qualification "as far as possible" is important. In this life, it is impossible to avoid all distractions and temptations. A person might even be tempted to a perverse pride in the very fact of following the evangelical counsels: "I am more pure and humble than those others! Why am I not made their spiritual director?" Needless to say, the spirit of the counsels militates against these forms of the pride of life too.

[12] St. Thomas explores how the evangelical counsels ground the consecrated religious life in more detail in his treatise *Defense of the Religious Orders against Their Opponents*, to which we return in the Discussion at the end of this Article.

One point needs to be clarified, because *castitatem* can refer to either chastity or virginity, and in view of contemporary English usage, the translation of *perpetuam castitatem* as "perpetual chastity" in the Blackfriars text is somewhat misleading. *All* persons are called to perpetual chastity in the sense of perpetual temperance regarding sex; chastity in this sense includes abstinence from premarital and extramarital intercourse, and it is not a matter of counsel but of command. In context, though, St. Thomas is speaking of the evangelical counsel of perpetual *celibacy*, which is the calling of only a few. To forestall confusion, I have rendered *perpetuam castitatem* not as "perpetual chastity" but as "perpetual virginity."

---

[13] *Now if a man observe these absolutely, this is in accordance with the counsels as they stand.*
[14] *But if a man observe any*

Here is the second way in which all of the various particular counsels may be boiled down to three general and perfect ones. The literal and unqualified meaning of fulfilling the counsels is

one of them in a particular case, this is taking that counsel in a restricted sense, namely, as applying to that particular case. [15] For instance, when anyone gives an alms to a poor man, not being bound so to do, he follows the counsels in that particular case. [16] In like manner, when a man for some fixed time refrains from carnal pleasures that he may give himself to prayer, he follows the counsel for that particular time. [17] And again, when a man follows not his will as to some deed which he might do lawfully, he follows the counsel in that particular case: [18] for instance, if he do good to his enemies when he is not bound to, [19] or if he forgive an injury of which he might justly seek to be avenged. [20] In this way, too, all particular counsels may be reduced to these three general and perfect counsels.

to follow them completely and in all situations. However, someone might follow them in a limited sense by doing as they invite only in particular cases. For example:

- If someone gives alms to a particular poor man, even though he is not obligated to do so, then he is acting in the spirit of the counsel of poverty just in the case of that man.
- If for a set time someone abstains from bodily pleasures in order to pray without distraction, then he is acting in the spirit of the counsel of virginity just for that time.
- If, for the sake of love, someone sets aside his own wishes concerning some matter even though he is not required to do so, then he is acting in the spirit of the counsel of obedience just in that matter – for example, if even though he is not inclined to do so, he does some good to his enemies which is not required of him, or he forgives an injury for which he would have been entitled to seek justice.

In both of these two ways we see that all of the counsels that apply to particular cases may be viewed as aspects of three more fully developed and comprehensive counsels.

---

[13] The counsel of poverty does not mean giving away some of one's wealth and keeping the rest, or putting one's wealth in a blind trust so that one can take over its management again at some future time. Rather the wording of the counsel is absolute: give it all away, completely, and for good. In the same way, literal observance of the counsel of obedience does not mean obeying curbing one's will in some things but in all things, subject to God's supreme direction, and literal observance of the counsel of perpetual virginity does not mean laying down the option of marriage only for a time, or laying down the option of getting married but reserving the option to smooch, but rather giving up such things unreservedly and forever.

[14] Even so, one could call it a *limited kind* of obedience to follow one of the counsels just with respect to a particular situation.

[15] I am not under command to make a voluntary donation to the homeless shelter, but suppose I do. Obviously, since I have not given up *all* that I have for the relief of the poor, I am not following the counsel of perpetual poverty. But it might be said that in a limited sense, I am acting in the spirit of the counsel just in the case of this donation.

[16] St. Paul writes to married Christians in Corinth, "Do not refuse one another except perhaps by agreement for a season, that you may devote yourselves to prayer; but then come together again, lest Satan tempt you through lack of self-control." He adds, "I say this by way of concession, not of command," meaning that although he permits such periods of abstinence for those who desire them, he does not require them.[22] Consider a husband and wife who agree not to enjoy each other's bodies during the season of Lent so that each of them can pray without distraction. Obviously, being married, they are not practicing perpetual virginity – in fact, St. Paul makes clear that just because they are married, they should *not* abstain from conjugal pleasure all of the time even though periods of abstinence are permitted. But it might be said that they are acting in the spirit of the counsel of perpetual virginity just for this season of abstinence.

[17] The point of the counsel of obedience is not to exalt someone else's personal will, but to set aside my own personal will, for when I vow obedience to authority that is exercised in the name of Christ, I am repudiating my privilege of making all of my decisions by myself. Suppose I do not lay aside my will completely, but only in a particular matter. Then it might be said that in a limited way I am acting in the spirit of the counsel of obedience. Apparently realizing that what he is trying to say may be obscure, St. Thomas gives two examples, to which we now turn.

[18] St. Paul urges his readers, "as we have opportunity, let us do good to all men."[23] The expression "all men" includes enemies, so we should do good to our enemies. But *which* acts of good should we do to them? Some such acts are required. For example, Christ commands "pray for those who persecute you."[24] But not all of them are required; in fact it would not even be possible to do *every* good to *every* enemy, because there is a vast number of such acts and our resources are limited. Suppose my enemy's car is in the shop, and he asks me to drive him to work. I do not want to do it because there are others whom he might ask, the favor would take me far out of my way, and it would make me late for my own job. But suppose I do it anyway, for the sake of love. Just because I have set aside my will to help out my neighbor, I am acting, in a limited way, in the spirit of the counsel of obedience.

[19] Contrary to common belief, the Gospel does not teach unconditional forgiveness, but *prompt and willing* forgiveness. Christ says, "If your brother sins, rebuke him, and if he repents, forgive him; and if he sins against you seven times in the day, and turns to you seven times, and says, 'I repent,' you must

---

[22] 1 Corinthians 7:5–6 (RSV-CE).
[23] Galatians 6:10 (RSV-CE).
[24] Matthew 5:44.

forgive him."[25] This is conditional: "If he repents." Thus John Paul II writes of a similar passage,[26]

> It is obvious that such a generous requirement of forgiveness does not cancel out the objective requirements of justice. Properly understood, justice constitutes, so to speak, the goal of forgiveness. In no passage of the Gospel message does forgiveness, or mercy as its source, mean indulgence towards evil, towards scandals, towards injury or insult. In any case, reparation for evil and scandal, compensation for injury, and satisfaction for insult are conditions for forgiveness.[27]

As this statement suggests, not only is forgiving unrepented injuries not commanded, it may even be wrong. For example, if my enemy shoots at me with a gun and I do not report him to the police, I am not being "more spiritual," but only foolish. On the other hand, forgiveness of an injury can *sometimes* be meritorious even when it is not required. Suppose my neighbor carelessly, but unintentionally, backs his truck into my fence and damages it. He ought to compensate me for the damage, but I decide to let the matter go. Just as in the previous case, I am curbing my will for the sake of love; thus, just as in the previous case, in a limited way I am doing what the counsel of obedience commends.

[20] It seems unlikely that when St. Thomas speaks of "particular counsels," he is thinking only of those counsels set down in words somewhere in Holy Scripture. Divine Wisdom may bid us to do many things that it does not command, some of them very specific: visit *this* sick person, give up *this* permitted thing, yield honor in *this* matter, set aside *this* allowable privilege. What St. Thomas suggests is that though not to the same degree, each of these more limited counsels points us in the same direction as the three evangelical counsels, which are comprehensive in scope:

- Any counsel to fast from a permitted bodily pleasure points toward the same goal as the counsel of perpetual virginity, or celibacy: Freedom from the lust of the flesh.
- Any counsel to refrain from a permitted enjoyment of wealth points toward the same goal as the counsel of perpetual poverty: Freedom from the lust of the eyes.
- Any recommendation to curb one's will, or yield honor to someone else, points toward the same goal as the counsel of obedience: Freedom from the pride of life.

---

[25] Luke 17:3-4 (RSV-CE).

[26] "Then Peter came up and said to him, 'Lord, how often shall my brother sin against me, and I forgive him? As many as seven times?' Jesus said to him, 'I do not say to you seven times, but seventy times seven.'" Matthew 18:21-22 (RSV-CE).

[27] Pope John Paul II, encyclical *Dives in Misericordia* ("Rich in Mercy"), section 14, http://w2.vatican.va/content/john-paul-ii/en/encyclicals/documents/hf_jp-ii_enc_30111980_dives-in-misericordia.html.

Did the New Law Really Need both Precepts and Counsels? 443

The purpose of these counsels is liberation from tyranny. If we are not serving God, then we are serving something less than God. Whenever we serve what is less than God, we are slaves. Only in serving Him are we perfectly free, for He made us in His image, for Himself.

Reply to Objection 1. [1] *The aforesaid counsels, considered in themselves, are expedient to all; but owing to some people being ill-disposed, it happens that some of them are inexpedient, because their disposition is not inclined to such things.* [2] *Hence Our Lord, in proposing the evangelical counsels, always makes mention of man's fitness for observing the counsels.* [3] *For in giving the counsel of perpetual poverty (Mt. 19), He begins with the words: "If thou wilt be perfect," and then He adds: "Go, sell all [Vulg.: 'what'] thou hast."* [4] *In like manner when He gave the counsel of perpetual chastity, saying (Mt. 19): "There are eunuchs who have made themselves eunuchs for the kingdom of heaven," He adds straightway: "He that can take, let him take it."* [5] *And again, the Apostle (1 Cor. 7), after giving the counsel of virginity, says: "And this I speak for your profit; not to cast a snare upon you."*	Reply to Objection 1. In themselves, the evangelical counsels are helpful to everyone. However, they are not helpful to those whose feelings are averse to them. This is why, whenever Our Lord proposes them, He always mentions that not everyone is able to follow them. For example, when He gives the counsel of perpetual poverty, He first says "*If you wish to be full and complete,*" only then instructing, "Go and sell your belongings." Similarly, when He gives the counsel of perpetual virginity, or celibacy, He first remarks that some have made themselves figurative "eunuchs" for the sake of the kingdom of heaven, then immediately adds, "*Those who can* receive this [counsel], let them receive it." St. Paul speaks in much the same way, for after giving the Christians at Corinth the counsel of perpetual virginity, he adds that he gives it to help them, not to entangle them in an obligation.

[1] The Objector had complained that although that which helps one person to attain an end may not be helpful to another, the New Law urges the same counsels to everyone. St. Thomas responds that the evangelical counsels do help everyone, if only he can follow them. For comparison, suppose the question before us had been not how to reach beatitude but how to get to Chicago, and someone had counseled, "Driving is faster than walking." Our Objector would have complained that driving is not faster for everyone but only for some people. St. Thomas would have responded, "It is faster for everyone *who can drive* – but of course not everyone can drive."

In the case of the evangelical counsels – perpetual poverty, virginity, and obedience – the difficulty is that although some people can follow them, most find themselves averse. A strong-willed couple of my acquaintance tell the story of a day early in their marriage when the wife was annoyed with the husband.

Earlier in life, she had considered a religious vocation. Half seriously, she exclaimed to her husband, "I should have joined the convent!" With affectionate mockery, he replied, "You? Poverty, yes. Chastity, yes. Obedience, never!" Amused, she admitted that the consecrated religious life wouldn't have worked for her unless she had been the superior.

[2] Just for this reason, when he offered the evangelical counsels Christ never simply said "Do this," but only "Do this if you can."

[3] For example, in advising the young man who asked "What do I still lack?", Christ did not simply say that the young man should sell his possessions, give the proceeds to the poor, and become one of those who traveled with Him, but that *if he desired to be perfect* – if he was determined to have no impediment or distraction – then he should do these things. It turned out that he didn't: "When the young man heard this he went away sorrowful; for he had great possessions."[28]

[4] St. Thomas's second example is that Jesus offered the counsel of perpetual virginity, or celibacy, only to those who could receive it. The context is a discussion in which Christ says that marriage is indissoluble, so that divorce and remarriage is really adultery. Astonished, the disciples say that if marriage is indissoluble, then it is better not to marry at all. Surprisingly, Christ agrees that it is better not to marry, but says that the counsel of not marrying is not for everyone:

The disciples said to him, "If such is the case of a man with his wife, it is not expedient to marry." But he said to them, "Not all men can receive this saying, but only those to whom it is given. For there are eunuchs who have been so from birth, and there are eunuchs who have been made eunuchs by men, and there are eunuchs who have made themselves eunuchs for the sake of the kingdom of heaven. He who is able to receive this, let him receive it."[29]

"Eunuchs who have been so from birth" means persons who are congenitally incapable of sexual intercourse; "eunuchs who gave been made eunuchs by men" means persons who have been castrated; and "eunuchs who have made themselves eunuchs for the sake of the kingdom of heaven" means those who have voluntarily given up the option of marriage and marital intercourse in order to follow a more perfect life. It seems likely that Christ chose the startling image of being a "eunuch" in order to emphasize the difficulty of following this way of life apart from the grace of God.

[5] St. Paul also recommends perpetual virginity, pointing out its spiritual advantages. But he emphasizes that he leaves his advice to the discretion of the individual Christian, because not everyone is able to practice this particular form of discipline:

I want you to be free from anxieties. The unmarried man is anxious about the affairs of the Lord, how to please the Lord; but the married man is anxious about worldly affairs,

---

[28] See again Matthew 19:16-22 (RSV-CE).
[29] Matthew 19:1–12, quoting the last three verses (RSV-CE).

how to please his wife, and his interests are divided. And the unmarried woman or girl is anxious about the affairs of the Lord, how to be holy in body and spirit; but the married woman is anxious about worldly affairs, how to please her husband. *I say this for your own benefit, not to lay any restraint upon you, but to promote good order and to secure your undivided devotion to the Lord.*[30]

Reply to Objection 2. [1] *The greater goods are not definitely fixed in the individual; but those which are simply and absolutely the greater good in general are fixed:* [2] *and to these all the above particular goods may be reduced, as stated above.*	Reply to Objection 2. True, the answer to the question "Which goods are better *for you*?" does vary according to the individual. But the answer to the question "Which goods are better *in themselves, universally*?" does not change. And as we saw earlier, all the particular counsels concern these three.

---

[1] This statement does not mean that for some persons salvation is not the greatest good, or that for some persons there might be salvation apart from Jesus Christ. What it means is that certain things that are good *in themselves* as aids to cooperation with the grace of Christ are not good *for everyone* as aids to this cooperation. This fact should not surprise us. In itself, rocket fuel is more powerful than gasoline, but rocket fuel will not work in my automobile. In itself, red meat contains more calories than beans and rice, but some people cannot tolerate red meat. In the same way, in itself the discipline of perpetual virginity is extremely beneficial, but not all people can sustain it, and those who would find themselves burning up with passion if they never married should seek grace in the married life instead.

[2] We have already seen that each of the more limited counsels points us in the same direction as the three comprehensive counsels. Thus, even though the person who fully observes the evangelical counsel of obedience is following a better way of life than the person who merely sets aside his will in a particular case for the sake of God, they are both seeking beatitude – just as, even though some people eat red meat while others eat beans and rice, they are both seeking nutrition.

Reply to Objection 3. Even the counsel of obedience is understood to have been given by Our Lord in the words: "And [let him] follow Me." For we follow Him not only by imitating His works, but also by obeying His	Reply to Objection 3. The Objector is mistaken in supposing that there was no counsel of obedience, for we understand Our Lord to have counseled obedience whenever he invited anyone, "follow me." Someone might think "follow me" is not about personal obedience – that it does not mean "Do as I tell you," but only "Do as you see me do." Actually, it means both, for in another place

---

[30] 1 Corinthians 7:32–35 (RSV-CE), emphasis added. See also the rest of the chapter.

commandments, according to Jn. 10:27: "My sheep hear My voice ... and they follow Me."	Christ remarks that His sheep *hear His voice* and follow Him – plainly implying that they hear what He tells them to do, and then do it.

Objector 3 had complained that although the New Law should have provided a counsel of obedience, it didn't. According to St. Thomas, however, it does provide such a counsel. Christ expected obedience to all of His commands, but He invited certain persons to do more – to leave everything and join in His ministry of teaching and healing under His personal direction. For example, His call to Peter, Andrew, Matthew, and Philip is worded "follow me," and so are his exhortations to the young man of whom we spoke above, as well as another whom he met on the road.[31] To follow Him does not mean merely traveling around with Him, although the disciples certainly did that, but to place themselves under His personal authority – and in later generations, under personal authority exercised in His name and by His commission.

So the point that St. Thomas is making in response to the Objector is not that some are called to obey Christ's commands, for everyone is called to do that. Rather his point is that some are called to curb their wills, abandon their former lives, and practice the more radical mode of personal obedience that we associate with the consecrated religious life – that this is a matter of counsel or invitation rather than command – and yes, that this did begin in the Gospels.

Reply to Objection 4. [1] *Those things which Our Lord prescribed about the true love of our enemies, and other similar sayings (Mt. 5; Lk. 6),* [2] *may be referred to preparation of the mind, and then they are necessary for salvation;* [3] *for instance, that man be prepared to do good to his enemies, and other similar actions, when there is need. Hence these things are placed among the precepts. But that anyone should actually and promptly behave thus towards an enemy when there is no special need, is to be referred to the particular counsels, as stated above.* [4] *As to those matters which are set down in Mt. 10 and*	Reply to Objection 4. In Matthew 5 (as well as Luke 6, which the Objector does not mention), Our Lord gave precepts about those preparations of the soul that are *necessary* for salvation. For example, we must love our enemies – we must be ready to do good to them when there is need. By contrast, such things as readiness to do good to our enemies even when there is *no* special need are matters of counsel, not of precept, because although they are helpful to salvation, they are not absolutely necessary. The Objector may be confused about the instructions that were set forth in Matthew 10 (and perhaps Luke 9 and 10, which the Objector does not mention), because although he considers them counsels, the explanation of counsels we have given does not account for them. The solution to this

---

[31] See Matthew 4:18–19, Matthew 9:9, John 1:43, Matthew 19:21, and Luke 9:59–60. See also Matthew 8:21–22, as well as what might be called the second call of Peter in John 21.

Lk. 9 and 10, [5] they were either disciplinary commands for that particular time, [6] or concessions, as stated above. [7] Hence they are not set down among the counsels.	puzzle is that they are *not* counsels. For as we found when we discussed them in a previous Article, some of them were permissions while others were disciplinary instructions just for that occasion.

[1] When St. Thomas speaks of those things Christ commanded about the true love of our enemies, he is thinking of the passage in the Gospel of Matthew which we saw previously,[32] and also the following closely parallel passage from the Gospel of Luke:

But I say to you that hear, love your enemies, do good to those who hate you, bless those who curse you, pray for those who abuse you. To him who strikes you on the cheek, offer the other also; and from him who takes away your coat do not withhold even your shirt. Give to everyone who begs from you; and of him who takes away your goods do not ask them again. And as you wish that men would do to you, do so to them. If you love those who love you, what credit is that to you? For even sinners love those who love them. And if you do good to those who do good to you, what credit is that to you? For even sinners do the same. And if you lend to those from whom you hope to receive, what credit is that to you? Even sinners lend to sinners, to receive as much again. But love your enemies, and do good, and lend, expecting nothing in return; and your reward will be great, and you will be sons of the Most High; for he is kind to the ungrateful and the selfish. Be merciful, even as your Father is merciful.[33]

Often this passage is misunderstood. Christ does not bid me not to protect myself if my enemy tries to stab me with a knife. Rather He bids me to offer no resistance if my enemy insults me by slapping my cheek. Even so, the daily standard set by this and His other instructions for loving enemies is staggeringly high. Apart from the grace of the Holy Spirit, it would be impossible.

[2] Even Plato, pagan though he was, recognized that there is something wrong with the common notion that justice requires doing good to our friends and harm to our enemies.[34] Yet Plato never required going beyond justice in order to *love* our enemies. Christ did. He presented love of enemies as absolutely necessity for friendship with God.

[3] There are *degrees* of perfection in love. Granted that I am required to love my enemy, how am I required to love him? Just as I love my wife and children? No. St. Thomas distinguishes between the readiness to do my enemy good when there is special need, and the readiness to do so when there is not. The former is the what one *must* do – it is a matter of precept. An example might be cheerfully giving my enemy assistance if I find that he has fallen off his roof and hurt himself: I *must not* walk on by. The latter goes beyond what one must do –

---

[32] That is, Matthew 5:43–48.
[33] Luke 6:27–36 (RSV-CE).
[34] See the words Plato assigns to Socrates, deep in conversation with Polemarchus, in *Republic*, book 1, 332a–334b.

although it may be good and praiseworthy, it is a matter of counsel. I do not have to send my enemy a birthday present.

The distinction between obeying and exceeding the precepts should not be misunderstood. Someone who does good to his enemy grudgingly, with the attitude "I just want to do what I have to in order to get by," is not really "getting by" at all. He does not grasp the *point* of loving his enemy, for love is not just a matter of outward acts but of the condition of the heart. I do not have to like my enemy or enjoy his company, and I certainly should not wish him success in doing wrong, but I must *will* his true good. I must desire that we could be reconciled in the truth, and that our love could be mutual, even if this is impossible. I must be willing to live with him forever in heaven, whatever profound changes in both of us that may require. If I am not willing to be reconciled with him, then God will not be willing to be reconciled with me.

[4] The indicated chapter in Matthew tells of Christ sending His twelve disciples out to spread His message, instructing them as follows:

And preach as you go, saying, "The kingdom of heaven is at hand." Heal the sick, raise the dead, cleanse lepers, cast out demons. You received without paying, give without pay. Take no gold, nor silver, nor copper in your belts, no bag for your journey, nor two tunics, nor sandals, nor a staff; for the laborer deserves his food.[35]

As Luke records, on another occasion He appoints seventy others, sending them out with similar instructions to areas He is about to visit Himself:

After this the Lord appointed seventy others, and sent them on ahead of him, two by two, into every town and place where he himself was about to come. And he said to them, "The harvest is plentiful, but the laborers are few; pray therefore the Lord of the harvest to send out laborers into his harvest. Go your way; behold, I send you out as lambs in the midst of wolves. Carry no purse, no bag, no sandals; and salute no one on the road."[36]

[5] The instructions of Christ just quoted are mentioned by St. Thomas in Question 108, Article 2, which is not included in this *Commentary*. In that Article, the third Objector takes these instructions to be New Law ceremonial precepts, analogous to the Old Law's rules about priests. St. Thomas replies that this is not the case. As he explains, however, they can be plausibly viewed in two other ways. The first way is that they were *temporary* precepts, commands not for all time but only for that time, a time when the disciples had not yet attained spiritual maturity:

For the disciples, being yet as little children under Christ's care, needed to receive some special commands from Christ, such as all subjects receive from their superiors: and

---

[35] Matthew 10:7–10 (RSV-CE).

[36] Luke 10:1–4 (RSV-CE).

especially so, since they were to be accustomed little by little to renounce the care of temporalities, so as to become fitted for the preaching of the Gospel throughout the whole world. Nor must we wonder if He established certain fixed modes of life, as long as the state of the Old Law endured and the people had not as yet achieved the perfect liberty of the Spirit.

These statutes He abolished shortly before His Passion, as though the disciples had by their means become sufficiently practiced. Hence He said (Luke 22:35–36) "When I sent you without purse and scrip and shoes, did you want anything? But they said: Nothing. Then said He unto them: But now, he that hath a purse, let him take it, and likewise a scrip." Because the time of perfect liberty was already at hand, when they would be left entirely to their own judgment in matters not necessarily connected with virtue.[37]

So by this first interpretation, yes, the disciples were commanded rather than counseled not to depend on their own property during their journeys. But this command did not concern the life of perfection, and it did not even approach the evangelical counsel of poverty. It was merely a temporary disciplinary measure, meant to *prepare* them for the later time when the evangelical counsels could be offered to them.

[6] The second plausible way in which the instructions can be viewed is as *concessions*, that is, permissions. From this point of view, the reason the Twelve and the Seventy were told that they need not take money on their missionary trips was that they were *permitted* to accept material support from those to whom they preached. It is not, then, that they were not *allowed* to provide their own support, but that they were not *required* to provide it. As St. Thomas puts it,

> For He permitted them to set forth to preach without scrip or stick, and so on, since they were empowered to accept their livelihood from those to whom they preached: wherefore He goes on to say: "For the laborer is worthy of his hire." Nor is it a sin, but a work of supererogation for a preacher to take means of livelihood with him, without accepting supplies from those to whom he preaches; as Paul did.[38]

St. Thomas points out that this second interpretation of the instructions had been offered by St. Augustine in his *Harmony of the Gospels*. Augustine expounds,

> [In both cases, therefore these][39] must be accepted as having been spoken by the Lord to the apostles; namely, at once that they should not take a staff, and that they should take

---

[37] I-II, Q. 108, Art. 2, ad 3.
[38] Ibid. The reference to St. Paul alludes to the fact that the Apostle supported himself during his own missionary trips by plying the tentmaking trade. "Do we not have the right to our food and drink?" Paul asked the Corinthians. "Nevertheless, we have not made use of this right, but we endure anything rather than put an obstacle in the way of the gospel of Christ." 1 Corinthians 9:4, 12b (RSV-CE).
[39] The translator has here "both these counsels," but the Latin, *utrumque ergo accipiendum*, does not refer to "counsels" (*consilia*), and the interpolation of this word is highly misleading since the instructions were *not* counsels.

nothing save a staff only. For when He said to them, according to Matthew, "Provide neither gold nor silver, nor money in your purses, nor scrip for your journey, neither two coats, neither shoes, nor yet a staff," He added immediately, "for the workman is worthy of his meat." And by this He makes it sufficiently obvious why it is that He would have them provide and carry none of these things. He shows that His reason was, not that these things are not necessary for the sustenance of this life, but because He was sending them in such a manner as to declare plainly that these things were due to them by those very persons who were to hear believingly the gospel preached by them; just as wages are the soldier's due, and as the fruit of the vine is the right of the planters, and the milk of the flock the right of the shepherds. For which reason Paul also speaks in this wise: "Who goes a warfare any time at his own charges? Who plants a vineyard, and eats not of the fruit thereof? Who feeds a flock, and eats not of the milk of the flock?" For under these figures he was speaking of those things which are necessary to the preachers of the gospel. And so, a little further on, he says: "If we have sown unto you spiritual things, is it a great thing if we shall reap your carnal things? If others are partakers of this power over you, are not we rather? Nevertheless we have not used this power." This makes it apparent that by these instructions the Lord did not mean that the evangelists should not seek their support in any other way than by depending on what was offered them by those to whom they preached the gospel (otherwise this very apostle acted contrary to this precept when he acquired a livelihood for himself by the labours of his own hands, because he would not be chargeable to any of them), but that He gave them a power in the exercise of which they should know such things to be their due. Now, when any commandment is given by the Lord, there is the guilt of non-obedience if it is not observed; but when any power is given, any one is at liberty to abstain from its use, and, as it were, to recede from his right. Accordingly, when the Lord spoke these things to the disciples, He did what that apostle expounds more clearly a little further on, when he says, "Do you not know that they who minister in the temple live of the things of the temple? And they which wait at the altar are partakers with the altar? Even so has the Lord ordained, that they which preach the gospel should live of the gospel. But I have used none of these things." When he says, therefore, that the Lord ordained it thus, but that he did not use the ordinance, he certainly indicates that it was a power to use that was given him, and not a necessity of service that was imposed upon him.[40]

[7] The Objector had complained that the New Law improperly addresses many aspects of the life of perfection by giving commands: not only the commands given to everyone about the love of enemies but also the commands given to the disciples before they were sent out to preach. We now see that he was mistaken.

For in the first place, although it is true that the exhortations to love enemies are commands, they are not *improperly* framed as commands rather than as counsels, because they express *necessities* of the life of grace rather than aspects of perfection. And in the second place, the instructions given by Christ to the disciples do not command the life of perfection either. Either they are

---

[40] St. Augustine of Hippo, *The Harmony of the Gospels*, book II, chapter 30, section 73, www.newadvent.org/fathers/1602.htm.

Did the New Law Really Need both Precepts and Counsels?

temporary disciplines just for the duration of the preaching trip, weaning them away from dependence on material goods just so that some day they *will* be able to consider such aspects of the perfect life as perpetual poverty – or else they are *not even* temporary disciplines but only permissions, allowing the disciples to accept material assistance from those to whom they preach, as any workman deserves his hire, so that they can preach without the distraction of wondering where their next meal is coming from. Of course these two interpretations cannot both be true, and St. Thomas does not offer any judgment about which of them is correct. But he does not need to, because neither interpretation would justify the Objector's complaint.

DISCUSSION

Does the Recommendation of Perpetual Virginity Imply that Marriage Is Bad?

The evangelical counsel of perpetual virginity is easy to misunderstand, for Christian theology has always been sensitive to the spiritual possibilities of marriage.[41] Marriage is good – it is very good. It is only that celibacy is better! From time to time throughout history, some misguided persons have taken a different view and tried to forbid marriage altogether. However, Holy Scripture condemns this attitude,[42] and Thomas Aquinas will have none of it. Marriage is a procreative partnership; the rock from which it rises is the hope of children and the willingness of the husband and wife to cherish and rear them. Considering this fact, it is most interesting that of the three aspects of the union of husband and wife – their joining in one flesh, their sharing in life, and their love – St. Thomas lists the "devotion of their love" first.[43]

But what exactly does the Angelic Doctor teach about this devotion? Much of what he thinks about the love of the husband and wife emerges not from his discussion of marriage itself but from his discussion of other kinds of love, especially the love of God and the love of friends. Needless to say, each of these loves has its own characteristics. However, whenever St. Thomas speaks of love in general, what he says is necessarily true of each particular love, including the marital kind.

---

[41] The following few paragraphs are adapted from my chapter "Thomas Aquinas on Marriage, Fruitfulness, and Faithful Love," in *Humanae Vitae 50 Years Later, Embracing God's Vision of Marriage, Love, and Life: A Compendium*, edited by Theresa Notare (Washington, DC: Catholic University of America Press, 2019).

[42] See 1 Timothy 4:1-5.

[43] Thomas Aquinas, *Commentary on St. Paul's Letter to the Ephesians*, translated by Matthew D. Lamb (Albany, NY: Magi Books, 1966), chapter 5, lecture 10 (referring to Ephesians 5:31-33 and Genesis 2:24).

We often say we love something when we mean only that we desire it. Considered closely, however, love is far more than desire. St. Thomas distinguishes a number of its features:

- The lover *wills the good* of the beloved.
- He wills it *as his own* good.[44]
- He wills it as his own good because it is the good of someone with whom he is *united*.
- He seeks the *perfection*, or complete development, of this union.
- The more closely he approaches union, and the more perfect his union becomes once attained, the more *intense* his love becomes.[45]

"Indeed," St. Thomas writes, "a person is loved in himself when the lover wishes the good for him, even if the lover may receive nothing from him."[46]

But there are different kinds of union. One is the kind of union that *causes* love. For example, because the lover is already one with himself, he loves himself. The second is the kind that is the *same thing* as love. For example, because the lover has a bond of affection with the beloved, he comes to have the same love for her that he has for himself. But finally, there is the kind that is *caused by* love. For example, the bond of affection induces the lover and beloved to seek the real union of matrimony. After getting married they live together, speak together, share the life of their household, share each other's bodies, and work together in bringing up their children.[47]

Feelings, by themselves, are not love. Certainly, however, strong feelings result from love. Which are these? St. Thomas writes that "in the hearts of those who love there are four feelings that usually arise from the good works which the lovers accomplish," four emotions that normally result from the lovers' freely willed partnership in a good life:

- The lovers experience *confidence* that what has begun well will get better.
- They experience *glory* because each one enjoys the splendor of the other's good.
- They are *consoled* because through delight in the good they share, each one possesses a remedy against sadness.
- They experience *exuberant joy* because not only is sadness absorbed, but their elation "overcomes every tribulation."[48]

---

[44] I-II, Q. 28, Art. 1.
[45] Thomas Aquinas, *Summa Contra Gentiles*, I, chapter 91.
[46] Thomas Aquinas, *Summa Contra Gentiles*, translated by Vernon Bourke (Notre Dame, IN: University of Notre Dame, 1975), III, chapter 153.
[47] I-II, Q. 28, Art. 1, ad 2.
[48] Thomas Aquinas, *Commentary on St. Paul's Second Letter to the Corinthians*, trans. Larcher, chapter 7, lecture 1 (referring to 2 Corinthians 7:4).

It is quite amazing how far St. Thomas is willing to go in describing the quality of loving union. He says, for example, that the lover and the beloved mutually indwell each other. "The beloved is contained in the lover, by being impressed on his heart" and becoming the object of his affections; the lover, in turn, "is contained in the beloved, inasmuch as the lover penetrates, so to speak, into the beloved."[49]

The power of will in general, he explains, is directed to the good. Love is a spontaneous act of the will, directed more particularly to the good of the beloved. But, since to will is itself a good, man can will himself to will. For this reason, love, by its own nature, "is capable of reflecting on itself." "Wherefore," says the Angelic Doctor, "from the moment a man loves, he loves himself to love."[50] This does not mean that he is infatuated with his feelings. It means that with all his heart, he concurs with the direction of his will. His attitude toward the beloved might be expressed, "I delight that you exist in this world, I seek all good for you, and I know it is good that I do."[51]

The Evangelical Counsels as the Foundation of the Consecrated Religious Life

We saw earlier that according to St. Thomas, every form of consecrated religious life is built upon the foundation of the evangelical counsels. He explains this idea in his *Defense of the Religious Orders against Their Opponents*, which is worth quoting at some length:[52]

Religion then bears a twofold meaning. Its first signification is that *re-binding*,[53] which the word implies, whereby a man unites himself to God, by faith and fitting worship. Every Christian, at his Baptism, when he renounces Satan and all his pomps, is made partaker of the true religion. The second meaning of religion is the obligation whereby a man binds himself to serve God in a peculiar manner, by specified works of charity, and by renunciation of the world. It is in this sense that we intend to use the word religion at present. By charity, fitting homage is rendered to God. This homage may be paid to Him by the exercise of either the active or the contemplative life. Homage is

---

[49] I-II, Q. 28, Art. 2, ad 1.
[50] I-II, Q. 25, Art. 2.
[51] The Thomist, Josef Pieper, remarks that charity wants to say "It is good that you exist" and "I *want* you to exist!" Josef Pieper, trans. Richard and Clara Winston, *About Love* (Chicago: Franciscan Herald Press, 1974), quoted in *Josef Pieper: An Anthology* (San Francisco: Ignatius Press, 1989), pp. 28–29, emphasis added.
[52] Thomas Aquinas, *Contra impugnantes Dei cultum et religionem*, translated by John Procter, OP (public domain), part 1, "What Is Meant by Religion? What Does its Perfection Consist In?"
[53] St. Thomas means that the word comes from *re*, back or again, plus *ligo*, binding or tying. This etymology is contested.

paid to Him by the various duties of the active life, whereby works of charity are performed towards our neighbor. Therefore, some religious orders, such as the monastic and hermetical, are instituted for the worship of God by contemplation. Others have been established to serve God in His members, by action. Such are the Orders wherein the brethren devote themselves to assisting the sick, redeeming captives, and to similar works of mercy. There is no work of mercy for the performance of which a religious order may not be instituted; even though one be not as yet established for that specific purpose.

As by Baptism man is re-united to God by the religion of faith, and dies to sin; so, by the vows of the religious life, he dies, not only to sin, but also to the world, in order to live solely for God in that work in which he has dedicated himself to the Divine service. As the life of the soul is destroyed by sin; so likewise the service of Christ is hindered by worldly occupations. For, as St. Paul says, "No man being a soldier to God, entangles himself with secular businesses."[54] It is on this account, that, by the vows of religion, sacrifice is made of all those things in which the heart of man is wont to be especially absorbed, and which are, consequently, his chief obstacles in the service of God.

That which, first and chiefly, engrosses man is marriage. Hence St. Paul writes, "I would have you to be without solicitude. He who is without a wife is solicitous for the things that belong to the Lord, how he may please God. But he who is with a wife, is solicitous for the things of the world, how he may please his wife; and he is divided."[55]

The second thing that fills man's heart is the possession of earthly riches. "The care of this world and the deceitfulness of riches chokes the word, and he becomes fruitless."[56] Hence the Gloss, commenting on the words of Luke, "But that which fell among thorns,"[57] etc., says, "Riches, although men seem to take pleasure in them, become as thorns to their possessors. They pierce the hearts of such as covetously desire, and avariciously hoard them."

The third thing on which man is inclined to center his heart, is his own will. He who is his own master has the care of directing his life. Therefore, we are counselled to commit the disposal of ourselves to Divine Providence, "casting all your care upon Him, for He has care of you."[58] "Have confidence in the Lord with all your heart, and lean not upon your own prudence."[59]

Hence perfect religion is consecrated to God by a threefold vow: By the vow of [virginal] chastity whereby marriage is renounced, by the vow of poverty, whereby riches are sacrificed, and by the vow of obedience, whereby self-will is immolated. By these three vows man offers to God the sacrifice of all that he possesses. By the vow of [virginal] chastity, he offers his body, according, to the words of St. Paul, "Present your bodies a living sacrifice."[60] By the vow of poverty, he makes an offering to God of

---

[54] 2 Timothy 2:4.
[55] 1 Corinthians 7:23.
[56] Matthew 13:22.
[57] Luke 8:14.
[58] 1 Peter 5:7.
[59] Proverbs 3:5.
[60] Romans 12:1.

all his external possessions, as did St. Paul, who says, "that the oblation of my service may be acceptable in Jerusalem to the Saints."[61] By the vow of obedience, he offers to God that sacrifice of the spirit of which David says, "the sacrifice to God is an afflicted spirit" etc.[62]

---

[61] Romans 15:31.
[62] Psalms 1:19.

Afterword

Implications of St. Thomas's Teaching for the World of the Present

If St. Thomas is right, then the relation between natural law, Divine law, sin, and grace has several clear consequences.

In principle, the human power of reason is quite adequate to work out the moral requirements for robust flourishing in the present life. For this reason, natural law provides a point of contact among all men. By its light, even nations that have never heard of Divine law may be able to achieve more or less decent rules of conduct and systems of civil law.

Yet apart from grace, in this fallen state we fall far short of admitting what in principle we are capable of knowing, and doing what in principle we are capable of doing. Our minds resist the natural law – resist, so to speak, their own natures – because it reminds us that we did not create ourselves and are not complete in ourselves. We resent God for being God. We want to be gods ourselves. Consequently, from earliest times the ability of our minds to command our emotions and desires has also been impaired, and our insistence on having no masters but ourselves is the very thing that keeps us from self-mastery. We deceive ourselves about our moral duties, employing our intellects to make excuses for our misdeeds, not because the wrong of them is obscure, but because we want it to be obscure. To be sure, conscience troubles us even then. Yet if we are unwilling to repent, the voice of conscience merely supplies us with a motive to put our fingers in our ears.

Consequently, natural law is not enough. We need Divine law to mend and correct us. And Divine law itself will not suffice without transforming grace, which by giving us back to God, gives us back ourselves – restoring us to peace not only with Him but with our healed natures.

Unfortunately, such is our rebellion against God that the very offer of this healing grace may appear to us an insult. This is why St. Paul remarks that although the grace of Christ is a fragrance from life to life among those who are

Afterword: Implications

receiving it, it is a fragrance from death to death among those who are perishing.[1]

These facts raise interesting questions about conversations with our neighbors in the public square.

Can natural law be invoked in such conversations? Yes, but it will often be resisted. If one wishes to have a reasonable conversation at all, then there is no alternative but to appeal to natural reason; yet the very appeal to natural reason unleashes a variety of irrational resentments.

Can natural law be invoked in such conversations without a willingness to discuss Divine law too? Probably not very effectively, because among the irrational sources of our resentment against natural law is that we lack the grace to obey it, and this resentment militates against Divine law as well.

Can resentment against natural and Divine law be removed, then, by invoking the Gospel's offer of redeeming grace? In the long run, among those who acknowledge their yearning for God, yes. But among those who resist their yearning for God, no, because the appeal to grace itself unleashes irrational resentments. We resist the natural law in part because we cannot obey it; but if we do not desire to obey it, then accepting the offer of Divine assistance may seem like ignominious surrender to a foe.

Not without reason, then, did St. Thomas follow his discussions of eternal, natural, human, and Divine law with his *Treatise on Grace*. For it is not enough to offer rational arguments to a mutinous world, expecting these arguments to be heard just because they are rational (the very thing careless readers think he is doing). A delicate diplomacy is needed, not only with the mind but also with the heart. More than that, the envoy must abandon himself to the Father of Lights, without whom all peacemaking fails, praying in love not only for the illumination of his readers but for his own. So, I believe, did Thomas Aquinas. So too must we.

---

[1] 2 Corintians 2:14–16 (RSV-CE).

Index of Scriptural References

Genesis 1:26–27, 170
Genesis 1:31, 404
Genesis 2:9, 289
Genesis 2:16–17, 289
Genesis 2:23–24, 127, 451
Genesis 15:6, 274
Genesis 17:10–12, 65
Genesis 18:23–25, 173
Genesis 22:16, 139
Genesis 27:29, 377

Exodus 3:16–17, 28
Exodus 3:21–22, 188
Exodus 6:6, 23
Exodus 6:23, 322
Exodus 12:13, 376
Exodus 12:48–49, 376
Exodus 17:8–16, 372
Exodus 18:17–24, 321–322
Exodus 19:10–13, 262
Exodus 20:2, 19
Exodus 20:3–17, *see* Decalogue in the Index of Persons and Topics
Exodus 20:13–14, 32
Exodus 20:18–21, 416
Exodus 21:12–25, 33, 242, 384
Exodus 21:28–29, 338
Exodus 22:1–2, 76, 337
Exodus 22:10–11, 337
Exodus 22:14–15, 337
Exodus 22:21, 362
Exodus 22:25–27, 254
Exodus 23, entire, 316

Exodus 23:1–2, 254
Exodus 23:6–9, 255, 317, 342, 362
Exodus 24:1, 322
Exodus 25:16–26, 130
Exodus 28, entire, 299
Exodus 32, entire, xliii, 83
Exodus 33:3–5, xliii
Exodus 34:9, xliii *see also* Book of the Covenant (Exodus 20:22-23:33) in the Index of Persons and Topics

Leviticus in general, 25, 51
Leviticus 15:38–39, 304–305
Leviticus 16, entire, 242
Leviticus 17:11, 306
Leviticus 18:1–5, 76, 77, 267, 280
Leviticus 18:6–18, 242
Leviticus 18:21–25, 77, 253
Leviticus 18:30, 77
Leviticus 19:2, 51
Leviticus 19:9–10, 242
Leviticus 19:13, 337
Leviticus 19:15–19, xxiv, 31, 32, 213, 240, 255, 299, 342, 349, 384
Leviticus 19:32, 251
Leviticus 19:34, xxiv
Leviticus 20:15–16, 338
Leviticus 22:9–11, 299
Leviticus 23:22, 242
Leviticus 23:26–32, 242
Leviticus 24:15–16, 251
Leviticus 25:2–7, 350
Leviticus 25:25–28, 337

459

Leviticus 25:35–37, 254
Leviticus 26, entire, 98 *see also* Holiness Code (Leviticus 17–26) in the Index of Persons and Topics

Deuteronomy in general, 280
Deuteronomy 1:13–15, 313, 322
Deuteronomy 1:16–17, 342
Deuteronomy 2:1–7, 413
Deuteronomy 4:5–8, xli, 54, 161, 173, 298
Deuteronomy 4:11–14, 121
Deuteronomy 5:1, 76
Deuteronomy 5:6–21, *see* Decalogue in the Index of Persons and Topics
Deuteronomy 6:1, 69, 76
Deuteronomy 6:4–12, xxiii, 31, 213, 267
Deuteronomy 7:6–9, 158, 172, 323
Deuteronomy 9:1–6, xliii, 174, 386
Deuteronomy 10:1–4, 133
Deuteronomy 10:12–13, 83
Deuteronomy 11:1, xxiii
Deuteronomy 11:13–21, xxiii, 422
Deuteronomy 13:1–5, 251, 261
Deuteronomy 14:23–26, 259
Deuteronomy 14:28–29, 351
Deuteronomy 15:1–15, 337
Deuteronomy 16:18–20, 198, 342–343
Deuteronomy 17:1–11, 337, 412
Deuteronomy 17:14–19, 313–314, 323–324, 337
Deuteronomy 18:9–12, 250
Deuteronomy 19:1–13, 242
Deuteronomy 19:15–21, 120, 337
Deuteronomy 20:1–8, 259, 365–367, 374
Deuteronomy 20:10–14, 374
Deuteronomy 20:16–20, 365–386
Deuteronomy 21:1–9, 338
Deuteronomy 21:18–21, 259, 337
Deuteronomy 22:1–4, 349
Deuteronomy 22:28–30, 242, 261
Deuteronomy 23:1–4, 362
Deuteronomy 23:7–8, 361
Deuteronomy 23:17–20, 253, 363
Deuteronomy 23:24–25, 11, 336, 349
Deuteronomy 24:1–4, xlv, 33
Deuteronomy 24:10–13, 337
Deuteronomy 24:19–22, 242, 349
Deuteronomy 25:13–16, 254
Deuteronomy 27:19–23, 226
Deuteronomy 27:26, 280
Deuteronomy 28–30 as a unit, 98
Deuteronomy 30:6, 65, 100
Deuteronomy 30:15–20, 27, 46, 80, 105

Deuteronomy 32:16–17, 168 *see also* Book of the Law (Deuteronomy 12–26) in the Index of Persons and Topics

Numbers 11:16–17, 312, 322
Numbers 14:17–19, 172
Numbers 15:32–36, 337
Numbers 22–24 as a unit, 360
Numbers 22:6, 360
Numbers 23:11–20, 361
Numbers 23:25, 361
Numbers 24:5–9, 318
Numbers 25:1–8, 366
Numbers 27:8–11, 336, 347
Numbers 27:15–20, 324
Numbers 29:7–11, 242
Numbers 33:53–54, 346
Numbers 35:1–8, 346
Numbers 35:9–34, 242
Numbers 36:2–3, 348

Joshua 22:5, xxiii
Joshua 22:31, 23
Joshua 23:11–12, xxiii

Judges 3:9–15, 324
Judges 11:2, 382
Judges 4–5 as a unit, 380

Ruth, entire, 378–379

1 Samuel 16:1–7, 205–207
1 Samuel 8, entire, 317–318, 324–325, 329, 331, 334–335

2 Samuel 11:2–12:23, 327–328
2 Samuel 12:1–23, 329
2 Samuel 22:3, 23

1 Kings 2:12–21, 380
1 Kings 11:31–33, 315–316

2 Kings 14:27, 23

2 Chronicles 30:8, xliii
2 Chronicles 36:14–21, xliii, 350

Ezra as a unit, 309

Judith 14, entire, 378

Job 31:29–30, 431

Index of Scriptural References

Psalm 4:7 (DRA 4:6), 292, 396
Psalm 7:8-10 (DRA 7:9-11), 207
Psalm 8:3-4 (DRA 8:3-4), 308
Psalm 18:3 (DRA 17:4), 23
Psalm 18:8-12 (DRA (17:7-11), 243
Psalm 19, entire (DRA 18, entire), 16, 175, 292
Psalm 31:23 (DRA 30:24), xxiii
Psalm 34:8 (DRA 33:9), xxxvi, 35
Psalm 37:4 (DRA 36:4), 130
Psalm 37:39 (DRA 36:39), 23
Psalm 44:11 (DRA 43:11), 414
Psalm 47:8-10 (DRA 46:8-10), 22–23
Psalm 49:16-19 (DRA 48:17-19), 94
Psalm 51, entire (DRA 50), 23, 328
Psalm 68:20 (DRA 67:21), 23
Psalm 69:5 (DRA 68:5), 302
Psalm 82:1-8 (DRA 81:1-8), 342
Psalm 93:14-15 (DRA 93:14-15), 67–68
Psalm 100, entire (DRA 99, entire), 201, 304
Psalm 104:14-15 (DRA 103:14-15), 259
Psalm 119, entire (DRA 118, entire), 6, 46, 66, 297
Psalm 130, entire (DRA 129, entire), 156
Psalm 137 (DRA 136), 432
Psalm 139:1-6 (DRA 138:1-6), 207
Psalm 147:12-20 (DRA 146:1-11), 338

Proverbs 1:7, 328
Proverbs 2:16, 23
Proverbs 3:1-5, 158–159, 422, 454
Proverbs 3:12, 392
Proverbs 6:6, 8, 308
Proverbs 7:1-4, 159
Proverbs 8, entire, 295, 368
Proverbs 11:14, 433
Proverbs 15:22, 433
Proverbs 17:3, 207
Proverbs 19:16, 267
Proverbs 19:25, 328
Proverbs 20:1, 260
Proverbs 23:10-22, 260
Proverbs 27:5-6, 434
Proverbs 27:9, 433
Proverbs 28:16, 326

Ecclesiastes 9:1-2, 86

Wisdom of Solomon 7:24-28, 398
Wisdom of Solomon 8:1, 295
Wisdom of Solomon 11:20-21, 159
Wisdom of Solomon 12:3-10, 391

Sirach (Ecclesiasticus) 13:15-20 (DRA 13:19-24), 50, 364
Sirach (Ecclesiasticus) 15:14, 4–5
Sirach (Ecclesiasticus) 17:8-11 (DRA 17:7-9), 48–49, 103
Sirach (Ecclesiasticus) 19:26-27, 303
Sirach (Ecclesiasticus) 31:29-30, 260

Isaiah 1, entire, 54, 87, 99
Isaiah 11:2-3, 140
Isaiah 24:5-6, 181, 288
Isaiah 29:13-14, 97
Isaiah 42:6, 376
Isaiah 44:13-20, 168
Isaiah 45:8, 23
Isaiah 49:5-6, 377
Isaiah 51:3, 61
Isaiah 52:7, 38, 410
Isaiah 52:10, 376
Isaiah 53:1, 410
Isaiah 56:1-8, 383
Isaiah 58:13-14, 138
Isaiah 60:2-3, 376

Jeremiah 12:10, 314
Jeremiah 17:1, 422
Jeremiah 17:9-10, 207, 403
Jeremiah 25:11, 350
Jeremiah 29:10, 350–351
Jeremiah 30:10, 23
Jeremiah 30:21, 314
Jeremiah 31:31-34, 6, 398, 422
Jeremiah 33:19-22, 175

Ezekiel 11:17-20, 422
Ezekiel 20:11-21, 267
Ezekiel 34:24, 314
Ezekiel 36:22-37, 422

Hosea 1-3 as a unit, 187, 189–190, 194–196
Hosea 6:6, 191
Hosea 8:4, 328–329
Hosea 13:11, 328–329

Amos 1, entire, 174
Amos 5:21-24, 96

Obadiah 1:5, 114

Habakkuk 1:4-5, 392
Habakkuk 2:4, 280, 414

Zechariah 2:8, 377
Zechariah 12:9, 377

1 Maccabees 2:41, 180

2 Maccabees 3:14-15, 337

Matthew 1:5, 379
Matthew 4:17-19, 27-28, 448
Matthew 5:8, 28
Matthew 5:21-24, 13, 32, 210, 252
Matthew 5:27-28, 32
Matthew 5:31-32, xlv, 33
Matthew 5:38-41, 384
Matthew 5:43-48, 32, 86, 431-432, 441, 446-447
Matthew 6:24-34, 92, 232
Matthew 7:1-5, 215
Matthew 7:12, xxiv
Matthew 8:21-22, 446
Matthew 9:9, 446
Matthew 10:7-11, 431-432, 446, 448
Matthew 12:1-8, 191, 349
Matthew 12:25-26, 315
Matthew 12:36-37, 409
Matthew 13:22-43, 15, 454
Matthew 15:7-9, 97
Matthew 16:24-25, 100
Matthew 19:1-12, xlv, 127, 194, 220, 444
Matthew 19:16-30, 220, 427, 444, 446
Matthew 22:13, 84
Matthew 22:34-40, xxiv, 213, 384
Matthew 23:23-24, 29
Matthew 24:43, 114
Matthew 25:29, 84

Mark 4:28, 113
Mark 12:28-31, xxiv, 384

Luke 6:27-38, xxiv, 432, 446-447
Luke 8:14, 454
Luke 9-10 as a unit, 432, 446-447
Luke 9:59-60, 446
Luke 10:1-4, 448
Luke 10:25-37, xxiv, 267, 384
Luke 12:16-31, 437
Luke 14:26, 404
Luke 17:3-4, 442
Luke 22:35-36, 449

John 1:43, 446
John 5:39-40, 91

John 7:25, 215
John 8:12-18, 353, 377
John 8:31-36, 131, 435
John 13:34, 30
John 14:12-17, 404
John 15:12-15, 418, 434
John 20:30-31, 395
John 21, entire, 61, 446

Acts 2:1-4, 416
Acts 4:12, 32
Acts 5:27-29, 124
Acts 10, entire, 288, 359
Acts 13:16-26, 371
Acts 13:42, 409
Acts 13:47, 377
Acts 17:23, xli
Acts 26:22-23, 377

Romans 1:14-17, 414
Romans 1:20, 110
Romans 2:2, 328
Romans 2:11-16, 106, 116, 247, 266, 396, 409, 422
Romans 2:25-29, 47, 65
Romans 3:8, 217
Romans 3:20, 288
Romans 3:27, 400
Romans 4:1-3, 274
Romans 4:15-16, 412
Romans 5:1, 409
Romans 5:5, 31, 157, 416
Romans 5:7-8, xliii, 434
Romans 7:7-14, 45, 73, 156, 269, 288
Romans 8:2, 401
Romans 8:7, 416
Romans 8:20, 140
Romans 8:24-25, 409
Romans 8:28-39, 100, 414
Romans 10:14-16, 38, 410
Romans 11, entire, 379
Romans 12:1, 455
Romans 13:1-2, 179, 295
Romans 13:8-10, xxiv, 416
Romans 14:10-12, 408
Romans 15:31, 455

1 Corinthians 1:21-24, 425
1 Corinthians 6:11, 409
1 Corinthians 7:5-6, 441
1 Corinthians 7:21-23, 222, 454
1 Corinthians 7:32-35, 445

Index of Scriptural References

1 Corinthians 9:4-12, 449
1 Corinthians 10, entire, 221, 272, 424
1 Corinthians 13, entire, 7, 287, 220, 419
1 Corinthians 15:19, 34

2 Corinthians 2:6-10, 179
2 Corinthians 2:17-3:6, 269
2 Corinthians 3:1-9, 46, 116, 417, 421, 423
2 Corinthians 5:10, 408
2 Corinthians 6:1, 409
2 Corinthians 7:4, 452
2 Corinthians 8:3, 366

Galatians 2:20, 33
Galatians 3:2, 288
Galatians 3:10-12, 279
Galatians 3:19, 423
Galatians 3:21-26, 26, 91, 156, 421, 435
Galatians 5:1-6, 47, 92, 104-105, 282, 409, 435
Galatians 5:14, xxiv
Galatians 6:10, 441

Ephesians 2:14-15, 286
Ephesians 5:28-29, 127
Ephesians 5:31-33, 451

Philippians 3:8-9, 92, 404
Philippians 3:13-15, 92
Philippians 3:20, 379
Philippians 4:11-12, 325

Colossians 3:23-24, 222
Colossians 3:55, 167

1 Thessalonians 5:21, xxxvi, 35, 192

1 Timothy 1:3-5, 118, 230
1 Timothy 1:8-11, 45
1 Timothy 2:4, 23
1 Timothy 3, entire, 320
1 Timothy 4:1-5, 451
1 Timothy 5:14, 321
1 Timothy 6:10, 84

2 Timothy 2:4, 454
2 Timothy 2:11-13, 185

Hebrews 4:6-15, 411, 434
Hebrews 5:1, 316-317
Hebrews 5:7-9, 410
Hebrews 6:13-16, 139
Hebrews 7:12, 24
Hebrews 8:8-13, 398, 422
Hebrews 10:29-31, 413
Hebrews 11:1, 28
Hebrews 11:13-16, 379
Hebrews 12:5-13, 48, 328, 392

James 1:8-12, 435
James 1:25, 435
James 2:8, xxiv
James 2:19-20, 410
James 5:20, 23

1 Peter 1:15-16, 51
1 Peter 2:9-11, 379
1 Peter 2:13-17, 123, 435
1 Peter 4:12-13, 100
1 Peter 5:7, 454

2 Peter 1:3-4, 100

1 John 2:15-17, 438
1 John 3:1, 434
1 John 4:1, 192
1 John 4:18, 82

Apocalypse of John (Revelation of John) 1:4, 140
Apocalypse of John (Revelation of John) 3:1, 140
Apocalypse of John (Revelation of John) 3:19, 328, 392
Apocalypse of John (Revelation of John) 4:5, 140
Apocalypse of John (Revelation of John) 4:11, 155
Apocalypse of John (Revelation of John) 5:6, 140
Apocalypse of John (Revelation of John) 6:9-11, 86
Apocalypse of John (Revelation of John) 9:20-21, 168
Apocalypse of John (Revelation of John) 21:22, 61

Index of Persons and Topics

Aaron, *see* Moses
abortion, 194, 247
Abraham
    and Melchizedek, 30
    covenants with God, 99, 139, 361, 386
    justified by faith, 274–275, 414
    protests to God, 173
    tested by God, 96, 192
Alexander of Hales, 61
Alighieri, Dante, xxix, 135
Amalekites, 369, 372–373, 375–376
Ambrose of Milan, Saint, 116, 129, 288–289, 291, 314
Ambrosiaster (Pseudo-Ambrosius), 288
angelism, 437
Anonymous Christian so-called, 36
Antiochus Epiphanes, 180
Aristotle
    had no knowledge of Divine law, 84
    infused virtue unknown to, 62, 214
    on authoritative elements, 399–400
    on causes, 292
    on charging interest, 363
    on children in relation to parents, 142, 144
    on citizenship, 369, 371–372, 380–382
    on constitutions, 312, 318–320, 333
    on direction to the end, 293–297
    on friendship, 127
    on general and particular justice, 276–278
    on impossibility of repayment, 162, 164, 169
    on perversion of the best, 320
    on pleasure in deeds, 213
    on property ownership, 337, 344–347, 349, 354
    on punishments, 82, 169, 205–206
    on rule among bees, 314
    on syllogisms, 89
    on the principle of a genus, 160
    on unexpected death, 387–388
    on variation in nature, 176–177
    on virtue, 52, 62–63, 84, 198–200, 203–204, 208, 325
    on voluntariness, 202–203
Augustine of Hippo, Saint
    on Atonement, 25
    on Creation, 137
    on definition of commonwealth, 338, 340, 355–356
    on evangelical counsels, 449
    on final judgment, 68
    on First Tablet, 129–131
    on first temptation, 287, 289–290, 301–302
    on four kinds of things to be loved, 132
    on four things to be considered in sacrifice, 309
    on heresy of Pelagius, 222
    on justification, 282
    on love and fear, 30, 81–84, 93, 156–157
    on lying, 193–194
    on measure, number, and weight, 160
    on murder, 186–187
    on punishment of evil, 14–15
    on spirit and letter of law, 57, 268–269, 401–404, 417–420, 422, 425

Augustine of Hippo, Saint (cont.)
  on symbolic precepts, 58, 64–65, 75, 270, 272, 353
  on temporal promises and threats, 27, 81
  on vice imitating virtue, 356–358
  on war and peace, 187, 333
Austin, John, 153
authority
  argument from, 161, 309
  Divine, xxxiv, 4, 12, 20, 54, 67, 78–79, 179, 188–190, 315, 317
  human, 12–14, 179, 180, 190, 429
  of family, 32
  two senses of, 243–244, 256, 260, 320

Balaam, 318, 360–361, 377
bastards, *see* children, illegitimate
Bastiat, Frédéric, 128
Bathsheba, 327–329, 380
beatitude, *see* happiness
Bellah, Robert N., 33
Benedict XVI, Pope Emeritus, 36
Berger, Peter, xxxiv
biases, of our own time, xxxviii, xlvi, 404
blessings and curses
  commemorated and foreshadowed, 135–138, 171
  cursing God, 96, 250
  generational, 172–173
  in the Law, 80–101, 105
  pronounced by Balaam, 318, 377
  pronounced by Isaac, 377
  see also punishment
Boethius, Anicius Manlius Severinus, 309
Book of the Covenant (Exodus 20:22–23:33), 370–371; *see also* Index of Scriptural References
Book of the Law (Deuteronomy 12–26), 370–371; *see also* Index of Scriptural References
bribes, *see* precepts about particular things

Caelestius, 222
Caesar, Julius, 246
Cassiodorus Senator, Flavius Magnus Aurelius, 66
cause or causes
  Aristotle's doctrine of, 292
  as explanations, 16, 292
  final, of Divine law, 16
  First, simply, xxxix
  First, of salvation, 409
  for change in human law, 80
  of justice, justification as, 272
  of love, 452
  of virtue, 281
  secondary, 163
chance or fortune, 95, 194–195, 293, 325, 388
charity or love
  and duty, 126
  as an infused virtue, 62, 200, 218–219, 238, 273
  as the purpose of the Commandments, 118
  characteristics of, xli, 82, 218
  covetousness the bane of, 81, 84, 93
  degrees of perfection in, 233–234
  destruction of, 16, 224–225, 235
  faith working through, 47, 92, 104–105
  for God's sake, meaning of, xli, 167, 214, 219, 221, 236
  four things to be loved, 132
  in relation to the New Law, 30, 32, 113, 157
  in relation to fear, 81–83
  in relation to merit, 211, 218, 220
  law of, 157
  not a feeling, 236, 453
  precepts of, xl–xli, 231–232
  precepts of Decalogue reducible to, 131
  toward friends, 213, 221, 344, 352, 363, 418–419, 434, 451
  toward God, xxiii–xxiv, 38, 93, 96, 100, 130, 149, 219, 227, 229, 235, 298, 404, 414, 451
  toward enemies, 32, 85–86, 431–432, 440–442, 448
  toward neighbors, xxiii–xxiv, xl–xli, 126, 145–150, 213, 219, 224, 245, 384, 431–432
  toward ourselves, 131–132, 134–135, 145
  toward parents or children, 86, 118–119, 125, 142, 172, 231, 328, 393, 404
  toward spouses, 50, 126–127, 219, 224, 252, 258, 275, 320–321, 438, 451–452
  toward those like us, 49–51, 364
  vices contrary to, xli
children
  as blessing, 389–391, 452
  delinquent or unruly, 337, 354
  illegitimate, 48, 361, 381–382
  in relation to parents, *see* charity or love
  led to school by *paidagogos*, 26, 90, 271, 278, 423
  not to be baptized against the parents' will, xliii–xliv, 263

Index of Persons and Topics

rewarded with trinkets, 88, 90, 96
ritual sacrifice of by pagans, 196, 250, 365, 391
to be taught God's law, xxiii, 422
treatment in war, 365, 373–374, 385
chimaeras, human–animal hybrids, 307
Christ, *see* Jesus Christ
Chrysostom, John, Saint, xlv, 113, 194
Cicero, Marcus Tullius, 337–338, 340, 355–356
citizenship
  and assimilation, 371
  in a qualified sense, 382
  in relation to family, 371
  in the full sense, 380
Clinton, William Jefferson, US President, 307
common good, *see* law
common ground, xlii–xliii
community or commonwealth
  considered ideally and in real life, 355–356
  definition of, 122, 338–340, 355
  excludes tyranny, *see* tyranny
  exile from, 337, 354, 379
  government of, 311–335, 379
  in relation to family, 30
  of heaven, 274, 279, 379
  of men in related with each other, with God, 52, 121–122, 183, 312
  whether dependably grounded on vice, *see* vice
Conrad, Richard, O.P., 43, 62, 141, 224, 370
conscience and remorse, xxxviii, 105, 114, 124, 158, 174, 192, 266, 287, 422, 429, 456
conspiracy to lie, 337, 343, 353
Cooke, Sam, 236
Cornelius, 288
counsel or counsels
  definition of, 5, 18, 235
  evangelical (poverty, celibacy, and obedience), 220, 235, 241, 427–451
  man left in the hand of his own, 4
  see also precepts
Cox, Harvey, xxxiii
Creation
  analogy between moral and material, 18
  commemoration of, 73, 135–136, 164, 166, 171
  not to be preferred to the Creator, 404
  pattern, design, or order of, xlv, 3, 35, 59, 111, 159–160, 174, 189, 253, 370, 406
  whether could have been arranged differently, 171, 174, 300, 308
  see also salvation
cross
  conformed to Christ through union with His suffering on, 36, 96, 306
  foreshadowed, 25, 30, 58, 61, 136, 138, 272, 299, 301, 306, 355
Crüsemann, Frank, 370

Darius, Persian king, 309
David, 6–7, 175, 316, 327–329, 380–381, 455
Deborah, 380
Decalogue
  its architecture, 148–150; *see also* individual commandments (by number)
Dekkers, Midge, 307
de Lubac, Henri, 37
duty or duties
  natural, 6, 18, 71, 103, 144
  to God, neighbor, and self, 132, 144–146

Edomites (Idumaeans), relations with, 359, 361, 369, 372, 375–376, 432
efficiency, *see* markets
Egyptians, relations with, 359, 361, 369, 372, 375–376
Eighth Commandment, false witness (Exodus 20:16, Deuteronomy 5:20), 125, 148, 219, 249, 254; *see also* lying
end, natural and supernatural, 8–9, 17, 19, 71, 407
Enlightenment project, xlii
Esau, 361, 369 *see* Jacob (later called Israel), essences
  divine, xlii, 8, 10, 131, 141, 293, 370
  essentialism, 177
  human, xlii, 177, 370
  of a people, 339
  of charity, 224
  of false swearing, 141
  of justice, 186, 188
  of law as such, 3, 153
  of love, 236
  of New Law, 15, 91
  substances or essential natures, 28, 145, 177
eunuchs, 361–362, 381, 383, 430, 443–444
evangelization, 36–37

faith
  beginnings of, 82
  implicit vs. explicit, 36–39

faith (cont.)
  infused, 62, 105
  substance of things hoped for, 28
  working through love, 47, 92, 105
  see also virtues
Fall
  disorders our nature, xxxviii, 10–11, 71, 132, 146, 239, 280–406; see also salvation
false teachers, 117–118, 139, 251, 262–264
false witness, see lying
family
  in relation to community membership, 371, 378, 382
  in relation to law, 31
  in relation to marriage, 127, 190, 258
  in relation to Old Law priesthood, 330
  in relation to property, 344, 346, 348, 352
  in relation to social order, 60, 257
in relation to transmission of faith, 389–391
fear
  carnal, 156
  filial or chaste, 82, 84, 328
  in relation to charity or love, 82, 84
  initial, 82–83
  law of, 155–157
  of God, as beginning of wisdom, 84
  servile or carnal, 156, 328
Fifth Commandment, murder (Exodus 20:13, Deuteronomy 5:17), 248, 252
First Commandment, worship of God alone (Exodus 20:3-6, Deuteronomy 5:7-10), 123, 129, 153, 157–158, 165–166, 171, 213, 238, 248, 250
First and Second Tablets, 20–21, 148–149, 183, 189, 239
forgiveness, 156, 225, 376, 244
  and repentance, 28, 38, 59, 100, 170, 225, 329, 391, 456
  and reconciliation, xxxviii, 25, 36, 38, 113, 210, 224, 252, 266, 402, 414, 448
  not unconditional, 441
fortitude or courage, see virtues
Fourth Commandment, honoring parents (Exodus 20:12, Deuteronomy 5:16), 248
Freddoso, Alfred J., 23, 347
Freeman, W.F.X.R., xxix
friendship, see neighbor, friendship with; God, friendship with

Gentiles
  metonymically called Greeks, 414, 425
  regenerate, 396
  unregenerate, see pagan practices forbidden
gifts of the Holy Spirit, 82, 140
Glossa Ordinaria, or Ordinary Gloss, 48–49, 140–141
God
  agnosticism about of disbelief in, 35, 206
  as Creator, 19, 60, 110–113, 170, 404
  as first cause, xxxix
  as uncreated source of good, 131, 137–138, 160, 178, 185, 233, 420, 424
  biblical portrayal of, 35
  does everything fittingly, 88, 293, 295–296, 308
  existence of demonstrable, xl, 10, 44
  friendship with, xxxv, 9, 49–51, 70, 85, 107, 221, 234, 241, 447
  future rest in, 63, 129, 136, 138
  His providential care, 161, 172, 321
  His Spirit, 46, 62, 82, 135, 155, 185, 283, 353, 360, 400, 402–403, 404, 415–420, 425, 447
  images of, 20, 72, 109, 129–130, 165–166, 170, 235
  inclination to seek the truth of, xxxvi, xli, 19, 145–146
  jealousy of, figurative, 153, 157–158, 168
  knowledge of, 19, 35, 110–111, 425
  love of, see Charity or love, toward God
  objection to "dragging Him into things," xxxiv
  one in Being, three in Person, 9, 53, 56, 131, 140–141, 185, 353
  ontological vs. practical dependence on, xxxv
  reconciliation with, see justification
  supremely lovable, 233
  unity, truth, and goodness of, 130
  virtues pre-exist in, 62
God-fearers, 288, 371
good
  as object of love, xxxv
  created, xxxix, 3, 48, 78, 140, 159, 170, 245, 295
  of all good, 131
  of obedience, 290, 301
  of the beloved, 452–453
  of this life, despising, 27, 83, 88, 92, 96, 100–101, 229
  see also God
Gospel
  primary and secondary element of, 415–416, 419, 436

Index of Persons and Topics

relevance of to philosophy, 406–407
scandal of, 425–426
teachings of, 425
see also law
government, see community or commonwealth, government of
grace
  as a gratuitous gift of God, 273
  cooperation with, 33, 62, 200, 219, 236, 403, 419, 426–427, 445
  definition of, 273
  heals, xlv, 71, 274, 281, 405–406, 415, 418, 456
  means, channels, or sacraments of, 21, 37, 216, 300
  offered to human race by Christ, 91, 407
  operating principles of, 407
  presupposes and uplifts nature, xl, xliv, 36, 53–54, 137, 233, 293, 406–407
  Treatise on, 457
Great Commandments (love God, love neighbor), xxiii–xxiv, xl, 213, 237
Gregory of Nazianzus, Saint, 262

happiness
  temporal vs. final, 7–10, 16, 18–19, 53
  in God, 7, 16, 70, 110, 137, 424, 436–437
  in union with beloved, 451–452
  very meaning of fulfillment, 137
harm
  "it doesn't hurt anyone," 257
  three ways to harm one's neighbor, 125
  whether wrong of act depends on, 256
Harrington, Michael, 406
Hart, H. L. A., 153
Hegel, G. W. F., 128
Hilary of Poitiers, Saint, 198–199
Hobbes, Thomas, xxix, 153, 331
Holiness Code (Leviticus 17–26), 370–371; see also Index of Scriptural References
hope, see virtues
humor
  what St. Thomas thinks of, 296
  whether God has a sense of, 306
  whether St. Thomas has a sense of, 308–310
  see also virtues, particular kinds of

idolatry
  motive for, 166–170
  of self, 124
  satirized, 168

why worship of one God incompatible with, 112, 124
see also First Commandment
inclinations, natural, xxxvi, 5–6, 18–19, 71, 103, 144–146
instinct, 19, 103, 145, 255
intrinsically evil acts
  doing evil that good will result, 194, 217
  in general, 167, 181–182, 184, 194, 217, 296, 299
Isaac, see Abraham
Isidore of Seville, 152–153
Islam, xxxvii, xliii, 22, 34–35
Israel (the nation)
  chosen, xliv, 22, 26, 34, 99, 123, 170, 262, 286, 323–324, 359, 376, 386, 407, 431
  distinguished from gentiles, 26, 262
  government of, 311–335
  reunited with gentiles in Christ, 286, 379
  through the Messiah, a light to the nations, 262, 377

Jacob (later called Israel), 361, 369, 377
Jephtha, 382–383
Jeroboam, 315–316
Jerome, Saint, 288
Jesus Christ
  atoning work of, xlv, 37, 299, 302, 306, 407; see also cross
  Divine and human natures of, 403
  Incarnation of, 21
  light to the nations, 262, 377
  Messiah, xliv, 30–31, 32, 140, 262, 270, 278, 282, 377, 398–399, 405, 411
  receiving, meaning of, 33
  reunites Jews and gentiles in Himself, 286, 379
Jethro, 312, 321–322
John of La Rochelle, 61
judgment and judgments
  distinguished from ceremonies and precepts, xlvii, 64–79
  divorced from truth, 261
  final, 14, 106, 209–210, 252, 266, 328, 408–409
  how reached, 109
  impairment of, 10–11, 56, 243–244, 246–247, 287, 316
  in sense of judicial precept, 47
  "in all your gates," **342**
  justice turned into, 67–68
  nonjudgmentalism, xxxiv, 215, 263

judgment and judgments (cont.)
  of judges, 198, 337, 339–340, 342, 351, 253
  reason as criterion of, 107–108
  speculative and practical, 106
  suspending, 15
  three ways to make, 108–110
  see also bribes; judges as rulers of Israel; justice
judges as rulers of Israel, 322–326, 334, 380, 382
Judith, 378
justification
  accomplished, being accomplished, and to be accomplished, 426
  forensic view of (as a legal fiction), 410–411
  in relation to sanctification, 281, 408
  in the view of the Reformers, 281–283, 408
  senses of, 265, 270–279, 409
justice
  characteristic act of, 67
  Divine, 171, 189, 268, 385, 392
  general vs. particular, 268, 276–278
  turned into judgment, 67–68
  see also virtues

Kelsen, Hans, 153
Kierkegaard, Søren, 188, 191
kings or kingship
  as form of government, 22–23, 313–314, 318–321, 325–326
  instructions to Israel concerning, *see* Israel the nation, government of
  meaning of, 332–334
knowledge
  certainty of, 10–11
  fear of Lord as beginning of, 328
  how attained, 90, 107, 249–250
  in relation to Divine illumination, xliii
  intelligence, science, wisdom, prudence, compared, 5, 85
  in this life and next, 7, 210
  natural, 10, 19, 35, 112, 173–175, 239
  of invisible movements of the heart, 206
  of first principles, 55, 106
  of God, 110–111
  revealed, 38, 110
  tree of, 289–290, 300–302
  uncertainty of, *see* judgment and judgments, impairment of
kritarchy, 333

language
  every-day, xxx
  police, 73
  so-called inclusive, xlvi–xlvii
  St. Thomas's, xlvi
  whole, 90
law
  and prophets, 213, 237–238
  as Divine pedagogy, xliv–xlv, 24–35, 78, 80–81, 88–93, 115, 287, 370, 390
  conclusions of vs. determinations of, 12, 21, 70–78
  conditions pertaining to, 26
  criteria of genuine, xxxviii, 6, 23, 27, 102, 109, 341
  constitutional, 61, 147, 311, 319, 321, 333, 357
  customary, 152–153
  discipline of, 12, 48–49, 98, 103–104, 218
  dispensation from, xlv, 176, 180, 183, 186, 189–196, 377
  doers vs. hearers of, 265–266, 276, 409
  eternal, xxxix, xl, 3–4, 7, 24, 102, 108, 160, 245, 396
  human, xxxix, xxliv, 3–21, 49–50, 53, 70–72
  in relation to common good, 23
  letter of, 46, 415
  natural, xxxix–xli, 3, 7–11, 16–21, 33–34, 52–53, 69–73, 102–114, 288
  of fear, *see* fear
  of love, *see* charity or love
  of revenge (*lex talionis*), 120, 385
  of sin, 3, 399
  philosophy of, 406
  what not to be attempted by human, 217
  whether arbitrary and unintelligible, 102, 115, 183, 260–261, 284, 293–298, 303
  whether to be distinguished from grace, 398, 400
  unwritten, *see* law, customary
  see also precepts in general; precepts, particular kinds of; "written on the heart"
legal maxims
  actus non facit reum nisi mens sit rea, the act does not make guilty unless the mind is also guilty, 13
  ex culpa non debet quis commodum reportare, no one may gain advantage from his own fault, 367

Index of Persons and Topics

lending
  viewed as act of charity, 59, 253–254, 352, 363, 384–385
  viewed as compensation for opportunity cost, 362–363
Levering, Matthew, 61
Levites, *see* priests or priesthood
Lewis, C. S., 38–39, 423–424
life
  and death set before the people, 28, 46, 80
  consecrated religious, 438–439, 444, 445, 454–455
  eternal, 27–28, 31, 62, 91, 219–221, 229, 241, 267, 427–428, 437
  pride of, 436–438, 442
  tree of, 289–290; *see also* knowledge, tree of
light
  Divine, xxxvi, xlii, 17, 54, 175, 229, 243, 292–293, 396
  to the nations, 262, 377
Live Action, 194
Locke, John, 128
Lombard, Peter, 8, 29–30, 63, 202–203, 274, 286
love, *see* charity or love
lust of the eye and of the flesh, 150, 438, 442; *see also* life, pride of
Luther, Martin, 281–282
lying, 115, 130, 146, 148, 170–171, 182, 193–194, 255; *see also* Eighth Commandment

MacIntyre, Alasdair, 215
Magna Glossatura (*Collectanea*) or Great Gloss, 202, 286
Maimonides (Moshe ben Maimon), xlvii, xliv, 58–61, 354
Marcion of Sinope, Marcionite heresy, 421
markets, 128, 342, 345
marriage (entrance into matrimony) and matrimony (state of being married)
  chief good of, 127, 383, 389
  compared with celibacy, 453–455
  divorce, xlv, 34, 195, 224, 261–262, 444
  see also Sixth Commandment
maturity, xlv, 82, 88, 91–92, 113, 177, 384, 448
Moabites, relations with, 174, 361, 365–366, 369, 373, 375–376
morality, enforcement of, 216
Moses
  advised by Jethro, 312, 321
  as a kind of king, 321, 326
  as an intermediary, 133, 244, 247, 413, 416
  calls heaven and earth to witness, 46
  commands execution of initiates to Moabite rites, 365
  commends God's commandments, xli, 55, 161, 294, 298
  explains why the nation was chosen, xliii
  implores God, 171–173
  instructed by God, 28, 77, 188, 262, 266, 313, 372
  instructs the people concerning judges, 341
  instructs the people concerning kings, 314, 324
  received the tablets of the Law, 116, 132
  reminds nation of past events, 81, 83, 168
  settles an inheritance dispute, 347–348
  testified to Messiah to come, 91
murder or bloodshed, 13, 193; *see also* Fifth Commandment

Nathan, 327
nature, human
  composite of soul and body, 437
  created good but fallen, 236, 274
  operating principles of, 407
  presupposed and uplifted by grace, *see* grace
  see also law, natural
neighbor
  duties to, xl, 20, 58, 78, 123
  friendship with, 85, 221, 144, 229, 352
  love of, xli, 49, 85–86, 111, 147
  three ways to harm, 125
neutrality, impossibility of, xliii, 264
Nietzsche, Friedrich, xxix–xxx
Ninth Commandment, coveting neighbor's wealth (Exodus 20:17a, Deuteronomy 5:21a), 149, 255; *see also* vices
Notare, Theresa, 127, 389, 451

obedience
  by natural powers, insufficient, 10–11
  evangelical counsel of, 428–433, 435, 438, 439–441
  pagan practices forbidden, 60, 77, 91, 158, 168, 180, 195, 250, 262, 262–264, 350, 365–366, 375, 391
  rewarded, 17, 31, 80–95, 153–154, 166, 211, 218, 227, 401–402, 447
  whether may be withheld from civil rulers, 124
  see also counsel or counsels, evangelical

paidagogos (guardian or child-leader), 26, 91, 271, 435
parents, honor to, 86, 125–126, 143, 149, 164, 230–231, 239, 260, 382; *see also* Fourth Commandment
parts
  in relation to wholes, 126, 144, 230, 245
  potential, subjective, and integral, 164
passions, *see* powers of the soul (concupiscible and irascible)
Passover, 30, 78, 136, 138, 272, 375–376
Pelagius, Pelagian heresy, 222, 234–235
perfection
  in love, degrees of, 83–84, 233–234, 447
  meaning of, 26, 90
  stages in development of, 89, 92–93
Pharisees and Scribes, 29, 191, 237, 315, 353
philosophy of religion, xxxiii, xxxvii
Phinehas, 365
Pieper, Josef, 453
Plato, 313, 328, 355, 447
polity (constitutionally mixed and balanced government), 319, 321, 333
positivism, legal, 153
positivism, logical, xxxiii
Posner, Richard A., 180, 186
powers of the soul (concupiscible and irascible), 114, 119–120, 146–147, 438; for the rational power, *see* reason and reasoning
precepts about particular things
  about blood, 138, 305–307
  about bribes, 90, 312, 316–317, 322, 334, 339, 342
  about clothing, 257, 303–305
  about foods other than blood, 59, 64, 350, 365, 386, 432, 448
  about misuse of the power of speech, 126, 139–141, 193; *see also* lying; Second Commandment; Eighth Commandment
  about sexual acts, *see* sexual acts
  about strangers in the land, 251, 359–392
  about the aged, 19, 108, 112, 134, 248, 251, 256; *see also* Fourth Commandment
  about the poor and vulnerable, 11, 59, 72, 242, 253–254, 341–342, 348–349, 351–353, 363, 366, 370, 379
  about the tree of knowledge, *see* knowledge, tree of
  see also Decalogue; sexual acts
precepts in general
  affirmative and negative, xli, 126, 151–152, 162–164, 226–227, 231, 233, 235
  as coercive, 205–206
  as embodying very idea of direction to the common good, 181
  as embodying the very idea of right relation to God or other men, 183–185, 189, 378
  as expressing idea of debt or duty, 125–126, 133–134, 142–143, 149, 162–164
  as taught by the wise, 20, 108–109, 133, 134–135, 251
  classification of, 43, 58–61
  dispensation from, xlv, 176–196, 377
  evangelical, *see* counsel or counsels, evangelical
  three grades of, 243
  whether anything can still be learned from those of Old Law, 306–307
  see also counsel or counsels; Decalogue; law
priests or priesthood
  change in, 24–25
  Levites assisted, 317
  levitical, 24–25, 30, 175, 327, 351
promises and threats
  in New Law, 100–101
  in Old Law, 80–100
  see also fear
property
  allotted to families, 344, 347, 351–352
  common vs. private use and ownership of, 128, 344–349, 352
  see also Seventh Commandment
Protestants and Protestantism, xxxvii, 30, 274, 398, 408, 428
  see also justification; Luther, Martin; Wright, N. T.
prudence or practical wisdom, *see* virtues
punishment
  as motive for obedience, 30, 31, 80–100, 156–157, 169–171, 200, 205–206
  capital, 179, 186–187, 279–280
  considerations in, 353–354
  generational, 158, 172–173
  in relation to disgrace, 170
  kinds of, 337, 354
  medicinal vs. retributive, 91, 287, 328–329
  see also blessings and curses; justice; suffering
Puritans, 15

Rabbi Moses, *see* Maimonides (Moshe ben Maimon)
Rahner, Karl, 36–37
reason and reasoning
  as criterion of conduct, 107–108
  first principles vs. remote implications of, xl, 56, 149, 255, 287

Index of Persons and Topics

from the less to the more difficult, 90, 249–250
historical vs. philosophical, 35
impairment of, *see* judgment
syllogisms, 85, 88–90
see also knowledge; Revelation
redemption, *see* justification; salvation
refuge, cities of, 242, 354
Rehoboam, 316
Revelation
 as Divine pedagogy, *see* law
 authority of, 4, 20, 54, 78, 121, 161, 189, 288
 data of, xxxvi, 21
 genuine vs. non-genuine, xxxvi, xliii, 4, 34, 35, 81, 192, 251, 262
 in relation to reason, xxxvi, xxxviii, xl–xli
 reason as preamble to, xl, 35
rhetorical devices
 allegory, 195, 291, 301
 analogy, xli, 18, 23, 34, 56, 88, 224, 270, 293, 321, 384, 448
 chiasmus or reversal, 16, 136
 foreshadowing (also called prefiguring, type and antitype, and promissory figure), 25, 30, 60–61, 64–65, 135–138, 263, 270–272, 278, 286, 299–301, 306, 316, 355, 360, 379, 417
 hyperbole, 269, 404
 metalepsis, 243
 metaphor, 82, 293
 metonymy, synechdoche, or antonomasia, 69, 332
 parable, 15, 365, 384, 437
 parallelism, 16, 23, 87, 136, 145, 178, 316, 317
 rhetorical question, 418
 transferred meaning, 271
Ruth, 350, 378–380

Sabbath
 every seven days, *see* Third Commandment
 of the land, every seven years, 348, 350
sacraments, *see* grace
sacrifice
 four things to be considered in every, 25
 perfect, of Jesus Christ, xliv, 25, 58, 61, 299, 306
salvation
 as God's purpose in all law, 23
 illegitimate pride in, 400
 Israel's role in, 377–378

meaning of, broad, 36, 414
 of Old Testament saints, 36
 phases of its history, 61, 406
 plan of, 112
 through Christ alone, 32–33, 35–39, 409, 445
 see also justification
Samuel, 205–207, 317–318, 324–325, 329, 330–331, 334–335
sanctification, *see* justification
Satan, 36, 315, 441, 453
Saul, *see* Samuel
scandal, 425–426, 428–429, 442
sciences, 84–85, 88, 89, 106–107
Scipio Africanus, 338, 355–356
Scribes, *see* Pharisees and Scribes
Second Commandment, empty speech about God (Exodus 20:7, Deuteronomy 5:11), 123–139, 148, 154–155, 158, 248, 250
 see also Eighth Commandment; lying; precepts about particular things
Second Tablet, *see* First and Second Tablets
secularization thesis, xxxiii–xxxiv
self
 duties toward, 36, 131–133, 135, 142–144
 lovers of, 400
Sermon on the Mount, 210
Seventh Commandment, stealing (Exodus 20:15, Deuteronomy 5:19), 149, 249
 see also stealing or theft
sexual acts
 disorder of natural desire for, 145, 167, 428, 439
 illicit, 45, 56, 59, 189, 249, 252, 261–262, 264, 303, 365
 natural vs. unnatural, 252, 307
 pleasure of, 242, 310
 sexual exploitation, 194, 250, 375
 see also counsel or counsels; eunuchs; marriage; Sixth Commandment; virtues, particular
Shapiro, Harold T., 307
Sheilaism, 33
Shiras, Wilmar H., xxix
sin
 alienates or separates from God, 16, 31, 36, 82, 101, 116–117, 158, 194, 404
 habitual, 55, 353
 unnatural, 143, 249, 252, 307
Singer, Peter, 307
Sixth Commandment, adultery (Exodus 20:14, Deuteronomy 5:18), 149, 249, 252

see also eunuchs; marriage; sexual acts; Tenth Commandment; virtues, particular
skepticism, xlii, 161, 177
slavery or bondservice, 20, 23, 98, 138, 166, 171, 188, 272, 307, 331, 334, 337, 349–350, 354, 375, 435–436, 443
socialism, 345, 406
  see also property
Sodom and Gomorrah, destruction of, 391
Solomon, 92, 159, 315–316, 380
stealing or theft
  among the German tribes, 246–247
  definition of, 12, 193
  see also Seventh Commandment
stoning
  figurative, 262
  literal, 250, 259, 262, 413
  see also punishment
strangers in the land, 359, 368
  see also God-fearers; precepts about particular things
Strauss, Leo, 174, 357–358
subsidiarity, 320
substances, *see* essences
suffering
  enduring, 68
  of Christ on our behalf, 25, 302
  reasons for, 95–97

temperance or moderation, *see* virtues
Temple
  desecration of, 180
  heavenly, 62
  of Jerusalem, 30
  pagan, 221, 252, 365
  regulations for, 60
  universe as, 170
Ten Commandments, *see* Decalogue
Tenth Commandment, coveting neighbor's wife (Exodus 20:17b, Deuteronomy 5:21b), 140, 249, 255
  see also marriage; sexual acts; Sixth Commandment; virtues, particular
theft, *see* stealing or theft
Theodosius, Macrobius Ambrosius, 63
Third Commandment, sabbath day (Exodus 20:8–11, Deuteronomy 5:12–15), 123, 148, 153, 158–159, 165–166, 171, 248
Tocqueville, Alexis de, 428
toleration, religious, *see* false teachers
Tranquillitas ordinis or rightly ordered peace, 333
tyranny, 124, 215–216, 317, 320–321, 325–328, 330–335, 436, 443

usury, *see* lending

verification criterion, *see* positivism, logical
vices
  acedia or sloth, 202
  avarice, covetousness, or greed, 14–15, 29, 45, 81–84, 93, 145, 269, 325, 437
  cowardice, 198, 205, 210, 214–215, 388
  cruelty, xxxviii, xliii, 59, 308, 325–326
  gluttony and drunkenness, 56, 256, 259–260, 337, 354, 378, 439
  ingratitude, 86
  malice, 120, 303–304, 343, 354, 419
  unchastity, 258
  whether community can be grounded on, 15, 356–358
virtues in general
  acquired vs. infused, 62–63
  as the aim of law, 14, 199–200, 268
  as the *honestum*, 74
  directed to the good, 20
  Hamburger Helper strategy about, 357
  in a qualified vs. an unqualified sense, 63, 218, 229
  neither by nature nor contrary to nature, 84
  related to excess or deficiency, 121, 147, 260, 296, 325–326, 330, 344, 367, 384, 440–441
  role of persuasion in forming, 88–89
  role of punishment in forming, 206
  social, cleansing, complete, and exemplar, 63
  trying or testing, 96, 251, 287
  whether less dependable than vice, *see* vices
virtues, particular
  chastity, 242, 256, 258
  "common good of," 366
  faith, *see* faith
  filial piety, 86, 125, 164, 210
  fortitude or courage, 52, 62, 140, 214–215, 229, 238, 257–259
  gratitude, xxxv, 9, 20, 67, 134, 136, 138, 173
  hope, xxxvi, xli, 28, 34, 62, 147, 156, 195, 220, 238, 275, 406, 409, 419, 437–438
  interconnection of, 424–425
  justice, 29, 52, 62, 64–79, 95, 149–150
  liberality, 241–242
  mercy, 242, 279–280, 442
  prudence or practical wisdom, 5, 52, 62, 135, 216, 229, 238, 295, 319, 407, 454
  religion, 20, 153, 164, 241–242, 257–258, 453–454

sapientia or Divine Wisdom, 272, 397, 442
self-control, 441
soberness, temperance, or moderation, 52, 59, 62, 242, 256, 259–260, 273, 439
wittiness, 257, 308
see also charity or love; obedience

war
  just vs. unjust, 56, 179, 186–187, 258–259, 332, 366–367, 373–374, 390–392
  on poverty, 406
  treatment of innocents in, 390–392
  treatment of women and children in, 365, 373–374, 385
Watts, Rikk, 170
will, reasonable, 11

William of Middleton, 61
women
  as inheritors, 344, 347, 352
  compared in power with wine, the king, and truth, 309–310
  role of queen mother, 380
  treatment of in war, 365, 373–374, 385
  see also Bathsheba; Deborah; Ruth
Wright, N. T., 408
"written on the heart"
  application of the phrase to Divine law, 401–402, 421–422
  application of the phrase to natural law, 106, 266, 396–397, 422
  senses in which phrase used in Holy Scripture, 421–422

CPSIA information can be obtained
at www.ICGtesting.com
Printed in the USA
LVHW111916030821
694401LV00001B/70